MICROSOFT EXAM OBJECTIVES
EXAM 70-240: MICROSOFT WINDOWS 2000 ACCELERATED EXAM
FOR MCPs CERTIFIED ON MICROSOFT WINDOWS NT 4.0

KV-638-376

Installing, Configuring, and Administering Windows 2000 Professional	See Chapter(s):
Installing Windows 2000 Professional	2, 15, 19, 21
Configuring Windows 2000 Professional	2, 12, 13, 21
Administering Windows 2000 Professional	6, 14, 16, 18, 20, 21

Installing, Configuring, and Administering Windows 2000 Server	See Chapter(s):
Installing Windows 2000 Server	2, 19
Installing, Configuring, and Troubleshooting Access to Resources	2, 12, 13, 18
Managing, Configuring, and Troubleshooting Storage Use	12, 18
Administering Windows 2000 Terminal Services	15, 17
Administering Windows 2000	14, 15, 17, 20
Securing a Windows 2000 Network	1, 13, 20

Implementing and Administering a Microsoft Windows 2000 Network Infrastructure	See Chapter(s):
Installing, Configuring, Managing, Monitoring, and Troubleshooting DNS in a Windows 2000 Network Infrastructure	3, 11
Installing, Configuring, Managing, Monitoring, and Troubleshooting DHCP in a Windows 2000 Network Infrastructure	11
Configuring, Managing, Monitoring, and Troubleshooting Remote Access in a Windows 2000 Network Infrastructure	16
Installing, Configuring, Managing, Monitoring, and Troubleshooting WINS in a Windows 2000 Network Infrastructure	11

Implementing and Administering a Microsoft Windows 2000 Directory Services Infrastructure	See Chapter(s):
Installing, Configuring, and Troubleshooting the Components of Active Directory	3, 4, 5, 6, 7, 8, 9, 10, 18
Designing and Modifying the Active Directory Schema	9
Installing, Configuring, Managing, Monitoring, and Troubleshooting DNS for Active Directory	3, 11
Installing, Configuring, Managing, Monitoring, Optimizing, and Troubleshooting Change and Configuration Management	2, 14, 15, 16
Managing, Monitoring, and Optimizing the Components of Active Directory	4, 6, 7, 8, 10
Configuring, Managing, Monitoring, and Troubleshooting Active Directory Security Solutions	1, 6, 14, 20
Installing, Configuring, Managing, Monitoring, and Troubleshooting Network Protocols and IP Routing in a Windows 2000 Network Infrastructure	2, 16, 20
Installing, Configuring, and Troubleshooting Access to Resources	2, 13
Managing, Monitoring, and Optimizing System Performance, Reliability, and Availability	2, 8, 12

MCSE™ Windows® 2000
Accelerated

Lance Cockcroft

Erik Eckel

Ron Kauffman

MCSE™ Windows® 2000 Accelerated Exam Prep
© 2000 The Coriolis Group. All Rights Reserved.

Limits of Liability and Disclaimer of Warranty

Trademarks

The Coriolis Group, LLC
14455 N. Hayden Road, Suite 220
Scottsdale, Arizona 85260

480/483-0192
FAX 480/483-0193
www.coriolis.com

Library of Congress Cataloging-in-Publication Data
Cockcroft, Lance.
    MCSE Windows 2000 accelerated exam prep / by Lance Cockcroft,
Erik Eckel, and Ron Kauffman.
        p. cm.
    ISBN 1-57610-690-X
    1. Electronic data processing personnel--Certification.   2.
Microsoft software--Examinations--Study guides.   3. Microsoft Windows
(computer file).   I. Eckel, Erik.   II. Kauffman, Ron.   III. Title.

QA76.3.C635   2000
005.4'4769--dc21

                                00-034062
                                CIP

President and CEO
Keith Weiskamp

Publisher
Steve Sayre

Acquisitions Editor
Shari Jo Hehr

Development Editor
Deborah Doorley

Marketing Specialist
Cynthia Caldwell

Project Editor
Sally M. Scott

Technical Reviewer
James F. Kelly

Production Coordinator
Meg E. Turecek

Cover Designer
Jesse Dunn

Layout Designer
April Nielsen

CD-ROM Developer
Michelle McConnell

CORIOLIS

Printed in the United States of America
10 9 8 7 6 5 4 3 2 1

The Coriolis Group, LLC • 14455 North Hayden Road, Suite 220 • Scottsdale, Arizona 85260

ExamCram.com Connects You to the Ultimate Study Center!

Our goal has always been to provide you with the best study tools on the planet to help you achieve your certification in record time. Time is so valuable these days that none of us can afford to waste a second of it, especially when it comes to exam preparation.

Over the past few years, we've created an extensive line of *Exam Cram* and *Exam Prep* study guides, practice exams, and interactive training. To help you study even better, we have now created an e-learning and certification destination called **ExamCram.com**. (You can access the site at **www.examcram.com**.) Now, with every study product you purchase from us, you'll be connected to a large community of people like yourself who are actively studying for their certifications, developing their careers, seeking advice, and sharing their insights and stories.

I believe that the future is all about collaborative learning. Our **ExamCram.com** destination is our approach to creating a highly interactive, easily accessible collaborative environment, where you can take practice exams and discuss your experiences with others, sign up for features like "Questions of the Day," plan your certifications using our interactive planners, create your own personal study pages, and keep up with all of the latest study tips and techniques.

I hope that whatever study products you purchase from us—*Exam Cram* or *Exam Prep* study guides, *Personal Trainers*, *Personal Test Centers*, or one of our interactive Web courses—will make your studying fun and productive. Our commitment is to build the kind of learning tools that will allow you to study the way you want to, whenever you want to.

Visit *ExamCram.com* now to enhance your study program.

Help us continue to provide the very best certification study materials possible. Write us or email us at **learn@examcram.com** and let us know how our study products have helped you study. Tell us about new features that you'd like us to add. Send us a story about how we've helped you. We're listening!

Good luck with your certification exam and your career. Thank you for allowing us to help you achieve your goals.

Keith Weiskamp
President and CEO

Look for these other products from The Coriolis Group:

MCSE Windows 2000 Server Exam Prep
By David Johnson and Dawn Rader

MCSE Windows 2000 Professional Exam Prep
By Michael D. Stewart, James Bloomingdale,
and Neall Alcott

MCSE Windows 2000 Network Exam Prep
By Tammy Smith and Sandra Smeeton

MCSE Windows 2000 Directory Services Exam Prep
By David V. Watts, Will Willis, and Tillman Strahan

MCSE Windows 2000 Security Design Exam Prep
By Richard Alan McMahon and Glen Bicking

MCSE Windows 2000 Network Design Exam Prep
By Geoffrey Alexander, Anoop Jalan,
and Joseph Alexander

MCSE Migrating from NT 4 to Windows 2000 Exam Prep
By Glen Bergen, Graham Leach, and David Baldwin

MCSE Windows 2000 Directory Services Design Exam Prep
By J. Peter Bruzzese and Wayne Dipchan

MCSE Windows 2000 Core Four Exam Prep Pack

MCSE Windows 2000 Server Exam Cram
By Natasha Knight

MCSE Windows 2000 Professional Exam Cram
By Dan Balter, Dan Holme, Todd Logan,
and Laurie Salmon

MCSE Windows 2000 Network Exam Cram
By Hank Carbeck, Derek Melber, and Richard Taylor

MCSE Windows 2000 Directory Services Exam Cram
By David V. Watts, Will Willis, and J. Peter Bruzzese

MCSE Windows 2000 Security Design Exam Cram
By Phillip G. Schein

MCSE Windows 2000 Network Design Exam Cram
By Kim Simmons, Jarret W. Buse, and Todd Halping

MCSE Windows 2000 Directory Services Design Exam Cram
By Dennis Scheil and Diana Bartley

MCSE Windows 2000 Core Four Exam Cram Pack

and...

MCSE Windows 2000 Foundations
By James Michael Stewart and Lee Scales

I would like to dedicate this book to my wife, Carol,
who has shown me that a positive attitude has positive results.
Without the support and confidence you have bestowed upon me,
I could have never finished this book.

I would also like to dedicate this book to my father, who through his own actions
has taught me how to persevere through difficult times.
—Lance Cockcroft

ॐ

To my father, who introduced me to punch card machines
and the world of computing back in the 1960s.
—Erik Eckel

ॐ

To my friends and crew. Without your help, this never would have been possible.
—Ron Kauffman

ॐ

ABOUT THE AUTHORS

Lance Cockcroft (MCP+I, MCSE, MCT, CCNA, CCA, Net+) recently brought his more than 11 years of networking experience to SENETS Broadband of Atlanta, an Internet Service Provider utilizing the very latest in state-of-the-art system architecture. He currently serves in that organization in the capacity of Manager of Technology and Deployment.

Combining recognized technical expertise with an eminently successful instructional style, Lance remains a highly sought-after instructor, delivering training for numerous North Georgia universities and colleges, including Kennesaw and Southern Polytechnic State universities and Floyd College.

Lance is a native of north Georgia and has a Bachelor of Sciences degree in Information Technologies Management from Kennesaw State University.

Erik Eckel (MCP+I, MCSE) considers himself fortunate to have had a first-wave IT professional as a father. He grew up with computers in the house, including portable systems that debuted in the early 1970s. Erik attended the University of Louisville, where he received a Bachelor of Arts degree in English. He also graduated from Sullivan College, where he earned network engineer accreditation. He currently serves as Editor-in-Chief of IT Communities at **TechRepublic.com**.

When he's not banging away at a keyboard, Erik enjoys spending time with his wife and daughter, racing bicycles both on-road and off, and listening to classic 1950s jazz.

Ron Kauffman (MCP+I, MCSE, MCT, A+, Net+) is an infrastructure architect for a large health insurance company and teaches Microsoft and CompTIA certification classes for a local private college on evenings and weekends.

He graduated from Webster University with a Master of Arts degree in Information Management, and he also has degrees in Information Systems and Computer Science. Ron started his career automating systems in the U.S. Army Medical Corps, where he served as a Defense Data network Consultant. He left the military in 1995 in order to begin a career as a programmer/analyst.

In his spare time, he is a freelance writer and is an IS management consultant for local companies.

ACKNOWLEDGMENTS

Thanks to everyone at The Coriolis Group for their assistance in building this text. It was a pleasure working with such a first-class team.

Several individuals must be recognized for their hard work and diligent efforts in helping to prepare this book. Thanks to Shari Jo Hehr, the Senior Acquisitions Editor, for assistance in getting the project off the ground. Development Editor Deb Doorley deserves credit for getting the author team up-to-speed.

The contributions of Project Editors Sharon McCarson and Sally M. Scott are certainly appreciated. Their energy and assistance helped three authors with full-time IT careers stay on deadline with the goal of getting the best book possible into your hands quickly. Thanks, too, to Meg Turecek, Production Coordinator, for her assistance.

While books shouldn't be judged by their covers, it sure helps to have a great one. Thanks Jesse Dunne, Cover Designer, for your graphic work.

Thanks, too, to Cynthia Caldwell, Marketing Specialist. We appreciate your spreading the word.

We also wish to recognize Michelle McConnell, CD-ROM Developer; Mary Milhollon, Copyeditor; Rachel Pearce Anderson, Proofreader; and Tim Griffin, Indexer. Their contributions add much to the quality of this Exam Prep.

A special thanks is in order for Technical Reviewer James F. Kelly. His painstaking attention to detail and technical accuracy, combined with our research and testing, ensures you can use this text with utmost confidence. We're very thankful to have had his fact-checking and editing expertise. Thanks, Jim, for all your help.

We also wish to thank our families for the support and sacrifices they made while we wrote and edited this book. Thanks for understanding the time and energy this project required.

Contents at a Glance

TABLE OF CONTENTS

EXAM INSIGHTS

Welcome to *MCSE Windows 2000 Accelerated Exam Prep*! This comprehensive study guide aims to help you get ready to take—and pass—Microsoft certification Exam 70-240, titled "Microsoft Windows 2000 Accelerated Exam for MCPs Certified on Microsoft Windows NT 4.0." This Exam Insights section discusses exam preparation resources, the testing situation, Microsoft's certification programs in general, and how this book can help you prepare for Microsoft's Windows 2000 certification exams.

Exam Prep study guides help you understand and appreciate the subjects and materials you need to pass Microsoft certification exams. We've worked from Microsoft's curriculum objectives to ensure that all key topics are clearly explained. Our aim is to bring together as much information as possible about Microsoft certification exams.

Nevertheless, to completely prepare yourself for any Microsoft test, we recommend that you begin by taking the Self-Assessment included in this book immediately following this Exam Insights section. This tool will help you evaluate your knowledge base against the requirements for an MCSE under both ideal and real circumstances.

Based on what you learn from that exercise, you might decide to begin your studies with some classroom training or some background reading. You might decide to read The Coriolis Group's *Exam Prep* book that you have in hand first, or you might decide to start with another study approach. You may also want to refer to one of a number of study guides available from Microsoft or third-party vendors. We also recommend that you supplement your study program with visits to **ExamCram.com** to receive additional practice questions, get advice, and track the Windows 2000 MCSE program.

We also strongly recommend that you install, configure, and fool around with the software that you'll be tested on, because nothing beats hands-on experience and familiarity when it comes to understanding the questions you're likely to encounter on a certification test. Book learning is essential, but hands-on experience is the best teacher of all!

HOW TO PREPARE FOR AN EXAM

Preparing for any Windows 2000 Server-related test (including "Microsoft Windows 2000 Accelerated Exam for MCPs Certified on Microsoft Windows NT 4.0") requires that you obtain and study materials designed to provide comprehensive information about the product and its capabilities that will appear on the specific exam for which you are preparing. The following list of materials will help you study and prepare:

➤ The Windows 2000 Server product CD includes comprehensive online documentation and related materials; it should be a primary resource when you are preparing for the test.

➤ The exam preparation materials, practice tests, and self-assessment exams on the Microsoft Training & Services page at **www.microsoft.com/ trainingandservices/default.asp?PageID=mcp**. The Testing Innovations link offers samples of the new question types found on the Windows 2000 MCSE exams. Find the materials, download them, and use them!

➤ The exam preparation advice, practice tests, questions of the day, and discussion groups on the **ExamCram.com** e-learning and certification destination Web site (**www.examcram.com**).

In addition, you'll probably find any or all of the following materials useful in your quest for Windows 2000 expertise:

➤ *Microsoft training kits*—Microsoft Press offers training kits on Windows 2000 topics. For more information, visit: **http://mspress.microsoft.com/ findabook/list/subject-category-T.htm.** This training kit contains information that you will find useful in preparing for the test.

➤ *Microsoft TechNet CD*—This monthly CD-based publication delivers numerous electronic titles that include coverage of Directory Services Design and related topics on the Technical Information (TechNet) CD. Its offerings include product facts, technical notes, tools and utilities, and information on how to access the Seminars Online training materials for TCP/IP. A subscription to TechNet costs $299 per year, but it is well worth the price. Visit **www.microsoft.com/technet/** and check out the information under the "TechNet Subscription" menu entry for more details.

➤ *Study guides*—Several publishers—including The Coriolis Group—offer Windows 2000 titles. The Coriolis Group series includes the following:

➤ *The Exam Cram series*—These books give you information about the material you need to know to pass the tests.

➤ *The Exam Prep series*—These books provide a greater level of detail than the *Exam Cram* books and are designed to teach you everything you need to know from an exam perspective. Each book comes with a CD that contains interactive practice exams in a variety of testing formats.

Together, the two series make a perfect pair.

➤ *Multimedia*—These Coriolis Group materials are designed to support learners of all types—whether you learn best by reading or doing:

➤ *The Exam Cram Personal Trainer*—Offers a unique, personalized self-paced training course based on the exam.

➤ *The Exam Cram Personal Test Center*—Features multiple test options that simulate the actual exam, including Fixed-Length, Random, Review, and Test All. Explanations of correct and incorrect answers reinforce concepts learned.

➤ *Classroom training*—CTECs, online partners, and third-party training companies (like Wave Technologies, Learning Tree, Data-Tech, and others) all offer classroom training on TCP/IP. These companies aim to help you prepare to pass the TCP/IP test. Although such training runs upwards of $350 per day in class, most of the individuals lucky enough to partake (including your humble authors, who've even taught such courses) find them to be quite worthwhile.

➤ *Other publications*—There's no shortage of materials available about Active Directory, Windows 2000 Professional, network configuration and management, and the other areas that are covered by the 70-240 exam. The complete resource section in the back of the book should give you an idea of where we think you should look for further discussion.

By far, this set of required and recommended materials represents a nonpareil collection of sources and resources for TCP/IP and related topics. We anticipate that you'll find that this book belongs in this company.

TAKING A CERTIFICATION EXAM

Once you've prepared for your exam, you need to register with a testing center. Each computer-based Windows 2000 Accelerated exam is free, but if you don't pass you will not be able to take the test again. In the United States and Canada, tests are administered by Prometric (formerly Sylvan Prometric), and by Virtual University Enterprises (VUE). Here's how you can contact them:

➤ *Prometric*—You can sign up for a test through the company's Web site at **www.prometric.com**. Or, you can register by phone at 800-755-3926 (within the United States or Canada) or at 410-843-8000 (outside the United States and Canada).

➤ *Virtual University Enterprises*—You can sign up for a test or get the phone numbers for local testing centers through the Web page at **www.vue.com/ms/**.

To sign up for a test, you must possess a valid credit card, or contact either company for mailing instructions to send them a check (in the United States). Only when payment is verified, or a check has cleared, can you actually register for a test.

To schedule an exam, call the number or visit either of the Web pages at least one day in advance. To cancel or reschedule an exam, you must call before 7 P.M. pacific standard time the day before the scheduled test time (or you may be charged, even if you don't appear to take the test). When you want to schedule a test, have the following information ready:

➤ Your name, organization, and mailing address.

➤ Your Microsoft Test ID. (Inside the United States, this means your Social Security number; citizens of other nations should call ahead to find out what type of identification number is required to register for a test.)

➤ The name and number of the exam you wish to take.

➤ A method of payment. (As we stated earlier; however, the Accelerated exam is free.)

Once you sign up for a test, you'll be informed as to when and where the test is scheduled. Try to arrive at least 15 minutes early.

THE EXAM SITUATION

When you arrive at the testing center where you scheduled your exam, you'll need to sign in with an exam coordinator. He or she will ask you to show two forms of identification, one of which must be a photo ID. After you've signed in and your time slot arrives, you'll be asked to deposit any books, bags, or other items you brought with you. Then, you'll be escorted into a closed room.

All exams are completely closed book. In fact, you will not be permitted to take anything with you into the testing area, but you will be furnished with a blank sheet of paper and a pen or, in some cases, an erasable plastic sheet and an erasable pen. Before the exam, you should memorize as much of the important material as you can, so you can write that information on the blank sheet as soon as you are seated in front of the computer. You can refer to this piece of paper anytime you like during the test, but you'll have to surrender the sheet when you leave the room.

You will have some time to compose yourself, to record this information, and to take a sample orientation exam before you begin the real thing. We suggest you take the orientation test before taking your first exam, but because they're all more or less identical in layout, behavior, and controls, you probably won't need to do this more than once.

Typically, the room will be furnished with anywhere from one to half a dozen computers, and each workstation will be separated from the others by dividers designed to keep you from seeing what's happening on someone else's computer. Most test rooms feature a wall with a large picture window. This permits the exam coordinator to monitor the room, to prevent exam-takers from talking to one another, and to observe anything out of the ordinary that might go on. The exam coordinator will have preloaded the appropriate Microsoft certification exam—for this book, that's Exam 70-240—and you'll be permitted to start as soon as you're seated in front of the computer.

All Microsoft certification exams allow a certain maximum amount of time in which to complete your work (this time is indicated on the exam by an on-screen counter/clock, so you can check the time remaining whenever you like). (Microsoft has announced that the Accelerated exam should take four hours, althoughsome testing centers are allowing six hours.) All Microsoft certification exams are computer generated. In addition to multiple choice, you'll encounter select and place (drag and drop), create a tree (categorization and prioritization), drag and connect, and build list and reorder (list prioritization) on most exams. Although this may sound quite simple, the questions are constructed not only to check your mastery of basic facts and figures about Windows 2000, but they also require you to evaluate one or more sets of circumstances or requirements. Often, you'll be asked to give more than one answer to a question. Likewise, you might be asked to select the best or most effective solution to a problem from a range of choices, all of which technically are correct. Taking the exam is quite an adventure, and it involves real thinking. This book shows you what to expect and how to deal with the potential problems, puzzles, and predicaments.

When you complete a Microsoft certification exam, the software will tell you whether you've passed or failed. Results are broken into several topic areas. Even if you fail, we suggest you ask for—and keep—the detailed report that the test administrator should print for you. You can use this report to help you prepare for another go-round, if needed.

In the next section, you'll learn more about how Microsoft test questions look and how they must be answered.

EXAM LAYOUT AND DESIGN

The format of Microsoft's Windows 2000 exams is different from that of its previous exams. For the design exams (70-219, 70-220, 70-221), each exam consists entirely of a series of case studies, and the questions can be of six types. For the Core Four exams (70-210, 70-215, 70-216, 70-217) and the Accelerated exam (70-240), the same six types of questions can appear, but you are not likely to encounter complex multiquestion case studies.

For design exams, each case study or "testlet" presents a detailed problem that you must read and analyze. Figure 1 shows an example of what a case study looks like. You must select the different tabs in the case study to view the entire case.

Following each case study is a set of questions related to the case study; these questions can be one of six types (which are discussed next). Careful attention to details provided in the case study is the key to success. Be prepared to toggle frequently between the case study and the questions as you work. Some of the case studies also include diagrams, which are called *exhibits*, that you'll need to examine closely to understand how to answer the questions.

Once you complete a case study, you can review all the questions and your answers. However, once you move on to the next case study, you may not be able to return to the previous case study and make any changes.

The six types of question formats are:

➤ Multiple choice, single answer

➤ Multiple choice, multiple answers

➤ Build list and reorder (list prioritization)

➤ Create a tree

➤ Drag and connect

➤ Select and place (drag and drop)

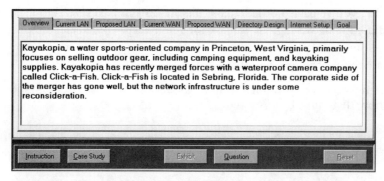

Figure 1 This is how case studies appear.

Note: Exam formats may vary by test center location. You may want to call the test center or visit **ExamCram.com** *to see if you can find out which type of test you'll encounter.*

Multiple-Choice Question Format

Some exam questions require you to select a single answer, whereas others ask you to select multiple correct answers. The following multiple-choice question requires you to select a single correct answer. Following the question is a brief summary of each potential answer and why it is either right or wrong.

Question 1

Andy Palmer is tasked with synchronizing his client's MS Exchange database with the client's Active Directory. The client needs to administer Microsoft Exchange objects from the Active Directory. What does Andy have to do to facilitate this type of administration?

○ a. Nothing; it is automatic.

○ b. An Exchange-to-Windows directory synchronization.

○ c. A Windows-to-Exchange directory synchronization.

○ d. Two-way directory synchronization.

Answer b is correct. To administer Exchange objects from Active Directory, Andy needs to create an Exchange-to-Windows directory synchronization.

This sample question format corresponds closely to the Microsoft certification exam format—the only difference on the exam is that questions are not followed by answer keys. To select an answer, you would position the cursor over the radio button next to the answer. Then, click the mouse button to select the answer.

Let's examine a question where one or more answers are possible. This type of question provides checkboxes rather than radio buttons for marking all appropriate selections.

Question 2

Andy is the architect for a Windows 2000 namespace. He needs to represent the zones on the plan. Which of the following are valid types of DNS zones? [Check all correct answers]

❑ a. Standard primary

❑ b. Standard secondary

❑ c. Incremental

❑ d. Active Directory integrated

Answers a, b, and d are correct. The standard primary, standard secondary, and Active Directory integrated are all valid DNS zone types in the Windows 2000 DNS service. Incremental is a type of zone transfer, not a type of zone.

> For this particular question, three answers are required. As far as the authors can tell (and Microsoft won't comment), such questions are scored as wrong unless all the required selections are chosen. In other words, a partially correct answer does not result in partial credit when the test is scored. For Question 2, you have to check the boxes next to items a, b, and d to obtain credit for a correct answer. Notice that picking the right answers also means knowing why the other answers are wrong!

Build-List-and-Reorder Question Format

> Questions in the build-list-and-reorder format present two lists of items—one on the left and one on the right. To answer the question, you must move items from the list on the right to the list on the left. The final list must then be reordered into a specific order.

> These questions can best be characterized as "From the following list of choices, pick the choices that answer the question. Arrange the list in a certain order." To give you practice with this type of question, some questions of this type are included in this study guide. Here's an example of how they appear in this book; for a sample of how they appear on the test, see Figure 2.

Question 3

From the following list of famous people, pick those that have been elected President of the United States. Arrange the list in the order that they served.

Thomas Jefferson

Ben Franklin

Abe Lincoln

George Washington

Andrew Jackson

Paul Revere

The correct answer is:

George Washington
Thomas Jefferson
Andrew Jackson
Abe Lincoln

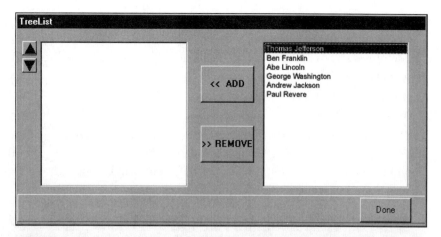

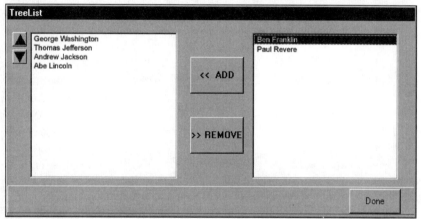

Figure 2   This is how build-list-and-reorder questions appear.

On an actual exam, the entire list of famous people would initially appear in the list on the right. You would move the four correct answers to the list on the left, and then reorder the list on the left. Notice that the answer to the question did not include all items from the initial list. However, this may not always be the case.

To move an item from the right list to the left list, first select the item by clicking on it, and then click on the Add button (left arrow). Once you move an item from one list to the other, you can move the item back by first selecting the item and then clicking on the appropriate button (either the Add button or the Remove button). Once items have been moved to the left list, you can reorder an item by selecting the item and clicking on the up or down button.

Create-a-Tree Question Format

Questions in the create-a-tree format also present two lists—one on the left side of the screen and one on the right side of the screen. The list on the right consists of individual items, and the list on the left consists of nodes in a tree. To answer the question, you must move items from the list on the right to the appropriate node in the tree.

These questions can best be characterized as simply a matching exercise. Items from the list on the right are placed under the appropriate category in the list on the left. Here's an example of how they appear in this book; for a sample of how they appear on the test, see Figure 3.

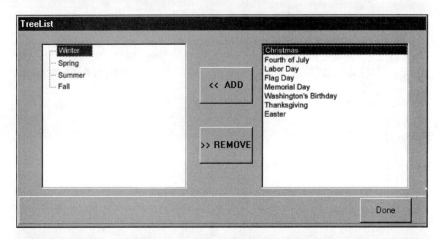

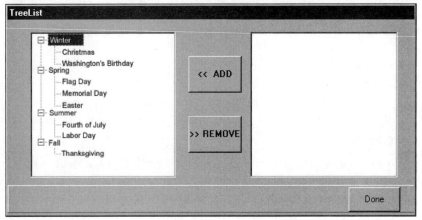

Figure 3   This is how create-a-tree questions appear.

Question 4

The calendar year is divided into four seasons:

Winter

Spring

Summer

Fall

Identify the season when each of the following holidays occurs:

Christmas

Fourth of July

Labor Day

Flag Day

Memorial Day

Washington's Birthday

Thanksgiving

Easter

The correct answer is:

Winter
    Christmas
    Washington's Birthday
Spring
    Flag Day
    Memorial Day
    Easter
Summer
    Fourth of July
    Labor Day
Fall
    Thanksgiving

In this case, all the items in the list were used. However, this may not always be the case.

To move an item from the right list to its appropriate location in the tree, you must first select the appropriate tree node by clicking on it. Then, you select the item to be moved and click on the Add button. If one or more items have been added to a tree node, the node will be displayed with a "+" icon to the left of the node name. You can click on this icon to expand the node and view the item(s) that have been added. If any item has been added to the wrong tree node, you can remove it by selecting it and clicking on the Remove button.

Drag-and-Connect Question Format

Questions in the drag-and-connect format present a group of objects and a list of "connections." To answer the question, you must move the appropriate connections between the objects.

This type of question is best described using graphics. Here's an example.

Question 5

The following objects represent the different states of water:

| Ice | Water Vapor | Water | Steam |

Use items from the following list to connect the objects so that they are scientifically correct.

Sublimates to form

Freezes to form

Evaporates to form

Boils to form

Condenses to form

Melts to form

The correct answer is:

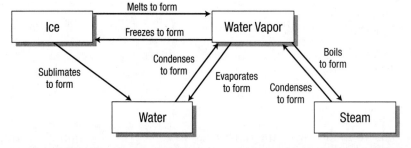

For this type of question, it's not necessary to use every object, and each connection can be used multiple times.

Select-and-Place Question Format

Questions in the select-and-place (drag-and-drop) format present a diagram with blank boxes, and a list of labels that need to be dragged to correctly fill in the blank boxes. To answer the question, you must move the labels to their appropriate positions on the diagram.

This type of question is best described using graphics. Here's an example.

Question 6

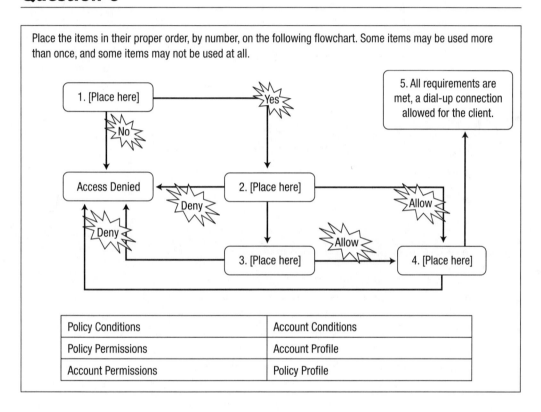

Place the items in their proper order, by number, on the following flowchart. Some items may be used more than once, and some items may not be used at all.

Policy Conditions	Account Conditions
Policy Permissions	Account Profile
Account Permissions	Policy Profile

The correct answer is:

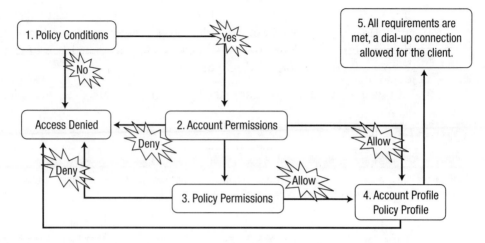

MICROSOFT'S TESTING FORMATS

Currently, Microsoft uses four different testing formats:

➤ Case study

➤ Fixed length

➤ Adaptive

➤ Short form

As we mentioned earlier, the case study approach is used with Microsoft's design exams. These exams consist of a set of case studies that you must analyze to enable you to answer questions related to the case studies. Such exams include one or more case studies (tabbed topic areas), each of which is followed by 4 to 10 questions. The question types for design exams, for Core Four exams, and for the Accelerated Windows 2000 exam are multiple choice, build list and reorder, create a tree, drag and connect, and select and place. Depending on the test topic, some exams are totally case-based, whereas others are not.

Other Microsoft exams employ advanced testing capabilities that might not be immediately apparent. Although the questions that appear are primarily multiple choice, the logic that drives them is more complex than older Microsoft tests, which use a fixed sequence of questions, called a *fixed-length test*. Some questions employ a sophisticated user interface, which Microsoft calls a *simulation*, to test your knowledge of the software and systems under consideration in a more or less "live" environment that behaves just like the original. The Testing Innovations link at **www.microsoft.com/trainingandservices/default.asp?PageID=mcp** includes a downloadable practice simulation.

For some exams, Microsoft has turned to a well-known technique, called *adaptive testing*, to establish a test-taker's level of knowledge and product competence. Adaptive exams look the same as fixed-length exams, but they discover the level of difficulty at which an individual test-taker can correctly answer questions. Test-takers with differing levels of knowledge or ability therefore see different sets of questions; individuals with high levels of knowledge or ability are presented with a smaller set of more difficult questions, whereas individuals with lower levels of knowledge are presented with a larger set of easier questions. Two individuals may answer the same percentage of questions correctly, but the test-taker with a higher knowledge or ability level will score higher because his or her questions are worth more.

Also, the lower-level test-taker will probably answer more questions than his or her more-knowledgeable colleague. This explains why adaptive tests use ranges of values to define the number of questions and the amount of time it takes to complete the test.

Adaptive tests work by evaluating the test-taker's most recent answer. A correct answer leads to a more difficult question (and the test software's estimate of the test-taker's knowledge and ability level is raised). An incorrect answer leads to a less difficult question (and the test software's estimate of the test-taker's knowledge and ability level is lowered). This process continues until the test targets the test-taker's true ability level. The exam ends when the test-taker's level of accuracy meets a statistically acceptable value (in other words, when his or her performance demonstrates an acceptable level of knowledge and ability), or when the maximum number of items has been presented (in which case, the test-taker is almost certain to fail).

Microsoft also introduced a short-form test for its most popular tests. This test delivers 30 questions to its takers, giving them exactly 60 minutes to complete the exam. This type of exam is similar to a fixed-length test, in that it allows readers to jump ahead or return to earlier questions, and to cycle through the questions until the test is done. Microsoft does not use adaptive logic in this test, but claims that statistical analysis of the question pool is such that the 30 questions delivered during a short-form exam conclusively measure a test-taker's knowledge of the subject matter in much the same way as an adaptive test. You can think of the short-form test as a kind of "greatest hits exam" (that is, the most important questions are covered) version of an adaptive exam on the same topic.

Note: *Several test-takers have reported that some of the Microsoft exams can appear as a combination of adaptive and fixed-length questions.*

Microsoft tests can come in any one of these forms. Whatever you encounter, you must take the test in whichever form it appears; you can't choose one form over another. If anything, it pays more to prepare thoroughly for an adaptive exam than for a fixed-length or a short-form exam: The penalties for answering incorrectly are built into the test itself on an adaptive exam, whereas the layout remains the same for a fixed-length or short-form test, no matter how many questions you answer incorrectly.

. . . .

Tip: The biggest difference between an adaptive test and a fixed-length or short-form test is that on a fixed-length or short-form test, you can revisit questions after you've read them over one or more times. On an adaptive test, you must answer the question when it's presented and will have no opportunities to revisit that question thereafter.

. . . .

STRATEGIES FOR DIFFERENT TESTING FORMATS

Before you choose a test-taking strategy, you must know if your test is case study based, fixed length, short form, or adaptive. When you begin your exam, you'll know right away if the test is based on case studies. The interface will consist of a tabbed Window that allows you to easily navigate through the sections of the case.

If you are taking a test that is not based on case studies, the software will tell you that the test is adaptive, if in fact the version you're taking is an adaptive test. If your introductory materials fail to mention this, you're probably taking a fixed-length test (50 to 70 questions). If the total number of questions involved is 25 to 30, you're taking a short-form test. Some tests announce themselves by indicating that they will start with a set of adaptive questions, followed by fixed-length questions.

. . . .

Tip: You'll be able to tell for sure if you are taking an adaptive, fixed-length, or short-form test by the first question. If it includes a checkbox that lets you mark the question for later review, you're taking a fixed-length or short-form test. If the total number of questions is 25 to 30, it's a short-form test; if more than 30, it's a fixed-length test. Adaptive test questions can be visited (and answered) only once, and they include no such checkbox.

. . . .

The Case Study Exam Strategy

Most test-takers find that the case study type of test used for the design exams (70-219, 70-220, and 70-221) is the most difficult to master. When it comes to studying for a case study test, your best bet is to approach each case study as a standalone test. The biggest challenge you'll encounter is that you'll feel that you won't have enough time to get through all of the cases that are presented.

Tip: Each case provides a lot of material that you'll need to read and study before you can effectively answer the questions that follow. The trick to taking a case study exam is to first scan the case study to get the highlights. Make sure you read the overview section of the case so that you understand the context of the problem at hand. Then, quickly move on and scan the questions.

As you are scanning the questions, make mental notes to yourself so that you'll remember which sections of the case study you should focus on. Some case studies may provide a fair amount of extra information that you don't really need to answer the questions. The goal with our scanning approach is to avoid having to study and analyze material that is not completely relevant.

When studying a case, carefully read the tabbed information. It is important to answer each and every question. You will be able to toggle back and forth from case to questions, and from question to question within a case testlet. However, once you leave the case and move on, you may not be able to return to it. You may want to take notes while reading useful information so you can refer to them when you tackle the test questions. It's hard to go wrong with this strategy when taking any kind of Microsoft certification test.

The Fixed-Length and Short-Form Exam Strategy

A well-known principle when taking fixed-length or short-form exams is to first read over the entire exam from start to finish while answering only those questions you feel absolutely sure of. On subsequent passes, you can dive into more complex questions more deeply, knowing how many such questions you have left.

Fortunately, the Microsoft exam software for fixed-length and short-form tests makes the multiple-visit approach easy to implement. At the top-left corner of each question is a checkbox that permits you to mark that question for a later visit.

Note: *Marking questions makes review easier, but you can return to any question by clicking the Forward or Back button repeatedly.*

As you read each question, if you answer only those you're sure of and mark for review those that you're not sure of, you can keep working through a decreasing list of questions as you answer the trickier ones in order.

Tip: There's at least one potential benefit to reading the exam over completely before answering the trickier questions: Sometimes, information supplied in later questions sheds more light on earlier questions. At other times, information you read in later questions might jog your memory about Windows 2000 facts, figures, or behavior that helps you answer earlier questions. Either way, you'll come out ahead if you defer those questions about which you're not absolutely sure.

Here are some question-handling strategies that apply to fixed-length and short-form tests. Use them if you have the chance:

➤ When returning to a question after your initial read-through, read every word again—otherwise, your mind can fall quickly into a rut. Sometimes, revisiting a question after turning your attention elsewhere lets you see something you missed, but the strong tendency is to see what you've seen before. Try to avoid that tendency at all costs.

➤ If you return to a question more than twice, try to articulate to yourself what you don't understand about the question, why answers don't appear to make sense, or what appears to be missing. If you chew on the subject awhile, your subconscious might provide the details you lack, or you might notice a "trick" that points to the right answer.

As you work your way through the exam, another counter that Microsoft provides will come in handy—the number of questions completed and questions outstanding. For fixed-length and short-form tests, it's wise to budget your time by making sure that you've completed one-quarter of the questions one-quarter of the way through the exam period, and three-quarters of the questions three-quarters of the way through.

If you're not finished when only five minutes remain, use that time to guess your way through any remaining questions. Remember, guessing is potentially more valuable than not answering, because blank answers are always wrong, but a guess may turn out to be right. If you don't have a clue about any of the remaining questions, pick answers at random, or choose all a's, b's, and so on. The important thing is to submit an exam for scoring that has an answer for every question.

Tip: At the very end of your exam period, you're better off guessing than leaving questions unanswered.

The Adaptive Exam Strategy

If there's one principle that applies to taking an adaptive test, it could be summed up as "Get it right the first time." You cannot elect to skip a question and move on to the next one when taking an adaptive test, because the testing software uses your answer to the current question to select whatever question it plans to present next. Nor can you return to a question once you've moved on, because the software gives you only one chance to answer the question. You can, however, take notes, because sometimes information supplied in earlier questions will shed more light on later questions.

Also, when you answer a question correctly, you are presented with a more difficult question next, to help the software gauge your level of skill and ability. When you answer a question incorrectly, you are presented with a less difficult question, and the software lowers its current estimate of your skill and ability. This continues until the program settles into a reasonably accurate estimate of what you know and can do, and takes you on average through somewhere between 15 and 30 questions as you complete the test.

The good news is that if you know your stuff, you'll probably finish most adaptive tests in 30 minutes or so. The bad news is that you must really, really know your stuff to do your best on an adaptive test. That's because some questions are so convoluted, complex, or hard to follow that you're bound to miss one or two, at a minimum, even if you do know your stuff. So the more you know, the better you'll do on an adaptive test, even accounting for the occasionally weird or unfathomable questions that appear on these exams.

. . . .

Tip: Because you can't always tell in advance if a test is fixed length, short form, or adaptive, you will be best served by preparing for the exam as if it were adaptive. That way, you should be prepared to pass no matter what kind of test you take. But if you do take a fixed-length or short-form test, remember our tips from the preceding section. They should help you improve on what you could do on an adaptive test.

. . . .

If you encounter a question on an adaptive test that you can't answer, you must guess an answer immediately. Because of how the software works, you may suffer for your guess on the next question if you guess right, because you'll get a more difficult question next!

QUESTION-HANDLING STRATEGIES

Based on exams we have taken, some interesting trends have become apparent. For those questions that take only a single answer, usually two or three of the answers will be obviously incorrect, and two of the answers will be plausible—of course, only one can be correct. Unless the answer leaps out at you (if it does, reread the question to look for a trick; sometimes those are the ones you're most likely to get wrong), begin the process of answering by eliminating those answers that are most obviously wrong.

Almost always, at least one answer out of the possible choices for a question can be eliminated immediately because it matches one of these conditions:

➤ The answer does not apply to the situation.

➤ The answer describes a nonexistent issue, an invalid option, or an imaginary state.

After you eliminate all answers that are obviously wrong, you can apply your retained knowledge to eliminate further answers. Look for items that sound correct but refer to actions, commands, or features that are not present or not available in the situation that the question describes.

If you're still faced with a blind guess among two or more potentially correct answers, reread the question. Try to picture how each of the possible remaining answers would alter the situation. Be especially sensitive to terminology; sometimes the choice of words ("remove" instead of "disable") can make the difference between a right answer and a wrong one.

Only when you've exhausted your ability to eliminate answers, but remain unclear about which of the remaining possibilities is correct, should you guess at an answer. An unanswered question offers you no points, but guessing gives you at least some chance of getting a question right; just don't be too hasty when making a blind guess.

Note: If you're taking a fixed-length or a short-form test, you can wait until the last round of reviewing marked questions (just as you're about to run out of time, or out of unanswered questions) before you start making guesses. You will have the same option within each case study testlet (but once you leave a testlet, you may not be allowed to return to it). If you're taking an adaptive test, you'll have to guess to move on to the next question if you can't figure out an answer some other way. Either way, guessing should be your technique of last resort!

Numerous questions assume that the default behavior of a particular utility is in effect. If you know the defaults and understand what they mean, this knowledge will help you cut through many Gordian knots.

MASTERING THE INNER GAME

In the final analysis, knowledge breeds confidence, and confidence breeds success. If you study the materials in this book carefully and review all the practice questions at the end of each chapter, you should become aware of those areas where additional learning and study are required.

After you've worked your way through the book, take the practice exam in the back of the book and the practice exams on the CD-ROM. Be sure to click on the Update button in our CD-ROM's testing engine to download additional free questions from **ExamCram.com**! Taking tests will provide a reality check and help you identify areas to study further. Make sure you follow up and review materials related to the questions you miss on the practice exams before scheduling a real exam. Only when you've covered that ground and feel comfortable with the whole scope of the practice exams should you set an exam appointment. Only if you score 85 percent or better should you proceed to the real thing (otherwise, obtain some additional practice tests so you can keep trying until you hit this magic number).

. . . .

Tip: If you take a practice exam and don't score at least 85 percent correct, you'll want to practice further. Microsoft provides links to practice exam providers and also offers self-assessment exams at **www.microsoft.com/trainingandservices/**). You should also check out **ExamCram.com** for downloadable practice questions.

. . . .

Armed with the information in this book and with the determination to augment your knowledge, you should be able to pass the certification exam. However, you need to work at it, because if you don't pass you will not be able to take the test again. If you prepare seriously, you should do well. We are confident that you can do it!

The next section covers the exam requirements for the various Microsoft certifications.

THE MICROSOFT CERTIFIED PROFESSIONAL (MCP) PROGRAM

The MCP Program currently includes the following separate tracks, each of which boasts its own special acronym (as a certification candidate, you need to have a high tolerance for alphabet soup of all kinds):

➤ *MCP (Microsoft Certified Professional)*—This is the least prestigious of all the certification tracks from Microsoft. Passing one of the major Microsoft exams qualifies an individual for the MCP credential. Individuals can demonstrate proficiency with additional Microsoft products by passing additional certification exams.

➤ *MCP+SB (Microsoft Certified Professional + Site Building)*—This certification program is designed for individuals who are planning, building, managing, and maintaining Web sites. Individuals with the MCP+SB credential will have demonstrated the ability to develop Web sites that include multimedia and searchable content and Web sites that connect to and communicate with a back-end database. It requires one MCP exam, plus two of these three exams: "70-055: Designing and Implementing Web Sites with Microsoft FrontPage 98,"

"70-057: Designing and Implementing Commerce Solutions with Microsoft Site Server, 3.0, Commerce Edition," and "70-152: Designing and Implementing Web Solutions with Microsoft Visual InterDev 6.0."

➤ *MCSE (Microsoft Certified Systems Engineer)*—Anyone who has a current MCSE is warranted to possess a high level of networking expertise with Microsoft operating systems and products. This credential is designed to prepare individuals to plan, implement, maintain, and support information systems, networks, and internetworks built around Microsoft Windows 2000 and its BackOffice family of products.

To obtain an MCSE, an individual must pass four core operating system exams, one core option exam, and two elective exams. The operating system exams require individuals to prove their competence with desktop and server operating systems and networking/internetworking components.

For Windows NT 4 MCSEs, the Accelerated exam, "70-240: Microsoft Windows 2000 Accelerated Exam for MCPs Certified on Microsoft Windows NT 4.0," is an option. This free exam covers all of the material tested in the Core Four exams. The hitch in this plan is that you can take the test only once. If you fail, you must take all four core exams to recertify. The Core Four exams are: "70-210: Installing, Configuring and Administering Microsoft Windows 2000 Professional," "70-215: Installing, Configuring and Administering Microsoft Windows 2000 Server," "70-216: Implementing and Administering a Microsoft Windows 2000 Network Infrastructure," and "70-217: Implementing and Administering a Microsoft Windows 2000 Directory Services Infrastructure."

The two remaining exams are electives. An elective exam may fall in any number of subject or product areas, primarily BackOffice components. To fulfill the fifth core exam requirement, you can choose from three design exams: "70-219: Designing a Microsoft Windows 2000 Directory Services Infrastructure," "70-220: Designing Security for a Microsoft Windows 2000 Network," or "70-221: Designing a Microsoft Windows 2000 Network Infrastructure." The two design exams that you don't select as your fifth core exam also qualify as electives. If you are on your way to becoming an MCSE and have already taken some exams, visit **www.microsoft.com/mcp/certstep/mcse.htm** for information about how to complete your MCSE certification.

In September 1999, Microsoft announced its Windows 2000 track for MCSE and also announced retirement of Windows NT 4.0 MCSE core exams on 12/31/2000. Individuals who wish to remain certified MCSEs after 12/31/2001 must "upgrade" their certifications on or before 12/31/2001. For more detailed information than is included here, visit **www.microsoft.com/mcp/certstep/mcse.htm**.

New MCSE candidates must pass seven tests to meet the MCSE requirements. It's not uncommon for the entire process to take a year or so, and many individuals find that they must take a test more than once to pass. The primary goal of the *Exam Prep* series and the *Exam Cram* series, our test preparation books, is to make it possible, given proper study and preparation, to pass all Microsoft certification tests on the first try. Table 1 shows the required and elective exams for the Windows 2000 MCSE certification.

➤ *MCSD (Microsoft Certified Solution Developer)*—The MCSD credential reflects the skills required to create multi-tier, distributed, and COM-based solutions, in addition to desktop and Internet applications, using new technologies. To obtain an MCSD, an individual must demonstrate the ability to analyze and interpret user requirements; select and integrate products, platforms, tools, and technologies; design and implement code, and customize applications; and perform necessary software tests and quality assurance operations.

To become an MCSD, you must pass a total of four exams: three core exams and one elective exam. Each candidate must choose one of these three desktop application exams—"70-016: Designing and Implementing Desktop Applications with Microsoft Visual C++ 6.0," "70-156: Designing and Implementing Desktop Applications with Microsoft Visual FoxPro 6.0," or "70-176: Designing and Implementing Desktop Applications with Microsoft Visual Basic 6.0"—*plus* one of these three distributed application exams—"70-015: Designing and Implementing Distributed Applications with Microsoft Visual C++ 6.0," "70-155: Designing and Implementing Desktop Applications with Microsoft Visual FoxPro 6.0," or "70-175: Designing and Implementing Desktop Applications with Microsoft Visual Basic 6.0." The third core exam is "70-100: Analyzing Requirements and Defining Solution Architectures." Elective exams cover specific Microsoft applications and languages, including Visual Basic, C++, the Microsoft Foundation Classes, Access, SQL Server, Excel, and more.

➤ *MCDBA (Microsoft Certified Database Administrator)*—The MCDBA credential reflects the skills required to implement and administer Microsoft SQL Server databases. To obtain an MCDBA, an individual must demonstrate the ability to derive physical database designs, develop logical data models, create physical databases, create data services by using Transact-SQL, manage and maintain databases, configure and manage security, monitor and optimize databases, and install and configure Microsoft SQL Server.

To become an MCDBA, you must pass a total of four exams and one elective exam. The required core exams are "70-028: Administering Microsoft SQL Server 7.0," "70-029: Designing and Implementing Databases with Microsoft SQL Server 7.0," and "70-215: Installing, Configuring and Administering Microsoft Windows 2000 Server."

Table 1   MCSE Windows 2000 Requirements

Core

If you have not passed these 3 Windows NT 4 exams	
Exam 70-067	Implementing and Supporting Microsoft Windows NT Server 4.0
Exam 70-068	Implementing and Supporting Microsoft Windows NT Server 4.0 in the Enterprise
Exam 70-073	Microsoft Windows NT Workstation 4.0
then you must take these 4 exams	
Exam 70-210	Installing, Configuring and Administering Microsoft Windows 2000 Professional
Exam 70-215	Installing, Configuring and Administering Microsoft Windows 2000 Server
Exam 70-216	Implementing and Administering a Microsoft Windows 2000 Network Infrastructure
Exam 70-217	Implementing and Administering a Microsoft Windows 2000 Directory Services Infrastructure
If you have already passed exams 70-067, 70-068, and 70-073, you may take this exam	
Exam 70-240	Microsoft Windows 2000 Accelerated Exam for MCPs Certified on Microsoft Windows NT 4.0

5th Core Option

Choose 1 from this group	
Exam 70-219*	Designing a Microsoft Windows 2000 Directory Services Infrastructure
Exam 70-220*	Designing Security for a Microsoft Windows 2000 Network
Exam 70-221*	Designing a Microsoft Windows 2000 Network Infrastructure

Elective

Choose 2 from this group	
Exam 70-019	Designing and Implementing Data Warehouse with Microsoft SQL Server 7.0
Exam 70-219*	Designing a Microsoft Windows 2000 Directory Services Infrastructure
Exam 70-220*	Designing Security for a Microsoft Windows 2000 Network
Exam 70-221*	Designing a Microsoft Windows 2000 Network Infrastructure
Exam 70-222	Migrating from Microsoft Windows NT 4.0 to Microsoft Windows 2000
Exam 70-028	Administering Microsoft SQL Server 7.0
Exam 70-029	Designing and Implementing Databases on Microsoft SQL Server 7.0
Exam 70-080	Implementing and Supporting Microsoft Internet Explorer 5.0 by Using the Internet Explorer Administration Kit
Exam 70-081	Implementing and Supporting Microsoft Exchange Server 5.5
Exam 70-085	Implementing and Supporting Microsoft SNA Server 4.0
Exam 70-086	Implementing and Supporting Microsoft Systems Management Server 2.0
Exam 70-088	Implementing and Supporting Microsoft Proxy Server 2.0

This is not a complete listing—you can still be tested on some earlier versions of these products. However, we have included mainly the most recent versions so that you may test on these versions and thus be certified longer. We have not included any tests that are scheduled to be retired.

* The 5th Core Option exam does not double as an elective.

The elective exams that you can choose from cover specific uses of SQL Server and include "70-015: Designing and Implementing Distributed Applications with Microsoft Visual C++ 6.0," "70-019: Designing and Implementing Data Warehouses with Microsoft SQL Server 7.0," "70-155: Designing and Implementing Distributed Applications with Visual FoxPro 6.0," "70-175: Designing and Implementing Distributed Applications with Visual Basic 6.0," and two exams that relate to Windows 2000: "70-216: Implementing and Administering Microsoft Windows 2000 Network Infrastructure," and "70-087: Implementing and Supporting Microsoft Internet Information Server 4.0."

If you have taken the three core Windows NT 4 exams on your path to becoming an MCSE, you qualify for the Accelerated exam (it replaces the Network Infrastructure exam requirement). The Accelerated exam covers the objectives of all four of the Windows 2000 core exams. In addition to taking the Accelerated exam, you must take only the two SQL exams—Administering and Database Design. Table 2 shows the requirements for the MCDBA certification.

➤ *MCT (Microsoft Certified Trainer)*—Microsoft Certified Trainers are deemed able to deliver elements of the official Microsoft curriculum, based on technical knowledge and instructional ability. Thus, it is necessary for an individual seeking MCT credentials (which are granted on a course-by-course basis) to pass the related certification exam for a course and complete the official Microsoft training in the subject area, and to demonstrate an ability to teach. MCT candidates must also possess a current MCSE.

This teaching skill criterion may be satisfied by proving that one has already attained training certification from Novell, Banyan, Lotus, the Santa Cruz Operation, or Cisco, or by taking a Microsoft-sanctioned workshop on instruction. Microsoft makes it clear that MCTs are important cogs in the Microsoft training channels. Instructors must be MCTs before Microsoft will allow them to teach in any of its official training channels, including Microsoft's affiliated Certified Technical Education Centers (CTECs) and its online training partner network.

Microsoft has announced that the MCP+I and MCSE+I credentials will not be continued when the MCSE exams for Windows 2000 are in full swing because the skill set for the Internet portion of the program has been included in the new MCSE program. Therefore, details on these tracks are not provided here; go to **www.microsoft.com/trainingandservices/** if you need more information.

Table 2   MCDBA Requirements

Core

If you have not passed these 3 Windows NT 4 exams	
Exam 70-067	Implementing and Supporting Microsoft Windows NT Server 4.0
Exam 70-068	Implementing and Supporting Microsoft Windows NT Server 4.0 in the Enterprise
Exam 70-073	Microsoft Windows NT Workstation 4.0
you must take this exam	
Exam 70-215	Installing, Configuring and Administering Microsoft Windows 2000 Server
plus these 2 exams	
Exam 70-028	Administering Microsoft SQL Server 7.0
Exam 70-029	Designing and Implementing Databases with Microsoft SQL Server 7.0

Elective

Choose 1 of the following exams	
Exam 70-015	Designing and Implementing Distributed Applications with Microsoft Visual C++ 6.0
Exam 70-019	Designing and Implementing Data Warehouses with Microsoft SQL Server 7.0
Exam 70-087	Implementing and Supporting Microsoft Internet Information Server 4.0
Exam 70-155	Designing and Implementing Distributed Applications with Microsoft Visual FoxPro 6.0
Exam 70-175	Designing and Implementing Distributed Applications with Microsoft Visual Basic 6.0
Exam 70-216	Implementing and Administering a Microsoft Windows 2000 Network Infrastructure

OR

If you have already passed exams 70-067, 70-068, and 70-073, you may take this exam	
Exam 70-240	Microsoft Windows 2000 Accelerated Exam for MCPs Certified on Microsoft Windows NT 4.0
plus these 2 exams	
Exam 70-028	Administering Microsoft SQL Server 7.0
Exam 70-029	Designing and Implementing Databases with Microsoft SQL Server 7.0

Once a Microsoft product becomes obsolete, MCPs typically have to recertify on current versions. (If individuals do not recertify, their certifications become invalid.) Because technology keeps changing and new products continually supplant old ones, this should come as no surprise. This explains why Microsoft has announced that MCSEs have 12 months past the scheduled retirement date for the Windows NT 4 exams to recertify on Windows 2000 topics. (Note that this means taking at least two exams, if not more.)

The best place to keep tabs on the MCP Program and its related certifications is on the Web. The URL for the MCP program is **www.microsoft.com/mcp/**. But Microsoft's Web site changes often, so if this URL doesn't work, try using the Search tool on Microsoft's site with either "MCP" or the quoted phrase "Microsoft Certified Professional Program" as a search string. This will help you find the latest and most accurate information about Microsoft's certification programs.

TRACKING MCP STATUS

As soon as you pass any Microsoft exam (except Networking Essentials), you'll attain Microsoft Certified Professional (MCP) status. Microsoft also generates transcripts that indicate which exams you have passed and your corresponding test scores. You can view a copy of your transcript at any time by going to the MCP secured site and selecting Transcript Tool. This tool will allow you to print a copy of your current transcript and confirm your certification status.

Once you pass the necessary set of exams (one for MCP, seven for MCSE), you'll be certified. Official certification normally takes anywhere from six to eight weeks, so don't expect to get your credentials overnight. When the package for a qualified certification arrives, it includes a Welcome Kit that contains a number of elements (see Microsoft's Web site for other benefits of specific certifications):

➤ A certificate suitable for framing, along with a wallet card and a lapel pin.

➤ A license to use the MCP logo, thereby allowing you to use the logo in advertisements, promotions, and documents, and on letterhead, business cards, and so on. Along with the license comes an MCP logo sheet, which includes camera-ready artwork. (Note: Before using any of the artwork, individuals must sign and return a licensing agreement that indicates they'll abide by its terms and conditions.)

➤ A subscription to *Microsoft Certified Professional Magazine*, which provides ongoing data about testing and certification activities, requirements, and changes to the program.

Many people believe that the benefits of MCP certification go well beyond the perks that Microsoft provides to newly anointed members of this elite group. We're starting to see more job listings that request or require applicants to have an MCP, MCSE, and so on, and many individuals who complete the program can qualify for increases in pay and/or responsibility. As an official recognition of hard work and broad knowledge, one of the MCP credentials is a badge of honor in many IT organizations.

ABOUT THE BOOK

Career opportunities abound for well-prepared Windows 2000 administrators. This book is designed as your doorway into Windows 2000 certification and administration. If you are new to Windows 2000, this is your ticket to an exciting future. Others who have prior experience with Windows 2000 will find that the book adds depth and breadth to that experience. Also, the book provides the knowledge you need to prepare for Microsoft's certification Exam 70-240, "Microsoft Windows 2000 Accelerated Exam for MCPs Certified on Microsoft Windows NT 4.0"

Because Windows 2000 is to closely tied to BackOffice and other Microsoft products, it is marvelously scalable and fits into both large and small organizations. It provides the cornerstone on which to build an Internet Web site, or an application server, while protecting the rest of your network from the outside world. The success of Windows 2000 Server is reflected in the huge number of software vendors and developers who develop in this environment or who have switched from other environments to Windows 2000 Server.

When you complete this book, you will be at the threshold of a Windows 2000 network administration career that can be very fulfilling and challenging. This is a rapidly advancing field that offers ample opportunity for personal growth and for making a contribution to your business or organization. The book is intended to provide you with knowledge that you can apply right away and a sound basis for understanding the changes that you will encounter in the future. It also is intended to give you the hands-on skills you need to be a valued professional in your organization.

The book is filled with real-world projects that cover every aspect of installing and managing Windows 2000 Server. The projects are designed to make what you learn come alive through actually performing the tasks. Also, every chapter includes a range of practice questions to help prepare you for the Microsoft certification exam. All of these features are offered to reinforce your learning, so you'll feel confident in the knowledge you have gained from each chapter.

Features

To aid you in fully understanding Windows 2000 concepts, there are many features in this book designed to improve its value:

➤ *Chapter objectives*—Each chapter in this book begins with a detailed list of the topics to be mastered within that chapter. This list provides you with a quick reference to the contents of that chapter, as well as a useful study aid.

➤ *Illustrations and tables*—Numerous illustrations of screenshots and components aid you in the visualization of common setup steps, theories, and concepts. In addition, many tables provide details and comparisons of both practical and theoretical information.

➤ *Notes, tips, and warnings*—Notes present additional helpful material related to the subject being described. Tips from the author's experience provide extra information about how to attack a problem, how to set up Windows 2000 for a particular need, or what to do in certain real-world situations.

Warnings are included to help you anticipate potential mistakes or problems so you can prevent them from happening.

➤ *Chapter summaries*—Each chapter's text is followed by a summary of the concepts it has introduced. These summaries provide a helpful way to recap and revisit the ideas covered in each chapter.

➤ *Review questions*—End-of-chapter assessment begins with a set of review questions that reinforce the ideas introduced in each chapter. These questions not only ensure that you have mastered the concepts, but are written to help prepare you for the Microsoft certification examination. Answers to these questions are found in Appendix A.

➤ *Real-world projects*—Although it is important to understand the theory behind server and networking technology, nothing can improve upon real-world experience. To this end, along with theoretical explanations, each chapter provides numerous hands-on projects aimed at providing you with real-world implementation experience.

➤ *Sample tests*—Use the sample test and answer key in Chapters 22 and 23 to test yourself. Then, move on to the interactive practice exams found on the CD-ROM. The testing engine offers a variety of testing formats to choose from.

WHERE SHOULD YOU START?

This book is intended to be read in sequence, from beginning to end. Each chapter builds upon those that precede it, to provide a solid understanding of Windows 2000. After completing the chapters, you may find it useful to go back through the book and use the review questions and projects to prepare for the Microsoft certification test for the Windows 2000 Accelerated exam (Exam 70-240). Readers are also encouraged to investigate the many pointers to online and printed sources of additional information that are cited throughout this book.

Please share your feedback on the book with us, especially if you have ideas about how we can improve it for future readers. We'll consider everything you say carefully, and we'll respond to all suggestions. Send your questions or comments to us at **learn@examcram.com**. Please remember to include the title of the book in your message; otherwise, we'll be forced to guess which book you're writing about. And we don't like to guess—we want to *know*! Also, be sure to check out the Web pages at **www.examcram.com**, where you'll find information updates, commentary, and certification information. Thanks, and enjoy the book!

SELF-ASSESSMENT

The reason we included a Self-Assessment in this *Exam Prep* book is to help you evaluate your readiness to tackle MCSE certification. It should also help you understand what you need to know to master the topic of this book—namely, Exam 70-240, "Microsoft Windows 2000 Accelerated Exam for MCPs Certified on Microsoft Windows NT 4.0." But before you tackle this Self-Assessment, let's talk about concerns you may face when pursuing an MCSE for Windows 2000, and what an ideal MCSE candidate might look like.

MCSEs in the Real World

In the next section, we describe an ideal MCSE candidate, knowing full well that only a few real candidates will meet this ideal. In fact, our description of that ideal candidate might seem downright scary, especially with the changes that have been made to the program to support Windows 2000. But take heart: Although the requirements to obtain an MCSE may seem formidable, they are by no means impossible to meet. However, be keenly aware that it does take time, involves some expense, and requires real effort to get through the process.

Increasing numbers of people are attaining Microsoft certifications, so the goal is within reach. You can get all the real-world motivation you need from knowing that many others have gone before, so you will be able to follow in their footsteps. If you're willing to tackle the process seriously and do what it takes to obtain the necessary experience and knowledge, you can take—and pass—all the certification tests involved in obtaining an MCSE. In fact, we've designed *Exam Preps*, the companion *Exam Crams*, *Exam Cram Personal Trainers*, and *Exam Cram Personal Test Centers* to make it as easy on you as possible to prepare for these exams. We've also greatly expanded our Web site, **www.examcram.com**, to provide a host of resources to help you prepare for the complexities of Windows 2000.

Besides MCSE, other Microsoft certifications include:

➤ MCSD, which is aimed at software developers and requires one specific exam, two more exams on client and distributed topics, plus a fourth elective exam drawn from a different, but limited, pool of options.

➤ Other Microsoft certifications, whose requirements range from one test (MCP) to several tests (MCP+SB, MCDBA).

THE IDEAL WINDOWS 2000 MCSE CANDIDATE

Just to give you some idea of what an ideal MCSE candidate is like, here are some relevant statistics about the background and experience such an individual might have. Don't worry if you don't meet these qualifications, or don't come that close—this is a far from ideal world, and where you fall short is simply where you'll have more work to do.

➤ Academic or professional training in network theory, concepts, and operations. This includes everything from networking media and transmission techniques through network operating systems, services, and applications.

➤ Three-plus years of professional networking experience, including experience with Ethernet, token ring, modems, and other networking media. This must include installation, configuration, upgrade, and troubleshooting experience.

Note: The Windows 2000 MCSE program is much more rigorous than the previous NT MCSE program; therefore, you'll really need some hands-on experience. Some of the exams require you to solve real-world case studies and network design issues, so the more hands-on experience you have, the better.

➤ Two-plus years in a networked environment that includes hands-on experience with Windows 2000 Server, Windows 2000 Professional, Windows NT Server, Windows NT Workstation, and Windows 95 or Windows 98. A solid understanding of each system's architecture, installation, configuration, maintenance, and troubleshooting is also essential.

➤ Knowledge of the various methods for installing Windows 2000, including manual and unattended installations.

➤ A thorough understanding of key networking protocols, addressing, and name resolution, including TCP/IP, IPX/SPX, and NetBEUI.

➤ A thorough understanding of NetBIOS naming, browsing, and file and print services.

➤ Familiarity with key Windows 2000–based TCP/IP-based services, including HTTP (Web servers), DHCP, WINS, DNS, plus familiarity with one or more of the following: Internet Information Server (IIS), Index Server, and Proxy Server.

➤ An understanding of how to implement security for key network data in a Windows 2000 environment.

➤ Working knowledge of NetWare 3.x and 4.x, including IPX/SPX frame formats, NetWare file, print, and directory services, and both Novell and

Microsoft client software. Working knowledge of Microsoft's Client Service For NetWare (CSNW), Gateway Service For NetWare (GSNW), the NetWare Migration Tool (NWCONV), and the NetWare Client For Windows (NT, 95, and 98) is essential.

➤ A good working understanding of Active Directory. The more you work with Windows 2000, the more you'll realize that this new operating system is quite different than Windows NT. New technologies like Active Directory have really changed the way that Windows is configured and used. We recommend that you find out as much as you can about Active Directory and acquire as much experience using this technology as possible. The time you take learning about Active Directory will be time very well spent!

Fundamentally, this boils down to a bachelor's degree in computer science, plus three years' experience working in a position involving network design, installation, configuration, and maintenance. We believe that well under half of all certification candidates meet these requirements, and that, in fact, most meet less than half of these requirements—at least, when they begin the certification process. But because all the people who already have been certified have survived this ordeal, you can survive it too—especially if you heed what our Self-Assessment can tell you about what you already know and what you need to learn.

Put Yourself to the Test

The following series of questions and observations is designed to help you figure out how much work you must do to pursue Microsoft certification and what kinds of resources you may consult on your quest. Be absolutely honest in your answers,. There are no right or wrong answers, only steps along the path to certification. Only you can decide where you really belong in the broad spectrum of aspiring candidates.

Two things should be clear from the outset, however:

➤ Even a modest background in computer science will be helpful.

➤ Hands-on experience with Microsoft products and technologies is an essential ingredient to certification success.

Educational Background

1. Have you ever taken any computer-related classes? [Yes or No]

   If Yes, proceed to question 2; if No, proceed to question 4.

2. Have you taken any classes on computer operating systems? [Yes or No]

   If Yes, you will probably be able to handle Microsoft's architecture and system component discussions. If you're rusty, brush up on basic operating system concepts, especially virtual memory, multitasking regimes, user mode versus kernel mode operation, and general computer security topics.

   If No, consider some basic reading in this area. We strongly recommend a good general operating systems book, such as *Operating System Concepts, 5th Edition*, by Abraham Silberschatz and Peter Baer Galvin (John Wiley & Sons, 1998, ISBN 0-471-36414-2). If this title doesn't appeal to you, check out reviews for other, similar titles at your favorite online bookstore.

3. Have you taken any networking concepts or technologies classes? [Yes or No]

   If Yes, you will probably be able to handle Microsoft's networking terminology, concepts, and technologies (brace yourself for frequent departures from normal usage). If you're rusty, brush up on basic networking concepts and terminology, especially networking media, transmission types, the OSI Reference Model, and networking technologies such as Ethernet, token ring, FDDI, and WAN links.

   If No, you might want to read one or two books in this topic area. The two best books that we know of are *Computer Networks, 3rd Edition*, by Andrew S. Tanenbaum (Prentice-Hall, 1996, ISBN 0-13-349945-6) and *Computer Networks and Internets, 2nd Edition*, by Douglas E. Comer (Prentice-Hall, 1998, ISBN 0-130-83617-6).

   Skip to the next section, "Hands-on Experience."

4. Have you done any reading on operating systems or networks? [Yes or No]

   If Yes, review the requirements stated in the first paragraphs after questions 2 and 3. If you meet those requirements, move on to the next section. If No, consult the recommended reading for both topics. A strong background will help you prepare for the Microsoft exams better than just about anything else.

Hands-on Experience

The most important key to success on all of the Microsoft tests is hands-on experience, especially with Windows 2000 Server and Professional, plus the many add-on services and BackOffice components around which so many of the Microsoft certification exams revolve. If we leave you with only one realization after taking this Self-Assessment, it should be that there's no substitute for time spent installing, configuring, and using the various Microsoft products upon which you'll be tested repeatedly and in depth.

5. Have you installed, configured, and worked with:

➤ Windows 2000 Server? [Yes or No]

If Yes, make sure you understand basic concepts as covered in Exam 70-215. You should also study the TCP/IP interfaces, utilities, and services for Exam 70-216, plus implementing security features for Exam 70-220.

Tip: You can download objectives, practice exams, and other data about Microsoft exams from the Training and Certification page at **www.microsoft.com/trainingandservices/ default.asp?PageID=mcp/**. Use the "Exams" link to obtain specific exam information.

If you haven't worked with Windows 2000 Server, you must obtain one or two machines and a copy of Windows 2000 Server. Then, learn the operating system and whatever other software components on which you'll also be tested.

In fact, we recommend that you obtain two computers, each with a network interface, and set up a two-node network on which to practice. With decent Windows 2000–capable computers selling for about $500 to $600 apiece these days, this shouldn't be too much of a financial hardship. You may have to scrounge to come up with the necessary software, but if you scour the Microsoft Web site you can usually find low-cost options to obtain evaluation copies of most of the software that you'll need.

➤ Windows 2000 Professional? [Yes or No]

If Yes, make sure you understand the concepts covered in Exam 70-210.

If No, you will want to obtain a copy of Windows 2000 Professional and learn how to install, configure, and maintain it. You can use *MCSE Windows 2000 Professional Exam Cram* to guide your activities and studies, or work straight from Microsoft's test objectives if you prefer.

Tip: For any and all of these Microsoft exams, the Resource Kits for the topics involved are a good study resource. You can purchase softcover Resource Kits from Microsoft Press (search for them at **http://mspress.microsoft.com/**), but they also appear on the TechNet CDs (**www.microsoft.com/technet**). Along with *Exam Crams* and *Exam Preps*, we believe that Resource Kits are among the best tools you can use to prepare for Microsoft exams.

6. For any specific Microsoft product that is not itself an operating system (for example, SQL Server), have you installed, configured, used, and upgraded this software? [Yes or No]

If the answer is Yes, skip to the next section. If it's No, you must get some experience. Read on for suggestions on how to do this.

Experience is a must with any Microsoft product exam, be it something as simple as FrontPage 2000 or as challenging as SQL Server 7.0. For trial copies of other software, search Microsoft's Web site using the name of the product as your search term. Also, search for bundles like "BackOffice" or "Small Business Server."

. . . .
Tip: If you have the funds, or your employer will pay your way, consider taking a class at a Certified Training and Education Center (CTEC) or at an Authorized Academic Training Partner (AATP). In addition to classroom exposure to the topic of your choice, you get a copy of the software that is the focus of your course, along with a trial version of whatever operating system it needs, with the training materials for that class.
. . . .

Before you even think about taking any Microsoft exam, make sure you've spent enough time with the related software to understand how it may be installed and configured, how to maintain such an installation, and how to troubleshoot that software when things go wrong. This will help you in the exam, and in real life!

Testing Your Exam-Readiness

Whether you attend a formal class on a specific topic to get ready for an exam or use written materials to study on your own, some preparation for the Microsoft certification exams is essential. The exam is free, but because it can only be taken once you want to do everything you can to pass it on your first try. That's where studying comes in.

We have included a practice exam in this book, so if you don't score that well on the test, you can study more and then tackle the test again. We also have exams that you can take online through the **ExamCram.com** Web site at **www.examcram.com**. If you still don't hit a score of at least 70 percent after the test, you'll want to investigate the other practice test resources we mention in this section.

For any given subject, consider taking a class if you've tackled self-study materials, taken the test, and failed anyway. The opportunity to interact with an instructor and fellow students can make all the difference in the world, if you can afford that privilege. For information about Microsoft classes, visit the Training and Certification page at **www.microsoft.com/education/partners/ctec.asp** for Microsoft Certified Education Centers or **www.microsoft.com/aatp/ default.htm** for Microsoft Authorized Training Providers.

If you can't afford to take a class, visit the Training and Certification page anyway, because it also includes pointers to free practice exams and to Microsoft Certified Professional Approved Study Guides and other self-study tools. And even if you can't afford to spend much at all, you should still invest in some low-cost practice exams from commercial vendors.

7. Have you taken a practice exam on your chosen test subject? [Yes or No]

If Yes, and you scored 70 percent or better, you're probably ready to tackle the real thing. If your score isn't above that threshold, keep at it until you break that barrier.

If No, obtain all the free and low-budget practice tests you can find and get to work. Keep at it until you can break the passing threshold comfortably.

Tip: When it comes to assessing your test readiness, there is no better way than to take a good-quality practice exam and pass with a score of 70 percent or better. When we're preparing ourselves, we shoot for 80-plus percent, just to leave room for the "weirdness factor" that sometimes shows up on Microsoft exams.

ASSESSING READINESS FOR EXAM 70-240

In addition to the general exam-readiness information in the previous section, there are several things you can do to prepare for the Microsoft Windows 2000 Accelerated exam. As you're getting ready for Exam 70-240, visit the Exam Cram Windows 2000 Resource Center at **www.examcram.com/ studyresource/w2kresource/**. Another valuable resource is the Exam Cram Insider newsletter. Sign up at **www.examcram.com** or send a blank email message to **subscribe-ec@mars.coriolis.com**. We also suggest that you join an active MCSE mailing list. One of the better ones is managed by Sunbelt Software. Sign up at **www.sunbelt-software.com** (look for the Subscribe To button).

You can also cruise the Web looking for "braindumps" (recollections of test topics and experiences recorded by others) to help you anticipate topics you're likely to encounter on the test. The MCSE mailing list is a good place to ask where the useful braindumps are, or you can check Shawn Gamble's list at **www.commandcentral.com**.

Tip: You can't be sure that a braindump's author can provide correct answers. Thus, use the questions to guide your studies, but don't rely on the answers in a braindump to lead you to the truth. Double-check everything you find in any braindump.

Microsoft exam mavens also recommend checking the Microsoft Knowledge Base (available on its own CD as part of the TechNet collection, or on the Microsoft Web site at **http://support.microsoft.com/support/**) for "meaningful technical support issues" that relate to your exam's topics. Although we're not sure exactly what the quoted phrase means, we have also noticed some overlap between technical support questions on particular products and troubleshooting questions on the exams for those products.

ONWARD, THROUGH THE FOG!

Once you've assessed your readiness, undertaken the right background studies, obtained the hands-on experience that will help you understand the products and technologies at work, and reviewed the many sources of information to help you prepare for a test, you'll be ready to take a round of practice tests. When your scores come back positive enough to get you through the exam, you're ready to go after the real thing. If you follow our assessment regime, you'll not only know what you need to study, but when you're ready to make a test date at Prometric or VUE. Good luck!

CHAPTER ONE

INTRODUCTION TO WINDOWS 2000

After completing this chapter, you will be able to:

✓ Describe the different Windows 2000 operating systems

✓ Discuss new features and improvements in Windows 2000 Professional

✓ Explain the capabilities of Windows 2000 Server

✓ Describe Active Directory Services, new security and communications enhancements, and enhanced administrative utilities

✓ Describe key technologies in Windows 2000 Advanced Server

✓ Discuss enterprise capacities possessed by Windows 2000 Datacenter Server

✓ Select the appropriate Windows 2000 operating system for specific applications and environments

This chapter examines the improvements and enhancements included in the family of Windows 2000 operating systems. New features and utilities make the OS a versatile, robust, secure, and scalable platform. The addition of powerful directory services capabilities will transform the manner in which many systems are administered and maintained.

In order for systems engineers to maximize Windows 2000, they must understand the importance of deploying Windows 2000 throughout their organizations, not just on their servers. Additionally, systems engineers must develop expertise with Windows 2000's features, consoles, and capabilities.

This chapter discusses Windows 2000's important innovations, utilities, and developments, including the enhancements made to Windows 2000 Professional, which is designed to replace Windows NT Workstation 4. Further, the chapter explains the improvements included in Windows 2000 Server, which replaces Windows NT Server 4. As you will see, Windows 2000 also offers two additional server platforms—Windows 2000 Advanced Server and Windows 2000 Datacenter Server. The platforms' strengths and differences are examined later in this chapter.

You should begin your study of Windows 2000 with explanations of the platforms' different features, even if you have no intention of using all of them. Windows 2000 relies on myriad technologies to support several new features, and you should be familiar with them before attempting any migration or installation. Without an understanding of LDAP compatibility and NTFS, for example, use of Active Directory Services is not possible. So, let's get started and look at what's new in Microsoft's Windows 2000 operating systems.

WHAT'S NEW?

Microsoft's Windows 2000 family of operating systems introduces numerous rich new features. In addition to strengthened security, enhanced reliability, improved capacities, and increased capabilities, the Windows 2000 platform boasts simplified ease of use.

Systems engineers can use new tools for administration and deployment. Support personnel can enjoy improved configuration and troubleshooting tools. End-users can benefit from increased reliability and bolstered security, as well as enhanced remote access capabilities and more. As a result, improved efficiencies made possible with the implementation of the new operating systems can be felt throughout an organization.

1

Picking up where Windows NT development left off, Windows 2000 aims to reduce an organization's total cost of ownership; provide a powerful, reliable, and scalable enterprise computing platform; and offer an adaptive infrastructure for information technology–based solutions deployment.

One of the most heralded new features of Windows 2000 is Microsoft's Active Directory. The new directory interface provides administrators the ability to exercise greater control of their networks with increased manageability. The platform's new Distributed file system permits the development of a single logical directory tree. Security, meanwhile, is enhanced with the introduction of Kerberos, IPSec (Internet Protocol Security), and Encrypting File System (EFS) technologies.

Despite the platform's increased potency, Microsoft's programmers have worked diligently to simplify the operating systems' usability. You will find Windows 2000's approachability similar to the NT 4 experience. Further, while many old functions, features, and menus have changed, Windows 2000 operators will find improved administration, configuration, and maintenance tools and utilities. You'll also find an abundance of new wizards, which simplify many processes that were once unintuitive and time-consuming. Additionally, Microsoft Management Console (MMC) is integrated into the client and server platforms, empowering administrators with a common management user interface. All Windows 2000 operating systems also offer the convenience of Plug and Play compatibility.

Many Windows 2000 features can be realized in a mixed environment in which other platforms operate. However, the new operating system's potential is maximized when it works in a native environment, or one in which Windows 2000 operating systems are used exclusively.

The Windows 2000 Family

Each Windows 2000 distribution possesses its own set of features and capabilities. The new Windows 2000 platform members are:

➤ Windows 2000 Professional

➤ Windows 2000 Server

➤ Windows 2000 Advanced Server

➤ Windows 2000 Datacenter Server

All the Windows 2000 operating systems have been built using Microsoft's New Technology (NT) platform and utilize the NT kernel.

WINDOWS 2000 PROFESSIONAL

Windows 2000 Professional combines the best user and consumer features from Windows 98 with the business-focused properties of Windows NT Workstation 4. Windows 2000 Professional supports upgrades from all of the operating systems it replaces, and it can replace the following in Microsoft's OS lineup:

➤ Windows 95

➤ Windows 98

➤ Windows NT Workstation 4

When compared to legacy Windows systems, Windows 2000 Professional provides:

➤ Enhanced user interface and setup

➤ Improved Internet and communications features

➤ Strengthened security

➤ Improved file management

➤ Improved configuration features

➤ Enhanced printing support

➤ Improved mobile computing platform

➤ New troubleshooting utilities

Enhanced User Interface

Windows 2000 Professional boasts several new user interface improvements, including a customized Start menu. The addition of a Use Personalized Menus option on the Taskbar And Start Menu Properties dialog box offers the option of activating Personalized Menus, which helps users to organize their most frequently used programs (less frequently used applications are subsequently hidden from view, thereby simplifying use of the Start menu). Individual settings can be customized, too, via the Advanced tab in the Taskbar and Start Menu Properties dialog box, as shown in Figure 1.1.

Note: Although less frequently used programs are hidden from view, they can still be easily accessed. No applications or programs are ever deleted from a machine. Users can expand customized Start menus via a single click at the bottom of the improved Start menu to view less frequently used applications.

IntelliMirror features are one of several benefits that can be realized when working within a native Windows 2000 operating environment. Similar to

Figure 1.1   You can easily customize Windows 2000's Start menu settings.

Windows NT 4's roaming profiles, IntelliMirror enables users to access their data, software, and preferences anywhere on a network. The technology uses policy definitions to deploy, recover, restore, or replace users' data, software, and personal settings when they move from one PC to another. Because IntelliMirror mirrors data between client machines and servers, users can continue working on their local machine when network outages occur.

The dialog boxes for the Logon and Shutdown options are smaller and easier to use in Windows 2000 than in Windows NT. In addition to being simplified, users' options are explained in greater detail than in past Windows versions.

Finally, scripts and programs can be run at specified times. The Scheduled Tasks applet permits you to configure applications to run at startup as well as schedule other tasks with the support of the Scheduled Task Wizard.

Enhanced Setup

New setup utilities simplify installation of the new OS. Working together, the setup utilities build a much smoother installation process. For example, while the Windows NT installation process often stops when it encounters errors, the Windows 2000 installation process continues unless an error is interpreted as being critical in nature. Further, assumptions are made regarding the manner in which a system should be set up, based on other information gained during the setup process. The result is improved reliability.

One of many new Windows 2000 wizards, the Setup Manager Wizard, helps you to customize an OS installation. You can select a system's configuration parameters and store the configuration details in a script file. Then, the script file can be used to automate installation on multiple machines.

Sysprep.exe is another new Windows 2000 setup tool. The system preparation utility improves the hard disk imaging process. With the use of third-party tools, hard disk images can then be copied to other systems.

In Windows 2000 Professional, configuring hardware devices is significantly easier than in Windows NT Workstation due to the extension of Plug and Play compatibility. Upon booting, Windows 2000 automatically detects new hardware and launches the Windows 2000 Hardware Wizard when necessary. The addition of automatically configured support for tens of thousands of hardware devices and drivers (including USB peripherals) helps to save administrators valuable time.

Improved Internet and Communications Features

Windows 2000 Professional includes enhanced Internet and communications functionality. Namely, Windows 2000 includes Internet Explorer 5 (IE5) and Outlook Express.

Internet Explorer 5

IE5 includes many new features that simplify use of the Internet. For example, IE5's Search Assistant improves searching by offering categories and enabling users to access multiple search engines without retyping queries. IE's AutoComplete feature activates a drop-down list of previously visited sites in the browser's Address bar, which can help to shorten the number of keystrokes needed when searching locations. The Windows 2000 desktop expands the AutoComplete feature by providing users with assistance when entering network addresses, URLs, folder names, and more. Another new feature offered in IE5 is that it can be configured to remember frequently used passwords.

Finally, automatic configuration is another benefit of IE5. The browser includes the ability to automatically locate and configure Internet connections through the use of the Internet Connection Wizard. It can also discover proxy settings automatically.

Outlook Express 5

Outlook Express offers Windows 2000 users a powerful client utility for managing email, contact information, and more. Using Outlook Express, users can send and receive HTML messages. In addition, multiple Outlook Express accounts can be hosted on the same machine. Finally, Outlook Express also includes an integrated Internet newsgroup client.

Strengthened Security

Several new security features and enhancements are incorporated in the Windows 2000 family of operating systems. Windows 2000 Professional benefits from almost all the additions.

1

Data stored on NTFS-formatted hard drives can now be stored in an encrypted format. The introduction of the Encrypting File System (EFS) strengthens security by requiring users who log on locally to also possess the appropriate public key for unlocking files. The EFS technology prevents thieves from accessing data on stolen hard drives, because merely accessing an NTFS partition via a third-party tool isn't sufficient for accessing the data. And, because EFS runs as an integrated system service, it's easy to manage, difficult to defeat, and virtually transparent to users.

Windows 2000 supports Internet Protocol Security (IPSec). IPSec encrypts Transmission Control Protocol/Internet Protocol (TCP/IP) traffic. As a result, Windows 2000 Professional enjoys the benefit of secure communications when packets traverse intranets and Internet virtual private networks (VPN).

The Layer 2 Tunneling Protocol (L2TP) provides a more secure version of the Point-to-Point Tunneling Protocol (PPTP). Thanks to the incorporation of the public key infrastructure in Windows 2000, L2TP can be used by the Windows 2000 desktop operating system.

Because Windows 2000 incorporates the Kerberos version 5 protocol into its distributed security model, users benefit from a single network logon for access to network resources, including files and printers. Windows 2000 relies on the Kerberos protocol, an industry standard, for user authentication. Advantages include strengthened security as well as improved authentication and network response times.

The need for transmitting sensitive authentication information and private keys over the public switched telephone network or other unsecured infrastructure is eliminated with support for smart cards. Further, smart cards are tamper-resistant and enable portability of personal information.

Note: Smart cards are credit-card like devices used to secure access to numerous resources. They can hold public-key certificates and private key information, as well as digital signatures. Smart card security is further increased through the requirement that passwords be supplied before they can be used. The password protection helps ensure a lost or misplaced smart card is not used without authorization.

Finally, an extensive public key infrastructure builds the foundation for many of the security options included in the Windows 2000 family of operating systems. Developers can leverage security mechanisms within an enterprise via the use of encrypted keys. A collection of cryptographic algorithms, incorporated into public keys and bolstered by the use of certificates of authority, help Windows 2000 protect against unauthorized intrusion. Applications that can benefit from the enhanced public key infrastructure include email, network authentication, and file access.

Improved File Management

Windows 2000 Professional's file storage and management capabilities are notably improved over the same capabilities found in earlier Windows operating systems. Windows 2000 maintains native NTFS file support while offering many new file management features:

➤ Windows 2000 provides support for the FAT32 file system, introduced in Windows with the Windows 95 Operating System Release 2 (OSR2).

➤ NTFS partitions no longer need third-party tools to ensure efficient file storage. Defragmentation software originally produced by Executive Software is now included as a native application within Windows 2000. Thus, Windows 2000 Professional possesses the ability to defragment any file system the operating system supports.

➤ Command-line backup scheduling is a tool of the past. Windows 2000's Backup utility is more powerful and more robust than its predecessor. Native support is now included for not just tape drives, but Zip drives, CD-RW devices, logical tape drives, and external hard drives. Backups can also be scheduled automatically.

➤ Windows 2000 introduces dynamic volumes to Windows. Machines no longer require rebooting after adjusting volumes. Additionally, volume administration can be performed via a network. Local drives and partitions can now be mounted at any empty folder as long as the target folder exists on an NTFS volume. In the past, volumes had to be mounted at the root of a drive letter.

Improved Configuration Features

Configuration tools have been strengthened within Windows 2000. New configuration programs and applets work to create a more consistent and simplified experience for users.

The Add/Remove Programs applet in Control Panel offers new features, including the ability to sort programs by name, frequency of use, size, and last date used. In addition, programs can now be installed simply by pointing to a resource from within the applet.

The Windows Installer provides a standard format for managing applications' installation, configuration, and removal. An application programming interface (API) enables you to manage applications and tools.

In Windows 2000, several computer management utilities have been consolidated into a single console. You can now manage computers from other machines on a network. Windows 2000's Computer Management utility includes the following features:

➤ *System Tools*—Includes diagnostic and service management tools, including the Event Viewer, Device Manager, and Services applets.

➤ *Storage*—Holds the disk management utilities, including Disk Defragmenter.

➤ *Services and Applications*—Allows manipulation of a system's Indexing Service, which provides data search capabilities, Routing and Remote Access, and more.

Figure 1.2 shows the Computer Management Disk Defragmenter utility.

The client desktop operating system offers support for the Microsoft Management Console. MMC can be customized to provide access from a single window to a variety of powerful tools and utilities, including the following:

➤ Device Management

➤ Disk Defragmenter

➤ Fax Service Management

➤ Indexing Service

➤ Performance Logs And Alerts

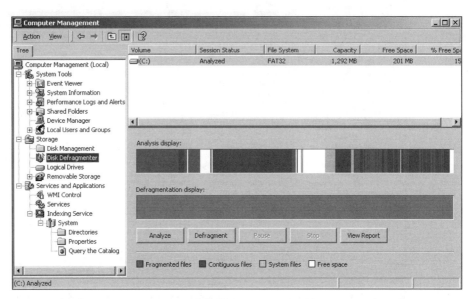

Figure 1.2 Windows 2000's Computer Management applet provides multiple utilities in a single interface.

➤ Security Configuration And Analysis

➤ System Information

Figure 1.3 shows a sample MMC configured to include the Event Viewer, among other utilities.

Enhanced Printing Support

With Windows 2000, you will probably notice an immediate improvement in printing processes. Ease-of-use has been greatly enhanced with the addition of browser-enabled printing support.

Internet Printing Protocol (IPP) enables browser-based printing via intranet and Internet connections. Users can now print to URLs, download and install printer drivers, and view printer-related information via their browsers.

The Add Printer Wizard simplifies printer installation, whether the printer is a local or networked device. Users no longer need to specify printer types, select ports, or choose print languages.

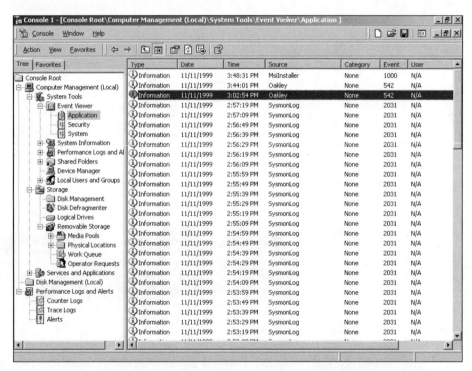

Figure 1.3   The customizable Microsoft Management Console integrated in Windows 2000 Professional offers users a powerful interface for managing disk space, security, performance, and much more.

1

Finally, high-quality color documents can be sent to printers and other computers with greater speed than in the past. Image Color Management 2 ensures images are reproduced on scanners and printers with the same colors as seen on users' monitors.

Improved Mobile Computing Platform

Windows 2000 includes numerous mobile computing improvements. The benefits aren't limited to software configuration enhancements and synchronization tools, either. Power consumption has also been significantly improved. The main mobile computing platform features and improvements are:

➤ Multiple network connections can be configured through a single utility, the Network Connection Wizard. Dial-up connections, VPNs, direct connections to other computers, and incoming calls can all be configured with the Network Connection Wizard.

➤ New support is included for securing virtual private networks that connect via the public switched telephone network.

➤ Users can store network-based documents in offline folders on their hard drives, enabling use of the documents when the network is unavailable.

➤ The Synchronization Manager can be configured to automatically update files and folders when logging on to the network. Changes made to files and folders, including Web pages and email messages, can be kept up-to-date using this utility.

➤ Power support is enhanced. Windows 2000 Professional supports the Advanced Configuration And Power Interface with the goal of extended battery life. New power management and suspend and resume capabilities contribute to improved battery performance, including Hibernate mode, which shuts off power but maintains programs' open states and hardware connections.

➤ Hot-swapping capabilities are enhanced. Portable computers no longer require rebooting when connecting to or disconnecting from docking stations. The reliability of Plug and Play is improved, and more hardware peripherals are natively supported by the operating system.

New Troubleshooting Utilities

Troubleshooting assistance comes in many forms in Windows 2000. In addition to improved Plug and Play reliability, Troubleshooting Wizards are available for solving common issues. Another improvement is enhanced Control Panel applets.

Several new Troubleshooting Wizards address common computer problems. Wizards are available for the following:

➤ *Client Service for NetWare (CSNW)*—Assists with accessing NetWare servers and Novell Directory Services objects, printing on Novell networks, using NetWare login scripts, and logging on to an NDS tree.

➤ *Display*—Assists with the configuration of video cards, drivers, and display adapters.

➤ *Hardware*—Helps troubleshoot issues with peripherals, such as CD-ROM drives, hard drives, input devices, and more.

➤ *Internet connections*—Helps users connect to Internet Service Providers (ISPs).

➤ *Modem*—Assists with modem setup and configuration.

➤ *MS-DOS programs*—Helps users to run MS-DOS programs in Windows 2000.

➤ *Multimedia and games*—Supports installation and configuration assistance for DirectX drivers and computer games.

➤ *Networking (TCP/IP)*—Troubleshoots Internet and intranet connections that use TCP/IP.

➤ *Print*—Assists in troubleshooting network and local printer setup and configuration.

➤ *Remote access*—Helps users link to remote computers using telephone connections.

➤ *Sound*—Provides sound card and speaker assistance.

➤ *System setup*—Helps users with problems related to Windows 2000 installation and setup.

➤ *Windows 3x programs*—Provides assistance to users running 16-bit Windows applications.

In addition to Troubleshooting Wizards, other available troubleshooting utilities include the following:

➤ *Windows 2000 Compatibility Tool*—When upgrading a Windows 95, Windows 98, or Windows NT Workstation 4 installation, the Windows 2000 Compatibility Tool warns users of any application and component incompatibilities.

➤ *Add/Remove Hardware applet*—Control Panel's Add/Remove Hardware applet includes the Add/Remove Hardware Wizard. The wizard offers troubleshooting assistance for error-ridden hardware devices. It can also be used to permanently or temporarily unplug or eject a locked-up device.

➤ *Plug and Play*—The improved functionality and reliability of Plug and Play support eliminates many troubleshooting situations common in older Windows operating systems.

➤ *Power Options applet*—New options aimed at preserving mobile computer battery life are available via Control Panel's Power Options applet, as shown in Figure 1.4.

➤ *Energy conservation features*—A variety of features, including selectable power schemes, user-configurable settings, and Advanced Power Management support, contribute to improved conservation of energy resources.

➤ *MMC*—MMC support in the client operating system provides powerful administration capabilities from client machines. MMC integration simplifies remote administration on enterprise networks, because multiple tools can be wrapped into a single window. Multiple MMC configurations can be stored and shared, further extending MMC's power.

➤ *Secondary Logon Service*—Network administrators no longer need to log users off a network in order to make system changes when sitting at a client machine. Windows 2000 includes a Secondary Logon Service for launching administrative programs and applications via a trusted administrator account.

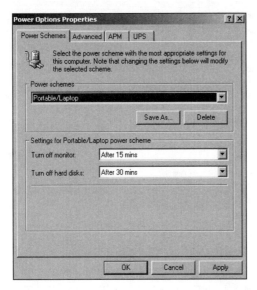

Figure 1.4   The new Power Options Properties dialog box includes preset power schemes as well as Advanced Power Management (APM) and uninterruptible power supply (UPS) support.

WINDOWS 2000 SERVER

The Windows 2000 Server platform includes Windows 2000 Professional's features and further extends the strengths developed in the Windows NT 4 Server operating system. The new OS performs functions faster, offers a much more reliable system architecture, boasts significantly increased scalability, and offers several new tools and utilities that simplify administration and help lower costs.

Windows 2000 Server is designed to provide small to medium-sized businesses with robust workgroup and department server functionality. The platform is ideal for powering file-and-print sharing services, running applications, accessing Web services, enabling remote communications, linking remote branches, and more.

In new installations, Windows 2000 Server supports up to two processors. However, the OS can support four processors when upgrading from the Windows NT 4 platform. Intel-based systems receive support for up to 4GB of memory.

In addition to reliable performance and ease of administration, Windows 2000 Server offers new and enhanced features in several areas, namely:

➤ The Active Directory changes the manner in which enterprise networks are administered.

➤ Management functions are simplified.

➤ Networking services and communications are improved.

➤ Web services are enhanced.

➤ Remote access services are improved.

➤ Security is strengthened considerably.

➤ File storage is enhanced.

➤ Configuration management is improved.

➤ Printing functions are expanded and simplified.

Introducing the Active Directory

Possibly the most important new Windows 2000 feature is the Active Directory service. The Active Directory Service simplifies the administration and maintenance of file, print, and Web services; user accounts; security; site management; email messaging; and other functions via a single directory tree.

Group policies, user accounts, and site management and resources can all be administered within Active Directory. Having access to several, frequently used tools within a single directory saves administrators valuable time. Further, Active Directory helps to eliminate the need for traveling to client machines for the purposes of configuration. These benefits all contribute to improved total costs of ownership.

The Active Directory, as shown in Figure 1.5, provides access to information about users, sites, and resources in a single directory tree. Multiple menus and consoles are no longer required. Simplified administration and management also make it easier for users to find the resources they seek on a network. Control of objects can be extended to users, as well, further reducing demands on a systems engineer's time.

In Windows NT 4, domains have practical limitations of 40,000 objects. This limitation can be problematic in large enterprise networks and can result in multiple domains and additional administrative headaches. These issues are nonexistent in Windows 2000, because Windows 2000 supports millions of objects.

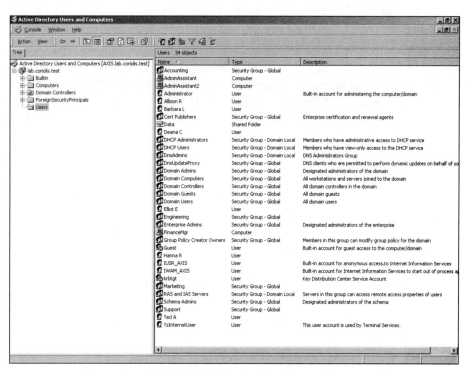

Figure 1.5   Active Directory provides a single console for the administration of shared folders, users, computers, printers, and more.

Active Directory's support of standards-based protocols, such as the Lightweight Directory Access Protocol (LDAP), and synchronization permits seamless integration with other vendors' systems, applications, directories, and services. Such integration enables you to control and manage multiple applications and programs from a single console.

New System Management Tools

Several new services contribute to simplified systems management in Windows 2000 Server. These services, combined with new remote installation and device reporting capabilities, assist administrators in improving their own operational efficiencies.

Dynamic Domain Name Service (DDNS) eliminates the need for manually editing DNS databases when client configurations change or new machines are added to a network. Windows 2000 Server's support for dynamic DNS means administrators can free time that was previously spent managing DNS databases.

Windows 2000 Professional can be installed on multiple client machines over the network from one location via Remote Installation Services (RIS). This saves valuable time by enabling administrators to install multiple client machines simultaneously from a central location.

Windows Management Instrumentation (WMI) supports the collection of data based on the Desktop Management Task Force's Web-based Enterprise Management (WBEM) standard. WMI helps keep administrators knowledge-able regarding the performance of vendors' peripheral devices and applications. Information, including performance data and failure notifications, can be collected from device drivers and fed to an application for the purposes of reporting.

Finally, the Terminal Services feature is bolstered in Windows 2000. Multiple client sessions are supported on the server, which powers applications for clients. The use of Terminal Services requires fewer resources to be made available on client machines and the use of thin clients.

Improved Network Protocol Support

Network services continue to grow in importance within Windows operating systems. Windows 2000 Server supports the following network protocol enhancements:

➤ Multiple protocol routing, including IP, IPX, AppleTalk, Open Shortest Path First (OSPF), and Routing Information Protocol (RIP).

➤ High-speed Asynchronous Transfer Mode (ATM). The primary benefit of ATM's exceptional bandwidth is its capacity for transmitting voice, data, and video signals simultaneously.

Enhanced Web Services

Web services in Windows 2000 include the widespread extension of Indexing Services, which originally appeared with Internet Information Server (IIS) 4. In Windows 2000 Server, server data is indexed automatically, providing enhanced search capabilities for users seeking resources on a network. Further, in Windows 2000, IIS is upgraded to IIS version 5. Internet Information Server 5 enables easy sharing of data over Internet and intranet networks. Among the most important new features is IIS' ability to plug into the Active Directory architecture. IIS 5 also offers Kerberos version 5, Windows Clustering support, and improved administrative capabilities.

Remote Access Refinements and Improvements

One of the most pressing challenges systems engineers face is the growing demand for remote access services. Windows 2000 Server introduces several new capa-bilities to help meet remote access requirements in enterprise environments.

In Windows 2000 Server, remote access policies and profiles allow admini-strators to control connection properties at a higher level of granularity. Remote access policies can be associated with profiles and pre-configured conditions, thereby enabling more secure use of network resources. You can configure remote access properties by using the Corporate User Properties dialog box, as shown in Figure 1.6, which is accessible via the Routing And Remote Access applet.

Long a staple of Internet Service Providers, support for the Remote Authentication Dial-In User Service (RADIUS) protocol is integrated in Windows 2000 Server. The protocol permits identification and authentication of dial-up users as well as accounting functions for tracking users' sessions.

The Connection Manager assists in configuring dial-up connections. The Configuration Manager can be configured to set up predefined connections, which can help to reduce the number of support calls an information technology department must field.

Strengthened Security

Next to Active Directory, security improvements are among the most important enhancements to the network operating system's platform. Support for new

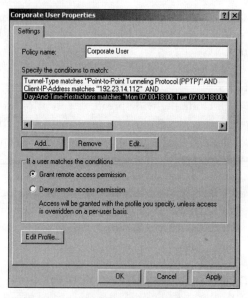

Figure 1.6   Connection settings can be edited by right-clicking on a username
in Routing And Remote Access.

protocols and changes to old processes strengthen security in Windows 2000
Server considerably in the following ways:

➤ Active Directory enables administrators to restrict access to resources
through the creation, implementation, and management of group policies.

➤ Security templates, as shown in Figure 1.7, collect all security attributes into
one location and can be used in their default states or customized.

➤ Windows 2000 Server permits the creation of computer-specific security
databases by enabling the use of security configurations among multiple
systems.

Enhanced File Management Features

File server capabilities received attention during Windows 2000 Server's
development. New file management features in Windows 2000 Server include
the Distributed File System (Dfs), disk quotas, and remote storage monitoring.

In Windows 2000 Server, a single directory tree consolidates files housed on
multiple servers, even if the files are located in different physical locations. Dfs
greatly simplifies users' access to files and resources, particularly on large
enterprise distributed networks.

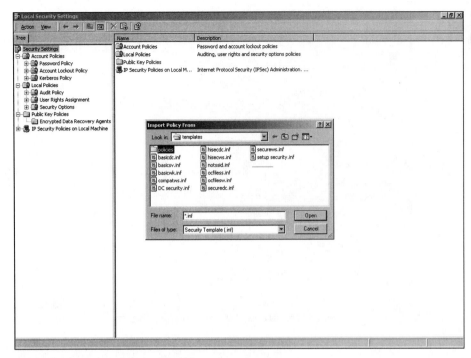

Figure 1.7   Windows 2000 offers administrators the use of built-in security templates.

Another long-running enterprise environment issue regarding Windows-based servers is addressed with the introduction of disk quotas. Using disk quotas, administrators can allot users preset storage space, as shown in Figure 1.8, which helps limit disk space use and maximize network storage.

Windows 2000 Server grants administrators the ability to manage local disk space automatically. Remote storage features permit data to be automatically transferred to network drives after a local disk reaches a preset limit.

Improved Configuration Management

In addition to the configuration tools found in Windows Professional 2000 and the Active Directory Service, several powerful new configuration management and administrative utilities are included in Windows 2000 Server, including MMC, enhanced group policies, Windows Scripting Host (WSH), and other specialized management services.

Once an add-on for Windows NT 4, MMC is a native administration tool in Windows 2000. While MMC serves as a powerful management utility within Windows 2000 Professional, its use is exponentially extended within Windows

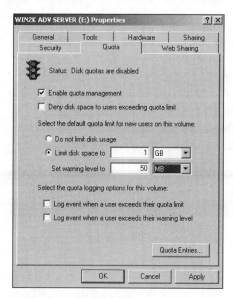

Figure 1.8 Disk quotas can help administrators limit the disk space users receive for storing files and other data.

2000 Server. Because the console can include Active Directory objects within it, network functions, resources, management, security, and other functions can be consolidated within a single MMC. Add the fact that MMC is highly customizable, and it becomes one of the most powerful management tools ever extended to network administrators.

Enhanced group policies provide administrators with increased control and granularity of user settings. Administrators can now control specific workstations, data, and applications via group policies.

Windows Scripting Host (WSH) extends the functionality of clunky batch files left over from the days of MS-DOS. WSH helps administrators and users save time by automating common processes and tasks.

Finally, in addition to the computer management capabilities found in Windows 2000 Professional, Windows 2000 Server adds extra features of its own. Support is also provided for Microsoft System Management Services (SMS) version 2 and a host of other server management services, including Indexing Services, WMI Control, Telephony settings, and more.

Bolstered Printing Support

Printing processes benefit from several improvements in Windows 2000 Server. In addition to the printing features found in Windows 2000 Professional, the server platform enjoys a few of its own improved capabilities. For example, in

Windows 2000 Server, printers and print permissions for multiple sites and domains can be administered from a single console through Active Directory. Printers can be published in Active Directory, making it easier for users to find the closest printer for print jobs. Further, print device compatibility is improved. Windows 2000 Server supports printing on more than 2,500 printers from a wide variety of manufacturers.

WINDOWS 2000 ADVANCED SERVER

Windows 2000 Advanced Server contains all the features of Windows 2000 Server in addition to other services that increase its capabilities. Windows 2000 Advanced Server's extra features contribute to its high scalability and reliability and make it ideal for line-of-business and e-commerce applications.

Windows 2000 Advanced Server is ideal for larger enterprises. It excels at powering database-intensive work, clustering, and load balancing. Instead of supporting two to four processors, Windows 2000 Advanced Server scales up to eight processors and supports up to 8GB of physical memory for Intel-based systems.

Windows 2000 Advanced Server provides the ability to link server clusters and have them work as a single system while also providing very high levels of availability. Cluster services includes support for MMC and Active Directory; rolling upgrades; WINS, Dfs, and DHCP; and a cross-platform API for the development and support of large-scale enterprise applications. Clustering is supported for up to two nodes.

Windows 2000 Advanced Server can network load balance (NLB) up to 32 clustered servers. Software scaling enables administrators to add NLB-configured servers to preexisting server farms as required to increase a system's capacity. NLB benefits include highly scalable performance and high-availability of applications and data.

Finally, commercial sorting of large data sets is optimized in Windows 2000 Advanced Server. This makes the Advanced Server ideal for data warehousing applications and large sort operations.

WINDOWS 2000 DATACENTER SERVER

The Windows 2000 Datacenter Server scales even higher than Windows 2000 Advanced Server. The Datacenter Server is the most powerful server operating system Microsoft has ever produced, and it has been built to meet the most demanding levels of availability and scalability for use by application service providers, ISPs, and large enterprises for the purposes of data warehousing, intensive online transaction processing, and applications service provisioning.

Windows 2000 Datacenter Server is designed for very large enterprises. The platform features scalability and availability for the largest of organizations. Windows 2000 Datacenter Server scales to provide support for up to 32 processors, and it supports 64GB of physical memory for Intel-based systems. Windows 2000 Datacenter Server also enhances the scalability of its clustering and load balancing services. As a result, the Datacenter Server is optimized for large, enterprise projects including data warehousing, econometric analyses, science and engineering simulations, online transaction processing, server consolidations, and Web site hosting. Clustering is supported for up to four nodes.

CHAPTER SUMMARY

Microsoft's Windows 2000 family of operating systems introduces numerous rich new features. In addition to strengthened security, enhanced reliability, improved capacities, and increased capabilities, the Windows 2000 platform boasts simplified ease of use. Despite the platform's increased potency, Microsoft's programmers worked diligently to simplify the operating systems' usability. Most administrators will find Windows 2000's approachability similar to that experienced with Windows NT Server 4.

Each Windows 2000 platform possesses its own set of new features and capabilities. The new Windows 2000 operating systems and their key features and capabilities are:

➤ *Windows 2000 Professional*—Windows 2000 Professional boasts several new user interface improvements. Workstation installation is simplified with the addition of new setup utilities. Working together, they build a much smoother and simplified installation process. Windows 2000 Professional includes enhanced Internet and communications functionality, compliments of Internet Explorer 5 and Outlook Express.

➤ *Windows 2000 Server*—The Windows 2000 Server platform includes Windows 2000 Professional's features and further extends the strengths developed in the Windows NT 4 Server operating system. The new OS performs functions faster, offers a much more reliable system architecture, boasts significantly increased scalability, and offers several new tools and utilities that simplify administration and help lower costs.

➤ *Windows 2000 Advanced Server*—Windows 2000 Advanced Server contains Windows 2000 Server features in addition to other features that increase its capabilities. Windows 2000 Advanced Server's extra features contribute to its high scalability and reliability and make it ideal for line-of-business and e-commerce applications.

➤ *Windows 2000 Datacenter Server*—The Windows 2000 Datacenter Server scales higher than Windows 2000 Advanced Server. The Datacenter Server is the most powerful server operating system Microsoft has ever produced, and it is designed to meet the most demanding levels of availability and scalability required by large-scale enterprise data warehousing, intensive online transaction processing, and applications service provisioning projects.

All Windows 2000 operating systems include several new security features and enhancements. Security improvements are among the most important enhancements to the network operating system's platform. Support for new protocols and changes to old processes strengthen security in Windows 2000 server platforms considerably.

File server capabilities received attention in Windows 2000, too. New file management features in Windows 2000 Server include the Distributed File System, the implementation of disk quotas, and the ability to monitor remote storage conditions. Several powerful new configuration management and administrative utilities are also included in Windows 2000 server platforms. The file storage and management capabilities in Windows 2000 Professional are notably improved over NT 4 file management capabilities.

In addition to security enhancements and file management improvements, Windows 2000 operators will find improved administration, configuration, and maintenance tools and utilities. Many users will also notice improvements in areas such as browser-enabled printing support, mobile computing, power consumption management, troubleshooting assistance, Plug and Play reliability, and Control Panel applets.

Possibly the most important new Windows 2000 feature is the Active Directory service. The Active Directory Service simplifies the administration and maintenance of file, print, and Web services, user accounts, security, site management, email messaging, and other functions via a single directory tree. Several new services contribute to simplified systems management under Windows 2000 server platforms. These services, combined with new remote installation and device reporting capabilities, assist administrators in improving their own operational efficiencies.

Network services continue to grow in importance within Windows 2000 server platforms, which feature two new enhancements of note. Web services are bolstered in Windows 2000 with the widespread extension of Indexing Services, which originally appeared with Internet Information Server. IIS also receives an upgrade.

Finally, one of most pressing challenges systems engineers face is the growing demand for remote access services. Windows 2000 server platforms introduce several new capabilities to help meet this requirement in the enterprise environment.

REVIEW QUESTIONS

1. Which computing platforms are supported by Windows 2000?
   a. Intel-based systems
   b. SPARC-based systems
   c. RISC-based systems
   d. Alpha-based systems
   e. All of the above

2. Which of the following Windows 2000 operating systems use NT technology?
   a. Windows 2000 Professional
   b. Windows 2000 Server
   c. Windows 2000 Advanced Server
   d. b and c
   e. a, b, and c

3. Which Windows 2000 feature assists an administrator in creating multiple groups and users quickly?
   a. Windows Scripting Host
   b. Active Directory
   c. Group Policies
   d. Secondary Logon Service
   e. Setup Manager

1

4. Windows 2000 Professional supports which of the following security features?

   a. IPSec

   b. Kerberos version 5

   c. Encrypting File System

   d. Smart card technology

   e. All of the above

5. For which problem does Windows 2000 Professional not provide a troubleshooting wizard?

   a. An improperly configured modem

   b. Execution of MS-DOS programs in Windows

   c. An incompatible CD-ROM drive

   d. Problems associated with Windows 2000 setup

   e. Errors experienced while attempting to print documents

6. Support for which new protocol permits Windows 2000 users to print documents in remote locations via a Web browser?

   a. IPP

   b. IPSec

   c. L2TP

   d. AppleTalk

   e. Kerberos version 5

7. Active Directory provides administration of which of the following resources via a single console?

   a. Printers

   b. Users

   c. Sites

   d. Security

   e. All of the above

8. Windows 2000 Server supports up to which of the following memory architectures?

   a. 2GB on Intel-based systems

   b. 4GB on Intel-based systems

   c. 8GB on Intel-based systems

   d. 16GB on Intel-based systems

   e. 32GB on Intel-based systems

9. Support for which industry-standard protocol enhances Active Directory's interoperation with other operating systems?

   a. LDAP

   b. IPSec

   c. L2TP

   d. EFS

   e. DFS

10. Windows 2000 Server supports dynamic DNS.

    a. True

    b. False

11. Active Directory requires which Windows 2000 protocol?

    a. Kerberos version 5

    b. IP

    c. IPX

    d. AppleTalk

    e. NetBIOS

12. Implementation of disk quotas requires which operating system?

    a. Windows Millennium Edition

    b. Windows NT Workstation 4

    c. Windows NT Server 4

    d. Windows 2000 Professional

    e. Windows 2000 Server

13. The Indexing Service helps users find which resources on a network?

    a. DNS servers

    b. Word processing documents

    c. Printers

    d. Spreadsheets

    e. b, c, and d

14. In Windows 2000 Server, the Microsoft Management Console can be customized to include Active Directory objects, computer management tools, and performance monitors.

    a. True

    b. False

15. What's the maximum number of multiprocessors that Windows 2000 Server can support?

    a. 1

    b. 2

    c. 3

    d. 4

    e. 6

16. What's the maximum physical memory configuration Windows 2000 Advanced Server can support?

    a. 2GB on Intel-based systems

    b. 4GB on Intel-based systems

    c. 8GB on Intel-based systems

    d. 16GB on Intel-based systems

    e. 32GB on Intel-based systems

17. Windows 2000 Advanced Server supports clustering for up to how many nodes?

    a. 1

    b. 2

    c. 3

    d. 4

    e. 6

18. What's the maximum physical memory configuration Windows 2000 Datacenter Server can support?

    a. 8GB on Intel-based systems

    b. 16GB on Intel-based systems

    c. 32GB on Intel-based systems

    d. 48GB on Intel-based systems

    e. 64GB on Intel-based systems

19. Windows 2000 Datacenter Server provides clustering support for how many nodes?

    a. 1

    b. 2

    c. 3

    d. 4

    e. 6

20. The Windows 2000 NTFS file system requires no defragmentation.

    a. True

    b. False

REAL-WORLD PROJECTS

At the end of each chapter in this book, you'll tag along with Andy Palmer as he completes real-world projects. You'll enjoy all the benefits of shoulder surfing while Andy troubleshoots networks, solves common problems, and works with many of the new features found in Windows 2000. From problem identification to the step-by-step solution implementation, you'll follow Andy as he installs Windows 2000, configures its utilities, and administers its services.

Andy is excited about his first opportunity to work for a new information technology consulting firm. He has recently signed on and is anxious to assist clients with their needs, prove his expertise, and move up within the company. After two weeks of shadowing the firm's other engineers, Andy is finally entrusted with keys to a company car of his own. At the very next weekly company meeting, Andy is given responsibility for three new clients.

His first three companies have drastically different needs, sizes, and budgets. The first is an insurance agency with 105 employees, the second is an advertising agency with 12 employees, and the third is a global multinational fast-food chain with 4,400 employees at its global headquarters.

Andy sets up and attends several meetings with representatives from the IT departments at each firm. He discusses the administrators' and end-users' needs. Then, he reviews each organization's budget, as well as their needs for remote communications and security.

His first client, the insurance agency, needs to replace an older NetWare system. The company has been recently purchased by a larger firm, and it has been asked to develop a network that provides standards-based support for end-user and resource administration. Andy must keep costs to a minimum. However, it is critical that the insurance agency's 105 employees have a dependable file and application server, because the agency will lose money if new premiums can't be processed.

Andy's second customer, the advertising agency, needs to replace an aging group of Macintosh computers. The company requires its users to have the ability to store large files on the server. Many of the firm's 12 employees also travel often, so they need laptops that can easily access email and files from different cities.

1

The third client, the multinational fast-food chain, maintains myriad systems. Andy has been asked to implement a data warehousing solution that will permit the company to store large volumes of files regarding its restaurants across the world. In addition, the chain needs the ability to administer vast SQL databases in order to track inventory and sales. The solution must also provide load balancing services for corporate resources.

To fulfill the companies' needs, Andy performs the following tasks. He begins by fulfilling the insurance company's needs first.

Project 1.1
To meet medium-sized business needs with Windows 2000 Professional and Windows 2000 Server:

1. Andy installs Windows 2000 Professional on all client desktops.

2. Andy replaces the older NetWare server with Windows 2000 Server.

3. Andy installs and configures Active Directory Services on the Windows 2000 Server.

As a result of Andy's changes, the insurance company's employees no longer have to worry about system downtime. In addition, Active Directory provides support for LDAP, enabling a standards-based utility for end-user and resource management.

With the first company satisfied with their new network, Andy upgrades the advertising agency's aging and inefficient Macs.

Project 1.2
To empower traveling employees and automate remote storage:

1. Andy replaces the advertising agency's employees' Macintosh computers with models featuring Windows 2000 Professional.

2. Andy configures the desktops for email and other network services, including remote storage.

3. Andy replaces the agency's server with Windows 2000 Server.

The upgrades Andy makes provide the agency's employees with a robust operating system featuring enhanced power management utilities and a full suite of communication tools, including email. In addition, Windows 2000 Professional enables secure VPN connections to the agency's main file server. Andy also uses Windows 2000 Server's remote storage feature, thereby automating the storage of large files on the agency's server.

With the advertising agency employees enjoying the features of their new desktop operating systems and network, Andy heads out to solve the fast-food operation's troubles.

Project 1.3
To implement a data warehousing, database administration, and load balancing solution:

1. Andy implements several Windows 2000 Datacenter servers at the chain's corporate headquarters.

2. The new servers are configured to provide data warehousing and database services, load balancing, and storage for thousands of files.

A few weeks later, Andy receives a promotion. It follows a telephone conversation Andy's boss had with the IT directory at the fast-food chain. The Windows 2000 Datacenter Server has done just the trick for the multinational corporation. The director reports the data warehousing capabilities are working fine and database applications are running faster than ever. Employees credit the change for improving response times when accessing resources on the firm's network.

CHAPTER TWO

WINDOWS 2000 INSTALLATION AND SETUP

After completing this chapter, you will be able to:

✓ Describe a proper preinstallation checklist

✓ List the minimum requirements for installing Windows 2000 Professional and Windows 2000 Server

✓ Select the appropriate file system for your Windows 2000 installation

✓ Explain the licensing options available with Windows 2000

✓ Discuss the five Windows 2000 installation methods and setup configurations

✓ Explain the prerequisites for installing Windows 2000 in a domain

✓ Troubleshoot faulty Windows 2000 installations

Before you can enjoy the new enhancements and features included in Windows 2000, you must install the new operating system. However, the setup process cannot be completed unless you are prepared to provide the necessary hardware and setup information required by the new operating system.

This chapter discusses the need for reviewing a pre-installation checklist and understanding Windows 2000's minimum requirements. In addition, it examines the different licensing options available to administrators, and the installation and setup processes.

Windows 2000's installation and set up routines are similar to the routines found on the Windows NT 4 platform. However, Windows 2000 enhancements improve the installation process, and new configuration tools and services make Windows 2000 easier to install, whether you're installing the new OS via CD-ROM, over the network, via disk duplication, or with the use of the new Remote Installation Services (RIS). By planning an installation in advance and ensuring necessary information is prepared beforehand, common difficulties can be avoided.

This chapter examines the installation options and common troubleshooting strategies. Once completed, you'll have a solid understanding of the pre-installation requirements, licensing choices, installation and setup configuration options, and troubleshooting strategies.

PREINSTALLATION CHECKLIST

Pilots always complete a checklist before taking to the skies. Administrators should do the same before installing or upgrading to Windows 2000. While much of the information needed prior to installing Windows 2000 is similar to that required for Windows NT 4, several important differences exist. For example:

➤ There are new installation options, including use of the new Remote Installation Services. You'll also find support for disk duplication.

➤ Windows 2000 boasts Plug and Play support.

➤ Windows 2000 requires more powerful hardware.

In addition to knowledge of these differences and others, administrators should properly design and plan an installation. Without a solid understanding of the new platform's requirements, improvements, and capabilities, it would be difficult to maximize the use of new features. Further, administrators must install Windows 2000 on systems with appropriate hardware to ensure trouble-free operation.

REVIEW HARDWARE REQUIREMENTS

The first step when preparing a Windows 2000 installation is to ensure that all of a system's devices are included on the Windows 2000 Hardware Compatibility List (HCL). The HCL file (HCL.TXT) can be found on the Windows 2000 CD-ROM in the Support folder. Microsoft also keeps an updated HCL on its Web site at **www.microsoft.com/hwtest/hcl**.

If a device isn't listed in the HCL, the vendor's Web site can be checked for the availability of an updated driver. Beware, though—third-party drivers sometimes prove unreliable. For this reason, you should only use hardware that's included on the HCL and known to be compatible with Windows 2000. Otherwise, performance can become erratic and failures and errors can be difficult to isolate and repair. And, if your hardware is not listed on the HCL, Microsoft technical support will not support it.

Along with all the powerful new enhancements and Windows 2000 services come increased system requirements. Administrators are well-advised to check the systems they're installing Windows 2000 on to ensure that the systems meet the minimum requirements demanded by the operating system. This step should be taken before the Windows 2000 installation process begins.

Administrators should strive to exceed the minimum requirements for operating the software, when possible. While the OS will operate on systems possessing the minimum hardware requirements, performance improves remarkably on systems configured with more powerful processors and additional RAM and disk storage space. Tables 2.1, 2.2, and 2.3 show the minimum hardware requirements for Windows 2000 Professional, Windows 2000 Server, and Windows 2000 Advanced Server.

Note: Microsoft no longer creates software builds for the 32-bit or 64-bit Alpha platforms. However, future 64-bit software products are being developed for Intel-based systems.

Table 2.1 Minimum hardware requirements for Windows 2000 Professional.

Component	Requirement
CPU	Pentium 133MHz or higher (supports up to 2)
Input devices	Keyboard and mouse or other input device
Disk space	650MB free space on 2GB hard disk
RAM	64MB minimum
Secondary drives	12X or better CD-ROM, 3.5 disk drive, or NIC
Display	VGA or better

Table 2.2   Minimum hardware requirements for Windows 2000 Server.

Component	Intel
CPU	Pentium 133MHz or higher (supports up to 4)
Input devices	Keyboard and mouse or other input device
Disk space	1GB free space on 2GB hard disk (additional space needed if installing over a network)
RAM	128MB (minimum), 256MB (recommended), 4GB (maximum)
Secondary drives	12X or better CD-ROM, 3.5 disk drive, or NIC
Display	VGA or better

Table 2.3   Minimum hardware requirements for Windows 2000 Advanced Server.

Component	Intel
CPU	Pentium 133MHz or higher (supports up to 8)
Input devices	Keyboard and mouse or other input device
Network connectivity	Network adapter card
Disk space	1GB free space on 2GB hard disk (additional space needed if installing over a network)
RAM	128MB (minimum), 256MB (recommended), 8GB (maximum)
Secondary drives	12X or better CD-ROM, 3.5 disk drive, or NIC
Display	VGA or better

After you've determined that a system possesses or exceeds the necessary hardware requirements, you're ready to move on to the next step—selecting a partition and file system for your installation.

SELECT A FILE SYSTEM

Upon loading, the Windows 2000 Setup program examines a system's hard disk. After determining a system's configuration, Windows 2000 then provides the option to install the OS on an existing partition or the opportunity to create a new partition for the installation.

A drive can include up to four primary partitions or three primary partitions and an extended partition. A Windows 2000 installation requires that a minimum of 650MB be available on a 2GB or larger hard disk. However, you should have even more disk space available for use with additional services, utilities, and features.

. . . .
Tip: During Windows 2000 setup, you should use the Setup program only to create the partition where you intend to install the new operating system.
. . . .

After you've selected the partition for the installation, you must select the file system. Windows 2000 supports the FAT, FAT32, and NTFS file systems. Microsoft recommends that you select NTFS for your entire system, because many of Windows 2000's features, including security enhancements, rely on the file system for their functionality. In fact, Windows 2000 Active Directory and domain controllers require NTFS partitions to be available. Table 2.4 shows the features of FAT, FAT32, and NTFS.

Tip: Don't select NTFS if your system must support other operating systems. While the need to support multiple operating systems on a server is unlikely, NTFS is only supported by Windows NT 4 Server and Workstation and the Windows 2000 family of operating systems.

You should remember that VFAT (originally introduced with Windows for Workgroups 3.11) is not natively supported in Windows 2000.

Note: VFAT, supported by the original releases of Windows 95, Windows NT 3.51, and Windows NT 4, essentially boasts the same file system features as FAT. However, VFAT provides long file-name support and carries no restriction on the number of files contained in non-root directories. In contrast, FAT is limited to 65,535 files in non-root directories.

Each file system supported by Windows 2000 possesses different strengths. The FAT and FAT32 file systems support easy dual-booting between operating

Table 2.4 FAT, FAT32, and NTFS capabilities and characteristics.

Feature	FAT	FAT32	NTFS
Total Volume Size	2GB	4TB	16EB
Maximum File Size	2GB	4TB	16EB
Maximum Files in Root Directory	512	No limit	No limit
Maximum Files in Non-root Directory	65,535	No limit	No limit
Maximum File Name Length	11	256	256
File-level Security	No	No	Yes
File Compression	Requires third-party utilities	Requires third-party utilities	Natively supported
Transaction Logging	No	No	Yes
POSIX Support	No	No	POSIX1
Dual-boot Support	Yes	Yes	No
Self-repairing	No	Limited	Yes

systems, but they don't offer compression. The NTFS file system offers support for file-level security and Active Directory services and compression.

The best file system for an installation depends largely on an administrator's needs and the environment in which Windows 2000 is being installed. If dual-booting is an important feature and security is not, you might elect for the FAT32 file system. Should Active Directory services and very large volumes be required in your organization, NTFS will be required.

FAT and FAT32 are supported in Windows 2000. While the two file systems don't provide the full-featured functionality of NTFS, they do offer several benefits.

FAT and FAT32 Strengths

Use of the FAT and FAT32 file systems in Windows 2000 restricts the new operating systems' capabilities. Features such as remote storage, Active Directory, security enhancements, and more rely upon NTFS.

One benefit of FAT and FAT32 is their dual-boot friendliness. The very features of NTFS that make it beneficial in a network environment where security is important make NTFS a poor host for dual-boot systems. Should you have the need to host multiple operating systems, or should you want to host redundant installations for purposes of recovery and high-availability, FAT or FAT32 might be required.

Warning: With Windows NT, many administrators load Windows NT Server on a FAT partition and store data on an NTFS partition. The storage method helps troubleshooting and recovery operations on errant systems. However, the practice should be discouraged, because it leaves the system registry and other critical account, user, and system information less than secure. Windows 2000 now includes the Recovery Mode Console, so FAT partitions should no longer be needed for this purpose. More information on the Recovery Mode Console can be found in Chapter 18.

NTFS Advantages

NTFS improves security and eliminates inefficiencies in Windows 2000. NTFS is known for its efficiency, security, and reliability, and it boasts the following benefits:

➤ Possesses superior compression capabilities compared to FAT and FAT 32

➤ Enables enhanced security, because it permits encryption and file- and folder-level security

➤ Permits the enforcement of disk quotas by user

➤ Enables several new Windows 2000 features, including use of the Active Directory

➤ Provides unlimited files in the root and non-root directories

➤ Offers support for long file names

➤ Features self-repairing characteristics

One of the few drawbacks of using NTFS is its dual-boot unfriendliness. The lack of dual-booting support has meant administrators who were worried about recoverability had to perform parallel installations of Windows NT. These parallel installations were used for recovery when the first installation failed. Windows 2000 addresses this issue with its Recovery Mode Console. The Recovery Mode Console permits command-line access to a non-booting system. Secured NTFS partitions can then be accessed, assuming the administrator possesses the appropriate rights. Windows 2000 also includes a Safe Boot option previously unavailable in Windows NT operating systems.

After the advantages and disadvantages are reviewed, and a file system is selected, the next step in installing Windows 2000 is to select a licensing mode.

SELECT A WINDOWS 2000 LICENSING MODE

Microsoft requires that every installed Windows 2000 Professional operating system possess a license. In addition, licenses are needed for every Windows 2000 Server product installed. However, licensing issues don't end there. Client Access Licenses (CALs) must exist for each client that accesses the Windows 2000 Server.

Just as in Windows NT, you can select from two licensing options in the Windows 2000 OS. Microsoft offers Per Seat and Per Server licensing options:

➤ *Per Seat licensing*—Requires each client accessing the server to have its own CAL. Clients with a CAL can access as many servers as they want, so this is the most commonly used licensing mode.

➤ *Per Server licensing*—Requires the server to possess a CAL for each concurrent connection it hosts. For example, if Per Server licensing is selected, and 25 concurrent licenses are purchased, 25 users can access the server at any time. This licensing mode works best when an organization uses a single server for Internet or remote access services.

Organizations with more than one server generally select Per Seat licensing, because this mode permits users to connect to as many different servers as they want without the requirement that they have a CAL for each of the different servers they access. Instead, just a single CAL is required. Smaller networks using a single server often opt for Per Server licensing. In Windows NT, you were given the option to upgrade to Per Seat licensing from Per Server mode, but you could only do so once.

In Windows 2000, you can change from Per Server to Per Seat if you discover that the number of CALs required to support the Per Server mode is greater than your number of client PCs. However, you can perform this conversion only once, and you can do so only for the following products:

➤ Windows 2000 Server

➤ Microsoft Exchange Server

➤ SQL Server

➤ SNA Server

. . . .
Tip: Per Seat licensing is commonly selected when using Windows 2000 Terminal Services. Per Server mode, however, must be selected when using Windows 2000 Terminal Services Internet Connector Licenses.
. . . .

Several services don't require licenses. Administrators need to recognize which applications require licenses and which do not require CALs. Connections that do not require CALs include anonymous or authenticated access to a Windows 2000 Server running Internet Information Services and Web servers providing HTML files via HTTP. CALs also are not required with Telnet and FTP connections.

Warning: You should be aware that Windows 2000 licenses cover their respective use of the desktop and server operating systems, and CALs cover access to Windows 2000 Servers, only. Windows 2000 licenses do not cover access to BackOffice products, such as Site Server Commerce Edition, Exchange Server, Proxy Server, BackOffice Server, SQL Server, Systems Management Server, SNA Server, and others.

After selecting the licensing mode that works best for your organization, you're ready to move on to the next Windows 2000 installation step. Before you can proceed, you must gather information about the domain or workgroup the server will be joining.

Determining a Namespace

When installing Windows 2000, you must specify the network security group that the new computer will be joining. The network security group will be either a domain or a workgroup.

Domain Membership

Before you can join a server to a domain, you must:

➤ Know the DNS name for the domain you want the new computer to join.

➤ Have a computer account in the existing domain or administrative privileges to create a computer account in the existing domain.

➤ Ensure that the domain controller and DNS server are online and available.

Joining an existing domain requires that you know the Domain Name System (DNS) name for the domain. For example, the DNS name for Microsoft Corp. is **microsoft.com**. If you were to add a server named Axis in the Microsoft Marketing domain, the FQDN would be **axis.marketing.microsoft.com**.

You'll also need to create a computer account for your new computer on the existing domain. If you possess administrative rights, you can create the necessary computer account during installation. Otherwise, you'll need to contact the network administrator and request that the computer account be created. Either way, the account must exist before your new computer can join the domain.

Finally, in order to complete the process of joining a domain, you'll also need an available domain controller as well as a server providing DNS service. While DNS can run on the domain controller, both must be available, or your new computer won't be able to join the domain.

Note: If you are installing the first server in a domain, you should select the No, This Computer Is Not On A Network, Or Is On A Network Without A Domain option from the Windows 2000 Server Setup dialog box and delete any text that appears in the Workgroup or computer domain box. For more information on domain configuration, please see Chapter 5.

Workgroup Membership

The process of joining a workgroup is the same as in Windows NT. You must simply know the name of the workgroup you are joining. You do not need a DNS server or a computer account when connecting a new computer to a workgroup. Rather than requiring a FQDN name, you'll merely use the 15-character network NetBIOS naming convention when adding a computer to a workgroup. This will identify your new machine to existing computers in the workgroup. After you've acquired the information necessary for domain or workgroup membership, you've wrapped up the final step of the pre-installation checklist.

Review the Checklist

After you've checked your systems' hardware for compatibility, selected a file system, reviewed Microsoft's licensing options, and acquired the information you need for joining a workgroup or domain, you should review the pre-installation checklist. Pay close attention to any systems or domain naming changes that could have occurred between the time you began the checklist and the time you approach a system for the actual installation of Windows 2000.

After reviewing the checklist and ensuring you've obtained the necessary information for proceeding, you're ready to install Windows 2000. All that remains is to select the installation method that's appropriate for your situation. Windows 2000 offers the following five installation options:

➤ Installation from a compact disk

➤ Installation over a network

➤ Automated installation using the Windows 2000 Setup Manager Wizard

➤ Automated installation using Disk Duplication

➤ Installation via Remote Installation Services

INSTALLING WINDOWS 2000 USING A COMPACT DISK

As with most operating systems, Windows 2000 can be installed using a compact disk. The compact disk installation can be initialized using floppy disks, or, if a computer's BIOS supports the option, you can select to boot directly from the CD. For upgrades, the Windows 2000 CD-ROM also offers an auto-run program.

Several new Windows 2000 wizards guide you through the setup and configuration processes. As in Windows NT, the winnt32.exe file is used to start an upgrade installation. The **Winnt.exe** command triggers the Windows 2000 Setup program to begin a new installation.

Winnt.exe Installation

When Winnt.exe is executed, a miniature version of Windows 2000 is loaded onto a system. Once the text-mode portion of the Setup program begins, you should press F6 to load third-party SCSI and RAID drivers.

Next, you'll need to select which partition will receive the new installation and the file system you'll be using. You'll also have an opportunity to format the partition. After copying files, the Setup program reboots the computer, and the Windows 2000 Setup Wizard takes over.

The Windows 2000 Setup Wizard will prompt you for the following information:

➤ Regional settings

➤ Name and organization

➤ Licensing mode

➤ Computer name and administrator account password

After regional settings are defined, a name and organization are provided, a licensing mode is chosen, and the computer name and administrator account password are entered, you're given the opportunity to install optional components. Table 2.5 shows the optional components that can be installed using the Windows 2000 Setup program.

Following the selection of optional components, the time and date must be supplied. Ensure that the time and date settings are accurate, because Windows 2000's replication processes rely on this information to perform properly.

Next, the Setup Wizard proceeds to the installation of several networking components. Setup first detects and configures a system's network adapter cards. Then it seeks the DHCP service on the network.

Note: *For more information on the DHCP service, please see Chapter 11.*

You'll then be presented with two options. You can select either a typical or a customized installation. Choosing a typical installation instructs Windows 2000 Setup Wizard to install the following:

➤ Client for Microsoft Networks

➤ File and Printer Sharing for Microsoft Networks

➤ TCP/IP

Table 2.5 Optional components that can be installed by the Windows 2000 Setup Wizard.

Component	Feature
Certificate Services	Permits the creation and enables requests for X.509 digital certificates used to verify identities.
Cluster Service	Available only in Windows 2000 Advanced Server and Windows 2000 Datacenter Server. Cluster Service lets two or more servers combine resources to maintain higher levels of system and application availability.
Internet Information Services	Provides and administers Web and FTP services. The option to install Internet Information Services is selected by default.
Management And Monitoring Tools	Installs utilities for network performance monitoring and maintenance.
Message Queuing Services	Permits communication across heterogeneous networks. Also provides application support for sending messages to queues, which control and verify data flow, and communicating with temporarily unavailable systems.
Microsoft Indexing Service	Permits full-text searches of resources stored on a system.
Microsoft Script Debugger	Installs a debugging utility for Microsoft ActiveX platforms, including Visual Basic, Visual Basic Scripting Edition, and Jscript. The option to install Microsoft Script Debugger is selected by default.
Networking Services	Installs DHCP, DNS, TCP/IP, print server, file and print server, and other networking services.
Other Network File And Print Services	Permits file and printer sharing services between Windows 2000 and Macintosh and Unix systems.
Remote Installation Services	Provides a server with the ability to install Windows 2000 Professional on remote clients over a network.
Remote Storage	Permits the automatic transfer of data from NTFS volumes to other media.
Terminal Services	Installs server support for Windows-based applications and virtual session support for Windows 95, Windows 98, Windows NT Workstation, Windows 2000 Professional, and Windows-based terminals.

After joining a workgroup or domain, Windows 2000 Setup copies additional files, applies the configuration settings you supplied earlier, saves the configuration settings, and removes temporary files created during the Setup process before rebooting.

At this point, for standalone and member servers, installation is complete. Domain controllers require additional configuration, which is covered in Chapter 5.

Winnt32.exe Installation

Executing Winnt32.exe starts the Windows 2000 upgrade installation. Inserting a Windows 2000 CD-ROM while a previously supported version of Windows is running can also trigger the auto-run file, which begins the upgrade installation program.

When the upgrade installation begins, a dialog box appears indicating that the CD-ROM contains a newer version of Windows than the one being used. Setup asks whether you would like to upgrade to Windows 2000. If you select Yes, you're guided by dialog boxes through a few questions. You must read and accept the licensing agreement and specify any upgrade packs required by your applications to work properly with Windows 2000. You are then presented with the opportunity to select a partition for installation, and then the Setup program examines your system's configuration. A Windows 2000 Setup dialog box monitors the examination's progress, as shown in Figure 2.1.

Potential software and hardware conflicts are then identified. The Windows 2000 Professional Setup program provides a report of potential system incompatibilities, as seen in Figure 2.2. Any incompatibilities should be addressed through the addition of new hardware, drivers, and/or patches. In many cases, Windows 2000 will operate properly, despite incompatibilities, while some features of software programs and hardware devices might be limited. Windows 2000 can also remove incompatible hardware after it is installed via the Add/Remove Hardware applet in the Control Panel.

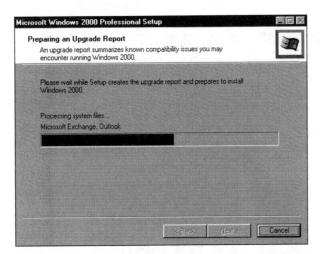

Figure 2.1 A dialog box tracks the progress while Windows 2000 examines your system.

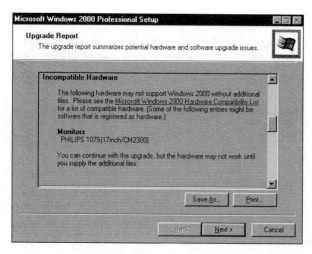

Figure 2.2   The Windows 2000 Professional Setup program checks a system for software and hardware incompatibilities, then lists the results of its search in its Upgrade Report.

After compatibility issues are resolved, the next step is to begin installing Windows 2000 files on your machine. One more dialog box, as shown in Figure 2.3, appears before the final Setup steps begin.

If several systems require new Windows 2000 installations, CD-ROM installation might not be the best method to use for deployment. A more efficient option might be to use network-based installations.

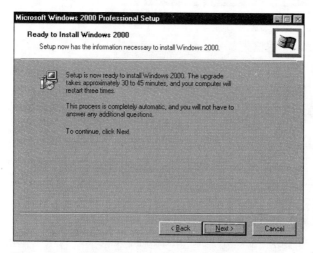

Figure 2.3   Windows 2000 Professional presents a dialog box before beginning the final phases of Setup to warn users how long the process could take and that the computer must restart several times.

INSTALLING WINDOWS 2000 OVER A NETWORK

2

Many administrators facing the prospect of multiple Windows 2000 installations prefer deploying the OS over a network. There's no requirement that all the machines receiving Windows 2000 share identical configurations. Windows 2000 network installations share many similarities with CD-ROM installations. The process begins with the execution of the Setup program from a shared folder. Setup then copies the necessary files to the client machine via the network. Several configuration options are available to administrators.

When preparing a network installation, you must:

➤ Ensure that the i386 directory is present on a shared folder

➤ Ensure that the target machine has a partition with 685MB of disk space

➤ Verify that the target machine has network client software loaded, enabling it to connect to the shared folder housing the i386 folder from the Windows 2000 CD-ROM

The following steps describe a Windows 2000 network installation:

1. Start the target machine using its network software.

2. Establish the connection between the target machine and the network share housing the i386 files.

3. Run Winnt.exe to begin the Windows 2000 Setup program. The Windows 2000 Setup program restarts the target machine and installation begins.

Windows 2000 network installations are highly configurable, whether performing fresh installations or upgrades. Several switches are available for modifying Winnt.exe-based installations. Table 2.6 lists Winnt.exe switches and their functions.

Switches used for creating Setup disks on the Windows NT 4 platform are no longer used. Instead, the Makeboot.exe program, which is found in the bootdisk folder on the Windows 2000 CD-ROM, replaces the old method.

Upgrades to existing Windows installations are conducted using Winnt32.exe. Several switches are available for modifying Winnt32.exe installations. Table 2.7 lists Winnt32.exe switches and their functions.

Another available Windows 2000 installation method is an automated installation using the Windows 2000 Setup Manager Wizard.

Table 2.6   Several switches are available for modifying Winnt.exe installations.

Switches	Function
/a	Turns accessibility options on.
/e:[command]	Executes the supplied command before Setup's final phase.
/i:[inf file name]	Specifies the information file name Setup is to use. Dosnet.inf is the default. Only the file name is required, not the path.
/r:[folder name]	Specifies an additional folder to be created during Setup.
/rx:[folder name]	Specifies an additional folder to be copied during Setup.
/s:[source path]	Specifies the location of Windows 2000 Setup files. Requires full path.
/t:[temp drive]	Specifies the drive where temporary files are to be copied. The default is the drive offering the most free space.
/u:[answer file name]	Specifies the use of an answer file for unattended installation. *Answer file name* indicates the name of the answer file to be used.
/udf:[identifier, UDF file]	Specifies a uniqueness database file, indicated by *UDF*, to be used during installation. *Identifier* specifies which parameter in the answer file should be replaced with information from the UDF file.

Note: *The* **/u:** *switch requires use of the* **/s:** *parameter to specify the answer file location.*

Table 2.7   Several switches are available for modifying Winnt32.exe installations.

Switches	Function
/checkupgradeonly	Checks a computer for incompatibilities. Saves a Winnt32.log report for NT upgrades and Upgrade.txt report for Windows 9x upgrades.
/copydir:[folder]	Creates an additional systemroot folder each time **/copydir** is used.
/copysource:[folder]	Creates additional folder in systemroot folder to be deleted upon completion of installation.
/cmd:[command]	Executes the supplied command before Setup's final phase.
/cmdcons	Installs files necessary for loading the file repair and recovery console.
/debug[level:file]	Creates a debug log at the level specified.
/s:[source path]	Specifies the location of Windows 2000 installation files. Multiple **/s:** switches can sometimes shorten transfer times.
/syspart:[drive letter]	Copies Setup files to the specified hard disk and marks the drive active.
/tempdrive:[drive letter]	Copies temporary Setup files to the specified drive for installation there and marks it active.
/unattend[number: answer file name]	Triggers an unattended installation. *Number specifies* the number of seconds between the time Setup finishes copying the files and when it restarts. *Answer file name* specifies the name of the answer file to be used during Setup.
/udf:[identifier, UDF]	Specifies a uniqueness database file, indicated by *UDF*, to be used during installation. *Identifier* specifies which parameter in the answer file should be replaced with information from the UDF file, which overrides the value supplied by the answer file.

Note: *The* **/syspart** *switch requires use of the* **/tempdrive** *parameter. Syspart permits installation of Windows 2000 on another computer, but stops before continuing to the next phase. This allows installation to start on a hard drive and then stop, allowing the hard drive to be moved to a different machine before Setup begins with the next phase of installation.*

INSTALLING WINDOWS 2000 USING THE SETUP MANAGER WIZARD

2

In Windows NT, administrators having to complete multiple Windows installations often turn to scripts to customize the installations for the various hardware configurations on the network. While you can still use installation scripts to deploy customized Windows installations, Windows 2000's Setup Manager Wizard can help eliminate many of the problems resulting from scripted installations.

The Windows 2000 Setup Manager Wizard helps you to quickly create customized scripts for the Windows 2000 installations. It works by creating a wizard interface that can be used to create the answers the Setup program needs as it customizes an installation.

Note: The option exists in Windows 2000 to manually edit the Unattend.exe file used to supply hardware configuration variables during unattended installations. However, you should use the Windows 2000 Setup Wizard to eliminate common syntax and keystroke errors.

In order to use the Windows 2000 Setup Manager, the Windows 2000 Resource Kit must be installed. The Resource Kit is included in the Support folder on the Windows 2000 CD-ROM. The kit itself is installed by running Setup.exe from the Support\Reskit folder.

The Windows 2000 Setup Manager possesses the ability to specify computer- and user-specific rights during setup. The distribution folder housing the Windows 2000 installation files can be specified via the wizard, too, and application setup scripts can be triggered to run from the answer file that the Setup Manager creates.

After the Windows 2000 Setup Manager starts, you must select from one of three options:

➤ Create A New Answer File

➤ Create An Answer File Using The Current System's Configuration

➤ Modify An Existing Answer File

If the first option is selected (Create A New Answer File), the type of answer file being created needs to be specified. Four types of answer files are available:

➤ Unattend.txt file for Windows 2000 Professional Setup

➤ Unattend.txt file for Windows 2000 Server Setup

➤ Remboot.sif file for Remote Installation Services use

➤ Sysprep.inf file for System Preparation Tool use

. . . .

Tip: The Sysprep.inf file can be used to specify that customized drivers should be loaded during the installation process.

. . . .

An answer file can be used when booting from a CD-ROM, too. Using the Windows 2000 Setup Manager, specify the installation folder, select the No, This Answer File Will Be Used To Install From A CD option on the distribution folder page, and save the newly created file to a floppy with the name Winnt.sif. Because the Winnt.exe program searches for this file when booting from a CD-ROM drive, it can be used to specify the answer file the Setup program needs for customizing an installation.

The Windows 2000 Setup Wizard also prompts you to specify the interaction level between users and the Setup program. The selection made determines how much expertise the user will require to complete the installation. Five setup interaction levels are available—Fully Automated, Provide Defaults, Hide Pages, Read Only, and GUI Attended. Table 2.8 describes the user interaction level options available in Windows 2000.

. . . .

Tip: When automating domain controller deployment, installation of a server can be automated with one answer file, and a second answer file can be used to promote the server to a domain controller. Domain controller promotion can be triggered by running the Dcpromo.exe command with the **/answer:**[answer file name] switch immediately after Setup completes.

. . . .

If you need to install Windows 2000 on multiple systems that share identical configurations, you might want to automate the installations by using disk duplication.

Table 2.8 The Windows 2000 Setup Wizard requires one of five possible user interaction levels to be selected during the Windows 2000 installation process.

Level	Description	Intended Use
Fully Automated	Uses the values provided in the answer file to completely automate the remaining steps of the Windows 2000 installation.	Best used when deploying multiple systems with the same configurations.
Provide Defaults	Requests that users confirm the values provided by the answer file when completing the Windows 2000 installation.	Best used for situations in which there might be just a few changes made to the configuration values supplied by the answer file.

(continued)

Table 2.8 The Windows 2000 Setup Wizard requires one of five possible user interaction levels to be selected during the Windows 2000 installation process *(continued)*.

Level	Description	Intended Use
Hide Pages	Automates the portions of the Setup process for which values are provided in the answer file but requires users to supply necessary information not provided in the answer file.	Best for preparing a system with a particular configuration when a user might also need the ability to configure a limited number of settings.
Read Only	Automates the sections of the Setup process for which values are provided in the answer file but requires users to supply information not provided in the answer file. With Read Only, only the portions of the dialog boxes are shown requiring more information.	Best when you want users to provide only the information not supplied by the answer file.
GUI Attended	Completely automates the text-based portion of the Setup process. A user completing the Setup program must then provide the remaining information needed by the Setup program to complete installation.	Best used when you want to completely automate the text-based portion of Setup but provide users with the ability to completely customize the GUI portion of the Setup process.

INSTALLING WINDOWS 2000 USING DISK DUPLICATION

The popularity of Norton Ghost and other disk duplication programs attest to the value administrators place on such utilities. The labor savings that result from the ability to duplicate, or clone, disk images for deployment of identically configured machines is significant. While the use of such third-party tools is still required, Windows 2000 includes additional support for disk duplication practices. Malfunctioning machines are sometimes most efficiently fixed by simply reinstalling the operating system as well as preconfigured software programs from a disk image created earlier when the computer was deployed.

The Role of Sysprep

The Sysprep.exe utility is one of the enhanced tools used for disk duplication by Windows 2000. Sysprep.exe, which is often used with the Windows 2000 Setup Manager Wizard, prepares a disk for the imaging process. After the Sysprep.exe program has run, the third-party tool can be used to capture an image and copy it to other systems.

In Windows NT, one of the major issues with disk duplication is security identifiers (SIDs), which contain user- and computer-specific information. A major new role for Sysprep.exe is its ability to strip the SIDs and other unit-specific information from an image before it's captured and duplicated.

Note: Systems receiving installation via disk duplication generate unique SIDs on their own following the disk duplication process.

Several switches, described in Table 2.9, are available for use. They can be used to customize the use of the System Preparation utility.

In order to maximize the use of the System Preparation Tool, you should have an understanding of the entire disk duplication process. The steps in the duplication process are as follows:

1. Install and configure Windows 2000 on a computer.

2. Install and configure applications, programs, and any proprietary software that you want to include in the automated deployment.

3. Run the System Preparation Tool—Sysprep.exe—on the master computer featuring the image you want to duplicate and later install on other machines. Or, run the Windows 2000 Setup Manager Wizard to create a Sysprep.inf file. This file, which the Setup Manager's Mini-Setup program seeks, is stored in the Sysprep folder created by the Setup Manager at the root of the drive image. It can also be stored on a floppy, which must be inserted into the destination computer's A: drive prior to the Mini-Setup program launching in Step 6.

4. Restart the master computer, and run a third-party disk-cloning program to create a master image, which should be stored on a shared folder (or burnt to a CD-ROM). Use a floppy disk created by the third-party disk imaging utility to boot the system on which you intend to install the image, then connect to the network share containing the drive image.

Table 2.9 The Sysprep.exe utility can be customized with four switches.

Switches	Function
-quiet	Instructs the Sysprep.exe utility to run with no user interaction
-pnp	Specifies that the Setup program detects Plug and Play devices on destination systems
-reboot	Specifies the destination system should restart instead of shut down
-nosidgen	Indicates that a security identifier should not be created on the destination system

5. Use the third-party disk imaging program to copy the image file onto the destination machine. Alternatively, you can load the destination machine using the CD-ROM.

6. Reboot the destination system. The Windows 2000 Mini-Setup program runs, and you'll be prompted for computer-specific information, such as an administrator password for the new computer, the computer name, and so forth. The Mini-Setup program then generates a new SID, and the system becomes operational.

Warning: Remember that, when using disk duplication, systems do not need to possess the same configurations. However, the mass storage controllers (SCSI controllers or IDE chipsets) and hardware abstraction layers (ACPI systems can't be mixed with non-ACPI systems) used on both the test and destination systems must be identical.

New to Windows 2000 is Remote Installations Services. In addition to possessing the capacity to deploy software installments throughout a network, Windows 2000 enables its servers to remotely install Windows 2000 Professional on other networked machines.

INSTALLING WINDOWS 2000 VIA REMOTE INSTALLATION SERVICES

One of the most important new features in Windows 2000 is Remote Installation Services (RIS), which enables systems engineers to install and configure Windows 2000 Professional throughout an entire network from a single location. Other benefits of using the Remote Installation Services for the widespread deployment of Windows 2000 Professional client desktop machines include:

➤ The requirement for maintaining hardware-specific images is eliminated, because RIS supports Setup's use of Plug and Play hardware detection.

➤ RIS provides another option for fixing networked computers that have failed due to corrupted operating systems.

➤ RIS contributes to improved total costs of ownership, because other technical staff can be entrusted to install Windows 2000.

Before an administrator can enjoy the benefits of deploying Windows 2000 Professional client installations using Remote Installation Services, several requirements must be met:

➤ A Windows 2000 server must be present on the network and running Remote Installation Services. RIS servers can be domain controllers or member servers.

➤ A Windows 2000 server must be running DNS service.

➤ A Windows 2000 server must be running DHCP service.

➤ A Windows 2000 server must be running Active Directory.

➤ Sufficient (2GB) hard disk or partition space must be available for holding the operating system images you plan to transfer to destination machines. (Group policies are used to control access to the different images housed here.) This partition must not be housed on the drive running the Windows 2000 Server operating system, and it must be formatted with NTFS.

➤ The destination machines must support remote boot or Preboot Execution Environment (PXE) network interface device cards.

➤ The client machines should be Network PC compatible.

The Net PC specification has further requirements of its own:

➤ The NIC must be set as the primary boot device within the system BIOS.

➤ The user account performing the installation must be able to log on as a batch job user.

➤ Users must be granted permission to create computer accounts in the domain they are joining, unless the computer account has already been created using Active Directory.

While all the required items do not have to be available on a single server, they must all be available on the network.

RIS works by permitting a destination machine to boot without Windows installed and request an IP address from the DHCP server, which also supplies the IP address of the closest RIS server. If a remote system doesn't support remote boot, a RIS boot disk can be created and inserted in the destination system. However, this requires an administrator to be physically present at the destination machine, which defeats one of RIS's chief advantages.

· · · · · · · · · · · · ·
Tip: The RIS boot disk can be created by running the Rbfg.exe command found in the
            RemoteInstall\Admin\i386 folder of the Windows 2000 Server CD-ROM.
· · · · · · · · · · · · · ·

If a destination computer has a computer account configured in Active Directory, the machine then contacts the RIS server. The RIS server queries Active Directory services for the unique Globally Unique Identifier (GUID) for the destination machine. Then the RIS server transmits the images that the destination machine has privileges to receive and installs automatically.

If a destination computer does not have a computer account configured, it must log onto Active Directory. The Client Installation Wizard is then run to select an operating system image.

In order to begin an RIS installation, Remote Installation Services must first be installed. As with many other new services in Windows 2000, a wizard is provided to assist with the installation. In fact, RIS must be installed using the Remote Installation Services Startup Wizard. Before the wizard can be run, the RIS component must be added using the Windows Components Wizard found in Control Panel's Add/Remove Programs applet. Then Remote Installation Services must be selected, as shown in Figure 2.4.

After the Windows Components Wizard completes its task, you need to restart the server. When Windows restarts, run Risetup.exe from a command prompt or the Start|Run command line. The command triggers the Remote Installation Services Setup Wizard, as shown in Figure 2.5. The first item the wizard calls for is the path to the Remote Installation Folder location, as shown in Figure 2.6.

Next, two options are provided regarding the initial RIS settings. You can enable the server to support client computers requesting service immediately, before the server has been configured to do so. In addition, you can configure

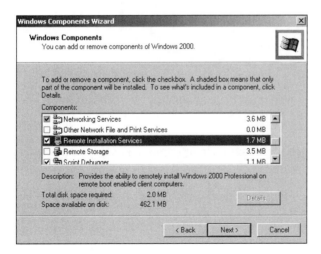

Figure 2.4 Remote Installation Services is installed using the Windows Components Wizard.

Figure 2.5   The Remote Installation Services Setup Wizard is used to install RIS.

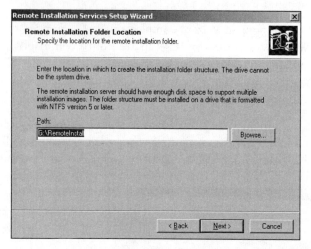

Figure 2.6   The RIS wizard requires the location for the Remote Installation Folder, which must have adequate free space available and be formatted with NTFS.

the server to respond to unknown client computers. By default, neither option is automatically supported.

The RIS wizard then requires that the path for the installation files be specified. The path can direct RIS to either a shared folder or a CD-ROM drive. The folder name should be supplied, too, or you'll be prompted to include it.

Tip: A full version of Windows 2000 Professional must be available when using RIS. RIS does not support upgrading from the Upgrade version of Windows 2000 Professional.

After providing a friendly description and help text language for the Windows 2000 Professional installation image, the wizard presents the installation settings for review, as shown in Figure 2.7. If the specified settings are accurate, click Finish to complete the installation. The wizard then completes the installation of RIS. The progress is tracked in a special dialog box, as shown in Figure 2.8. Upon completion, RIS is started. Click Done, and you're ready to begin imaging client machines on your network.

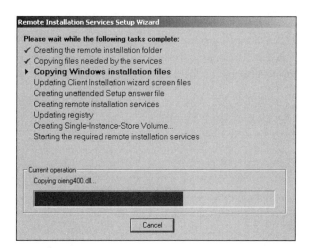

Figure 2.7   As with many of the new wizards and utilities in Windows 2000, a Review Settings dialog box is presented for final review before changes are made to your system.

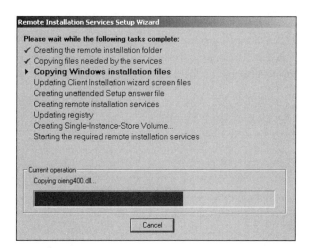

Figure 2.8   Installation progress is monitored as the wizard completes the process.

TROUBLESHOOTING WINDOWS 2000 SETUP

Despite the best planning and preflight preparations, Windows 2000 installations sometimes experience trouble. Therefore, you must have an understanding of common setup problems and their appropriate solutions. Following are a few troubleshooting pointers for various setup problems:

➤ *Windows fails to install or start*—Check the HCL to ensure you don't have an incompatible device that's foiling the Setup program.

➤ *Windows 2000 Setup locks up midway through the installation process*—Attempt to reboot the system using Ctrl+Alt+Delete. If there is no response, try the "three-finger salute" again. If there is still no response, press your system's reset button. If a boot menu appears, select Windows 2000 Server Setup. If you don't see a boot menu, try executing Setup again.

➤ *Setup fails or freezes while copying files*—Check your BIOS and ensure IDE controllers are configured properly. Also, check to ensure another peripheral isn't interfering with your hard disk controller. While inconvenient, this can simplify troubleshooting exponentially. Simply remove all unneeded peripherals in an attempt to eliminate the offending device.

➤ *Multiple faults are experienced*—Forcibly reboot the machine as many times as faults are encountered. The Windows 2000 Setup program can learn from previous faults it experiences.

➤ *Installation trouble due to scratched or faulty CD-ROMs*—Contact Microsoft or your vendor. Replacement media can eliminate the trouble.

➤ *Windows 2000 doesn't support your CD-ROM drive*—Reach for the requisition requests, because you'll need to replace the CD-ROM drive with a compatible device. In a pinch, resorting to a network-based installation can circumvent this problem.

➤ *Setup program finds insufficient disk space for the Windows 2000 installation*—Specify another drive or partition. Should no other drives or spaces be available, either purchase new drives or delete data you no longer need in order to free up space.

➤ *A dependent service fails to start*—Check the Network Settings page and ensure the correct protocol and adapter are installed. Also check that the network adapter is properly configured and has the correct transceiver type specified, and verify that the local computer name is unique.

➤ *After installing Windows 2000, you can't connect to a domain controller*—Perform the following procedures:

> Ensure you've entered the correct domain name.

> Verify you've entered the correct DNS and DHCP server addresses and that both services are online.

> Verify that the network card and protocol settings are configured correctly.

> If Windows 2000 is being reinstalled and is using the same computer name, delete and then re-create the computer account on the server.

> *No domain controller is available, or the DNS or DHCP services are unavailable—* Complete the installation by joining a workgroup instead. Later, when the failed services come online or a domain controller becomes available, you can join the domain.

CHAPTER SUMMARY

The installation and setup routines used by Windows 2000 are similar to those found on the Windows NT 4 platform. However, Windows 2000 enhancements improve the installation process, and new configuration tools and services have been added to make Windows 2000 easier to install, whether you're installing the new OS via CD-ROM, over the network, via disk duplication, or with the use of the new Remote Installation Services. By planning an installation in advance and ensuring necessary information is prepared beforehand, you can avoid common difficulties.

Administrators, like pilots, should always complete a checklist before undertaking their duties. This is especially true for IT professionals installing Windows 2000. While much of the information needed prior to installing Windows 2000 is similar to that required with Windows NT 4, several important differences exist.

In addition to gaining knowledge of these differences, administrators must properly design and plan an installation. To maximize the use of Windows 2000's features, administrators should have a solid understanding of the new platform's requirements, improvements, and capabilities. Further, administrators must install Windows 2000 on systems with appropriate hardware to ensure trouble-free operation.

The first step when preparing a Windows 2000 installation is to ensure that all of a system's devices are included on the Windows 2000 Hardware Compatibility List. Along with all the powerful new enhancements and Windows 2000 services come increased system requirements. Administrators are well-advised to ensure that the systems they're installing Windows 2000 on meet the minimum requirements demanded by the operating system.

After an installation partition is selected, you must select the file system you'll use. Windows 2000 supports FAT, FAT32, and NTFS. Microsoft recommends you select NTFS for your entire system, because many Windows 2000 features, including security enhancements, rely on NTFS for their functionality. In fact, Windows 2000 Active Directory and domain controllers require that NTFS partitions be available.

As in Windows NT, the Winnt32.exe file is used to start an upgrade installation. The **Winnt.exe** command triggers the Windows 2000 Setup program to begin a new installation.

Many administrators facing the prospect of multiple Windows 2000 installations prefer deploying the OS over a network. There's no requirement that all the machines receiving Windows 2000 share identical configurations. A network installation of Windows 2000 is highly configurable, whether performing fresh installations or upgrades.

In Windows NT, administrators having to complete multiple Windows installations often use scripts to customize the installations for the various hardware configurations on the networks. While you can still use installation scripts to deploy customized Windows installations, Windows 2000's Setup Manager Wizard can help eliminate many of the problems resulting from scripted installations. The Windows 2000 Setup Manager also possesses the ability to specify computer- and user-specific rights during setup.

The labor savings that result from the ability to duplicate, or clone, disk images for deployment of identically configured machines is significant. The popularity of Norton Ghost and other disk-duplication programs attest to the value administrators place on such utilities. While the use of such third-party tools is still required, Windows 2000 includes additional support for disk duplication practices. Malfunctioning machines are sometimes most efficiently fixed by simply reinstalling the operating system and any pre-configured software programs from a disk image created earlier when the computer was deployed. The Sysprep.exe utility is one of the enhanced tools used for disk duplication by Windows 2000. Sysprep.exe, which is often used with the Windows 2000 Setup Manager Wizard, prepares a disk for the imaging process.

One of the most important new features in Windows 2000 is Remote Installation Services, which provides systems engineers with the ability to install and configure Windows 2000 Professional throughout an entire network from a single location. Before an administrator can enjoy the benefits of deploying Windows 2000 Professional client installations using Remote Installation Services, several requirements must be met. They include Windows 2000 Servers must be present on the network and running Remote Installation Services, DNS, DHCP, and Active Directory Services.

Despite the best planning and preflight preparations, Windows 2000 installations sometimes experience trouble. Therefore, you should have an understanding of common setup problems and their appropriate solutions.

REVIEW QUESTIONS

1. Which steps should be taken prior to installing Windows 2000 Professional?

   a. Confirm your system meets or exceeds the minimum hardware requirements

   b. Ensure the hardware devices on your system are listed in Microsoft's HCL

   c. Stop the Remote Installation Service on the server

   d. Secure a CAL for the destination computer

   e. a, b, and d

2. What are the minimum hardware requirements for running Windows 2000 Server?

   a. Pentium 166 processor, 64MB RAM, 500MB hard disk space

   b. Pentium 166 processor, 64MB RAM, 685MB hard disk space

   c. Pentium 166 processor, 128MB RAM, 1GB hard disk space

   d. Pentium 200 processor, 64MB RAM, 685MB hard disk space

   e. Pentium 200 processor, 64 MB RAM, 1GB hard disk space

3. Which is not a feature of the NTFS file system?

   a. Enables file- and folder-level security

   b. Supports disk compression

   c. Enables support of disk quotas

   d. Supports dual booting with Windows 98

   e. Supports file encryption

4. Which of the following are required when joining a domain? [Check all correct answers]

   a. IP address

   b. Valid domain name

   c. Computer account

   d. Available domain controller

   e. Server running DNS service

5. Valid methods of installing Windows 2000 include which of the following? [Check all correct answers]

    a. Disk duplication

    b. Remote Installation Services

    c. Installing from a CD-ROM

    d. Installing over a network

    e. Typing "Winnt.exe/o" to create installation floppy diskettes

6. The Windows 2000 Setup Wizard prompts you for what information? [Check all correct answers]

    a. The file system to be used

    b. The partition to receive the Windows installation

    c. Regional settings

    d. The IP address of the new system

    e. Which mode will be used to license the Windows 2000 system

7. Which Windows 2000 component enables dynamic full-text searches of data stored on a system or network?

    a. Microsoft Indexing Service

    b. Networking Services

    c. Internet Information Services

    d. Other Network File And Print Services

    e. Remote Storage

8. Which switch is used with the **Winnt.exe** command to specify an optional folder during installation?

    a. **/r**

    b. **/i**

    c. **/a**

    d. **/rx**

    e. **/f**

9. Which command is run to create Windows 2000 boot disks?

    a. **Winnt.exe/o**

    b. **Winnt.exe/ox**

    c. **Rdisk.exe**

    d. **Makeboot a:**

    e. Boot disks cannot be created for Windows 2000

2

10. The Per Server licensing mode should usually be used when clients need to access multiple servers.

   a. True

   b. False

11. Which Winnt32.exe switch specifies the location of Windows 2000 installation files?

   a. **/s**

   b. **/w**

   c. **/i**

   d. **/sysfile**

   e. **/installfiles**

12. The purpose of the Windows 2000 Setup Manager is to fulfill which function?

   a. Complete the installation of Windows 2000

   b. Prepare a system for Windows 2000 installation to begin

   c. Automate the creation of an Unattend.txt file

   d. Begin a CD-ROM-based installation

   e. Run a system check to ensure all hardware devices are compatible with Windows 2000

13. Which of the following is not a benefit of the Windows 2000 Setup Manager?

   a. Provides a graphical interface for creating answer files

   b. Simplifies installation of multiple deployments

   c. Creates a distribution folder used for installation files

   d. Eliminates errors in syntax and scripts

   e. Eliminates SIDs

14. A third-party disk imaging utility is no longer needed when using disk duplication to install Windows 2000.

   a. True

   b. False

15. Which switch is used with the Sysprep.exe utility to specify that no SID should be generated?

   a. **-quiet**

   b. **-negsid**

    c. **-reboot**

    d. **-nosidgen**

    e. **-removesid**

16. Which of the following items are required before RIS can be used to install Windows 2000 Professional? [Check all correct answers]

    a. DNS server

    b. DHCP server

    c. Active Directory Services

    d. WINS

    e. Destination system that is Network PC compatible

17. RIS must be installed on a hard disk that is not running Windows 2000 Server.

    a. True

    b. False

18. Which utility is often used with the Windows 2000 Setup Manager to assist with customized configurations of Windows 2000?

    a. Sysdiff.exe

    b. Sysprep.exe

    c. Unattend.txt

    d. Answer.txt

    e. Winnt.exe

19. A remote system must be Network PC compliant in order to benefit from remote installation.

    a. True

    b. False

20. Which of the following should be checked when experiencing trouble connecting to a domain controller? [Check all correct answers]

    a. NIC settings

    b. Protocol configuration

    c. Domain controller availability

    d. DNS server availability

    e. Whether the computer account has been used before, in which case it should be deleted and re-created

REAL-WORLD PROJECTS

2

Andy Palmer, our trusty consultant, has arrived back at work following a holiday weekend. After grabbing a cup of coffee and checking his email, he sits down to review the projects he's been assigned. He finds three new clients need Windows 2000 installed. However, two of the clients have special needs. Only one of the installations can be solved simply by booting from the CD-ROM.

The first client is a publishing firm requesting installation of another Windows 2000 Server. New manuscripts are arriving daily, but the firm is running out of disk storage space, and it doesn't want to overload its pair of domain controllers. The firm has no unusual needs for the new server. It will be used simply to provide file and print services. But the company needs the server operational as quickly as possible, and they want to ensure its installation will impose as little disruption to daily operation as possible.

The second customer is a law firm that already has two Windows 2000 Servers in place, but needs 22 Windows 2000 Professional desktops installed. The company wants to make use of new collaboration features in Office 2000, but it doesn't want to load it on the Windows 95 units currently installed throughout the organization. Instead, the IT director has prepared those units for a fresh installation. Andy notes that the office's IT director says some of their computers are three to four years old while others are brand new. As always, the sooner the machines are installed, the better.

The third client is a local library. The non-profit organization needs six desktops installed, but the computers feature a complex configuration due to the use of proprietary catalog services software. The institution's librarian usually performs the installation herself, but recent budget cuts have reduced staff and eliminated the time she is able to spend performing such tasks. As a service to the community, Andy's firm will provide pro bono consulting for the library, so he needs to meet their needs quickly and efficiently, thereby enabling him to return to the office and pick up new projects from paying customers.

Project 2.1
To install Windows 2000 from a CD-ROM:

Andy meets with the publishing company's single IT person and reviews the client's needs to be sure he has all the information he needs to complete the project appropriately. Andy then ensures that the new system that will be receiving Windows 2000 meets the minimum hardware requirements and all of its devices are supported by Windows 2000. He also checks to ensure he has the company's DNS and DHCP IP addresses available. Before beginning the installation, he verifies that a computer account has been created on the network using Active Directory and that he has the correct name and password for the administrator account.

Next, Andy installs Windows 2000 Server by performing the following steps:

1. Start the Windows Setup program by inserting the Windows 2000 CD-ROM and instructing the system's BIOS to boot from the CD-ROM drive.

2. Press Enter at the Setup Notification screen.

3. Press Enter at the Welcome To Setup screen.

4. Press C when the message is received indicating the computer's startup disk is new or has been erased.

5. Press F8 to accept the licensing terms.

6. Press C to select the C: partition to house the Windows 2000 installation, and press Enter to format the partition with the NTFS file system. Windows 2000 completes copying files to the hard disk, restarts the system, and begins the Windows 2000 Setup Wizard.

7. Press Next when the Setup Wizard appears, and the Setup program begins installing devices.

8. Select the Regional Settings and personalized software settings preferred by the publishing company.

9. Next, select Per Seat as the licensing option, because that's the licensing mode the client selected.

10. Enter the computer name and the password for the administrator account.

11. Because the server is to be used simply for file and printer services, Andy does not select any additional Windows 2000 components.

12. Andy is then prompted to enter the time and date, which he verifies is accurate on the publisher's other servers.

13. Select to proceed by installing networking components with their typical settings after Windows 2000 detects the system's network interface card.

14. Enter the domain name. The Setup program then completes the remainder of the installation by finishing with the transfer of files, applying the configuration settings, saving the configuration settings to the C: drive Andy had selected earlier, removing temporary files that had been placed on the hard drive during Setup, and restarting the system.

15. Create a Manuscripts folder on the new server, and share it to the Editors group. Andy then reviews what he has done with the publisher's IT director.

Under direction from the IT director, Andy then places a new manuscript in the folder and confirms that users in the Editors group can access it. After he is assured the server is functioning properly and can be used as intended by the publishing group, Andy heads to lunch.

Project 2.2
To install Windows 2000 using Remote Installation Services:

Several of the computers at Andy's next client, the law firm, feature different IDE controllers and BIOS programs. Therefore, he cannot elect to use disk duplication to roll out the 22 new Windows 2000 Professional machines. However, the law firm, anticipating growth, has implemented a 100MB Ethernet LAN.

Andy decides the best method for installing Windows 2000 Professional is by deploying the new operating system with the help of Remote Installation Services. All the requirements are in place on the server and destination machines, and the network boasts plenty of bandwidth for such an install.

Andy ensures he had the correct username and password for the administrator account, as well as the right domain name for the new system computers. Andy also verifies that computer accounts have been created, using Active Directory, for all 22 of the new machines.

Andy's first step is to install RIS on the law firm's Windows 2000 Server.

Installing RIS
To install RIS, Andy performs the following steps:

1. Open Add/Remove Programs in Control Panel and click Add/Remove Windows Components to launch the Windows Component Wizard.

2. Check the Remote Installation Services box and click Next to begin installing the service.

3. After permitting the system to reboot, select Add/Remove Programs again from the Control Panel and click Configure next to Configure Remote Installation Services.

4. Select Next, enter the folder path to be used as the root of the RIS, then click Next again.

5. Accept the default entries to not permit RIS to respond to client requests until it is configured to not respond to unknown clients.

6. Enter the path to the Windows 2000 Professional CD-ROM and click Next.

7. Enter the folder name where the Windows 2000 Professional image will be stored.

8. Enter a user-friendly name for the image in the dialog box.

9. Enter a detailed description of the operating system image in the Help Text section of the RIS Setup Wizard dialog box.

10. Review the settings in the Review Settings dialog box, then click Finish to complete the installation.

If DHCP were installed on another server, Andy would open the Microsoft Management Console, add the DHCP snap-in, right-click the DHCP root and select Manage Authorized Servers, click the Authorize button, enter the IP address of the RIS server, and then click OK.

With RIS installed on the server, which also provides DHCP services, Andy is ready to create the Windows 2000 Professional image for installation on destination machines.

Creating a RIS Image

To create the RIS image, Andy performs the following steps:

1. Open the Active Directory's Users And Computers view.

2. In the law firm's domain, right-click Server1, which houses the RIS service. Select Properties and then click the Remote Install tab.

3. Click Advanced Settings, then click the Images tab.

4. Click Add to start the Add Wizard.

5. Skip the Associate A New Answer File To An Existing Image option, because there are no existing images, and click Next.

6. Select the Add A New Installation Image option, and click Next.

7. Using the Add Installation Image Wizard, create the new Windows 2000 Professional image and the option to associate it with an answer file, and then click Finish to complete the wizard.

8. Specify the location of the answer file (prepared by the IT director), and click Next.

9. Select the Windows 2000 Professional image just created to apply the answer file to, then click Next.

10. Supply the name of the answer file.

11. Enter a user-friendly name and a more detailed description of the image in the Help Text box, then click Finish to complete the RIS image creation process.

After the RIS image is created, Andy is ready to move ahead with installation. First, though, he needs to quickly make the RIS boot disk for use by the destination machines that aren't Net PC–compliant. Because they aren't Net PC–compliant, they cannot boot directly to the network, thereby necessitating the need for the boot floppy.

Creating a RIS Boot Disk

To create the RIS boot disk, Andy performs the following steps:

1. Place a floppy disk in the destination machine's A: drive.

2. Connect to the RIS server and execute the **RBFG.EXE** command from the RemoteInstall\Admin\i386 folder.

3. Select the A: drive as the floppy drive to be used in the Remote Boot Disk Generator dialog box.

4. Click the Adapter List button to quickly ensure that the NIC the machine has is supported.

5. Click Create Disk to build the remote RIS boot disk.

Now, Andy is ready to transfer the Windows 2000 Professional image from the server to the destination machines.

Transferring an Image from the Server to Destination Machines

To transfer the Windows 2000 Professional image from the server to the destination machines, Andy performs the following steps:

1. Take a boot disk, created using the **RBFG.EXE** command found in the RemoteInstall\Admin\i386 folder of the Windows 2000 server CD-ROM, and place it in the floppy drive of the units not featuring the remote boot capability. Press F12 when prompted to boot from the network.

2. Select Enter from the first screen to trigger the Client Installation Wizard.

3. Enter the name of the law firm's domain that the system should join, and then tab to the password box.

4. Enter the password for the administrator account and press Enter.

5. Enter the IP address for the law firm's DNS server.

6. After selecting Custom Setup, press Enter.

7. Enter the appropriate computer name for the system, as supplied by the law firm's IT director, then indicate the path to the share created on the server housing the Windows 2000 Professional image the destination system was to use. Then press Enter.

8. Select the image that is intended to transfer to the destination system.

9. Finally, verify the settings are correct and press Enter, triggering the Windows 2000 Professional installation.

Andy has the law firm's employees log on with their Windows 2000 machines to ensure that they have network access, and then he heads for his last appointment of the day.

Project 2.3

To install Windows 2000 using disk duplication:

Driving across town to the public library, Andy thinks about the options that are available to the librarian. He can set up RIS, but he wants to ensure the librarian doesn't have to go behind the installation of each Windows 2000 Professional installation in the future and add all the complex proprietary software members used to reserve books, check card catalogs, and view upcoming events.

He thinks about creating a single disk image she can use to clone systems, and that seems to make the most sense. That will probably be her best bet, because the library often receives new computers donated by other corporations, and he may not always be available to swing by and set up her new units.

In order to install Windows 2000 and configure software programs using disk duplication, Andy first needs to build the master disk image. There is already a new Windows 2000 Professional installation available, so he uses it as his master.

Creating a Master Image for Disk Duplication

To create a master image for disk duplication, Andy performs the following steps:

1. Find the desktop machine the librarian says is configured exactly as she'd like the others set up.

2. Install a third-party disk cloning utility.

3. Run Sysprep.exe on the machine.

4. Reboot the machine.

5. Using the third-party utility, transfer the image from the desktop across the network to a shared folder on the librarian's server.

After Andy has prepared the disk image for transfer and located the image on the library's only Windows 2000 server, he is ready to clone the six new systems.

2

Closing a Machine Using Disk Duplication

To clone a machine using disk duplication, Andy performs the following steps:

1. Take the six new client desktops out of their boxes and set them up in the library. All Andy has to do is plug them in and attach the category five cabling that had been run earlier by another firm.

2. Use a boot floppy to connect to the network and the share with the disk image.

3. Execute the image setup, which then automates the Windows 2000 Professional installation.

Before leaving, he instructs the librarian on the use of the network boot disk, shows her where the Windows 2000 Professional image resides on her server, and tells her that when future machines arrive with the same configuration, she should just install the image over the network.

The day's work done, our tired consultant heads for home.

CHAPTER THREE

DNS AND THE ACTIVE DIRECTORY

After completing this chapter, you will be able to:

✓ Define the Domain Name System

✓ Describe a DNS server and its role in the system

✓ Describe zone types and explain their uses

✓ Describe record types and explain their uses

✓ Describe DNS resolvers and lookup query types

✓ Configure zone transfers

✓ Integrate zones with the Active Directory

✓ Install and configure the DNS service

✓ Troubleshoot the DNS service using nslookup and other tools

This chapter's goal is to provide information that will help you to plan, implement, and administer the Domain Name System (DNS) for Windows 2000–based networks of any size and complexity. Specifically, this chapter examines DNS and its implementation in Windows 2000, and it looks at different server types and the zone files that reside on them. Furthermore, the types of records in DNS zone files are defined, and their uses are briefly described.

In addition, overall DNS concepts are discussed, including the mechanics involved with resolving names on a LAN and the Internet, communication between servers and the methods servers use to transfer zone information, integration between DNS and the Active Directory, and the basic installation and configuration of the DNS. That's a lot to cover, so let's get started.

WHAT'S IN A NAME?

When the Internet was young, it was composed of a few high-end time-sharing systems, so there was no need for name servers. There was one master HOSTS file maintained at the network information center that was distributed via the FTP protocol to every host on the Internet. As the topology changed from a few centralized processing systems to many smaller client/server systems, bandwidth was saturated with the traffic from host files. A few schemes, such as multilevel FTP and time-differentiated transfers, were devised, but many system administrators complained that having to wait for the Network Information Center to change the host file just wasn't acceptable. To resolve this issue, the Domain Name System, or DNS, was devised.

INTRODUCTION TO THE DNS SERVICE

DNS is often referred to as "the phone book of the Internet." Just as the telephone book translates a familiar name into a seven-digit number, DNS translates a user-friendly fully qualified domain name (FQDN) into a 32-bit TCP/IP address. Just as the telephone system is composed of many kinds of devices, there are many types of DNS servers on the Internet. Windows 2000 uses the DNS service as the primary method of name resolution on a LAN also. Enhancements to the service make legacy name resolution services like WINS all but obsolete.

The DNS system that we know today is the result of many experimental systems in which the only common theme was an extensible hierarchical structure that could represent an organization. The originators also knew they would have to balance the requirement for fresh data with the limitation of bandwidth available for DNS queries.

Today's DNS system is composed of four major entities:

➤ The structure

➤ The zone files

➤ The records

➤ The DNS clients (resolvers)

The Structure

The Internet has millions of DNS servers that act as the authority for one or more domains. The servers also have pointers to other name servers that eventually lead to records for every domain on the Internet. A domain is represented by a zone, which is an area of the internetwork represented by a file that lists the FQDNs and TCP/IP address for a particular resource. As shown in Figure 3.1, the namespace for the DNS looks like an inverted tree. The root of the namespace is the null record, represented by a period (.). Root servers are administered by one of a few registrars, which are listed in Table 3.1, and contain entries in their primary zone files for the top-level domains listed in Table 3.2.

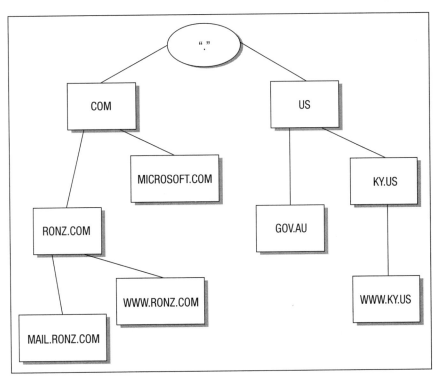

Figure 3.1 Graphic representation of the DNS namespace.

Table 3.1 Internet domain registrar names.

Second-Level Internet Domain Registrar Name	Web Page URL
Asian Pacific Network Information Center	http://www.apnic.net
American Registry for Internet Numbers	http://www.arin.net
Reseaux IP Network Coordination Center	http://www.ripe.net
Internet Information Center	http://www.internic.net
A+ Net	http://www.names4ever.com
AW Registry	http://www.awregistry.net
Alabanza	http://www.bulkregister.com
America Online	http://whois.compuserve.com
CORE	http://www.corenic.net
Domain Bank	http://www.domainbank.com
Domain Discover	http://www.domaindiscover.com
Domain Info	http://www.domaininfo.com
Domain People	http://www.domainpeople.com
Domain Registration Services	http://www.dotearth.com
Dotster	http://www.dotster.com
Easyspace	http://www.easyspace.com
Enames	http://www.easynames.org
E-Nom	http://www.enom.com
Enter Price Multimedia	http://www.epag.de
French Teleco	http://www.oleane.com
Gandi	http://www.gandi.net
Global Knowledge Group	http://register.gkh.net
Hangang Systems	http://www.doregi.com
Interaccess	http://www.interaccess.com
Internet Domain Registrars	http://www.registrars.com
InterQ	http://www.discount-domains.com
Melborne IT	http://www.internetnamesww.com
NameIT	http://www.nameit.net
Name Secure	http://namesecure.com
Network Solutions	http://www.networksolutions.com
Nominalia Internet	http://www.nominalia.com
NordNet	http://www.nordnet.net
PSI-Japan	http://www.psio-domains.com
Register	http://www.register.com
Secure GMBH	http://www.domainregistry.de
Signature Domains	http://www.signaturedomains.com
Tucows	http://www.opensrs.org

Table 3.2   Listing of top-level domains.

Domain	Description
.ARPA	Original domain
.COM	Commercial entities
.GOV	Government organizations
.US	United States
.ORG	Non-profit entities
.MIL	Military institutions
.EDU	Educational institutions
.NET	Network

3

Top-level servers are also maintained by a limited number of registrars, and their zone files contain entries for second-level domains. These second-level zone files are maintained by a local authority and can be updated in a matter of minutes. Second-level domains are smaller and easier to administer. An example of a second-level domain is *Microsoft.com*. Second-level zone files usually hold host records, but they can also contain records for subdomains like *sales.microsoft.com*. In that case, the subdomain zone files contain host records. To become a second-level domain, there must be a responsible person, called the *authority*. If an issue arises with the domain or one of its members, the authority is responsible for resolving the matter. Additionally, if an issue arises with a subdomain, the second-level domain authority is responsible for resolving the problem. Technically, a domain must have at least one name server, though most organizations have one primary and one secondary name server.

Combining all the zone files creates a huge distributed database that spans the world. The database is indexed by domain name, which creates a hierarchical index of the name space. This makes the database, though extremely large, an efficient mechanism for resolving queries.

The Zone Files

As mentioned, the DNS system is composed of zone files scattered throughout the Internet. These zone files break the DNS namespace into manageable pieces. Zones allow not only distribution of data but also the administration of a DNS database. Local DNS administrators define the zone boundaries, maintain the zone files, and provide settings that affect how resource records are maintained. As demonstrated in Figure 3.2, dividing a large second-level domain into zones can improve performance and manageability. In this example, the zone file for the first zone contains entries for the *.KY* and the *.Louisville* subdomain. The zone file for the *.Lexington* subdomain, however, resides on a server in a separate zone.

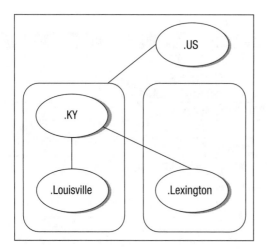

Figure 3.2 Dividing a domain into zones.

Standard Primary and Standard Secondary Zones

A *standard primary zone* is the first zone set up for a new domain and the zone on which administration takes place. The standard primary zone server is also the master server in the zone replication model. A copy of the primary zone is distributed to one or more servers with standard secondary zones. Secondary zone servers provide fault tolerance and load balancing to the DNS by maintaining mirror copies of the primary zone file on a separate server. Secondary zones are updated by zone transfers, which use a function that DNS provides called *Notify*. With DNS Notify, the primary zone server contains a list of servers that it will automatically notify when the zone file is updated. This list is located in the Zone Properties dialog box on the Zone Transfer tab. When the file is updated, the primary server increments the serial number of the file and notifies its secondary servers of the change. The secondary servers then check the serial number on the primary. If the serial number is higher, the file is newer, and a zone transfer is initiated. Figure 3.3 demonstrates this process.

Two types of zone transfers can occur—*full* or the new *incremental* zone transfer. In a full zone transfer, when a secondary server's refresh interval expires, it sends an AXFR query to the primary server. The primary compares its zone file's serial number to the one on the secondary server. If the serial number doesn't match, the entire zone file is copied. An incremental zone transfer follows the same pattern, but the query issued is an IXFR query and only new or updated records are copied.

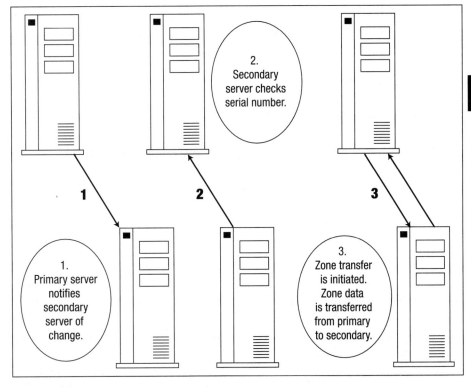

Figure 3.3 The DNS Notify process.

Active Directory-Integrated Zones

Active Directory-Integrated zones perform the same function as standard zones with improved distribution and administration. Active Directory-Integrated zones are stored in and replicated with the Active Directory. This means the data is fresher and there is no one master and no one point of failure. Also, access control lists can be built for the zones using Windows 2000 integrated security.

Caching Zones

To expedite the name-resolution process, special zones called *caching zones* can store the results of forward lookup queries (a forward lookup query is the process a client uses to resolve a fully qualified domain name to a TCP/IP address). Most servers provide both forward lookup and caching services by serving as an authority for a zone, and caching resolutions the server has gotten from the rest of the Internet. These servers begin their caching zones with a root hints file that contains entries for the Internet root name servers. A caching zone keeps all name resolutions for the amount of time specified in the Start of Authority (SOA); this amount of time is commonly referred to as the TTL, or Time To Live. These servers can also provide negative caching, or caching of negative responses to queries. By caching both positive and negative responses, DNS server loads can be reduced. The price you pay for this reduced load is that DNS data are not real time, and can be incorrect.

Forwarders

Some servers do not actually contact Internet servers to resolve queries for Internet hosts; they merely forward all requests to a forwarder, which in turn contacts Internet name servers to resolve them. Any Windows 2000 Server connected to the Internet can be a forwarder with no additional configuration. The servers that use the forwarders will need the address of the forwarder in their configuration settings. Sometimes the forwarder server cannot resolve a DNS query. If the requesting server is in exclusive mode, it will not attempt to resolve the query for itself and is referred to as a *slave server*. Otherwise, the original server will attempt to resolve the query itself.

Although Windows 2000's implementation makes it the only method of name resolution necessary, WINS can still be used to assist with this crucial task. If the WINS service is integrated with the DNS service, it is very important that the NetBIOS name and the host name for all resources be the same, or the results of queries might not be accurate. To facilitate this, two additional records must be in the forward lookup zone. The WINS-type DNS record maps the TCP/IP address of the WINS server, and it is used for forward lookup queries that the DNS record cannot resolve on its own. The WINS-R record is similar to the WINS record, but it is used for reverse lookups that the DNS server cannot resolve for. The client, or resolver, is not aware of the source of the resolution. All that matters to the client is whether a name can be resolved.

The Records

The Windows 2000 DNS service has Unicode support built in for international compatibility. Computers with the TCP/IP protocol are called *hosts*. Each host must have a unique 32 bit TCP/IP address. The address consists of four octets, each eight bits in length. There are three commonly used classes of network on the Internet: Class A networks are the largest because the network ID consists of the first octet only; class B networks use the first and second octet for the network ID; and class C networks use the first three octets to identify the network ID. Class B networks can be divided into networks smaller than a class B yet bigger than individual class Cs. This is accomplished using a process called *supernetting*. A class C network can be divided into smaller networks using a process called *subnetting*. The most common way to represent an address is in decimal format (192.168.0.1), but at the machine level the binary representation is used to determine a network ID and host ID. An FQDN can then represent an address. An FQDN begins at the left with the host name followed by the subdomain, if applicable, and second-level domain. The last piece of the FQDN is the top-level domain, which is shared with all entities of the same type. Domain names can be up to 63 characters long, while host names can be only 24 characters. Names can contain letters, numbers, or dashes (-). Sections are separated by a period, or *dot*. An example of an FQDN for a host called *domestic* in the *sales* zone of the *Microsoft* domain would be *domestic.sales.Microsoft.com*.

The DNS system provides flexibility, fault tolerance, and redundancy. A host address can resolve to more than one name. For instance, a company with one Internet host for Web hosting and email could add Alias records for **mail.X.com** and **www.X.com,** which both resolve to the same TCP/IP address. An Alias type record also allows one name to resolve to more than one address, in round-robin fashion. For example, if company *Y* has two Web servers hosting the same Web site, the company could add an Alias record for each server to resolve to *www.Y.com*. Redundancy is also built into other record types. For instance, electronic mail servers are represented by an *MX record*. If a company has more than one email server, both can have MX records with different precedence. A precedence is assigned to each of the MX records in the DNS console, and the MX record with the lowest precedence is processed first.

The system offers much flexibility, but some guidelines should be followed. Namely you should:

➤ Create at least one secondary zone for each primary one. This ensures that name resolution is not interrupted, and it balances the load on the servers so that the primary zone doesn't bear the brunt of the use.

➤ Create reverse lookup zones to allow clients to download certain software through the Internet. Due to export restrictions, some software can be downloaded only if the server can verify a client's location.

➤ Create subdomains only for performance or administrative reasons. Adding too many subdomains can make a system difficult to manage and difficult for users to navigate.

➤ Ensure that domain names are short and to the point. One of the main benefits of the DNS is its ability to describe a resource in the name.

➤ Keep the records in your zone up to date and set reasonable configuration parameters, such as a relatively short TTL for the zone records, to ensure accurate data.

Inside zone files are records of many types. Two mandatory records are the SOA and the NS types. An SOA type record is the Start of Authority for a particular domain. SOA records contain zone configuration parameters including zone serial number; responsible person; primary server; minimum TTL; and secondary server parameters for retry interval, refresh interval, and expiration period. An NS type record resolves for the name servers in the domain. Normal hosts are represented by A type records, and mail servers are represented MX records. A new record type is the SRV, or service, records. These records perform network service location much like the sixteenth character of a NetBIOS name. (NetBIOS names are actually 16 characters in length, but the administrator can assign only the first 15. The sixteenth character is assigned by the system to identify the type of resource that is represented by the NetBIOS record.) Clients query the DNS server for all records matching a particular service rather than a particular host name.

There are also some less frequently used record types that might be of use to many administrators. In the DNS console, right-click the forward lookup zone and select Other New Record to reveal a list of these record types. For example, the HINFO type record details the processor type and operating system for a particular host. The AAAA type record maps a TCP/IP version 4 (current implementation) address to a TCP/IP version 6 (proposed next version) address. The RP record identifies the responsible person, or the person who should be contacted with issues for a particular zone or domain. There is also a record type called TXT, which can be used for any textual information an administrator would like to provide.

The Resolvers

Any DNS client can use the services of a Windows 2000 DNS server, but Windows 2000 clients reap the most benefits from the service's new features. Configuring a Windows 2000 client is much the same as configuring other systems. Addresses for DNS servers are listed in the DNS tab of the network properties in order of preference. The lookup process can be optimized by specifying domain search order. As shown in Figure 3.4, at the bottom of the window, one checks the box to register the connection and to register the domain with the DNS server.

Once a client is configured, that client is able to perform DNS queries, including forward and reverse lookups.

Forward Lookups

Clients issue forward lookup queries to their local primary or secondary DNS servers to retrieve a TCP/IP address that corresponds to an FQDN. The local name server checks its cache and, if necessary, queries a root name server for the address of a server that maintains the appropriate top-level domain.

Then the local server queries a server in the top-level domain to get the address of the server with authority for the second-level domain in question. At this point, it is possible that the local server will have to query another server for a local subdomain, but most of the time the address of the host in question is returned. The local server returns the address to the client, and communication

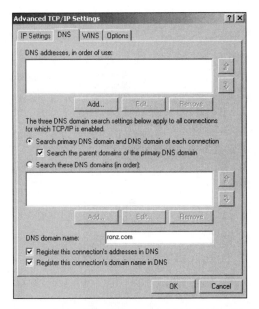

Figure 3.4   The Windows 2000 DNS client configuration screen.

begins between the source and the destination hosts. If the client receives more than one record for a resource, it will choose records with addresses on a directly connected subnet first. By default, a client will accept resolutions from any DNS server, whether it is in the local system or on the Internet, but this can be disabled to enhance security. The forward lookup process facilitates FQDNs, because addresses are difficult to remember and might have to change, while an FQDN can be user friendly and remain the same during network changes. The flow of a forward lookup query can be seen in Figure 3.5.

Reverse Lookups

The reverse lookup process is much the same as a forward lookup, but the result is reversed. Rather than requesting an address from a name, a reverse lookup supplies the name and queries for the address of the host. This improves a client's level of accountability by tracing the client back to a specific address space for which someone has authority. The DNS namespace is indexed by address through the use of reverse lookup zones, called *in-addr.arpa zone files*.

Planning a DNS Namespace

The DNS namespace for a Windows 2000 network can be integrated with the Internet or maintained separately. The domain name used on the Internet can also be used for the root server of your Active Directory. If this is the case, some precautions should be taken to protect the Active Directory from the Internet. A subdomain of your Internet domain can also be used. This offers the

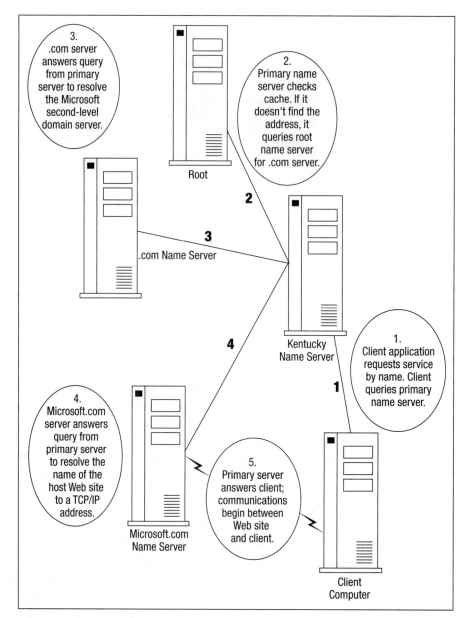

Figure 3.5 A forward lookup query.

flexibility of Internet integration without the commitment of the entire
organization falling under the Active Directory. Finally, your Active Directory
domain can be totally separate from your Internet domain. In this case,
however, no resources from the directory will be available to the Internet.

TESTING AND TROUBLESHOOTING DNS

The DNS console has an interface built in to help test the DNS service. A Monitoring tab displays the properties of the DNS server. Figure 3.6 displays the interface.

3

The Monitoring Utility

The DNS server can be tested any time by using the Monitoring utility in the properties of the DNS console server. During server testing, the server computer also acts as the client (resolver). The first test is a simple query to the DNS server. A simple, or iterative, query requests that the server resolve a name, but not necessarily authoritatively. The second test is a recursive test, meaning that the client asks the server to recurse through the namespace to the name server for the target domain. Any queries answered by the authority, such as a recursive query, are said to be recursive. The test can be run continuously at a specified interval or on the spot with the Test Now button. After the test concludes, the results are displayed at the bottom of the Monitoring dialog box.

The nslookup Utility

nslookup is another tool designed for testing the DNS service. To start nslookup, type "nslookup" from the command prompt. To test the local DNS server, type:

```
Ip_address 127.0.0.1
```

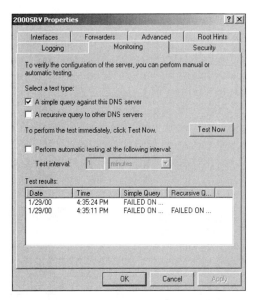

Figure 3.6   Monitoring the DNS server.

If the service is running properly, the name *localhost* is returned. Another useful command in nslookup is the query type. Setting the query type to MX will return the mail exchanger records for a particular domain. To set the query type, issue the following commands:

```
SET Q=MX <ENTER>

Domain Name
```

Other record types, such as SRV, can be queried using nslookup as well. To end the program, type "Exit". For more information about DNS, Table 3.3 lists the Internet Request For Comments (RFC) relating to DNS.

IPCONFIG and PING

A number of diagnostic tools can be used to help troubleshoot the service, although they are not directly related to DNS. For example, the IPCONFIG utility can be used with the **/ALL** switch to display the current TCP/IP settings for all adapters on a machine. It can also be used with the **/RELEASE** and **/RENEW** switches to verify DHCP communications. Two more switches to the IPCONFIG utility that apply to the DNS service in particular are the **/REGISTERDNS** switch that ill refresh all DHCP leases and reregister the DNS names for the host, and the **/FLUSHDNS** switch that will purge the DNS resolvers cache. Our old friend PING proves invaluable for name resolution verification. If you can PING a host by address but not by name, and the DNS server settings on the client are correct, DNS is a good place to start looking for an answer.

Netmon

Another useful tool to troubleshoot the DNS service is Network Monitor, or Netmon. Netmon captures packets from the network and allows administrators to view the data inside the packets. Though Netmon can be very powerful, the volume of packets captured can easily overwhelm an administrator. To limit the kinds of packets Netmon captures, a capture filter must be configured to capture IP. This eliminates a large amount of spurious packets. After that, a display filter can be configured to specifically display only DNS packets.

Table 3.3   Internet RFCs relating to DNS.

RFC	Subject
1034	Concepts and facilities
1035	Implementation and specifications
1996	DNS Notify
2052	DNS SRV
2065	DNS Security Extensions
2136	Dynamic DNS

CHAPTER SUMMARY

Windows 2000 depends on the Domain Name System (DNS) for name resolution both on the Internet and on LANs. The DNS provides translation from user-friendly fully qualified domain names to 32 bit TCP/IP addresses. The system is based on the cooperation of many DNS servers from the root of the Internet to a subdomain at the bottom level. Each domain must have one or more primary zone files, and some provide fault tolerance with secondary zone files that are mirror copies of the primary. The process of updating a secondary zone file is called a *zone transfer*. Zone transfers can be controlled with DNS notify, based on a list of servers to notify. Inside these zone files are records of many types. Host records, or A type records, identify normal TCP/IP hosts. Electronic mail servers are identified by MX record. Name servers have NS records, the most important of which is the Start of Authority (SOA).

The implementation of the DNS server in Windows 2000 has many enhancements, but the fundamental name resolution method remains the same. In previous versions of the DNS service, all records had to be manually entered. Clients can now automatically register with the DNS server when they receive an address from DHCP. The most common type of resolution is the iterative forward lookup. When a client queries a primary server for a record that is not in its zone or cache, the server queries its parent for the parent of the destination. The destination parent answers the query, and the results are kept in cache for future queries. Through the use of reverse lookup zones, DNS also provides a mechanism to resolve a name from an address if necessary.

After the DNS service is set up, it must be tested and monitored. Testing DNS usually involves a utility called nslookup. This interactive utility can verify DNS servers, records, and configuration settings. There is also a tool built into the zone properties to verify a DNS server's functionality with both standard and recursive lookups. Enhancements, such as the incremental zone transfer, service type records, and dynamic DNS, make the DNS service in Windows 2000 a robust and reliable name resolution mechanism. With such a system in place, this service will be the premier name resolution method for most Windows 2000 networks.

REVIEW QUESTIONS

1. How long is a TCP/IP V4 address?

   a. 8 bytes

   b. 8 bits

   c. 32 bytes

d. 32 bits

e. None of the above

2. The acronym FQDN stands for

    a. Fixed quantity distinctive name

    b. Full query domain name

    c. Fully qualified domain name

    d. Fixed quality domain name

3. The first zone created for a domain must be which of the following?

    a. Primary zone

    b. Secondary zone

    c. Caching zone

    d. In-addr.arpa zone

4. A mirror copy of the primary zone is the _____ zone.

    a. Backup

    b. Tertiary

    c. Secondary

    d. Duplicate

5. The record type that represents a standard host is the _____ record.

    a. Alias type

    b. H type

    c. A type

    d. Node type

6. The standard that supports foreign character sets is which of the following?

    a. ASCII code

    b. ANSI code

    c. Unicode

    d Versacode

7. To distinguish a mail server, assign it a(n) _____.

    a. SRV record

    b. MS record

    c. MSRV record

    d. MX record

8. What is resolving a name to a TCP/IP address called?

a. Lookup query

b. Reverse lookup

c. Forward lookup

d. Name lookup

9. To implement an intranet with Windows 2000 that requires the least amount of administration, which of the following services are required? [Check all correct answers]

a. DHCP

b. DNS

c. WINS

d. PPTP

e. Simple TCP/IP services

10. Which of the following are required to implement Dynamic DNS? [Check all correct answers]

a. DNS

b. FTP

c. DHCP

d. WINS

e. All of the above

11. AXFR represents a(n) _____.

a. Active transfer

b. Full zone transfer

c. Forward lookup

d. Alternate transfer

12. Which of the following is required by DNS with redundancy? [Check all correct answers]

a. Setting up a primary zone server and a caching-only zone server

b. Configuring the forwarder in zone configuration

c. Setting up a secondary zone server

d. Configuring replication in the zone properties

13. As the administrator for a small company, Pam changes the TCP/IP address of the email server. Now, Internet email doesn't come in. What must be done?

   a. Create an A record for the new server and delete the MX record for the old server.

   b. Create an MX record for the new server and delete the A record for the old server.

   c. Create an MX record for the new server, and delete the MX record for the old server.

   d. Create the MX record for the new server with a precedence of 1, and set the precedence for the MX record for the old server to 99.

14. When resolving for a domain controller, the client looks for a(n) _____ type record.

   a. A

   b. DOM

   c. SRV

   d. CTL

15. What type of clients can use Windows 2000 DNS server? [Check all correct answers]

   a. Windows 2000

   b. Linux

   c. Windows 9x

   d. Win NT

16. Users complain that they are not receiving electronic mail from Internet users but they can receive mail from other users of the internal email system. What tool can be used to determine whether the DNS records for the electronic mail server are correct?

   a. Network Monitor

   b. ARP

   c. Nslookup

   d. DNS Domain Administrator

17. You want the LAN for a small four-year college to link to the Internet and use friendly names for resources and electronic mail. What must be done to accomplish this? [Check all correct answers]

    a. Register a top-level domain within the EDU namespace, set up a primary DNS server, and create an MX record for the electronic mail server.

    b. Register a primary-level domain within the EDU namespace, set up a secondary DNS server, and create an MX record for the electronic mail server.

    c. Register a second-level domain in the EDU namespace, set up a primary DNS server, and create an MX record for the electronic mail server.

    d. Register a subdomain with the InterNIC and point the resolvers to their servers for hostname resolution.

18. Which of the following does DNS use to help balance the demand for fresh data and the limitations on bandwidth? [Check all correct answers]

    a. Secondary zone

    b. Caching zones

    c. Time To Cache

    d. Time To Live

19. Before the Domain Name System was devised, what was name resolution based on?

    a. HOSTS files maintained by local administrators

    b. LMHOSTS files maintained by local administrators

    c. HOSTS files maintained by a central Network Information Center

    d. LMHOSTS files maintained by a central NIC

20. If a DHCP client cannot access a resource by name but it can access the resource by address, where should the DNS settings being verified?

    a. In the DNS manager

    b. In the network properties

    c. From a command prompt using NBTSTAT

    d. From a command prompt using IPCONFIG

REAL-WORLD PROJECTS

Note: This exercise assumes a test Windows 2000 Advanced Server with Active Directory installed. Read the instructions carefully and do not perform this install on your production machine unless you understand the options presented. If you are unsure about an option, cancel the installation and read the Books On Line about the option to be installed.

As a consultant for an IT firm, Andy Palmer has been assigned a new client. This client is a travel agency that has been in the area for many years. The agency has a number of new standalone personal computers with local printers, and they often share files using floppy disks. During the initial assessment, the owner expressed interest in connecting the company to the Internet for e-commerce.

Andy has installed two Windows 2000 advanced servers for the company, but he knows that without a DNS server the functionality of the system would be severely limited. He sits down at both servers and begins to install the service.

Project 3.1
To install the DNS service:

1. Start the Add/Remove Programs applet in Control Panel.

2. Click the Components button and follow the prompts until a list including Networking Services appears.

3. Click the details of Networking Services and check the box for the Domain Name System service, as shown in Figure 3.7.

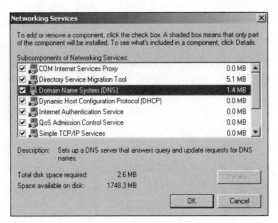

Figure 3.7 Installing the DNS service.

4. Click OK and supply the path for the Windows 2000 source files if necessary.

5. The DNS service is started automatically after installation without rebooting.

3

There is a new shortcut to the DNS console under the Administrative Tools menu. Also, the following key is added to the registry:

```
\\HKEY_LOCAL_MACHINE\System\CurrentControlSet\Services\DNS
```

A folder is created at:

```
\<SystemRoot>\System32\DNS
```

With the service installed, Andy lays out a plan of the necessary steps to implement the service on the network. The next thing to be done is to set up the zones that will host the records.

Project 3.2
To create and configure zones:

1. The first time the DNS console is opened on the primary DNS server, the question of whether to configure a root server is presented, as shown in Figure 3.8. Create a root server.

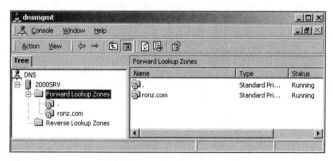

Figure 3.8 The DNS console.

2. Right-click the Forward Lookup Zones folder and select New Zone.

3. Select Standard Primary zone from the dialog box shown in Figure 3.9.

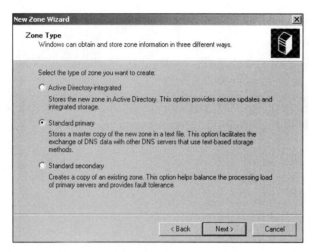

Figure 3.9   Creating a new primary zone.

4. Supply the domain information.

5. Right-click the Reverse Lookup Zones folder and select New Zone.

6. Supply the network ID and subnet mask when prompted, as shown in Figure 3.10.

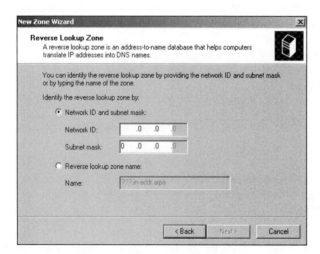

Figure 3.10   Configuring a reverse lookup zone.

7. On the secondary server, right-click the Forward Lookup Zones folder and select New Zone.

8. Select Standard Secondary Zone and click Next.

9. Provide the domain name when prompted, and click Next.

10. Provide the address for the primary server, click ADD, and then click Next.

11. Click Finish.

12. Right-click the Reverse Lookup Zones and select New Zone.

13. Select Standard Secondary Zone and click Next.

14. Provide the Network ID when prompted, and click Next.

15. Provide the address for the Primary server when prompted, click ADD, and then click Next.

16. Click Finish.

Now that Andy has a primary server and a secondary server for both the forward lookup zone and the reverse lookup zone, it is time to set up the zone transfers with DNS Notify.

Project 3.3
To configure zone transfers and DNS Notify:

1. Figure 3.11 shows the zone transfer settings. Right-click the Forward Lookup Zone and select Properties.

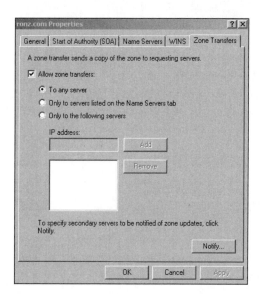

Figure 3.11   Configuring DNS zone transfers.

2. On the Zone Transfer tab, check the box that toggles zone transfers.

3. Choose Only To The Following Servers, and add the address for axis2.

4. Click the Notify button on the Zone Transfers tab in the Zone Properties dialog box.

5. Check the box to turn on DNS Notify.

6. Choose The Following Servers, and add the address for axis2. Figure 3.12 shows the DNS Notify configuration dialog.

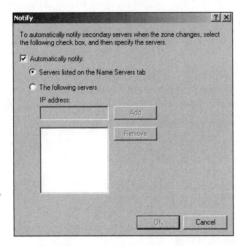

Figure 3.12   Configuring DNS Notify for zone transfers.

The servers are now set up, but with no records in the zone files they are of little use to anyone. Andy begins by entering standard host records for the servers themselves.

Project 3.4
To create a standard host record:

1. Figure 3.13 displays the interface for creating a host record. Right-click the Forward Lookup Zone in the DNS console and select New Host.

2. Provide the name and TCP/IP address of the host.

3. Check the box labeled Create Associated Pointer Record to create a reverse lookup record for the host.

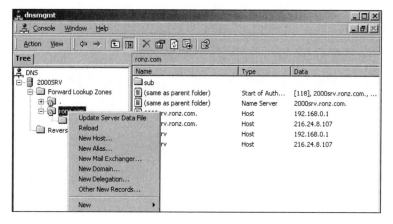

Figure 3.13   Creating a new DNS record.

Andy also has to enter special records for the two Web servers that the company has. The servers are clustered together and have the exact same information on each. Andy knows that these servers need the special record type called *Alias records*.

Project 3.5
To create an Alias type record:

1. Right-click the Forward Lookup Zone in the DNS console and select New Alias.

2. Provide the alias name for the host.

3. Either type in the host name, or click the Browse button to find the host record.

The company's electronic mail system also need a record to exchange email with other email servers on the Internet. The mail server needs an MX record for this purpose.

Project 3.6
To create a mail exchanger type record:

1. Right-click the zone in the DNS console and select New Mail Exchanger.

2. Usually the host or domain is left blank to indicate the current parent domain. If the record is for a subdomain, type in the subdomain name.

3. Either type in the name of the mail server or click the Browse button to select it from the zone file.

4. If there is more than one mail server, two MX records can be entered with different priorities. In this case, the server with the lowest priority will be the first MX record used.

To facilitate the logon process, Andy has to add Kerberos service type records to the zone files.

Project 3.7
To create a service type record:

1. Select the Other New Records menu.

2. Highlight Service Location in the Record Type list box and click Create Record. Figure 3.14 shows the resulting dialog box.

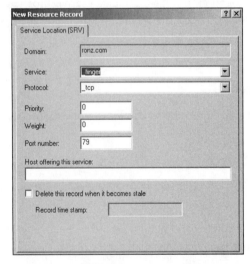

Figure 3.14   Creating a new service type record.

3. Select the Kerberos Service from the drop-down box and the protocol used for the service.

4. If there is more than one server providing the service, it is possible to assign a priority to this record much like the MX record.

5. If there is more than one server with the same priority, the record with the highest weight will be returned first.

6. The default port for the service is provided, but services can reside at different ports if necessary.

With the records for the servers complete, Andy has to add records for all the clients on the network. This could be a daunting task were it not for the new features of Windows 2000 that allow dynamic updates of the Host and Ptr type records. First he has to set the server up to receive dynamic updates.

Project 3.8
To configure a zone for dynamic updates:

Note: Configuring a zone for automatic client registration must take place in both the DNS console and the DHCP console.

1. Figure 3.15 shows the DNS console. Right-click the zone and open its properties.

2. On the General tab, drop down the Allow Dynamic Updates box. If the zone is integrated with the Active Directory, select the option to Allow Only Secure Updates; otherwise, select Yes.

3. In the DHCP console, right-click the server and open its properties.

4. As shown in Figure 3.15, dynamic DNS is enabled on the DNS tab by checking the box to automatically update DHCP client information to DNS.

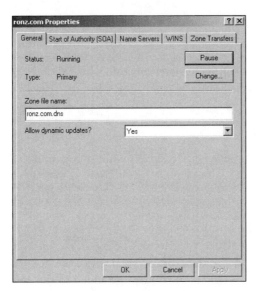

Figure 3.15   Configuring dynamic DNS updates in the DNS service.

5. Figure 3.16 shows that selecting Update According to Client Request means that the client will update the A type record while the DHCP server will update the PTR type record. Selecting Always Update DNS uses the DHCP server to update both records in DNS.

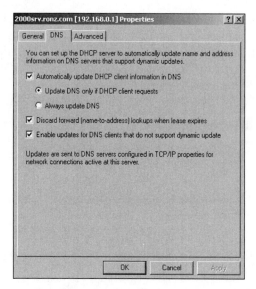

Figure 3.16   Configuring the DHCP service for dynamic DNS updates.

Finally, Andy is ready to set up the clients. He goes to each client and performs the following operation.

Project 3.9
To set up the client:

1. Open the Network And Dialup Connections folder, right-click the connection that needs to be configured, and open its properties.

2. Select Internet Protocol (TCP/IP) from the components dialog box and click the Properties button.

3. On the General tab, click the Advanced button and select the DNS tab.

4. The first box on the DNS tab is the DNS Servers To Query, in the order of use.

5. Below that is a set of radio buttons to tailor the DNS search order to specific needs. If a query is issued that does not contain the entire FQDN, this setting determines how the operating system should respond. The primary suffix (COM, EDU, and so forth) can be added to the name, and, optionally, the parent of this node (Coriolis.test in this case) can be appended. The second option allows a listing of domains to append.

6. As seen in Figure 3.17, the last item on the DNS tab is the current DNS domain and the options to register the machine and/or domain automatically. Setup for other operating systems remains the same, with the exception of dynamic DNS settings.

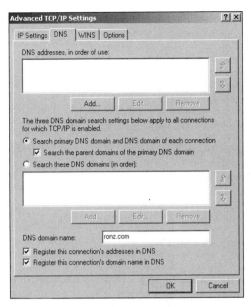

3

Figure 3.17   Setting up the Windows 2000 client for dynamic DNS update.

Note: *If the client receives its configuration from a Windows 2000 DHCP server, it is possible for the server to automatically register the client in the DNS zone file. This makes a migration from Windows 9x and NT participate in the Active Directory.*

CHAPTER FOUR

ACTIVE DIRECTORY DEFINED

After completing this chapter, you will be able to:

✓ Understand network directories

✓ Describe the Active Directory and its role in a Windows 2000 network

✓ Explain Active Directory's structure, including sites and replication

✓ Describe the schema, trust relationships, and Global Catalog Server

✓ Plan directory namespaces, sites, and Organizational Units

✓ Install and test the Active Directory services with various domain modes

✓ Create and configure sites, links, replication, and Global Catalog Servers

A directory service catalogs network objects and provides a method for network clients to find resources. Prior to Windows 2000, Windows depended on the domain model for directory services, but Windows 2000 introduces a new directory service method called *Active Directory services*. Active Directory provides a convenient single point of administration for networks, and it's compatible with other directory services, such as LDAP and NDS. The Active Directory is the biggest and possibly the most beneficial new feature that Windows 2000 adds to Microsoft networking. This chapter discusses Active Directory's features as well as briefly explores the history of directory services, and it points out some key features that make the Active Directory the next logical next step in enterprise directory development.

NETWORK DIRECTORIES EXPLORED

To understand the Active Directory fully, you must understand what a network directory is. This first section explores network directories and their role in the network environment. The X.500 directory, which is the basis for the Active Directory, will be explained; and the history of the X.500, its evolution, and the current state of the standard will be detailed.

The Network Directory Explained

The network directory is much like the directory in a shopping mall. If you know that you need a particular item from a particular store, simply asking a stranger for the location of nearest one will probably lead you to the local shopping mall. However, the mall is likely to be quite large, with many shops. The directory at the mall will likely contain a listing of all the stores in the mall, separated by category, as well as their locatons within the mall. Knowing this, you can now look at the directory for not only the location of the store you are looking for, but also the location of the directory that you are standing before.

The network directory has a similar structure to the mall directory. If you know the resource you are looking for, simply asking a co-worker where that resource is will probably lead you to the nearest server with that resource. However, the network is likely quite large, with many servers. The network directory is a listing of all the resources in the network, separated by category, and gives their location by domain and domain component. Knowing this, you can now look at the graphic representation of the directory, which will identify not only the location of the resource in which domain and component, but also your own domain and component.

The development of the network directory has led to the X.500 standard, which started as a directory of electronic mail addresses and also a separate directory of resources and applications. The X.500 standard was proposed to merge these two directories into a complete network directory. Initially, this new directory seemed like a surreal, unattainable goal, but the X.500 directory has grown to accommodate the needs of the originators and has extended to include functions that could not have been anticipated by the brave inventors of the standard. Table 4.1 lists some major milestones in the X.500 directory history.

4

The first X.500 systems, implemented in 1988, were fairly limited in scope. In the United States, the Defense Advanced Research Projects Agency funded a directory with fewer than 20 organizations. By the time the 1992 standards extensions were published, this directory held almost half a million records from more than 100 companies and universities. During the same period in the United Kingdom, a directory was built that grew to more than 100,000 entries from public and private organizations. In 1990, there was an effort to link these two directories and create new directories in different nations. By 1993, this global directory had 26 members and 1 million records. Though the system was quite large, its text-based interface and limited resources made it less popular than other systems such as Whois Gopher.

The X.500 directory can be separated into two systems—a local directory and a distributed directory—that depend heavily on each other. Local administrators maintain the local directory, which has a user view with limited data and an administrators view with completed details for all records. This local directory is extensible so that new types of records, called *classes*, can be added to satisfy local needs. A portion of each record in the local directory is available to the distributed directory. The distributed directory is not extensible, however, because interoperability with other directory systems is necessary.

Classes are objects that serve as models for other objects. Classes contain attributes that further define the class. More than one class can use an attribute, and classes can be used as a basis for subclasses.

Table 4.1   Milestones in the X.500 standards development.

Event	Year
X.500 Draft Presented	1988
Standard Editing	1989
X.500 Recommendations Presented	1990
X.500 Standard Published	1991
X.500 Extensions Published	1992

INTRODUCTION TO THE ACTIVE DIRECTORY

Because the Active Directory is the backbone of a Windows 2000 network, a network administrator must have a thorough understanding of the Active Directory and the role it plays in a Windows 2000 network.

In general, a directory service organizes all the resources on a network and makes the resources available to network clients. Resources include data, printers, servers, and any other objects found on a network. A directory not only maintains information about network resources, but it also makes resources available to network clients. Clients query the directory that contains enough information about every object to locate the object. After a client can locate an object, other details can be retrieved directly from the object itself. Previous versions of Windows used the NetBIOS browser service for directory services, but Windows 2000 Server uses the Active Directory services.

Active Directory Benefits

Active Directory services is a major enhancement to the administrative model for Windows-based networks for many reasons. For example, the domain model has been improved for scalability and reliability; standards-based protocols have been adopted into the technology to improve interoperability; and the name resolution process has been improved and standardized to use the Internets Domain Name System.

Improvements to the Domain Model

Domains are the building blocks of the Active directory. Domains can have peer relationships with each other, or they may have a parent/child relationship. This allows domains to be used that mimic the structure of your organization, no matter how small or large it may be. Domains are the foundation of a network, and each domain must have one or more servers running Windows 2000 Server to function as domain controllers. Domain controllers are special because they contain a copy of the domain directory called a *replica*.

All domain controllers have a replica, so changes to the directory can be made from any controller. All domain controllers are peers, and there is no master. When changes are made, they are replicated to all other domain controllers. This architecture makes it possible to log on to any machine in the network and administer any object in the directory. With the directory partitioned into domains, it can also grow to any size—from a few objects to a few million objects.

Use of Standards-Based Protocols

Active Directory supports many standard protocols. When a client requests a resource, the directory service facilitates the name resolution process. Active Directory uses the Domain Name System (DNS) to resolve names, which is the standard for the Internet. The Active Directory also supports the Internet standard directory service Lightweight Directory Access Protocol (LDAP). Many other directory services, including Novell NDS, also use Internet standards, thereby making it possible to manage a heterogeneous system through the use of namespaces.

As mentioned earlier, LDAP is an Internet standard for directory access. Like Active Directory, LDAP can organize the objects in a network. LDAP uses another standard called HyperText Transfer Protocol (HTTP) to display accumulated data in a Web page, which is accessible from a standard browser. HTTP is a protocol used to display pages coded in HTML on a TCP/IP network. The X.509 standard and Kerberos are used for authentication and authentication certificates. The Dynamic Host Control Protocol (DHCP) administers client configuration settings, and Simple Network Time Protocol helps synchronize time on all network nodes. Table 4.2 contains the Internet Requests for Comments (RFCs) associated with the protocols. The full text of these RFCs can be found at **http://www.ietf.org**.

Active Directory Namespace and DNS

The entire Active Directory is actually a namespace. Active Directory uses DNS as its sole method for name resolution, so DNS is a required piece of the Active Directory. Furthermore, the implementation of DNS in Windows 2000 makes the service full featured and easier to administer. Dynamic DNS (DDNS) is an enhancement to the DNS service that helps to replace the automatic client registration features in the WINS service. DDNS-enabled clients can automatically register their hostnames with the DNS server. If the client does not directly support DDNS, using the services of a Windows 2000 DHCP server can still automatically register the clients with the DNS server.

Table 4.2 Internet RFCs for standard protocols supported by Windows 2000.

RFC	Protocol
205 2,2163	DDNS
2131	DHCP
1769	SNTP
1777	LDAP
1510	Kerberos 5
822	User Principal Names

Unlike previous Windows networks that required a NetBios namespace for the LAN and a DNS namespace for the Internet, standardizing on DNS cuts the administrative requirements in half. A new record type, called *service* (or *SRV*) *records*, resolves services rather than TCP/IP addresses. The use of SRV records replaces an equivalent function in WINS, which used the sixteenth character of a NetBIOS name for this purpose. WINS can still be used in conjunction with DNS for clients and applications that require NetBIOS names, but it is no longer a required component.

Another feature that makes the DNS system attractive is its hierarchical nature. While NetBIOS networks are flat, DNS networks can be navigated by level. As you can see in Figure 4.1, a namespace can be divided into zones to form an internal hierarchy that fits into the Internet hierarchy. In this figure, the *Win2kPro* client is in the *ADS* subdomain of the second-level *coriolis* domain, which is part of the fictitious top-level *test* domain. In this scenario, the *Win2kPro* client and users of the machine could be referenced in a number of ways. Table 4.3 demonstrates different ways to reference a resource or a user.

Locating Objects in the Active Directory

In Active Directory, every object can be referenced by a *distinguished name*, which contains the name of the object as well as the complete path to the object. A distinguished name has three attributes:

➤ Domain Component (DC)

➤ Organizational Unit (OU)

➤ Common Name (CN)

This setup extends the namespace to include many layers of administration. For example, the workstation shown in Figure 4.1 could be in the OU named *Computers* so that its distinguished name would be:

```
/DC=test/DC=coriolis/DC=ADS/OU=Computers/CN=Win2kPro
```

In addition to the distinguished name, an object can be referred to by its *relative distinguished name*. In the preceding example, the object could be referred to simply as *Win2kPro*. More than one object can be named *Win2kPro* as long as the objects do not have the same distinguished name.

Internally, Windows 2000 refers to objects by their Globally Unique Identifier (GUID) rather than using distinguished names. A GUID is a 128-bit identifier that is generated when an object is created, and it is guaranteed to be unique. Providing a 128-bit identifier ensures that there can be millions of objects in a directory without running out of GUIDs.

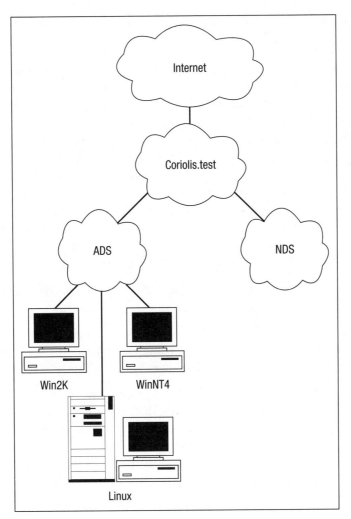

Figure 4.1   A hierarchical DNS system.

Table 4.3   Naming conventions supported by Windows 2000.

Format	Use	Example
User Principal Name	User	**Win2kpro@ADS.Coriolis.test**
HTTP	Resource	**http://win2kpro.ads.Coriolis.test/ResourceName**
LDAP	User	**LDAP://ADS.Coriolis.test/CN=Win2kPro CN=JDoe**
UNC	Resource	**\\Win2kPro.ADS.Coriolis.test\ResourceName**

Active Directory Structure

Determining the structure of an Active Directory is an important step in planning a Windows 2000 network. When planning your network, you must consider Active Directory's logical structure as well as its physical layout. The flexibility of Active Directory makes it a viable solution for networks of all sizes.

The Logical Structure

The logical structure of the Active Directory can be completely separate from the physical layout of the network, thereby making it possible to build systems based on organizational structure or geographic relationships. To facilitate this abstraction, Active Directory provides *objects*. An object and its attributes represent the smallest unit of administration. Many types, or *classes*, of objects exist in the default schema of a directory (schemas are discussed in more detail later in this chapter). Table 4.4 lists some examples of object classes.

Larger objects are used to build the structure of the Active Directory. These objects include the following:

➤ *Organizational Units* (OU)—Special objects that have the ability to hold other objects without the overhead of being a separate domain. An OU allows other objects to be grouped logically within a domain.

➤ *Domains*—The backbone of an Active Directory. Grouping objects into organizational units is convenient, but all objects in a directory must exist within a domain. Domains can hold more than a million objects, but 1 million is the recommended maximum. The main function of a domain is to control access to the network objects. Because all objects must be members of a domain, domains can control access to all objects.

➤ *Tree*—A hierarchical group of one or more domains that can be peers or arranged in a parent/child structure. A tree is a contiguous namespace in which the name of a parent is always part of the name of a child domain.

Table 4.4   Examples of objects.

Object Class	Attribute	Sample Values
User Accounts	First Name	Ron
	Last Name	Kauffman
	Logon Name	Rkauffman
Groups	Members	Rkauffman
Computers	Computer Name	WS-Rkauffman
Printers	Printer Name	PRN-Rkauffman

➤ *Forest*—A structure in which one or more trees are peers. The forest is a disjointed namespace, because the name of one tree is not part of the name of another tree. Because the namespace is disjointed, trees in a forest provide the structure for different types systems to interact in a heterogeneous environment. Figure 4.2 shows an example of a simple forest with one tree containing a root domain with two child domains. The root domain is named *Coriolis.test*, and it contains two child domains named *Sales* and *Corp*. One child contains printer, computer, and user objects.

4

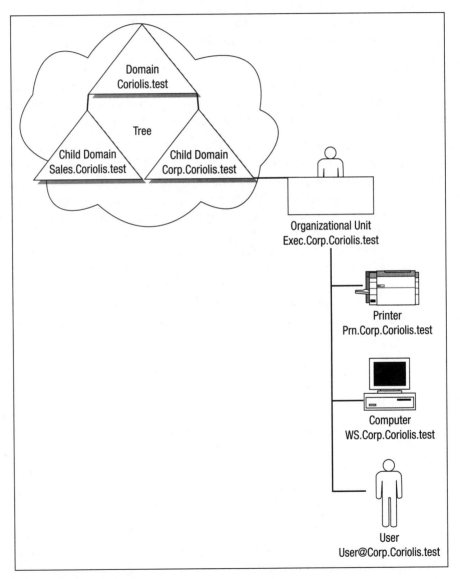

Figure 4.2   A simple forest.

The Physical Layout

The physical structure of an Active Directory consists of *sites* and *site links*. A site is one or more TCP/IP subnets. If more than one subnet exists within a site, the subnets must be connected by a reliable link of at least 512Kbps with at least 128Kbps available bandwidth. These sites are not part of the namespace, so users do not see the sites in the directory. Sites determine the manner in which domains and domain controllers will exchange information, making sites and domains dependent on each other. A site can contain one or more domains. A domain can span one or more sites. The main purpose of a site is to manage communication within the directory, which is called *replication*. Figure 4.3 illustrates the possible relationships between sites and domains.

Remember that all domain controllers are peers, and each controller maintains a copy of the domain's Active Directory information. Multiple domain controllers not only provide a local point of authentication and resource allocation, but they also add fault tolerance to the domain structure.

All domain controllers must be able to replicate changes to all other domain controllers in a reliable and efficient manner. Although some changes are stored and replicated at specific times, other information (such as disabled user accounts) replicates immediately. The planned replication is controlled by the frequency of replication as well as by the amount of data replicated during each session. All controllers in a domain are placed in a logical ring. Data is replicated following this ring topology so that there are always at least two physical connections between domain controllers. If a link fails, the data simply turns around and follows the reverse path. If a domain controller is removed, the Active Directory automatically rebuilds the ring without the controller in it. When a domain controller is added, the ring is rebuilt to accommodate the new controller.

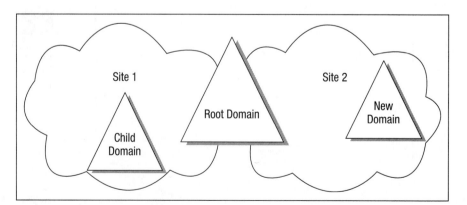

Figure 4.3 Possible relationships between sites and domains.

ACTIVE DIRECTORY CONSIDERATIONS

The Active Directory uses many familiar concepts, as well as a few new ones. Although the domain remains the core unit for administration, the network is now a hierarchical structure. The forest and its trees reside above the domain structure, while child domains and organizational units provide granularity below the parent domain. All of these new concepts are governed by a set of rules that are contained in the schema.

4

The Schema

The *schema* maintains a list of all classes and attributes in an entire forest. The schema is created when Active Directory services install the first domain controller in a forest. The default schema defines many common classes, such as users, groups, computers, printers, and organizational units. The schema also contains classes for internal use by Active Directory services. A class is the template for an object. Think of a class as a cookie cutter, and objects as the cookies. A user named jsmith would be an object derived from the class User.

The schema lists and defines classes with both required and optional attributes. You can extend the schema to accommodate new classes as well as new attributes for existing classes. You can modify the schema with the Active Directory Services Interface (ADSI) snap-in from the Windows 2000 Resource Kit. Figure 4.4 graphically represents the schema.

All the schema information is stored in the *Global Catalog*. When an administrator or a process modifies the schema, the Global Catalog is automatically updated.

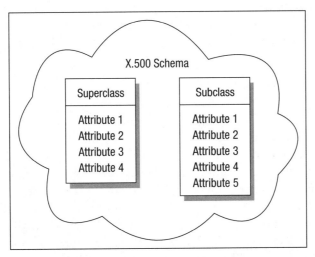

Figure 4.4   A graphic representation of the schema.

Global Catalog

The Global Catalog provides a method for users to find resources quickly and reliably in a system that can potentially manage millions of objects. In Active Directory services, the Global Catalog handles resource allocation. The Global Catalog is a service, and its related files identify resources for the entire Active Directory. To help limit the size of the directory, only the subset of the attributes necessary to identify and locate an object are stored in the catalog. This set of attributes differs for each class of object, but it always includes the fields that are necessary to find a full replica of any object, as well as the fields that are used most often to search for objects of this class. For instance, a user's logon name would be placed in the catalog because it not only identifies that user object, but it also is a field that others would use to search for that user. All objects in a forest share a common catalog.

The Global Catalog is created automatically on the first domain controller with Active Directory services in the forest. This server stores the catalog and processes queries to the catalog. When more than one domain exists or multiple controllers exist in a domain, they can replicate the subset of information necessary to the Global Catalog Server. You can have more than one Global Catalog Server in a directory, and having multiple Global Catalogs can speed up forestwide searches. However, numerous Global Catalog Servers translates into more replication traffic, which can slow down the network as a whole.

Note: Each site should have one Global Catalog Server. Remember, a site is one or more TCP/IP subnets connected by a fast link.

Trust Relationships

A *trust* is a mechanism that makes resources on one domain available to another domain. Trusts are also useful for *pass-through authentication*, in which a user in domain A can log in from a computer in domain B. Windows 2000 supports two types of trusts:

➤ One-way non-transitive trusts

➤ Two-way transitive trusts

Figure 4.5 illustrates both trust models. In Figure 4.5, the left side of the figure shows a three-domain system with two one-way non-transitive trusts. One of the trusts is between domain A and domain B, with the point at B. This indicates that domain A is trusting domain B, and domain B is trusted by domain A. The other trust indicates domain C is trusting domain B. The domain at the end with the arrow is called the *trusted domain*, while the other domain is called the *trusting domain*. Because the trusts are one way, resources can be shared only from A to B or from C to B. The non-transitive nature of

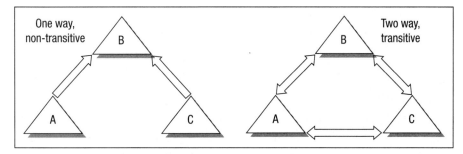

Figure 4.5   Comparison of trust relationship types.

the trusts dictates that there is no implied relationship between domains A and C. A one-way non-transitive trust can be used to connect to Windows NT 4 domains as well as trees within a forest.

The right side of the diagram in Figure 4.5 illustrates domains with two-way transitive trusts. The points at both ends of the connector lines mean that resources can be shared between the domains at both ends of the trust. Furthermore, users from any domain can log in from any other domain in the system. Because the trusts are transitive, an implied trust exists between domains A and C. Two-way transitive trusts are the default type in Windows 2000, and they are automatically created to accommodate the domain models built in the Active Directory.

New domains and migrated Windows NT 4 domains are referred to as being in a state called *mixed mode*. This means that the domains can still communicate with domain controllers from previous versions of Windows NT. The mode should be changed to *native mode* only when there are no more domain controllers running previous versions of Windows, and none will be added. After changing to native mode, the primary domain controller from the original domain becomes a peer with all other domain controllers.

Warning: Once a domain changes to native mode, it cannot be changed back to mixed mode.

The Database and Shared Volume

The directory database and system volume provide storage for the directory data and log files as well as serve as a point of storage and replication for group policies and scripts. The directory database is stored in the folder *<system root>\NTDS*. Changes to the Active Directory database are temporarily stored in the log files until the changes are committed and replicated to other domain controllers. The database log files are also stored in this folder; however, for optimum performance, the logs should be moved to a separate physical disk.

Every Windows 2000 domain controller has a shared system volume to store the domain's public files. The shared system volume must be stored on an NTFS partition, which, by default, is located in the *<system root>\SysVol* folder.

PLANNING THE ACTIVE DIRECTORY

Planning the Active Directory is the most critical phase of Windows 2000 implementation. Planning the Active Directory involves planning the namespace, replication paths, and Organizational Units.

Determining a Namespace

The first step in planning for your Active Directory is to decide which type of DNS to implement for the directory. Specifically, you have three choices:

➤ Convert an existing namespace

➤ Extend an existing namespace

➤ Create a new internal namespace

To convert an existing namespace, you must already be the authority for that namespace, as documented with the appropriate registrar. In most cases, there will already be a primary and secondary DNS server established for the second-level domain. If the DNS servers are using the Windows NT 4 implementation of DNS, they can be upgraded to Windows 2000. In all other cases, you need to either assign the address already registered as name servers to the Windows 2000 Servers or change the address for the name servers at the registrar level. Building a new Windows 2000 Server as the DNS and Active Directory root converts the entire second-level domain to Active Directory.

Extending an existing namespace is almost the same as converting a namespace, except that the Active Directory occupies only a portion of the namespace. When extending a namespace, the root of the Active Directory is not the root of the second-level domain. Rather, the Active Directory occupies a subdomain within the second-level domain. As shown in Figure 4.6, the Active Directory can reside in only a portion of the DNS namespace.

In contrast to converting or extending an existing namespace, you can also create a new internal namespace. In other words, you can completely separate the Active Directory from the external DNS namespace. This provides a clear division between internal and external resources, and it allows for completely separate administration. In this case, the first domain controller created in the Active Directory will also be the DNS root server.

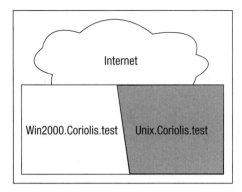

Figure 4.6   Extending a namespace to accommodate Active Directory.

Planning for Replication Traffic

As previously mentioned, sites and domains are completely separate entities. The single biggest factor in site planning is replication traffic, which is the traffic associated with communication between domain controllers. Any subnets that are linked together with at least 512Kbps links and a minimum of 128Kbps available bandwidth can be combined into one site. Once sites have been identified, replication traffic must be tailored to meet the business needs. Replication should be scheduled to keep the directory information fresh and to occur only when network utilization is low.

Identifying Organizational Units

Domains can be divided into Organizational Units for a number of reasons. For example, domains can be used to reflect an organization's structure. Since objects can be moved from one OU to another, they can accommodate changes within a company. They can also be used to delegate authority to a user for objects within an OU without implying any special permissions for that user outside of the OU. Users can see only those objects that they have permissions to access, so an OU can be used to conveniently group resources for users. Finally, administrators can use an OU to group similar resources together to ease administration.

CHAPTER SUMMARY

The Active Directory provides a Windows 2000 network with a scalable and reliable method of identifying resources and making them available to network clients. The service is scalable, because it allows many layers of administration without any single point of failure. Furthermore, the directory can contain millions of objects in different types of container objects to delineate both security and organizational structure. Active Directory supports many common standards used on the Internet to provide a highly interoperable directory service.

The logical structure of the directory is extensible, and the nature of its separation from the physical structure makes it flexible enough to accommodate systems of any size. There are many predefined classes of objects in the logical structure of the directory, including common network objects such as users and computers. The tree is a familiar structure to many people in the computer industry, and it is implemented using a domain model similar to Windows NT 4. Below the tree layer and above the individual user level, Organizational Units offer a level of administrative grouping.

The physical structure of the directory remains separate from the logical structure. The basic physical unit is the TCP/IP subnet. Any subnets connected by high-speed links can be grouped into a site, which is an autonomous unit of replication. Replication between sites is facilitated by site links that should contain no one point of failure.

Planning the Active Directory is an important undertaking, because the Active Directory affects system performance as well as the network's usability. Properly planning a system's forest and trees impacts the way in which name resolution takes place on the Internet as well as the local area network. Creating domains and organizational units tailors the way in which users access resources and the way administrators control the resources. A properly planned directory leads to an efficient and effective information system.

REVIEW QUESTIONS

1. The Active Directory uses _____ for name resolution.

   a. LDAP

   b. DNS

   c. HTTP

   d. WINS

2. The naming format used in email addresses comes from which of the following?

   a. RFC 1777

   b. MS Exchange

   c. RFC 822

   d. LDAP

3. An Organizational Unit can contain which of the following? [Check all correct answers]

   a. User

   b. Computer

   c. Universal group

   d. Domain

   e. Tree

   f. Forest

4

4. What is the core unit in the Active Directory structure?

   a. User

   b. Computer

   c. Universal group

   d. Domain

   e. Tree

   f. Forest

5. Which of the following represents a contiguous namespace?

   a. User

   b. Computer

   c. Universal group

   d. Domain

   e. Tree

   f. Forest

6. Which of the following represents a disjointed namespace?

   a. User

   b. Computer

   c. Universal group

   d. Domain

   e. Tree

   f. Forest

7. A _____ can contain many _____, and a _____ can span many _____.

   a. site, domains, tree, subnets

   b. domain, sites, tree, subnets

   c. site, domains, domain, sites

d. domain, sites, domain, sites

e. domain, sites, site, domains

8. A _____ is one or more _____ connected by high-speed links.

   a. site, subnets

   b. domain, sites

   c. subnet, sites

   d. subnet, sites

9. A high-speed link is at least _____ with _____ available bandwidth.

   a. 128Kbps, 64Kbps

   b. 256Kbps, 128Kbps

   c. 512Kbps, 256Kbps

   d. 512Kbps, 128Kbps

   e. 512Kbps, 64Kbps

10. A domain controller contains a replica of the _____.

   a. active directory

   b. domain directory

   c. LDAP directory

   d. tree structure

11. All domain controllers within a domain are peers.

   a. True

   b. False

12. Because the replication path forms a _____, it is fault tolerant.

   a. star

   b. bus

   c. ring

   d. chain

13. The schema defines classes and the attributes for them.

   a. True

   b. False

14. New schemas must be downloaded regularly, because this is the only way to extend the schema.

   a. True

   b. False

15. All _____ within a _____ share a common _____.

    a. domains, forest, global schema

    b. domains, forest, Global Catalog

    c. forests, tree, global schema

    d. forests, tree, Global Catalog

16. Only a domain controller can house the Global Catalog.

    a. True

    b. False

17. Only one server can house the Global Catalog.

    a. True

    b. False

18. What protocol is used for authentication in Windows 2000?

    a. NTLM

    b. CHAP

    c. Kerberos

    d. SLIP

19. If a two-way transitive trust exists between domains A and B and another exist between domains B and C, which of the following is true? [Check all correct answers]

    a. Domain A trusts B, but domain B doesn't trust A.

    b. Domain B trusts domain C, but domain C doesn't trust domain B.

    c. Domain A trusts domain C.

    d. Domain C trusts domain A.

20. Which of the following types of trust is available to support Windows NT 4 domains?

    a. Two-way non-transitive

    b. Two-way transitive

    c. One-way non-transitive

    d. One-way transitive

21. In a distinguished name, what does DC represent?

    a. Domain controller

    b. Domain component

    c. Distinguished controller

    d. Distinguished component

22. How long is a Globally Unique Identifier?

    a. 32 bits

    b. 128 bits

    c. 32 bytes

    d. 128 bytes

23. What does Active Directory support to provide backward compatibility?

    a. Native format

    b. Mixed format

    c. Native mode

    d. Mixed mode

REAL-WORLD PROJECTS

Andy Palmer has been assigned the job of planning and implementing a Windows 2000 network for a client named Coriolis. After interviewing a number of employees and examining documents such as the organization chart, he has collected the following information.

The company has two locations. The first location is a suite in a downtown office building that houses the Corporate, Finance, and Sales departments. The second location is a standalone building in a suburban office park that houses the IT, Engineering, and Research departments. The two locations are connected by a 256Kbps WAN link.

Andy determines that the downtown location should have one server, numerous workstations, and a few printers. The resources are allocated as follows:

➤ The Corporate department consists of the president of the company, the vice president of finance, the vice president of sales, the vice president of technology, and an administrative assistant. The president and vice presidents use notebook computers. The administrative assistant uses a desktop computer. All corporate employees share a network-connected printer.

➤ The Finance department has one accountant and one assistant. The accountant uses a notebook computer, and the assistant uses a desktop computer. Both employees share a network-connected printer.

➤ The Sales department has three salespeople who use notebook computers, and an administrative assistant who has a desktop computer. They all share a network-connected computer.

Andy determines that the suburban location should also have one server, numerous workstations, and a few network-connected printers. The resources are allocated as follows:

➤ The IT department has one system administrator, one developer, and one assistant who all use desktop computers and share one network-connected printer.

➤ The Engineering department has one system administrator, two developers, and an administrative assistant. The system administrator and the assistant use desktop computers, while the developers use notebook computers. The engineering department shares two network-connected printers.

➤ The Research department consists of one system administrator, one developer, one sales researcher, and one assistant. All research employees use notebook computers, and they all share one network-connected printer.

Project 4.1
To plan an Active Directory:

1. Determine the number and names of forests. The department needs only one tree in one forest.

2. Create a forest change control policy. All changes will be documented and processed through the IT department's system administrator.

3. Determine the number and hierarchy of the domains. For this situation, choose one root domain.

4. Determine domain names and DNS server requirements. The domain for this organization will be *coriolis.test*.

5. Determine the number and placement of domain controllers. For this project, two domain controllers will be necessary, one at each site.

6. Determine the number and placement of Global Catalog Servers. One Global Catalog Server will be sufficient for this organization.

7. Determine the number and placement of sites and site links. This scenario will require one downtown site and one suburban site.

8. Determine replication paths and replication intervals.

9. Create sites and connect them with the site links that are appropriate for the organization.

10. Finally, assign cost to links, configure the replication schedule interval, and pick either RPC or SMTP for the transport. RPC will suffice for this situation because there is enough bandwidth.

Project 4.2

To name and organize resources for the Active Directory:

1. Identify the OUs that will yield the greatest amount of flexibility without adding unnecessary complexity. Table 4.5 lists one possible combination.

2. List the TCP/IP nodes that will be necessary along with their address and host names.

3. Define the DHCP scope along with scope options and exclusion ranges for statically assigned address. Table 4.5 leads to the scope 1 range 192.168.0.1 through 192.168.0.254. Scope 2 range is 192.168.1.1 through 192.168.1.254. Global options for Primary DNS 192.168.0.1 and secondary 192.168.1.1. Scope 1 router 192.168.0.1 and scope 2 router 192.168.1.1.

Table 4.5 Network nodes for the domain *Coriolis.test*.

Organiza-tional Unit	User/Computer Name	IP Address	Function
Information—Technology	Axis1.Coriolis.test	192.168.0.1	DC, Primary DNS
Corporate	PresPrinter.Coriolis.test	192.168.0.5	President's Printer
Corporate	VPPrinter1.Coriolis.test	192.168.0.6	Vice President's Printer
Sales—Marketing	SMPrinter1.Coriolis.test	192.168.0.7	Sales Printer
Finance—Accounting	FAPrinter1.Coriolis.test	192.168.0.8	Finance Printer
Corporate	President.Coriolis.test	192.168.0.9	President's Workstation
Corporate	VPFinance.Coriolis.test	192.168.0.10	Vice President's Workstation
Corporate	VPTechnology.Coriolis.test	192.168.0.11	Vice President's Workstation
Corporate	VPSales.Coriolis.test	192.168.0.12	Vice President's Workstation
Corporate	VPAssistant1.Coriolis.test	192.168.0.13	Assistant's Workstation
Sales—Marketing	SMEast1.Coriolis.test	192.168.0.14	Salesperson's Workstation
Sales—Marketing	SMWest1.Coriolis.test	192.168.0.15	Salesperson's Workstation
Sales—Marketing	SMInternat1.Coriolis.test	192.168.0.16	Salesperson's Workstation
Sales—Marketing	SMAssistant1.Coriolis.test	192.168.0.17	Assistant's Workstation
Finance—Accounting	FAAccountant1.Coriolis.test	192.168.0.18	Accountant's Workstation
Finance—Accounting	FAAssistant1.Coriolis.test	192.168.0.19	Assistant's Workstation

(continued)

Table 4.5 Network nodes for the domain *Coriolis.test (continued)*.

Organizational Unit	User/Computer Name	IP Address	Function
Information Technology	Axis2.Coriolis.test	192.168.1.1	DC, secondary DNS, router
Information Technology	ITPrinter1.Coriolis.test	192.168.1.5	Information Technology Printer
Engineering	EngPrinter1.Coriolis.test	192.168.1.6	Engineering Printer
Engineering	EngPrinter2.Coriolis.test	192.168.1.7	Engineering Printer
Research	RDPrinter1.Coriolis.test	192.168.1.8	Research Printer
Information Technology	ITSysadmin1.Coriolis.test	192.168.1.9	Sysadmin Workstation
Information Technology	ITDeveloper1.Coriolis.test	192.168.1.10	Developer Workstation
Information Technology	ITAssistant1.Coriolis.test	192.168.1.11	Assistant's Workstation
Engineering	EngSysadmin1.Coriolis.test	192.168.1.12	Sysadmin Workstation
Engineering	EngDeveloper1.Coriolis.test	192.168.1.13	Developer Workstation
Engineering	EngDeveloper2.Coriolis.test	192.168.1.14	Developer Workstation
Engineering	EngAssistant1.Coriolis.test	192.168.1.15	Assistant's Workstation
Research	RDSysadmin1.Coriolis.test	192.168.1.16	Sysadmin Workstation
Research	RDDeveloper1.Coriolis.test	192.168.1.17	Developer Workstation
Research	RDSM1.Coriolis.test	192.168.1.18	Salesperson's Workstation
Research	RDAssistant1.Coriolis.test	192.168.1.19	Assistant's Workstation

Project 4.3
To represent graphically the physical structure of the Active Directory:

1. Assess the proposed system, and then break the system down into a very superficial diagram for physical structure. Use circles for the sites involved and straight lines for site links, as illustrated in Figure 4.7.

2. Drill down to the subnet level for the Active Directory physical structure diagram. Use dotted circles to represent the subnets, as shown in Figure 4.8.

3. Drill down one more level to add the domain controllers and connections to the Active Directory physical structure diagram. Use rectangles to represent the domain controllers and dotted lines to represent the connection paths, as shown in Figure 4.9.

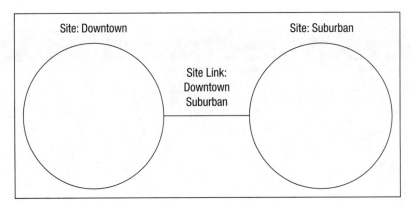

Figure 4.7   The sites for the Active Directory physical structure diagram.

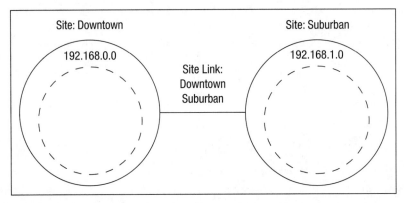

Figure 4.8   The subnets for the Active Directory physical structure diagram.

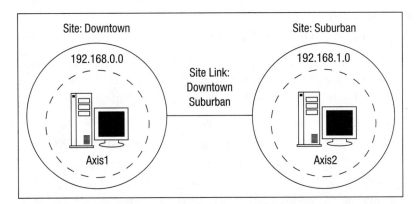

Figure 4.9   The domain controllers for the Active Directory physical structure diagram.

Project 4.4

To represent graphically the logical structure of the Active Directory:

1. Assess the proposed system, and then break the system down into a very superficial diagram for logical structure. Use clouds for the DNS domains involved, as illustrated in Figure 4.10.

4

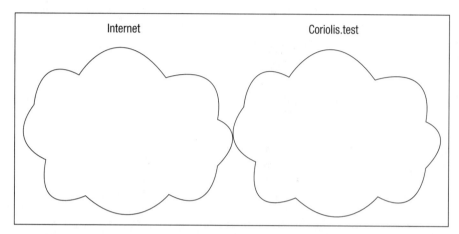

Internet   Coriolis.test

Figure 4.10   The namespace for the Active Directory logical structure diagram.

2. Drill down to the domain level for the Active Directory logical structure diagram. As shown in Figure 4.11, use triangles to represent the domains and dotted lines to represent the trusts between them.

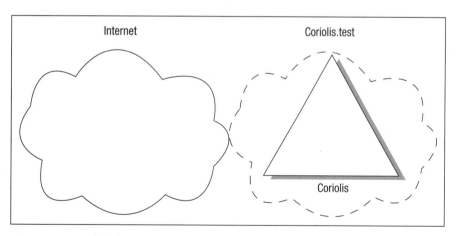

Internet   Coriolis.test

Coriolis

Figure 4.11   The domain level for the Active Directory logical structure diagram.

3. Drill down one more level to the Organizational Units for the Active Directory logical structure diagram. Represent Organizational Units as a tree structure within the domain, as illustrated in Figure 4.12.

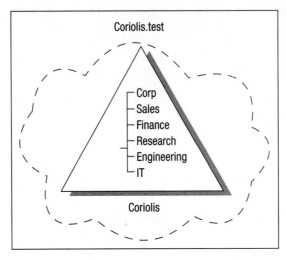

Figure 4.12 The Organizational Units for the Active Directory logical structure diagram.

CHAPTER FIVE

DESIGNING AND CONFIGURING THE FIRST DOMAIN

After completing this chapter, you will be able to:

✓ Describe the new features of Windows 2000 domains

✓ Define and explain the purpose of Organizational Units

✓ Learn ways to distribute administrative authority

✓ Install a first domain controller

✓ Install Active Directory

All previous versions of Windows NT as well as Windows 2000 networks revolve around the basic network unit named the *domain*. Windows 2000 networks incorporate the same domain structure as NT; however, many new features have been added and many limitations have been removed. This chapter introduces the new features of the Active Directory domain.

One limitation of NT was that the function of servers (such as PDCs, BDCs, and member servers) had to be defined during installation and could not be changed. Windows 2000 Servers can be promoted to domain controllers and then demoted without reinstalling the software.

This chapter introduces the requirements and steps necessary to install an Active Directory Domain Controller, describes what Organizational Units are, and discusses how to delegate authority to an Organizational Unit.

DOMAIN STRUCTURES

Even with all the changes and new features in Windows 2000, the basic concept of the domain remains the same. The domain represents the logical grouping of computers, users, and resources for the purposes of administration, security, and replication. Although Active Directory is a technology that groups all objects into one manageable unit, the domain is still the core component of Windows 2000 networks.

Creating the First Domain

The first domain created in the Active Directory is called the *forest root domain*. All domains defined after the initial domain become *child domains* to the forest root. For example, if the first domain is **examcram.com**, then a subsequent domain named Europe becomes **europe.examcram.com**. Great care should be taken before creating and naming the first domain. Because all domain names are Domain Name System (DNS) domains, a domain name should be registered with an Internet naming authority, such as Network Solutions.

The administrators group, in the parent domain, automatically has administrative authority in all child domains. Administrative permissions can be removed for the domain admins group, but the enterprise admins group will continue and should always have administrative permissions in all domains within the tree.

All Windows 2000 Servers are installed as member servers and can be promoted to domain controllers only after installation. Windows 2000 has many requirements that must be properly planned before any server can be promoted to a domain controller.

Creating the First Windows 2000 Domain Controller

Any computer running Windows 2000 Server can be promoted to become the first domain controller. If you are currently working on an existing Windows NT 4 network, the PDC should be the first computer that is upgraded to an Active Directory domain controller. A Windows 2000 domain controller will continue to emulate a Windows NT 4 PDC while running in mixed mode. This provides backward compatibility and allows the network to be upgraded in gradual steps.

Planning Active Directory Installation

Before you can effectively implement an Active Directory network, you will need a plan that defines the network structure you plan to create. This information includes the number of domains that will be present in the network, the specification of which domains will be child domains and which will be parent domains, a description of which servers will be DNS servers, and a DNS strategy for each domain.

The installation of Active Directory and subsequent promotion to a domain controller can be accomplished only if the following components are installed and working properly:

➤ A computer running Windows 2000 Server, Advanced Server, or Datacenter Server.

➤ TCP/IP installed and configured to use DNS. The IP address must be statically configured on the server that will become a domain controller. Domain controllers cannot use Dynamic Host Configuration Protocol (DHCP).

➤ At least one partition formatted with NTFS file system.

➤ A DNS server that supports SRV records and DNS dynamic update.

➤ Correct system time and zone information.

In addition to the above-mentioned components, you must also have the proper credentials to install Active Directory on a Windows 2000 server if this new domain controller is joining an existing domain. Proper credentials include a user account logon name, password, and the domain name where the user account resides.

Active Directory Installation Options

When you install Active Directory on a Windows 2000 server, you must specify whether this is going to be a domain controller in an existing domain, or whether this domain controller is creating a new domain.

If a server is going to create a new domain, you must specify if this new domain controller is going to be a member of an existing Active Directory Tree and become a child domain, or if the server is going to create a new tree in the forest. If a domain controller is going to start a new tree, you must specify if it is going to become a member of the same Active Directory forest or if that domain controller is going to create a new forest as well. See Figure 5.1 for installation options. Active Directory trees and forests are explained in Chapter 6.

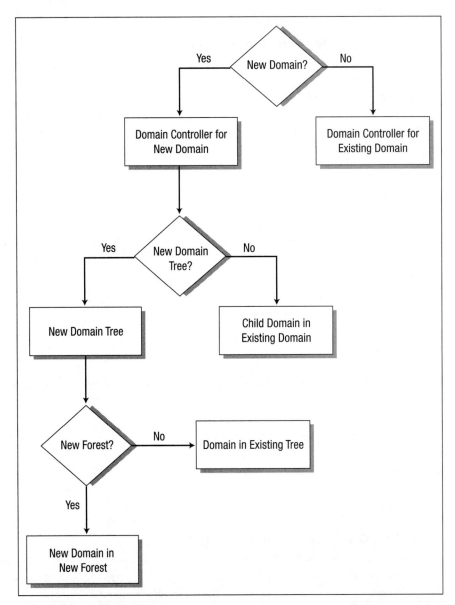

Figure 5.1 Installation options.

Once you have determined and selected the appropriate check boxes to install an additional domain controller in an existing domain, a child domain, a domain in a new forest, or a domain in an existing forest, the Active Directory installation wizard will then prompt you for the appropriate information regarding your choice.

Active Directory Installation

You can create the first domain by simply running the Windows 2000 Active Directory Wizard or running Dcpromo.exe. Dcpromo installs Active Directory and promotes the server to a domain controller.

All domain controllers are peers in a multi-master relationship, and there is no longer a question of primary and backup domain controllers. Before promoting the first server to a domain controller, you should have a DNS server installed. After the DNS server is installed, you should set up Active Directory integrated zones as well as allow dynamic updates via DHCP.

The following steps can assist you when you install Active Directory and create the first domain:

1. In the Run dialog box, type "dcpromo.exe".

Tip: Dcpromo.exe can be used to add or remove Active Directory.

2. In the Run dialog box, click OK. The Active Directory Installation Wizard appears, as shown in Figure 5. 2. Click Next.

Figure 5.2   Viewing the Active Directory Installation Wizard.

3. In the Active Directory Installation Wizard, select a domain controller type. If this is the first domain controller or the first domain controller in a new domain, select the Domain Controller For A New Domain radio button, as shown in Figure 5.3.

4. Click Next, and then select the Create A New Domain Tree radio button, as shown in Figure 5.4.

5. Click Next, and then enter the domain name for the new domain name in the Full DNS Name For The New Domain text box (see Figure 5.5).

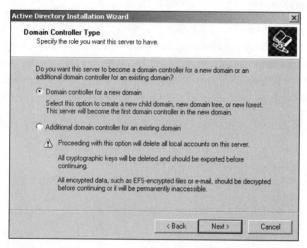

Figure 5.3   Selecting a domain controller type.

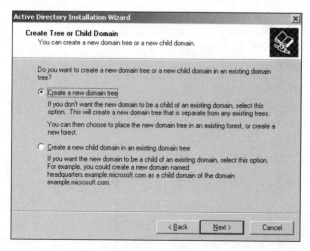

Figure 5.4   Specifying to create a new domain tree.

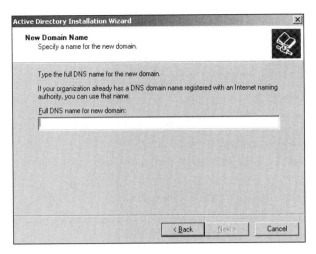

Figure 5.5   Providing a new domain name.

6. Click Next. The NetBIOS Domain Name screen in the Active Directory Installation Wizard displays, as shown in Figure 5.6. This screen enables you to specify the NT 4 domain name that existing clients expect to log into. The Windows 2000 domain controller will emulate an NT 4 Server and authenticate users attempting to log into a PDC. Enter the NetBIOS domain name in the Domain NetBIOS Name text box.

7. Click Next. The Database And Logs Locations screen appears, as shown in Figure 5.7. This screen enables you to specify the location in which the actual Active Directory database and log files will be stored. Keep in mind

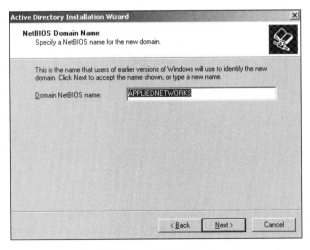

Figure 5.6   Specifying a NetBIOS domain name.

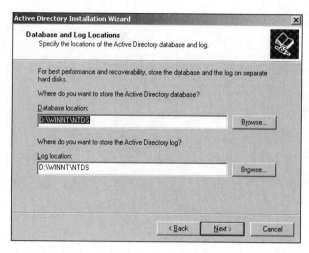

Figure 5.7 Choosing locations for the database and log files.

that the location must be an NTFS partition. Enter pathnames in the Database Location and Log Location text boxes, and then click Next.

8. In the Shared System Volume screen, shown in Figure 5.8, specify where the SYSVOL folder should be located. The SYSVOL folder contains a copy of the domain public files. The SYSVOL folder replaces the use and functionality of the NETLOGON folder within Windows NT 4.

As you may recall, the NETLOGON folder was used for standard and pass-through authentication, folder replication, and a storage location for logon scripts and policy files. This data is replicated to all domain controllers within the domain. Click Next.

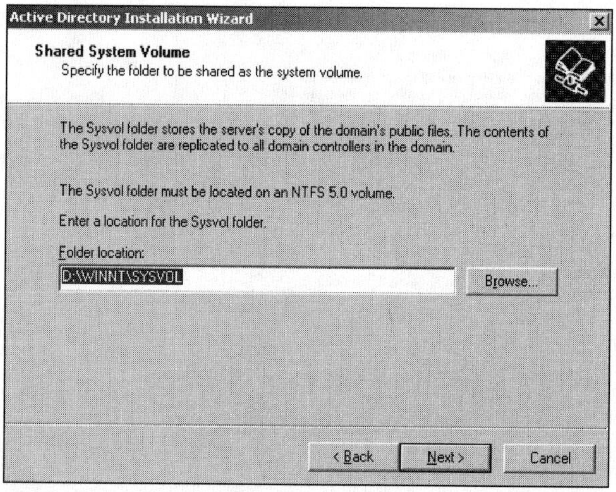

Figure 5.8 Assigning a location for the SYSVOL folder.

9. At this point, you will see a message box, as shown in Figure 5.9. If DNS is already installed, ignore the message. If DNS is not installed, then it must be installed before Active Directory will function properly. Click OK.

10. On the Configure DNS screen (see Figure 5.10), click the Yes option to install DNS, or click the No option if DNS is already installed, and then click Next.

11. The Permissions screen displays, as shown in Figure 5.11. If you are still running Windows NT 4 Servers on your network, choose the Permissions Compatible With Pre–Windows 2000 Servers option. Otherwise, select the Permissions Compatible Only With Windows 2000 Servers option. The Permissions Compatible With Pre–Windows 2000 option allows current users with dial-in permission to gain access to the Windows 2000 network without the use of Group Policy permissions. This function is provided for networks that are upgraded to Windows 2000 from Windows NT 4. Then, click Next.

12. In the Directory Services Restore Mode Administrator Password screen, shown in Figure 5.12, enter and confirm a password that can be used with

Figure 5.9   Reviewing the DNS warning.

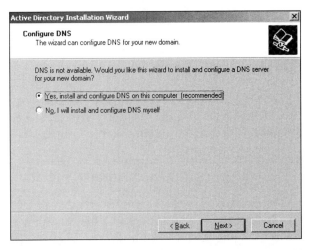

Figure 5.10   Opting to install DNS if necessary.

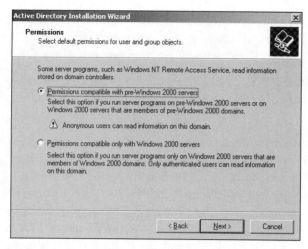

Figure 5.11 Setting permissions.

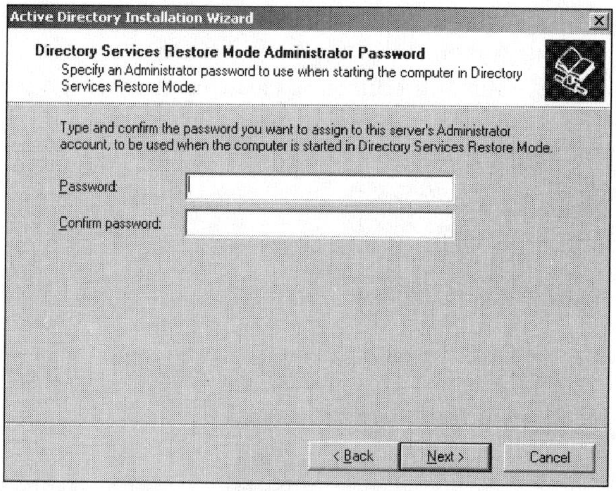

Figure 5.12 Creating a restore mode password.

the Administrators account in order to restore the Active Directory. This password is necessary whenever someone attempts to restore the Active Directory. Active Directory restoration is discussed in Chapter 18.

13. Click Next twice. At this point, the Configuring Active Directory window appears while the Active Directory is set up (see Figure 5.13).

14. When the Active Directory installation is complete, the Active Directory Installation Wizard displays a screen indicating that the procedure is completed, as shown in Figure 5.14. Click Finish.

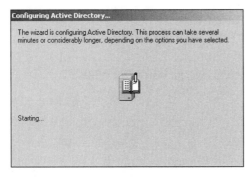

Figure 5.13 Writing the Active Directory database.

Figure 5.14 Completing the Active Directory installation.

Once Active Directory has been installed, the Active Directory Wizard adds three new management consoles to the administrative tools menu for managing the Active Directory. These tools are:

➤ *Active Directory Users and Computers*—an administrative tool that is used to create and modify user accounts, group accounts, and Organizational Units. This tool is also used to publish information to the directory.

➤ *Active Directory Domains and Trust*—an administrative tool that can be used to administer domain trusts and user principal names, and that is used to convert the domain model from mixed to native mode.

➤ *Active Directory Sites and Service*—an administrative tool that is used to create and manage subnets, sites, site links, and site link bridges. This tool is also used to control replication traffic within the local domain as well as remote domains within the forest.

Improvements to the Domain

Although the core component of the network is still the domain, Windows 2000 is not hindered by the same limitations as NT 4. The following NT 4 domain limitations have been corrected in Windows 2000:

➤ *Domains in Windows 2000 are not limited by a 40,000-object limit*—Domains in Windows 2000 can theoretically support up to 10 million objects each.

➤ *Domains are no longer the most basic unit of administration*—Windows 2000 and Active Directory introduce Organizational Units (OUs), which allow administration to be broken up according to business units.

➤ *Trust relationships between domains is a concept of the past*—Two-way transitive trusts are automatically created between parent and child domains. Non-transitive one-way trusts can still be created between domains in different trees.

ORGANIZATIONAL UNITS

Now that size limitations and administrative issues have been resolved, many companies that have medium to large multidomain networks might choose a single domain model in order to simplify administration. One of the most notable changes in Windows 2000 when compared to NT 4 is Window 2000's ability to break up administrative responsibilities within the domain. Organizational Units provide this function.

Organizational Units allow administrative responsibilities to be delegated to distinct areas of a network. For example, a company that has locations in both Atlanta and Los Angeles could implement one domain and then divide administrative authority according to two top-level OUs (named Atlanta and Los Angeles). Several questions must be answered before determining whether to implement multiple domains or multiple OUs. Reasons for creating multiple domains include:

➤ *Security requirements*—Multiple business units or geographic locations might have different security requirements that cannot be implemented with OUs.

➤ *Network traffic*—Using multiple domains can reduce replication traffic. Domain controllers automatically replicate all changes to all other domain controllers within the domain. By creating multiple domains, only changes to the Global Catalog are replicated.

➤ *IS organization*—IS management might not be centralized. Multiple domains will be necessary in cases where information technology is driven from the bottom up and the company has no centralized IT department, or the company does not have control over how information technology is implemented in all departments. They are also needed in cases where each business unit plans and manages a separate information systems infrastructure.

Administrators have the ability to create and delete an OU within the Active Directory. OUs are container objects. Container objects are special Active Directory objects that can contain other objects that reside in the same domain. They can simplify administration and searching, because they can organize Active Directory objects according to business unit and/or logical administrative units.

Organizations Units allow you to create the logical structure of your network. To ensure efficiency, you should fully plan and document your OU structure before adding a single OU to the Active Directory. You can use OUs to do the following:

➤ *Group objects of the same type together logically*. For example, you could create a printers OU that contains all the printers in the entire enterprise or all the printers in each office. By grouping all printers together into one OU, users will find it easier to locate the resources they need to perform their job.

➤ *Break the network into logical units*. While the network is still managed on a domain-by-domain basis, you can create a logical structure by locating resources in their respective Organizational Unit. By creating a sales and engineering OU, you have effectively broken different parts of the domain into a logical structure that resembles the business model.

➤ *Delegate*. Once the OU structure has been designed to mimic the business model, you can then delegate administrative functions to each OU. Administrative permissions can be assigned at the OU level.

Planning OUs

The single purpose of OUs is to make management and administration easier. Users will be able to see OUs when they browse the network; however, OUs are administrative tools, and they are not designed to facilitate organization for the purpose of browsing.

Administrative functions within the OU, such as user and object creation, can be delegated to administrators and managers at the OU level. While there might be only one domain, multiple administrators and department heads can manage separate pieces of the domain. Because of this, your OU design should mirror your administrative model.

Many of Windows 2000's features—such as Group Policies, security settings, and administrative functions—can be implemented at the OU level. Part of the OU planning process is to be aware of what features and benefits of Windows 2000 you plan to implement before designing the OU structure. Only after all the benefits of Windows 2000 are known and the features to be used are understood can you begin to plan your OU strategy. Before finalizing that strategy, you must first understand that one of the most powerful features of OUs is their ability to create logical domains or subdomains.

Using OUs as Subdomains

In previous versions of Windows NT, if departments or offices wanted to manage their own resources and maintain their own domain, the network engineer was forced to design a master or multi-master directory database. With Windows 2000, administrators can simply set up multiple OUs for each office and then delegate control of the OU to the appropriate office personnel.

Security policies can also be applied to individual OUs. An entire domain is no longer affected by one security policy. With Active Directory and Windows 2000, different security policies can be placed on separate OUs. This setup allows companies that once separated their network into multiple domains to simplify administration by managing just one domain.

Administrators can establish different security policies for different groups or business units. For example, an administrator could require that all users change their passwords every 60 days; however, the administrator could also require that users in the Sales department that have remote access privileges change their password every 30 days. Another powerful feature of OUs is the ability to nest one OU into another OU.

Nesting OUs

Nesting OUs is the process of creating additional OUs inside other OUs, much like creating subfolders within folders. Nesting provides the ability to build your OU structure to match your administrative model while making administration and management easier.

Although there is no practical limit to how many levels of OUs you can build, the deeper the OU structure, the slower object discovery will be. Microsoft recommends never having more than 10 levels of OUs; however, 10 levels of nest OUs could easily become confusing and difficult to administer, so common practice dictates that there be no more than 3 or 4 levels. Proper planning will help to ensure a proper balance between speed and OU organization.

First-level OUs, or *root OUs*, provide the base of your network organization. For this reason, root-level OUs should be based on a static feature within your network, such as geographic locations. In a single location networked environment, you might consider creating just one root-level OU and multiple OUs below the one root level. This strategy will provide consistency as more root level OUs are added as the network expands. Another good strategy is to create an OU for every network unit for which you would have created another domain in Windows NT 4, as shown in Figure 5.15. This figure shows multiple nested OUs.

Additional levels of OUs can be created to organize users, groups, printers, and other network objects. In some cases, you might find it beneficial to create the same root-level OUs for each separate domain within a tree or forest. Below the root-level OU, you can define additional organizational OUs, such as Sales and Marketing, or an OU to contain objects, such as a Users OU and a Groups OU. The remaining OU levels depend greatly on the administrative model of the network. As mentioned earlier, administrative permission can be delegated to users and groups at OU levels; therefore, you should consider who is going to be allowed administrative functions as well as what OUs they will have control over.

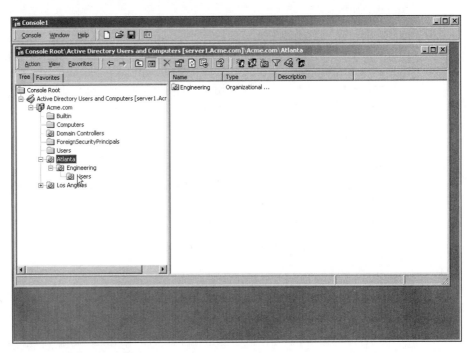

Figure 5.15 Nested OUs.

PLANNING FOR DELEGATION OF AUTHORITY

As mentioned previously in this chapter, domains can be split into separate administrative units or OUs. After an OU is created, administrative responsibilities can be delegated to the OU. Administrative responsibilities can be assigned at the OU, object, or object-attribute level.

The ability to grant administrative authority gives you a great amount of flexibility in how you manage your network. When using OUs, all administrative functions—such as creating users, assigning permissions, and managing group membership—no longer have to be handled by just one administrator or group of administrators.

Through the proper design of your Active Directory and delegation, you can allow project leaders, managers, secretaries, and other employees to manage different objects within the Active Directory. For example, a project manager might be granted the ability to add new members to a project group. The administrator can simply delegate control of the project group to the project manager and allow the project manager to add and remove users from the project group. As another example, the Human Resources department might be granted permissions to alter user object attributes such as phone number, home address, and department.

Understanding delegation and your delegation strategy is a prerequisite to planning your Active Directory and OU design. Before promoting the first domain controller, you should have a delegation plan to identify the OU that will be created, as well as which individuals will be granted administrative privileges to those OUs.

Part of the job of recognizing which user accounts will be granted permissions is to document which administrative privileges will be granted—which accounts will be allowed full control and which accounts will be allowed only to reset passwords. Designing the delegation policy within Windows 2000 is much like designing global and local groups within a Windows NT 4 single or multiple-master domain model.

Permissions that can be delegated to groups or individuals include the following tasks:

➤ *Create, delete, and manage user accounts.* By delegating this common task, you are allowing the individual or group to create additional user accounts within the OU. By delegating this permission, you are also allowing the person to whom you delegate the permission to delete and modify existing and new user accounts.

➤ *Reset passwords on user accounts.* This permission allows an individual to reset the passwords on all user accounts that reside in the OU. This will not allow anyone to reset passwords on client server applications such as SQL or Exchange server.

➤ *Read all user information.* With this permission, anyone can read all the attributes (other than password) of any user account within the OU.

➤ *Create, delete, and manage groups.* This permission allows an individual to create, delete, and manage groups within the OU. Any user with the permission to manage the group can modify the membership of any group.

➤ *Modify the membership of a group.* This allows the user or members of the group to add and remove user accounts from a group, but it does not allow anyone to create additional groups or to delete groups.

➤ *Manage group policy links.* This allows the user or members of the group to modify the group policies that are assigned at the OU level. Group policy Objects are explained in Chapter 14.

Within the Delegation Of Control wizard, as seen in Figure 5.16, you can select to create a custom task to delegate rather than use the default administrative permissions. Once Create A Custom Task To Delegate has been selected, you can specify for what object types you would like to delegate control. With this option, you can delegate control of specific object types within the OU while not allowing control of other object types. The common object types that you can specify include the following objects:

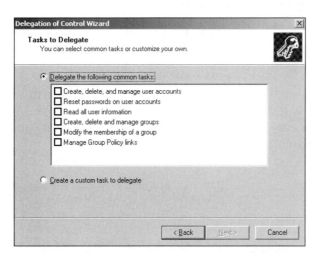

Figure 5.16   Delegating administrative authority.

➤ Computer objects

➤ Connection objects

➤ Contact objects

➤ Group objects

➤ Organizational Unit objects

➤ Printer objects

➤ Shared folder objects

➤ Site objects

➤ Site link objects

➤ Site link bridge objects

➤ Site settings objects

➤ Site container objects

➤ Subnet objects

➤ Subnet container objects

➤ Trusted domain objects

➤ User objects

Steps to Delegate Permissions

1. Right-click the OU to which you want to delegate administrative permissions.

2. Select Delegate Control. This will start the delegation wizard.

3. Click Next.

4. Click the Add button and select the users or groups to which you want to delegate authority.

5. Click OK and Click Next.

6. Select the permissions you wish to delegate, as was shown in Figure 5.16.

7. Click Next and Finish.

Note: Keep in mind that regardless of users' permisions to manage objects, the administrators' group maintains ultimate control of all objects.

To manage permission delegation, you must understand how Active Directory manages security.

Active Directory Security

Active Directory Security is made up of three components:

➤ *Security Principles*—Security principles are user, computer, and group objects. Any objects that can be assigned permissions are considered security principles. All security principles have security identifiers (SIDs).

➤ *Security Identifiers (SIDs)*—SIDs uniquely identify security principles. Every security principle has a unique SID. Windows 2000, like NT 4, uses the security principle's SID to identify and assign permissions to users. SIDs are unique and never duplicated within a forest. A SID is made up of two parts: The first part identifies the domain in which the security principle was created, and the second part, known as the *relative identifier (RID)*, identifies an account object within the domain in which the object was created.

➤ *Security Descriptors*—Security descriptors define the permissions that can be assigned to a particular object type. Just as every security principle has a SID, so too does every object have a security descriptor. The security descriptor for a printer specifies that there is a print permission that can be assigned; however, the security descriptor for a file does not include the print permission. The security descriptor also contains the object's *owner SID* and any *group SIDs*:

   ➤ *Owner SID*—This security identifier identifies the security principle that owns an object. The owner of any object automatically has full control of the object and is allowed to assign permissions to the object.

   ➤ *Group SID*—This security identifier is used for compatibility with non-Microsoft network operating systems.

Security descriptors also contain discretionary access control lists (DACLs) and security access control lists (SACLs):

   ➤ *Discretionary access control list (DACL)*—This contains all the SIDs for the security principles that have been given permissions for an object, as well as the SIDS of all users that have been denied access to a particular object. The DACL is what controls access to any object on Windows 2000. It contains the access control lists (ACLs) for a particular object and the object's attributes.

   ➤ *Security access control list (SACL)*—This stipulates auditing services. The SACL defines what events can be audited for a particular object. Auditing must be enabled on the domain controller in order to use the SACL. If auditing is enabled, the administrator can audit an OU for object creation. Whenever an object is created in an OU, an event will be written to the security log. The SACL works much like the security descriptor: The security descriptor defines what permissions can be assigned to an object, and the SACL does the same for auditing.

5

Every user account and group account is considered a security principle because permissions can be assigned to any user or group account. The operating system identifies security principles by their SID. Each SID is unique to the forest and is made up of two distinct parts: a string of numbers that represents the domain in which the object was created, and the RID that identifies the particular object within the domain. By examining any SID, the operating system can identify what domain each object belongs to.

Every object within Windows 2000 contains a security descriptor. This security descriptor defines what permissions can be assigned to the object. Printers and files, for example, have different security descriptors because the permissions that can be established on a file are different from permissions that can be set on a printer. Contained within each security descriptor are the DACL and SACL.

Each object within Windows 2000 therefore contains a list of users and groups (security principles) that have been allowed or denied access to the object (DACL). The list of users and groups that have been assigned permissions do not contain the group or user names; instead, it lists the SIDs of each user and group. If a user or group SID is not listed in the DACL or has been denied access in the DACL, then that user or group cannot access the object.

In Active Directory, every object and every object attribute has a unique identifier that allows an administrator to assign permissions to that object or attribute. When designing Active Directory security, you need to understand the concept of *permission inheritance*, in which the permissions set on one object can be inherited by one or many lower-level objects.

Permission Inheritance

Within the Active Directory, permissions can be inherited from parent objects. By default, objects inherit the permissions of the OU in which they are created. Although inheritance can be blocked, it is a useful function that eases administration by limiting the issuance of permissions to just the parent object. When assigning permissions to a container object, permissions can be applied to:

➤ Just the container object

➤ The container object and all child objects

➤ Only child objects

➤ Only specific types of child objects (such as printers, users, groups, and so forth)

There may be times when you want to block permissions assigned to a parent object from being inherited by child objects. For example, the administrator may have full control to a directory that contains the payroll database, but the payroll department may require that the administrator not have full control to files contained within the payroll directory. In situations such as this, you must block inheritance to prevent the administrator's full-control permission from being inherited to all files within the directory.

Blocking Inheritance

Blocking permission inheritance is shown in Figure 5.17. When inheritance is blocked, child object permissions have to be explicitly set. When you disable permission inheritance, you must specify what should happen to the permissions that have already been inherited. Two options can be used when blocking permission inheritance:

➤ *Copy previously inherited permissions to the objects*—When this option (shown in Figure 5.18) is used, the previous permissions of a parent object are copied to all existing child objects. New objects created after inheritance

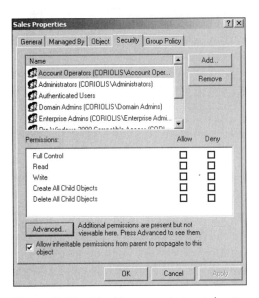

Figure 5.17   Blocking permission inheritance.

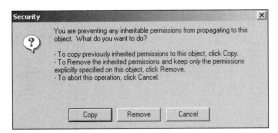

Figure 5.18   Copying or removing inherited permissions.

blocking will not contain permissions that were previously inherited by the directory. Any new permissions assigned to the parent object will not be inherited by the child objects. After blocking is enabled, permissions will have to be manually set on all child objects.

➤ *Remove previously inherited permissions from the child objects*—When this option (also shown in Figure 5.18) is used, any permissions the child objects had inherited are removed. Permission will have to be manually set on all child objects.

CHAPTER SUMMARY

Windows 2000 was designed with the intention of creating a more enterprise-ready network operating system while simplifying administrative functions. Microsoft developed Active Directory to address these issues. Active Directory provides a centralized location for managing every object in the entire network. Organizational Units (OUs) allow administrators and engineers to customize the Active Directory according to their administrative model.

Microsoft Windows NT 4 multidomain network administrators might now find that it makes more sense to upgrade to Windows 2000 and create just one domain and use OUs to copy the logical structure of the company. After OUs are in place, administrative functions and permissions can be delegated at the OU, object, or object-property level. Because Windows 2000 is not plagued by NT 4 limitations (such as the 40MB limit on the SAM database and the reliance of administrative permissions on the domain model), Windows 2000 provides much more flexibility in how your network is designed and administered.

In this chapter we discussed the planning and installation requirements that must be made prior to installing the Active Directory database. Additionally, we learned how to delegate permissions to Organizational Units within the domain in order to simplify administration. Finally, this chapter described how security is implemented in Windows 2000 through the use of SIDs, the security descriptors, and the DACL.

REVIEW QUESTIONS

1. What is the name of the first domain created in an Active Directory network?

   a. Tree domain

   b. Primary domain

   c. Forest root domain

   d. Parent domain

2. How do you refer to the domains created after the first domain?

   a. Child domains

   b. Branch domain

   c. Forest member domains

   d. Secondary domains

3. Which of the following can be promoted to an Active Directory domain controller? [Check all correct answers]

   a. Windows 2000 Server

   b. Windows 2000 Professional

   c. Windows 2000 Advanced Server

   d. Windows 2000 Datacenter

4. When upgrading a Windows NT 4 network, which computer(s) should be upgraded to Windows 2000 first?

   a. Backup domain controllers

   b. Primary domain controller

   c. Member servers

   d. Application servers

5. What components are required in order to promote a Windows 2000 Server to a domain controller?

   a. DNS, TCP/IP, WINS

   b. TCP/IP, DNS, DHCP

   c. TCP/IP, DNS, NTFS

   d. DHCP, NTFS, TCP/IP

6. What program is used to promote a Windows 2000 Server to a domain controller?

   a. promote.exe

   b. dcpromo.exe

   c. promo.exe

   d. dcpromo.bat

7. Multiple domain controllers within the same domain behave in what type of relationship?

   a. Single master

   b. Multi-master

   c. Complete trust

   d. One-way trust

8. How do you demote a Windows 2000 Active Directory domain controller back to a member server?

    a. Choose Demote in Server Manager

    b. Promote another server to the primary domain controller

    c. Reinstall Windows 2000

    d. Run dcpromo.exe

9. Which of the following can be contained within an Organizational Unit? [Check all correct answers]

    a. Users

    b. Computers

    c. DNS zones

    d. Organizational Units

10. Organizational Units provide the ability to create logical:

    a. Domains

    b. Sites

    c. Administrative units

    d. Subdomains

11. What are Organizational Units?

    a. Container objects

    b. Administrative objects

    c. Primary objects

    d. Control objects

12. All domains within a single Active Directory tree:

    a. Must be configured with two-way trusts

    b. Are automatically configured with non-transitive two-way trusts

    c. Are automatically configured with transitive two-way trusts

    d. Must be configured with transitive two-way trusts

13. What functions do Organizational Units serve? [Check all correct answers]

    a. Organize users and other objects

    b. Make network browsing easier

    c. Simplify administration

    d. Divide the network into subdomains

14. Which of the following are examples of security principles? [Check all correct answers]

    a. Windows 2000 Servers

    b. Enterprise Admins Group

    c. Windows 2000 domain controllers

    d. Shared network printers

15. Which of the following security elements contain the DACL and SACL?

    a. Security descriptors

    b. Security identifiers

    c. Security principles

    d. SIDs

16. What does the discretionary access control list define?

    a. Usernames of all permitted users

    b. Security identifiers of both permitted and denied users

    c. Security identifiers of only permitted users

    d. Security identifiers of only denied users

17. Which ACL is responsible for auditing?

    a. DACL

    b. MACL

    c. AACL

    d. SACL

18. Which administrative permission would you delegate if you wanted to allow a user to view the membership of a group?

    a. Modify group membership

    b. Create, delete, and manage groups

    c. Manage group policy links

    d. Read all user information

19. Which application is used to demote a Windows 2000 domain controller?

    a. dcdemote.exe

    b. demote.exe

    c. dcpromo.exe

    d. memserv.exe

20. Which of the following is contained within the security descriptor?
    a. ACL
    b. DCL
    c. DCLA
    d. SACL

21. Which of the following groups allows administrative control to all domains within a tree?
    a. Enterprise Admins
    b. Domain Admins
    c. Local Admins
    d. Local administrator account of the first domain

22. In order to install Active Directory, you should first have a DNS server that supports which of the following?
    a. Integrated Zones
    b. MX records
    c. Reverse ARPA records
    d. Dynamic updates

23. Windows 2000 Domain Controllers that are not DHCP or DNS servers can obtain their TCP/IP configuration from a DHCP server.
    a. True
    b. False

24. The SYSVOL folder is a replacement of the:
    a. NETLOGON shared folder
    b. WINNT$ shared folder
    c. IPC$ Share
    d. %Systemroot%\system32\repl\scripts\export folder

25. The Active Directory Log files must be stored on which type of partition?
    a. NTFS partition
    b. The system partition
    c. The boot partition
    d. Any partition that does not contain the page file

26. The NETBIOS name specified during Active Directory installation is used for which of the following?

    a. The naming of the local domain and future child domains

    b. Backward compatibility

    c. Registering the DNS name with the WINS server

    d. Allowing dynamic updates to the DNS server

27. Microsoft recommends never nesting OUs more than _____ levels deep.

    a. 3

    b. 5

    c. 6

    d. 10

28. You can delegate administrative privileges for which of the following?

    a. The entire Organizational Unit

    b. The entire domain

    c. To specific types of objects within a container object

    d. All of the above

29. Security identifiers are assigned to which of the following?

    a. Organizational Units

    b. Security principles

    c. User accounts

    d. Group accounts

30. When permission inheritance is blocked, what happens to existing permissions?

    a. They are automatically retained on all child objects.

    b. They can be copied and removed automatically.

    c. They can be automatically copied but cannot be manually removed.

    d. They can be automatically removed but must be manually copied.

REAL-WORLD PROJECTS

Note: Although the character set and overall Real-World Project setup carries over from Project 4.1 (in Chapter 4), the project presented in this chapter does not require any reference to Project 4.1 in order to be completed successfully. The planning performed in Project 4.1 continues to be relevant throughout the next few chapters as different parts of the network are implemented.

Andy Palmer, now working with his client Coriolis, has developed what he thinks is a good design for their new Windows 2000 network. Because the IT department manages the entire network and the network is relatively small, Andy has decided to implement only one domain. Eventually each office will contain at least one domain controller.

To allow both locations to be separated into multiple sites, each location will have to have its own subnet network address. Later, the decision will have to be made regarding whether to configure the network with a single site or multiple sites. This decision will be based on the amount of replication traffic that is generated.

Andy decides that the logical placement for the first domain controller is at the IT department offices. Here, Andy will install the first Windows 2000 Server and upgrade this server to become an Active Directory domain controller.

Project 5.1
To install Active Directory:

1. Log into the server as Administrator.

2. Then, click Start|Run.

3. In the Run dialog box, type "Dcpromo.exe" and click on OK.

4. When the Active Directory Installation Wizard begins, click Next.

5. Select Domain Controller For A New Domain, and click Next.

6. Select Create A New Domain Tree, and click Next.

7. Then select Create A New Forest Or Domain Trees, and click Next.

8. Enter "Coriolis.test" for the DNS name for the new domain.

9. Click Next.

10. Then enter "Coriolis" as the NT 4 compatible NetBIOS domain name, and click Next.

Idongが

11. Select the drive and location for the Active Directory database and log, and click Next.

12. Select the location for the shared volume (this must be an NTFS partition), and click Next.

13. When the DNS warning dialog box appears, click OK—DNS is already installed.

14. Select Permissions Compatible With Pre–Windows 2000 Servers, and then click Next.

5

15. Enter a password twice to create and confirm the password to be used with the administrators account if the computer is ever started in restore mode, and then click Next.

16. After reading and verifying the summary, click Next, click Finish, and then restart the computer.

Andy must now develop the OU structure as well as the delegation strategy he will use. The office is a standalone building in a suburban office park that houses the IT, Engineering, and Research departments. It is connected to the other office via a 256kb leased line. The following is a list of users and their departments.

➤ The IT department has one system administrator, one developer, and one assistant who all use desktop computers and share one network-connected printer.

➤ The Engineering department has one system administrator, two developers, and an administrative assistant. The system administrator and the assistant use desktop computers, while the developers use notebook computers. The engineering department shares two network-connected printers.

➤ The Research department consists of one system administrator, one developer, one sales researcher, and one assistant. All research employees use notebook computers, and they all share one network-connected printer.

Project 5.2
To plan Organizational Unit structure:

1. Based on the information just given, determine how many first-level OUs should be created and why. (Why do you think?)

2. Then determine what second-level OU should be created and where. (Where do you think?)

3. As shown in Table 5.1, define which OU each object will belong to.

4. Using Table 5.2, define which OU each user will belong to.

Table 5.1 Coriolis.test objects.

OU Name	Object Name	Object Type and Location
_____	ITPrinter1.Coriolis.test	Information Technology Printer
_____	EngPrinter1.Coriolis.test	Engineering Printer
_____	EngPrinter2.Coriolis.test	Engineering Printer
_____	RDPrinter1.Coriolis.test	Research Printer
_____	ITSysadmin1.Coriolis.test	Sysadmin Workstation
_____	ITDeveloper1.Coriolis.test	Developer Workstation
_____	ITAssistant1.Coriolis.test	Assistant's Workstation
_____	EngSysadmin1.Coriolis.test	Sysadmin Workstation
_____	EngDeveloper1.Coriolis.test	Developer Workstation
_____	EngDeveloper2.Coriolis.test	Developer Workstation
_____	EngAssistant1.Coriolis.test	Assistant's Workstation
_____	RDSysadmin1.Coriolis.test	Sysadmin Workstation
_____	RDDeveloper1.Coriolis.test	Developer Workstation
_____	RDSM1.Coriolis.test	Salesperson's Workstation
_____	RDAssistant1.Coriolis.test	Assistant's Workstation

Table 5.2 OUs and users.

Username	Job Title	OU Name
Mmeier	IT Department Sys Admin	_____
JTbaker	IT Department Developer	_____
Jmachaude	IT Department Assistant	_____
Lcockcroft	Research Department Sys Admin	_____
Jlanford	Research Department Developer	_____
Agates	Research Department Developer	_____
Mgallow	Research Department Assistant	_____
Ccrosby	Engineering Department Sys Admin	_____
Tmorton	Engineering Department Developer	_____
Kmorton	Engineering Department Developer	_____
Ksergi	Engineering Department Assistant	_____

Project 5.3

To delegate control:

1. Which users listed in Tables 5.1 and 5.2 will have permissions delegated to them?

2. Which OUs should Andy plan to delegate control to? Which users?

CHAPTER SIX

ACTIVE DIRECTORY ADMINISTRATION

After completing this chapter, you will be able to:

✓ Create and manage user objects

✓ Create and manage computer objects

✓ Create and manage group objects

✓ Create Organizational Units

✓ Move objects

✓ Secure access to Active Directory

✓ Delegate administrative authority to Organizational Units

Administration is the process of creating, maintaining, and managing all objects within the Active Directory. An administrator is responsible for creating users, groups, and shares, as well as managing permissions for those objects. All these tasks can be managed using Windows 2000's new administrative tools that access and modify the Active Directory database.

After the structure of the Windows 2000 network is created, you must begin creating objects, such as users and groups. For the most part, user and computer accounts are the same in Windows 2000 as they were in Windows NT4; however, how and where objects are created has changed.

In this chapter, you will learn where to create new user and computer objects, how to modify those objects, and how to find objects in the Active Directory database. Groups have changed significantly with Windows 2000, and this chapter will document and explain these changes.

ADDING OBJECTS TO THE ACTIVE DIRECTORY

Administration of Windows 2000 revolves around the new directory service, *Active Directory*. All network components that make up a network—such as users, groups, computers, and servers—reside within the Active Directory as *objects*. Objects within Active Directory can be organized into container objects known as *Organizational Units (OUs)*. Organizational Units provide the ability to organize network objects and your logical network structure according to the business structure.

Organizational Units

As mentioned in Chapter 5, Organizational Units are special Active Directory objects that have the ability to contain other objects, including other OU objects. OUs can contain any object residing in the same domain but not objects from other domains. OUs should be used to organize network objects to match the administrative or business hierarchy. If you use OUs to represent your network hierarchy, you could create first-level OUs to represent geographic locations and second-level OUs to represent business departments. For example, if you had offices in both Los Angeles and Atlanta, you could create an OU for each location. Below the Atlanta and Los Angeles OUs, you could then create additional OUs, such as a sales OU and an engineering OU.

In order to create OUs, you must have permission to do so. The two permissions required are Read and Create Organizational Unit Objects for the domain or container object in which you are adding an OU. The administrators group has these permissions by default.

Viewing Organizational Units

To view, create, and move objects, including OU objects within the Active Directory, you must use the new Active Directory Users And Computers administrative tool. You can run this tool directly from administrative tools, or you can run the Microsoft Management Console (MMC) and add the Active Directory Users And Computers snap-in, as shown in Figure 6.1.

When you open Active Directory Users And Computers, each OU is represented by a folder, as shown in Figure 6.2. When this application is opened for the first time, you will notice that there are already five existing folders that appear to be OUs. These are built-in container objects that provide backward compatibility with previous versions of Windows NT. Although they look and operate just like Organizational Units, Microsoft refers to these folders as *pre-installed container objects*. The following is a list of the pre-installed container objects:

> *Builtin*—Contains all the built-in local groups from Windows NT 4.

> *Computers*—Contains all computer accounts that were created on a previous version of Windows NT. During the upgrade process, all computer accounts that were held in Server Manager are moved to the Computer's container object in Active Directory.

> *Domain Controllers*—Contains a list of all the domain controllers.

> *ForeignSecurityPrinciples*—Provides assistance when a trust relationship exists between one domain and another domain that resides outside the current forest. Users from the external domain can be granted access to resources in

Figure 6.1   Adding the Active Directory Users And Computers snap-in.

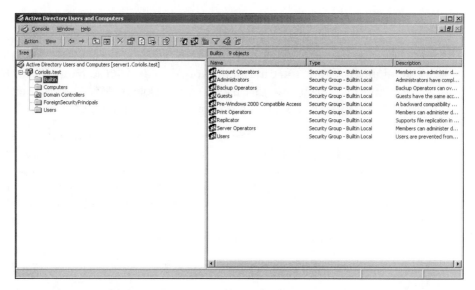

Figure 6.2 Organizational Units in Active Directory Users And Computers.

the forest. Active Directory creates a Foreign Security Principle object to represent each user from the trusted external domain. Each foreign security principle can then become a member of any domain local groups.

➤ *Users*—Contains all users from a previous version of Windows NT that was upgraded to Windows 2000. All the accounts in the security accounts database of a Windows NT Server are copied to the Users container object. The Users container also contains any global built-in groups from the previous Windows NT domain as well as any groups that existed in the previous operating system.

Note: *The pre-installed container objects viewed within Active Directory Users And Computers are not Organizational Units and cannot be moved or deleted.*

Creating Organizational Units

Creating OUs is a simple process:

1. In Active Directory Users And Computers, right-click the domain or container object where you want to create an OU.

2. Choose New, then choose Organizational Unit.

3. Name the OU.

4. Click OK.

Moving Organizational Units

To move an OU, follow these steps:

1. In Active Directory Users And Computers, right-click the OU that you want to move, and click Move.

2. Select the container object where you want to move the OU to, and click OK.

User Accounts

User and computer accounts represent users and computers, respectively, within the Active Directory. Furthermore, users, computers, and groups are all examples of security principals. All security principals are assigned a security identifier (SID) at creation. Security identifiers are unique and are never reused. Because of this, when a user, computer, or group account is deleted, it cannot be recovered by simply re-creating the account using the same name as the deleted account. Only security principals have the ability to log on and access resources on a domain. A user or computer account is used to:

➤ Identify and authenticate a security principal

➤ Manage permissions on network resources

➤ Access resources in a domain, tree, or forest

➤ Identify users for auditing purposes

Creating and Managing User Accounts

All user accounts within Windows 2000 contain three unique names. User account naming is shown in Figure 6.3. Each user account contains the following:

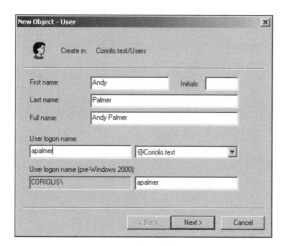

Figure 6.3   User account naming.

➤ *Logon name*—The name used for logon validation and to identify the user on the network.

➤ *Pre-Windows 2000 username*—The username preceded by the NetBIOS domain name (chosen during the promotion to a domain controller) and a forward slash.

➤ *User principle name (UPN)*—The UPN name is the username followed by the user principle suffix. The administrator must enter the user's first and last name as well as the logon name. After the logon name is entered, the user principal suffix can be chosen. The suffix is simply the domain name preceded by an *@* symbol.

For example, Andy Palmer's account may contain the following:

➤ *Logon name*—apalmer

➤ *Pre-Windows 2000 name*—CORIOLIS\apalmer

➤ *UPN name*—apalmer@Coriolis.test

Keep in mind that a Windows 2000 username must conform to the following rules:

➤ A username must be unique to the domain in which it resides.

➤ A username must be different from any group or domain names.

➤ A username can be no more than 20 characters.

➤ A username cannot contain any of the following:

" / \ [ ] ; : | , + * ? < >

➤ A username can include spaces and periods; however, any usernames that are referenced in scripts or at the command line that contain spaces will have to be enclosed in quotes.

The process of creating a user account is the same as creating an OU. To create a user account, follow these steps:

1. In Active Directory Users And Computers, right-click the container object that will hold the user account.

2. Select New, and then select User.

3. Enter the user's first, last, and logon names.

4. Click Next, and enter the password in the Password and Confirm Password fields. In this window, you can select among four options:

➤ User Must Change Password At Next Logon

➤ User Cannot Change Password

➤ Password Never Expires

➤ Account Disabled

Creating user accounts on Windows 2000 non-domain controllers is performed with the Computer Management tool. The Computer Management tool can be located by clicking Start | Settings | Control Panel | Administrative Tools, and then clicking Computer Management. Right-click Local Users And Computers, and select New User.

User Account Properties

Unlike Windows NT, you cannot assign group membership or other user properties until after the account is created. After an account exists for a user, you can then right-click on the user object and modify its properties. The User Properties dialog box contains several tabs:

➤ *General tab*—Contains general information about a user, such as name, department, office, email address, and Web page.

➤ *Addresses tab*—Contains addressing information about a user.

➤ *Account tab*—Lists information such as the username, pre–Windows 2000 logon name, and UPN suffix. The Account tab is where logon hours as well as which computers a user can log into are set. Account options also reside within the Account tab. Account options include:

➤ *Store Password Using Reversible Encryption*—Used for systems that do not support Windows 2000 encryption. This option is not new to Windows NT, but in previous versions of NT it could be set only by modifying the registry. If you have users logging on to your Windows 2000 network from Apple computers, select this option for those user accounts.

➤ *Smart Card Required For Interactive Logon*—Specifies that before users can log on using the account, they must first be issued a smart security card. Any computers that this account will use must have a card reader. Smart cards are generally used in high-security environments.

➤ *Account Is Trusted For Delegation*—Allows a user to assign responsibility for management and administration of a portion of the domain to another user, group, or organization.

➤ *Account Is Sensitive And Cannot Be Delegated*—Stipulates that the account cannot be assigned for delegation by another account.

➤ *Don't Require Kerberos Preauthentication*—Disables Kerberos preauthentication when the account uses a different implementation of the Kerberos protocol than the one supplied with Windows 2000.

➤ *Use DES Encryption Types For This Account*—Allows you to use other security measures that follow the Data Encryption Standard (DES).

➤ *Profile tab*—Serves the same purpose as the Profile button in the application User Manager For Domains included in Windows NT. The Profile tab stores the path and name of the account's profile and logon script. Home directory path information is also stored on the Profile tab. The information on this tab is used for backward compatibility with previous versions of Windows NT. Windows 2000 clients use group policies, which are discussed in Chapter 14.

➤ *Telephones tab*—Contains fields to hold a user's telephone numbers. Each field can contain multiple numbers.

➤ *Organization tab*—Contains fields that indicate a user's title, department, company, and manager, as well as any direct reports to the user.

➤ *Member Of tab*—Provides options used to assign and remove a user to and from groups.

➤ *Dial-In tab*—Enables an administrator to grant or deny dial-in privileges. The Dial-In tab also is where callback options are set.

Note: *A user's password cannot be changed in the User Properties dialog box. To change a user's password, you must right-click the user object and select Change Password.*

If you have terminal services installed, you will have four additional tabs in the User Properties dialog box. They are:

➤ Environment tab

➤ Sessions tab

➤ Remote Control tab

➤ Terminal Services Profile tab

These tabs will be discussed in more detail in Chapter 17.

Every tab in the User Properties dialog box contains a unique list of account attributes. These attributes can be searched using the Active Directory. For example, if an administrator wants to find out how many user accounts are in the sales department, he or she could perform an Active Directory search to list all users who have the department attribute set to *sales*. For this reason, you should ensure that all account attributes are completed.

Computer Accounts

Every computer running Windows 2000 or Windows NT that joins a domain must have a computer account. Like user accounts, computer accounts allow for authenticating and auditing a computer's access to a network as well as access to domain resources. Every Windows 2000/NT computer participating on a network should have its own unique computer account. Computer accounts are created using the Active Directory Users And Computers utility.

Computer accounts must be created for all Windows NT or Windows 2000 computers that are going to participate on a network. Windows 9*x* computers do not share the same advanced security features of NT or 2000 and, therefore, are not required to have a computer account. Users will not be able to log into a Windows 2000 network from any computer that does not have a computer account.

Adding a Computer Account

Windows 2000's default domain policy settings allow only members of the domain admins group to add a computer account to a domain. Once an account is created, only users with the appropriate rights can then add the computer to a domain. Figure 6.4 shows how to add a computer account. Members of domain admins can create a computer account and then specify a user account that is allowed to join the client computer to the domain.

Figure 6.4   Adding a computer account.

To create a computer account, follow these steps:

1. Launch the Active Directory Users And Computers utility.

2. Right-click the container object that will contain the computer account, select New, and then select Computer. A dialog box will appear. By default, only the domain admins can add the computer to the domain. To allow other users to add this computer to the domain, click Change, and select the users or group of users that will be allowed to join the computer to the domain.

3. Click Next, click Next again, and then click Finish.

GROUPS

Windows NT 4 supported two forms of groups: local groups and global groups. Both global and local groups were considered security groups, because they were both used only to assign permissions to the member users. The difference between the two groups was their scope. Local groups could contain local user accounts and other global groups within the local domain or a trusted domain. Furthermore, local groups were confined to the domain in which they were created. Global groups could contain only users in the local domain; however, global groups could be used to cross trusts. The scope of a group determines who can be a member and whether a group can be used throughout the forest or locally within the local domain only.

In contrast, Windows 2000 provides greater flexibility, because you can define the type of group you want to create as well as the scope of the group. Windows 2000 provides two types of groups: security groups and distribution groups. Microsoft has also added the ability to define the scope for each type of group. Figure 6.5 shows the Add Group dialog box.

Group Types

As mentioned, Windows 2000 provides security groups and distribution groups. Security groups are the only groups used by the operating system and are the only groups that can be assigned permissions. Security groups are used to assign permissions to users for network resources. Security groups serve the same purpose as local and global groups in Windows NT 4. When creating security groups, an administrator must define the scope of the group, as shown in Figure 6.5. Group scope is discussed below.

Distribution groups are used to group together users for application and searching purposes. Distribution groups can be used by applications, such as Microsoft Exchange, to send email to all the members of one or more distribution groups. If there is a requirement to group users together for a

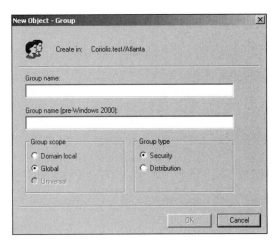

Figure 6.5   Adding a group.

purpose other than for assigning permissions, then you should use distribution groups. Distribution groups cannot be assigned permissions.

When a user logs onto a network, the domain controllers generate and send the client an access token containing the user's permissions and a list of all the security groups a user belongs to. Distribution group membership is not sent in the token. Therefore, you should use distribution groups rather than security groups whenever possible to reduce the size of tokens.

Group Scope

The group scope attribute can be assigned to both security and distribution groups. The scope determines which users and other groups can become members of a group. Also, the group scope determines which groups a group can become a member of. Finally, the scope defines which groups can cross into other domains. Three scope attributes can be assigned to a group:

➤ *Domain Local Groups*—Contains user accounts, global groups, and universal groups from any domain in the forest. Domain local groups can also contain other domain local groups residing within the same domain. If the domain controllers are still running in mixed mode, however, the domain local groups can contain only user accounts and global groups from any domain in the forest. Domain local groups should be used when there is no requirement to cross domains.

➤ *Global Groups*—Contains user accounts and global groups from the local domain while running in native mode. If domain controllers are running in mixed mode, then the global groups can contain only user accounts within the same domain, but not other global groups.

➤ *Universal Groups*—Contains user accounts, global groups, and other universal groups that reside within the forest. Only distribution groups can be universal groups while the network is running in mixed mode. Universal security groups can be created in native mode.

Table 6.1 lists group scopes and what objects each group scope can contain.

Groups and Replication

To allow groups created in one domain to access resources in another domain, all domain controllers must be aware of all groups within the forest. For example, to allow a universal group in the domain **sales.examcram.com** to access resources in the domain **marketing.examcram.com**, the domain controller(s) for the marketing domain must be aware of the universal group *sales* that resides in the *sales* domain. Each domain controller discovers the existence of all groups by querying the Global Catalog Server (GCS).

Every group that is created is automatically replicated to the Global Catalog Server; however, the amount of information that is replicated depends on the group scope. Domain local and global groups replicate only their names to the GCS. Membership information for domain local and global groups is held only within the domain in which the group resides. Universal groups replicate both their name and their membership. Therefore, the number and size of universal groups directly affect the size of the global catalog. The larger the global catalog, the more time searches take. Therefore, the number of universal groups should be kept to a minimum.

Care should be taken when creating universal groups. Universal group names and membership are replicated to the Global Catalog Server. Any changes to a

Table 6.1 Group scopes and membership limitations.

Group Scope	Mixed Mode Can Contain	Native Mode Can Contain	Allowed To Be A Member Of	Can Be Granted Permissions For
Domain Local	User Accounts*, Global Groups*	User Accounts*, Global Groups*, Universal Groups*, Domain Local**	Domain Local**	Local Domain
Global	User Accounts**	User Accounts**, Global Groups**, Universal Groups*, Domain Local*, Global**	All Domains	
Universal	None	Any Group*	Domain Local*, Universal Groups*	All Domains

*   From any domain
** From Local Domain only

universal group cause the group to be replicated again to the GCS. In order to reduce replication traffic, universal groups should contain only global groups, not user accounts. Changing the membership of global groups that are members of the universal group will not cause replication to occur.

Assigning Permissions and Membership

The purpose of groups is to simplify the assignment of permissions and policies. Managing permissions is much easier for a few groups than it is for a few hundred or a few thousand users. Permissions should always be assigned to domain local groups rather than individual user accounts or to global groups. Groups can be created to represent groups of users with similar jobs and similar permissions. For example, you could create a *sales* group to represent all the sales personnel. The sales local group would then be assigned all the permissions that the sales users would need.

Microsoft's recommended strategy for implementing groups and permissions is to place user accounts in global groups, place global groups in domain local groups, and assign permissions to the domain local groups.

Tip: Remember the acronym *AGDLP*: Accounts (A) are placed in global (G) groups, global groups are made members of domain local (DL) groups, and permissions (P) are assigned to domain local groups.

Built-In Groups

The default groups are contained in the Builtin container object of the Active Directory Users And Computers utility. The default groups are:

➤ Account Operators

➤ Administrators

➤ Backup Operators

➤ Guests

➤ Print Operators

➤ Replicator

➤ Server Operators

➤ Users

All built-in groups have domain local scope and are used to assign default sets of permissions to user accounts that will have some administrative rights or permissions. For example, the domain administrators group in a domain has authority over all accounts and resources in the domain. Table 6.2 shows the default rights held by the default groups, and it introduces each built-in group as well as what rights have been assigned to each group.

Table 6.2 User rights.

User Right Name	Grants The Right To	Groups With This Right By Default
Access This Computer From The Network	Connect to the computer over the network.	Administrators, Everyone, Power Users
Back Up Files And File Folders	Back up files and folders, regardless of NTFS or permissions.	Administrators, Backup Operators
Bypass Traverse Checking	Traverse folders, even when permissions to those folders may be denied.	Everyone
Change The System Time	Change the system time.	Administrators, Power Users
Create A Pagefile	Can change pagefile size and location.	Administrators
Debug Programs	Debug various low-level objects, such as threads.	Administrators
Force Shutdown From A Remote System	Shut down a remote computer.	Administrators
Increase Scheduling Priority	Boost the execution priority of a process.	Administrators, Power Users
Load And Unload Device Drivers	Install and remove device drivers.	Administrators
Log On Locally	Ability to log on to a server locally.	Administrators, Backup Operators
Manage Auditing And Security Log	Enable auditing on network resources and view audit logs.	Administrators
Modify Firmware Environment Variables	Modify firmware held in Nonvolatile RAM, such as the BIOS.	Administrators
Profile Single Process	Monitor a specific performance counter on a system.	Administrators, Power Users
Profile System Performance	Monitor system performance.	Administrators
Restore Files And File Folders	Restore files and folders, regardless of NTFS permission.	Administrators, Backup Operators
Shut Down The System	Shut down the operating system.	Administrators, Backup Operators
Take Ownership Of Files Or Other Objects	Take ownership of files, folders, printers, and other objects on (or attached to) the computer. This right supersedes permissions protecting objects.	Administrators

Predefined Groups

The Active Directory Users And Computers utility includes predefined groups in the Users folder. The predefined groups are:

➤ cert publishers

➤ domain admins

➤ domain computers

➤ domain controllers

➤ domain guests

➤ domain users

➤ enterprise admins

➤ group policy admins

➤ schema admins

These groups are all global in scope and can be used to hold user accounts in the domain. These groups can then be placed in groups with domain local scope in any domain.

All created user accounts are automatically made members of the domain users group, and all created computer accounts are made members of the domain computers group. Because the domain users and domain computers groups already contain all users and all computers in the domain, there is no need to create an "all users" or "all computers" group. For example, if you have an employee handbook document file that you want all users to have permissions to, you could grant permission to the users domain local group that contains the domain users global group.

The domain admins group should contain any user accounts that will have administrative privileges throughout the domain. By default, the only member of the domain admins is the administrators account. Only accounts that need administrative authority throughout the entire domain should be placed in the domain admins group. Because Windows 2000 supports delegation, any user accounts that need administrative authority over a specific part of the network can have the authority delegated to them without being members of any administrative group.

Microsoft follows the AGDLP rule by placing all predefined global groups into their corresponding domain local group. For example, the domain admins group is a member of the administrators local group, and the domain guest group is a member of the local guests group. Permissions are assigned to the local groups, and user membership is assigned to the global groups.

WORKING WITH ACTIVE DIRECTORY OBJECTS

As a network grows and new servers, users, and groups are added to the directory, there might be a problem with locating individual objects within the directory. Networks always seem to become larger, not smaller, and a system once designed for a few hundred users could soon be supporting thousands of users and hundreds of servers. Locating particular objects within the directory could become a job in and of itself. Thankfully, Active Directory is not a static database. Within Active Directory, you can always create new objects and remove old objects as well as rename and move existing network objects.

Locating Objects within the Directory

Active Directory provides tools to assist users in easily locating any object within the directory. Because all domain controllers replicate the directory to all other domain controllers, the physical location of an object is not an issue. For example, if you are looking for a particular shared folder, you do not have to search for the folder on the server on which it resides. The folder is an object of the Active Directory and, therefore, can be found on any server that has an updated copy of the Active Directory.

To find an object within the Active Directory, use the Active Directory Users And Computers administrative tool or MMC snap-in. Click Find on the Actions drop-down menu, and the Find option displays.

The Find utility in Active Directory Users And Computers is a powerful utility. You can choose to search a particular computer or the entire directory. Notice in Figure 6.6 that you can choose to search for specific types of objects. The Find drop-down menu contains the following selections:

➤ Users, Contacts, And Groups

➤ Computers

➤ Printers

➤ Shared Folders

➤ Organizational Units

➤ Custom Search

While most of the search categories are obvious, what is not is the Custom Search option. Custom Search enables you to design powerful searches. With Custom Search, you can search the Active Directory and locate objects according to their attributes. For example, you can search for a user or a list of

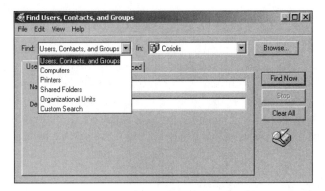

Figure 6.6   Find Users, Contacts, And Groups dialog box.

users by searching for all users that reside at a particular address, or you can locate a user by phone number. Any object attribute is searchable. If you need to find a printer that supports stapling in your network, you could perform a custom search for the stapling attribute in the Printer field.

Moving Objects

When organizational, administrative, or business requirements change, you can move objects between Organizational Units. For example, if there is a business reorganization, you can move users and groups into existing or new OUs where administration is managed by another administrator or manager. Furthermore, you can move multiple objects at the same time by selecting each object while holding down the Shift or Ctrl key.

To move an object, follow these steps:

1. Right-click an object, and select Move.

2. In the Move dialog box, select the destination container object. To move multiple objects at the same time, select each object while holding down the Shift or Ctrl key.

3. Click OK.

Permissions on Moved Objects

Any permission that is directly assigned to an object remains there if the object is moved. Any inherited permission that an object has received from a parent object will be lost if the object is moved to a new container/parent object. Furthermore, moved objects inherit permissions from their new parent container.

SECURING ACCESS TO ACTIVE DIRECTORY OBJECTS

Active Directory service objects have a security descriptor that defines who has permission to access an object and the type of access allowed. These security descriptors are used by Active Directory to control access to objects within the directory. By grouping objects with the same security requirements into one OU, you can reduce the number of times permissions have to be granted, because Active Directory permissions can be granted at the OU level and then inherited to all child objects in the OU.

Active Directory Object Permissions

Active Directory permissions allow an administrator to control who can access objects or object attributes as well as what actions can be performed on any object. Active Directory permissions can also be used to delegate administrative authority over any OU or hierarchy of OUs as well as any object to any specific user or group of users.

Before users can access objects within the Active Directory, the administrator must first assign the appropriate permissions to the user or to a group of users. All permissions for each object are stored in the discretionary access control list (DACL). Each object has a corresponding DACL that lists all the users who are allowed to access the object. The DACL for each individual object lists the SIDs of all security principles that are allowed or denied access to the object as well as the specific actions that each user can perform on the object.

Each object class has a unique set of actions that can be performed with or on it. For example, a shared file object will have a Write permission that can be assigned; however, a printer will not have a Write permission.

Taking Ownership

All objects in Active Directory have an owner attribute. A user who creates an object automatically becomes the owner of the object. The owner of an object has Full Control permissions and is responsible for assigning permissions to the object.

Any member of the administrators group has the special Take Ownership permission on all objects. If a member of the administrators group creates an object, the group becomes the object owner, not the individual account. For example, if Andy (a member of the admins group) creates a shared file, the owner of the file is the admins group, not Andy's user account.

Anyone who has Full Control permissions to a file, such as the owner, can grant the Take Ownership permission to the object. Once this permission has been granted to a user, the user can then take ownership of the object. Ownership cannot be assigned to another user.

Allowing or Denying Access

Anyone with Full Control permissions can allow or deny access to an object. Deny permissions always supersede any permission that grants permissions to an object. If you deny permissions to a user for a specific object, the user will not be able to access the object even if she or he is a member of a group that is allowed to access the object. The Deny permission should be used only in cases where a specific user must be denied access because he or she is a member of a group that has access permissions.

Effective Permissions

The *effective permissions* that a user has is a combination of all permissions assigned directly to the user as well as any permissions assigned to any groups of which the user is a member. If a user has been assigned the Read permission for a file and is a member of a group that has been assigned the Change permission, then the user's effective permissions are Read and Change. If a user has been assigned the Deny permission or is a member of any group that has been assigned the Deny permission, then the user will not have access to the object, regardless of any other permissions.

Special Permissions

Windows 2000 provides a common set of permissions that are sufficient for most administrative tasks and security needs. This common set of permissions is known as *standard permissions*. Examples of standard permissions include Full Control, Read, and Write permissions for a file or folder object. Standard permissions are created by combining special permissions. You can assign the more common standard permissions to any object; however, if more granular control is needed, you might want to assign individual special permissions to an object. Figure 6.7 shows the special permissions that make up the Read permissions for a shared folder.

Setting Permissions

Setting or changing permissions is done in the Active Directory Users And Computers utility. To set or change permissions, follow these steps:

1. On the View menu, select Advanced Features.

2. Right-click the object or container object that you want to set permissions for, and select Properties.

3. To add new permissions, click Add, select the user or group account that you want to add, and click Add again.

4. To view or add special permissions or to change how these permissions are inherited, click the Advanced button. In Figure 6.8, the Allow Inheritable Permissions From Parent To Propagate To This Object special permission is selected.

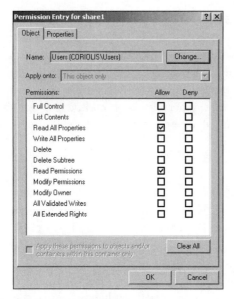

Figure 6.7 Special permissions.

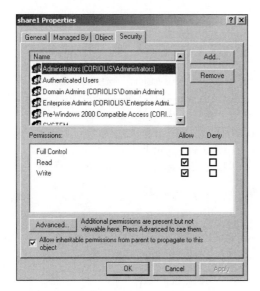

Figure 6.8 Share properties.

Delegation of Administrative Authority

Part of administering a Windows 2000 Active Directory is planning for and configuring delegation of administrative responsibilities. Through delegation, you can allow managers, department heads, or any user account to administer a specific set of objects within the Active Directory. As an administrator, you determine which administrative functions you will grant to each subadministrator. Figure 6.9 shows a list of basic administrative functions that can be delegated to a user account.

After you create subadministrators and delegate control to them, you can then create customized read-only MMC tools for them. These read-only tools will allow the subadministrators to perform only the functions they are allowed and will prevent the users from adding additional snap-ins.

The Delegation Of Control Wizard is used to grant permissions at the OU and domain level. To maintain a finer degree of control, you can set permissions manually at the object level. To use the Delegation Of Control Wizard, follow these steps:

1. To start the Delegation Of Control Wizard, right-click the domain or OU that you want to delegate control to, and select Delegate Control.

2. Click Next, and then click Add to select the user or group of users that you want to delegate control to.

3. Select the user(s) or group, click Add, and click OK.

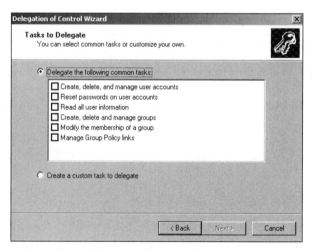

Figure 6.9   Delegating administrative privileges.

Inheritance

When permissions are delegated to a container object, such as an Organizational Unit or a domain, the permissions are automatically assigned to any child objects within the container. Inheritance can be blocked, so the permissions do not flow down to child objects. For more information on inheritance, see Chapter 5.

4. Select the administrative permissions you want to delegate. The permissions that you can delegate are:

➤ Create, Delete, And Manage User Accounts

➤ Reset Passwords On User Accounts

➤ Read All User Information

➤ Create, Delete, And Manage Groups

➤ Modify The Membership Of A Group

➤ Manage Group Policy links

5. After you have selected the permissions, click Next, and click Finish. Or, if you do not wish to allow control over all objects, you can select the Create A Custom Task To Delegate option, and select Next. (See Figure 6.9.) In the Custom Task dialog box, you can specify which objects within the OU or domain you want to delegate control to. Then, click Next, select the permissions you want to delegate, click Next, and click Finish.

CHAPTER SUMMARY

The new Windows 2000 Active Directory Users And Computers administrative tool provides the ability to create user, computer, and group objects within the Active Directory. This tool is also used to search for and move objects in the Active Directory.

All computer, user, or group accounts are known as *security principals*. Security principals are assigned a security identifier (SID) at creation. Each object within the Active Directory contains a discretionary access control list (DACL) that contains the SIDs of any security principal that has been granted or denied access to the object.

Windows 2000 introduces a new group type used for nonsecurity purposes named *distribution groups*. Distribution groups are used for distribution purposes and cannot be assigned permissions. Groups now have a new property known as the group scope. The group scope determines where a group can be used as well as what types of accounts the group can contain.

REVIEW QUESTIONS

1. In the Active Directory Users And Computers utility, Builtin and Users folders are examples of what?

    a. Organizational Units

    b. Shared folders

    c. Pre-installed container objects

    d. Dfs

2. The Builtin folder in Active Directory Users And Computers provides a location for groups that were created in previous versions of Windows NT.

    a. True

    b. False

3. The ForeignSecurityPrinciples is used for what?

    a. To hold user accounts from trusted domains

    b. To hold user accounts from trusted forests

    c. To hold group accounts from trusted forests

    d. To hold group accounts from child domains

4. All new user accounts should be placed in the users container object.

    a. True

    b. False

5. Organizational Units cannot contain user accounts from a domain other than their own.

    a. True

    b. False

6. Which of the following is the proper structure of a UPN name?

    a. Fred Pumpkin

    b. Pumpkinf

    c. ACME/pumpkinf

    d. Pumpkinf@Acme.com

7. Which of the following is a valid username?

    a. @!%&.

    b. !@\$$

    c. %$#*

    d. None of the above

8. Usernames can contain spaces.

    a. True

    b. False

9. Which administrative tool is used to create user accounts on Windows 2000 member servers?

    a. User Manager

    b. Computer Management

    c. Active Directory Users And Computers

    d. Local Directory Users And Computers

10. A user's password can be changed in the User Properties dialog box.

    a. True

    b. False

11. What is the user principle name suffix?

    a. Last name and first initial of the full username

    b. Pre–Windows 2000 username

    c. Logon name proceeded with the domain name

    d. Domain name

12. What does the Account Is Trusted For Delegation option in the User Properties dialog box allow users to do?

    a. Have administrative functions delegated to them

    b. Delegate administrative functions to other users

    c. Set permissions on Active Directory objects

    d. None of the above

13. Which of the following client operating systems must have a computer account before joining a domain? [Check all correct answers]

    a. Windows 2000 Professional

    b. Windows 2000 Datacenter

    c. Windows NT Workstation 4

    d. Windows 98

14. After a computer account is created, who can join the computer to a domain by default?

    a. Members of the power users group

    b. Members of the account operators group

    c. Members of the domain admins group

    d. Only the enterprise admins group

15. What are the two types of groups in Windows 2000?

    a. Universal and security

    b. Domain local and distribution

    c. Security and distribution

    d. Global and universal

16. Which type of group cannot be assigned permissions?

    a. Distribution

    b. Domain local

    c. Security

    d. Universal

17. A group's _____ defines which user accounts can become members.

    a. Type

    b. Scope

    c. Domain

    d. None of the above

18. Which group scope can contain any other group from any other domain?

    a. Domain global

    b. Domain local

    c. Universal

    d. Security

19. Which of the following group's members are replicated to the Global Catalog Server?

    a. Global groups

    b. Domain local groups

    c. Distribution groups

    d. Universal groups

6

20. Global groups can contain which of the following groups while running in native mode?

    a. Universal

    b. Domain local

    c. Global

    d. Distribution

21. Distribution groups are used for:

    a. Security purposes

    b. Auditing purposes

    c. Administrative functions

    d. Applications and searching

22. Which of the following acronyms describes the proper group strategy for Windows 2000?

    a. AGLP

    b. AGDLP

    c. AGPDL

    d. ADLGP

23. Who can set permissions on an object?

    a. Administrators

    b. The object's owner

    c. Server operators

    d. Account operators

24. What happens to the permissions assigned to an object if the object is moved to another container object?

    a. The permissions are erased.

    b. The permissions remain.

    c. The permissions remain only if they do not conflict with the permissions on the new container object.

    d. None of the above.

25. The DACL contains the SIDs of which security principles?

    a. All user accounts in the domain

    b. All groups that have been granted permissions

    c. All user accounts that have been granted permissions

    d. All user accounts that have been granted or denied permissions

REAL-WORLD PROJECTS

Note: *This project assumes that Active Directory is installed and running properly on a Windows 2000 Server. Installing Active Directory is covered in Project 5.1 (in Chapter 5). You must be logged on as the administrator to perform the following projects or be a member of the administrators group.*

Andy Palmer, having installed Active Directory, is ready to start creating computer, user, and group accounts. User accounts will follow the popular last-name-first-initial naming convention for usernames. The planning information created in Project 4.1 (in Chapter 4) will be used to create the Active Directory objects in this lab.

6

In this project Andy has been assigned the task of populating the new Windows 2000 network with the appropriate network objects. The Active Directory structure should be configured to match the Coriolis management and department structure. In order to create an Active Directory model that reflects the company's management and departmental structure, Andy will create OUs for each department, place the correct users in each OU, and delegate control of each OU to the appropriate user accounts.

Project 6.1
To create Organizational Units:

1. Click Start, then select Programs | Administrative Tools | Active Directory Users And Computers.

2. If not already expanded, click the plus sign next to the domain name to expand the Active Directory.

3. Right-click the domain name (Coriolis.test), and select New-Organizational Unit.

4. Enter "Corporate" as the name of the first Organizational Unit.

5. Click OK. The new OU should appear at the bottom of the structure.

Repeat the preceding steps to create the following OUs (the names can be abbreviated):

➤ Corporate

➤ Information Technology (IT)

➤ Sales-Marketing (Sales)

➤ Finance-Accounting (F&A)

➤ Engineering

➤ Research-Development (R&D)

Project 6.2
To create user accounts:

1. If it is not already started, start Active Directory Users And Computers.

2. Right-click the Corporate OU, and select New-User.

3. In the New Object–User dialog box, enter your first name, last name, and logon name, and then click Next.

4. Enter "password" for the password, click Next, and then click Finish.

5. Select the Corporate OU by clicking it once. The user account object should appear in the window to the right.

6. Right-click the user object, and select Properties. The User Properties dialog box should appear.

7. On the General tab, enter "Corporate" as the office name.

8. Click the Organization tab, and enter "Owner" as the title.

9. Click OK.

Repeat the preceding steps to create the accounts shown in Table 6.3. Each user's department is also the OU that they should be placed in.

Table 6.3 User properties.

Name	Logon Name	Department	Phone	Title
Carol Croft	Croftc	Corporate	555-1111	President
Lauren Meier	Meierm	Corporate	555-2222	Vice President
Chris Matthew	Matthewc	Sales	555-3333	Sales Executive
CB Hackworth	Hackworthc	Engineering	555-4444	Engineer
Ashley Gates	Gatesa	IT	555-5555	Administrator
Amy Enriquez	Enriqueza	Sales	555-6666	Sales

Project 6.3
To create and modify groups:

1. If it is not already started, start Active Directory Users And Computers.

2. Right-click the Corporate OU, and select New-Group.

3. Enter "Executives" as the name.

4. Select Domain Local as the scope and Security as the type of group.

5. Click OK. The new group should appear in the left window.

6. Right-click the group, and select Properties.

7. In the Description box, enter "Corporate Executives".

8. Click the Members tab.

9. Click Add.

10. Select and add Carol Croft and Lauren Meier.

11. Click OK, and click OK again.

Follow the preceding steps to create the groups shown in Table 6.4.

Table 6.4   Group and member information.

Group Names	Members
Sales&Marketing	Amy Enriquez, Chris Matthew
Research&Development	Lauren Meier, Ashley Gates
Engineering	CB Hackworth, Carol Croft

Project 6.4
To move an object:

1. If it is not already started, start Active Directory Users And Computers.

2. View the Corporate OU by clicking the OU once.

3. Right-click the group object Executives, and select Move.

4. Select the Sales OU, and click OK.

5. View the Sales OU by selecting it.

6. Right-click the Executives group, and select Move.

7. Select the Executive OU, and click OK.

Project 6.5
To locate an object:

1. If it is not already started, start Active Directory Users And Computers.

2. Display the Action drop-down menu, and select Find.

3. In the Find field, select Custom Search.

4. Click the Field button.

5. Select User and Telephone Number.

6. In the Value field, enter "555".

7. Click Find Now.

8. Click Yes.

9. All users whose telephone number begins with 555 should now appear.

Project 6.6
To delegate administrative control:

1. If it is not already started, start Active Directory Users And Computers.

2. Right-click the sales OU.

3. Select Delegate Control.

4. Click Next.

5. Select Add.

6. Select the Ashley Gates user account, click Add, and click OK.

7. Click Next, and then select the Create, Delete, And Manage Users Accounts selection box.

8. Click Next, and click Finish.

CHAPTER SEVEN

PLANNING LARGER WINDOWS 2000 NETWORKS

After completing this chapter, you will be able to:

✓ Recognize when to use multiple domains

✓ Describe new server roles in Windows 2000 networks

✓ Plan an Active Directory tree consisting of multiple domains

✓ Plan an Active Directory forest consisting of multiple trees

✓ Plan an Active Directory network that has multiple forests

One of the main objectives underlying Microsoft's Windows 2000 initiative is to create a more enterprise-ready network operating system. Windows 2000 addresses this objective by introducing many new features and server roles that facilitate communication in a large networking environment. One of the new features included in the Active Directory is the introduction of trees and forests to the once-isolated domain.

Trees and forests allow you to combine multiple domains into one or more administrative units while still maintaining the network as a single entity. In order for you to plan and implement a network utilizing multiple domains, trees, or forests, you must first understand the interactions among domains, trees, and forests. This chapter discusses the new features and server roles as well as addresses planning and implementation considerations when building large Windows 2000 networks.

WHEN TO USE MULTIPLE DOMAINS

The simplest domain model to create, understand, and administer is the single domain model. With the proper planning, most companies can create a single Windows 2000 domain and still meet all their networking infrastructure requirements. Some international companies, or companies that have technology driven from the bottom up (that is, each department runs its own IT department), might require separate domains to meet their networking-infrastructure challenges. Reasons why you might decide to design and implement multiple domains include the following:

➤ *Business partnerships*—Often, businesses enter a limited partnership for a number of reasons. Each company might want to allow limited network access to their partner companies. In these cases, multiple domains can isolate one domain from another but still allow each domain to share resources with another.

➤ *Decentralized administration*—In companies or government agencies, departments or smaller offices sometimes purchase and manage their own computer and networking equipment and must retain complete admin-istrative control. Although this type of setup could still be implemented logically with Organizational Units (OUs), administrators at the domain level can't be blocked from accessing any OU within the domain. Because many agencies and departments want to prevent anyone from accessing their network, a multidomain environment would be required.

➤ *Different user account level policies*—User account policies are defined and maintained at the domain level. Policies, such as password policies, are created at the domain level. If you need separate user account policies, you will have to create multiple domains.

➤ *Isolation of administrative control*—Administrators of one domain cannot cross into another domain unless they have explicitly been granted permissions to do so.

➤ *Reduced replication traffic*—All domain controllers within a single domain replicate any changes to all other domain controllers. Only Global Catalog, schema, and configuration information is replicated to domain controllers in other domains.

➤ *Upgrade path*—Upgrading an existing Windows NT 4 multiple master or complete trust directory service to a multidomain Windows 2000 network might be the easiest way to implement Windows 2000 in an established NT 4 environment.

7

Just as in Microsoft Windows NT 4, the smallest and simplest directory service model is the single domain. By upgrading a Windows 2000 server to a domain controller, you are in effect creating a single domain tree.

UNDERSTANDING ACTIVE DIRECTORY TREES

The first domain controller in the Active Directory is known as the *forest root*. In some instances, a single domain will not meet a network's infrastructure requirements, so child domains must be added to the tree.

You should understand the implications of creating a multidomain tree before setting up any additional domains. Creating multiple domains affects hardware costs, because each domain requires at least one domain controller. Adding domains to a tree also creates additional replication traffic, which might require faster networking components or higher bandwidth for wide area connections. Figure 7.1 displays the tree hierarchy, and, as you can see, every domain within a tree shares a common tree root.

Tree Root

The tree root is the first domain created within a tree. Each subsequent domain created within the tree must belong to the contiguous namespace created by the tree root domain. Every child domain has a parent domain. The child domain must belong to the same contiguous namespace as the parent.

The Active Directory naming and logical structure follow the Domain Name System (DNS) naming hierarchy structure. Each child domain inherits the name of its parent domain. For example, if a child domain called *marketing* is

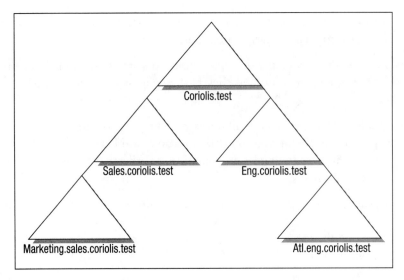

Figure 7.1 Tree hierarchy.

created below the parent domain *sales.coriolis.test,* then the child domain name will be *marketing.sales.coriolis.test.* In this way, you can see the path of domains from the bottom of the tree to the top. The marketing domain is a child of the sales domain which is a child of the coriolis domain. Because all these domains share the same namespace, they must all be within the same tree.

Transitive and Cross-Link Trusts

All domains within an Active Directory tree automatically participate in two-way transitive trusts with their child and parent domains. The trusts are transitive, so any user in any domain can access resources in any other domain within the tree as long as they have the appropriate permissions.

Transitive Trusts

Transitive trusts ensure that all domains within a tree trust each other. *Transitive* simply means that if domain A trusts domain B and domain B trusts domain C, then domain A also trusts domain C. Windows NT 4 did not permit transitive trusts and used only explicit (i.e., manually created) trust relationships. Direct trusts between domains can be created manually.

Cross-Link Trusts

In a large tree or forest environment, explicit trusts can be created between domains that reside in the same or different trees. This means that one domain can trust another domain outside its own namespace. The purpose of cross-link trusts is to speed searching and authentication from one domain to another.

When a Windows 2000 domain controller needs to communicate with or access another domain controller, the server must follow the trust path in order to get to the remote domain controller. A domain controller for a child domain must communicate with another domain in the same tree (other than the DC child or parent domain) through the tree root domain. By creating a trust between one domain and another within the same tree or forest, you provide a shortcut communications path between the two domains. See Figure 7.2 for an example of cross-link trusts.

For example, let's say you have a large number of users from the sales.coriolis.test domain physically located at the accounting.coriolis.test domain. You could create a cross-link trust between the two domains to speed up the authentication process. With such a trust, each domain will be able to communicate directly with the other domain that it trusts and not have to communicate through the coriolis.test domain.

Cross-link trusts must be manually configured as two-way trusts where both domains trust each other. Furthermore, the trusts must be configured in a transitive trust relationship.

Creating Additional Domains within a Tree

When planning for a multiple domain tree, each domain should be planned separately. As each new domain is added, you can then plan how each domain will change the overall structure of the tree.

In order to add a child domain to an existing tree, you must first create a subdomain on the DNS server. The DNS zone file can be created on a new DNS server within the child domain or can become part of the parent domain's zone file. If your DNS

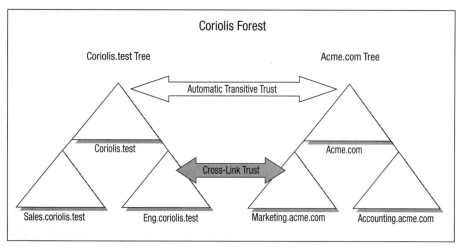

Figure 7.2   Cross-link trusts.

server supports dynamic updates, then the subdomains will be created during the Active Directory installation on the new domain controller.

Only members of the Enterprise Admins group can add domains to an existing tree. Members of the Enterprise Admins group can use the **ntdsutil** command at the command prompt to add new domains to the tree. In order to create a new domain, you must promote a server to a domain controller in a new domain. When prompted during Active Directory installation, choose the Join An Existing Tree and Create New Child Domain options.

An Active Directory tree can become very large in size and contain millions of objects. Simply browsing through the multiple domains and OUs to find the needed resources could take an unacceptable amount of time and lead to high administrative overhead. To simplify the process of locating resources, Windows 2000 utilizes the Lightweight Directory Access Protocol (LDAP) to accelerate the searching process.

Locating Resources within a Tree

Windows 2000 uses LDAP queries to search and find objects within the Active Directory. An LDAP query passes from one domain controller to another until it reaches the server on which the object resides. The object must reside within the current tree for LDAP to locate the object. LDAP queries are contained within the tree and cannot be used to search for objects outside the local tree even though the tree might be part of a larger forest.

PLANNING A FOREST

The combination of one or more trees combined by two-way transitive trusts is known as a *forest*. The trust between two or more trees is automatically established between the tree roots of each tree in order to create a forest. As mentioned earlier, the tree root is the first domain created within a particular tree. All domains within a forest share a common Global Catalog, schema, and configuration. The presence of a two-way transitive trust and the sharing of common information is what separates a forest from a set of unrelated trees.

Isolated trees or trees that are part of a forest are named or identified by the root domain name. Because all trees within a tree share the same namespace, a tree is easily described by the name of the first domain created in the tree. The forest is named and identified by the DNS name of the forest root. The forest root is the DNS name of the first domain created in the forest.

Forests become a part of a single network that is divided into separate hierarchal units as displayed by their DNS names. The Active Directory within

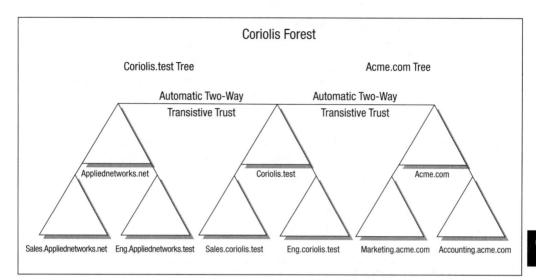

Figure 7.3   Coriolis forest.

any domain or tree can resolve names of objects contained in any of the trees within the forest, because the trees of a forest all share a common Global Catalog Server. (See Figure 7.3 for an example of a forest.)

When to Use Multitree Forests

Forests allow separate DNS-named networks to be combined into one large network. Each forest can retain its own unique namespace and administrative organizations while still allowing information and resources to be shared across the entire organization. The main purpose behind combining multiple trees into a forest is to allow for a distinctive and unique namespace. This reasoning might be important in the following situations:

➤ In a large corporation made up of smaller and dissimilar business units, each business unit may want to retain their individual namespace while still participating in the corporation's wide area network. For example, the General Good Foods corporation owns the restaurants Red Lobster Claw and Green Olive Garden. Both of them might want to maintain their own networks and namespace but still be connected to the General Good Foods worldwide email system.

➤ Companies that are in partnership with another company may have business reasons for creating a shared network environment.

➤ Companies that purchase other business may want to keep the purchased company's namespace and network intact.

7

Searching Multiple Trees

As mentioned earlier, LDAP queries are limited to a single tree and cannot cross into other trees. Windows 2000 does not use LDAP for searching through the entire forest. Instead, the Global Catalog Server can be used. By default, the Global Catalog Server is the first domain controller installed in the forest.

Additional Global Catalog Servers can be created using the Active Directory Sites And Services administrative tool. If you suspect the network might need to support a large number of intra-tree searches, you should consider placing a Global Catalog Server at each site to reduce global catalog queries across wide area connections. Keep in mind that creating multiple Global Catalog Servers will increase the replication traffic.

CREATING A FOREST

You can create a forest simply by installing a new domain controller and specifying that the domain controller is part of a new tree. During the promotion, you can then specify the root domain of the initial tree. During the installation of Active Directory on the new domain controller, a two-way transitive trust will be created between the new tree root and the original tree root. Each new tree added to the forest will be set up with a two-way transitive trust between the new tree root and the initial tree root. This logically builds a star topographical view of the trusts between the original tree root and all others. Because the trusts are transitive and bidirectional, resources in any tree can be accessed from any other tree. Before you create a new tree, though, you should understand the structure of a multitree forest.

Forest Structure Planning

You need to plan a forest before you add trees. First, because each new tree requires its own namespace, the DNS structure should be configured and the namespace should be registered with the proper organizations if the namespace is going to be accessible from the Internet. Any additional subdomains, or child domains, should be planned and configured accordingly.

When creating a new domain controller that will become the tree root of a new domain, select the Create New Domain Tree In An Existing Forest option during Active Directory installation. Additionally, during the installation, you must specify the root domain of the initial tree so that the trust relationships can be created.

UNDERSTANDING MULTIPLE FORESTS

The Windows 2000 Active Directory does not support the configuration of a multiple forest network infrastructure. Although multiple forests can be created manually, you cannot create a single Active Directory hierarchy that includes multiple forests. Each forest will maintain its own separate Active Directory database, completely separated from the Active Directory databases in other forests.

You cannot join an existing Windows 2000 Active Directory to another. In order to combine multiple domains into a tree or multiple trees into a forest, each domain or tree must be built after the first domain controller is installed. The reason for this is simple. No matter how large an Active Directory you build—a single domain, multidomain tree, or multitree forest—the Active Directory will always contain just one schema and one schema master server. If two networks are built separately from one another, each will have its own schema and schema master server. The schema of one Active Directory cannot be merged with another Active Directory. In the future, third-party tools might provide this function.

When to Use Multiple Forests

Multiple forests environments are usually very difficult to understand, and administration can become very complex. Creating multiple forests doesn't offer any advantages over creating multiple trees within one forest. Creating multiple trees within a single forest accommodates the connecting of separate and diverse organizations within one Active Directory hierarchy. Regardless, some situations might arise that require multiple forests, including:

➤ *Company acquisitions*—A company might purchase another company that already has a Windows 2000 Active Directory forest in place. Although the domain controllers could be reinstalled and joined to the original company's initial forest, this might not be practical.

➤ *Limited partnerships*—Two companies might enter into a joint venture in which each company already has an existing Windows 2000 Active Directory forest in place. The only way to provide access from one forest's domain to another domain in a remote forest is to create a trust relationship.

Tip: You should not purposely plan to build a multiple forest environment as your first choice.

CREATING MULTIPLE FORESTS

Because Windows 2000 Active Directory does not support the creation of multiple forests into one hierarchy, the only way to provide resource sharing between two forests is to set up explicit one-way trusts between one or more domains from one forest to the other. If users from each forest will access resources in both domains, you must create trusts in both directions. This scenario is much the same as creating a trust relationship between domains in a Windows NT 4 environment. Trusts created between non-related domains must be non-transitive, so, in many cases, you might have to configure multiple trusts between multiple domains.

Planning Multiple Forests

Before creating or planning a multiple forest organization, you need to understand how and where the trust relationships will be configured. Multiple trust relationships will create additional administrative overhead for both forests. Through trust relationships, you can assign permissions, monitor access, and limit the scope of authorized access to user accounts that are accessing domains from domains in remote forests.

PLANNING FOR INFRASTRUCTURE SERVICES IN A MULTIDOMAIN ENVIRONMENT

Just as with Windows NT 4, Windows 2000 networks rely on a number of services to enable proper network communications. For example, because Windows 2000 incorporates multiple domain controllers cooperating in a peer fashion, the presence of the Global Catalog Server and the domain name servers are examples of critical services that must remain operational for proper operation of the Active Directory and network devices. This section lists many of the infrastructure services that you need to consider as well as where to locate these services when building large-scale enterprise networks. Namely, this section discusses:

➤ Domain naming systems

➤ Global Catalog Servers

➤ Operation masters

➤ Replication issues in large network environments

➤ SYSVOL

Domain Naming Systems

As mentioned in previous chapters, the DNS system replaces WINS as the primary name resolution method for Windows 2000 and is critical for the proper operation of the Active Directory. Windows 2000 provides an improved DNS service by adding RFC 2052 compliance. RFC 2052 introduces SRV records that are used in much the same way as MX records are used to locate servers running SMTP. SRV records allow you to identify the services a server is providing, much like the sixteenth character in a NetBIOS name. (SRV and MX records are discussed in more detail in Chapter 3.) Client computers can now query a DNS server to find services such as LDAP servers, the Global Catalog, or domain controllers on a network. For these reasons, ensure that you plan for highly available DNS servers in your enterprise network.

Windows 2000 supports three different zone file types. All DNS servers support the two common primary and secondary zone types, but Windows 2000 also supports a third type, the Active Directory integrated zone.

7

Planning for Enterprise Zone Types

As described in Chapter 3, three types of zone files are held by DNS servers—primary, secondary, and integrated:

➤ *Primary zone file*—Primary zone files are the most prevalent type of zone files. A primary zone file is the master file containing IP address and computer name mappings for a particular domain name.

➤ *Secondary zone file*—A secondary zone file is used to provide fault tolerance in case a primary server is unavailable. A secondary zone file is simply a copy of the primary zone file that is kept updated by the process of zone transfers.

➤ *Active Directory integrated zone file*—This is the third and newest type of zone file. With integrated zone files, the IP address and computer name information is stored within the Active Directory and is therefore replicated to all domain controllers. In order for a domain controller to read the zone file information within the Active Directory and respond to a name resolution request, it must have the DNS service installed.

Note: *Windows 2000 DNS service supports all three zone file types.*

Replication of Integrated Zone Files

All DNS information (zone files) is replicated to all domain controllers within a domain. DNS information is not replicated to domain controllers in other domains, even if the domains are all part of the same tree. This concept is important to understand because it affects how name resolution will be configured on clients in other domains.

Because all DNS information is contained within one domain, you have to decide whether the zone file for all domains will be contained in one domain or if each domain will maintain its own copy of its zone file. If the DNS information is all contained in one domain, then administration of the DNS system will be much less complex. Whether you created one zone file for all domains or have each domain maintain its own copy dictates how client computers are configured.

Clients have to know the IP address of the DNS server. If the DNS server is in another domain and possibly another site, you have to consider that all name resolution requests will have to cross domains and possibly site boundaries. If you have slow links between child domains and the domain containing the DNS information, allowing DNS requests to cross into other sites is not a good idea. On the other hand, if each domain maintains its own zone file, the bandwidth consumed by name requests should not be a problem.

In another possible setup, you can create a *caching DNS server*. Caching DNS servers do not hold the zone file or even a copy of the zone file. Caching DNS servers simply cache previous results to name query requests. For example, a caching DNS server could be installed in each domain while all DNS information is contained in the forest root domain. Client computers at each domain will point to the caching DNS server for requests, and the caching server will pass the name query to the proper DNS server (if not already cached) in the forest root domain.

Locating Service Resources with DNS

Windows 2000 client computers must have the IP address of a DNS server in order to participate and interoperate with the Active Directory. Without DNS servers, Windows 2000 clients will be unable to locate objects within the directory, and, more specifically, they will not find the Global Catalog Server. If a client cannot find the Global Catalog Server, the client will not be able to log into the network

Global Catalog Servers

By default, the first domain controller becomes the Global Catalog Server for the domain. The Global Catalog Server maintains a list of all Active Directory objects within the domain as well as a list of some of the objects' attributes (properties). Because a multitree forest contains only one Active Directory, the Global Catalog Server maintains a list of all objects within the forest.

Note: Global Catalog SRV records within DNS are recognized by _msdcs.gc, as seen in Figure 7.4.

As well as controlling a list of all objects, the Global Catalog also maintains an index of the objects, which enables faster searching. The purpose of the Global

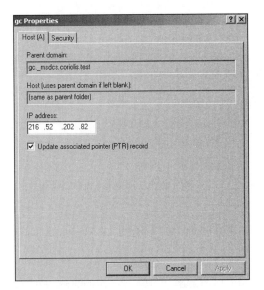

Figure 7.4   Global Catalog host record.

Catalog is to allow searching for specific objects without requiring searches to traverse all the domain controllers. Because the Global Catalog already contains a list of all objects and their locations, each domain controller does not have to be queried during the creation of the object list.

Global Catalog Servers also contain a list of all universal groups within the forest and the group members. The Global Catalog Server contains a list of all universal, domain local, and global groups, but it contains the *membership* of only universal groups. Although each forest by default only has one Global Catalog Server, you can create more as needed. Global Catalog Servers replicate changes to one another; therefore, as the number of Global Catalog Servers increases, the more replication traffic will be increased.

Global Server Replication and Placement

Global Catalog replication is separate from the Active Directory replication that takes place between domain controllers. When planning for bandwidth requirements, don't forget to include the Global Catalog replication. The more Global Catalog Servers that are running, the faster searching will be, but the Global Catalog Servers will consume more precious bandwidth.

Client computers will attempt to find a Global Catalog Server within their own site. A client finds a Global Catalog Server by issuing a DNS query for a list of Global Catalog Servers. One way to limit search traffic across wide-area networks (WAN) links is to place a Global Catalog Server at each site. If a given site contains a domain controller, it might be a good idea to also make the domain controller a catalog server.

Creating a Global Catalog Server

You can create a Global Catalog Server within the Active Directory Sites And Services administrative tool or Microsoft Management Console (MMC) snap-in. To create a Global Catalog Server, follow these steps:

1. Open the Active Directory Sites And Services administrative tool or MMC snap-in.

2. Select the site where the server resides, and then select the server that you want to make a Global Catalog Server.

3. Right-click the NTDS Services folder under the server you want to create, and select Properties.

4. Check the Global Catalog checkbox (see Figure 7.5).

Operation Masters

Windows 2000 does not contain a primary domain controller (PDC) as Windows NT 4 did. In Windows 2000, all domain controllers are essentially peers on the network, so there has to be some way to distribute the services for which the PDC was responsible. Basically, the role of the PDC has been divided into five server roles within Windows 2000. Servers performing these functions are known as *operation masters*. The following is a list of the five types of operation masters and the services that each one provides.

➤ *Domain naming*—Not to be confused with the DNS service, the domain naming operation master is responsible for ensuring that domain names are unique.

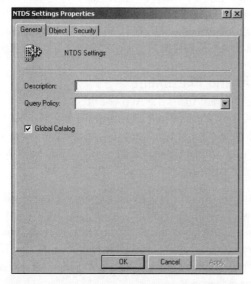

Figure 7.5 Adding a Global Catalog Server in Active Directory Sites And Services.

➤ *Infrastructure role*—The purpose of the infrastructure server is to hold configuration information for the domain. This server contains configuration information for Active Directory objects that cross domain boundaries. Sites, for example, are objects that can cross domain boundaries. There is one infrastructure server per domain.

➤ *PDC*—Although there is no real primary domain controller in Windows 2000, there is always one domain controller per domain that will emulate the PDC for legacy Windows clients. The PDC emulator also acts as a storage location for group policy objects (GPOs).

➤ *RID (relative ID) pool*—One server within the domain must be the RID pool master. The RID master is responsible for keeping track of sequential numbers (called the *relative identifier numbers*) that are assigned to objects within the Active Directory. Because any domain controller can create objects within the directory, one server must be responsible for assigning unique identification numbers. The RID is the unique portion of the security ID (SID). The RID master assigns a pool of RIDs to each domain controller.

➤ *Schema master*—Only one schema is defined within a forest, and only one server can contain and modify the schema. The schema master maintains the only copy of the schema within any domain, tree, or forest.

Replication Issues in Large Network Environments

Many of the new features as well as critical network services rely on proper replication of data throughout the network. In order for a large network environment to operate consistently and reliably, the network infrastructure must allow for proper replication of network data. Replication of the Global Catalog, Dfs, and the SYSVOL data all must be performed and all have an impact on network performance.

Any discussion of replication leads to the concept of naming contexts. A naming context consists of an area and path in which information is replicated. Windows 2000 includes three naming contexts—domain, schema, and configuration:

➤ *Domain naming context*—Replicates only within the local domain and does not cross domain boundaries.

➤ *Schema naming context*—Replicates objects throughout the domain forest.

➤ *Configuration naming context*—Replicates configuration information related to replication topology and is replicated across the entire forest.

Sites and site links act as boundaries for the three naming contexts. Windows 2000 also builds directory service connection objects between domain controllers within a forest through the use of the Knowledge Consistency

Checker (KCC). The KCC builds connection objects that define which domains will replicate to which other domains, as well as the time replication will take place.

Using tools included in the Windows 2000 Resource Kit might assist in improving and troubleshooting replication between and within domains. The Windows 2000 Resource Kit tool Replmon.exe can be used to monitor, trigger, and troubleshoot replication. Another tool—Repadmin.exe—can be used for diagnosing replication problems.

SYSVOL

All the functions of the NETLOGON share on Windows NT 4 are now handled by the SYSVOL. The SYSVOL share is replicated to all domain controllers within a domain. The SYSVOL share holds information regarding group policy objects and legacy NETLOGON information for downlevel client operating systems.

The SYSVOL share is replicated to all domain controllers utilizing the file replication service (FRS). By default, the FRS replicates on the same schedule as the Active Directory. The FRS service will obey site boundaries just as the Active Directory service does. You can change the replication schedule for the FRS service within the Active Directory Users And Computers administrative tool (see Figure 7.6).

CHAPTER SUMMARY

This chapter examined how to connect multiple domains into trees and forests. Many of the issues in creating a large multidomain Windows 2000 network were touched on. This chapter also documented the new Windows 2000 server functions and described the role each server can provide throughout a network

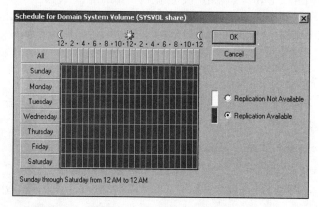

Figure 7.6 SYSVOL replication schedule.

infrastructure. The schema operations master server is responsible for maintaining the integrity of the schema information for the active directory. The infrastructure operations master maintains site and connection information for the network. The PDC emulator provides backward compatibility with downlevel Microsoft operating systems. This chapter also discussed the RID operations master, whose responsibility it is to ensure that all objects and security principals within the directory have a unique security identification number (SID).

In addition, the chapter looked at DNS in the enterprise environment and discussed how you can design an efficient DNS infrastructure. DNS server placement is crucial to resolving host names efficiently as well as proper operation of the Active Directory. DNS strategies should be developed before any servers are upgraded or installed on the network.

This chapter explained replication in the enterprise and issues that network engineers must consider when planning a large network infrastructure. As the network becomes larger, the network engineer must take into consideration the amount of replication traffic and query traffic that will cross expensive and slow WAN links. Global Catalog Servers can be added at each site to improve search times and reduce the amount of queries that cross WAN links; however, by adding more Global Catalogs, you increase the amount of replication traffic crossing the same WAN links. The placement of network resources is not always an easy decision to make and should be justified by performing network utilization and traffic pattern tests.

REVIEW QUESTIONS

1. At a minimum, how many domains and domain controllers does a forest require?

   a. Two domains and two controllers

   b. One domain and two controllers

   c. Two domains and four controllers

   d. One domain and one controller

2. Which of the following is a valid reason to create a multiple domain tree? [Check all correct answers]

   a. Administrative control needs to be divided among each department.

   b. The Security Accounts Manager database needs to be prevented from exceeding 40MB.

   c. Administrative control must be isolated among departments.

   d. Replication traffic needs to be reduced between locations.

3. What is the first domain in an Active Directory network infrastructure called?

   a. Forest root

   b. Domain root

   c. Active Directory root

   d. Enterprise root

4. Adding multiple domains to an Active Directory tree produces what effect?

   a. It increases replication traffic over the WAN.

   b. It slows network performance.

   c. It increases hardware costs.

   d. It decreases administrative overhead.

5. The amount of replication traffic between domains is less than the amount of replication traffic within a domain.

   a. True

   b. False

6. All domains within an Active Directory Tree share a common _____.

   a. Infrastructure server

   b. Relative identifier server

   c. Domain controller

   d. Tree root

7. Each domain name within a tree must adhere to which of the following?

   a. It must be listed on the DNS server in the tree root domain.

   b. It must share the same contiguous namespace as the tree root domain.

   c. It must contain 15 or fewer characters.

   d. It must be registered with a naming authority.

8. How is the forest root domain different from all other domains in a tree?

   a. The forest root does not have a parent domain.

   b. The forest root domain does not have a child domain.

   c. Only the forest root can have more than one parent domain.

   d. Only the forest root can have more than one child domain.

9. Transitive trust relationships exist only between separate trees in a forest.

   a. True

   b. False

10. Which statement best describes transitive trust relationships?

    a. If domain A trusts domain B and domain B trusts domain C, then users from domain A can be assigned permissions to resources in domain B.

    b. If domain A trusts domain B and domain B trusts domain C, then users from domain C can be assigned permissions to resources in domain A.

    c. If domain A trusts domain B and domain B trusts domain C, then domain C automatically trusts domain A.

    d. If domain A trusts domain B and domain B trusts domain C, then domain C automatically trusts domain B.

11. Where are Lightweight Directory Access Protocol queries confined?

    a. Forest

    b. Tree

    c. Local Domain

    d. Active Directory

12. What type of trust relationship does a cross-link trust create?

    a. Trust relationship between trees

    b. Trust relationship between forests

    c. Trust relationship between two separate sites

    d. Trust relationship between two domains residing in the same or different trees

13. What is the main purpose of a cross-link trust?

    a. It creates a trust where no trust relationship currently exists.

    b. It reduces replication traffic.

    c. It provides faster access to resources between separate domains.

    d. It replaces Windows NT 4 non-transitive trusts with transitive trust relationships.

14. Cross-link trusts must be transitive.

    a. True

    b. False

15. In order for two domains to establish a cross-link trust, they must both reside in the same namespace.

    a. True

    b. False

7

16. Which statement best describes how to join two preexisting Windows 2000 domains into one Active Directory tree?

   a. Within the Active Directory Users And Computers administrative tool, select the domain and then select Join Existing Domain.

   b. Within the Active Directory Sites And Services administrative tool, select the domain and then select Join Existing Domain.

   c. You must reinstall a domain controller when you want to join it to an existing domain.

   d. You must reinstall both domain controllers in both domains before they can become part of the same domain.

17. What is the combination of two or more trees configured automatically with a two-way transitive trust called?

   a. POD

   b. Forest

   c. Multitree domain

   d. Multitree POD

18. When adding a domain to an existing forest, what do you need to specify?

   a. IP address of the root domain controller

   b. Computer name of the root domain controller

   c. Forest Active Directory name

   d. Full DNS name of the root domain controller

19. Each tree requires its own _____.

   a. Subnet

   b. Schema master

   c. Global Catalog Server

   d. Unique namespace

20. In a multiple forest network, an automatic two-way transitive trust is configured.

   a. True

   b. False

21. Request For Comments (RFC) 2052 provides what additional functionality?

   a. SRV records to DNS

   b. Dynamic updates to DNS servers

   c. Active Directory Integrated DNS

   d. DNS zone transfers

22. Active Directory integrated zones are automatically replicated to all domain controllers within which of the following?

   a. Tree

   b. Forest

   c. Domain

   d. Entire Active Directory

23. A caching DNS server is responsible for which zone file?

   a. Primary zone file

   b. Secondary zone file

   c. Integrated zone file

   d. None of the above

24. The Global Catalog Server contains a(n) _____ to allow for faster searching?

   a. List

   b. Index

   c. Copy of all objects

   d. Copy of all objects and their attributes

25. A Global Catalog Server can be created using which of the following administrative tools?

   a. Active Directory Sites And Services

   b. Active Directory Computers And Users

   c. Computer Management

   d. Server Manager

26. Which of the following operation master server roles acts as a storage location for group policy objects?

   a. Schema

   b. Domain naming

   c. Infrastructure

   d. PDC

27. The RID pool server is responsible for what?

   a. Assigning relative identification numbers to clients

   b. Assigning pools of relative identification numbers to domain controllers

c. Assigning replication identification numbers to objects

d. Pooling identification numbers of all objects in the directory

28. The infrastructure server holds configuration information for which of the following?

a. Domain

b. Forest

c. Tree

d. Entire Active Directory

29. What does the naming context of an object define?

a. How the object/data is named

b. How the object/data is addressed

c. How the object/data is replicated

d. None of the above

30. Which Windows 2000 feature replaces the functionality of NT 4's NETLOGON share?

a. Dfs

b. SYSVOL

c. RIDs

d. Active Directory Users And Computers

31. Creating multiple Global Catalog Servers throughout a forest will increase which of the following network attributes?

a. Replication and administration

b. Administration and Active Directory size

c. Search speed and replication traffic

d. Search speed and administration

32. Which statement is true concerning a multiforest network?

a. Multiforest networks are a good solution for dividing networks into administrative units.

b. Multiforest networks are a good solution for combining two separate networks into one manageable namespace.

c. Multiforest networks allow for simpler administration.

d. Multiforest networks make administration difficult and should only be used when no other possible solutions exist.

33. How can trust relationships be created between forests?

    a. Manually

    b. Automatically

    c. With a transitive relationship

    d. Without a transitive relationship

34. Which of the following describes trust relationships between forests?

    a. Transitive

    b. Non-transitive

    c. Two-way trusts

    d. Complete trusts

35. Trusts between forests must be configured between the root domains of each forest only.

    a. True

    b. False

7

REAL-WORLD PROJECTS

For his next assignment, Andy Palmer has been assigned the task of creating a multiple domain network for the Coriolis Company. The Sales department requires that they be removed from the coriolis.test parent domain and placed in their own sales.domain.

In this project, Andy installs additional domain controllers in order to create child domains, trees, and forests. For this, he determines that at least one additional computer is necessary to meet the minimum requirements to run Windows 2000 Server (minimum of two computers total).

Andy determines that in order to complete this project, the Server1 domain controller (installed in Chapter 5's Real-World Projects section) must be in place, and the second computer (Server2) must have Windows 2000 Server installed and configured as a member server for the coriolis.test domain. Both servers must be members of the same TCP/IP subnet. Server1.coriolis.test will act as the DNS server for Server2 and the new sales.coriolis.test domain.

Note: See Chapter 2's Real-World Projects section for directions on how to install Windows 2000 Server.

Warning! Before the projects in this section can be completed, the Organizational Unit named *sales* must be deleted. You cannot have a domain name that is the same as an OU.

Project 7.1

To prepare DNS for additional domains, complete the following steps:

1. On Server1, open DNS in Administrative Tools.

2. Click the Plus next to Server1 and Forward Lookup Zones.

3. Right-click the coriolis.test folder, and select Properties.

4. In the Properties dialog box, under Allow Dynamic Updates, click Yes, as shown in Figure 7.7

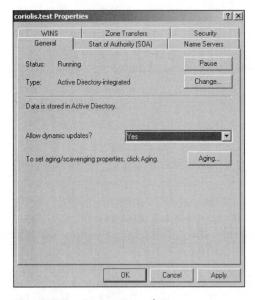

Figure 7.7 Dynamic updates.

5. Click the Change button, and select Active Directory–Integrated, as shown in Figure 7.8

6. If prompted to implement integrated zone files, click Yes.

7. Click OK in the Change Zone Dialog box and OK again in the coriolis.test dialog box.

8. Click the Plus next to Reverse Lookup Zones.

9. Right-click the Reverse Lookup Zone, and select Properties.

10. Under Allow Dynamic Updates, select Yes.

11. Click the Change button, and select Active Directory–Integrated.

12. If prompted to implement integrated zone files, select Yes.

13. Click OK in the Change Zone Dialog box and OK again in the properties box.

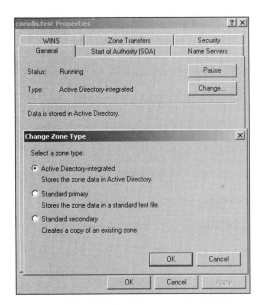

Figure 7.8   Active Directory–Integrated zone type.

Note: By allowing Dynamic updates, you allow the DNS zones for new domains to be created automatically when new domains are added to the tree.

14. If not already completed, install Windows 2000 Server on the second computer, and name the server Server2.

15. Right-click My Network Places and then right-click Local Area Network under TCP/IP Properties; ensure that Server1 and Server2 are on the same subnet. Server2's DNS settings should point to the IP address of Server1, and Server2 should be a member of the coriolis.test domain.

Note: If Windows 2000 was already installed, Server2 might have to be restarted after changing the settings in Steps 14 and 15.

16. To verify DNS configuration, from Server1, ping the IP address of Server2.

17. From Server1, ping Server2.coriolis.test.

18. From Server2, ping the IP address of Server1.

19. From Server2, ping Server1.coriolis.test.

Project 7.2

To create a child domain, complete the following steps:

1. From Server2, click Run, type "dcpromo.exe", and click OK.

2. In the Active Directory Installation Wizard window, click Next.

3. Select Domain Controller For A New Domain, and click Next.

4. Select the Create New Child Domain In An Existing Domain Tree option, and click Next.

5. Enter an administrator name and password for the coriolis.test domain.

Note: Only members of the Enterprise Admins group can add domains to the tree.

6. Enter "coriolis.test" as the domain name.

7. Click Next.

8. Enter "coriolis.test" in the Parent Domain field.

9. Enter "sales" as the child domain.

10. Verify that the complete DNS name of the new domain is sales.coriolis.test.

11. Click Next.

12. Verify that sales is the NetBIOS name, and click Next.

13. Accept the defaults for database and log storage locations.

14. Click Next.

15. Accept the default location for the SYSVOL folder.

16. Click Next.

17. Select the Permissions Compatible With Pre-Windows 2000 Servers option.

18. Click Next.

19. Leave the password field blank, and click Next.

20. Click Next.

21. When Active Directory installation is finished, click Restart Now.

Project 7.3
To verify domain configuration, complete the following steps:

1. From Server1, run Active Directory Domains And Trusts from Administrative Tools.

2. Click the Plus next to coriolis.test. Notice that sales.coriolis.test is below coriolis.test.

3. Close Active Directory Domains And Trusts.

4. Open DNS from Administrative Tools.

5. Expand Forward Lookup Zones.

6. Expand coriolis.test.

7. Select the sales folder below coriolis.test. Notice the host record entry for Server2 in the right pane.

Project 7.4

To view automatic trust configuration, complete the following steps:

1. Log into the sales.coriolis.test domain from Server2.

2. Open Active Directory Domains And Trusts from Administrative Tools.

3. Right-click the coriolis.test domain and select Properties, as seen in Figure 7.9

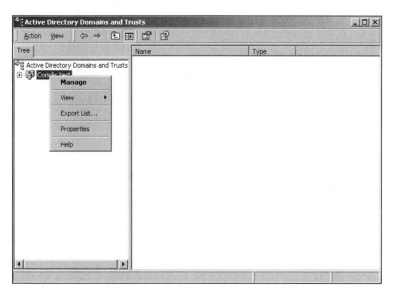

Figure 7.9   Domains and trusts.

4. Select the Trusts tab. Notice that two one-way trusts are established and both are transitive.

Project 7.5

To create objects in child domains, complete the following steps:

1. Log onto the coriolis.test domain on Server1.

2. Open Active Directory Users And Computers.

3. Right-click the coriolis.test domain, and select Connect To Domain.

4. In the Connect To Domain box, click Browse.

5. Select the sales.coriolis.test domain below the coriolis.test domain.

6. Click OK, and then click OK again.

7. Click the Plus next to the sales.coriolis.test domain.

8. Right-click on sales.coriolis.test, select New, then click Organizational Unit.

9. In the Name field, enter "Marketing".

10. Click OK.

11. Right-click the Marketing OU, select New, and select User.

12. Enter "Sam" as the first name.

13. Enter "Slug" as the last name.

14. Enter "Sslug" for the logon name.

15. Verify or change the suffix to @sales.coriolis.test.

16. Select Next in the New user dialog box and click Next again.

17. Select Finish.

Project 7.6
To view operation master roles, complete the following steps:

1. Log onto the sales.coriolis.test domain from Server2.

2. Open Active Directory Users And Computers.

3. Right-click the sales.coriolis.test domain, and select Operation Masters.

4. Select the PDC and Infrastructure tabs to view which servers are configured.

Note: By clicking the Change button in the operations master dialog box, you can change which servers are operation masters, but you must first connect to another domain controller within the domain. See Figure 7.10 for an example of an operations master.

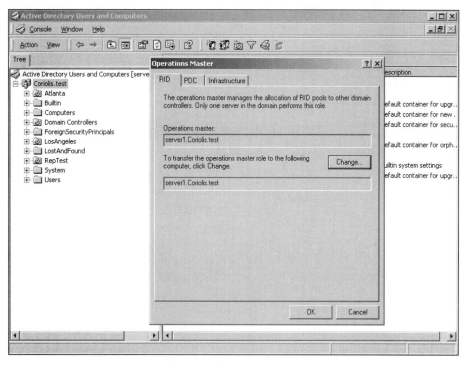

Figure 7.10   Operations master.

Project 7.7

To search the Global Catalog, complete the following steps:

1. Log onto the sales.coriolis.test domain from Server2.

2. Open Active Directory Users And Computers from the Administrative Tools menu.

3. Right-click the sales.coriolis.test domain, and select Find.

4. In the Find dialog box, select Computers, as seen in Figure 7.11.

5. In the In box, select your domain, and click Find Now.

6. Change the In box to coriolis.test.

7. Click Find Now again. Notice that you can opt to search your domain, another domain, or the entire directory.

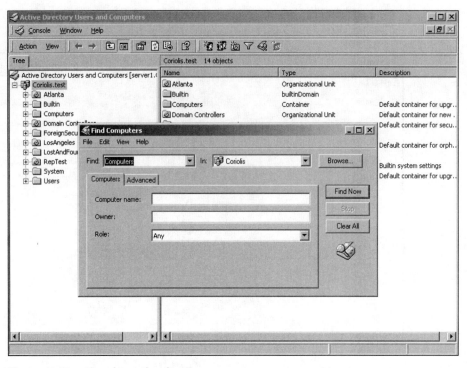

Figure 7.11   Searching the directory.

CHAPTER EIGHT

UNDERSTANDING AND CONFIGURING REPLICATION

After completing this chapter, you will be able to:

✓ Explain how domain controllers identify changes to the directory

✓ Identify differences between directory replication and directory synchronization

✓ Configure intersite replication

✓ Configure intrasite replication

✓ Use sites and site links

In Windows NT 4, the directory database is contained on one server, called the *primary domain controller* (PDC). Any changes made to the directory are made only on the PDC and then replicated to all *backup domain controllers* (BDCs), regardless of which computer made the changes. In contrast, in Windows 2000, each domain controller maintains a working copy of the Active Directory, and changes can be made on any domain controller.

Windows 2000 domain controllers are peers, organized in a multi-master replication model. Because any domain controller can make changes to the Active Directory, changes made at any domain must be replicated to all other domain controllers. This chapter explains how replication takes place, as well as what you can do to control and optimize replication traffic.

REPLICATION DEFINED

Windows 2000 networks can contain any number of domain controllers, each with its own copy of the Active Directory database. Each domain controller is responsible for maintaining the database, managing changes to the database, and ensuring that any changes made to its own copy of the database are sent to the replication partners. Because changes can be made to any copy of the Active Directory database, some mechanism must be in place to ensure that changes are made to all copies of the database on all domain controllers. The process of notifying and updating each domain controller of any changes is called *replication*.

To provide efficient and consistent network operation, all domain controllers must have a directory database that is an exact copy of all other domain controllers' directory databases. For example, if a user's password is changed on one domain controller and the change is not properly replicated to other domain controllers, the user might be unable to log on to the network because each domain controller might have a different password for the user.

Each object within the Active Directory contains attributes that can be changed. For example, a user's password is an attribute of the user object. When a password is changed, the entire user object is not replicated—only the user's password is replicated.

Note: Directory replication and directory synchronization are not the same, although the terms are sometimes used interchangeably. Directory replication takes place between directory databases of the same type. Directory synchronization takes place between different directories. Copying changes from the Active Directory database to the NetWare Directory Service (NDS) is an example of synchronization, not replication. (See Figure 8.1.)

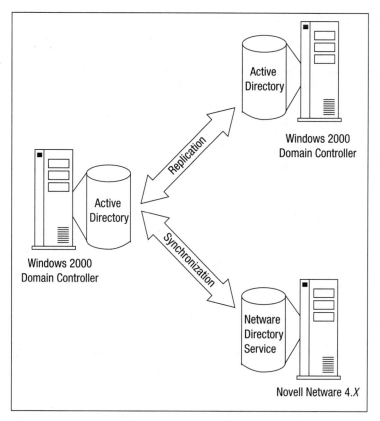

Figure 8.1   Directory replication and synchronization.

UNDERSTANDING ACTIVE DIRECTORY REPLICATION

The replication process depends on the interaction of various components. When a change is made to the directory database on a domain controller, a change notification is sent from the domain controller that made the change to each replication partner. After a change notification is received, an update request is sent back to the original domain controller. The update request contains an *update sequence number* (USN) that identifies the current replicated state of the domain controller requesting changes to the directory.

Update Sequence Numbers

Update sequence numbers are used to track changes to objects within the Active Directory. When a change is made to an object, the change is assigned a USN. The USN is incremented for each change made to the Active Directory. Every domain controller contains a USN table that is used to store and track the domain controller's own USNs. In Figure 8.2 you can see the original and current USNs.

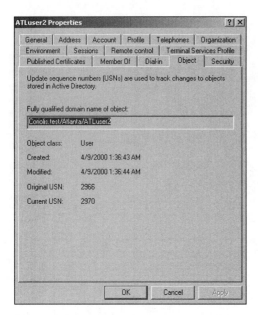

Figure 8.2 Universal sequence numbers.

When a change is made to the directory database, the attribute of the object that changed as well as the USN for the change are stored. This is referred to as an *atomic operation*, because both writes either succeed or fail.

Each domain controller notified of a change compares its own highest USN to the USN on the domain controller that sent the change notification. If the sending domain controller's USN is higher than the locally stored USN, replication must occur to ensure a consistent directory database.

Update sequence numbers eliminate the need for all domain controllers to have their time synchronized perfectly, because timestamps are not used for standard replication. Many replication techniques use timestamps to determine what needs to be replicated. This is a difficult situation to manage, however; when replication relies on timestamps, each domain controller has to be perfectly synchronized with all other domain controllers. Timestamps are used in Windows 2000 replication for tie-breaking only.

If a domain controller is repaired and then added back to the network, it will request changes from its replication partners. The repaired domain controller has to request only the USNs greater than the last USN it received from each domain controller. The repaired domain controller is fully replicated when all USNs from all domain controllers are received.

To facilitate efficient replication, the server that performed the update is not responsible for sending change notification to all domain controllers. Domain controllers that receive the change from the originating server via replication can send out change notifications and replicate the change to its replication partners as well. How a replica is updated (by the originating server or through a secondary server) is called the *directory update type*.

Directory Updates

Each update to the directory can either be committed or not committed. After an update is committed (by clicking OK or Apply), the change and the new USN identifying the change are stored. Windows 2000 supports two types of updates to the directory database—originating updates and replicated updates.

Originating Updates

An originating update is a change made at the local domain controller. For example, if an administrator makes a change at serverA, then the originating update is created at serverA.

Four types of originating updates are available:

➤ *Add*—Adding an object to the directory database. For example, creating a user account creates an add update.

➤ *Delete*—Deleting an object from the directory database. For example, deleting a user account creates a delete update.

➤ *Modify*—Modifying the attributes of an object. For example, changing a user's phone number or password creates a modify update.

➤ *ModifyDN*—Changing the name of an object or moving the object into another container. For example, moving a user account from the **coriolis.test** domain to the **sales.coriolis.test** domain creates a modifyDN update.

Replicated Updates

A replicated update is a change to a directory database that is made as a result of replication. For example, if an administrator makes a change to the directory database at serverA and serverA replicates the change to serverB, then the change to serverB is known as a replicated update (see Figure 8.3). The change takes place on the directory database of serverA and the change is then replicated and applied as a replicated change to serverB's directory database.

Each replicated update is performed as a result of an originating update performed on a directory database. Originating updates create stamps for each change to the directory. This stamp is attached to the data that has been created or changed and is replicated along with the new data. The stamp, which is

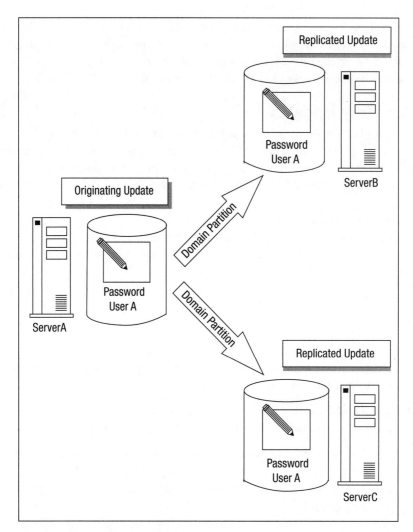

Figure 8.3 Replicated updates.

represented by a number, is always different from all other stamps. If the change is made to an attribute, then the new stamp will always be greater than the existing stamp for the changed attribute.

Because updates are replicated from one domain controller to another eventually, one domain controller will attempt to replicate a change to another domain controller that has already received the change. Replication of information to a replica that has already received the new data should be prevented so as to reduce unneeded replication traffic. Windows 2000 implements *propagation dampening* to prevent unneeded replication and replication traffic.

Understanding Propagation Dampening

Propagation is the process of replicating data from one domain controller to another throughout the entire domain. The time it takes for a change made on one directory to propagate to all other directories in the network is known as *propagation delay*. To decrease propagation delay (increase the speed of replication), Active Directory replication creates a fully meshed or looped replication topology. For example, serverA replicates to serverB. ServerB replicates to serverC, and serverC notifies serverA that there are changes. This looping topology helps to increase replication speed and provide fault tolerance. Increasing speed and providing fault tolerance helps to provide consistency; however, this process might also create redundant replication traffic. Propagation dampening helps to reduce unwanted traffic by ensuring that replication traffic is not sent to servers that have already received the updated information.

To allow propagation dampening, each domain controller stores a pair of vectors. Each vector includes an array of numbers. These arrays include the globally unique identifiers (GUIDs) for each Active Directory replica as well as the USN. The two vectors used by each domain controller to determine their replicated state are the up-to-date vector and the high watermark vector, as seen in Figure 8.4.

8

Up-to-Date Vector

The up-to-date vector is made up of the server GUID and the highest originating update's USN number received from any particular server. The up-to-date vector contains only the USN for the last originating update it received from each server. Originating updates are changes that occurred on a particular server. For example, if a user's password is changed on serverA, and serverA writes the change to its own directory, serverA has performed an originating

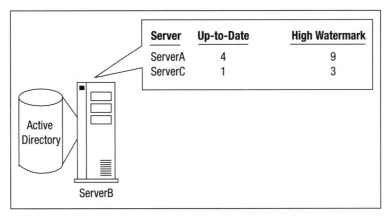

Server	Up-to-Date	High Watermark
ServerA	4	9
ServerC	1	3

Active Directory

ServerB

Figure 8.4 Up-to-date and high watermark vectors.

update. When serverB receives the changes from serverA and applies the changes, then serverB has performed a replicated update.

Each domain controller keeps a table listing all other known domain controllers and a list of the last originating update they received from each domain controller. For example:

1. ServerA performs an originating update and assigns a USN number of 10 to the update. ServerA stores the following information as metadata with the change (see Figure 8.5):

   ➤ Updated password

   ➤ GUID of the server that performed the original update (serverA)

   ➤ Local USN number assigned to the change (USN 10)

   ➤ USN assigned by the originating update server (USN 10)

2. ServerA then sends a change notification to serverB.

3. ServerB responds with an update request that includes the last known originating USN number that it received from serverA.

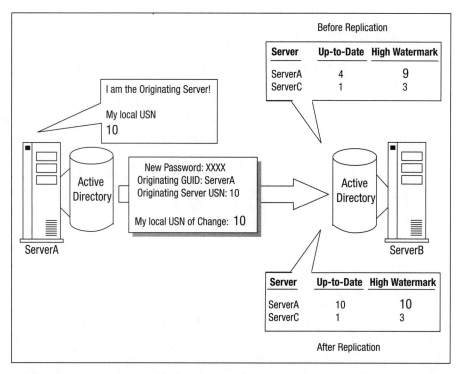

Figure 8.5   Up-to-date vector.

4. ServerB sees that serverA's USN number is now 10.

5. Server B performs a replicated update and changes the up-to-date vector for serverA to 10.

Because serverB's up-to-date vector for serverA is 10 and serverA's local USN is 10, you know that the directories on both servers are consistent. If serverB's local USN were 4 before replication took place, then serverB would increment its own local USN to 5.

High Watermark Vector

Each Windows 2000 domain controller maintains its own USN number, which is known as the *local USN*. All domain controllers are aware of all other domain controllers' local USN numbers. The highest USN replicated from each domain controller is recorded as the *high watermark* for the server.

The USN is incremented each time an object attribute is added or changed in the directory database regardless of whether it is an originating or replicated update. The USN is stored as metadata with the changed or added attribute. Any time an object's attributes are changed, the USN is incremented, and the USN is also stored as that object's usnChanged parameter. Each time an object's attribute is changed, the object's usnChanged parameter also is changed to match the USN. This allows a requesting domain controller to request any usnChanged values that are higher than the high watermark recorded for the domain controller. The USN identifies how many changes have been made, and the usnChanged identifies what object was changed for each USN.

Returning to the previous example, serverB performed a replicated update from the originating update performed on serverA. Because serverB replicated with serverA, serverB will change the high watermark for serverA to 10. The entry for serverA in serverB's table will contain a high watermark and up-to-date vector of 10. Remember that the high watermark represents the highest USN received from each server, and the up-to-date vector is the highest USN received from any originating server. Because serverB replicated with the originating server (serverA), the high watermark and up-to-date vector are the same.

Now, let's suppose that serverB replicates to serverC. ServerC's high watermark entry for serverB is 4; however, serverB's local USN is 5. ServerB will now send the following information to serverC (see Figure 8.6):

➤ Updated password

➤ GUID of the server that performed the originating update (serverA)

➤ Local USN of the update on the password attribute (USN 5)

➤ The USN of the server that performed the original update (USN 10)

8

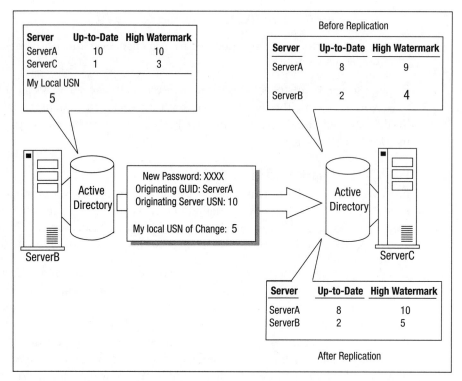

Figure 8.6 Transitive replication.

ServerC can now see that serverB received the information from serverA, because the update contains the GUID of serverA. Furthermore, serverC now knows that serverA's local USN is 10. ServerC will update its high watermark for serverB to 5 and the high watermark for serverA to 10. Because serverC did not receive the update from serverA, serverC will not increment its up-to-date vector for serverA to 10. Only its high watermark will be incremented to 10.

Now, suppose serverA sends serverC a change notification. ServerC will request the update by sending serverA its own current vectors in the update request. ServerA will see that serverC has a high watermark entry (for serverA) of 10 that matches serverA's local USN, and therefore serverA will not send the replicated information to serverC.

Because changes can be made at any domain controller, there is the possibility that changes could be made to the same object attribute on different domain controllers. If an object attribute is changed on serverA and the same attribute is changed on serverB before it has had a chance to replicate with serverA, there will be a replication conflict.

Replication Conflicts

Another issue associated with a multi-master directory service is that changes can be made at any location to any attribute at the same time. When more than one change is made to the same attribute before replication of one of the changes can be propagated throughout the domain, a collision is created. Both changes cannot be made at the same time. This was not a problem with Windows NT 4 because there was only one directory database that would accept changes, the PDC. As you have already learned, only changes to an object or attribute, not the entire object, are replicated. Different attributes of the same object can be changed at the same time without creating a collision of replication traffic. So, one administrator can change a user's password and at the same time another administrator can change the user's phone number without causing any problems.

Resolving Conflicts

8

Every change made to a directory database is stored with information regarding the change. This information describing the change is called *metadata*. Part of the metadata stored for a change to a directory includes a timestamp and the version number of the attribute that was changed. The timestamp and version number metadata are used to prevent and resolve replication conflicts.

Version Numbers and Timestamps

When an attribute is created for an object, the attribute is initialized with a version number. The version number is unique within the forest and is never duplicated. The attribute number is the same regardless of which domain controller you use to view the attribute. Do not confuse this with USN numbers, which are different for each domain controller.

Timestamps, as the name implies, simply specify the time that an update was made to an attribute.

Detecting Collisions

Collisions are created whenever a domain controller receives a replicated update and either of the following occurs:

➤ *The attribute's current version number is equal to the replicated attribute's version number.* In cases where the version numbers are the same yet the values are different, timestamps are used to resolve the conflict. If the version numbers are not the same, then the attribute with the highest version number is used.

➤ *The version number and the timestamp are the same.* When version numbers and timestamps are the same on domain controllers that are sending updates, the update coming from the server with the highest GUID is used.

THE REPLICATION MODEL

The Active Directory replication model manages many events by using different processes for each event. Events that are managed include:

➤ Replicating from partition to partition

➤ Tolerating the effects of replication delay

➤ Allowing concurrent updates of mission-critical items to more than one domain controller

➤ Counteracting the effects of slow network performance as a result of replication traffic

Before designing your enterprise-wide Active Directory strategy, you should be aware of the aforementioned issues and how you can design a directory to resolve these issues. Each of these issues revolve around the process and time it takes for a change made to one replica to traverse the network to all domain controllers. The time and process of replicating a change to all domain controllers is called *replication propagation*.

Replication Propagation

Changes made to the directory database are replicated from one controller to the next until all domain controllers are updated. In large network environments with low-speed wide-area network (WAN) links, this process can take a considerable amount of time. *Latency* and *convergence* are terms used to describe the replicated state of all domain controllers and the amount of time is takes for this replication to occur.

Latency

The Active Directory is a distributed system in which any directory database can change at any time. Changes to any database must be replicated to all other databases. Propagation of changes throughout an enterprise takes time. The time it takes for changes to replicate to all directories is called *latency*. The term *high latency* is used to describe a network in which changes to the Active Directory take a long time to replicate to all domain controllers.

Convergence

Convergence describes an environment in which replication has taken place and all domain controllers have an exact replica of the directory database. At any point in time, however, each domain controller might have a different replica of the database than all other servers. The term used to describe an environment in which all changes have not yet converged is *loose consistency*. That is, each directory is loosely consistent with all other directories in the domain or forest.

Understanding Replication Partitions

The Active Directory is made up of many parts that are concerned with different functions of the server and the network. Different partitions of the directory are replicated in unique ways, while some of the partitions follow the replication path of other partitions. Some partitions are replicated only within the local domain, while others are replicated throughout the entire forest.

The directory is made up of three major partitions—the domain partition, the configuration partition, and the schema partition. The domain partition can be used to create a fourth partition, the partial domain directory partition, for replication to Global Catalog Servers.

Domain Partition

The *domain partition* contains information that is specific to the domain only. Objects that are part of the domain partition include groups, users, Organizational Units, and computers, to name just a few. Any objects that reside within or are part of a domain are members of the domain partition. The domain partition is replicated to all domain controllers within the domain.

Partial Domain Directory Partition

The *partial domain directory partition* contains a partial copy of the domain partition. The partial domain directory contains a list of all objects in the directory but only a limited number of attributes for each object.

Global Catalog Servers use the partial domain directory partition. The partial domain directory is replicated to all Global Catalog Servers within a forest. So, each Global Catalog Server contains a partial domain directory for every domain in the forest and a full replica copy of its local domain partition. Replication of the Global Catalog's partial directory follows the same replication topology as the domain partition within the domain; however, each Global Catalog Server can act as a replication partner for other catalog servers outside the local domain.

Configuration Partition

The *configuration partition* stores forest-wide information that includes specifying which domains are a part of the forest as well as which sites each domain is a member of. The configuration partition is replicated to all domain controllers within the forest.

Schema Partition

The *schema* is like a data dictionary file. It contains information (metadata) that describes what can be created, the rules for creation, and the actions that can be performed on all objects that make up the Active Directory. Schema information must remain constant throughout the entire forest. For example, you can modify the schema to add a new field to the user object, such as a nickname field. If the information is not consistent throughout the forest, then replication of the nickname attribute will fail, because the nickname field will not be a part of the user object in domains with independent schemas.

The schema and configuration partitions are known as *enterprise partitions*, because both are replicated to all domains within the forest. Each domain controller has the same schema and configuration information as all other domain controllers in the forest.

Operation Master Replication

Although Active Directory uses a multi-master directory service, some of the directory information must be contained and controlled by only one server. The reason why only one server controls some tasks is because critical parts of the directory must always remain the same at all times and must never be different in separate directories. Servers that perform these roles are called *operation masters*. The operation master's roles are:

➤ Primary Domain Controller Emulator

➤ Domain Operations Master

➤ Relative Identifier Operations Master

➤ Infrastructure Operations Master

➤ Schema Operations Master

Tip: For more information on operation masters, see Chapter 7.

Replication Topology

The *replication topology* is the path that replicated data travels through an enterprise. As mentioned earlier in this chapter, three directory partitions are replicated—schema, configuration, and domain. Domain controllers can replicate different partitions with different replication partners. For example, serverA could replicate the configuration partition with serverB and serverC; however, serverA might replicate the schema partition with yet another server. Replication between servers takes place through the use of *connection objects*.

Connection Objects

A connection object is a potential replication path between one domain controller and a direct replication partner. When a connection object exists connecting one domain controller with another domain controller, the domain controllers become potential replication partners. Connection objects are unidirectional, meaning that data is replicated only in one direction across a connection object. Each server maintains its own connection objects in Active Directory Sites and Services. Two types of replication partners are available—direct partners and transitive partners. Direct replication and transitive replication takes place as follows:

Note: Connection objects can be viewed using the Active Directory Sites and Services Administrative Tool in the NTDS object (see Figure 8.7).

➤ *Direct replication*—Occurs when partners are domain controllers that represent a direct source for replicated data. Direct replication means that changes to the local Active Directory of a server are replicated to any direct partners. The Active Directory examines all connection objects and uses a process known as the *Knowledge Consistency Checker* (KCC) to determine whether a domain controller will become a direct replication partner.

➤ *Transitive replication*—Defines replication data that is gathered from a secondhand source. For example, if data is replicated from serverA to serverB and serverB replicates the information to serverC, then serverC and serverB are transitive replication partners. Transitive replication partners can be viewed using the Active Directory Replication Monitor utility, which is discussed in the upcoming section, "Replication Traffic." Connection objects are established between domain controllers, not the directory partitions; therefore, replication of each directory partition can use the same connection object to replicate information.

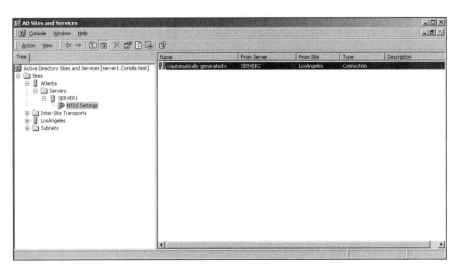

Figure 8.7   Active Directory Sites and Services.

Creating the Replication Topology

The replication topology within a site is created automatically, although the administrator can manually configure connection objects. If an administrator or network engineer wants to ensure that one server always replicates with another, then connection objects can be created within Active Directory Sites and Services. Automatic generation of connection objects will not be affected by manually creating additional connection objects. The KCC is the service that analyzes current information and automatically creates connection objects.

The KCC determines the best connections between servers based on information supplied by a network administrator. The administrator, using Active Directory Sites and Services, must provide information regarding sites, subnets, cost of sending data between the sites, and the network transport protocol to be used to send data between each site. If a replication or server failure occurs within a site that prevents the flow of information, the KCC attempts to modify the current topology in order to continue replication.

By default, the KCC creates a ring replication topology, as shown in Figure 8.8. Replication can travel in both directions around a ring topology. A ring is created so that there are an average of three or less hops between any two domain controllers.

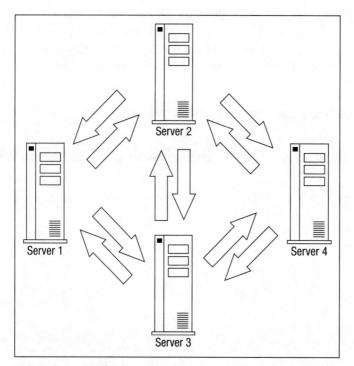

Figure 8.8 Replication topology.

After a change is made to a directory database, the replication engine waits five minutes to ensure that no more changes are being made to the directory. After the directory has remained stable for five minutes, the replication engine notifies the first replication partner that directory changes exist. Every 30 seconds, the originating server sends a change notification to one replication partner. The server sends only one change notification at a time to prevent being overwhelmed by replication requests. If no changes occur in any six-hour period, each domain controller will begin replication procedures to ensure that the domain controller has not missed any changes.

REPLICATION TRAFFIC

One of the few reasons an administrator might want to delete or create additional connection objects is to reroute or reduce replication traffic within a site. Using Performance Monitor, Replication Monitor, and Network Monitor, you can analyze and measure network replication traffic.

8

Performance Monitor

Performance Monitor can be used to monitor and measure traffic that is destined to or from a particular server. Common counters used by Performance Monitor to measure replication efficiency include:

➤ *DRA Inbound Bytes Not Compressed*—Specifies the number of replicated bytes received that were not compressed. Noncompressed bytes usually indicate that the bytes originated from a Directory Services Agent within the same site (intrasite replication).

➤ *DRA Inbound Bytes Compressed (Before Compression)*—Identifies the number of replicated bytes received that were compressed. The true number of bytes is recorded, meaning that the bytes are measured after decompression.

➤ *DRA Inbound Bytes Compressed (After Compression)*—Specifies the number of replicated bytes received that were compressed. The number of compressed bytes is recorded or measured.

➤ *DRA Inbound Bytes Total*—Specifies the number of replicated bytes received that were compressed (after compression) and the number of noncompressed bytes (never compressed).

➤ *DRA Outbound Bytes Not Compressed*—Identifies the amount of replicated data (in bytes) sent out that were not compressed. If data is sent out not compressed, it usually means that the Directory Service Agent destination is within the local site. Replication data sent between sites is compressed.

Replication Monitor

The Replication Monitor is used to analyze the replication topology within a site. Replication Monitor is included in the Windows 2000 Resource Kit. You can perform the following tasks using Replication Monitor:

➤ Display objects within a domain controller's directory that have not yet been replicated.

➤ Force replication between two particular domain controllers.

➤ Monitor and log the current replicated state and current statistics. The time intervals that Replication Monitor uses to poll each server can be configured by an administrator.

➤ List the USN numbers of attributes, reasons for failed replication attempts, and flags used between two direct replication partners.

➤ Display a domain controller's direct and transitive replication partners.

➤ Configure replication failure thresholds. Send mail and/or write to the event logs if those thresholds are broken.

Network Monitor

You can use Network Monitor to capture and isolate replication packets as they travel between one domain controller and another. Active Directory supports two transport mechanisms that can be used for replication—Simple Mail Transfer Protocol (SMTP) and Remote Procedure Calls (RPC).

SMTP traffic is easily isolated, because SMTP always uses TCP port 25 for communication. Once Network Monitor is capturing packets, you can force replication using Active Directory Sites and Services. After you receive a message that replication has completed, stop the capture and then apply a filter to show only packets destined for port 25. By filtering on TCP port 25, you eliminate any traffic that was captured other than replication traffic. The SMTP protocol is used only for replication among sites, not intrasite.

Filtering captured RPC replication is a bit more difficult. Replication using RPC always uses dynamic port assignment for security purposes. Because there is no static port to filter on, isolating RPC replication traffic is almost impossible without modifying the Windows 2000 registry.

One way to isolate RPC communication is to configure RPC communication traffic to use a static port number. By adding the following key to the registry, you can force RPC replication to use a specific TCP port number, and you can then configure filtering on the TCP port number to isolate RPC replication traffic:

```
HKEY_LOCAL_MACHINE\System\CurrentControlSet\Services\NTDS\Parameteres\
TCP/IP Port
```

By adding the preceding key and setting the key to a value such as 1350, you can filter your captured data. Any unused port number will work, but you should ensure that you do not configure replication to occur on any used port number.

The amount of replication taking place between domain controllers on the local network is usually not as much of a concern as the amount of replication traffic traveling over expensive WAN links. Domain controllers that are connected only by WAN technologies should normally be configured to reside in separate sites. Administrators and network engineers have more control over the amount of time replication occurs between sites.

REPLICATION AMONG SITES

In order to maintain a consistent directory throughout an enterprise, replication must constantly take place between domain controllers. Replication should be automatic between domain controllers where there is no bandwidth restrictions, such as in a local area network (LAN); however, replication across WAN connections needs to be controlled as well. Replication between domain controllers that are connected with slower and more expensive WAN links is controlled through the use of Active Directory sites. Separate sites are connected together with logical connections called site links. Site links represent paths for replication traffic.

Sites

Sites consist of one or more TCP/IP subnets and are completely independent of the domain structure. A single site can contain multiple domains, a single domain, or only part of one or more domains. For example, a company might have a network consisting of one domain yet still have offices in Atlanta and Los Angeles. The network administrator can define two sites—one in Atlanta and another in LA—and add the subnet of each location to the associated site. Because the sites represent connection boundaries between domain controllers, replication between sites must be configured manually.

In general, sites are used to:

➤ *Control replication traffic*—How and when changes are replicated between domain controllers in separate sites can be controlled.

➤ *Control authentication*—When a user attempts to log onto the domain, the client (Windows NT/Windows 2000) attempts to find a domain controller within the site first.

➤ *Control and house the Distributed File System (Dfs)*—Dfs is discussed in Chapter 13.

Sites are not tied to the Active Directory namespace or domain layout in any way. Sites represent the physical structure of the network, and the namespace, domain, and OUs represent the logical structure. Each site is a collection of domain controllers that reside within one or more subnets. Two types of replication apply to sites—intrasite and intersite—as illustrated in Figure 8.9.

Intrasite Replication

Domain controllers within the same site should have constant high-speed connections to the network (such as a LAN). Replication between domain controllers in the same site is known as intrasite replication. Directory replication within a site is focused on reducing latency and CPU load, and depends on high-speed connections. The replication topology within a site forms a ring topology and is automatically generated by the KCC. Connection objects (as viewed from Active Directory Sites and Services) that list IP as the transport protocol use RPC communications. Intrasite replication uses RPC communication as well as the file replication service (FRS).

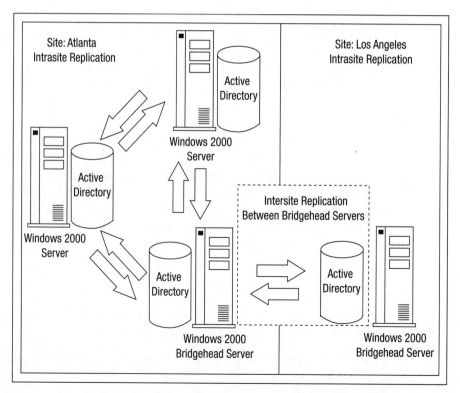

Figure 8.9 Intrasite and intersite replication.

Intersite Replication

Replication that takes place between domain controllers in separated sites is known as intersite replication. Replication between sites focuses on reducing network load. Domain controllers separated by slow WAN connections should be placed in separate sites. Because the connections between LANs are expensive and slow, replication between sites can be configured to take place during slower network periods. Replication between sites must be manually configured. Connection objects (as viewed from Active Directory Sites and Services) that list IP as the transport protocol use RPC communications.

Site Links

A site link represents a connection between two or more sites that is used for replication traffic. Within Active Directory Sites and Services, one site link, named DEFAULTIPSITELINK, is configured during setup. The administrator must manually create additional site links if needed. Any time an additional site is added to the directory, the administrator must specify which site link the site will use. To create a site link, the administrator must specify which sites are going to be connected, during what times those sites will be allowed to be replicated, the cost associated with the site link, and the transport mechanism that will be used for replication over the site link (see Figure 8.10).

Member Sites

Member sites list sites that will be connected with the site link. Every site requires at least one site link in order to replicate outside the site. Furthermore, a network connection must be in place in order to create a site link. Each site

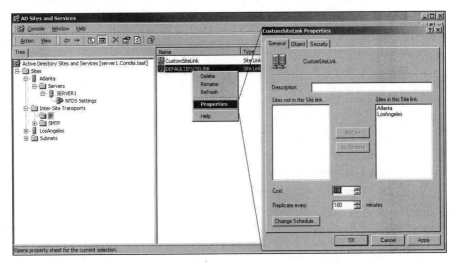

Figure 8.10   Site link properties.

in the enterprise must contain at least one site link connecting it with another site. Without a site link configured, a site's domain controllers will be unable to replicate with any domain controllers outside their local site.

Schedule

A *schedule* specifies the times that replication should take place over a site link. For overly expensive or slow network connections, replication should be configured when network utilization is at its lowest—at night, for example.

Cost

Cost is assigned by an administrator and can be used to prioritize which links get used over others. The higher the cost, the lower the priority is on a site link. If more than one site link connects any two or more sites, the link with the lowest cost will be used. An administrator might wish to create multiple site links to provide fault tolerance.

Transport

When creating a site link, the administrator must specify which *transport mechanism* will be used to carry the data. The administrator can specify whether to use RPC or SMTP as the transport method for replicated data:

➤ SMTP transport mechanisms send email messages between each site to perform replication. The SMTP transport supports schema and global catalog replication; however, SMTP cannot be used for replication between domain controllers in the same site. SMTP replication is known as *asynchronous* replication.

➤ The RPC transport will appear as the IP transport within Active Directory sites and services. RPC communications typically require large amounts of bandwidth and therefore should be used only between domain controllers within the same site or sites connected with high-speed connections. Some intrasite replication requires the use of the file replication service. Because the file replication service does not support asynchronous transport mechanisms, RPC is required.

Bridgehead Servers

In a multisite enterprise network, one server at each site must act as a *bridgehead server*. A bridgehead server is a domain controller linked to another domain controller from a remote site that is configured to receive replicated data from the remote site. A bridgehead server can participate in replication with more than one other site. Because the longest theoretical replication time is 15 minutes, each bridgehead server should receive any changes in its local site within 15 minutes.

After the bridgehead server receives an update, it replicates the data with the remote site's bridgehead server. After the remote bridgehead server receives the update, it can take as long as 15 minutes again for the entire remote site to receive the update. Therefore, the maximum amount of time it should take for data to converge completely between two joined sites is 30 minutes.

CHAPTER SUMMARY

Windows 2000 domain controllers all participate in a multi-master directory structure where each domain controller maintains its own replica of the directory database. Because a domain controller can make changes to its own replica, there has to be some mechanism to ensure that each domain controller can send those changes to all other domain controller database replicas. Windows 2000 provides this mechanism in a network service called *replication*, the topic discussed in this chapter. The replication service ensures that changes made to any replica of the database are also propagated to all other replicas in the domain, tree, and forest.

8

Replication between domain controllers is accomplished through the use of universal sequence numbers (USN) that are used to identify changes to the local replica of the database. Each domain controller maintains its own USN numbers and tracks the local USN numbers of each replication partner. Replication conflicts occur when the same attribute of the same object is changed on separate database replicas.

Replication conflicts are resolved using timestamp information. A timestamp is placed on all changes to the directory database. Timestamps are not used for normal replication, but they are used to resolve replication conflicts. When a conflict occurs, the change with the latest timestamp is applied to the replica and the conflicting change is discarded.

This chapter also discussed how propagation dampening prevents data from being replicated to domain controllers that have a current replica of the Active Directory. The high watermark vector is used to discover the current replicated state of a domain controller.

Sites are a collection of one or more TCP/IP subnets connected with high-speed inexpensive network connections. Sites are used to control replication traffic between domain controllers that reside in separate sites and to control login traffic. This chapter concluded by discussing replication traffic between sites and the use of site links. Site links are connection objects used to connect sites for the transport of replication traffic.

REVIEW QUESTIONS

1. Each Windows 2000 domain controller contains a _____ copy of the Active Directory database.

    a. Read-only

    b. Compressed

    c. Working copy

    d. Archived

2. Which utility ensures that all directory databases receive any changes to any replicas?

    a. Synchronization

    b. Replication

    c. Administrative process

    d. File replication service

3. Domain controllers in Windows 2000 are organized in a _____ type of relationship?

    a. Single master

    b. Complete trust

    c. Cooperative

    d. Multi-master

4. Changing a user's password will not cause replication to occur.

    a. True

    b. False

5. When the properties of an object change, the object must be replicated to all domain controllers.

    a. True

    b. False

6. What does the acronym USN represent?

    a. Universal serial number

    b. User security number

    c. Universal sequence number

    d. Update sequence number

7. What controls USNs?

   a. The RID single operations master

   b. The first domain controller in the root domain

   c. Each domain controller maintains its own USN

   d. The Global Catalog Server in each domain

8. How are timestamps used in Active Directory replication?

   a. Break replication ties

   b. Standard replication method

   c. Timestamps are never used in replication

   d. Synchronize time between domain controllers

9. When a change is made to an object of the directory, the attribute of that object as well as the USN for that change are stored simultaneously. The simultaneous storing of this information is referred to as a(n) _____.

   a. Dependent operation

   b. Atomic operation

   c. Circular logging operation

   d. Inclusive operation

8

10. Which of the following replication properties eliminates the need for all domain controllers to have their time synchronized perfectly?

    a. Timestamps

    b. Global time master

    c. Local time network service

    d. USN

11. What process must a repaired domain controller perform to receive changes to the directory?

    a. The repaired domain controller must copy the entire directory from the schema operations master.

    b. The repaired domain controller must copy the entire directory from the forest root domain controller.

    c. The Global Catalog Server must copy any directory changes to the repaired domain controller.

    d. The repaired domain controller must request all USNs greater than the last USN it received from all replication partners.

12. Identify the two types of directory updates supported by Windows 2000. [Check all correct answers]

   a. Originating

   b. Primary

   c. Secondary

   d. Replicated

13. Changing the name of an object or moving an object to another container is described as what type of change?

   a. Add

   b. Modify

   c. ModifyDN

   d. Move/Rename

14. A change is made to a user object on serverA. The change is written to serverA's replica and then replicated to serverB. ServerB performs what type of update?

   a. Replicated

   b. USN

   c. ModifyDN

   d. Originating

15. A change is made to a user object on serverA. The change is written to serverA's replica and then replicated to serverB. ServerA performs what type of update?

   a. Replicated

   b. Primary

   c. Modify

   d. Originating

16. Which of the following causes a replicated update to be performed?

   a. ModifyDN

   b. Server failure

   c. Originating update

   d. Replication conflict

17. An originating update attaches a _____ to the new or changed data.

    a. Stamp

    b. GUID

    c. RID

    d. Schema modifier

18. What is propagation dampening used for?

    a. Reduce replication traffic

    b. Eliminate redundant replication traffic

    c. Speed replication traffic

    d. Speed propagation

19. How do the Active Directory and KCC attempt to provide fault tolerance for replication?

    a. Using USN numbers for replication

    b. Creating a looped or fully meshed replication topology

    c. Using timestamps for conflicts

    d. Maintaining high watermark vectors

20. To allow propagation dampening, what does each domain controller store?

    a. Their own USN table and vectors

    b. Only their replication partner's GUID

    c. Every local domain controller's GUID

    d. The GUID and USN for each directory replica

21. The up-to-date vector contains the GUID and which of the following?

    a. USN of the replicated update

    b. Lowest USN of the originating update

    c. Originating server's highest local USN number

    d. Originating server's highest universal USN number

22. Which of the following is not an example of metadata stored as part of a change?

    a. Domain in which the change occurred

    b. GUID of the server that performed the original update

    c. Local USN number assigned to the change

    d. Changed data

8

23. What does the high watermark vector contain?

    a. Last USN replicated to another server

    b. Highest USN replicated from any server

    c. Highest USN for an originating update from all servers

    d. Highest USN for an originating update from each server

24. The up-to-date vector gets incremented only when _____.

    a. Replication occurs with the originating server

    b. Replication occurs with a server other than the originating server

    c. The local server performs the originating update

    d. Replication occurs with another domain controller

25. What is the usnChanged parameter?

    a. The last USN received from a replication partner

    b. The highest USN number for any object

    c. The highest USN number assigned to each attribute of an object

    d. A Boolean property that identifies whether an object's attributes have been changed

REAL-WORLD PROJECTS

*Note: The domain controller (server2) from the Real-World Projects in Chapter 7 can be removed and reinstalled for use in this chapter's projects. Server2 should be installed as a member server initially. The first project in this section provides the steps necessary to promote the server to a domain controller in the **coriolis.test** domain.*

Additionally, to complete the upcoming tasks, you need to configure the servers with the IP addresses listed in Tables 8.1 and 8.2. Both servers will be in the same subnet (192.168.0.0); however, the subnet will be split into two subnets (192.168.1.0 and 192.168.2.0) within Active Directory Sites and Services. In order to create two sites, Active Directory Sites and Services requires each site to be a unique subnet. Configuring each server to belong to the same subnet, yet configuring Active Directory Sites and Services to split the subnets, enables you to create logical subnets and perform the following projects without the use of a router.

Today, Andy Palmer must install a domain controller as a member of the **coriolis.test** domain. The new server will be a member of a new site named LosAngeles.

Once the server is installed and connection to the network has been verified, Andy must promote server2 to a domain controller by installing the Active Directory. Active Directory is installed with the Dcpromo.exe application.

Table 8.1   Server2 installation and configuration properties.

Name	Server2
IP address	192.168.2.10
Subnet mask	255.255.0.0
DNS	IP address of server1 (192.168.1.10)
Domain	coriolis.test

Table 8.2   Server1 configuration properties.

Name	Server1	
IP address	192.168.1.10	
Subnet mask	255.255.0.0DNS	192.168.1.10

Tip: Dcpromo.exe can also be used to demote a domain controller to a member server by removing the Active Directory.

8

Project 8.1

To install Active Directory on server2, complete the following steps:

1. Click Start|Run.

2. Type "dcpromo.exe" in the Run dialog box, and click OK.

3. Click Next.

4. Select Additional Domain Controller For An Existing Domain.

5. Click Next.

6. Enter "Administrator" in the username field, enter the Administrator password (for server1), and enter "coriolis" as the domain name.

7. Click Next.

8. Enter "coriolis.test" as the full DNS name of the domain.

9. Click Next.

10. Retain the default database and log locations, and click Next.

11. Retain the default SYSVOL location, and click Next.

12. Leave the password text box blank, and click Next.

13. In the Summary dialog box, click Next.

14. Click Finish.

15. Click Restart Now.

The first site is automatically created when a computer is promoted to a domain controller and the site is named Default-First-Site. Andy wants to rename the Default-First-Site to something more descriptive.

Project 8.2
To rename a site, complete the following steps:

1. Open Active Directory Sites and Services.

2. Expand the Sites folder.

3. Right-click the Default-first-site, and select Rename.

4. Enter "Atlanta" as the new name.

5. Press Enter.

Andy must now create and configure the new site and site links.

Project 8.3
To create a new site, complete the following steps:

1. Open Active Directory Sites and Services.

2. Right-click the Sites folder, and select New Site.

3. Enter "LosAngeles" as the new site name.

4. Select DEFAULTIPSITELINK.

5. Click OK twice to close the dialog boxes.

Project 8.4
To create and assign a subnet to a site, complete the following steps:

1. Open Active Directory Sites and Services.

2. Expand the Sites folder.

3. Right-click the Subnets folder.

4. Click New|Subnet.

5. Enter the IP address "192.168.1.10".

6. Enter "255.255.255.0" as the subnet mask.

7. Select the Atlanta site.

8. Click OK.

9. Right-click the Subnets folder.

10. Click New|Subnet.

11. Enter the IP address "192.168.2.10".

12. Enter "255.255.255.0" as the subnet mask.

13. Select the LosAngeles site.

14. Click OK.

Project 8.5

To move a server to a new site, complete the following steps:

1. Open Active Directory Sites and Services.

2. Expand the Sites folder.

3. Expand the Atlanta site.

4. Expand the Servers folder.

5. Right-click Server2, and click Move.

6. Select the LosAngeles site, and click OK.

Note: *Depending on the order in which each project is completed, server2 may already be listed in the LosAngeles site. If this is the case, you can move server2 to the Atlanta site and then back to the LosAngeles site.*

Project 8.6

To create a connection object, complete the following steps:

1. Open Active Directories Sites and Services.

2. Expand the Sites folder.

3. Expand the LosAngeles site.

4. Expand the Server folder.

5. Expand the server2 object.

6. Click the NTDS settings object. A connection object should not be located in the display panel.

7. Right-click NTDS settings.

8. Select New Active Directory Connection.

9. Select server1, and click OK.

10. View the new connection object in the display panel.

11. Verify that the configuration in Active Directory Sites and Services is the same as the one in Figure 8.11, which shows the completed project.

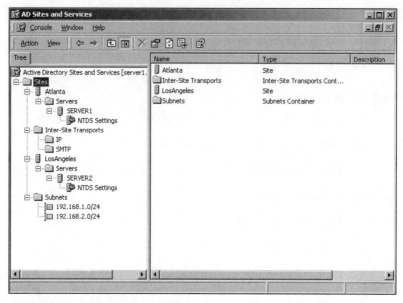

Figure 8.11 The completed project.

Project 8.7
To force replication, complete the following steps:

1. On server1, open Active Directory Users and Computers.

2. Right-click coriolis.test, and select New|Organizational Unit.

3. Type the name "RepTest" as the new Organizational Unit.

4. Click OK.

5. Right-click the RepTest Organizational Unit, and select New|User.

6. Enter the appropriate information to create a new user.

7. Close Active Directory Users and Computers.

8. Open Active Directory Sites and Services.

9. Expand the Sites folder.

10. Expand the Atlanta site.

11. Expand the server1 Object.

12. Select the NTDS settings object.

13. In the display panel, right-click the Automatically Generated Connection Object. and select Replicate Now.

14. Click OK in the Replicate Now dialog box.

15. From server2, open Active Directory Users and Computers.

16. Notice that the RepTest and User object has been replicated to server2 from server1. You might have to wait up to 15 minutes for replication to occur. If the RepTest Organizational Unit is not present, close Active Directory Users and Computers, wait a few minutes, and reopen Active Directory Users and Computers on server2.

8

CHAPTER NINE

THE ACTIVE DIRECTORY SCHEMA

After completing this chapter, you will be able to:

✓ Describe the Active Directory schema

✓ Locate the schema container and related files

✓ Define the schema objects and their functions

✓ Define the schema cache's purpose and function

✓ Describe the security of the Active Directory objects

✓ Extend the schema to accommodate organizational needs

✓ Deactivate unused administrator-created schema objects

✓ Describe some of the issues involved with extending the schema

T he Active Directory is a highly complex combination of data and related code. The *schema* helps control the Active Directory while maintaining the scalability and extensibility necessary for an enterprise directory service. The schema can be thought of as a set of rules. As discussed later in this chapter, the schema classes dictate the types of objects the schema can hold, and the schema attributes dictate the details of each class.

The schema contains objects, much like the directory. In fact, every object in the directory is created as an instance of a schema object called a *class*. Essentially, a class defines an object, the data that can describe an object, and the actions that can be performed on an object. A user is an example of a class. The data an object contains is called the object's *attributes*. Different types of attributes exist for different types of objects. For a user class object, a telephone number is a common attribute. In addition, a class can have the same attributes as another class. In this case, the original class is called the *superclass* because it was used as the basis for the new class, and the new class is called a *subclass*. A subclass inherits all the attributes from its superclass. For instance, if a firm routinely uses contract employees, a subclass, contractUser, could be created from the superclass user. Then a new attribute, contractAgency, could be added to the class contractUser. As a result, the agency for whom a contract employee works could be quickly determined by looking at the properties of the contract employee's user account. The set of inherited attributes can be extended in the subclass that has more attributes after inheritance without affecting the original class.

The schema keeps track of the attributes associated with a class. Classes have mandatory attributes and optional attributes. The schema defines the syntax, or valid data types, for attributes. With these fundamental pieces in place, the schema can support a basic enterprise directory.

The schema provides not only the classes for the Active Directory, but also the relationships that can exist between objects based on the classes. For instance, an Organizational Unit (OU) is a container that can contain other objects, like users and computers. A user and a computer are both leaf objects, however, which means they cannot contain other objects. The attributes of a user could be items such as display name, department, and telephone number. The telephone number would have a syntax of 19 alphanumeric characters. This means that a user with the display name Andy Palmer could have a telephone number like (555) 555-5555, ext 555. Furthermore, his department could be Information Technology, and he could be a member of the OU IT.

Windows 2000 is shipped with a default schema with all the classes needed to set up a Windows 2000 network. The default schema is represented in the Active Directory as a number of schema objects. For each class, a **classSchema** object displays in the directory. Similarly, each attribute has an

attributeSchema object. Administrators, drivers, and applications can refer to the directory for the list of classes and attributes that can be used in the network. The schema's design is extensible, so new classes and attributes can be created to accommodate the needs of any network environment.

The schema is a crucial piece of the Active Directory. It maintains the list of classes and their attributes that makes the Active Directory a stable, scalable directory service for networks of any size. To help familiarize you with the schema, this chapter discusses some of the schema's key points (including its location and contents) and describes how you can customize the schema.

THE SCHEMA'S LOCATION

As mentioned, the schema is part of the Active Directory. The Active Directory stores its objects in the *Directory Information Tree* (DIT). The base DIT contains enough information to get Windows 2000 up and running, and it is automatically installed with the first Windows 2000 domain controller in the forest. Part of this base DIT is the base schema.

The DIT is broken into directory partitions that can be discretely replicated. One of the directory partitions is the *schema partition*, and at the top of the schema partition is a special container called the *schema container*. The schema container is located at **cn=schema,cn=configuration,dc=forest root <domain name>**, and it contains all the class and attribute information necessary to locate directory objects. Although the schema partition appears to be part of the **configuration** partition, the **schema** partition is kept separately to ensure the latter's integrity.

You can view the schema container using either of the following two tools:

➤ Active Directory Schema console in the Microsoft Management Console (MMC)

➤ Active Directory Services Interface (ADSI) Edit utility in the Support Tools directory on the Windows 2000 Server CD-ROM

A schema can be referred to by its distinguished name, using the following syntax:

```
cn=schema,cn=configuration,dc=forest root <domain name>
```

You don't need to know a schema's domain name to view the schema, however. Instead, you can access the special entry at the top of the Lightweight Directory Access Protocol (LDAP) search tree named the **RootDSE**. The attributes of the **RootDSE** that identify the domain, schema, forest root, and configuration partitions in the DIT are used by scripts and applications to navigate the directory. One attribute in particular—**schemaNamingContext**—directs a query to the location of the schema.

. . . .

Tip: By using the **RootDSE** in scripts and applications, rather than a schema's distinguished name, the scripts and applications remain portable.

. . . .

Another important attribute in the **RootDSE** is the **subSchemaSubEntry** attribute. The **subSchemaSubEntry** attribute contains the location of the sub-schema, which contains all the attributes and classes in the Active Directory schema. This is a convenient location for client applications to connect to by using the following distinguished name syntax:

```
cn=aggregate,cn=schema,cn=configuration,dc=<domain name>,
dc=<domain root>
```

The actual files that contain the schema data are distributed to each domain controller. Therefore, no single domain controller has all the directory data, although every domain controller holds a complete copy of the schema. The directory data and the schema data are kept on the domain controller in a file named *Ntds.dit*. In addition, the *schema.ini* file contains the information necessary to create and populate the default directory and control security for the schema. Both these files together are called the *directory database*, and they are stored along with the directory database logs in the <systemroot>\ Ntds directory.

THE SCHEMA'S CONTENTS

The schema container is an object instantiated from the **directory Management Domain (dMD)** class. (The dMD is a class that represents a schema container.) Schema classes and attributes are stored as schema objects in the schema container. These objects are aptly called the **attributeSchema** and **classSchema** objects.

The **attributeSchema** Object

All attributes in the schema are derived from the **attributeSchema** object. As previously mentioned, attributes define classes. Because attributes are stored separately from classes, there can be a one-to-many or many-to-one relationship between attributes and classes. Attributes have specific pieces of information in common. To ensure that each attribute is unique and accessible, the LDAP display name, object identifier, and GUID are specified for each attribute object. The syntax and range for the attribute provide data validation.

Attributes can contain a single value or multiple values. Table 9.1 lists the attributes that are mandatory for all **attributeSchema** objects.

Notice in the table that the **attributeSchema** has a bit named **isSingleValued**. Turning off **isSingleValued** allows multiple values for an attribute. Though multiple values can be configured, they all must follow the correct syntax and range for the attribute. Multiple values are stored in no particular order, so there is no method to control the retrieval order for these values. The LDAP supports only retrieval of a single value for an attribute, which means that the retrieval of multiple values is actually many single value retrievals. This adds a great amount of overhead to transactions that attempt to retrieve multiple values. The Internet Engineering Task Force recognized the shortcomings of the LDAP multiple value retrieval process and devised a special control called *ranges* (not related to attribute syntax ranges) to assist with multiple value retrievals. By using a range, it is possible to retrieve multivalued attributes in increments rather than one at a time.

Attributes can be *indexed*, or sorted in a particular order. Indexing makes searching for the attribute of a particular record easier and less resource intensive than simply searching the attributes sequentially. A bit named **searchFlags** can be set to 1 to indicate that an attribute should be indexed. An index is automatically created when the **searchFlags** bit is turned on, and the index is deleted when the bit is turned off. The most gain can be found by indexing single value attributes that have nearly unique values. Keep in mind that, while indexing attributes speeds up searching a field, it also adds overhead to the creation or deletion of records because the index has to be rebuilt with each transaction.

Table 9.1 Mandatory attributes for all **attributeSchema** objects.

Attribute	Syntax	Description
cn	Unicode	Relative distinguished name for the attribute
attributeID	Object Identifier	Uniquely identifies the attribute
LDAPDisplayName	Unicode	Display name for LDAP directory
SchemaIDGUID	String	Globally Unique ID
attributeSyntax	Object Identifier	Syntax object identifier for the object
OMSyntax	Boolean	Syntax of object specified by the open object model
isSingleValued	Boolean	Identifies object as a single value or multivalue
ObjectClass	Object Identifier	Class for the object, always **attributeSchema**
NTSecurityDescriptor	NT Security DES	Security descriptor for the object

The **classSchema** Object

All classes in the Active Directory are derived from the **classSchema** object. This object controls the attributes for a class and the hierarchy of classes in the Directory Information Tree. The **classSchema** object is the mold from which all objects are made. This ensures that all objects of a particular class are standard. The **classSchema** object dictates the LDAP display name, object identifier, and GUID for a class, all of which combine to uniquely identify the class in the DIT. The **classSchema** object also specifies the mandatory and optional attributes for a class and any other classes from which it can inherit attributes. Table 9.2 lists the mandatory and system attributes for the **classSchema** objects. Finally, the **classSchema** identifies a class type.

Class Types

Classes can belong to one of four class types:

➤ *Structural classes*—The objects that populate the directory are structural type classes. Structural classes are based on other structural objects or an abstract object type. A structural class can also include many auxiliary type classes. A structural class has the **objectClassCategory** attribute set to 1.

➤ *Abstract classes*—Abstract classes do not actually exist as objects; instead, this type exists only to give attributes to structural classes. This means that a structural class is actually a subclass that holds all the attributes from one or more abstract classes. Given this relationship, abstract classes are like building blocks for structural classes. An abstract class has the **objectClassCategory** attribute set to 2.

➤ *Auxiliary classes*—Auxiliary classes exist only to provide structural classes with attributes, but they can also provide abstract classes with attributes. This makes auxiliary classes useful as the building blocks for other classes. The **objectClassCategory** attribute is set to 3 for an auxiliary class.

Table 9.2   Mandatory attributes for all **classSchema** objects.

Attribute	Syntax	Description
cn	Unicode	Relative distinguished name for the attribute
GovernsID	Object Identifier	Uniquely identifies the class
LDAPDisplayName	Unicode	Name LDAP uses to identify the object
SchemaIDGUID	String	GUID that uniquely identifies the class
SubClassOf	Object Identifier	Parent class of object
ObjectClassCategory	Integer	Class type for the object
ObjectClass	Object Identifier	Object's class, always **classSchema**
NTSecurityDescriptor	NT-Sec_Desc	Security descriptor for the object
DefaultObjectCategory	Distinguished Name	Default object category

➤ *Type 88 classes*—Type 88 classes are classes that do not have a type, because the 1988 X.500 standard did not require that classes be part of a class type. The X.500 standard that supports class types was not ratified until 1993. This means that objects created before 1993 were dubbed as type 88. For a type 88 class, the **objectClassCategory** bit is set to 0.

Inheritance

Inheritance, or derivation, is the process of creating new classes that contain the attributes from one or more existing classes. This process also creates a parent/child relationship between two classes. Another way to state this relationship is to say that the new class is a subclass and the original class is the superclass. Inherited information includes the mandatory and optional attributes as well as the parent object for the class. For example, if an attribute is added to a parent class, all related subclasses automatically inherit the attribute. This process of inheritance builds structural classes in the directory that relate to objects in the network environment.

Tip: Remember, when discussing inheritance, *Top* refers to the object at the top of every Directory Information Tree. All classes in the DIT are based on the Top, which is discussed in more detail later in this chapter.

9

The Directory System Agent

Windows 2000 protects the Active Directory schema by making some attributes *system only*, which means they can be changed only by the *directory system agent* (DSA). These system attributes usually have nonsystem counterparts that can be changed by administrators, who maintain the flexibility of the directory structure. Some of the system-only attributes include:

➤ *systemMustContain*—Specifies the mandatory attributes that are protected by the system. In contrast, the **mustContain** attribute lists the mandatory attributes that can be changed by administrators.

➤ *systemMayContain*—Specifies the optional attributes that are protected by the system. The **mayContain** attribute lists the optional attributes that can be changed by administrators.

➤ *systemPossSuperiors*—Identifies the parent classes that are protected by the system, whereas the **possSuperiors** are not protected by the system.

➤ *systemAuxiliaryClass*—Identifies the protected auxiliary classes that make up the class. Windows 2000 protects the attributes it needs to properly function. In contrast, the **auxiliaryClass** attribute is modifiable.

All objects in the Active Directory have certain mandatory attributes. If an attribute is left blank, the attribute will be filled in with a default value, or the object will not be created. The Top object provides certain mandatory attributes through inheritance.

Attribute Syntax

The syntax for an attribute dictates the type of data that it can contain. Syntaxes are not objects—rather, they are rules for objects. Syntaxes cannot be created, nor can they be deleted. Active Directory has a number of syntaxes built in, and these are the only allowable syntaxes. Every attribute must have a syntax, and creating a new attribute requires the definition of its syntax. Table 9.3 lists the allowable syntaxes along with the codes for the **attributeSyntax** and **oMSyntax** that must be provided when new attributes are created.

Object Identifiers

An object identifier is a string of numbers listed in dot notation, such as **1.2.840.113556.1.5.9**. Object identifiers allow objects to be identified in the directory, no matter how large the directory becomes. A number of authorities issue object identifiers, and each authority has its own ID to help ensure that all objects it creates have a unique ID. The International Standards Organization (ISO)

Table 9.3 Attribute syntaxes and related parameters.

Syntax	attributeSyntax	oMSyntax	Description
Undefined	2.5.5.0		Not a legal syntax
Object (DN-DN)	2.5.5.1	127	Fully qualified name of the object
String(object ID)	2.5.5.2	6	Object identifier
Case-sensitive string	2.5.5.3	27	General string
Case-ignore string	2.5.5.4	20	Teletex, no case
Printable string	2.5.5.5	19, 22	Printable string
Numeric string	2.5.5.6	18	Numeric string
Binary object	2.5.5.7	127	Distinguished name for object
Boolean	2.5.5.8	1	True or False
Integer, enum	2.5.5.9	2, 10	32-bit number or enumeration
Octet string	2.5.5.10	4	String of bytes
Time string	2.5.5.11	23, 24	UTC time
Unicode string	2.5.5.12	64	Unicode string
Presentation address	2.5.5.13	127	Presentation address
DN string object	2.5.5.14	127	Object address
NT-sec-desc	2.5.5.15	66	Win NT security descriptor
Large integer	2.5.5.16	65	64-bit integer
Security ID	2.5.5.17	4	Win NT SID

is the root authority, and it has the identifier "1." The ISO issued the identifier "2" to the American National Standards Institute (ANSI). ANSI dedicated the number "840" to the United States, which in turn issued Microsoft the number "113556." Microsoft assigned the number "1" to its Active Directory, the number "5" to the classes in the Active Directory, and the number "9" to the class User within the Active Directory. This means that the class User in the Active Directory has the object identifier listed previously: 1.2.840.113556.1.5.9.

The OSI model, X.500, SNMP, and many other applications use object identifiers. LDAP uses object identifiers to locate and find attributes of objects in the directory. The Active Directory is a mixture of X.500 objects and objects created by Microsoft Corporation. Autonomous systems, or standalone networks, have a local authority for issuing object identifiers. Most nations also have a *National Registration Authority* (NRA) that provides root object identifiers that can be expanded by local authorities. In the United States, the organization is the *American National Standards Institute*. You can add objects to the NRA; however, there may be a fee to do so.

Schema Structure Rules

The rules that govern the structure of the schema are contained in the **possSuperiors** and **systemPossSuperiors** attributes of the classes. These attributes contain the parent classes for the current class, because, as you will recall, all classes have a parent all the way up to class Top, which is at the root of the tree. The possSuperiors and systemPossSuperiors attributes ensure that objects are not created unless they are based on another class, and *orphan objects* are dealt with appropriately (an orphan object is an object whose classes have been deleted).

We've already discussed the attribute rules contained in **mustContain** and **mayContain attributes**, but now let's discuss further rules instituted by the *security access manager* (SAM). The SAM sets the following attributes as read only:

- ➤ **badPasswordCount**
- ➤ **badPasswordTime**
- ➤ **creationTime**
- ➤ **domainReplica**
- ➤ **isCriticalSystemObject**
- ➤ **lastLogoff**
- ➤ **lastLogon**

➤ **LockoutTime**

➤ **modifiedCount**

➤ **ntPwdHistory**

➤ **PrimaryGroupName**

➤ **revision**

➤ **SAMAccountName**

➤ **SAMAccountType**

Queries to the Schema

To expedite queries to the schema, a copy of the schema, called the *schema cache*, is stored in memory. The schema cache is loaded into memory at boot time and updated every five minutes if necessary. A special attribute, named **schema-UpdateNow**, immediately triggers a schema cache update when the attribute is added to the **RootDSE**. This ability to reload the cache on demand, by adding this attribute, is convenient, but it can adversely affect system performance, so its use should be limited.

Initial Security Mode

When Active Directory is being installed, it is in its initial security mode and will not allow changes. After Active Directory is installed, the default security is applied to directory partitions separately. The domain directory partition and the configuration directory partition both set the permissions for enterprise administrators, domain administrators, and the system to full control, but only enterprise domain controllers and administrators can replicate directory changes, topology changes, and synchronization. Authenticated users and the legacy Everyone group have read and audit access to the partition. The schema partition has basically the same permissions with a couple of exceptions. Write permissions for the **fsmoRoleOwner** attribute are necessary to enable the group schema administrators to transfer the domain forcibly. Finally, the permission to *change schema master control* is given to the group schema administrators, so they can change the domain controller at which schema changes can be made.

CUSTOMIZING THE SCHEMA

The schema is the framework for all objects and rules in the Active Directory. The default schema provides most of the functionality needed by the network environments currently in implementation. However, there may be times when the schema does not provide a particular object or attribute that is necessary for the proper operation and scalability of a system. Fortunately, you can modify the schema to accommodate new objects and attributes dynamically on production systems. Additionally, there may be times when objects that have been added need to be removed or disabled to provide the controls that a particular implementation requires. In those instances, objects in the schema can be deactivated or disabled on the fly, with certain ramifications.

Warning: Changing a schema can have severe implications. Some modifications cannot be reversed, so changes should be thoroughly examined before being implemented.

Keep in mind that the default schema is a rich tool for use in network administration, and care should be taken to avoid making unnecessary changes. Some changes could create inconsistencies in the schema, and that might lead to a nonfunctioning system.

Preparing to Modify the Schema

You can add new classes and attributes to the Active Directory schema as well as modify existing classes, modify attributes, and deactivate classes and attributes. Classes can be added by:

➤ *Adding new attributes to an existing class*—Classes need to be extended when additional attributes are needed, when no reason exists to separate the class with no attributes from the original, and when you want to administer the new attributes from the MMC.

➤ *Deriving a new class from an existing class*—Deriving a new class from an existing class is necessary when there is an existing class that closely meets your needs, when the new class must be separate from the existing class, and when you want to use an existing MMC console to administer it.

➤ *Creating an entirely new class*—Creating an entirely new class is necessary when no existing class closely matches the new requirements.

After analyzing a situation and determining that extending the schema is absolutely necessary and that your modifications are possible, you are ready to begin the modifications. Windows 2000 protects the schema by implementing the following three controls on schema modification:

➤ Schema modification must be enabled in the Schema console.

➤ Windows 2000's security model sets permissions on schema objects.

➤ Only the schema operations master domain controller can modify the schema.

Extending the schema is recommended only when absolutely necessary. Schema modifications can be accomplished via the Lightweight Directory Interchange Format (LDIF) scripts or by using an application programming interface (API).

When extending the schema, you should create documentation that details the following aspects of each change:

➤ Object identifier and its issuing authority

➤ Common name

➤ LDAP display name

➤ Class hierarchy

➤ NT security descriptor

➤ All attributes for the class with their descriptions

Common names, or relative distinguished names, must follow a specific format when adding new classes. The first part of the common name is the company prefix, which consists of the registered DNS domain name for the company followed by a hyphen and the current year (consisting of four digits). The next section consists of a hyphen and a product prefix that is unique for your company and that begins with an uppercase letter. The third section is the name of the class, separated by hyphens. See the following for an example of syntax for a common name:

```
Coriolis-Test-2000-CL-Class-1
```

The LDAP display name is a derivation of the common name, in which instance the product prefix begins with a lowercaser letter and the name of the class is closed up. See the following for an example of an LDAP display name:

```
Coriolis-Test-2000-cLClass1
```

Now that we know how to name a new class, we need to know how to add one. Although the Active Directory has no master domain controller, schema updates follow the Flexible Single Master Operation model. The domain controller that is designated as the schema master in Active Directory's **fsmoRoleOwner** attribute performs all changes to the schema, regardless of where changes are initiated. The schema master coordinates update transactions to the schema to ensure the integrity of the system and the updates made to the system. Project 9.6 in the Real-World Projects section at the end of the chapter will show you how to determine the operations master.

Modifying the Schema—Checks, Ramifications, and Tools

Modifying the schema can have a serious impact on the forest as a whole. Therefore, Windows 2000 places certain checks on changes to ensure that they will not render the system unusable. When a change is allowed by the system, it can still have certain ramifications, such as orphan attributes and dead classes, that must be considered. Finally, with all the other factors considered, there are specific tools for use in modifying the schema.

Active Directory Checks

Whenever a change is applied to the schema, Active Directory checks the transaction. Namely, the Active Directory conducts a consistency check and safety checks:

➤ *Consistency check*—The consistency check is applied when either a class or an attribute is modified. When a class is modified, the check ensures that the LDAP display name, the GUID, and other important attributes are unique. Then it makes sure that all the mandatory and optional attributes for that class exist in the schema, and that the superclass also exists within the schema. If the change is occurring on an attribute, then the consistency check ensures that attribute names such as **attributeID** and **MAPIID** are unique. (The MAPIID is a unique ID used for the Messaging API.) The **rangeUpper** (upper-range boundary) and **rangeLower** (lower-range boundary) must exist, and the **rangeLower** must be less than the **rangeUpper**. Finally, the syntax of the object and the **oMSyntax** (expected syntax of the attribute) must match correctly.

➤ *Safety checks*—Safety checks help you to avoid making changes that might impact existing functionality. Schema objects fall into one of two categories—category 1 and category 2. Category 1 objects are supplied with the base schema and, as such, are completely necessary for the directory to function properly. Category 1 objects are identified by the second low-order bit set on the **systemFlags** attribute. Category 1 objects cannot be deactivated or renamed. The attributes **defaultObjectCategory**, **attributeSecurityGUID**, **objectClassCategory**, **lDAPDisplayName**, **rangeLower**, and **rangeUpper** cannot be modified on a category 1 object. Category 2 objects are added to the schema after installation of the default schema. For both category 1 and category 2 objects, new **mustContain** attributes cannot be added or deleted through the console or new auxiliary classes.

Ramifications of Modifying the Schema

Although the schema provides methods for modifications, certain ramifications must be considered when modifying the schema. When modifying a schema, keep the following points in mind:

➤ When a schema object is deactivated, no new objects of the class can be created.

➤ The error codes for failed object creation are the same ones that would result if the class never existed.

➤ Searches for objects of a class or attribute will still return any instances of an object, making cleanup of these objects easier. Deactivating an attribute does not delete all the attribute values.

➤ Deactivated objects cannot be modified, and future checks will treat the object as if it does not exist.

The only exception to the preceding rules is that the relative distinguished name is still active after you delete an object, which prohibits the creation of duplicate distinguished names.

Tools for Schema Modification

Windows 2000 provides administrators with two tools for bulk schema modification—LDIFDE tool and CSVDE utility. The LDIFDE tool is an Internet standard method for updating an LDAP directory in bulk. LDIFDE can be used to add objects to the directory, delete objects from the directory, and even modify objects in the directory using text files. Listing 9.1 shows a sample record in the text file for the LDIFDE tool along with the command to import the file named adduser.ldf:

Listing 9.1   A sample record from LDIFDE tool's text file.

```
dn: cn=aPalmer, cn=users, dc=coriolis, dc=test
changetype: add
cn: aPalmer
description: Importing a user with LDIFDE
objectClass: user
sAMAccountName: aPalmer

C:\>LDIFDE -I -f adduser.ldf -v
```

Table 9.4 provides some of the parameters that can be used with the LDIFDE tool. Additional instruction can be found by issuing the **LDIFDE ?** command from the command prompt.

Table 9.4   Parameters for the **LDIFDE** command.

Parameter	Values
-?	Help for command
-i	Mode for command stated as import, export, or modify (export is the default mode)
-f	File name for the action (including path)
-v	Verbose operation statistics
-p	Port for socket (the LDAP default port is 389)

As mentioned, the CSVDE utility can also be used for additions and deletions with a comma-delimited text file (CSV), but, at the time of this writing, the CSVDE tool does not offer modifications to the directory. Listing 9.2 illustrates the format for adding a user by using a comma-delimited file with the CSVDE utility.

Listing 9.2   Adding a user by using a comma-delimited file in the CSVDE utility.

```
mode, dn, objectClass, cn, sAMAccountName
add, "cn=aPalmer, cn=users, dc=coriolis, dc=test", user, aPalmer
```

In Listing 9.2, notice that the first line of the file details the fields that will be in each record. The second line presents the actual record to add (which is the same user who was added in Listing 9.1 using the LDIFDE tool). The parameters for the command are the same as those for LDIFDE. Therefore, the command would appear as:

```
C:\>CSVDE -I -f adduser.ldf -v
```

Both the LDIFDE tool and the CSVDE utility can be used to migrate from another directory service, publish directory data to other sources, and perform periodic maintenance for the directory. However, sometimes it is necessary to use applications to modify the directory due to the improved error trapping and reusability. As Windows 2000 matures, there will undoubtedly be numerous third-party tools for such needs.

CHAPTER SUMMARY

The Active Directory combines the data and the code necessary to organize complex network environments. The schema acts as the mold for all the objects in the Active Directory and, by its very flexible nature, maintains the scalability and extensibility necessary for any size network. The schema provides the Active Directory with all the base objects necessary as well as the rules that govern objects' interrelationships in the directory. Windows 2000 provides administrators with a schema that contains the fundamental building blocks, called *classes*, and class properties, called *attributes*. Without the schema, the Active Directory cannot function and, as such, neither can a Windows 2000 network.

When the first domain controller in the first tree of the forest is installed, the Active Directory provides it with a Directory Information Tree (DIT). The DIT is considered a base of information from which will evolve a completed tree. The Microsoft Management Console (MMC) has two snap-ins that can be installed to view the schema container—Active Directory Schema console (which can be made available through snap-in registration) and Active Directory Services Interface (ADSI) Edit utility (which can be found on the Windows 2000 Server CD-ROM). The schema container stores an important object called the **RootDSE**. The **RootDSE** object has an attribute called the **subSchemaSubEntry**, which points to the location of the sub-schema. The sub-schema lists all of the attributes and classes in the Active Directory schema. The physical location of the schema data is fault tolerant, because every domain controller has a full copy of the schema. The Ntds.dit and schema.ini files reside in the NTDS share on each domain controller. The Ntds.dit file has the actual schema data, while the schema.ini file contains the parameters necessary to install the base schema.

All objects in the directory are stored in containers, and the schema is no exception. The schema containers are the **attributeSchema** and the **classSchema**. The schema container is an object, also, and it's instantiated from the **directory Management Domain (dMD)** class. Separating the containers for classes and attributes allows relationships to exist among them, such as one attribute for many classes and vice versa. To ensure that every object can be properly addressed in the directory, each object must have a unique LDAP display name, object identifier, and GUID. For attributes to be of any use, rules must be in place for the type of data and boundaries for the value of the attribute. These rules provide syntax and range values. Some attributes lend themselves to multiple values, which the schema can accommodate. However, the LDAP protocol treats multivalue attributes as numerous single values, which can be inefficient. To make searching for an attribute value more efficient, attribute fields can be indexed. However, the gain realized in searching is paid for in additional processing for every addition or deletion of an indexed item.

As mentioned, the schema consists of a number of classes. All classes are based on a single object named the **classSchema**, which specifies all mandatory and optional attributes for a class as well as any other classes from which attributes are inherited. One attribute that the **classSchema** provides is the class type. Four basic class types exist—abstract, structural, auxiliary, and type 88. Abstract classes are the basis for all structural classes. Structural classes populate the directory. Auxiliary classes provide attributes to structural and abstract classes. Type 88 classes were made before the official 1993 X.500 standard was ratified, and actually represent classes with no valid type. Classes can inherit certain attributes from their parent class, which makes them a child, or subclass, to the parent or superclass.

Windows 2000 protects some attributes because they are critical to system functioning. These protected attributes can be changed only by a system process named the Directory Service Agent. To facilitate administrative changes to these parameters, the directory pairs every system attribute with one that can be changed by administrators. Object identifiers are a string of numbers listed in dot notation, like 1.2.840.113556.1.5.4. A number of authorities can issue object identifiers, and each authority has its own ID to help ensure that all objects they create have a unique ID. The rules that govern the structure of the schema are contained in the **possSuperiors** and **systemPossSuperiors** attributes of the classes. Remember that all classes have a parent all the way up to Top. To expedite queries to the schema, a copy of the schema is stored in memory called the schema cache. The schema cache is loaded into memory at boot time, and updated every five minutes if necessary. When Active Directory is being installed, it is in its initial security mode, but, after it's installed, the default security is applied to directory partitions separately.

Windows 2000 provides a default schema, but the schema can be modified to add or deactivate objects. You must take care when you modify the schema, because some changes cannot be undone and others can render a system unusable. New classes can be added, and existing classes can be modified. Similarly, attributes can be added, disabled, and modified. This makes the schema an extensible and scalable solution. Schema modification relies on enabling registry keys, access control lists, and protected objects to ensure functionality. Any changes to the schema should be fully documented for future reference. Attributes such as the object identifier and its issuing authority, common name, LDAP display name, class hierarchy, and NT security descriptor must be available for future reference.

Although technically no one domain controller is a master with Windows 2000, the schema master is **fsmoRoleOwner**. Though changes to the schema can occur from any computer with the appropriate console, all schema changes are executed by the schema master. This master applies checks to a proposed change to verify the consistency and safety of the change. After deactivating an object, new instances cannot be created. To assist with the cleanup of deactivated classes, however, the objects of a deactivated class can be searched.

REVIEW QUESTIONS

1. Which of the following holds a subset of the information in the Active Directory that provides enough information to start and run the service?

   a. Directory system agent

   b. Directory Information Tree

   c. Directory Management Domain

   d. Schema Management Interface

2. Which of the following is the part of the Active Directory that represents a discrete unit of replication and contains parameters necessary for the schema to function properly?

   a. Schema container

   b. Object identifier

   c. Schema master

   d. Common name (CN)

3. Which of the following is the part of the Active Directory that represents a discrete unit of replication and contains parameters necessary for the Active Directory to function properly?

   a. Object identifier

   b. Schema container

   c. Common name (CN)

   d. Configuration partition

4. Which of the following is an application programming interface (API) that provides access to the Active Directory?

   a. Active Directory Services Interface

   b. Directory Information Tree Console

   c. Directory System Agent Interface

   d. Directory Management Domain Console

5. The _____ object is at the top of every LDAP tree that contains the attributes necessary to extract critical directory data. This object is used to maintain portability in LDAP scripts and applications.

   a. Ntds

   b. schemaNamingContext

   c. searchFlags

   d. RootDSE

6. Which attribute directs a query to the location of the schema?

   a. schemaNamingContext

   b. RootDSE

   c. searchFlags

   d. Ntds

7. Which attribute resides in the **RootDSE** and contains the location of the sub-schema that contains all the attributes and classes in the Active Directory?

   a. Ntds.dit

   b. RootDSE

   c. schemaNamingContext

   d. subSchemaSubEntry

8. The _____ is a file that contains the domain directory data for a domain and resides in the NTDS share on the domain controllers.

   a. RootDSE.dat

   b. Ntds.dit

   c. schema.ini

   d. LDIF.ini

9. The _____ is a file used to create and populate a schema.

   a. schemaNamingContext.ini

   b. RootDSE.dit

   c. schema.ini

   d. attributeSchema.dit

10. Which of the following is an object that, through inheritance, is the parent for an attribute in the Active Directory?

    a. attributeSchema

    b. RootDSE

    c. searchFlags

    d. schemaNamingContext

11. What is the name of the object that specifies the attributes and hierarchy for a class in the Active Directory?

    a. classSchema

    b. RootDSE

    c. schemaNamingContext

    d. attributeSchema

12. The _____ is a class used to create the schema container in the Active Directory.

    a. Directory Management Domain

    b. Directory Information Tree

    c. Directory system agent

    d. Directory Information Domain

13. The _____ bit is used to indicate that an attribute should be indexed.

    a. RootDSE

    b. attributeSchema

    c. searchFlags

    d. schemaNamingContext

14. The _____, also called the relative distinguished name, is an attribute for an object within the Active Directory that uniquely identifies the object.

    a. Object identifier

    b. Common name (CN)

    c. Schema container

    d. Object container

15. What is the name of the system process that controls access to Active Directory information?

    a. Directory Information Tree

    b. Directory Management Domain

    c. Schema Management Agent

    d. Directory system agent

16. The _____ is a code that uniquely describes an object within the directory. Issuing authorities' hierarchical systems regulate object ID codes while allowing local administrators to create local object identifiers.

    a. Schema Manager

    b. Common name (CN)

    c. Object identifier

    d. Schema container

17. What is the name of the regulatory body that sets standards, including X.500 object identifiers?

    a. American National Standards Institute

    b. Directory Information Tree Institute

    c. Directory Management Domain Institute

    d. X.500 National Standards Institute

18. What utility does the Active Directory use to ensure certain changes occur only on one particular machine in a domain?

    a. Directory Information Tree Master

    b. Directory System Agent Manager

    c. Flexible Single Master Operations

    d. Directory Management Domain Operation

19. Which utility can be used only for bulk additions and deletions in the directory?

    a. LDIFDE

    b. ADSI Edit

    c. Schema console

    d. CSVDE

20. Which utility can be used for bulk additions, deletions, and modifications in the directory?

    a. LDIFDE

    b. ADSI Edit

    c. Schema console

    d. CSVDE

21. Which of the following is a snap-in that can be installed from the Windows 2000 Server CD?

    a. Schema Manager

    b. CSVDE utility

    c. ADSI Edit

    d. LDIFDE utility

22. Which of the following is a snap-in that is present in the Active Directory by default and only needs to be registered?

    a. Schema console

    b. CSVDE utility

    c. ADSI Edit

    d. LDIFDE utility

23. Which utility is used to view the **RootDSE**?

    a. Schema Manager

    b. CSVDE utility

    c. ADSI Edit

    d. LDIFDE utility

24. Schema modifications can be enabled using the _____.

    a. Schema console

    b. CSVDE utility

    c. ADSI Edit

    d. LDIFDE utility

25. Which group has permissions to modify the schema?

    a. schema operators

    b. schema administrators

    c. server operators

    d. server admins

REAL-WORLD PROJECTS

Andy Palmer has been assigned to a new customer who claims that the default schema does not have the necessary classes and attributes to accommodate their business needs. Andy knows that modifying the schema can have serious consequences, so he decides to assess the situation before committing to any requested changes.

Project 9.1
To install the ADSI Edit utility:

Andy needs to view the properties of the rootDSE for the client's schema. He would like to use the ADSI Edit utility to do this, so he installs the utility on the domain controller.

1. Insert the Windows 2000 Server or Advanced Server CD-ROM.

2. Browse to the \support\tools directory on the CD.

3. Double-click setup.exe.

4. Click Start|Run, and type "MMC" in the Run dialog box.

5. In the blank MMC, click Console|Add/Remove Snap-in.

6. Click the tab labeled Standalone, and click the Add button.

7. Select ADSI Edit from the list of snap-ins, click Add, then click Close.

8. Click OK on the Add/Remove Snap-in tab.

9. Click Console|Save As. The display box should default to the Administrative Tools folder.

10. In the File Name text box, type "ADSI Edit", and click Save. Figure 9.1 shows the ADSI Edit utility.

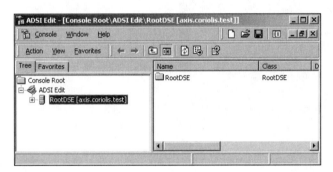

Figure 9.1   The ADSI Edit utility.

Project 9.2
To find the schema directory partition using ADSI Edit:

With the ADSI Edit utility installed, Andy now needs to find the schema directory partition for possible use in Windows Scripts.

1. Open the ADSI Edit console from the Administrative Tools menu.

2. Right-click ADSI Edit, then click Connect To.

3. In the Connection Point check box, ensure Naming Context is selected.

4. Select RootDSE in the Naming Context box, and click OK.

5. In the console tree, double-click RootDSE. The RootDSE folder is displayed.

6. Right-click the RootDSE folder, and select Properties.

7. In the Select A Property To View box, select ConfigurationNamingContext. As you can see in Figure 9.2, the Attribute Values section displays a Value(s) text box, which shows the distinguished name of the schema directory partition.

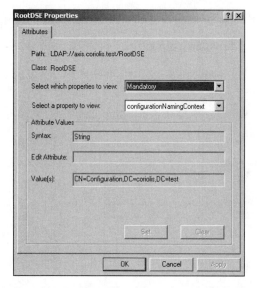

Figure 9.2   Revealing the schema directory partition.

Project 9.3
To register and install the Active Directory Schema console:

To get a better view of the classes and attributes in the current schema, Andy would like to use the Schema Console. To create a new console with the appropriate snap-in, he follows these steps:

1. From a command prompt, change to the <%systemroot%>\System32 folder.

2. Type "Regsvr32 Schmmgmt.dll". A prompt confirming the registration should appear.

3. Click Start|Run, and type "MMC".

4. In the blank MMC, click Console | Add/Remove Snap-in.

5. Click the tab labeled Standalone, and then click the Add button.

6. Select Active Directory Schema from the list of snap-ins, click Add, then click Close.

7. Click OK on the Add/Remove Snap-in tab.

8. Click Console | Save As. The display box should default to the Administrative Tools folder.

9. In the File Name text box, type "Active Directory Schema", and click Save. Figure 9.3 shows the completed Schema console.

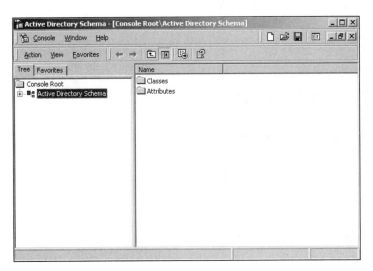

Figure 9.3   The completed Schema console.

Project 9.4
To enable schema modifications using the Schema console:

Having decided that the company may need new classes or attributes, Andy needs to enable modifications for the schema. To do this, he does the following:

1. Open the Active Directory Schema console from the Administrative Tools menu.

2. Right-click the Active Directory Schema, and click Operations Manager.

3. In the Change Schema Master dialog box, check the box labeled The Schema May Be Modified On This Domain Controller, and click OK. The checkbox (shown in Figure 9.4) actually adds the following registry key:

```
Hkey_Local_Machine\System\CurrentControlSet\Services\Ntds\Parameters\
SchemaUpdateAllowed
```

However, care should be taken not to add this key manually with the Regedit utility, because Regedit bypasses all system checks and balances.

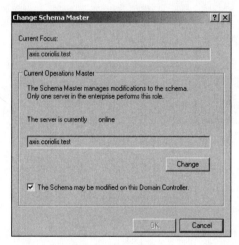

Figure 9.4   Enabling schema modifications.

Project 9.5
To verify the permissions on the account used to modify the schema:

At first, Andy cannot modify the schema. To verify that his user account has the appropriate permission, he performs the following tasks:

1. Open the Active Directory Users And Computers console.

2. Expand your domain by clicking the plus (+) sign.

3. Double-click the Users folder, and double-click the Schema Admins security group.

4. In the Schema Admins Properties dialog box, click the Members tab. As you can see in Figure 9.5, you can use the Members tab to ensure whether an account is in the Schema Admins group. To add an account, click Add, and select the account from the resulting dialog box. Click Add, and then click OK.

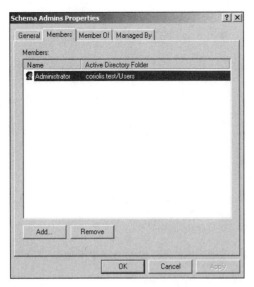

Figure 9.5   Verifying membership in the Schema Admins group.

9

Project 9.6

To view and change the current schema master using the Schema console:

Andy needs to make sure he is connected to the schema master to commit changes to the schema. To view the current master, and change it if necessary, he takes the following actions:

1. Open the Active Directory Schema console from the Administrative Tools menu.

2. Right-click the Active Directory Schema, and click Operations Manager. The current Operations Master (part of the FSMO) is listed in the Current Operations Master dialog box.

3. To change the current Operations Master, close the Operations Master dialog box, right-click the Active Directory Schema, and select Change Domain Controller.

4. Select the Any Domain Controller option or the Specify Name option for the target domain controller, and click OK.

5. Right-click the Active Directory Schema, and select Operations Master.

6. Click the Change button, and select the desired domain controller from the list of controllers.

Project 9.7
To change the schema master using Ntdsutil:

When a co-worker, Jeff, approaches Andy with a question about using the command prompt to change the schema master, Andy demonstrates the procedure for Jeff.

1. From a command prompt, type "ntdsutil". The Ntdsutil utility opens.

2. At the **ntdsutil** prompt, type "roles".

3. At the **FSMO maintenance** prompt, type "connections".

4. Type "connect to server <servername>". (See Figure 9.6.)

5. To display current information, type "info".

6. To return to the FSMO maintenance mode, type "quit".

7. To transfer the FSMO, type "transfer schema master".

8. At the confirmation prompt, click Yes.

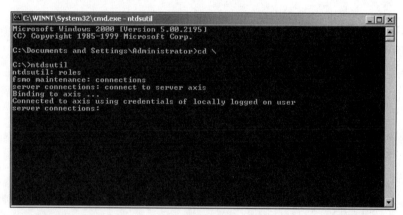

Figure 9.6 Changing the schema master from the command prompt.

Project 9.8
To seize the schema master using Ntdsutil:

While demonstrating the procedure, Andy notices that the schema master will not change. He decides to seize the role from the command prompt forcibly, as follows:

1. From a command prompt, type "ntdsutil". The Ntdsutil utility opens.

2. At the **ntdsutil** prompt, type "roles".

3. At the resulting **FSMO maintenance** prompt, type "connections".

4. At the **server connections** prompt, type "connect to server <servername>".

5. To display current information, type "info".

6. To return to the FSMO maintenance mode, type "quit".

7. To change the FSMO, type "seize schema master".

8. At the confirmation prompt, click Yes.

Project 9.9
To add a class using the Active Directory Schema console:

Andy has identified that the company indeed needs a new class. He performs the following steps to add the class to the schema.

1. Open the Active Directory Schema console from the Administrative Tools menu.

2. Ensure that you are connected to the current FSMO Operations Master by right-clicking Active Directory Schema, and selecting Operations Master.

3. Verify that the current focus is the same as the current Operations Master, and then click Cancel.

4. Verify that the Schema can be updated (see Project 9.4).

5. Verify that your account has permissions to update the registry (see Project 9.5).

6. To reveal the dialog box shown in Figure 9.7, right-click Classes, click Create Class, and click Continue at the prompt.

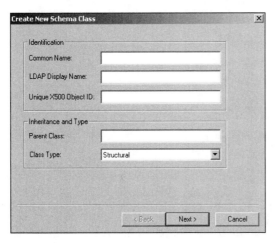

Figure 9.7   Adding a class using the Schema console snap-in.

7. Provide the common name, LDAP display name, object ID, parent class, and class type. Then, click Next.

8. Provide the mandatory and optional attributes by using the Add button next to the appropriate list boxes in the resulting dialog box.

9. Click Finish.

Project 9.10
To add an attribute using the Active Directory Schema console:

With the new class in place, Andy needs to add an attribute to the class that does not yet exist. To create the attribute, he performs the following steps:

1. Open the Active Directory Schema console from the Administrative Tools menu.

2. Ensure that you are connected to the current FSMO Master by right-clicking Active Directory Schema, and selecting Operations Master.

3. Verify that the current focus is the same as the current Operations Master, and click Cancel.

4. Verify that the schema can be updated (see Project 9.4).

5. Verify that your account has permissions to update the registry (see Project 9.5).

6. To reveal the Create A New Attribute Object dialog box shown in Figure 9.8, right-click Attributes, click Create Attribute, and click Continue at the prompt.

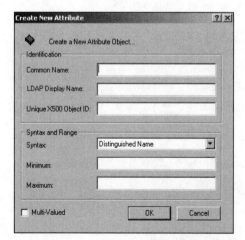

Figure 9.8 Adding an attribute using the Schema console snap-in.

7. Provide the common name, LDAP display name, object ID, syntax, minimum range, and maximum range settings. Then, check the Multi-Valued checkbox if necessary and click Next.

8. Click Finish.

Project 9.11
To modify a class using the Active Directory Schema console:

Now that the new attribute exists, Andy must modify the class he created to add the new attribute to it.

1. Open the Active Directory Schema console from the Administrative Tools menu.

2. Ensure that you are connected to the current FSMO Master by right-clicking Active Directory Schema and selecting Operations Master.

3. Verify that the current focus is the same as the current Operations Master, and click Cancel.

4. Verify that the Schema can be updated (see Project 9.4).

5. Verify that the account has permissions to update the registry (see Project 9.5).

6. Expand the Classes folder by clicking the plus (+) sign, and select the target class from the list.

7. To reveal the Properties dialog box shown in Figure 9.9, right-click the class, and select Properties.

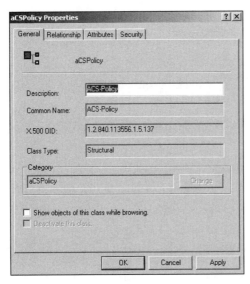

Figure 9.9   Modifying a class using the Schema console snap-in.

8. Click the General tab in the Properties dialog box if necessary. You can change the policy's description on the General tab.

9. Click the Relationship tab to access options that enable you to modify the Auxiliary classes and Possible Superiors settings.

10. Click the Attributes tab to modify the attributes associated with the class.

11. Click the Security tab to view a brief list of permissions for the class as well as the users and groups that possess them. At the bottom of the Security tab is a button that you can click to view the Advanced Security settings and a checkbox to allow inheritable permissions from the parent of the class.

12. Click OK after completing modifications to the class.

Project 9.12
To modify an attribute using the Active Directory Schema console:

While adding the new attribute to the new class, Andy realizes that the description is not accurate. He completes the following steps to modify the new attribute:

1. Open the Active Directory Schema console from the Administrative Tools menu.

2. Ensure that you are connected to the current FSMO Master by right-clicking Active Directory Schema, and selecting Operations Master.

3. Verify that the current focus is the same as the current Operations Master, and click Cancel.

4. Verify that the schema can be updated (see Project 9.4).

5. Verify that the account has permissions to update the registry (see Project 9.5).

6. Expand the Attributes folder by clicking the plus (+) sign, and select the target Attribute from the list.

7. To reveal the dialog box shown in Figure 9.10, right-click the Attribute, and select Properties.

8. Click the General tab in the Properties dialog box to change the Attribute's description. There are also checkboxes that enable you to index the attribute, replicate the attribute, and show objects based on the attribute's class when browsing.

9. Click OK to end the modification of the Attribute.

Figure 9.10   Modifying an attribute using the Schema console snap-in.

9

Project 9.13
To deactivate and reactivate classes and attributes:

During this procedure, Andy notices that a class and an attribute had been incorrectly added before he arrived. He decides to deactivate both so that new objects of their type cannot be created.

1. Open the Active Directory Schema console.

2. Right-click the target class or attribute, and select Properties.

3. Check the Deactivate This Class/Attribute checkbox to deactivate the class or attribute. To reactivate the class or attribute, you simply clear the Deactivate This Class/Attribute checkbox.

4. Click OK.

CHAPTER TEN

ACTIVE DIRECTORY CONNECTOR ADMINISTRATION AND EXCHANGE SERVICE INTEROPERABILITY

After completing this chapter, you will be able to:

✓ Describe the Active Directory Connector service

✓ Install the Active Directory Connector service

✓ Configure Connection Agreements using the Active Directory Connector

✓ Manage directory synchronization on different servers using the Active Directory Connector

✓ Monitor the Active Directory Connector

✓ Plan for integration between Active Directory services and Exchange Server 5.5 services using the Active Directory Connector

Among the new utilities included in Windows 2000 is the *Active Directory Connector* (ADC). ADC is a configuration and maintenance tool designed to simplify administration between multiple directory services. ADC's directory synchronization and import/export utilities enable systems engineers to replicate objects such as mailbox recipients and users between a Microsoft Exchange Server 5.5 directory and Windows 2000's Active Directory. The Active Directory Connector can be particularly helpful when rolling out Windows 2000 in environments in which Exchange Server 5.5 is already deployed. ADC also plays a role in Exchange 2000 migrations. Don't be surprised if ADC technology is later extended to support other directories, such as the Netscape Directory Server or DCL X.500. In this chapter, we'll examine the role Active Directory Connector plays in connecting different databases in Windows 2000.

ROLE OF THE ACTIVE DIRECTORY CONNECTOR

The Active Directory Connector comes in two versions:

➤ *Windows 2000*—The Windows 2000 ADC is used to replicate directory information between Windows 2000 Active Directory and Exchange Server 5.5. The Windows 2000 ADC is included with Windows 2000.

➤ *Exchange 2000*—An update, the Exchange 2000 ADC is included with Exchange 2000 Server. In fact, Exchange 2000 does not include directory services of its own, as does Exchange 5.5. Instead, Exchange 2000 uses the Windows 2000 Active Directory service.

Most likely you'll be called upon to use the Windows 2000 ADC to help manage replication and synchronization between Active Directory and Exchange 5.5 directory services. Implementing ADC helps the two directory services live in harmony and prevent duplication of objects. The Windows 2000 component can be used in production environments to synchronize applicable directory services. It can also be implemented on test networks to help determine whether an Active Directory design is efficient and manageable. Furthermore, the ADC also plays a critical role in achieving coexistence between Exchange Server 5.5 and Exchange 2000 Server.

According to Microsoft, ADC works in the following ways:

➤ Uses the LDAP API to perform fast replication between directories

➤ Hosts all active replication components in the Active Directory

➤ Replicates changes only between the two directories

➤ Maps objects for replication (the Active Directory Users object maps to the Exchange mailbox recipient object)

➤ Hosts multiple connections on a single Active Directory server

As a result of ADC's synchronization ability, administrators can make configuration changes to Exchange Server 5.5 objects using Active Directory. The ability to perform basic management functions using Active Directory can help maximize the investments many institutions have already made in an Exchange Server infrastructure.

Four items must be in place for effective coexistence between Active Directory and Exchange directory services:

➤ *Microsoft Windows 2000 Server platform*—Beware of placing the Active Directory Connector on inadequately powered domain controllers, because ADC can increase network traffic considerably and overwhelm available bandwidth and processor capacity.

➤ *TCP port*—ADC must have access to a TCP port to function properly.

➤ *Microsoft Exchange Server*—Microsoft Exchange Server 5.5 and Exchange 2000 Server are supported by ADC connections.

➤ *LDAP 3*—LDAP version 3 is used by ADC as the standard protocol for communication between Active Directory and Exchange directory services, and it is installed with ADC.

Connection Agreements are used to configure directory synchronization between Active Directory and Exchange.

CONNECTION AGREEMENTS

The Active Directory Connector service is used to configure and manage Connection Agreements. Connection Agreements are used to establish and maintain synchronization between Active Directory and Exchange. Four items must be provided when configuring Connection Agreements:

➤ Server name

➤ The objects to be synchronized

➤ Target containers

➤ A synchronization schedule

An Active Directory Connector can host a single Connection Agreement or multiple Connection Agreements. A single Exchange site recipient container can be defined to synchronize with multiple Active Directory containers, or multiple Exchange site recipient containers can be defined to synchronize with a single Active Directory container.

Multiple object types, or a single object type, can be configured for synchronization via a single Connection Agreement. As a result, an administrator could create two Connection Agreements that synchronize a single Exchange container holding users and groups with two separate Active Directory containers. One container could hold users, and the second could hold groups.

Like other services, the Active Directory Connector can be started and stopped. The service is configured by default using a Microsoft Management Console snap-in. As with many new features in Windows 2000, a wizard assists with the installation of ADC.

INSTALLING ACTIVE DIRECTORY CONNECTOR

Before the ADC setup program is begun, two items should be prepared in advance:

➤ *The location in which you plan to install ADC*—The default location is *systemroot*\Program Files\ADC.

➤ *A service account and password that must be provided to install ADC*—ADC setup automatically assigns the account the following rights: Logon As Service, Restore Files And Directories, Act As Part Of The Operating System, and Audit.

The Active Directory Connector is installed using the Active Directory Connector Installation Wizard. To install ADC, follow these procedures:

1. Insert the Windows 2000 server platform CD-ROM, navigate to the Valueadd\MSFT\Mgmt\ADC folder, and then double-click Setup.exe. After Setup.exe is triggered, the wizard in Figure 10.1 appears.

2. Click Next to begin the installation. You'll be asked to select the components you want to install (or remove). Two options are presented, as shown in Figure 10.2. The Microsoft Active Directory Connector Service Component option should be selected to install the ADC services. The Microsoft Active Directory Connector Management Components option should be selected to install the administrative components used to manage the ADC service.

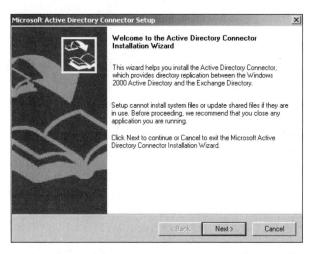

Figure 10.1   The Active Directory Controller Installation Wizard guides you through the installation of the Active Directory Connector.

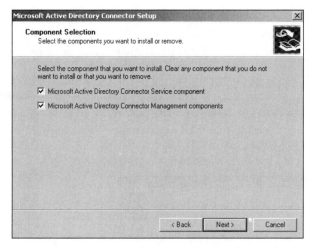

Figure 10.2   The Active Directory Controller Installation Wizard presents you with the option of installing or removing the two Active Directory Connector components.

3. After you check the components you want to install, click Next. A dialog box, as shown in Figure 10.3, directs you to specify the location where you want to install the ADC software.

4. Enter the folder location manually or select a location by browsing, and then click Next to continue the installation.

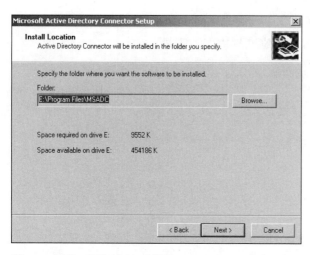

Figure 10.3 Windows 2000 generates a dialog box prompting you to specify the installation location.

5. The next installation step involves providing the account name and password for the service account that will be used to run the ADC service, as shown in Figure 10.4. An account name can be entered manually or by browsing.

6. After the service account name and password are specified, click Next to proceed. A dialog box appears, as shown in Figure 10.5, that monitors the progress of the installation. This step can take several minutes while the ADC installation wizard copies files, updates the system registry and schema, and installs the ADC service.

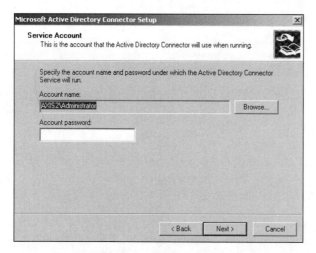

Figure 10.4 The ADC installation requires that a service account name and password be provided.

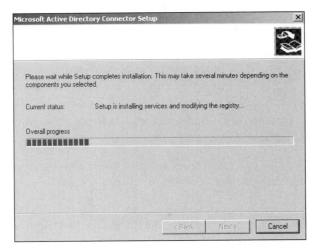

Figure 10.5   The ADC setup program monitors the installation progress.

7. After the process completes, click Next to continue. A dialog box confirms the successful completion of the installation, as shown in Figure 10.6. Click Finish to exit the ADC installation wizard.

In addition to installing ADC on the servers from which you plan to administer Connection Agreements, workstations that you plan to use for administering Active Directory users possessing mail attributes will also need the ADC management components installed on them. ADC setup can be used to install those components, as shown earlier in Figure 10.2. After the installation is completed, you're ready to configure ADC properties.

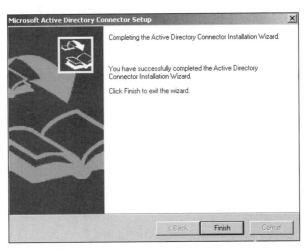

Figure 10.6   A dialog box confirms the successful installation of ADC.

Configuring ADC Properties

Configuring ADC properties is necessary for specifying which attributes are synchronized. Additionally, ADC properties must be configured to specify in which direction synchronization should occur. For example, administrators must specify whether Active Directory will receive updates from Exchange directory services or whether Exchange directory services will be synchronized according to changes made in Active Directory.

Note: All user attributes from each directory are synchronized by default. You must specify from within ADC properties the attributes that should not synchronize, if that need exists.

The relationship between Active Directory and Exchange directory services is defined through the use of Connection Agreements, which can be configured after ADC is installed.

Configuring Connection Agreements

To create a Connection Agreement, follow these procedures:

1. Click Start | Programs | Administrative Tools | Active Directory Connector Management.

2. Select the Active Directory Connector for the appropriate server in the left pane, or *tree*, of the ADC Management snap-in, as shown in Figure 10.7.

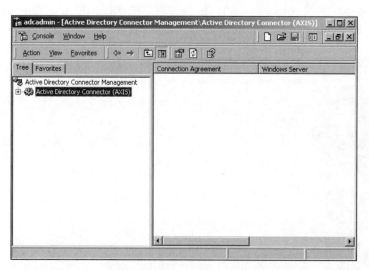

Figure 10.7 Connection Agreements can be configured from within the ADC Management snap-in.

3. Right-click the server you wish to configure, and select Properties. The Properties dialog box opens. Using the Properties dialog box, you can configure six components for Connection Agreements:

➤ Synchronization direction

➤ Bridgehead servers

➤ Synchronization schedules

➤ Source and destination containers

➤ Object deletion settings

➤ Advanced settings

Configuring Synchronization Direction

Directory synchronization can be configured to occur in one direction or in two directions. The General tab in the Properties dialog box, shown in Figure 10.8, is used to establish one-way or two-way configuration.

The first piece of information you can add to the General tab is the connection's name. To provide a name for a connection, complete the Name text box.

Depending on your firm's requirements, directory synchronization is configured in the Replication Direction section of the General tab. Two-way

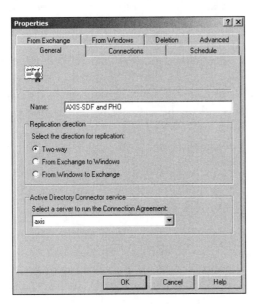

Figure 10.8   The General tab in the Properties dialog box is used to label a connection and configure directory synchronization direction.

should be selected if you want changes in either the Active Directory or Exchange directory to replicate to one another. This option should be selected when you intend to perform administrative tasks from within both Active Directory and Exchange. The From Exchange To Windows option should be selected when you desire changes made in Exchange to replicate to Active Directory. You should select this option when you prefer all object administration to be performed within Exchange. The From Windows To Exchange option should be selected when you want to use Active Directory for administration. All object administration conducted within Active Directory will be synchronized to Exchange when this option is selected.

The last item of information that needs to be provided on the General tab is the selection of the service to run the Connection Agreement. The server that should run the service should be named in the Select A Server To Run The Connection Agreement text box. The server can be entered manually or selected from the drop-down list box.

Configuring Bridgehead Servers

Every Connection Agreement requires that a bridgehead server be specified. Bridgehead servers must be defined for both directories being synchronized, because ADC uses the bridgehead servers' directories to synchronize Exchange and Active Directory directories.

Note: Active Directory requires that its bridgehead server be a domain controller. The Exchange directory must have an Exchange Server defined as its bridgehead server.

Several factors should be considered when selecting bridgehead servers:

➤ Do the bridgehead servers possess adequate resources for the traffic they will receive? Two calculations can be used to predict bridgehead server resource requirements. To determine the Active Directory to Exchange synchronization requirements, calculate 121K per bind or connection plus 11K per changed object. For Exchange to Active Directory synchronization, calculate 140K per bind or connection plus 14K per changed object.

➤ Is the bridgehead server centrally located in the network? The bridgehead server shouldn't be physically located at a remote location; instead, it should be located at the distributed network's hub.

Because each recipient object in Exchange has multiple attributes modified by Active Directory, when configuring a Connection Agreement to modify Exchange, you should be prepared for considerable replication to occur when initial synchronization takes place. For this reason, initial synchronization should occur during an off-peak time.

You can use the Connections tab in the Properties dialog box (see Figure 10.9) to configure your bridgehead servers. Server, Authentication, and Connect As information must be provided for both the Windows Server and the Exchange Server. A TCP port must also be specified for the Exchange Server. The ADC server seeks the Exchange directory on the bridgehead server on port 389. Port 379, meanwhile, is used by Exchange's Site Replication Service.

Generally, Connection Agreements are usually configured between the Active Directory and Exchange 5.5 directory service. If you're using a slow network link between bridgehead servers, however, you can also direct the agreement to use Exchange's Site Replication Service (SRS) in Exchange 2000 Server.

You should supply the name of the Windows Server on which ADC resides as well as the permissions account you want to connect with. The desired authentication method must also be entered. You can specify the authentication method manually or use the drop-down list to select an available option.

Note: *Remember that the bridgehead servers receiving updates require only the Write permission.*

After the bridgehead servers are configured, you're ready to schedule ADC synchronization.

10

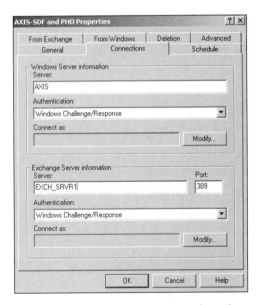

Figure 10.9   The Connections tab in the Properties dialog box is used to configure bridgehead server information.

Configuring Synchronization Scheduling

By default, the ADC checks for changes in directories every five seconds within the polling time frames you configure; polling times are completely customizable, however.

You can use the Schedule tab in the Properties dialog box (see Figure 10.10) to specify a Connection Agreement's synchronization schedule. Synchronization can overcome a server's capacities, so you should ensure that the server hosting the feature possesses the necessary resources (particularly network bandwidth). If your network is particularly busy during normal business hours, it might be best to configure polling to occur at off-peak hours.

Notice also that the option to replicate the entire contents of a directory is available on the Schedule tab.

According to Microsoft, if the default polling schedule creates excessive load, you can decrease that load by reducing the following values in registry key HKEY_ LOCAL_MACHINES\System\CurrentControlSet\Services\MSADC\Parameters:

➤ *Name*—Sync Sleep Delay (specify the delay, in seconds, that the service waits to check for updates)

➤ *Type*—DWORD

➤ *Data*—Specify the number of seconds to wait between cycles

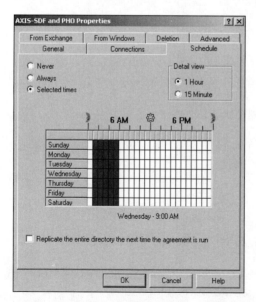

Figure 10.10   The Schedule tab in the Properties dialog box is used to specify when synchronization should occur as well as whether the entire directory should be replicated.

Now that you've scheduled polling, you're ready to proceed. The next step involves specifying synchronization source and destination containers.

Configuring Source and Destination Containers

The source and destination containers for each directory specified in the Connection Agreement must be configured. The From Windows and From Exchange tabs are used to specify the containers to be synchronized, which container should receive updates, and which objects actually are subject to synchronization.

The From Windows tab, shown in Figure 10.11, also includes settings for specifying objects to be filtered using discretionary access control lists (DACLs). The option is enabled when you select the Replicate Secured Active Directory Objects To The Exchange Directory checkbox. On the From Windows tab, you should select the objects you want to replicate, such as users, contacts, and groups. The default destination should also be supplied.

The From Exchange tab is used to specify the Exchange recipient containers, the default destination, and the objects to be replicated, as shown in Figure 10.12. You can choose which objects replicate on the From Exchange tab, including mailboxes, custom recipients, and distribution lists. Table 10.1 shows the object mappings between Active Directory and Exchange.

10

The next step involves configuring object deletion settings.

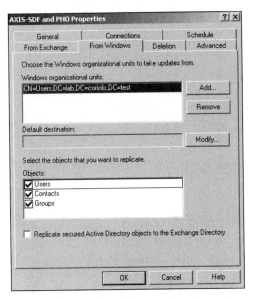

Figure 10.11   The From Windows tab is used to configure synchronization settings from Windows directories to Exchange directories.

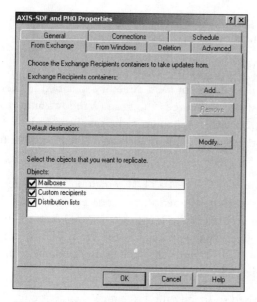

Figure 10.12   The From Exchange tab is used to configure synchronization settings from Exchange directories to Windows Active Directory.

Table 10.1   Microsoft Active Directory/Microsoft Exchange object mappings.

Active Directory Object	Exchange Object
Mailbox-enabled User	Mailbox
Mail-enabled User	Custom recipient in the target container
Non-mail-enabled User	Not replicated
Mail-enabled Contact	Custom recipient in the target container
Non-mail-enabled Contact	Not replicated
Mail-enabled Group (type: Distribution)	Distribution List in the target container
Mail-enabled Group (type: Security)	Distribution List in the target container
Non-mail-enabled Group (type: Distribution)	Not replicated
Non-mail-enabled Group (type: Security)	Not replicated

Configuring Object Deletion Settings

When objects are deleted in one directory, they are not deleted in the partner directory. For example, if you were to delete a user in Active Directory, the mailbox would remain in the Exchange directory by default. Deletions are stored in a file on the server operating the Active Directory Connector service. This file is located in *systemroot*\System32\MSADC\Connection Agreement Name\NT5.LDF or Ex55.CSV.

Note: *Active Directory deletions are kept in the NT5.LDF file, while Exchange deletions are logged in the Ex55.LDF file.*

Changes to modify this behavior can be configured using the Deletion tab in the Properties dialog box, as shown in Figure 10.13. Four options exist, two for each directory. From within Windows Active Directory, you can elect to delete the Exchange mailbox or keep the Exchange mailbox and store the deletion list in the temporary CSV file for future reference. From within Exchange, you can elect to delete the Windows account or keep the Windows account and store the deletion list in the temporary LDF file.

Several Advanced settings are also available for configuring synchronization settings.

Configuring Advanced Settings

Advanced settings can be configured to optimize Connection Agreements. Three settings can be configured on the Advanced settings tab in the Properties dialog box, as shown in Figure 10.14. The following items are configured from the Advanced tab:

➤ Paged results

➤ Primary Connection Agreements

➤ Directions for replicating a nonexistent Windows account mailbox

10

The Paged Results settings specify the number of entries to be synchronized per request. Larger page sizes result in fewer server requests, but they also require more memory. For Exchange, the page size setting should not exceed

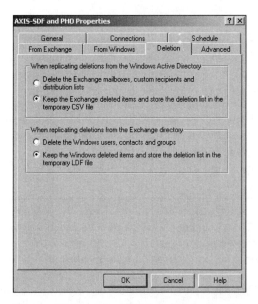

Figure 10.13   The Deletion tab in the Properties dialog box is used to configure ADC deletion settings.

Figure 10.14 Advanced settings are used to optimize Connection Agreements.

the LDAP search result value specified on the Exchange Server. No synchronization occurs when the Paged Result is set to 0.

The primary Connection Agreement settings specify how the directory services synchronize. You need to understand the implications of both primary Connection Agreement options if synchronization is to occur properly. The two options are:

➤ *This Is A Primary Connection Agreement For The Connected Exchange Organization*—This option should be selected to specify which Connection Agreement will synchronize new non-homed Active Directory objects. Such objects are mail-enabled but don't have mailboxes.

If the This Is A Primary Connection Agreement For The Connected Exchange Organization checkbox isn't chosen, the Connection Agreement won't generate new objects in the Exchange directory. However, synchronization between existing objects still occurs.

Warning: Be careful when associating more than one Connection Agreement with Active Directory, because duplicate objects could result. When creating new non-homed Active Directory container objects, objects are synchronized to the Exchange recipient container you've specified as the primary Connection Agreement for the connected Exchange organization. If you've specified two Connection Agreements, with each as primary, duplicate Exchange objects will result because the objects will synchronize with each Exchange recipient container.

➤ *This Is A Primary Connection Agreement For The Connected Windows Domain—* This option should be selected to specify which connection agreement will synchronize new Exchange Directory objects to Active Directory. These new Exchange objects can be mailboxes, distribution lists, or custom recipients. Such objects are mail-enabled but don't have mailboxes.

If the This Is A Primary Connection Agreement For The Connected Windows Domain checkbox isn't chosen, the Connection Agreement won't generate new objects in Active Directory. However, synchronization between existing objects still occurs.

Warning: Take care when associating more than one Connection Agreement with one Exchange recipient container. When creating new Exchange objects, these objects are synchronized to the Active Directory container you've specified as the primary Connection Agreement for the connected Windows organization. If you've specified two Connection Agreements, with each as primary, duplicate Active Directory objects will result, because the objects will synchronize with each Active Directory container.

The last option on the Advanced tab involves replicating mailboxes that don't have a corresponding account in the Windows domain. Using this option, you can specify the action to be taken when a mailbox being synchronized from the Exchange directory to Active Directory Services doesn't have a corresponding primary Windows Account.

By default, a mail-enabled contact is created in such situations, but you might want to perform another action instead. Three choices are available on the Advanced tab:

➤ Create a Disabled Windows User Account

➤ Create a New Windows User Account

➤ Create a Windows Contact

After the configuration of the Connection Agreement is completed, you're ready to manage the synchronization of objects in Exchange and Active Directory.

Managing Synchronization

Your organization's system architecture should determine the manner in which you manage synchronization of Exchange and Active Directory objects. While you can do so from either Exchange or Active Directory, the direction in which you intend replication to occur should dictate the console you use to administer the management of the two directories' synchronization.

If you plan to manage user accounts from within Active Directory, you should configure your Connection Agreement to synchronize from Active Directory to Exchange only. You would not want to synchronize from Exchange to Active Directory, because changes made within Exchange would replicate to Active Directory objects. To manage Exchange mail recipients from within Active Directory, you should use the Active Directory Users And Computers interface to configure changes in Active Directory, which will then be synchronized to Exchange directories. Such integrated management is possible thanks to the installation of mailbox properties within Active Directory. These properties are provided when ADC is installed. In Active Directory, you can configure the same mailbox objects managed by the Exchange Administrator.

Warning: When you opt to configure Exchange objects from within Active Directory, several Exchange items must continue to be managed from within the Exchange Administrator, including connectors, address book views, public folders, and queues.

Mailbox-related properties are added by ADC installation, and new options are created in Active Directory, as shown in Figure 10.15. The options include Add Exchange Mailbox and Enable Exchange Mail.

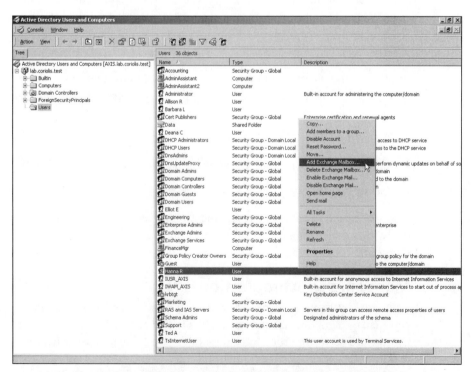

Figure 10.15 Additional configuration options are added to the Active Directory Users And Computers console with the addition of Active Directory Connector services.

As mentioned earlier, you can also opt to manage objects from within Exchange. In such an environment, you'd synchronize only in the direction from Exchange to Active Directory. Synchronizing in such a manner means changes made within Exchange replicate to Active Directory objects. You would not want Active Directory to synchronize in the direction of Exchange in this case, because any changes made in Active Directory would affect Exchange objects.

To configure Exchange to synchronize objects, you should use the Exchange Administrator to configure changes in Exchange directories that are then synchronized to Active Directory objects.

Now that you're up to speed on the installation and configuration of ADC, you're ready to examine the models and configurations that can be used within different computing environments.

ACTIVE DIRECTORY CONNECTOR PREPARATION

Just as with Windows 2000 installation, several preparatory steps should be taken when planning an Active Directory Connector installation. Among the items to review are Microsoft's deployment recommendations, the development of a test environment, the selection of a deployment model, and resource requirements. (The latter was discussed earlier in this chapter in the "Configuring Bridgehead Servers" section.)

Deployment Recommendations

Microsoft recommends upgrading primary domain controllers to Windows 2000 when preparing to populate Active Directory with user accounts. Furthermore, Microsoft recommends using Active Directory only to backfill directory data from Exchange to preexisting Active Directory accounts.

If your organization is using connector servers to enable communication between Exchange sites on its network, you should also use the servers as the Exchange bridgehead servers. Using them to host the Connection Agreements improves network efficiency.

For best performance, you should locate the server running the ADC service on the same physical subnet that hosts the Exchange and ADC service bridgehead servers. Doing so helps eliminate synchronization traffic over WAN links. When forced to pass synchronization traffic over WAN links, be sure to place the bridgehead servers strategically. Centralized, or hub, locations are best for optimizing bridgehead server performance.

Finally, be sure to review your planned network architecture. You probably don't want to create duplicate and redundant objects when synchronizing between Active Directory and Exchange directory services.

Preparing a Test Environment

Before rolling out an ADC implementation, you should ensure that the network design, architecture, and synchronization design are tested properly. Therefore, you should build and deploy a test environment. The results experienced from the deployment of this test should then be used to fine-tune the ADC service's configuration and verify that the ADC architecture will, indeed, work as planned.

> **Warning:** Implementing an ADC service without first testing it properly could prove disastrous in a production environment.

Test environments should be built so that they mimic your production environment. Your test environment should mirror the following items of your production network:

➤ Locations and bandwidth restrictions

➤ Server and client structures

➤ Exchange directory size and complexity (Microsoft recommends making a copy of your existing Exchange directory)

> **Tip:** If the development of a mirrored production environment isn't feasible, configure one-way Connection Agreements from your production Exchange directory to the test lab. Microsoft recommends this action, because it synchronizes the Exchange objects to your test lab.

When testing the Active Directory Connector design, be sure to monitor system performance and ensure that disaster-recovery plans are in place.

Selection of an ADC Deployment Model

When the time arrives for ADC service deployment, three production models are available to systems engineers:

➤ Single Site, Single Domain

➤ Single Site, Multiple Domains

➤ Multiple Sites, Multiple Domains

Single Site, Single Domain

In an environment in which a single Exchange Server and a single Active Directory domain exist, all Exchange users and custom recipients are synchronized with the Active Directory Users container. A single site, single domain configuration also requires that the Exchange Distribution List recipient container be synchronized with Active Directory's Groups organizational unit.

Just one ADC possessing two Connection Agreements is required to fulfill these requirements. Table 10.2 describes a sample configuration for the first Connection Agreement, and Table 10.3 shows a sample configuration for the second Connection Agreement for a single site, single domain.

Single Site, Multiple Domains

A second model available to systems engineers is the single Exchange site, multiple Active Directory domains configuration. Table 10.4 describes the sample configuration for the first Connection Agreement in such an environment, and Table 10.5 describes the sample configuration for the second Connection Agreement in a single Exchange site, multiple Active Directory domains model.

Table 10.2   Values and settings for the first Connection Agreement in a single site, single domain model.

Value	Setting
Direction	Two-way
From Exchange	Exchange Users and Custom Recipients to Active Directory Users
From Active Directory	Active Directory Users to Exchange Users
Primary Connection Agreement for the connected Exchange organization?	Yes
Primary Connection Agreement for the connected Active Directory domain?	Yes

Table 10.3   Sample configuration for the second Connection Agreement in a single site, single domain model.

Value	Setting
Direction	Two-way
From Exchange	Exchange Distribution Lists to Active Directory Groups
From Active Directory	Active Directory Groups to Exchange Distribution Lists
Primary Connection Agreement for the connected Exchange organization?	Yes
Primary Connection Agreement for the connected Active Directory domain?	Yes

10

Table 10.4 Values and settings for a single site, multiple domains model.

Value	Setting
Direction	Two-way
From Exchange	Exchange Recipient Container to Active Directory Users
From Active Directory	Active Directory Users to Exchange Recipient Container
Primary Connection Agreement for the connected Exchange organization?	Yes
Primary Connection Agreement for the connected Active Directory domain?	Yes

Table 10.5 Second Connection Agreement in a single site, multiple domains model.

Value	Setting
Direction	Two-way
From Exchange	Exchange Recipient Container to Active Directory Users
From Active Directory	Active Directory Users to Exchange Recipient Container
Primary Connection Agreement for the connected Exchange organization?	Yes
Primary Connection Agreement for the connected Active Directory domain?	No

Multiple Sites, Multiple Domains

The third model available to systems engineers is the multiple Exchange sites, multiple Active Directory domains configuration. In this model, proper synchronization requires that an ADC be configured for each connection between an Exchange site and a Windows 2000 domain.

For illustrative purposes, let's say that you have two Active Directory domains: Coriolis and CertPress. Furthermore, you've got three Exchange sites with mailbox recipients in three locations: Toledo, Louisville, and Phoenix. Under normal circumstances, you'd implement primary Connection Agreements between each site and the relevant domain in which Active Directory is used to administer the appropriate users.

For example, if the mailbox recipients in Toledo and Louisville were associated with Active Directory users in the Coriolis domain, you'd form primary Connection Agreements between Toledo and Coriolis and between Louisville and Coriolis. Then, if mailbox recipients in Phoenix were associated with Active Directory users in the CertPress domain, you'd create a primary Connection Agreement between the Phoenix Exchange site and the CertPress domain.

Network administration doesn't always work so cleanly, however. Suppose you've got the same network structure, but with the following caveats:

➤ Mailbox recipients in Toledo are associated with Active Directory users in the Coriolis domain.

➤ Mailbox recipients in Phoenix are associated with Active Directory users in the CertPress domain.

➤ Mailbox recipients in Louisville are associated with both domains. Furthermore, suppose there's a need to create a Connection Agreement between Louisville and the Coriolis domain that synchronizes groups and mailboxes with accounts hosted in the Coriolis domain, but there is also the need to synchronize mailboxes only for mailbox recipients with user accounts hosted by Active Directory in the CertPress domain.

How could you best configure the preceding situation? In this scenario, you might want to structure the ADC service by configuring two primary Connection Agreements. One would be between Exchange recipients in Toledo and Active Directory users in the Coriolis domain. The second primary Connection Agreement would exist between Exchange recipients in Phoenix and Active Directory users in the CertPress domain.

For Louisville, simple Connection Agreements could be implemented between its Exchange directory and each Active Directory domain (Coriolis and CertPress). You'd then configure the Connection Agreements appropriately, as shown in Tables 10.6 through 10.9.

After the Active Directory installation, configuration, and management features are in place and running, you'll want to ensure that the service is monitored properly.

Table 10.6 Sample configuration for the Connection Agreement between the Toledo Exchange site and the Coriolis domain.

Value	Setting
Direction	Two-way
From Exchange	Exchange Recipient Containers to Active Directory Users
From Active Directory	Active Directory Users to Exchange Recipient Container
Primary Connection Agreement for the connected Exchange organization?	Yes
Primary Connection Agreement for the connected Active Directory domain?	Yes

Table 10.7 Sample configuration for the Connection Agreement linking the Louisville Exchange site and the Coriolis domain.

Value	Setting
Direction	Two-way
From Exchange	Exchange Recipient Container to Active Directory Users (groups and mailbox objects)
From Active Directory	Active Directory Users to Exchange Recipient Container
Primary Connection Agreement for the connected Exchange organization?	No
Primary Connection Agreement for the connected Active Directory domain?	Yes

Table 10.8 Sample configuration for the Connection Agreement between the Louisville Exchange site and the CertPress domain.

Value	Setting
Direction	Two-way
From Exchange	Exchange Recipient Container To Active Directory Users (mailbox objects only)
From Active Directory	Active Directory Users To Exchange Recipient Container
Primary Connection Agreement for the connected Exchange organization?	No
Primary Connection Agreement for the connected Active Directory domain?	No

Table 10.9 Sample configuration for the Connection Agreement linking the Phoenix Exchange site and the CertPress domain.

Value	Setting
Direction	Two-way
From Exchange	Exchange Recipient Container To Active Directory Users
From Active Directory	Active Directory Users to Exchange Recipient Container
Primary Connection Agreement for the connected Exchange organization?	Yes
Primary Connection Agreement for the connected Active Directory domain?	Yes

MONITORING THE ACTIVE DIRECTORY CONNECTOR SERVICE

As with most services, specific events can be logged when using the Active Directory Connector. Four levels of event logging can be set for five categories. The four levels of event logging are:

➤ *None*—Logs only critical events and error events. This setting provides the best server performance, and it is the default logging level.

➤ *Minimum*—Logs the success and failure of user accounts that are added or removed, LDAP session errors, and directory update errors.

➤ *Medium*—Logs events associated with specific directory objects and proxy error warnings.

➤ *Maximum*—Logs all events and provides a complete record of the operation of the ADC service and replication. This option can require significant server resources.

The five categories that can be logged are:

➤ *Replication*—Logs events that occur during replication.

➤ *Account Management*—Logs events that occur while attempting to write or delete a Windows object during replication.

➤ *Attribute Mapping*—Logs events that occur while mapping attributes between the Active Directory and Exchange.

➤ *Service Controller*—Logs events that occur when the ADC service is started or stopped.

➤ *LDAP Operations*—Logs events that occur when LDAP is used to access the directory.

Note: Use the Performance Monitor MSADC performance object to track ADC activity.

To log events, follow these steps:

1. Click Start | Programs | Administrative Tools | Active Directory Connector Management.

2. Select Active Directory Connector in the left pane of the adcadmin Microsoft Management Console screen and click Action, or right-click it and select Properties. The Properties dialog box appears. You can specify the logging properties you want to set on the Diagnostic Logging tab in the Properties dialog box.

CHAPTER SUMMARY

Windows 2000's Active Directory Connector can be used in production environments to synchronize directory services. It can also be implemented within test networks to help determine whether an Active Directory design is efficient and manageable. In Windows 2000, you'll most likely use ADC to manage synchronization between Active Directory and your Exchange Server 5.5 directory services.

As a result of ADC's synchronization ability, administrators can make configuration changes to Exchange Server 5.5 objects using Active Directory. The ability to perform basic management functions using Active Directory can help maximize the investments many institutions have already made in Exchange Server infrastructure.

The Active Directory Connector service is used to configure and manage Connection Agreements. Connection Agreements are used to establish and maintain synchronization between Active Directory domain containers and Exchange site recipient containers. Four items must be provided when configuring Connection Agreements: server name, objects that will be synchronized, target containers, and a synchronization schedule.

The Active Directory Connector is installed using the Active Directory Connector Installation Wizard. Configuration of ADC properties is necessary for specifying which attributes are synchronized. Additionally, ADC properties must be configured to specify in which direction synchronization should occur. Advanced settings can also be configured to optimize Connection Agreements.

Every Connection Agreement requires that a bridgehead server be specified. Active Directory requires that its bridgehead server be a domain controller.

You should take care when associating more than one Connection Agreement with one Exchange recipient container. Your organization's system architecture should determine the manner in which you manage synchronization of Exchange and Active Directory objects.

Just as with Windows 2000 installation, several preparatory steps should be taken when planning an Active Directory Connector installation. Among the items to review are Microsoft's deployment recommendations, the development of a test environment, the selection of a deployment model, and resource requirements.

As with most services, specific events can be logged when using the Active Directory Connector. Four levels of event logging can be set for five categories.

REVIEW QUESTIONS

1. The Active Directory Connector is a utility designed to fulfill which function?

   a. Connect and synchronize Active Directory services from multiple domains

   b. Connect and synchronize multiple Exchange sites

   c. Connect and synchronize Active Directory with other network services, such as DHCP and DNS

   d. Serve as a configuration and maintenance tool designed to simplify administration between multiple directory services

2. The Windows 2000 Active Directory Connector can be used to establish a connection between the Active Directory service and which of the following? [Check all correct answers]

   a. Microsoft Exchange Server 5

   b. Microsoft Exchange Server 5.5

   c. Microsoft Exchange 2000 Server

   d. DHCP and DNS service

3. Connection Agreements perform which function? [Check all correct answers]

   a. Create and maintain connections for the purpose of synchronizing Active Directory and Exchange site directories

   b. Link Active Directory services from different sites

   c. Link Windows 2000 Active Directory services with other directory services

   d. Create replication paths for database synchronization

4. An Active Directory Connector can support multiple Connection Agreements.

   a. True

   b. False

5. Connection Agreements can be configured to synchronize how many objects per connection?

   a. 2

   b. 3

   c. 4

   d. Single or multiple objects

10

6. The Active Directory Connector service is stopped and started, similar to other services.

   a. True

   b. False

7. Which of the following is the preferred installation location for installing the Active Directory Connector service when trying to optimize network bandwidth?

   a. Windows 2000 Workstation

   b. Windows 2000 standalone server

   c. Windows 2000 domain controller

   d. Microsoft Exchange site server

8. Which protocol does the Active Directory Connector service use to communicate with Microsoft Exchange directory services?

   a. NetBIOS

   b. IPX

   c. Kerberos

   d. LDAP

9. Which of the following is not required for defining Active Directory and Exchange connections when using the Active Directory Connector service?

   a. The IP addresses of each server hosting directory services to be synchronized

   b. A synchronization schedule

   c. Bridgehead server configuration

   d. Synchronization direction settings

10. Directory synchronization can occur only one way.

    a. True

    b. False

11. When implementing the Active Directory Connector service, bridgehead servers need to be defined for which connections? [Check all correct answers]

    a. The Exchange sites being synchronized

    b. All Exchange sites in a network

    c. Only the Active Directory domain directories being synchronized

    d. All domains within an enterprise

12. Which systems can be configured as bridgehead servers? [Check all correct answers]

    a. Exchange Servers

    b. Domain controllers running Active Directory

    c. Standalone servers

    d. Any server running Windows 2000 and Microsoft Exchange 5.5

13. How are object deletions synchronized?

    a. Upon deletion, all objects that are synchronized are deleted.

    b. Upon deletion, all objects that are synchronized are held in a swap file for 45 minutes, then deleted.

    c. Object deletions are configured using the setting provided on the Deletions tab in a Connection Agreement's Properties dialog box.

    d. Synchronized objects cannot be deleted.

14. The Advanced tab in a Connection Agreement's Properties dialog box is used to configure which settings? [Check all correct answers]

    a. Primary Connection Agreements

    b. Paged results

    c. Mailbox replication settings

    d. Deleted object settings

15. Exchange recipient objects can be administered using which Windows 2000 tool?

    a. Active Directory Connector

    b. Active Directory Sites And Services

    c. Active Directory Users And Computers

    d. Active Directory Exchange Administration Interface

16. The Active Directory Connector Service supports which of the following site/domain models? [Check all correct answers]

    a. Single site, single domain

    b. Multiple sites, single domain

    c. Single site, multiple domains

    d. Multiple sites, multiple domains

10

17. The deployment of Active Directory Connector services and Connection Agreements with Exchange sites should occur all at one time to ensure that synchronization occurs properly.

    a. True

    b. False

18. The Active Directory Connector can be used in which environments? [Check all correct answers]

    a. Test environments

    b. Production environments

    c. Heterogeneous environments

    d. Native environments

19. By default, which objects are synchronized when using the Active Directory Connector with Exchange Server 5.5?

    a. All objects

    b. No objects

    c. Only those objects specified during ADC installation

    d. Only those objects specified in Active Directory

20. Since the Active Directory Connector service uses LDAP to communicate with Exchange Servers, little network overhead is required, and synchronization can be scheduled during normal working hours.

    a. True

    b. False

REAL-WORLD PROJECTS

It's the beginning of a three-day weekend for our consultant, Andy Palmer. Before he heads out of the office for the holiday, however, he has to make one last stop at a client's headquarters to install and configure the Active Directory Connector service.

The client, a bicycle manufacturer called FastWheels Inc., has its corporate offices located across town. The FWWest domain hosts all of the headquarters' 45 users and computers.

FastWheels Inc. also has an Austin, Texas, location, where its products are manufactured. An Exchange Server (running version 5.5) is located there. Andy's job is to configure the FWWest domain's Active Directory service to synchronize all objects at the Exchange site in Texas. The sites are linked via a fractional T-1 circuit.

Project 10.1
To install the Active Directory Connector service on a Windows 2000 Server:

After a brief meeting with the bicycle company's IT director, Andy sits down at the company's bridgehead server, which is the domain controller, and pops in the Windows 2000 Server CD-ROM.

Andy proceeds to install the ADC service by completing the following steps:

1. Navigate to the Valueadd\MSFT\Mgmt\ADC folder.

2. Double-click on Setup.exe to start the Active Directory Connector Installation Wizard.

3. After the wizard appears, click Next to begin.

4. Select both ADC components (ADC Service and ADC Management) for installation, then click Next to continue with the wizard.

5. Then provide a location where the wizard will install the ADC service files, then select Next.

6. Provides the account name and password for the ADC service. Then, click Next and watch the installation's progress on the screen.

7. When the installation completes, click Finish and exit the installation wizard.

Andy is now ready to move on to configuring a primary Connection Agreement and the appropriate synchronization settings.

Project 10.2
To configure a primary Connection Agreement and synchronization settings for Active Directory Connector service:

As mentioned earlier, a connection needs to be constructed between the FW West domain and the Exchange service at the Austin plant. Changes made to user accounts in Active Directory are supposed to synchronize at the Texas Exchange site.

Andy draws a quick network diagram. He starts by drawing a line down the middle of a sheet of paper and writing FW West (for the domain and its users directory) on the left-hand side. On the right-hand side of the paper, he scribbles ExcSrvr1, the name of the Exchange Server.

Just to help guide him through the configuration, he draws a line between FW West and ExcSrvr1 to represent the Primary Connection Agreement he needs to implement. As the fractional T-1 circuit is used only for mail

10

synchronization, he quickly calculates that adequate bandwidth exists for synchronizing all users and groups. He jots "Users and Groups" on the sheet of paper and puts his pen down.

With the diagram in hand, Andy proceeds to configure the Connection Agreement, which will also serve as the Primary Connection Agreement:

1. First, select Start | Programs | Administrative Tools | Active Directory Connector Management. Then, select the Active Directory Connector (FWWest, the server name, too) and right-click it. Then select New | Connection Agreement.

2. Enter a Connection Agreement name, and select the From Windows To Exchange radio button. Doublecheck to ensure the correct bridgehead server is selected in the Select A Server To Run The Connection Agreement box.

3. On the Connections tab, ensure that the correct server name and authentication method are selected (FWWest and Windows Challenge/Response, respectively).

4. In the Exchange Server Information section, enter the Exchange Server name (ExcSrvr1). Then enter the port, 389, chosen by the company and recommended by Microsoft, and doublecheck that the authentication method for the Exchange Server is Windows Challenge/Response.

5. In the Schedule area, set synchronization to occur always.

6. On the From Windows tab, add the appropriate Windows Organizational Units and fill in the Users and Groups checkboxes in the Select The Objects That You Want To Replicate box.

7. Select Delete The Exchange Mailboxes, Custom Recipients, And Distribution Lists radio button to synchronize deletions at the Exchange site that are made in Active Directory.

8. On the Advanced tab, select This Is A Primary Connection Agreement For The Connected Exchange Organization.

9. Select OK and then close the adcadmin Microsoft Management Console snap-in.

After instructing the IT director to keep him appraised of the ADC's performance, Andy heads out to start his long weekend—a well-deserved one at that.

CHAPTER ELEVEN

MANAGING DHCP AND WINS

After completing this chapter, you will be able to:

✓ Use the Dynamic Host Control Protocol (DHCP)

✓ Create and configure DHCP scopes and leases

✓ Avoid address conflicts and set up scope and global options

✓ Troubleshoot DHCP and maintain the DHCP database

✓ Discuss the Windows Internet Naming Service (WINS)

✓ Create and configure WINS servers and clients

✓ Control WINS servers and WINS replication

✓ Troubleshoot WINS and the WINS database

This chapter provides a review of the Dynamic Host Control Protocol and the Windows Internet Naming Service. Additionally, it covers new features that Windows 2000 has added to these services, and it performs some common tasks related to these services.

INTRODUCTION TO THE DYNAMIC HOST CONTROL PROTOCOL

The very nature of a TCP/IP network necessitates that each node should have a number of configuration settings. Early in the history of the Internet, the task of setting up nodes manually was realistic; as TCP/IP networks grew to thousands and even tens of thousands of nodes, however, an automated client configuration process had to be developed. Therefore the *Dynamic Host Control Protocol* was developed. The Dynamic Host Control Protocol (DHCP) was rapidly deployed throughout the Internet, and it continues to be used today.

The DHCP responds to client requests for TCP/IP configuration settings. Each node on a TCP/IP network needs an IP address, which is an obvious use for the DHCP. For the IP address to be of any use, a subnet mask and gateway address must also be assigned to DHCP clients. In addition to the IP address, primary and secondary name servers such as the Domain Name System (DNS) and the Windows Internet Naming System (WINS) can be assigned to the clients. If the WINS server address is specified, the NetBIOS node type must also be specified. These are the basic parameters that most DHCP servers issue to clients. If any of these settings need to be changed, that can be done on the DHCP server rather than having to visit each client machine.

In a TCP/IP network, the administrator sets up the DHCP server and configures the DHCP client to use the server. Within the DHCP server, one or more *scopes* represents a TCP/IP subnet. Each scope has a pool of TCP/IP addresses that can be assigned to clients as well as optional exclusion ranges, which will not be given to clients because they are reserved for hosts that are or will be manually configured. Clients request configuration settings from the DHCP server during bootup, and the server issues a lease that allows a client to keep an address for a specified amount of time so that the client doesn't have to obtain an address every time it boots. The DHCP server can also reserve an address for a client, so that a client, and only that client, can use a particular address consistently.

In addition to assigning TCP/IP addresses, DHCP servers can assign other configuration parameters called *options*. Basically, DHCP options are settings provided by the DHCP server that enable a DHCP client to participate on the TCP/IP network. Options can be specifically applied to a scope or applied globally to all scopes on a particular server. For example, the gateway (or router) option is typically set to the last router interface that the DHCP packet traversed before getting to the client. This is best defined as a scope, not a global option.

A typical example of a global option, which applies to all clients for a DHCP server, is the primary and secondary DNS server address. This option is often a global option for small to medium-sized networks that have only one primary and secondary server. If, however, the network is larger and contains multiple DNS subdomains, then the DNS server option would be particular to a scope. The DHCP service is actually less prone to errors than manually assigning parameters. Using a DHCP server is a good thing because changes to TCP/IP settings can be committed on the server without physically visiting each node on the network. Also, address conflicts seldom occur when using a DHCP server because the server maintains a database of address mappings and exclusion ranges. Finally, most network infrastructure devices recognize DHCP, and they can be configured to restrict or permit DHCP traffic through their interfaces.

The process that a client uses to obtain an address from a DHCP server involves certain costs. For example, the client boot process is prolonged because negotiating the settings is time consuming. Additionally, the server is loaded because it has to process address requests. Third, the traffic caused by the DHCP negotiation can overburden a network. To avoid these costs, a DHCP address is actually leased from a DHCP server. The lease allows the client to use the address for a specified duration rather than having to negotiate for an address during every boot.

DHCP Leases

The DHCP lease ensures that the address given to a client machine will not be reissued to another client for a specified time period. The default lease duration is eight days, but this setting can be tailored to meet the network environment. For instance, a network with more TCP/IP addresses than TCP/IP nodes might have a longer lease, which reduces DHCP traffic on the network. In the same scenario, if the options in DHCP change frequently, the lease duration might need to be reduced to ensure proper client configuration. Although an address can be leased to a client indefinitely, this is not recommended. Clients change and TCP/IP parameters change in every network environment, so a long lease is better than an indefinite lease for almost all DHCP implementations.

Leases are important, because the DHCP information is stored on the client and used during the boot process, before the client can communicate with the server to ensure that its address is unique. The first step in the process is for a client to announce that it needs an address, which is done by the DHCPDiscover message.

The *DHCPDiscover* is a broadcast message sent from a client with no TCP/IP configuration information. Because the client doesn't have an address yet, the source for the DHCPDiscover packet is 0.0.0.0, and the DCHPDiscover's destination address is the broadcast address.

All DHCP servers that the DHCPDiscover packet reaches answer with a *DHCPOffer* packet containing the necessary TCP/IP parameters for the client. The client will use only the first *DHCPOffer* packet it receives.

After the client receives the DHCPOffer, it returns a *DHCPRequest* to the offering server to express an acceptance of the address and lease. At this point, the server can issue either a *DHCPAcknowledge*, allowing the client to use the address, or a *DHCPNak* to instruct the client that the address was accepted by another client before the DHCPRequest was received. The *DHCPDecline* message can be sent from the client if it realizes the parameters sent by the server are not appropriate. The last conversation between client and server is the *DHCPRelease* in which the client releases the address for use by other clients.

The preceding process can be divided into the following client states:

➤ *Initialization state*—When the client is issuing the DHCPDiscover packets, it is in a state of initialization. This state instructs the client to use the source address 0.0.0.0 and destination of 255.255.255.255, and selects the packets for use in the selecting state.

➤ *Selecting state*—In the selecting state, the client has received one or more DHCPOffer packets. If no offers have been made, the client resends the discover messages numerous times at increasing intervals. Because the client has no address, most communication takes place at the Media Access (MAC) layer through User Datagram Protocol (UDP) ports 67 and 68. The most important function of the selecting state is to enable the client to decide which DHCPOffer it will use.

➤ *Requesting state*—After the selecting state, the client enters the requesting state. The requesting state deals primarily with the DHCPRequest message. Because the entire transaction has not been completed, the address at the Network layer still uses the broadcast destination address. After the DHCP server with authority for the address in the DHCPRequest gets the packet, the server issues either a DHCPAcknowledge or a DHCPNak, and the other DHCP servers expire their DHCPOffers.

➤ *Binding state*—The binding state involves the server sending a DHCPNak, which resets the entire process, or a DHCPAcknowledge, which allows the client to bind the address and parameters to the TCP/IP stack. As mentioned, the client receives a lease on a particular address.

➤ *Renewing state*—The default lease duration is eight days. When the lease has half expired, after four days, the client enters the renewing state. During the renewing state, the client sends a DHCPRequest to the server, which automatically renews the lease and updates any parameters that have changed since the last request. If the client cannot renew its address with the issuing server before 87.5 percent of the lease time expires, the client broadcasts a DHCPRequest to any available server. When a DHCP client is rebooted, it sends a DHCPRequest rather than starting over with a DHCPDiscover. A client will restart a process with a DHCPDiscover only if the client receives a DHCPNak.

Setting Up the DHCP Scope

Scopes are the fundamental unit of administration in DHCP. For DHCP to be effective, at least one TCP/IP scope must be created, and it must be activated for clients to receive addresses from the server. A scope is commonly a TCP/IP subnet, but it can be any group of contiguous addresses. A scope must also have a subnet mask to identify the boundaries of the scope. Scopes help the DHCP with maintenance and flexibility, provide fault tolerance, reserve addresses for particular clients, avoid address conflicts, and simplify administration.

Maintenance and Flexibility

For DHCP to remain a flexible service, certain facilities have to be provided, including:

➤ Certain types of nodes—DHCP servers, for example—need to have their addresses assigned statically. The DHCP service provides exclusion ranges so that one or more addresses within one or more ranges within a scope will not be handed out to DHCP clients.

➤ Lease durations can be customized for each scope to meet the needs of the network environment.

➤ Deleting records from DHCP is necessary, and can be a complicated task. The lease for the address first must be deleted, then the address must be excluded from the scope before the client reboots and requests the address again. To ensure that the client releases the address, the IPConfig/Release command can be issued on the client.

Fault Tolerance

The Windows 2000 implementation of DHCP does not provide a mechanism for fault tolerance. Therefore, the administrator must manually provide fault-tolerance services, using the following procedures. When multiple subnets exist, you should have a DHCP server on each subnet. The server not only provides a scope of addresses on the local subnet, but it also contains a scope for the remote subnet. The client will always prefer DHCPOffers from the local subnet, so the scope in the remote subnet will be used only if the DHCP server in the home subnet is not functioning properly. A common formula for this implementation is 80 percent of an address for a subnet on its home server, and 20 percent in a scope on the server in the remote subnet.

Reserving Addresses for Particular Clients

Some node types should always receive the same address from the server, even though they can have dynamically assigned addresses. For this purpose, a reservation system allows administrators to reserve a particular TCP/IP address for a node with a particular MAC address. However, making a reservation does not ensure that the address is not already being used by a different client. Testing the TCP/IP address with the ping command can verify whether the address is currently in use. If a DHCP client is using the address, issuing the IPConfig/ Release command on the client frees the address. Reservations do not automatically configure the client that is receiving the address, either. This can be accomplished by issuing the IPConfig/Release command on the target client. Reservations can be tricky to implement, but they are very useful for any clients that require the same address and need an automatic way to receive the latest configuration parameters.

Avoiding Address Conflicts

The DHCP server avoids address conflicts through the following processes. Namely, a DHCP server will not issue an address that is excluded, reserved, or issued to another client. Additionally, when conflict detection is enabled the server will ping an address a specified number of times before issuing it to a client. If the server receives a response to the ping, then the address is taken and marked as a BAD_ADDRESS for the length of the scope lease. However, you should take care when using conflict detection due to the obvious overhead involved. If the client has Windows 98 or later as an operating system, the client will also perform conflict detection and return a DHCPDecline if a conflict is detected.

Using Super-scopes to Simplify Administration

From time to time, scopes might need to be combined or deleted entirely. A group of scopes on a DHCP server that all serve the same network segment is called a *super-scope*. Super-scopes are outside the scope of this book and are not directly related to Exam 70-240, the Microsoft Windows 2000 Accelerated Exam, but they are important because they can be used when one network segment must be broken down into multiple TCP/IP subnets. They can also be used when a scope has allocated all its addresses and new nodes need to be added. Deleting scopes can cause some network interruption if clients are actively using the scope. Rather than deleting the scope immediately, deactivate the scope for at least half the duration of its lease so that its clients can perform a DHCPDiscover for a new scope or server.

Identifying Client Options and Using Multicast DHCP

As mentioned earlier in this chapter, DHCP options are settings that a DHCP server provides for a DHCP client to enable the client to participate on the TCP/IP network. Windows 2000 ships with a number of options, and additional options using the DHCP console can be installed as the need arises. (This is discussed in more detail in Project 11.2 in the Real-World Projects section at the end of this chapter.) DHCP options are used at the following various levels:

➤ *Client level*—The most specific level is the client level, which means that an option exists only for a specific client.

➤ *Class level*—The class level options are applied to clients that identify themselves with a particular class ID.

➤ *Scope level*—Above the class level is the scope level, which applies only to a particular scope.

➤ *Server level*—The server level applies to all scopes on a DHCP server.

If a conflict occurs between options at two different levels, the option more specific to the client takes precedence. Although not required, a number of options prove extremely useful in the network environment.

The most common options are settings that administrators statically assign to clients. The most commonly used options are subnet mask, router (gateway), DNS servers, WINS servers, and WINS node type. The DHCP settings can be customized with the lease time and renewal time options. Additionally, options can be used for a specific class of vendor equipment or a certain class of user. When these classes are necessary, the client will supply the server with the class ID, and the server will respond with the appropriate options. Classes can be useful, but many clients don't support them. Clients that do not support classes fall into the default user class on the DHCP server.

A special type of scope—a *multicast scope*—can be configured in Windows 2000 DHCP. Multicast scopes are in the range 224.0.0.0 through 239.255.255.255, and they are set up as regular scopes in the DHCP console. A multicast scope assigns a secondary TCP/IP address to a client. Once assigned a multicast address, all clients in the multicast scope participate in a multicast group, similar

11

to being part of a distribution list in Microsoft Exchange. Packets can then be sent to a multicast group, and all clients within the group will receive the packet.

Keeping the DHCP Database Reliable

The DHCP service requires certain files for proper operation. All the files are located in the %systemroot%\system32\dhcp directory. This directory contains a number of log files that record the activities of the DHCP service. Additionally, the address mappings and options are stored in the DHCP database. When records are deleted from the database, empty spaces are created. Compacting the database gets rid of the empty space and improves the performance of the database.

Compacting the DHCP Database

The addresses assigned by the DHCP server are kept in a database. Networks change frequently, and, as a network changes, the DHCP database grows. The database can become quite large, and some records within the database might be outdated. Even though it is possible to delete records through the DHCP console, the space that deleted records held in the database is still present in the database. Therefore, Windows 2000 periodically compacts the database while it is online, but some offline compaction should also be performed. (This is discussed in more detail in the Real-World Projects at the end of this chapter.)

The DHCP protocol is used for the TCP/IP configuration of standard client machines. However, the bootstrap protocol can be used for diskless workstations that need TCP/IP configuration before the start of their operating system.

Using the Bootstrap Protocol

The bootstrap protocol, also known as BOOTP, is used to assign the parameters necessary to participate in a TCP/IP network to diskless workstations. BOOTP provides many of the same services as DHCP. The packet types and port numbers are the same, and even the communication between client and server is the same for both services. However, a couple of characteristics of BOOTP differ from DHCP, specifically:

➤ BOOTP clients not only receive TCP/IP parameters, but they also download an image file from the server to assist them in the boot process.

➤ BOOTP doesn't support as many TCP/IP options as DHCP, and the clients renew their address only when the client boots.

The Windows 2000's implementation of DHCP provides the ability to support both DHCP clients and BOOTP clients effectively. Table 11.1 lists the most common options used with BOOTP clients.

Table 11.1   Common options for BOOTP clients.

Option Code	Description
1	Subnet Mask
3	Router
5	Name Server
12	Computer Name
15	Domain Name
44	WINS Server
46	NetBIOS Node Type
55	Additional Options
69	SMTP Server
70	POP Server
N/A	Boot Image Type
N/A	Boot Image Path
N/A	Boot Image Server

Special Considerations with DHCP Implementation

Although the DHCP service can be straightforward, a few issues need to be considered. If the DHCP server is to be upgraded from a previous version of Windows NT to Windows 2000, a special procedure exists for that conversion.

Converting to the Windows 2000 Database Format

If a DHCP database from a previous version exists, Windows 2000 will automatically convert it to the Windows 2000 database format. This process not only stops the DHCP service temporarily, but can also require a large amount of disk space depending on the size of the database. Keep in mind that once a database is converted, it cannot be changed back to its old format.

Preventing Rogue DHCP Servers

Another consideration associated with DHCP implementations are rogue DHCP servers. A rogue DHCP server is a server that is not authorized in the Active Directory. To prevent rogue servers, all DHCP servers should be on a domain controller or member server in an Active Directory. Furthermore, it is critical that the first DHCP server be a domain controller or member server when DHCP is implemented. Changing from a standalone server after DHCP is implemented can cause problems. Rogue servers can be detected by sending DHCPInform messages between servers or by using vendor-specific options designed for the task.

Providing Fault Tolerance

The DHCP service provides fault tolerance and integration with name resolution services. Windows 2000 clustering services will allow two servers—

a primary and a backup—to offer the same DHCP services and configuration at the same time. During normal operations, the primary DHCP server provides clients with their configuration. If the primary server fails, the backup server services requests so clients do not experience any significant downtime.

Integration with DNS

The DHCP service in Windows 2000 can provide Windows 2000 DNS servers with the data necessary to update both A type (host) and PTR type (reverse) records (which are discussed in Chapter 3). Windows 2000 clients can register themselves dynamically with the DNS server, but downlevel operating systems (such as NT 4 and Windows 9x) cannot register themselves. If NT 4 and Windows 9x clients receive their TCP/IP configuration from a Windows 2000 DHCP server, the server will handle the dynamic registration for these NT 4 and Windows 9x clients so dynamic DNS can be implemented.

DHCP and APIPA Interaction

The Windows 2000 DHCP service has features designed for both small and large networks. Beginning with Windows 98, all Windows operating systems (including Windows 2000) provide Automatic Private IP Addressing (APIPA) (169.254.0.0) for small networks. This means that systems receive their TCP/IP configuration from an APIPA server without needing to implement DHCP. After a network grows to more than 25 nodes, however, a DHCP server should be implemented. If an APIPA server detects a DHCP server, that DHCP server will automatically cease to serve clients on the network. A single Windows 2000 DHCP server can be multihomed and serve all segments to which it is connected. The service binds to the primary TCP/IP address on each NIC in the server, and scopes can be configured for each subnet that the server is connected to. These features make Windows 2000 DHCP an effective service for networks of all sizes and complexities.

Maintaining the DHCP Service

Maintaining the DHCP service involves monitoring both the server and the clients. Two tools are available on the client depending on which operating system it is running—IPCONFIG and WINIPCFG.

If a client is Windows NT or Windows 2000, the IPCONFIG utility can be used with switches from the command prompt to display the TCP/IP settings for the client and release or renew a DHCP lease. If a client is Windows 9x, the utility can be run using the **WINIPCFG** command. This utility is a window that displays the TCP/IP configuration and has buttons to release and renew a DHCP lease. Though these utilities can be useful, the connectivity of the machine (Physical layer) is often the problem. To test client connectivity, checking the link light on the NIC and pinging to and from a client are the two best tests to run.

If the problem appears to be with the DHCP server, you have a few tools you can use to narrow down the problem. The first functionality to check is whether the service is actually running. To start the service from the command prompt, issue the following command:

```
NET START DHCPSERVER
```

If the service still does not appear to be working, the Event Viewer can be used to uncover additional details or specific error codes. One common error is placing a DHCP relay and a DHCP server on the same machine. If a DHCP relay exists, it can't be on the same server as the DHCP service. Because the DHCP service and the DHCP relay service both use the same UDP ports, the services will conflict with each other; they should reside on separate computers.

A few other useful tools can be used to keep track of statistical data about the DHCP service. The *System Monitor* (sysmon), formerly Performance Monitor, can be used to capture performance data from the DHCP service. When DHCP is installed, a number of counters are also installed, including:

➤ *packets received per second*—Assists in troubleshooting a server that might be overwhelmed by DHCP traffic.

➤ *requests per second*—Specifies whether the lease time for a scope is long enough. If the lease time is not long enough, the *requests per second* will far outweigh the expected number for the clients on the network.

➤ *declines per second*—Indicates that the scope contains addresses that are being used for statically assigned clients if there's a high number of *declines per second*.

Finally, log files can be used to record all activity for a DHCP service. The audit log settings can be found in the properties of the DHCP server. For the log files to be of any use, they must be customizable. The path for log files can be customized along with the size of the logs. To avoid filling the disk, the amount of space available on disk and the interval at which the server will check for free space can be set. The name of the log is based on the day of the week that the service starts, such as *dhcpsrvlog.mon*. If the existing log has not been updated in the last 24 hours, it is overwritten; otherwise, it is appended. The log records each event ID, date, time, description, client IP address, client computer name, and client MAC address. Table 11.2 lists the common event IDs for the DHCP service.

Table 11.2   Common event IDs for DHCP service.

Event ID	Description
00	Log started
01	Log stopped
02	Log paused (due to disk limit)
10	New IP leased
11	Lease renewed
12	Lease released
13	Conflict detected

INTRODUCTION TO THE WINDOWS INTERNET NAMING SERVICE

The WINS service provides NetBIOS names to TCP/IP address resolution so that network resources can be referred to by their 15-character NetBIOS names without using excessive broadcasts or lengthy LMHOSTS files. NetBIOS is a protocol used at the Session layer of the OSI model. It can be used with numerous compatible Transport layer protocols, such as NetBEUI, TCP/IP, and IPX/SPX. While the assignable names are only 15 characters, NetBIOS names are actually 16 characters. The last character of a NetBIOS name is reserved and identifies the type of record, such as computer name, service, workgroup, and so forth. The NetBIOS namespace is flat, meaning that there is no hierarchy of domains like the DNS namespace.

The NetBIOS name resolution process can occur in a few ways, and the network engineer is responsible for tailoring NetBIOS to the needs of the environment. In addition to a NetBIOS name server (WINS), LMHOSTS files that list the NetBIOS name and TCP/IP addresses can be placed on each client machine. Also, broadcasts can be performed by the resolver to query particular machines or machines with particular services. To a great extent, the node or client type will dictate the NetBIOS name resolution methods and the order in which they are used. Node types include the following:

➤ *B-node*—The B-node is strictly a broadcast-based resolver. Microsoft Windows clients can be B-nodes; however, this is not the most efficient method of name resolution.

➤ *P-node*—The P-node uses a point-to-point method of communication, such as WINS client to WINS server.

➤ *M-node*—The M-node, or mixed node, first tries to broadcast, then tries the point-to-point method.

➤ *H-node*—Most Windows clients are hybrids of the other nodes, or H-node. H-nodes first check their NetBIOS name cache, then the WINS server, followed by a broadcast. If the broadcast doesn't resolve the name, the LMHOSTS, HOSTS, and DNS servers are checked, in that order.

The WINS registration process is straightforward, but some complexities can arise depending on the network environment. During the boot process, the client attempts to register with a name registration request. Not only is the name registered, but every NetBIOS process attempts to register itself. If unable to register, the client will retry at 10-minute intervals. If the server returns a positive response, the client is registered. If a duplicate name is on the network, the server will return a *WACK* (wait for acknowledgment). During the wait, the server sends a challenge to the client that is already using the name. The results of the challenge determine which client gets the registration, and the other client must change names and restart the process.

Two mechanisms necessary for WINS are the *renew* and *release* functions. When the client reaches half of its renewal interval, it must renew its registration. The client sends a refresh request to the primary server. If the client doesn't receive a reply, it continues to try every 10 minutes, for 60 minutes; then it switches to the secondary WINS server. If the secondary server cannot accommodate the request (again using 10-minute intervals for one hour), the client moves back to the primary server to repeat the routine. This continues either until the client is registered or the refresh interval expires. If the refresh interval expires, the server releases the name for use by other clients. Releasing a name occurs whenever a client or name is taken offline. This release marks the record on the server, and the record remains released for the extinction interval (the amount of time the record remains after it is released). However, the record will continue to exist until the extinction timeout period expires and it is finally scavenged from the jet database that contains the WINS data.

If a conflict is detected during the registration process, a server can react in a few ways. For example:

➤ If the record is a normal group record or a static mapping, the server returns a negative response.

➤ If the record is dynamic and the client address is the same as the existing record, the registration is completed and the appropriate timestamps are reset.

➤ If the record's address is different than the registering client and the record is tombstoned (as described later in this chapter) or released, the registration is successful.

➤ If the record and the client address are different for an active record, the server verifies the record with a name query. If the query is returned by the original host, a negative response is returned and the registering client is responsible for rectifying the situation by changing names. If the query is not successful, however, the new registrant gets the name.

Controlling traffic due to existing WINS clients can be tricky. When a client is turned off, it releases its name, but the records for that machine remain until the extinction interval expires. If it is turned on again within a reasonable period (set by the administrator), the record will not be pushed to other servers. This ensures that traffic for most clients will not be voluminous. If a number of clients move between subnets, however, the overhead can flood the network. After moving, the client will attempt to register with a different address, which will cause the server to perform a name query. Then, the server will acknowledge the registration, which causes more traffic.

Exploring WINS

WINS servers are an effective means of providing NetBIOS name resolution without the overhead of broadcast traffic or complex maintenance of LMHOSTS files. To ensure enterprise-wide NetBIOS name resolution, WINS servers replicate their databases to other servers. Since the service provides dynamic registration, administrators are not involved in the daily operation of the servers. The WINS implementation of NetBIOS name services (NBNS) is compatible with Internet standards, thereby enabling a limited amount of interaction with other NBNS systems. Previous versions of WINS required building and breaking down connections whenever a replication was necessary, but Windows 2000 WINS maintains persistent connections with its replication partners. The new version also has automatic discovery of replication partners.

Most records in a WINS server are unique, but some records can be duplicates. Normal group names are one type of record that can have multiple entries; they are registered, but not associated with any TCP/IP address. Multiple normal group registrations are allowed on WINS servers across the network, but they all share a common timestamp, which is set to the last time a client registered the group. When a client looks for a group registration, it broadcasts on the local subnet and is answered by the WINS server. As described later in this chapter, there are mechanisms to scavenge old records, but the server will return the record until it is scavenged even if it's released or tombstoned. Internet groups are created by users and registered with up to 25 TCP/IP addresses of the groups' members. Internet groups can file for registration with a sixteenth character of 0x20, workgroup registration 0x0, or the messenger service identified by 0x3. The domain record is used to identify domain controllers.

Up to 25 records with a domain name and TCP/IP address can identify domain browsers. Records are overwritten if there are more than 25 records. Similarly, there can be only 25 records identifying multihomed computers.

WINS traffic can be fairly extensive, so mechanisms are built in to help control traffic. The broadcast only, or B-node type, of node is not the most efficient means of NetBIOS name resolution. However, sometimes broadcasts are the only method available for the client's operating system. To limit the broadcast traffic and expedite the name resolution process for broadcast nodes, Microsoft introduced the *WINS proxy*.

The WINS proxy is a WINS-enabled node that resides on the same subnet as one or more B-node clients. When the B-node client broadcasts for a resolution, the WINS proxy intercepts the request. If an entry is in the proxy cache, the proxy will immediately resolve the name. If the name is not in the cache, the proxy agent will query the WINS server for resolution and then return the results to the B-node. By its very nature as a name service, WINS traffic occurs in large bursts. To accommodate this traffic, the Windows 2000 implementation of WINS has burst-handling capabilities. When the burst queue becomes full, the server begins to respond positively to all requests without the normal collision and error checking. The Time To Live on these records is offset by five minutes so that records will reregister at staggered intervals. If the number of registrations exceeds 25,000, the server stops servicing registrations and queries.

11

Keeping the WINS Database Reliable

The WINS service requires certain files for proper operation. All the files are located in the %sysroot%\system32\WINS directory.

The WINS server maintains a database named WINS.MDB, which contains the NetBIOS name to TCP/IP address mappings. This database is the same type used by Windows 2000 and Microsoft Exchange. This database format places no restrictions on the number of records or the size of the database. As entries in the database become unusable, they can be scavenged manually or the WINS service will scavenge them from the database. Windows 2000 automatically performs a certain amount of online compaction, but this does not free the space in the database. To solve this problem, the database should be compacted offline periodically by following the directions given in the Real-World Projects at the end of this chapter.

Because the WINS.MDB database holds information that is crucial to WINS, Microsoft includes a method of repairing and backing it up. Namely, the WINS service provides a parameter that you can use to indicate a backup path, and the service will back up the database every three hours by default. To repair minor corruption in a database, you can use version numbers. Setting the version number to a higher level on the server with good records will force replication of the good records. The version number settings are decribed further in the Real-World Projects. Care should be taken, though, because the version number can only be incremented and the WINS database must be deleted to decrement the value. These methods are very cumbersome, and there is an easier way to restore WINS data; forcing a replication from a WINS partner that has a valid database usually solves most corruption problems.

Managing Servers, Records, and Replication

Replication allows many servers to maintain an accurate database with records from other servers. WINS servers exchange data among themselves in a process called *replication*. The WINS server that registers a record owns the record. Periodically, based on administrative parameters, a server will send the records it owns to the other servers that are configured as its replication partners. Consistency checking forces a WINS server to obtain periodically all the records in its database directly from the owning server. If a local record's version ID is the same on the owning server record's ID, the record is simply timestamped. If the record's version ID is higher on the owning server than the local record's version ID, the record is updated.

The records in the database are governed by a few timer settings. For example:

➤ The *renewal interval*, also known as Time To Live, is the amount of time that a client has to reregister a name before the name is released. If a name is released and another client wants to register the name with a different TCP/IP address, the server will allow the transaction to occur.

➤ The *extinction interval* is the amount of time that a released name can exist before it is tombstoned.

➤ The *extinction timeout* is the amount of time a tombstoned record will exist before it is deleted.

➤ The *verification interval* is the amount of time an active record exists before it will be verified with its owner server.

All these timer settings help ensure that the WINS database records are accurate and that the WINS database stays as small as possible.

Records can be removed in a few ways. First, you can simply delete a record. When a record is deleted, however, it is removed only from the current server. All replicated copies of the record will still exist and need to be dealt with further. A better option to deleting a record is to tombstone the record. When a record is tombstoned, the tombstone is replicated so that other servers have the tombstone record as well. After all the servers have a tombstone, the name will no longer resolve, and the record will eventually be removed from the databases of all WINS servers.

Replication for WINS servers can be triggered by time or a number of other changes. Furthermore, WINS servers can take advantage of both push and pull replication:

➤ *Push replication*—Based on the number of changes to the version number of a record or set of records. When the push replication is triggered, the server sends the records with newer versions to all its push replication partners.

➤ *Pull replication*—Based on a start time and an interval at which the server should pull records from its pull partners.

To ensure reliable WINS databases, primary and secondary servers should be configured as both push and pull partners. Both replication types can be triggered by service startup, and the settings for these replications depend on the speed of the links between the servers. The time of convergence, or period of time between client registration and server replication, is called *latency*. Latency can sometimes cause problems, because client registrations might conflict with records that are being replicated or the replica on the server might conflict with a replica from another server. If the conflict is between a record that the server owns and a replica, the record can be overwritten only if it is not active. If the conflict is between two replicas, the newest replica takes precedence.

11

CHAPTER SUMMARY

All nodes on a TCP/IP network need certain configuration parameters to function properly. On smaller networks, these settings can be handled manually; on larger networks, however, an efficient means of managing these settings is needed. The Dynamic Host Control Protocol (DHCP) service gives administrators a tool to deal with the volume of configuration parameters and nodes for any size of network. In addition to the address, clients can receive some parameters that are considered to be options. Options can be assigned based on the scope, class, or individual client. Common options are addresses for DNS and WINS servers, the router or gateway address, a time server address, and many others. Though it can introduce a certain amount of overhead, conflict detection can be used to ensure that address conflicts do not occur. The Windows 2000 DHCP service also supports the bootstrap protocol, or BOOTP. This protocol is used for clients that must receive their address immediately to download their operating system to memory through the network.

The DHCP server has a multifaceted job. The DHCP service is assigned one or more ranges of contiguous TCP/IP addresses, called scopes, that it can offer to clients, as well as specified exclusion ranges within the scopes that will not be handed out. After a client receives an address from a DHCP server, it can keep using the address for an amount of time, called a lease, that can be adjusted by the administrator. The mechanics behind a DHCP process is actually quite involved, as described in the chapter. The default lease duration is eight days, but that can be tailored to meet the network environment. On a network with more TCP/IP addresses than hosts, the lease can be longer so that it just renews optional parameters. In a network with more hosts than TCP/IP address, the lease should be shorter so that nodes without an address have a chance to get one. Halfway through the lease, the client begins the renewal process to ensure that it has enough time to renew before the lease expires.

The DHCP service should be engineered with certain considerations in mind. Windows 2000 DHCP eliminates rogue DHCP servers by requiring servers to be authorized in the Active Directory. This authorization might also affect downlevel servers, so they must be considered. To provide a limited amount of fault tolerance, more than one DHCP server should be available. A DHCP server should contain a scope containing 80 percent of the address for the local subnet, and 20 percent of the address for another subnet in case the server in the other subnet should fail. Additionally, sufficient addresses should be available in the exclusion ranges to accommodate any nodes that should have static address, such as servers and printers. If a scope runs out of addresses, or two scopes need to be combined, super-scopes can be formed to group scopes for administrative purposes. (As noted earlier in this chapter, super-scopes are beyond the coverage of this book, but interested readers are encouraged to learn more about them.) Multicast scopes allow clients to receive a secondary address that is part of a subscription-based group for special types of network traffic called multicast.

Periodically, the DHCP service requires maintenance. The mappings are kept in a database in \<sysroot>\system32\dhcp. This database is automatically compacted online, but offline compacting with the jetpack utility (discussed in more detail in the Real-World Projects at the end of this chapter) is sometimes necessary. To take the service offline from the command prompt, issue the **net stop dhcpserver** command. Log files in this directory can be used for troubleshooting, and the Event Viewer records some events for the service. Both DHCP and DHCP relays use the same ports, so ensure that both the services are not running on the same server. The System Monitor has some counters for the DHCP service, and SNMP can be used for realtime statistical management of the service. The client provides a few tools that can help troubleshoot the functionality of DHCP. On Windows 9x clients, the WINIPCFG utility displays the current TCP/IP configuration and provides buttons to release and renew the DHCP settings. On Windows NT and Windows 2000, the same functionality can be found in the **IPCONFIG** command with command-line switches.

Downlevel systems often use a Session level protocol named NetBIOS for application communication. The WINS service resolves NetBIOS names to TCP/IP addresses much like LMHOSTS files do. NetBIOS clients can be B-node (broadcast based), P-node (server based), M-node (broadcast and server), or H-node (server, broadcast, and static file based). All Windows operating systems are H-node. When a WINS client boots, it registers its name as well as any NetBIOS process with the WINS service automatically. If no response is received, the client continues to attempt registration, and, if a duplicate name is on the network, the server responds with a WACK message and attempts to verify the other computer before denying the request. Some records are not unique. Normal groups can have unlimited members, because client addresses are not registered with the group name. Internet groups register the client addresses with the computer name, so they are limited to 25 members. To support clients that are not WINS enabled, a WINS proxy can be placed on the local subnet to capture broadcast requests and resolve the name for the client.

Like the DHCP service, the WINS service requires maintenance. The mappings are kept in a database in \\<sysroot>\system32\WINS. This database is automatically compacted online, but offline compacting with the jetpack utility is sometimes necessary. Log files also reside in this directory, and they can be used for troubleshooting. Additionally, the Event Viewer records some events for the WINS service, and the client provides the **WINIPCFG** or **IPCONFIG** command to assist with maintenance.

11

REVIEW QUESTIONS

1. After creating a DHCP scope, the scope is automatically available to clients.

   a. True

   b. False

2. A(n) _____ is a type of network traffic sent to all nodes on a TCP/IP subnet.

   a. Unicast

   b. Broadcast

   c. Telecast

   d. Multicast

3. A(n) _____ is a computer on a network that provides the DHCP service to clients.

   a. Normal group

   b. WINS Proxy

   c. Internet group

   d. DHCP server

4. What type of message is sent by a DHCP client to identify DHCP servers on the network?

   a. DHCPRequest

   b. DHCPNak

   c. DHCPDiscover

   d. DHCPDecline

5. A _____ is a response from a DHCP client wanting to accept parameters.

   a. DHCPDiscover

   b. DHCPNak

   c. DHCPDecline

   d. DHCPRequest

6. A DHCPNAK is a message sent by a DHCP server denying a DHCPRequest message.

   a. True

   b. False

7. A(n) _____ is a range of addresses in a DHCP scope that will not be offered to clients by the server.

   a. Normal group

   b. Exclusion range

   c. Internet group

   d. WINS Proxy

8. Which utility is used from the Windows 2000 client command prompt to display, release, and renew DHCP parameters?

   a. WINIPCFG

   b. IPCONFIG

   c. IPACTIVATE

   d. IPSET

9. _____ is a type of network traffic sent to select clients based on their multicast TCP/IP address.

   a. Unicast

   b. Broadcast

   c. Multicast

   d. Telecast

10. The _____ is the DHCP state in which the client sends a DHCPRequest message halfway through the lease duration.

   a. Normal group

   b. Renewing state

   c. Internet group

   d. WINS Proxy

11. _____ are a contiguous range of TCP/IP addresses, usually a TCP/IP subnet, available for use on a DHCP server.

   a. Scopes

   b. Super-scopes

   c. Subscopes

   d. IPScopes

12. A(n) _____ is a group of DHCP scopes combined to reduce administrative overhead.

   a. Normal group

   b. Internet group

   c. WINS Proxy

   d. Super-scope

13. The Session layer protocol used by applications on a LAN is _____.

   a. IPX/SPX

   b. DLC

   c. NetBEUI

   d. NetBIOS

11

14. A static file that contains the NetBIOS name to TCP/IP address mappings is _____.

    a. HOSTS

    b. NBHOSTS

    c. LMHOSTS

    d. WINHOSTS

15. The type of NetBIOS node that uses another host as its primary name resolution mechanism is _____.

    a. P-node

    b. B-node

    c. H-node

    d. M-node

16. The type of NetBIOS node that can use broadcast, point-to-point (WINS and DNS), as well as HOSTS and LMHOSTS files is _____.

    a. B-node

    b. H-node

    c. P-node

    d. M-node

17. The process a client initiates to enter its record(s) into a WINS server database is _____.

    a. Broadcast

    b. Deactivation

    c. Activation

    d. Registration

18. The server acknowledgement that a record has been entered into the WINS database is _____.

    a. DACK

    b. WACK

    c. RACK

    d. LACK

19. The process a WINS client uses to free up a record temporarily is _____.

    a. Release

    b. Renew

    c. Config

    d. Tombstone

20. The process a server uses to mark a WINS record available, but not yet ready for scavenging, is _____.

    a. Renew

    b. Release

    c. Config

    d. Tombstone

21. The process a server uses to remove records from a WINS server is called _____.

    a. Scavenging

    b. Scrubbing

    c. Ravaging

    d. Parsing

22. A record that identifies a common name for multiple nodes but does not list TCP/IP addresses is a(n) _____.

    a. DHCP server

    b. Internet group

    c. Normal group

    d. WINS Proxy

23. The type of record that identifies a common name for multiple nodes and lists TCP/IP addresses is a(n) _____.

    a. Internet group

    b. Normal group

    c. DHCP server

    d. WINS Proxy

24. A(n) _____ is a WINS-enabled client that intercepts and resolves broadcast queries from non-WINS clients.

    a. DHCP server

    b. Normal group

    c. WINS Proxy

    d. Internet group

11

REAL-WORLD PROJECTS

Andy Palmer has been assigned a new client with an existing network. Andy's client has migrated most of its clients and member servers to Windows 2000, and all their domain controllers are using Windows 2000. Now Andy needs to implement DHCP for the client to automate the assignment of TCP/IP configuration settings and WINS to support NetBIOS name resolution for their downlevel clients.

Project 11.1
To install the DHCP service:

The first thing Andy needs to do is install the DHCP service. He decides to do this on a member server that has already been upgraded to Windows 2000.

1. Start the Add/Remove Programs applet in the Control Panel.

2. Select Add/Remove Windows Components, and click the Components button. Figure 11.1 shows the resulting dialog box.

3. Select Networking Services, and click Details.

4. Select Dynamic Host Control Protocol, and click Next.

5. Restart the computer if necessary.

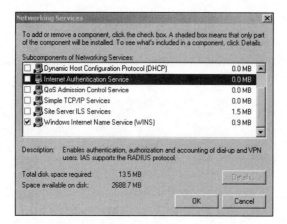

Figure 11.1 Installing the DHCP service.

Project 11.2
To set up the DHCP service:

Once the DHCP service has been installed, Andy needs to configure the server to meet the client's needs. He must set the server configuration parameters and create a new scope of address for the client to use.

1. Open the DHCP console from the Administrative Tools menu.

2. Right-click DHCP in the left pane, and select Add Server.

3. Select This Server, and click Browse. Select your server from the dialog box, and click OK. Click OK in the Add Server box.

4. Right-click the server in the left pane, and select New Scope. Click Next.

5. Provide a name and description for the new scope, and click Next.

6. Provide the start address and end address parameters, verify that the length and subnet mask are correct, and click Next.

7. Provide the start address and end address for the exclusion range, click Add, then click Next.

8. Provide a lease duration that suits the situation, and click Next.

9. Select the Yes, I Want To Configure These Options Now option.

10. Provide the router address, click Add to insert the routers to the list, then click Next.

11. Provide the parent domain (such as **coriolis.test**), add the IP address of the DNS servers, then click Next.

12. Add the IP address of the WINS servers, and click Next.

13. If there is no other configuration necessary, select Yes, I Want To Activate The Scope Now, click Next, then click Finish.

14. On the Action menu, select Authorize to ensure Active Directory will allow the server to provide addresses. Figure 11.2 shows a DHCP console with a completed scope that is not yet activated.

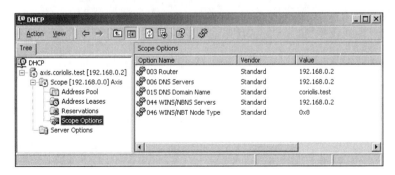

Figure 11.2   A DHCP console with a completed but inactive scope.

Project 11.3
To compact the DHCP or WINS database:

After a few weeks of use, many changes have been committed to the DHCP and WINS databases. Andy decides that compacting the databases will improve performance. He uses the following procedure for each database.

1. Open a command prompt, as shown in Figure 11.3.

2. Change to the %systemroot%\system32\wins directory for the WINS database, or the %sysroot%\system32\dhcp directory for the DHCP database.

3. Issue the **net stop wins** command for the WINS database, or the **net stop dhcpserver** command for the DHCP database.

4. Compact the database by issuing the **jetpack wins.mdb tmp.mdb** command for the WINS database, or the **jetpack dhcp.mdb tmp.mdb** command for the DHCP database.

5. Finally, issue the **net start wins** command to restart the WINS service, or the **net start dhcpserver** command to restart the DHCP service.

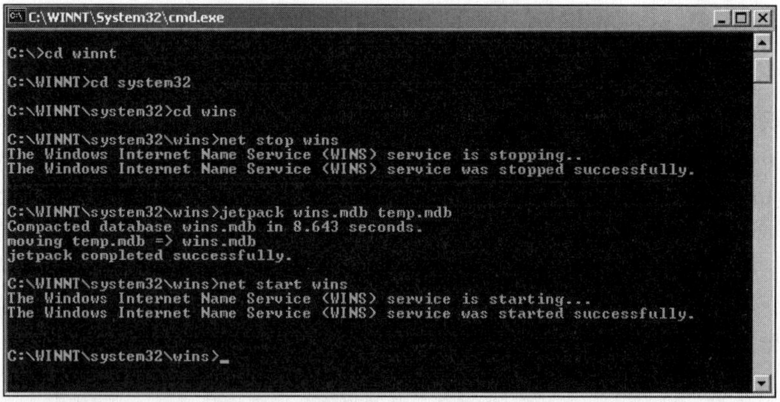

Figure 11.3   Compacting the WINS database from the command prompt.

Project 11.4
To set up Windows 2000 Professional as a WINS client:

After installing the WINS service, Andy needs to configure his client and its own clients to use the service. Some clients can be configured by changing options on the DHCP server, but a few of the client machines have statically assigned address. Andy takes the following steps on each statically configured client to enable the WINS service.

1. Open Control Panel, then open Network And Dialup Connections.

2. Right-click the desired connection, and click Properties.

3. Select Internet Protocol (TCP/IP), and click Properties.

4. Click the Advanced button, and select the WINS tab, as shown in Figure 11.4.

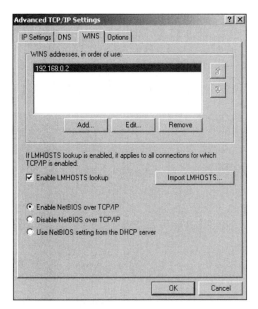

Figure 11.4 Configuring a Windows 2000 Professional WINS client.

5. Click Add, enter the TCP/IP address of the secondary WINS server, then click Add again.

6. Click Add, enter the TCP/IP address of the primary WINS server, then click Add again.

7. If you will use an LMHOSTS file for special mappings, select the Enable LMHOSTS Lookup option. This action will use the LMHOSTS file in the %sysroot%\system32\drivers\etc directory, or you can import an LMHOSTS file using Import LMHOSTS button.

8. Choose the Enable NetBIOS Over TCP/IP option.

9. Click OK three times to close the dialog boxes. This procedure should not require a reboot.

Project 11.5
To install the WINS service:

Andy has configured the clients, but then he notices that the WINS service is not actually installed on the secondary WINS server. He takes the following actions to install the service on the secondary server.

1. Start the Add/Remove Programs applet in Control Panel.

2. Select Add/Remove Windows Components, and click the Components button.

3. Select Networking Services, and click Details.

4. Select Windows Internet Name Service (WINS), and click Next.

5. Restart the computer if necessary.

Project 11.6
To add a static mapping in WINS:

Andy's client has complained that their downlevel clients cannot access the Unix server by its NetBIOS name. Andy knows that this feature will require a static mapping for the Unix host on the WINS server, so he takes the following steps to enter the static mapping.

1. Start the WINS console from the Administrative Tools menu.

2. Right-click the Active Registrations, and select New Static Mapping. Figure 11.5 shows the resulting dialog box.

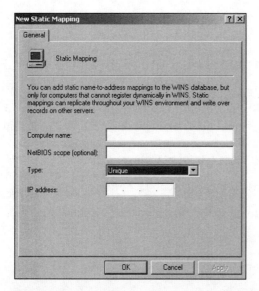

Figure 11.5   Adding a new static mapping in WINS.

3. Enter the computer name.

4. Enter the NetBIOS scope, if necessary (not commonly used).

5. In the Type drop-down box, select the appropriate mapping type.

6. Enter the TCP/IP address, and click OK.

Project 11.7
To configure burst mode for WINS servers:

While troubleshooting a helpdesk ticket for the client, Andy notices that during peak periods the WINS server stops responding to client requests. He knows that the burst mode support in the Windows 2000 WINS service will help alleviate this problem. He follows this procedure to implement burst mode support on the WINS server.

1. Open the WINS console.

2. Right-click the server, and select Properties.

3. On the Advanced tab (shown in Figure 11.6), check the box for the burst mode settings.

4. Check the Enable Burst Handling checkbox, select the appropriate level, and then click OK. Low will start burst handling at 300 queries, Medium starts at 500, High starts at 1,000, and Custom allows you to enter the number of queries manually before burst handling starts. Then click OK.

11

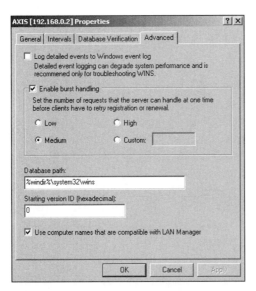

Figure 11.6   Configuring the WINS server for burst mode.

UNDERSTANDING AND ADMINISTERING DISK MANAGEMENT FUNCTIONALITY

After completing this chapter, you will be able to:

✓ Differentiate between basic disk storage and dynamic disk storage

✓ Explain differences between Windows NT and Windows 2000 disk storage

✓ Configure the Disk Management MMC snap-in

✓ Create, administer, and extend simple volumes

✓ Implement, manage, and extend spanned volumes

✓ Create and administer stripe volumes

✓ Describe and administer the Disk Defragmenter utility

✓ Manage disks on other systems

✓ Configure drive letters and drive paths

✓ Create and administer Windows NT 4 disk sets

W hile the concepts are the same as in Windows NT Server 4, the creation, implementation, and administration of disk storage and management functions are enhanced in Windows 2000. New disk storage alternatives exist, and the Disk Defragmenter utility has been improved. Furthermore, Windows 2000 includes support for the FAT32 file system.

Unlike with Windows NT, Windows 2000 administrators and support personnel can now make use of dynamic disks and profit from the new efficiencies the new storage functionality creates. Prior to sitting for Microsoft Exam 70-240, the Windows 2000 Accelerated exam, you should ensure you have a grasp of all the new disk management utilities in Windows 2000 as well as the new interfaces you'll encounter when performing tasks once completed on the Windows NT 4 Server platform.

Windows 2000 offers complete disk management functionality using another Microsoft Management Console (MMC) snap-in titled, appropriately enough, Disk Management. Before we discuss its usage, it's best to quickly review differences between the old Windows NT and new Windows 2000 disk storage options.

DISK STORAGE OPTIONS

Windows 2000 supports two disk storage options—basic storage and dynamic storage. Although you may be familiar with basic storage, or basic disk configurations, dynamic storage, or dynamic disk configurations, is a new feature of Windows 2000.

Basic Storage

Basic storage disks contain primary disk partitions. Basic disks can also house extended partitions that house logical drives. Hard disks featuring basic storage support up to four primary partitions. Alternatively, a basic disk can contain three primary partitions and one extended partition.

By default, Windows 2000 disks typically feature basic storage. The Windows NT platform also makes use of basic storage. When using basic storage, partitions can be created, formatted, and deleted from within Windows 2000 without requiring that the system be rebooted.

. . . .

Tip: When using a disk with the basic storage format, be sure to leave 1MB of unallocated space free on the disk. This shouldn't be a problem, even for administrators with the tightest of budgets. Maintaining a free MB of space ensures the disk possesses sufficient space to calculate a conversion to a dynamic disk, should you choose to upgrade.

. . . .

Dynamic Storage

Dynamic storage types include the following:

➤ Simple volumes

➤ Spanned volumes

➤ Mirrored volumes

➤ Stripe volumes

➤ RAID (Redundant Array of Independent Disks) 5 volumes

Windows NT administrators will be familiar with dynamic storage volume types, albeit by another name, as shown in Table 12.1.

With the dynamic storage method, disk configuration information is stored on the hard disk instead of in the registry or as another file. As a result, disk failures are less likely to result in lost data, because dynamic storage synchronizes disk configuration information across multiple disks.

Tip: Disks cannot share basic storage and dynamic storage features. A disk supports only a single disk storage type, although multiple disks can mix the use of basic storage and dynamic storage on the same system.

Other advantages of dynamic storage include the fact that the use of available hard disk space is maximized and that volumes can span multiple disks. Additionally, a disk isn't limited to just four partitions when using dynamic storage.

12

Simple Volumes

Windows NT volumes are now known as simple volumes. Simple volumes are composed of free space on a single hard drive. You might hear some administrators refer to simple volumes as partitions. Volumes provide no fault tolerance, and they make excellent use of available hard disk space.

Table 12.1   Dynamic volume types carry new names in Windows 2000.

Windows NT	Windows 2000
Volume	Simple Volume
Volume Set	Spanned Volume
Mirrored Set	Mirrored Volume
Stripe Set	Stripe Volume
Stripe Set With Parity	RAID 5 Volume

Spanned Volumes

Known as volume sets in Windows NT, Windows 2000 spanned volumes collect and include space from two or more hard disks. Spanned volumes support a maximum of 32 hard disks. Don't be surprised if many IT professionals call spanned volumes *extended volumes*. Spanned volumes provide no fault tolerance, and they make excellent use of available hard disk space.

Mirrored Volumes

Windows NT mirrored sets, in which a disk is duplicated for fault tolerance purposes, are known as mirrored volumes in Windows 2000. When using mirrored volumes, if the original disk fails, the duplicate can be pressed into live production quickly to minimize downtime and data loss. You might hear many administrators refer to mirrored sets and volumes as RAID 1 or disk duplexing configurations.

. . . .

Tip: Traditionally, disk duplexing means separate hard disk controllers are used for each hard drive. Disk duplexing provides increased fault tolerance, because it eliminates the single point of failure weakness with the addition of the second hard disk controller. Performance is also enhanced, because writes to both the production disk and the mirror disk, or backup, can occur simultaneously.

. . . .

Mirrored sets provide fault tolerance. Mirrored sets do not maximize the use of available disk space. In fact, because a mirror is an identical disk copy, only 50% of the available disk storage space can actually be used.

Stripe Volumes

Stripe sets are used on Windows NT platforms for high-speed read performance. By writing data across a minimum of two hard disks, file retrieval time is enhanced. Windows 2000 refers to such disk sets as stripe volumes. Stripe volumes support anywhere from 2 through 32 hard disk drives and consolidate them into a single volume. Sometimes, administrators call this configuration *RAID 0*. Stripe volumes provide no fault tolerance, but they do maximize the use of available hard disk space.

RAID 5 Volumes

Stripe sets with parity offer the speed benefits of stripe sets, but they also include a fault-tolerant element, because parity and recovery information is included on each disk. Thus, they don't maximize the use of available hard disk space. Should one member of the array fail, the parity information on the surviving disks is used to regenerate the information from the failed disk. A loss of two or more disks will require data restoration from a backup. Stripe sets with parity are referred to as RAID 5 volumes in Windows 2000. RAID 5 volumes provide fault tolerance, as shown in Table 12.2.

Table 12.2 Properties of the disk storage options supported by Windows 2000.

Disk Storage Option	Supports Multiple Disks	Maximum Use of Hard Disk Space	Fault Tolerant	Performance Rating
Simple Volumes	No	Yes	No	Normal
Spanned Volumes	Yes	Yes	No	Normal
Mirrored Volumes	Yes	No (50%)	Yes	Slow (duplexing improves speed to normal)
Stripe Volumes	Yes	Yes	No	Fastest
RAID 5 Volumes	Yes	No (1/partitions)	Yes	Fast

Tip: RAID 5 volumes can play a crucial role in protection against data loss. For more information on complete fault tolerance and disaster protection, see Chapter 18.

Now that you're up to speed on the new disk storage options in Windows 2000, you're ready to learn how to configure disk management.

CONFIGURING AND ADMINISTERING DISK MANAGEMENT

Windows 2000's Disk Management MMC console is used to configure and administer the disk storage options and disk capabilities. Several options are available to trigger its use:

➤ Select Start | Programs | Administrative Tools | Computer Management. Then, expand Storage, and select Disk Management.

➤ Select Start | Run, type "Diskmgmt.msc", then click OK.

➤ Right-click the My Computer icon on the desktop, and select Manage.

➤ Double-click Diskmgmt.msc in the sysroot\Winnt\System32 directory.

➤ Click Start | Run, type "mmc", and click OK. Then, click Console, select Add/Remove Snap-in (or press CTRL+M), click Add, select Disk Management (or Computer Management), select the local or a remote computer, click Finish, click Close, and then click OK.

➤ Add Disk Management within any MMC console by clicking Console, select Add/Remove Snap-in (or press CTRL+M), click Add, select Disk Management (or Computer Management), select the local or a remote computer, click Finish, click Close, and then click OK.

If you've used MMC snap-ins in the past, you'll immediately be familiar with the look of the Disk Management console, as shown in Figure 12.1.

12

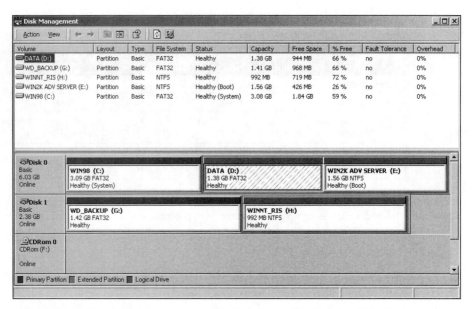

Figure 12.1   The Disk Management application, also found within the Windows 2000 Computer Management utility, is configured from an MMC interface.

The Disk Management console is configured from an MMC interface. One benefit of using the MMC interface is that multiple incidences of the Disk Management utility can be loaded as MMC snap-ins. As a result, you can load Disk Management as many times as you have disks, meaning all drives can be administered from a single console.

The Disk Management application lets you view the properties of your systems' hard drive partitions, volumes, and disks. For example, to view volume properties, select a volume from the volume pane, shown in Figure 12.2. Then, right-click the respective volume, and select Properties. The following tabs appear on volumes formatted with the FAT32 file system, as shown in Figure 12.3:

➤ General

➤ Tools

➤ Hardware

➤ Sharing

➤ Web Sharing

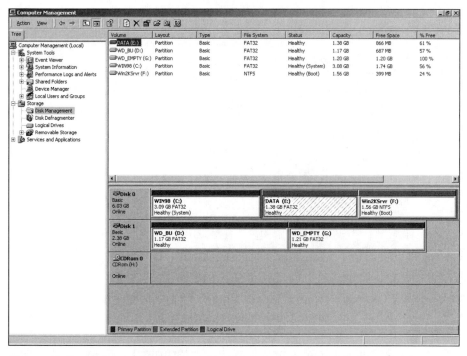

Figure 12.2   Volumes are displayed in the top portion of Windows 2000 Disk Management.

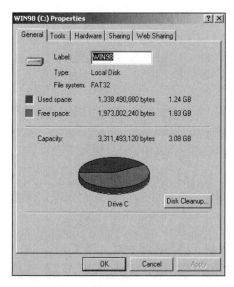

Figure 12.3   Options for configuring FAT32-formatted volumes are provided on five tabs.

12

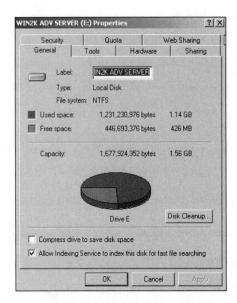

Figure 12.4   Options for configuring NTFS-formatted volumes are provided on seven tabs.

The following tabs appear on volumes formatted with the NTFS file system, as shown in Figure 12.4:

➤ General

➤ Tools

➤ Hardware

➤ Sharing

➤ Security

➤ Quota

➤ Web Sharing

Much information can be learned from viewing volume and partition properties, as described in Table 12.3.

Table 12.3   Volume and partition properties can be easily identified from within Windows 2000's Disk Management utility.

Property	Value
General	Displays volume label, volume type, the file system in use, used space, free space, capacity, and an option for Disk Cleanup. A graphic representation of the volume's used space versus free space is also provided.
Tools	Houses error-checking, backup, and defragmentation utilities for the volume.

(continued)

Table 12.3 Volume and partition properties can be easily identified from within Windows 2000's Disk Management utility *(continued)*.

Property	Value
Hardware	Provides a listing of the names and types of the disk drives installed, as well as device property information. This tab is identical for all of a systems' volumes. There are also Troubleshoot and Properties buttons (which display information for the selected drive) housed on the Hardware tab.
Sharing	Presents options for sharing a volume, setting the share name and user limits, setting permissions, configuring settings for Offline access through Caching, and creating a new share.
Security	Appears only on volumes formatted with the NTFS file system. Permits the addition of computers, users, and groups permissions. An Advanced button permits further permissions settings, configures auditing, and names the owner of a volume.
Quota	Indicates whether disk quotas are enabled and presents settings for disk quota administration.
Web Sharing	Presents options for sharing a volume on a Web site and configuring Aliases.

Similar to volume and partition information, disk configuration settings can also be found by clicking Properties for a disk. Disks reside in the lower pane of the Disk Management utility, as shown in Figure 12.5. Much information can be learned from disk properties, as described in Table 12.4.

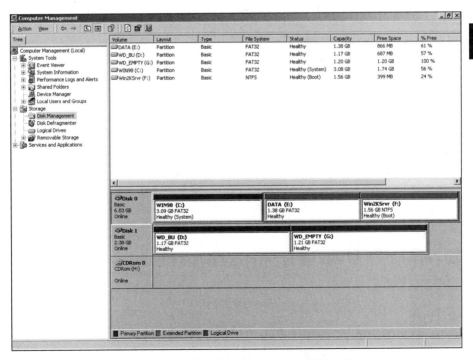

Figure 12.5 Disks are displayed in the lower pane of Disk Management.

Table 12.4   Disk properties can be easily identified from within Windows 2000's Disk Management utility.

Property	Value
Disk	Indicates the disk number (Example Disk 0).
Type	Describes the type of disk (basic, dynamic, or removable).
Status	Indicates whether the disk is online, offline, foreign (on another system), or unknown.
Capacity	Reveals the total capacity of the disk.
Unallocated Space	Indicates unallocated, or available, space on the disk.
Device Type	Describes whether the device is an IDE (integrated device electronics) drive, SCSI (small computer system interface) drive, or EIDE (enhanced IDE) drive. Such device type information as Target ID and LUN are also provided.
Hardware Vendor	Reveals the vendor and model of the disk drive.
Adapter Name	Describes the disk's controller type.
Volumes Contained On This Disk	Lists the volumes that exist on the selected disk and each volume's capacity. A Properties button enables you to display the volume and partition information for a highlighted volume.

Whenever changes are made to a volume, partition, disk configurations, or hardware, you need to refresh the MMC interface.

Refresh and Rescan Disks

If changes are made to a disk or volume, and the Disk Management MMC interface is left open while the changes are made, you need to refresh the Disk Management MMC view. This is done by clicking Action|Refresh or Action|Rescan Disks.

Refresh updates the drive letter, file system, volume, and removable media settings displayed in the Disk Management MMC. Selecting Rescan Disks updates all the respective hardware and controller information.

Now that you have an understanding of the new Disk Management MMC administrative interface, you're ready to move on to the configuration and administration of disk configurations.

DYNAMIC DISK ADMINISTRATION

The Disk Management utility is used to configure and administer disks. You can use it to create and extend simple volumes.

Simple Volume Administration

Simple volumes, of course, contain disk space from a single drive. While a partition also contains space from a single disk, simple volumes are not bound by the size limits or restrictions inherent with partitions. And, unlike partitions, you can later add, or *extend* in Microsoft parlance, space to a simple volume from another volume on the same disk.

While simple volumes aren't fault tolerant, they make the most efficient use of disk space. In addition, you can mirror simple volumes if fault tolerance is important for the data housed on the volumes.

Creating and Extending Simple Volumes

You can create a simple volume on dynamic disks formatted with the FAT, FAT32, or NTFS file systems. Follow these steps to create a simple volume:

1. Open Disk Management.

2. Right-click unallocated space where you want to create the simple volume.

3. Click Create Volume, and follow the on-screen wizard to complete the process.

Extended Volume Administration

You can add space to, or extend, a simple volume only if it is formatted with the NTFS file system. The available space added to the preexisting volume must be on the same disk, but it need not be contiguous. In other words, you can add available space located immediately before or after the volume you want to expand, or from other physical locations of the same hard disk not immediately adjacent to it.

12

Extending a Simple Volume

You extend simple volumes by following these steps:

1. Open Disk Management.

2. Right-click the simple volume you want to extend.

3. Click Extend Volume.

4. Follow the on-screen instructions.

Warning: System and boot volumes cannot be extended.

Should you run out of available space on a disk and want to extend it, you can do so by creating a spanned volume. The simple difference between simple volumes and spanned volumes is that spanned volumes include space from multiple disks.

Spanned Volume Administration

Like simple volumes, spanned volumes make excellent use of available dynamic disk space. However, spanned volumes do not offer fault-tolerant benefits.

A single spanned volume can include space from 2 through 32 dynamic disks formatted with the FAT, FAT32, and NTFS file systems. Windows 2000 completely fills the first disk in a spanned volume before writing to the next disk in a spanned volume. Should all the space on the disks composing a spanned volume become full, administrators can extend the spanned volume as long as they haven't already made use of all the available volumes on 32 disks. If all the volumes available on a system have been filled, but there are less than 32 disks, another can be added.

> **Warning:**   Should any one disk in a spanned volume fail, all your data will be lost! In addition, you cannot delete any portion of an extended simple volume without deleting the entire volume.

Creating a Spanned Volume

You add space from another disk to a volume, or create a spanned volume, by following these steps:

1. Open Disk Management.

2. Right-click the unallocated space on the dynamic disk where you want to create the spanned volume.

3. Click Create Volume.

4. Select Next in the Create Volume Wizard.

5. Click Spanned Volume.

6. Follow the on-screen wizard instructions.

You can add space to, or extend, spanned volumes formatted with the NTFS file system. Because Disk Management is sufficiently smart to format the new disk space without overwriting other data, you can extend volumes without losing existing files on the original volume.

> **Warning:**   You cannot delete any portion of a spanned volume or extended spanned volume without deleting the entire volume.

Stripe Volume Administration

When performance is the name of the game, stripe volumes can't be beat. Stripe volumes provide the best read/write performance of any disk storage option due to its use of multiple drives.

In a stripe volume configuration, each drive head needs to read only a fraction of the data needed to access a file versus single-disk systems. For example, if you're using a five-disk stripe volume set, and you're attempting to open a 10MB file, each disk head needs to read only 2MB, because the other disks will also be simultaneously reading 2MB. With a single disk system, the disk head must read the entire 10MB file, which of course takes exponentially longer. Consider that disk heads read countless bits per day, and you can begin to understand how beneficial the use of stripe volumes can be in environments in which quick performance is required.

Remember, however, that stripe volumes offer no fault tolerance. If fault tolerance is required, you should choose to implement a RAID 5 configuration, in which parity information is stored on each disk. In the event that a disk goes bad in a RAID 5 set, the parity information is used to rebuild the failed member. The use of parity lessens the maximization of hard disk storage space, an area in which stripe volumes excel.

Tip: For more information about configuring and administering RAID 5 volumes, see Chapter 18.

12

Creating a Stripe Volume

Stripe volumes are created by following these steps:

1. Open Disk Management.
2. Right-click unallocated space on the dynamic disk where you want to create the stripe volume.
3. Click Create Volume.
4. Select Next in the Create Volume Wizard.
5. Click Stripe Volume.
6. Follow the on-screen wizard's instructions.

ADMINISTERING COMMON DISK MANAGEMENT TASKS

In order to complete the Windows 2000 Accelerated exam successfully, you'll need an excellent understanding of common disk management tasks. Among the tasks you'll need to master, you need to know how to:

➤ Defragment hard disks and partitions

➤ Create partitions

➤ Add local and remote disks to your Disk Management interface for administration

➤ Manage drive letter assignments and drive paths

➤ Administer Windows NT Server 4 mirrored sets, volume sets, stripe sets, and stripe sets with parity

➤ Convert disk storage types

Administering Disk Defragmenter

Most Windows NT administrators are quite familiar with the trials and tribulations of disk fragmentation. The more a system is used, the more fragmented a disk becomes. This is true not only of FAT and FAT32 file systems, but of the NTFS file system, too.

As files and folders are added and deleted, hard drives often store small pieces constituting a single file across multiple physical locations on a hard disk. Recalling the file or folder then takes longer, because the hard drive head requires multiple reads. The multiple reads are necessary because the entire file or folder isn't located in a single contiguous space on the hard disk.

For years, Microsoft has included disk defragmentation utilities with its Windows 9x operating systems. However, NT administrators previously had to rely on third-party software for such assistance. No more.

Windows 2000 now includes disk defragmentation utilities for the Windows 2000 operating systems. The tool analyzes hard disk drives and presents a report on the fragmentation state of the drive. A graphic representation is also provided. This graphic interface can help an administrator determine in a glance whether defragmentation is advisable.

The defragmentation program works by rearranging contents of the hard drive. It moves data around the physical surface of the drive so that files and folders are stored contiguously. As a result of having data consolidated on the disk, performance increases. For this reason, frequent drive defragmentation is recommended.

Using the Disk Defragmenter

The new Disk Defragmenter included with Windows 2000 can be found by clicking on Start | Programs | Administrative Tools | Computer Management. Alternatively, the utility can be loaded as a Microsoft Management Console (MMC) snap-in or run from within the Disk Management utility. To run Disk Defragmenter from within the Disk Management utility, click on the volume or disk you want to defragment, right-click it, select Properties, click Tools, and select Defragment Now under Defragmentation. After Disk Defragmenter is selected, the interface shown in Figure 12.6 appears.

Note: Disk Defragmenter, Disk Management, and Computer Management snap-ins include the use of the defragmentation application.

Tip: If you elect to create a new MMC using Computer Management, you'll find the Disk Defragmenter housed under Storage.

Administration of the Disk Defragmenter is straightforward. Select the disk you want to check under Volume, then select Analyze. The Disk Defragmenter

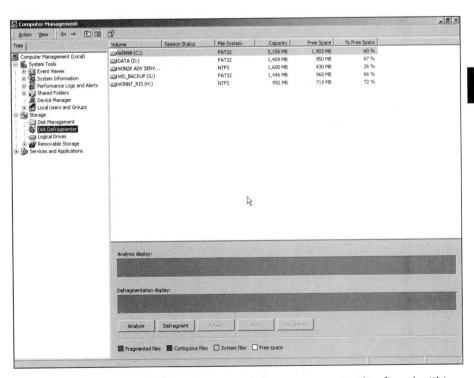

Figure 12.6   The Disk Defragmenter is a disk management utility found within the Computer Management application.

utility will provide a graphic representation of your hard drive, as shown in Figure 12.7. The utility also informs you, with a pop-up dialog box, whether defragmentation is recommended for the drive you've analyzed, as shown in Figure 12.8.

The defragmentation utility uses color-coding to indicate the state of drive information:

➤ *Red*—Represents fragmented files that can be relocated to help increase a system's performance

➤ *Blue*—Represents files that aren't fragmented

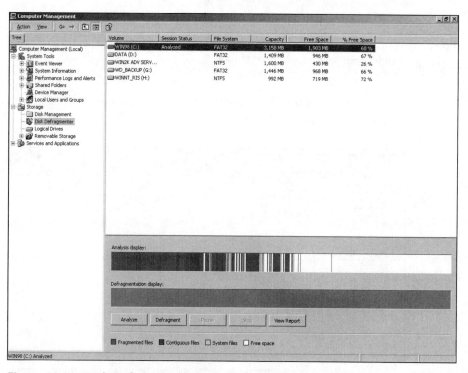

Figure 12.7   Disk Defragmenter provides a graphic representation of a hard disk's defragmentation.

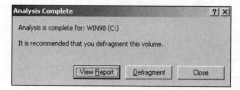

Figure 12.8   The Disk Defragmenter eliminates guesswork as to whether disk defragmentation is recommended.

➤ *Green*—Represents system files, which cannot be moved

➤ *White*—Shows free space

To defragment drives, click Defragment. The Defragmentation Display tracks the utility's progress, as shown in Figure 12.9.

Disk Defragmenter can also be used to create an analysis report, as shown in Figure 12.10. To create a report, simply select View Report to review volume information as well as a list of the drive's most fragmented files. The report provides much information, including the following:

➤ Name of the drive

➤ Volume size

➤ Cluster size

➤ Used space

➤ Free space

➤ Percent of free space

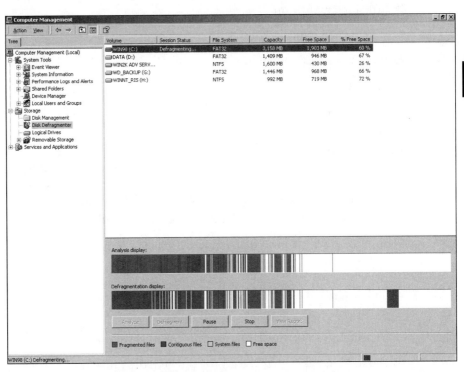

Figure 12.9   Disk defragmentation progress is monitored in the Defragmentation Display section.

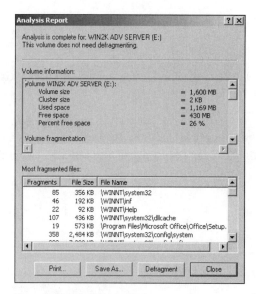

Figure 12.10 Disk Defragmenter can produce a detailed analysis report for each drive.

➤ Total fragmentation

➤ File fragmentation

➤ Free space fragmentation

➤ Total files

➤ Average file size

Managing Partitions

Basic disk types are selected in Windows 2000 by default. Basic disks possessing unallocated space must be partitioned and formatted before they can be used. The process of partitioning and formatting is improved in Windows 2000 thanks to the inclusion of the Disk Management utility.

You can create a partition in Windows 2000 by following these steps:

1. Open Disk Management.

2. Right-click the unallocated space where you want to create a new partition.

3. Select Create Partition to start the Create Partition Wizard.

4. Follow the on-screen wizard to complete the process.

Several options are available in the Create Partition Wizard. Table 12.5 describes the options and their purposes.

Table 12.5   The Create Partition Wizard simplifies disk partition creation with the use of a graphic interface used to specify disk changes to be made.

Option	Purpose
Select The Type Of Partition You Want To Create	Allows you to specify whether the partition being created is to be a primary partition, an extended partition, or a logical drive.
Amount Of Disk Space To Use	Enables sizing of the partition to be created. By default, the Create Partition Wizard selects the entire available space.
Assign A Drive Letter Or Path	Lets you specify the drive letter and path that the new partition should receive. If you neglect to provide a drive letter or path, the partition will be unavailable.
Format This Partition With The Following Settings	Lets you select the file system with which the partition will be formatted. Partitions must be formatted in order to store files, folders, programs, and applications.
Perform A Quick Format	Allows you to save time by eliminating the bad sector scan during formatting.
Enable File And Folder Compression	Lets you specify that data on the partition should be compressed, thereby increasing the amount of data that a partition can hold. However, compression results in slower read/write performance.

Adding Local and Remote Disks to Disk Management

As your data storage needs increase, you can add new disks to your Windows 2000 systems. Unless your systems support hot swapping, or the addition of hard drives while the server is running, you need to power down your system.

After the new disks are physically added to your machine, you can then power up the machine and make use of the new disk space. After the system boots, the new disks should appear in the Disk Management utility.

Adding Local Disks

If your system supports hot swapping, here are the steps to follow when adding new local disks:

1. Insert the new hard disk(s).

2. Open Disk Management.

3. Select Action.

4. Click on Rescan Disks, and the new disks should appear in the MMC snap-in.

12

Adding Remote Disks

Often, other computer disks are imported automatically by Windows 2000. Sometimes, however, disks will appear as foreign in Disk Management. You can import these disks by right-clicking them and selecting Import Foreign Disk from the pop-up menu. A wizard will then guide you through the process.

When importing multiple disks from other computers, they will be grouped by the name of the computer from which they were moved. Microsoft recommends using the following process when importing multiple disks from remote computers:

1. Right-click the new disks.

2. Select Import Foreign Disk.

3. Highlight the disks you want to add.

4. Click Select Disk.

Tip: If you have no dynamic disks installed, all of the disks are added.

If you import a disk that includes a spanned volume or a stripe volume, and you don't import the disks containing the remainder of the spanned volume or stripe volume, you'll receive a Failed: Incomplete Volume error. You can correct this situation easily. All you need to do is import all the members of the entire volume.

Should you receive a Failed Redundancy error, then you'll need to import the remaining disks in a mirrored volume or RAID 5 volume, because this is the cause of the error. While you'll still be able to access the disk's data, your fault tolerance will have been eliminated, unless you also import the redundant volume member.

Drive Letter and Drive Path Management

Windows 2000 relies on the Disk Management utility to assign permanent drive letters to volumes, partitions, and CD-ROM drives. Disk Management can also be used to mount local drives to empty folders on an NTFS volume or partition on the local computer.

Unlike drives, mounted folders aren't limited to 26 occurrences, because recognizable names are used instead of letters. For example, instead of naming a connection E:\, you can name it Payroll Forms, Marketing Brochures, or some other name. A chief benefit of mounting folders instead of drives is that users' shortcuts and file associations will continue to work, even if disk drive letter assignments change.

Drive Letter Administration

Twenty-four drive letters are available for use. A and B are reserved for floppy drives, but C through Z are up for grabs. If you're using just a single floppy drive, however, you can select drive letter B for a network connection.

When adding new disks to a system, previously assigned configurations will not be impacted. Instead, you can configure drive letters using the following steps:

1. Open Disk Management.

2. Right-click the volume, partition, or logical drive you want to change.

3. Select Change Drive Letter And Path.

4. A dialog box appears in the graphical user interface (GUI), as shown in Figure 12.11, and you're prompted to add, edit, or remove a drive letter assignment. In order to add a drive letter, you should click Add. If you want to remove a drive letter, click Remove. If you want to modify a drive letter, highlight the letter you want to change, and select Edit. After you've made your selection, click OK.

Drive Path Management

Drive paths are assigned in Windows 2000 when you mount a drive on the local computer to an empty folder on a local NTFS-formatted partition or volume. Drive paths can be created for partitions and volumes. Mounted drives can be formatted with any of the file systems supported by Windows 2000.

12

Tip: See Chapter 2 for more information on file systems supported in Windows 2000.

Drive paths can be administered using the following steps:

1. Open Disk Management.

2. Right-click the partition or volume you want to change.

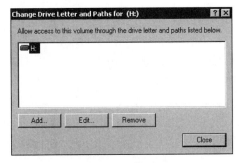

Figure 12.11   A GUI guides you through drive letter and path changes.

3. Click Change Drive Letter And Path.

4. A dialog box appears, as shown in Figure 12.11, and you're prompted to add, edit, or remove a drive letter assignment. Select Add to create a new drive path. You can use Browse to locate the local path you want to use. All available drive paths can be viewed by clicking View | All Drive Paths. Paths must be manually entered for remote systems. After you've provided the path, click OK.

Warning: Drive paths, unlike drive letter assignments, cannot be edited.

Administering Windows NT Server 4 Disk Sets

After Windows NT Server 4 systems are migrated to the Windows 2000 platform, many basic disk sets will be present on Windows 2000 Servers, including the following:

➤ Mirrored sets

➤ Volume sets

➤ Stripe sets

➤ Stripe sets with parity

You should be prepared for a few questions on the exam asking you to administer these legacy disk sets. In the following sections, we'll discuss the tasks with which you should be familiar.

Working with Mirror Sets

Windows NT Server 4 mirror disk sets are, by default, loaded as basic disks. Disk Management enables you to repair, resynchronize, break, and delete existing mirror sets. However, you cannot create new basic mirror sets using Disk Management. Instead, you can use Windows 2000 to create mirrored volumes.

When a basic disk that operates as part of a mirror set fails or disconnects, a Failed Redundancy error occurs, because the mirroring process can no longer work properly. Only a basic disk can be used to repair a mirrored set. A dynamic disk is, of course, used to repair a mirrored volume.

Although a Failed Redundancy error occurs, data does not immediately become unavailable. Instead, the disk remains online, but the fault tolerance is no longer in place.

In order to repair a Windows NT Server 4 mirror set on a Windows 2000 Server, you must have another basic disk available that possesses sufficient free space for creating a new mirror. If a basic disk is not available with the sufficient free space, you're out of luck. Your options are to purchase a new disk or convert the mirror set to a mirror volume.

If you do, indeed, have another basic disk with sufficient free space available, you can follow these steps to repair the failed mirror set:

1. Open Disk Management.

2. Right-click the mirror set you want to repair.

3. Select Repair Volume.

4. Follow the on-screen wizard's instructions.

Tip: Keep an eye on the mirror set in Disk Management while the repair occurs. The mirror set's status should change from Regenerating to Healthy. If it does not, you should right-click the mirror set and select Resynchronize Mirror.

Resynchronizing mirror sets ensures each member of the mirror set reflects the same data and that identical images are created. After a mirror set is broken for repairs, you should always select Resynchronize Mirror to ensure the new member is updated.

Breaking a mirror set results in two separate partitions or logical drives that are no longer operating in a fault-tolerant manner. While no information is destroyed when a mirror set is broken, any new changes made to the first member of the set will not be copied to the mirror, or backup, copy.

Breaking a mirror set is a simple process. All you need to do is open Disk Management, right-click the mirror set you want to break, and select Break Mirror. The mirror set is then broken. If you want to delete a mirror set entirely, select Delete Volume instead of Break Mirror. Deleting a mirror set should be done only when you're sure you no longer want any of the data kept on the mirrored set. Deleting a mirror set deletes not only the data the set holds, but the partitions as well.

Deleting Volume Sets and Stripe Sets

When a disk housing a volume set or stripe set experiences trouble or fails, you can delete it within Windows 2000. You might also want to delete volume sets and stripe sets created with Windows NT following an upgrade to Windows 2000. Windows 2000, by default, sets up such disk sets as basic disks.

12

. . . .
Tip: While Disk Management will let you delete Windows NT volume sets and stripe sets, it
            will not let you create such disk configurations. Instead, you can create simple volumes,
            spanned volumes, and stripe volumes.
. . . .

When you delete a volume set or stripe set, you delete all the data the entire volume or stripe set contains—not just the data created in the single volume, partition, or disk you delete. All the partitions are deleted, as well. To delete a volume set or stripe set, follow these steps:

1. Open Disk Management.

2. Right-click the volume set or stripe set you want to delete.

3. Select Delete Volume.

Managing Stripe Sets with Parity

You're likely to find many stripe sets with parity operating on a Windows 2000 system following migration from a Windows NT 4 Server platform. From within Windows 2000, you can use the Disk Management MMC snap-in to repair and delete RAID 5 configurations.

As with mirror sets, volume sets, and stripe sets, Windows 2000 initializes legacy Windows NT Server 4 disk sets as basic disks, by default. Disk Management lets you repair, regenerate, and delete stripe sets with parity. However, you cannot use Disk Management to generate new stripe sets with parity. Instead, you can create RAID 5 volumes.

If a member of a stripe set with parity fails or becomes disconnected, a Failed Redundancy error occurs. While the disks remain online, you should try to repair the stripe set with parity. In order to repair a Failed Redundancy error on a stripe set with parity, you need another basic disk with enough free space to take over the duties of the failed disk member. Dynamic disks cannot be used. Should another basic disk not be available, you're again out of luck. Your options are to either purchase a new disk or convert the set to a RAID 5 volume.

Disk Management repairs a stripe set with parity by moving part of the stripe set with parity to the new disk you've selected, where it regenerates the data the disk held. The disk is then ready to be pressed back into service.

Follow these steps to repair a Failed Redundancy error on a stripe set with parity:

1. Open Disk Management.

2. Right-click the stripe set with parity you want to repair.

3. Select Repair Volume.

Tip: Keep an eye on the stripe set with parity in Disk Management while the repair occurs. The stripe set with parity's status should change from Regenerating to Healthy. If it does not, you should right-click the stripe set with parity and select Regenerate Parity.

When you delete a stripe set with parity, all the data is lost. After all, that's the purpose of deleting the set. In addition, all the partitions that composed the set are deleted. Deleting a stripe set with parity is straightforward. Simply select the stripe set with parity from within Disk Management, right-click it, and select Delete Volume.

Converting Disk Types

Following migrations from Windows NT Server 4 to Windows 2000, or as your network's needs change, you will have occasion to convert basic disks to dynamic disks. There may be occasions when you also want to revert to a basic disk from a dynamic disk.

While no data is lost when converting from a basic disk to a dynamic disk, all volumes must be deleted from a dynamic disk before it can revert to a basic disk. Thus, you should keep this in mind when creating dynamic disks, because it could take time to restore data housed on dynamic disks when you must revert a disk to basic disk storage.

Upgrading from Basic Disk Storage to Dynamic Disk Storage

Upgrading from basic disk storage to dynamic disk storage is easy. A Windows 2000 wizard is provided to help you through the upgrade. Follow these steps to upgrade a basic disk to a dynamic disk, after ensuring that the disk you're going to upgrade contains a minimum of 1MB of unallocated space:

1. Open Disk Management.

2. Right-click the disk you want to upgrade.

3. Select Upgrade To Dynamic Disk, as shown in Figure 12.12.

4. Indicate the disk you want to upgrade, as shown in Figure 12.13.

Converting a basic disk to a dynamic disk results in existing partitions becoming volumes. Other results of converting basic disks to dynamic disks include:

➤ System and boot partitions and primary partitions become simple volumes.

➤ Extended partitions and logical drives become simple volumes.

➤ Free space from extended partitions and logical drives becomes unallocated space.

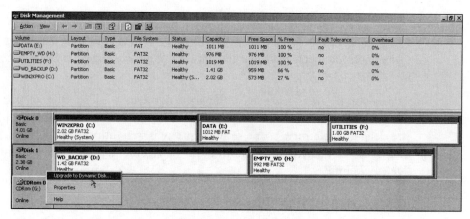

Figure 12.12   You can upgrade a basic disk simply by right-clicking on it in Disk Management and selecting Upgrade To Dynamic Disk.

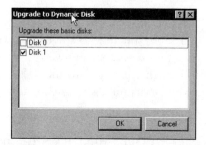

Figure 12.13   When upgrading to dynamic disk storage from basic disk storage, you need to confirm the disks you want to upgrade.

Reverting to Basic Disk Storage from Dynamic Disk Storage

The process of reverting to basic disk storage from dynamic disk storage is straightforward. Simply follow these steps:

1. Open Disk Management.

2. Right-click the dynamic disk you want to revert to basic disk management.

3. Select Revert To Basic Disk.

CHAPTER SUMMARY

Whereas the concepts are the same as in Windows NT Server 4, the creation, implementation, and administration of disk storage and management functions are enhanced in Windows 2000. New disk storage alternatives exist, and the disk defragmenter utility has been improved. Furthermore, Windows 2000 includes support for the FAT32 file system.

Unlike with Windows NT, Windows 2000 administrators and support personnel can now make use of dynamic disks and profit from the increased efficiencies the new storage functionality creates. Windows 2000 offers complete disk management functionality using another MMC snap-in titled, appropriately enough, Disk Management.

Basic storage disks contain primary disk partitions. Basic storage types include volume sets, mirror sets, stripe sets, and stripe sets with parity. Dynamic storage types include simple volumes, spanned volumes, mirrored volumes, stripe volumes, and RAID 5 volumes.

Windows NT volumes are now known as simple volumes. Called volume sets in Windows NT, Windows 2000 spanned volumes collect and include space from two or more hard disks. Windows NT mirrored sets, in which a disk is duplicated for fault tolerance purposes, are known as mirrored volumes in Windows 2000. Windows 2000 refers to disk sets without parity as stripe volumes. Stripe sets with parity are referred to as RAID 5 volumes in Windows 2000.

Windows 2000's Disk Management MMC console is used to configure and administer the disk storage options and disk capabilities. Several options are available to trigger the Disk Management console's use.

The Disk Management utility is used to configure and administer disks. In order to complete the Windows 2000 Accelerated exam successfully, you'll need an excellent understanding of common disk management tasks. Among the techniques you'll need to master, you'll need to know how to:

12

➤ Defragment hard disks and partitions

➤ Create partitions

➤ Add both local and remote disks to your Disk Management interface for administration

➤ Manage drive letter assignments and drive paths

➤ Administer Windows NT Server 4 mirrored sets, volume sets, stripe sets, and stripe sets with parity

➤ Convert disk storage types

Following migrations from Windows NT Server 4 to Windows 2000, or as your network's needs change, you will have occasion to convert basic disks to dynamic disks. There may be occasions when you also want to revert to a basic disk from a dynamic disk. While no data is lost when converting from a basic disk to a dynamic disk, all volumes must be deleted from a dynamic disk before it can revert to a basic disk.

REVIEW QUESTIONS

1. Which disk types are supported by Windows 2000? [Check all correct answers]

   a. Basic disks

   b. Dynamic disks

   c. Hybrid disks

   d. Traditional disks

2. Basic disks include which disk types? [Check all correct answers]

   a. Mirror volumes

   b. RAID 5 volumes

   c. Mirror sets

   d. Volume sets

3. Stripe sets with parity are known as what in Windows 2000?

   a. RAID 0 volumes

   b. RAID 1 volumes

   c. RAID 5 volumes

   d. Stripe volumes with parity

4. Stripe volumes provide fault tolerance.

   a. True

   b. False

5. Jessica works for an ISP that provides newsgroup access to its subscribers. As a product manager, Jessica wants to ensure subscribers can access newsgroups as quickly as possible. She's not concerned with data loss, because she can download newsgroup information if her system crashes. Which disk configuration should Jessica select?

   a. Volume sets

   b. Mirrored volumes

   c. Stripe volumes

   d. RAID 5 volumes

6. Mike needs to format a drive on his Windows 2000 Server. Which utility can he use to administer his disk configuration? [Check all correct answers]

   a. Computer Management

   b. Disk Administration

   c. Disk Management

   d. System Disk Management

7. John is an administrator for an insurance company. He has added a new hard drive to his system so users can store customer documents on the server. He must first format the drive before it can be used to store files. Which commands will provide access to Disk Management by default? [Check all correct answers]

   a. Select Start | Programs | Administrative Tools | Computer Management. Then, expand Storage, and select Disk Management.

   b. Select Start | Run, type "Diskmgmt.msc", then click OK.

   c. Double-click Diskmgmt.msc in the sysroot\Winnt\System32 directory.

   d. Click Start | Programs | Administrative Tools | Disk Management.

8. Disk Management provides system information on which of the following? [Check all correct answers]

   a. Partitions

   b. Volumes

   c. Controllers

   d. Disks

9. Which of the following items cannot be configured on volumes formatted with FAT32?

   a. Web Sharing

   b. Quotas

   c. Security

   d. b and c

10. Hannah is trying to determine which controller Disk 1 is using on her system. Which property should she check within Disk Management to answer her question?

   a. Disk

   b. Type

   c. Device Type

   d. Adapter Name

11. Jim has just changed the formatting on a disk on his Windows 2000 Advanced Server. Which command must he enter before he can view his changes?

    a. Refresh

    b. Refresh Disks

    c. Rescan

    d. Rescan Disks

12. Kevin is having trouble adding a new volume to a spanned volume. He upgraded the new disk to dynamic disk storage and formatted it with the FAT32 file system. What must he do to add the new disk to his spanned volume?

    a. He must Commit Changes.

    b. He must stop the Disk Management Service, and then select Add New Volume from the Action menu.

    c. He needs to select Span Current Volume.

    d. He cannot add the disk, because it is not formatted with the NTFS file system.

13. Volumes formatted with NTFS and containing system files can be extended.

    a. True

    b. False

14. Windows 2000 spanned volumes include support for how many disks?

    a. 12

    b. 16

    c. 26

    d. 32

15. If one disk in a spanned volume fails:

    a. No data is lost.

    b. Data is lost until the failed disk is replaced, upon which the lost data is regenerated.

    c. Only the data on the volume or volumes contained on the disk is/are lost.

    d. All data is lost.

16. Disk Defragmentation is required with which of the following file systems in Windows 2000? [Check all correct answers]

    a. FAT

    b. VFAT

    c. FAT32

    d. NTFS

17. What information does a Disk Defragmenter report not provide? [Check all correct answers]

    a. Volume size

    b. Used space

    c. Total files

    d. Estimated defragmentation time

18. Kerry's Windows 2000 Server triggers a Failed Redundancy error. After reviewing Disk Management, Kerry realizes an old Windows NT Server 4 legacy mirror set has triggered the error, because one of the drives has failed. After replacing the new disk, what steps must Kerry take to restore the mirror set?

    a. She must upgrade the basic disk to a dynamic disk.

    b. She must select Repair Volume and follow the on-screen instructions.

    c. She must select Repair Mirror Set and follow the on-screen instructions.

    d. She must right-click on the mirror set and select Resynchronize Mirror if Disk Management doesn't display the mirror set as being Healthy.

19. Scott just added a new disk to his Windows 2000 Server, but he has many shortcuts on his desktop. Users also use shortcuts to connect to shared folders on the server. What actions can Scott take to ensure the new drive doesn't throw off his and the users' shortcuts? [Check all correct answers]

    a. Nothing, because the only drive letters added by default are A and B

    b. Create his own drive letter assignments using Disk Management

    c. Create his own drive letter assignments using Drive Letter Administrator

    d. Select the Use Custom Drive Letter option in Disk Management

12

20. Sheila needs to revert a disk to basic disk storage from dynamic disk storage, because she needs some of its space to complete a volume set. However, she has a few files on the dynamic disk, and she needs to keep them. What action should she take? [Check all correct answers]

    a. Right-click the disk in Disk Management and select Revert To Basic Disk

    b. Back up the data from the volume she's going to revert to another disk

    c. Reformat the disk

    d. Commit changes

REAL-WORLD PROJECTS

Waiting in line at the local coffee shop, Andy Palmer's pager alerts him to a new project awaiting him back at the office. Fresh mocha java in hand, Andy sits down to review the next client task he's been requested to perform.

Piece-of-cake, he thinks, as he reads the client's request list. A small pool company needs a few changes made to its two Windows 2000 Servers, which support a handful of users. The company doesn't need a full-time administrator, so it outsources its information technology operations.

Recently, Andy's company has installed a mirror volume to help ensure customer databases and warranty information aren't lost forever in the event a hard disk crashed. Here are the most recent tasks Andy has been asked to perform:

➤ Create a partition on one of the server's hard drives

➤ Convert another hard disk from a basic disk to a dynamic disk

➤ Create a volume

Project 12.1
To create a partition using Disk Management:

1. Begin by opening Disk Management on the first computer by selecting Start|Run, typing "Diskmgmt.msc", and clicking OK. Andy sees the console shown in Figure 12.14.

2. Right-click on unallocated space on the disk where a partition is to be created, as shown in Figure 12.15.

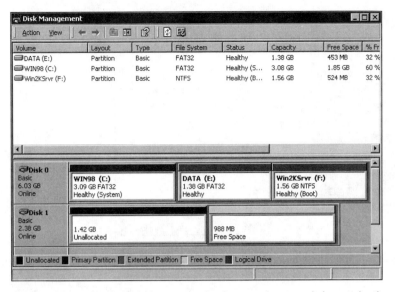

Figure 12.14   Disk Management displays partitions, disks, and other information.

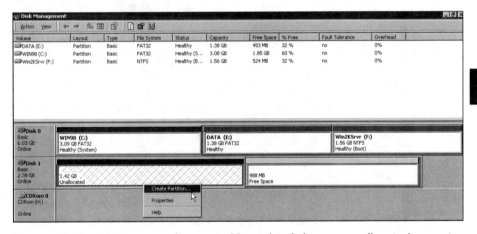

Figure 12.15   Partitions can be created by right-clicking an unallocated space in Disk Management.

3. Upon selecting Create Partition, the Create Partition Wizard appears, as shown in Figure 12.16.

4. Select Next, upon which the user is prompted to select the type of partition to be created. Specify a primary partition, as shown in Figure 12.17.

12

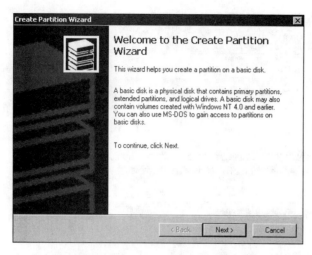

Figure 12.16 The Create Partition Wizard guides you through the partition creation process.

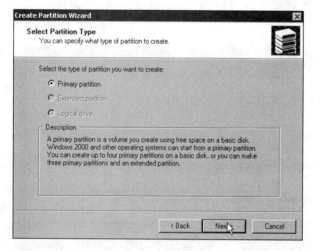

Figure 12.17 A partition type must be supplied when formatting a partition.

5. After selecting the partition type and clicking Next, the user is asked to specify the size of the partition, as shown in Figure 12.18.

6. After entering 750MB and selecting Next, the user is prompted to supply a drive letter or path, as shown in Figure 12.19.

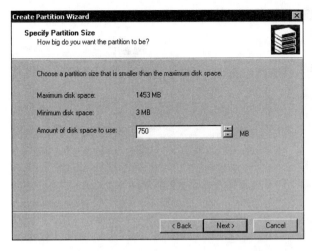

Figure 12.18   The size of the partition to be created must be supplied.

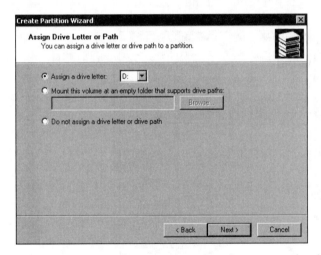

Figure 12.19   You must enter a drive letter or path when creating a partition.

7. After entering D as the drive letter and selecting Next, the Create Partition Wizard asks which file system the partition should be formatted with, as shown in Figure 12.20.

8. Select FAT32, and click Next. That triggers a box in which the user can review the settings that were just provided. If they're correct, select Finish, as shown in Figure 12.21.

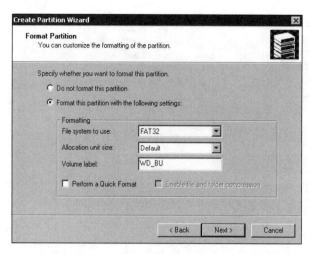

Figure 12.20   You must select a file system with which to format the partition, or elect not to format the partition.

Figure 12.21   Click Finish to create the partition with the settings you've supplied.

Having completed the first task, Andy polishes off his mocha java and proceeds to the second project for the client.

Project 12.2
To create a dynamic disk using Disk Management:

1. On the second computer, open Disk Management and select the disk to be upgraded to dynamic disk storage. Right-click on it, and select Upgrade To Dynamic Disk, as shown in Figure 12.22.

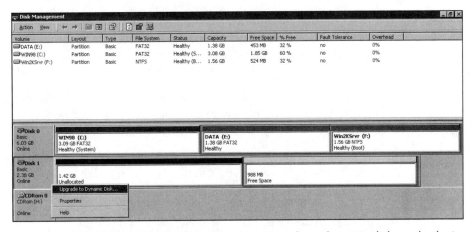

Figure 12.22 Right-click the disk you want to make a dynamic disk, and select Upgrade To Dynamic Disk.

2. The first thing that appears is a dialog box asking the user to confirm the disks to be upgraded, as shown in Figure 12.23.

3. After clicking OK in the box, and indicating that Disk 1 is to be upgraded, a screen appears confirming which disks will be upgraded. All the user needs to do to start the process is click Upgrade, as shown in Figure 12.24.

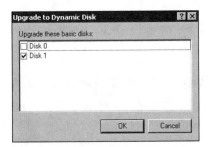

Figure 12.23 You must confirm the disks to be upgraded and click OK.

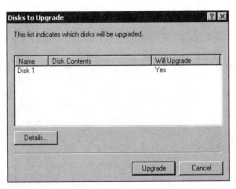

Figure 12.24 Click Upgrade to proceed with the disk upgrade.

4. A dialog box appears informing the user that, once he upgrades the disk to dynamic disk storage, he will not be able to boot previous versions of Windows from any volume on the affected disk. Continue by selecting Yes, as shown in Figure 12.25.

5. Next, the user is asked whether he wants to continue the operation, because all filesystems on any of the impacted disks will be force dismounted. Select Yes, as shown in Figure 12.26.

6. The process then completes, and the new dynamic disk appears in Disk Management as Dynamic and Online, as shown in Figure 12.27.

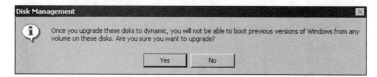

Figure 12.25   You must acknowledge that previous versions of Windows will not boot from the affected disk.

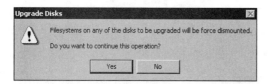

Figure 12.26   You must confirm that it's OK to proceed, even though impacted disks will be force dismounted.

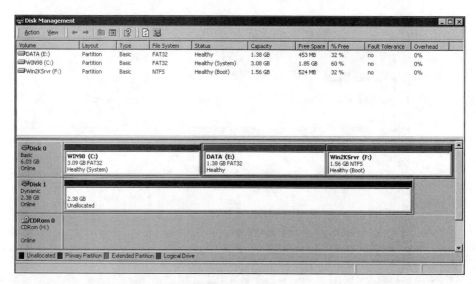

Figure 12.27   Windows 2000 completes the process and creates a dynamic disk with unallocated space.

Project 12.3
To create a volume using Disk Management:

1. With Disk Management still open on the second computer, right-click the disk where a new volume should be created, and select Create Volume, as shown in Figure 12.28. The Create Volume Wizard appears, as shown in Figure 12.29.

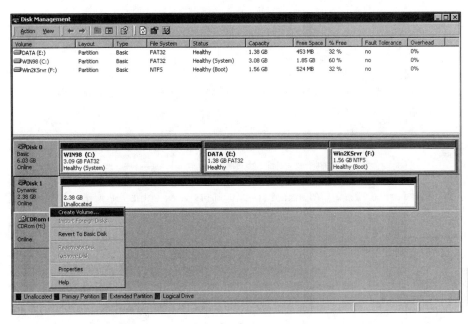

Figure 12.28   Right-click the disk where you'd like the new volume created.

Figure 12.29   The Create Volume Wizard is used to create a volume.

2. After clicking Next to continue, the user is prompted to select the type of volume he wants to create. Select Simple Volume, and click Next, as shown in Figure 12.30.

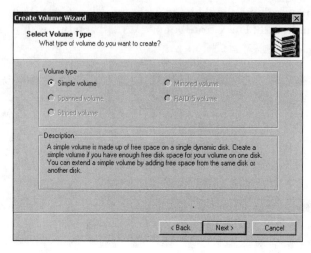

Figure 12.30 You must specify the type of volume you want to create.

3. Next, the user is prompted to select the disk and the size of the volume he wants to create. Figure 12.31 depicts the box in which this information is provided.

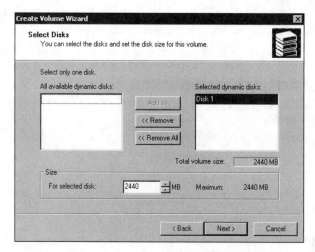

Figure 12.31 You must specify the disk and the size of the volume.

4. After selecting Disk 1, entering 2.4GB as the size for the volume, and clicking Next, the Wizard requests that a drive letter or drive path be supplied. Enter D as the drive letter, as shown in Figure 12.32.

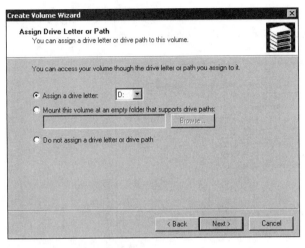

Figure 12.32   When creating a volume, you must assign a drive letter or drive path for the volume, or you can elect not to assign a drive letter or drive path.

5. After clicking Next, the user is prompted to specify whether the volume should be formatted, and, if so, which file system should be used. Indicate that the volume should be formatted NTFS, as shown in Figure 12.33.

12

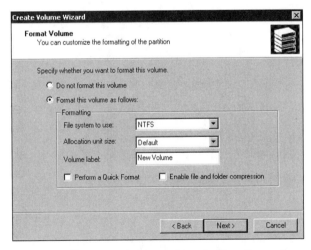

Figure 12.33   You must specify whether the volume is to be formatted.

6. After clicking Next, the user can view a dialog box providing a review of changes that will be made. Clicking Finish, as shown in Figure 12.34, completes the process.

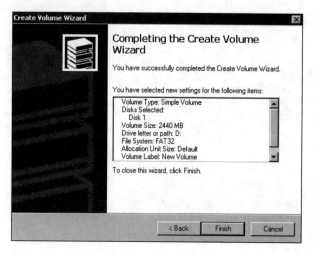

Figure 12.34 A dialog box allows you to review the settings you have supplied before making the changes.

Now that these three projects have been completed, Andy's day is now over and he can go home.

CHAPTER THIRTEEN

ADMINISTERING WINDOWS 2000 FILE SYSTEM

After completing this chapter, you will be able to:

✓ Share and publish shared folders

✓ Use the Computer Management Administrative Tool

✓ Create and manage the Distributed files system (Dfs)

✓ Plan and implement NTFS permissions

✓ Plan and implement disk quotas

✓ Manage the Encrypting File System (EFS)

This chapter looks at the many enhancements that Microsoft has added to the NTFS and FAT file systems. The chapter begins by looking at how to share and publish a folder in the Active Directory. Publishing files in the Active Directory allows users to search the directory to locate the resources they need.

This chapter also discusses the new Distributed file system (Dfs). Dfs allows an administrator to share files on multiple servers throughout an enterprise yet organize all the shares within one directory tree. Dfs allows users to look to a single source for network resources, without having to know on which server a shared folder is located.

Additionally, this chapter describes how to plan and implement NTFS permissions, as well as how to manage storage resources more effectively by implementing disk quotas. Disk quotas allow an administrator to set limits on how much space a user can consume on a server hard drive.

Finally, this chapter wraps up by explaining the new Encrypting File System (EFS). The new EFS provides a much higher degree of security for files stored on a Windows 2000 computer.

PUBLISHING FOLDERS

Publishing a folder within the Active Directory allows the folder to be accessed from a central location, without requiring users to remember on which server each share is published. If a file is published within the Active Directory, the user must simply search the directory for the share or browse the directory using My Network Places.In order to map a network drive to a share, the user must know the name of the server on which the share is located. Publishing a folder within the Active Directory is accomplished using the Computer Management Administrative Tool.

Computer Management Administrative Tool

To allow access to files or folders, you must first share the resources. You can use the Computer Management console to share folders that reside on any Windows 2000 Server. The Computer Management Administrative Tool is the primary configuration tool used to configure Windows 2000 Servers and clients. You can use the Computer Management tool to connect to any Windows 2000 computer. After you are connected to another Windows 2000 computer, you can use the Computer Management tool to view or change the remote computer's configuration.

The Computer Management Administrative Tool includes three nodes used to view and configure separate parts of the Windows 2000 system (see Figure 13.1). The three nodes are the System Tools node, the Storage node, and the Services and Applications node.

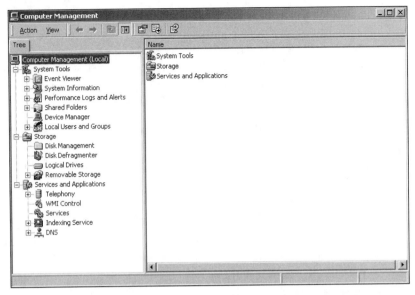

Figure 13.1   The Computer Management Administrative Tool.

System Tools

The System Tools node is used to view the Event Viewer logs, services, and Device Manager. The System Tools node is included on all versions of Windows 2000. Using the System Tools Computer Management node, you can view the following information.

➤ *Event Viewer*—The Event Viewer is used to connect to and view Windows 2000 Security, Application, DNS, System, File Replication, and Directory Replication logs. This node replaces the Windows NT 4 Event Viewer Administrative Tool.

➤ *System Information*—The System Information folder lists important configuration information regarding the computer's hardware and software. This tool replaces Windows NT 4's Diagnostics Administrative Tool. The System Information tool contains six topic-specific folders. These folders are:

➤ *System Summary*—The System Summary folder contains general information about the computer, such as the processor type, OS version number, installed service packs, total memory, and page file size.

➤ *Hardware Resources*—The Hardware Resources folder holds information regarding the computer's hardware configuration. Information includes IRQ (interrupt request line) usage, DMA (direct memory access) usage, any forced hardware (non-PNP), I/O address usage, base memory usage, and any detected system conflicts or shared IRQs.

➤ *Components*—The Components folder contains information regarding the hardware peripherals installed on the system. The listed components are Multimedia, Display, Infrared, Input, Modem, Network, Ports, Storage, Printing, Problem Devices, and Universal Serial Bus (USB). Each component folder listed contains detailed information regarding the installed hardware associated with the component.

➤ *Software Environment*—The Software Environment folder contains information regarding all software installed on the system. This includes drivers and services. The modules listed within Software Environment include Drivers, Environment Variables, Jobs, Network Connections, Running Tasks, Loaded Modules, Services, Program Groups, Startup Programs, and Object Linking and Embedding (OLE) Registration.

➤ *Internet Explorer*—The Internet Explorer folder contains configuration information for Internet Explorer, Microsoft's browser. This information includes the version number, how the browser should connect to the Internet, cached pages, browser version information, and certificate and security information.

➤ *Applications*—The Applications folder contains information regarding applications that have been installed on the system. This folder, for the most part, contains only information regarding Microsoft products, such as Microsoft Office. As of this writing, this folder contains only information on applications written specifically for Windows 2000.

➤ *Performance Logs and Alerts*—The Performance Logs and Alerts tool contains three subcategories—Counters, Trace Logs, and Alerts. The Counters category is a set of objects and counters that can be monitored and logged in order to monitor system performance. This supplements the Performance Monitor tool's logging feature within Performance Monitor. Performance Monitor can still be installed and used as well. The Trace Logs and Alerts nodes allow you to create trace logs and alerts, respectively.

➤ *Shared Folders*—The Shared Folders tool lists information about shared folders on the local system. The Shared Folders tool includes the following three categories relating to shared folders:

  ➤ *Shares*—The Shares folder lists all shares on the system and is used to create new shares. By right-clicking the Shares folder, you can select New File Share. You will then be prompted to enter the share name and path to the folder that you want to share, as shown in Figure 13.2.

  ➤ *Sessions*—The Sessions folder displays all open sessions. Any connections from the local computer to another computer or any connections to the local system are listed.

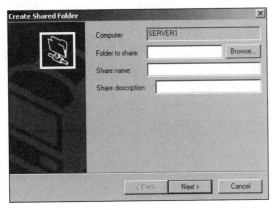

Figure 13.2   The Create Shared Folder Wizard.

> *Open Files*—The Open Files folder lists all open files on the system. This folder does not list operating system files that are open, only files that users or other computers have open on your system.

> *Device Manager*—The Device Manager application, shown in Figure 13.3, allows you to view graphically the hardware resources installed on the system. Device Manager looks and operates much like the Device Manager in Windows 95 and Windows 98. You can use Device Manager to view the properties of all hardware installed on a system, including IRQ, DMA, and memory resources used by any installed peripheral.

> *Local Users and Groups*—The Local Users and Groups application is used to create user and group accounts for the local accounts database. Because

13

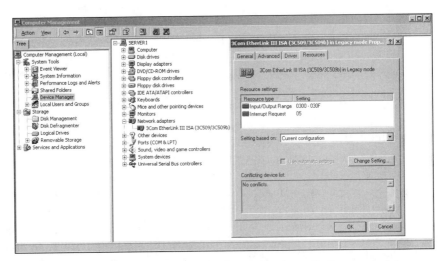

Figure 13.3   Device Manager (with the network card's Resources tab displayed).

servers that are installed as domain controllers do not have a local accounts database, this icon will be disabled. Windows 2000 member servers and Windows 2000 Professional computers can use this application to create user and group accounts.

Storage

The Computer Management Administrative Tool's Storage node is used to view and configure storage resources. Storage resources include hard drives, removable media, and logical drives. The Storage node can also be used for disk defragmentation. The information and applications in the following list can be found within the Storage node.

Note: Chapter 12 discusses disk defragmenting in more detail.

➤ *Disk Management*—The Disk Management application can be used to manage your hard drive resources. This tool replaces Windows NT 4's Disk Manager Administrative Tool. Using Disk Management, you can partition, format, assign drive letters, and configure RAID. Chapter 12 presents more detail regarding this application.

➤ *Disk Defragmenter*—The Disk Defragmenter application is new to the Windows NT/2000 operating systems. Disk Defragmenter is used to defragment hard drives. Removing and writing files to a drive causes file fragmentation.

➤ *Logical Drives*—The Logical Drives folder lists all drives installed on the system, including network drives. From this folder, you can view the properties of the system drives as well as set permission to each drive.

➤ *Removable Storage*—The Removable Storage application allows an administrator to create media pools for removable storage. The information configured within this application can be shared with Windows 2000's backup application. Media pools are often used to organize large numbers of tapes used in backup. Microsoft advises not to create media pools with more than 1,000 pieces of removable media.

Services and Applications

The Services and Applications node is installed only on Windows 2000 Servers. This node contains information that is dynamically built, depending on which applications are installed on the server. For example, if Internet Information Server (IIS) is installed on the local server, the properties for IIS can be viewed and changed with this node. Other applications that can be listed are Indexing, DHCP, DNS, and Telephony. All installed BackOffice applications are listed and configurable from this node. Services that are installed on this local server are listed as well. Services can be started and stopped using the Services and Applications node.

Sharing a Folder

Before files can be accessed over a network, the folders that contain the files must be shared. Sharing a file is a simple process, performed by the network administrator, which allows the folder to be accessed by users with the appropriate permissions.

When administrators share files, they can assign share permissions to the shared folder. Share permissions that can be assigned to a share include Read, Change, and Full Control. Additional NTFS permissions can also be assigned to a share. NTFS permissions are discussed later in this chapter.

The steps to share a folder are:

1. Open Computer Management from the Administrative Tools menu.

2. Expand the Shared Folder by clicking the plus symbol.

3. Right-click the Shares folder, and select New File Share. The Create Shared Folder Wizard appears, as shown earlier in Figure 13.2.

4. Enter the full path to the folder you want to share. The folder does not have to be created in order for the wizard to work. If you enter a path to a folder that does not exist, the wizard will ask if you want to create the folder.

5. Click Next.

6. Select the appropriate radio button for the permission that you want to apply to the share. If none of the options list the appropriate permissions, you can select Customize and set the permissions manually.

7. Click Next, and you will be asked if you want to create another share. If not, select No, and the Create Shared Folder Wizard ends.

13

Once a folder has been shared, you can publish the shared folder in the Active Directory to provide a centralized point of administration and access.

Publishing Shares to the Active Directory

The purpose of the Active Directory is to provide a central storage location for network resources. The Active Directory stores all network objects that are created on the network. Administrators can choose to publish shared folders within the Active Directory or not to store shared folders within the Active Directory. If shared folders are published in the Active Directory, all users throughout the enterprise will be able to view the shares.

Like Windows NT 4, Windows 2000 clients rely on browse lists to find shares within My Network Places. In most cases, browse lists do not cross subnet boundaries, so shares created on one subnet will not appear in the browse list of other subnets. Administrators can avoid this issue by publishing shared folders in the Active Directory. The Active Directory is replicated to all domain controllers, and, therefore, all clients will be able to view all shares throughout the enterprise.

The steps to publishing a share are as follows:

1. Open Active Directory Users and Computers.

2. Open the domain where you want to publish the share.

3. Right-click the domain name or Organizational Unit that will contain the published share, and select New | Shared Folder.

4. Enter the share name and the path to the shared folder.

5. Click OK.

Note: A share can be published before there is even a shared folder located at the path specified. If there is no shared folder as specified during publishing, a published folder will still appear in the Active Directory; however, a published folder will not be accessible until the folder is created and shared.

UNDERSTANDING AND CONFIGURING DISTRIBUTED FILE SYSTEMS

The Distributed file system (Dfs) allows an administrator to combine multiple shares from multiple locations as well as multiple servers into one manageable directory tree. This feature was available in Windows NT 4; however, it was troublesome to manage and was not normally discussed in texts dealing with NT 4. In this section, you will learn the benefits of setting up Dfs as well as how to manage Dfs.

Why Use Dfs

In large enterprise networks, users and administrators might find that it's difficult to locate network resources. Dfs solves this problem by not involving the use of specific locations for network resources or, more specifically, shared folders. Dfs hides the specific location of shared folders and allows administrators to publish shares within one directory tree regardless of the number of shares or where the shares are physically located. Dfs also eases administration by combining shares into one manageable unit and providing fault tolerance.

Note: Computers running Windows 95 do not have the ability to connect to Distributed file systems without the installation of additional software available from Microsoft's Web site.

Some of the benefits of implementing Dfs are that it does the following:

➤ Enables you to organize resources

➤ Preserves network permissions

➤ Provides fault tolerance

➤ Simplifies network navigation

Organize Resources

The Dfs uses a hierarchy of root nodes and child nodes. The root node represents the beginning of the Dfs tree, while the child nodes are shared folders below the root. In this way, you can create a virtual file system made up of shared folders. Each child node can be located on any server within the enterprise. Users will be able to access the shared folders by connecting to the Dfs, not the server on which each share resides (see Figure 13.4).

Shared files and folders in the same general category can be shared within the same Dfs. In this way, you can organize your shares according to function or purpose. For example, you could have an application Dfs that stores child nodes consisting of shared application folders or, just as easily, you could have an accounting Dfs that contains child nodes containing payroll, accounts receivable, accounts payable, and so forth.

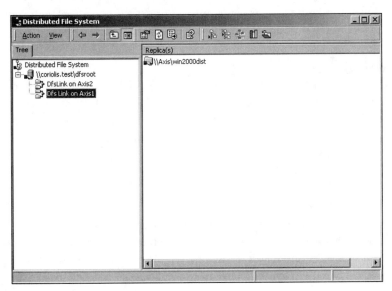

13

Figure 13.4   Distributed file system.

Network Permissions

Network permissions assigned to shared folders or files are still effective when those shares are made part of a Dfs. Dfs does not change or have any effect on share or NTFS permissions.

Fault Tolerance

Because the physical locations of shares are hidden from users, administrators can set up fault tolerance within the Dfs directory structure. Shares that contain important information can be replicated to multiple servers within the domain. If, for example, a server fails that contains vital data, the administrator can simply redirect the Dfs root to point to a duplicate share on another server, and the users are none the wiser that the share they are connecting to has changed. Additionally, if the Dfs is created as a fault-tolerant Dfs, each node can point to multiple shares. While most of this could be implemented without Dfs, the administrator would have to inform all users that they need to connect to another server to collect necessary information as well as walk users through the remapping of network drives.

Network Navigation

Users and administrators no longer have to browse through endless lists of servers to find resources they need to perform their jobs. The actual locations of child nodes are transparent to users and administrators after Dfs is configured. After Dfs is configured, users can simply connect to the appropriate root and browse all the child nodes regardless of physical location.

Creating Dfs

To begin the process of creating a Dfs, you must first create the Dfs root. The root represents the beginning location of the Dfs. Dfs roots can be created on either a FAT or NTFS partition, although NTFS partitions provide the ability to assign permissions on files as well as folders. Dfs allows you to create one of two types of root for each Dfs—standalone and domain (also referred to as fault-tolerant Dfs)—as shown in Figure 13.5.

Standalone Dfs

In a standalone Dfs, the Dfs topology is stored on a single computer. The shares might be located on multiple servers; however, the path to the shares and the Dfs reside on only one server. This scenario provides no fault tolerance. If the server that stores the topology fails, then the entire Dfs is unusable.

The following steps describe how to create a standalone Dfs root:

1. Start the Distributed File System console by clicking Start | Programs | Administrative Tools | Distributed File System.

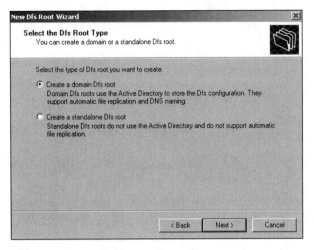

Figure 13.5 Dfs roots.

2. Start the New Dfs Root Wizard by right-clicking Distributed File System, and selecting New Dfs Root.

3. Click Next, and then select Create A Standalone Dfs Root. Click Next.

4. Enter the name of the server that will host the Dfs. Click Next.

5. Click the drop-down box to select an existing share or enter the name and path to a new share.

6. Enter a descriptive comment, and click Next.

7. Click Finish.

Fault-Tolerant Dfs

With a domain or fault-tolerant Dfs, the topology is stored as part of the Active Directory. This allows the nodes within the Dfs to point to multiple, yet identical, shares to provide fault-tolerance. Fault tolerant Dfs also supports DNS, FRS, and mult-iple levels of child volumes. To create a fault-tolerant Dfs, follow these steps:

1. Start the Distributed File System console by clicking Start | Programs | Administrative Tools | Distributed File System.

2. Start the New Dfs Root Wizard by right-clicking Distributed File System, and selecting New Dfs Root.

3. Click Next, and then select Create A Fault-Tolerant Dfs Root. Click Next.

4. Enter the name of the domain that will host the Dfs. Click Next.

5. Enter the name of the server that will host the Dfs. Click Next.

6. Click the drop-down box to select an existing share or enter the name and path to a new share.

7. Enter a descriptive comment, and click Next.

8. Click Finish.

Adding Dfs Links

Dfs links are shares published within the Dfs root. Each Dfs root can contain multiple links to multiple shares throughout an enterprise. The only restriction on Dfs links is that the path to any link cannot be more than 256 characters.

Each link can point to more than one shared folder. This provides redundancy as well as fault tolerance. For example, one Dfs link named *Word* could point to a share on server1 as well as another identical share on server2. In Figure 13.6, the MS Word Dfs link points to a share named *Word* on both server1 and server2. Both shares on both computers could be configured for manual or automatic replication to ensure they both are copies of one another. In the event that one server or share fails, the users would automatically be rerouted to the other identical share.

Each time a client computer connects to a Dfs root, the client caches the path information for each Dfs link. You can modify the default cache time of 1,800 seconds for each link. If each link points to multiple identical shares, each client attempts to connect to the first link until the timeout period expires. After the timeout period of 1,800 seconds expires, the client rereads the path information from the Dfs root and then attempts to connect to the next link.

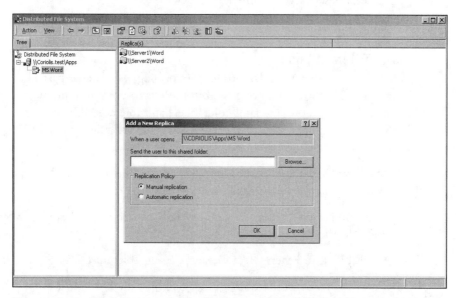

Figure 13.6 Dfs links using multiple shares for fault tolerance.

Before creating Dfs links, a Dfs standalone or fault-tolerant Dfs root must be configured. Each link is listed below the root.

Creating Dfs Links

To create Dfs links, follow these steps:

1. Open the Distributed File System Administrative Tool.

2. Right-click the Dfs root, and select New Dfs Link.

3. Enter the name, path, and description of the link (see Figure 13.7).

4. If needed, change the default client cache timeout period.

5. Click OK.

Adding a Share to an Existing Link

To add another share to an existing link, follow these steps:

1. Right-click the link to which you want to add a replica, and select New Replica.

2. Enter the UNC (Universal Naming Convention) path to the replica share.

3. Select automatic or manual replication.

4. If automatic replication is chosen, select the master replica, and click Enable. Select the second share, and select Enable to allow file replication.

5. Click OK.

13

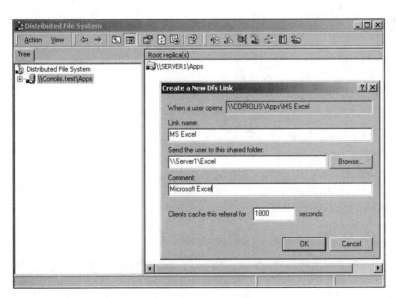

Figure 13.7   Creating Dfs links.

NTFS PERMISSIONS

As with Windows NT 4, NTFS permissions allow network administrators to control access to folders as well as files being accessed either locally or over the network. NTFS permissions can be configured only on NTFS partitions. FAT or FAT32 partitions can rely only on shared folder permissions to control access. NTFS permissions come in two types—standard and special.

Note: NTFS partitions allow for file encryption and compression.

Standard Permissions

Standard permissions are the most common permissions assigned to users for accessing files and folders. Standard permissions provide all the general permissions needed for everyday network administrative needs. The six standard NTFS permissions are:

➤ *Read*—Allows a user to list the contents of a directory as well as read the contents of a file. The Read NTFS standard permission also allows a user to view the attributes and extended attributes of a file or folder.

➤ *Write*—Allows a user to read and make changes to a file or directory. The Write permission also allows a user to delete a file, but it does not allow a user to delete a folder. Anyone assigned the Write permission can also change file attribute properties.

➤ *List Folder Contents*—Allows a user to view the files and subfolders contained in the folder. This permission is available only for folders.

➤ *Read and Execute*—Grants a user the default Read permission as well as permission to execute application files.

➤ *Modify*—Grants a user Read, Write, List Folder Contents, and Read and Execute permissions on a folder. The Modify permission grants all permissions except for three special permissions—Delete Subfolders, Take Ownership, and Change Permissions.

➤ *Full Control*—Grants a user all the previously mentioned permissions. Full Control permission also grants the user the Take Ownership and Change Permission special permissions.

Special Permissions

Special permissions allow administrators to gain more control over the file permission process. Thirteen special permissions combine to create standard permissions. For example, the standard Read permission is made up from the List Folder/Read Data, Read Attributes, Read Extended Attributes, and Read NTFS Special Permissions. Two of the most powerful special permissions are the Take Ownership and Change Permissions permissions.

Take Ownership

The Take Ownership permission allows a user to take ownership of a file or folder and become the owner creator of the file. Any user that is the owner creator of a file automatically has full control of the file or folder. Ownership of a file or folder cannot be assigned. For example, if an administrator wants to grant ownership of the payroll database to the new CIO, the administrator must assign the CIO the Take Ownership permission and show the CIO how to take owner-ship of the file. The administrator cannot assign the CIO ownership directly.

Change Permissions

The Change Permissions permission gives a user account the ability to change permissions on a file or folder. The user account does not have to have any other permission for the file or folder. For example, you might not want to allow the administrator to view or change the payroll database; however, you do want the administrator to have the ability to change permissions on the database file. Therefore, you could assign the administrator only the special Change Permis-sions permission, which would allow the administrator to change permissions on the file, yet would not allow the administrator to view or change the file.

Viewing NTFS Special Permissions

You can view and assign NTFS permissions by clicking the Security tab in the file's Properties dialog box (see Figure 13.8). To view NTFS special permissions, follow these steps:

1. Right-click the file or folder you want to view or set permissions on.

13

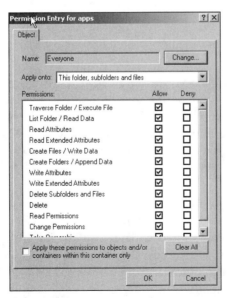

Figure 13.8 Viewing NTFS special permissions.

2. Select Properties.

3. Select the Security tab (available only on NTFS partitions).

4. Click Advanced.

5. Click View/Edit.

Modifying NTFS Special Permissions

To modify the standard or special NTFS permissions on a file, you must remove the checkmark in the Allow Inheritable Permissions From Parent To Propagate To This Object option on the Security tab. To modify permissions, follow these steps:

1. Right-click the file or folder you want to view or set permissions on.

2. Select Properties.

3. Select the Security tab (available only on NTFS partitions).

4. Clear the Allow Inheritable Permissions From Parent To Propagate To This Object checkbox.

5. Select Copy to copy existing permissions or Remove to erase all existing permissions.

6. From this screen, you can add and remove users as well as standard NTFS permissions.

7. Click Advanced.

8. Click View/Edit.

9. Select the permissions you want to allow or deny.

NTFS Permission Inheritance

By default, files and folders inherit the permissions of their parent folder. Any and all permissions assigned to a parent object propagate to all child objects unless specifically blocked by the administrator. Any new files or folders created with a folder also automatically inherit the permissions of the folder in which they are created. You can block and reset permissions on files and folders.

Blocking Permission Inheritance

Permissions assigned to a parent folder can be blocked from affecting the permissions of files and folders within the original folder. The folder that blocks the flow of permissions down into the file structure becomes a parent folder. Permission assigned to the new parent folder will be inherited by any files or folders created below the new parent folder.

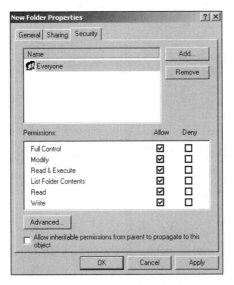

Figure 13.9 Preventing inheritance.

Preventing permission inheritance is accomplished by clearing the Allow Inheritable Permissions From Parent To Propagate To This Object checkbox on the Security tab of the folder's Properties dialog box, as shown in Figure 13.9. When clearing the checkbox, a message appears asking what you would like to do with the existing permissions already inherited from the parent object. You can either remove all existing permissions or copy the existing permissions to the new parent folder.

Resetting Permissions on Child Objects

After a new parent folder is created by blocking inheritance to a folder, you can allow the new permissions on the parent folder to flow down to any subfolders or files contained in that parent folder. After the Reset Permissions On All Child Objects And Enable Propagation Of Inheritable Permissions option is set, as shown in Figure 13.10, any permission set on the parent folder will automatically take effect on all child objects.

MANAGING DISK QUOTAS

One of the long-awaited features of Windows NT/2000 is the ability to set and manage disk quotas. Disk quotas allow administrators to set and enforce maximum disk resource usage. Using Windows 2000's new disk quota system, you can monitor user disk usage, configure the OS to send warnings to users automatically when they cross set thresholds, and send the administrator a message when users exceed their configured quota. Disk quotas can be configured only on NTFS partitions.

13

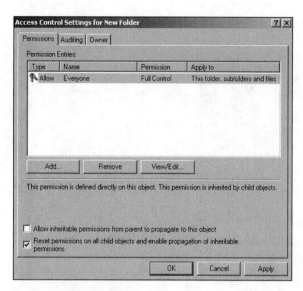

Figure 13.10 Allowing inheritance on child objects.

How Quotas Work

User quota limits are tracked on a per-user and per-partition basis. Quotas are based on the amount of information a user account has written to a partition, not a folder. Quotas cannot be established for folders. Quotas measure the amount of space within a volume or partition, not the physical drive, because a physical drive can contain multiple partitions.

Disk resources used by a particular user account are measured based on file and folder ownership. If a user takes ownership of a file or folder, then the user's account will be charged with the disk resources used by the file or folder.

Many applications query the operating system during installation to discover how much available space is left on the hard drive. When an application queries Windows 2000 to find the available space, Windows 2000 reports only the amount of space remaining within the user's disk quota limit.

Compression has no effect on the disk quotas system. Compressed files are measured according to their uncompressed values. One reason for this is that before a file can be used, it must be uncompressed, which means that all files will eventually take up more space.

The disk quota system can be configured to deny additional disk resources to users who exceed their quota limit. If you do not want to prevent users from writing additional data to the drive, you can have the disk quota system generate an event and/or send the user a warning instead.

Configuring Disk Quotas

Disk quotas can be configured for all users or on a per-user basis. You can enable disk quotas by viewing a drive's properties and selecting the Quota tab in the Properties dialog box, as shown in Figure 13.11. To enable quotas for all users, check the Enable Quota Management checkbox. Table 13.1 lists the option that can be configured using the Quota tab in the Properties dialog box.

Using the Quota Entries and Properties Dialog Boxes

You can monitor all aspects of the disk quota system using the Quota Entries dialog box (see Figure 13.12). The properties that can be viewed in the Quota Entries dialog box include the following:

➤ Users who have surpassed their warning levels are identified. After a user passes the warning level, a yellow triangle displays next to the user's name in the Quota Entries dialog box.

➤ A red circle identifies users who have surpassed their quota limit.

➤ The dialog box enables you to view the current warning and quota limits for each user.

➤ The current amount of disk resources consumed by each user are specified.

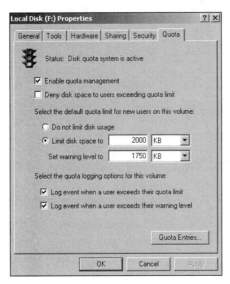

13

Figure 13.11 The Quota tab in the Properties dialog box.

Table 13.1 Configuring disk quotas.

Option	Description
Enable Quota Management	Select this option to enable quotas for all users.
Deny Disk Space To Users Exceeding The Quota Limit	If this option is set, users receive an Out Of Disk Space message when they attempt to write a file to the affected partition.
Do Not Limit Disk Usage	Select this option when you do not want to enforce disk limits.
Limit Disk Space To	Use this option to set the amount of space each user is allowed to consume.
Set Warning Level To	Use this option to set the amount of space each user is allowed to consume before a warning message is sent to the user.
Quota Entries	Click this button to open the Quota Entries
Log An Event When Users Exceed Their Quota Limit	This option configures the quota service to log and event to the Event Log when users exceed their quota.
Log An Event When Users Exceed Their Quota Warning	This option configures the quota service to log and event to the Event Log when users exceed their quota warning.
Quota Entries dialog box, where each entry can be viewed, added, or deleted	With this dialog box, you can create different limits for specific users, as shown in Figure 13.12.

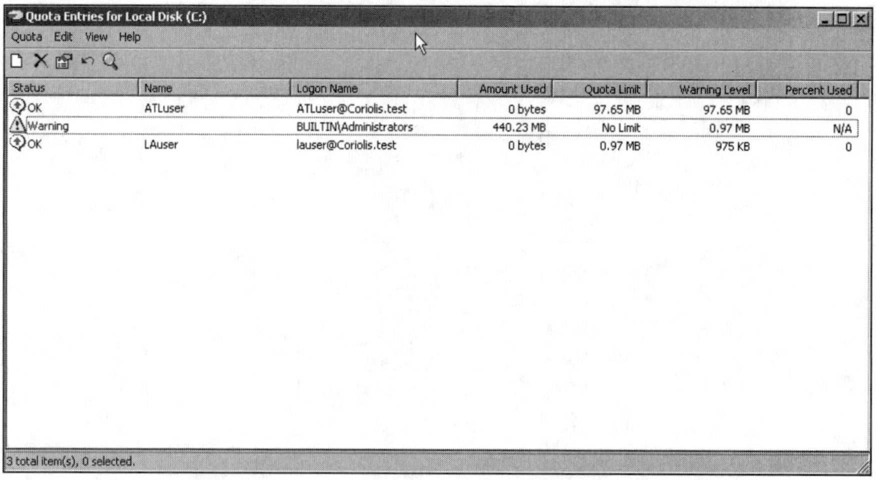

Figure 13.12 Quota Entries dialog box.

Determining the status of the entire disk quota system for a given drive can be viewed using the Properties dialog box, as shown in Figure 13.13. The Properties dialog box uses the following identifiers to provide information:

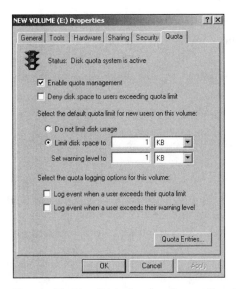

Figure 13.13   Disk Quotas Properties dialog box.

➤ *Red light*—Indicates that disk quotas are not enabled.

➤ *Yellow light*—Signifies that the disk quota information is being rebuilt.

➤ *Green light*—Signifies that the disk quota system is working properly.

ENCRYPTING FILE SYSTEM

The Encrypting File System (EFS) provides file encryption services on Windows 2000 NTFS partitions. EFS for Windows 2000 uses a strong public/private key system to encrypt and decrypt files. The EFS runs as a Windows service and is transparent to the user.

Integrated into the overall Windows 2000 security policy is a recovery method that can be used to recover files that were encrypted by users who are no longer on the network. Corporate security policies can be implemented that delegate control of encrypted files to trusted individuals within the company. The trusted personnel could be given recovery authority (called a *recovery agent*) for some or all encrypted files. Microsoft provides many safeguards to ensure that no data is lost due to files that cannot be decrypted.

All files within a folder are encrypted together. Files that are backed up or moved to new NTFS partitions remain encrypted. EFS cannot be used to encrypt files transferred over the network. Windows 2000 provides Secure Sockets Layer (SSL) to encrypt network transmissions.

13

How EFS Works

EFS is a public/private key technology used to encrypt and decrypt personal files. Users can choose to encrypt any files or folders that are contained on an NTFS partition. After a file is encrypted, the file can be moved to any NTFS partition.

Encrypting a File

Encrypted files are encrypted using multiple symmetric keys that are designed for high-speed bulk encryption. The file is broken into blocks, and a different key is used to encrypt each block. The keys used to encrypt a file are stored in the Data Decryption Field (DDF) and the Data Recovery Field (DRF) within the file's header. The header of the file that contains the encryption keys is then encrypted and can be unlocked only with the user's private key or a recovery agent.

Any new files that are created or moved into an encrypted folder are automatically encrypted as well. The encryption property works like permissions in that all child objects within the parent object inherit the encryption property.

Decrypting a File

When an encrypted file is opened, EFS automatically detects the file as being encrypted and locates the certificate and private key needed to unlock the file header. All the encryption keys used to encrypt the file are located in the header, so EFS needs only to unlock the header to locate all the encryption keys. After the header is decrypted, the file can be opened easily. The entire process of decrypting the file is transparent to the user.

EFS Features

Any user who is listed as the owner of a folder can encrypt the contents of the folder. To gain access to an encrypted file, a user would have to possess the private key. If a user has the private key, then the user would be able to transparently access, write to, and save the file. Anyone without the private key will be unable to access the file. Additional EFS features include:

➤ *Simplicity*—Users do not have to be trained to encrypt and decrypt a file as they would with third-party tools, such as PGP. Users simply open and save files, and the EFS service performs encryption and decryption in the background. The EFS system is built into the operating system, so there is no additional software or training costs.

➤ *Prevention of lost data*—The EFS system provides a recovery method that can be used to decrypt files when the user who encrypted the files is unavailable. The recovery agent's public key can be used to decrypt the DDF and DRF headers so any file can be opened if needed. The recovery agent's public key must be present before any files can be encrypted.

➤ *Protection of encryption keys*—The keys used to encrypt files are themselves encrypted with the user account's X.509 v3 certificate and then stored as part of the file. The user's certificate must be present to decrypt the encryption keys. The list of keys used to encrypt each file is unique. The encryption keys used to encrypt a file are not used on another file; therefore, copies of keys used to encrypt one file cannot be used to decrypt another file.

➤ *Temporary file protection*—Many applications, such as Microsoft Word, create temporary files as a user works with the application. With many encryption applications, the temporary files stored on the hard drive while the user is working with the application are not protected. Because EFS works with directories, any files within the directory are protected.

➤ *Keys stored in non-paged RAM*—The encryption keys used by Windows 2000 are never written to the page file where someone could gain access to them. Encryption keys reside in the Windows 2000 kernel, which always resides in non-paged memory.

➤ *Additional security*—If the administrator takes ownership of a file or changes permissions to a file, the file remains inaccessible to anyone other than the owner or the recovery agent. If the recovery agent is used to recover a file, the keys used to encrypt the file are not exposed and, therefore, cannot be copied.

The Recovery Agent

The recovery agent can be used to unlock files that were locked by users who are unavailable. The recovery agent can use the public key to unlock the DRF portion of the header to decrypt the encryption keys used to encrypt the file. The file should be sent to the recovery agent rather than having the recovery agent copy a public key to any foreign machine.

Recovery keys can be used to decrypt any files that were encrypted after the recovery key was created, but the recovery key cannot decrypt files that were created before its creation. Therefore, a recovery key must be generated before anyone can encrypt files. Recovery keys should be protected and backed up regularly.

Encrypting and Decrypting at the Command Prompt

The command-line utility Cipher.exe can be used at the command prompt to encrypt and decrypt files and folders. To provide additional functionality, the Cipher utility has six switches that can be used to modify the default behavior of the encryption process. Table 13.2 lists each switch as well as the functionality added by each switch.

Table 13.2   Cipher command-line switches.

Switch	Description
/s	Encrypts all files and subfolders within a folder.
/e	Encrypts the folder and marks the folder so any new files written to the folder are also encrypted.
/d	Decrypts the folder and marks the folder so any new files written to the folder are not encrypted.
/i	Causes Cipher.exe to ignore errors and continue to encrypt files after errors have been generated.
/f	Causes all files to be encrypted. Normally, files that are already encrypted are skipped. If this switch is used, then files that are already encrypted are re-encrypted.
/q	Reduces reporting information. Only essential information is reported.
Filename	A required parameter, rather than a switch, that specifies the name of a file, pattern, or folder to encrypt. A pattern is a string, such as *proposal*, in which case any files that include "proposal" anywhere in the file or folder name would be encrypted.

CHAPTER SUMMARY

This chapter examined the new features of Windows 2000 file system as well as some file system functions that are an improvment over Windows NT 4. To provide centralized access and administration, you can publish shared folders in the Active Directory. By publishing shared resources in the Active Directory, you are allowing users to access the resource from anywhere in the forest without requiring that each user memorize the server name that hosts the share. The Distributed file system provides the same functionality while providing even more benefits and functionality.

The Distributed file system (Dfs) allows you to publish shared folders throughout the domain to one or more virtual file systems. Multiple shares that reside on different servers can be published within shared folders on any server. Dfs provides additional benefits by allowing administrators to organize similar shares throughout the enterprise into virtual file systems.

The Computer Management Administrative Tool was reviewed and described. Standard and special NTFS permissions allow administrators and users to control access to private and/or sensitive data on the network. Using the NTFS Take Ownership Permission, administrators can recover files that have been accidentally excluded from use to everyone or files that contain permissions that must be modified. To further protect files, Windows 2000 has included the ability to encrypt files with the Encrypting File System.

The Encrypting File System (EFS) allows users and administrators to include an extra layer of security through the use of encryption. Sensitive data can be encrypted to secure files even in the event that they are physically copied or moved to a new location and the NTFS permissions are bypassed. Laptop users are very susceptible to theft, but with the proper administration of EFS any data on the laptop is protected.

REVIEW QUESTIONS

1. Creating a shared folder is accomplished using which of the following Administrative Tools?

   a. Active Directory Users and Computers

   b. Computer Management

   c. Active Directory Computer Management

   d. Active Directory Sites and Services

2. To publish a folder to the directory, the folder must first be shared.

   a. True

   b. False

3. Shared folders must be published to the Active Directory before users can access the share.

   a. True

   b. False

4. What can the Computer Management Administrative Tool connect to?

   a. Only the local computer

   b. Only domain controllers

   c. Only computers within the local domain

   d. Any computer on the network where the user has appropriate permissions

5. Which tool within the Computer Management application allows you to view all current hardware installed on the system as well as the properties of each peripheral?

   a. Diagnostics Manager

   b. Local System Hardware (LSH) editor

   c. Device Manager

   d. The hardware resources folder within the system node

13

6. Which of the following Administrative Tools can be used to create local accounts on a domain controller?

    a. Computer Management

    b. Active Directory Users and Computers

    c. User Manager

    d. None of the above

7. Which node within the Computer Management Administrative Tool is used to view disk resources?

    a. Drive Resources

    b. Storage

    c. System

    d. Services and Applications

8. Which of the following is not a shared folder permission?

    a. Take Ownership

    b. Write

    c. Change Permissions

    d. None of the above

9. Which of the following statements is true regarding publishing a share in the Active Directory?

    a. Provides a centralized location for accessing the folder

    b. Allows all users in the forest to view the share

    c. Eliminates the need to memorize which servers contain which shares

    d. All of the above

10. Publishing a share to the Active Directory is accomplished with which of the following Administrative Tools?

    a. Computer Management

    b. Active Directory Users and Computers

    c. Windows Explorer

    d. The Publish Share MMC snap-in

11. What does the Distributed file system allow administrators to do?

    a. Centrally locate multiple shares into one virtual directory structure

    b. Format a partition for the purpose of sharing the drive

    c. Publish shares to the Active Directory

    d. All of the above

12. Which of the following client operating systems can connect to Dfs without additional software?

    a. Windows 3.1

    b. DOS

    c. Windows 95

    d. None of the above

13. Dfs can be created on which of the following?

    a. Domain controllers only

    b. Member servers only

    c. Domain controllers or member servers

    d. The forest root domain controller only

14. Permissions assigned to a shared folder are _____.

    a. Overridden by Dfs permissions

    b. Not affected by Dfs

    c. Erased when used in a Dfs

    d. Combined with Dfs permissions

15. Where can a Dfs be created?

    a. NTFS partitions only

    b. Fat partitions only

    c. NTFS and FAT partitions

    d. FAT32 and NTFS partitions only

13

16. Dfs is created by defining a _____.

    a. Root

    b. Leaf

    c. Link

    d. Directory structure

17. What is a Dfs link?

    a. A pointer to any shared folder

    b. A shared file that has been configured as the root

    c. A pointer to a shared file on another server

    d. None of the above

18. What are the two types of Dfs?

    a. Fault tolerant and published

    b. Member server and isolated

    c. Standalone and fault tolerant

    d. Standalone and published

19. What type of Dfs topology is stored on a server?

    a. Member

    b. Fault tolerant

    c. Published

    d. Standalone

20. What type of Dfs topology is stored in the Active Directory?

    a. Member

    b. Fault tolerant

    c. Published

    d. Standalone

21. How can Dfs links be made fault tolerant?

    a. Store the shares in the Active Directory

    b. Publish the shares in the Active Directory

    c. Create replica shares

    d. Create replica shares and add multiple links

22. By default, how long will a client computer cache the path to Dfs links?

    a. 18 minutes

    b. 180 minutes

    c. 30 minutes

    d. 1,800 minutes

23. Which of the following standard NTFS permissions includes all permissions except Take Ownership and Change Permissions?

    a. Change

    b. Write

    c. Full Control

    d. Modify

24. Which of the following statements is true?

    a. Ownership of a file must be assigned to a user.

    b. Ownership of a file must be taken and cannot ever be assigned.

    c. Ownership of a file can be taken only by the administrator.

    d. The owner of a file can assign ownership.

25. By default, NTFS permissions are _____.

    a. Inherited from the parent folder to the subfolder, although files do not inherit file permissions

    b. Inherited from parent folder to all subfolders and files

    c. Not inherited, because inheritance is blocked

    d. None of the above

REAL-WORLD PROJECTS

Andy Palmer, while continuing to spend endless hours studying for the Windows 2000 Accelerated exam (70-240), gets an email informing him that there is yet another project waiting for his attention. The customer, Coriolis, has already started upgrading their network to Windows 2000; however, users are now complaining that, with all the turmoil, they can no longer find the resources they need to perform their jobs.

During the confusing upgrade process, some of the shared folders that were on the original Windows NT 4 network were moved to the new Windows 2000 Server. Permissions were not properly configured, however. Due to the oversight, someone managed to download the payroll database and email it to everyone in the company.

All the users were informed to copy all their files to the backup server while their computers' operating systems were being upgraded. Many users became confused and copied the entire contents of their hard drive to their home folder. This quickly filled the hard drives containing the home folders to capacity and now no one can save any files to their home folders. Coriolis is at a standstill until these issues can be corrected.

Andy shakes his head as he reads the email and wonders why he was not hired to upgrade the network in the first place. Andy's first priority is to create the shares that are needed by the employees. All the files were copied from the NT 4 server but were not shared. Andy plans to share the files and then create a Distributed file system to allow users to easily find needed resources.

13

Project 13.1

To share a file using Computer Management, complete the following steps:

1. Andy starts the Computer Management Administrative Tool.

2. Expand the Shared Folders folder.

3. Right-click the Shares folder, and select New File Share.

4. Enter "C:\Apps" in the Folders To Share field.

5. Enter "Applications" as the share name.

6. Click Next.

7. Click Yes to allow the folder to be created.

8. Select the Administrators Have Full Control; Other Users Have Read-Only Access radio button, as shown in Figure 13.14.

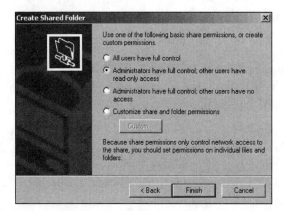

Figure 13.14 Creating and setting permissions on a shared folder.

9. Click Finish, and select No in the dialog box asking if you want to create another share.

10. Right-click the Shares folder again, and select New File Share.

11. Enter "D:\Word" in the Folder To Share field.

12. Enter "Word" as the share name.

13. Click Next.

14. Click Yes.

15. Select the Administrators Have Full Control; Other Users Have Read-Only Access radio button, as was shown in Figure 13.14.

16. Click Finish.

17. Select Yes to share another folder.

Andy completes Steps 10 through 16 again in order to share another folder. This folder should be named Excel and should be located on the D: drive.

Andy now wants to publish the Word share in the Active Directory so users can easily find the share without having to know which server it is located on.

Project 13.2
To publish a share in the Active Directory, complete the following steps:

1. Open Active Directory Users and Computers.

2. Right-click the domain name, and select New | Shared Folder.

3. Enter "Word" as the name of the share.

4. In the Path field, enter the UNC path to the shared folder.

5. Click OK.

Project 13.3
To verify a published share, complete the following steps:

1. Double-click Network Neighborhood.

2. Double-click Entire Network.

3. Click the Hyperlink Entire Network.

4. Double-click Directory.

5. Double-click the domain name.

6. Ensure that the published share Word is present, as shown in Figure 13.15.

13

Andy now will configure a Dfs called *Applications* and establish links to all the application-shared folders. This setup will make finding shared resources easier for the users as well as provide a centralized location of shares for the purposes of administration.

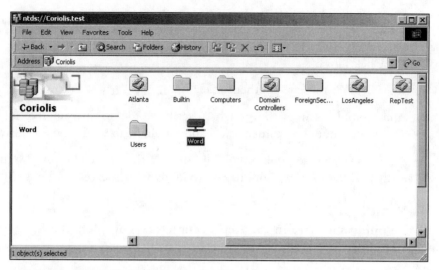

Figure 13.15 Viewing a published share.

Project 13.4
To configure a Dfs root, complete the following steps:

1. Open the Distributed File System manager within Administrative Tools.

2. Click the Action drop-down menu, and select New Dfs Root.

3. Click Next after the wizard starts.

4. Select Create A Domain Dfs Root, and click Next.

5. Select the coriolis.test domain, and click Next.

6. Enter the name of the server where the root Dfs share resides.

7. Click Next.

8. Select Use An Existing Share, and select the Applications share.

9. Click Next.

10. Enter "Applications" as the Dfs root name.

11. Add any comments, and click Next.

12. Click Finish.

Project 13.5
To add Dfs links, complete the following steps:

1. Open the Distributed File System manager within Administrative Tools.

2. Right-click the Applications Dfs Root, and select New Dfs Link.

3. Enter "Word" as the link name.

4. In the Send The User To This Shared Folder , enter the UNC path to the Word share. For example, enter "\\server1\Word".

5. Click OK.

6. Repeat Steps 2 through 5 to add the Excel share as a Dfs link (see Figure 13.16).

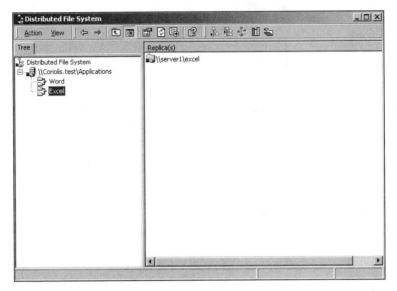

Figure 13.16   Dfs links.

13

Project 13.6
To add replica links, complete the following steps:

1. Create a folder on the same or a different server called Word2.

2. Share the Word2 folder with the share name Word2.

3. Open the Distributed File System manager within Administrative Tools.

4. Right-click The Word link, and select New Replica.

5. Enter the UNC path to the new shared folder, Word2.

6. Select Automatic Replication, as shown in Figure 13.17, and click OK. (If both shares are on the same machine, you must choose Manual Replication. Replication between two directories on the same server is not possible.)

7. Highlight each entry, and click Enable.

8. Click OK.

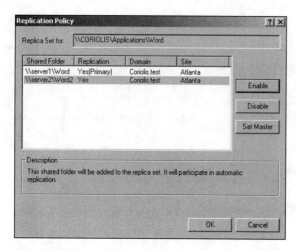

Figure 13.17 Configuring automatic replication.

Project 13.7
To verify Dfs configuration, complete the following steps:

1. Double-click Network Neighborhood.

2. Double-click Entire Network.

3. Click the Hyperlink Entire Network.

4. Double-click the Microsoft Windows Networks icon.

5. Double-click the coriolis domain.

6. Double-click Server1.

7. Double-click the Applications folder.

8. Both the Word and Excel folders should be present.

Andy is now going to encrypt the payroll folder. This will prevent data copied from this folder from being read by anyone other than the owner. Even if the shared and NTFS permissions are bypassed and the file is stolen, the file will remain encrypted and inaccessible to anyone other than the owner. Because encrypted files can be decrypted only with the user's or the recovery agent's public key, Andy will have to sign on as the user who will own the directory.

Project 13.8
To encrypt a folder, complete the following steps:

1. Log in as the user who will own the folder.

2. Right-click the payroll folder.

3. Select Properties.

4. Click Advanced.

5. Select the Encrypt Contents To Secure Data checkbox.

6. Click OK, and click OK again.

7. Select the Apply To This Folder, Subfolders And Files option.

8. Click OK.

Now that all is well at Coriolis, Andy can go back to studying for the Windows 2000 Accelerated exam.

13

CHAPTER FOURTEEN

CONTROLLING THE USER ENVIRONMENT WITH GROUP POLICIES

After completing this chapter, you will be able to:

✓ Use group policies with Active Directory

✓ Create and control group policy objects and links

✓ Process group policies in networked and standalone environments

✓ Support downlevel clients and use downlevel policy templates

✓ Plan group policy implementations

Group policies are used to customize and control a user's environment. Unlike customizations controlled by users (such as desktop color schemes and Favorites folders), policies are implemented by administrators. Windows 2000 ensures a reliable enforcement of policies and improves on existing policy technologies in previous versions of Windows, called downlevel systems. Policies are applied to sites, domains, and Organizational Units. This structure allows inheritance to take place, which means that each user's or computer's ultimate policies are a combination of policies from sites, domains, and Organizational Units. For further flexibility, inheritance can be blocked by administrators, or it can be enforced with the No Override switch by an administrator at a higher level. In addition, security groups, like Windows NT local and global groups, can be used to filter policies but not implement them.

Windows NT 4 and Windows 9x both incorporate system policies that can perform some of the same tasks as a group policy. In Windows NT 4 and Windows 9x, policies were created by Poledit.exe and held in the NETLOGON share as NTCONFIG.POL or CONFIG.POL. This approach presents the following three basic problems:

➤ Users can change the registry keys that are modified by the policy, thereby making the keys less secure.

➤ After the policy updates the registry, the changes stay and often have to be manually removed.

➤ Policies are limited to items that can be changed with registry keys.

Windows 2000's group policy rectifies the preceding shortcomings, and it adds the Active Directory site and Organizational Unit container applicability to make policies more flexible. Let's look at how group policies apply to the Active Directory.

GROUP POLICIES AND ACTIVE DIRECTORY

When planning and implementing the Active Directory, group policies should be a major consideration. You configure group policies using group policy objects. A *group policy object* includes the nodes and extensions along with their settings. The main types of group policies include the following:

➤ Local policy—A group policy object that resides locally on every machine.

➤ Site linked policies—A group policy object that requires a guaranteed fast link.

➤ Domain linked policies—Policies that apply to all objects in a domain, such as account policies.

➤ Organizational Unit policies—Policies that are used for granularity and delegation of policies.

Group policies' order of precedence is very important, because the last policy processed has the net effect on the target object (computer or user). When policies are applied to a user or computer, the local policy is applied first. Then site linked policies are applied. After the site linked policies, the domain linked and Organizational Unit (OU) policies are applied. As mentioned, these policies exhibit inheritance. Therefore, the settings in a policy at one level can be contradicted by a policy at a level closer to the target user or computer. This behavior can be modified with the No Override setting in the Group Policy tab at the higher level, as seen in Figure 14.1 (the No Override setting is discussed in more detail later in this chapter).

A policy can also be blocked with the Block Policy Inheritance setting, as seen in Figure 14.2. These settings can be powerful, but their use should be limited to avoid unnecessary complexity.

In Windows 2000, group policy objects must be applied or blocked as a whole, so, aside from disabling the entire computer or user configuration node within a policy, you cannot accept some settings and reject others within a group policy object. Even the filtering of policies based on security group membership must be applied by entire group policy objects. In the Windows 2000 environment, every machine has a local group policy object, but the majority of administra-tive policies should be implemented through non-local group policy objects. Non-local policy objects are linked to sites, domains, or OUs. Some exceptions to the policy linking rule are the generic containers, which are identified in Active Directory Users and Computers by a normal folder instead of an Active Directory type folder. Group policies cannot be linked directly to generic folders, but generic folders can inherit group policies from parent domains or sites.

14

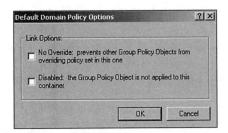

Figure 14.1   The No Override setting.

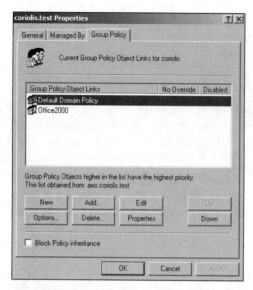

Figure 14.2   The Block Policy Inheritance setting.

With all this in mind, now we'll look at the methods of linking a group policy to a particular container, such as an OU or domain.

GROUP POLICY OBJECTS AND LINKS

Group policy objects are created from the settings configured in the Group Policy Console. When you initially open the console, it is focused on the root node, which uses the following syntax:

<policy object> <server>

Group policy objects are updated in real time. This means that after a policy is linked, any change to the policy is effective when the computer boots or when a user logs on as well as when the policy is refreshed, without the need for saving or reapplying the policy.

Although group policy has its own Microsoft Management (MMC) snap-in, users more commonly spawn group policies from either Active Directory Users and Computers or Active Directory Sites and Services. Using the Group Policy snap-in from either of the consoles mentioned makes it easier to link a policy to the desired site, domain, or OU immediately.

Tip: A Group Policy tab is found in the properties of all sites, domains, and non-generic OUs.

> **Warning:**   The permission to change group policies is a very powerful permission, and you should
> delegate the power carefully within the Active Directory.

You can filter policies via security group membership by using a discretionary access control list (DACL) for the policy (filtering is discussed in more detail later in this chapter). A DACL contains all the permissions for a particular user or group of users. Administrative access to a policy can be delegated to a security group or an individual user at the level where the policy is linked. The first requirement of policy administration delegation is that the group or user must have Read and Write permissions to the system volume (SYSVOL) of the domain controller. Furthermore, the user or group must have Modify rights to the site, domain, or OU in question.

The Group Policy Console, and other default consoles provided with Windows 2000, are extensive enough for most networks. For example, the default console can be customized and delegated in user mode to administrators of the container affected. Also, customized extensions to the console can be developed to accommodate any needs not immediately satisfied by the default console. Finally, because the console is merely a snap-in for the MMC, you can combine it with other snap-ins to encompass all the necessary functionality needed for day-to-day administrative tasks. When there are no extensions or snap-ins added to the Group Policy Console, it is known as the Default Console. Every container also has a default policy that is linked to the container but has no parameters set within it. The default policy has two basic nodes—Computer Configuration and User Configuration. Both nodes are broken down into three extensions:

➤ Software Settings

➤ Windows Settings

➤ Administrative Templates

Usually, Computer Configuration policies take precedence over contradictory User Configuration policies. In the Computer Configuration Node, there are a number of extensions, the first of which is Software extensions.

Software Settings Extensions in the Computer Configuration Node

As shown in Figure 14.3, the Computer Configuration node's Software Settings extensions apply application settings for a machine regardless of which user is logged on. Applications can be assigned to a computer, which means that the application will be installed on the machine without user intervention. If an

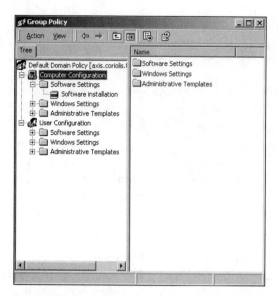

Figure 14.3 Software Settings extensions.

application is assigned to a machine but the entire application is not installed, a stub that advertises the application is installed instead. The first time the application is run, the most common components will be installed on the computer. If the user chooses a feature that is not installed, the feature will be automatically installed. Users can remove assigned applications, but the application will be reinstalled the next time the computer is logged onto or the next time the user logs on. In addition to assigned applications, software can also be published. Published software is software that is available to a user but not forcibly installed on a computer. Published software can be installed through the Add/Remove Programs applet in Control Panel.

Windows Settings Extensions in the Computer Configuration Node

The Windows Settings extensions, shown in Figure 14.4, enable you to customize selected Windows components' behavior. For example, the Computer Configuration's Scripts node can be applied at startup, shutdown, or both. These scripts can be simple command-line batch files, or they can be more complex scripts written for the Windows Scripting Host (WSH).

The Windows Scripting Host is an integral part of Windows 2000, as well as Windows 98. The WSH includes an interpreter for the command prompt called CSCRIPT.EXE as well as an interpreter for the GUI called WSCRIPT.EXE. By default, scripts written for WSH can use the VBScript and JScript languages, although other scripting languages, such as Perl, can be installed.

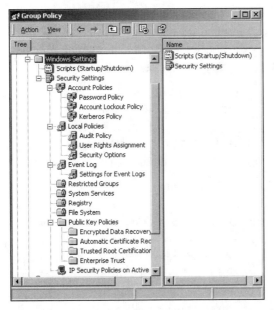

Figure 14.4   Windows Settings extensions.

The Windows Settings node also contains many nodes. Each node within the Windows Settings has a specific purpose.

The Security Settings Node

The Security Settings node is more extensive in the Computer Configuration node than in the User Configuration node. Namely, the Security Settings node in Computer Configuration encompasses:

➤ Account Policies—Settings that must be set at domain level.

➤ Local Policies—Settings that affect local machines.

➤ Public Key Policies—Settings that relate to the public key infrastructure.

➤ IP Security Policies—Settings for communications across the network.

Account Policies Extension for Computer Configuration

The Account Policies extensions apply only to the domain level, and they are ignored if they are applied at the OU level. Account Policies extensions include the Password policy, Account Lockout policy, and Kerberos policy:

➤ *Password Policy*—Sets the password history and remembers one password by default. The maximum password age is set to 42 days by default, while the minimum password age is set to 0. The minimum length defaults to 0 and password complexity requirements are disabled. The ability to store passwords in reversible encryption is disabled by default.

14

➤ *Account Lockout Policy*—Sets the duration of lockout threshold before locking out and the reset interval for logon attempts. The duration of the lockout and counter reset is not defined by default, which renders the default threshold of 0 failed logon attempts useless.

➤ *Kerberos Policy*—Affects logon restrictions, service ticket lifetime, ticket renewal lifetime, and clock synchronization tolerance.

Local Policies Extension for Computer Configuration

The Local Policies extensions includes the Audit Policy, User Rights Assignments, and Security Options:

➤ *Audit Policy*—The Audit Policy captures events to the system's Event Log to track the failure or success of designated activities. For example, an event can be registered for account logons to help identify brute force attacks. To help control the activities of support personnel, any account management and policy change events can be audited. Effectiveness of the Active Directory structure can be tested by logging any directory services access. With further configuration on the object itself, object access can be monitored. Some more advanced settings that might be needed by software developers or server administrators are privileged use, process tracking, and system events.

➤ *User Rights Assignments*—User Rights Assignments determine which actions a user can commit, unlike permissions that determine what resources they can access. User rights are very extensive, although some are used more than others. For example, authenticated users need the right to add workstations to the domain and access the domain controller from the network, but you can also assign a right that explicitly denies access to the domain controller from the network. Backup operators need to be able to log on locally as well as have the rights to back up files, restore files, and shut down the system. Server operators need the same rights as backup operators as well as the right to change the system time and shut down the system remotely. Administrators are assigned all the rights of server operators and the rights to create a page file, debug programs, increase quotas, increase scheduling priority, load and unload device drivers, manage auditing and security logs, profile system performance, and take ownership of objects. These are all default settings for the security of a domain, and they can all be changed at the site, domain, or OU level using group policies.

➤ *Security Options*—The Security Options control activities that, by their very nature, are powerful and can be detrimental to your enterprise if they fall into the wrong hands. Security Options are not configured or disabled by default, so the available options are not listed here. Administrators should ensure that they are familiar with the Security Options. Some standard policies can be applied to a domain by using one of the incremental security templates found in the *%systemroot%/*security/templates folder. Windows 2000 systems that were upgraded from Windows NT 4 can use only the basic templates, however.

Configuring the Security Options for the Event Log is a convenient method to control event logs in the entire enterprise with group policies. By using these settings, you can set the maximum size for the application, security, and system logs. Restricting guest access to the logs is a good practice. The number of days to retain logs as well as the method of retaining the logs by overwriting can be configured individually for each log. Finally, the system can be shut down when the security log is full.

Restricted groups—Restricted groups are a new feature in Windows 2000. By adding a group to the list of restricted groups and explicitly adding members to the group, an automatic process for group management can be implemented. For example, the Administrators group should be a restricted group. When the Administrators group is added to the restricted group list, the members of all permanent administrators are added. If any other users are added to the group temporarily, Windows 2000 will remove them from the group during the next security audit. If new members should be added to the restricted group permanently, they can be added using the restricted groups settings in group policy.

14

System Services, Registry, and File System Policies for Computer Configuration

The System Services, Registry, and File System extensions of all computers in a container that a group policy is linked to can be controlled via the Group Policy Editor. The manner in which a service starts can be set to automatic, manual, or completely disabled. Care should be taken and testing performed any time a service is set to start automatically. Some services require intervention during startup, and this can stall a system when it starts. The permissions for registry keys can be managed using these policies. Use these policies sparingly, because incorrect permissions on registry objects can render a system unusable. Finally, file system objects can be managed using a policy. However, all computer file systems to which a File System policy applies must be configured with the same settings for the policy to be effective.

Public Key Policies for Computer Configuration

The Public Key Policies tailor the public key encryption settings for the objects in a selected container. The public key infrastructure, which these settings govern, control the manner in which X.509 certificates are used to encrypt files on the network. The public key infrastructure includes a fallback agent that can decrypt any files on the network, as well as trusts with other domains within the Active Directory.

The Encrypted Data Recovery Agents within the computer's Public Key Policies have the ability to decrypt any files or folders encrypted by other users. This ability can be useful when employees are unavailable to retrieve files or when keys have been lost.

The Automatic Certificate Request within the Public Key Policies allows clients to query a certificate authority to receive the certificates that facilitate public key cryptography. Public Key Policies is also the place where you can import lists of Trusted Certificate Authorities and distribute the lists to the objects in a selected container. Trusted Certificate Authorities can issue the certificates necessary for public key cryptography.

Another setting in the Public Key Policies is the Enterprise Trust Settings, which contains settings for certificate authorities that will be trusted at the enterprise level. Windows 2000 certificate authorities do not need to be listed in these settings because they are automatically trusted, but any external certificate authorities that need to be trusted can be entered in the Enterprise Trust Settings.

IP Security Policies for Computer Configuration

The last configuration in the Security Settings extensions in the Computer Configuration node is the IP Security Policies On Active Directory. Three default policies are included here:

➤ *Client Policy*—Allows communication without a secure channel for most situations. However, the Client Policy also allows a client to negotiate with servers that request a secure channel. If a secure channel is negotiated, only the traffic on the selected port is secure.

➤ *Secured Server Policy*—States that communication should always be secure. Secure communication should take place with the Kerberos security protocol, and unsecured communication should not be allowed.

➤ *Server Policy*—States that a secure channel should be requested by the server. However, if the client does not respond to the secure channel request, unsecured communication can take place.

Administrative Templates Extensions in the Computer Configuration Node

Figure 14.5 shows the Administrative Templates extensions for the Computer Configuration node. This node can be added using Unicode files with the .adm extension, which are standalone templates usually provided by the software manufacturer. These .adm files contain modifications to the registry key *HKEY_LOCAL_MACHINE*. The extensions provide group policies with an additional level of control over software and hardware behavior. The default nodes present are Windows Components, System, Network, and Printers.

Windows Component Extension for Computer Configuration

The Windows Components extension contains settings for NetMeeting, Internet Explorer, Task Scheduler, and Windows Installer. Notable settings for the extensions include the following:

➤ *NetMeeting*—Allows you to disable remote desktop sharing to remove possible network intrusions.

➤ *Internet Explorer*—Enables you to customize security zones and provides the ability to prevent users from changing the security zone settings. Proxy server settings can also be set and locked, and the splash screen can be disabled. The last setting for Internet Explorer is the ability to disable the Windows and the Internet Explorer update feature.

➤ *Task Scheduler*—Enables you to prevent users from adding, deleting, browsing, running, or stopping tasks.

➤ *Windows Installer*—Allows you to customize the install scripts, patch updates, and priorities of Windows Installer–based rollouts.

14

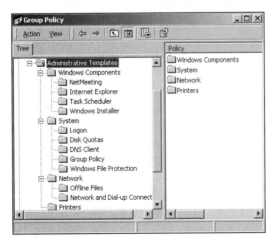

Figure 14.5   The Administrative Templates extensions.

System Extension for Computer Configuration

The System extension contains settings for logons, disk quotas, DNS clients, group policy, and Windows file protection:

➤ *Logon*—Logons can be customized to run startup and shutdown scripts synchronously or asynchronously as well as visible or invisible. Additionally, the way the scripts are processed can be customized. For instance, users can wait a specified period of time for group policy scripts and user profiles before timing out. Furthermore, cached profiles can be deleted, and a user can be logged off if a roaming profile is not available.

➤ *Disk Quotas*—Disk quotas can be enabled and the warning and exceeded levels set. Disk quotas can also be selectively applied to removable media.

➤ *DNS Clients*—The primary DNS suffix can be set with the DNS client settings.

➤ *Group Policy*—Group policy processing can be customized and certain portions of group policies can be disabled here.

➤ *Windows File Protection*—Windows system files can be scanned, and the cache location for these can be changed.

Network Extension for Computer Configuration

The Network extension contains the Offline Files settings as well as the Network and Dial-up parameters. Using the Offline Files setting, you can lock users out of offline files, or you can disable offline files entirely. Furthermore, file synchronization can be forced at logoff, or the local copy of the files can be deleted at logoff. In addition, administrators can set certain files to be available offline or prevent the use of offline files. Finally, reminder balloons can be disabled or their timing can be set through the policy. Using the Network and Dialup settings, you can lock users out of their configuration.

Printers Extension for Computer Configuration

The last extension in Computer Configuration is the Printers extension. Policies can be set to allow local printers to be published or to publish them automatically so that they are automatically available in the Active Directory. Settings also enable you to allow or force pruning printers from the Active Directory. Furthermore, Web-based printing can be enabled with a URL set by the policy. Finally, the Printers folder can be forced to open in a particular location.

Software Settings Extensions in the User Configuration Node

The User Configuration node Software Settings extensions apply application settings for users regardless of the computer they are logged onto. As seen in

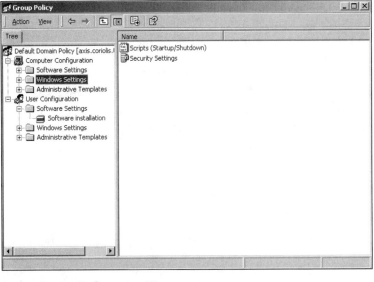

Figure 14.6   Software settings.

Figure 14.6, the software extensions for the User Configuration node are the same as the extensions for the Computer Configuration node.

Windows Settings Extensions in the User Configuration Node

The Windows extensions for the User Configuration node differ from those in the Computer Configuration node. As seen in Figure 14.7, particular settings

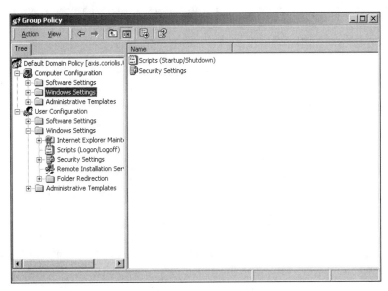

Figure 14.7   The Windows Settings extensions.

exist for Internet Explorer Maintenance and Remote Installation Services. These settings facilitate significant Windows customization that was previously implemented through separate applications like the Internet Explorer Administration Kit.

Internet Explorer Maintenance Extensions for User Configuration

The Internet Explorer Maintenance extension contains settings for the browser user interface, connection, URLs, security, and programs.

➤ *Browser user interface settings*—Allow customization of the browser title, bitmaps, and toolbar buttons.

➤ *Connection settings*—Contain proxy settings, connection settings, and the user agent string.

➤ *URLs section*—Allows policy-driven Favorites, channels, and important URLs.

➤ *Security zones*—Allow zone configuration, content ratings, and Authenticode code signature settings.

➤ *Programs settings*—Contain a facility in group policy to import custom programs to accompany Internet Explorer.

User Configuration Scripts

The User Configuration scripts can be applied at logon, logoff, or both. These scripts can be simple command-line batch files, or they can be more complex scripts written for the WSH.

The user Public Key Policies are slightly more limited than the Computer Configuration's Public Key Policies. The only parameter present in the User Configuration node is the list of certificate trusts based on the user.

The Remote Installation Services (RIS) settings determine the options that a user has during an RIS procedure. Both automatic and manual setup can be allowed or disallowed as well as the ability to restart an RIS procedure.

Folder Redirection Settings

Folder redirection is a feature that is new to Windows 2000. Group policy can control where users must point their systems to find specific types of files. For each folder, you can point all users to the same location or specify a location based on user groups. If the location is group based, the following options are available:

➤ Users can be granted exclusive rights to the My Documents folder, and the contents can be immediately moved to a new location.

➤ If the policy is removed, a folder can stay in the new location or be redirected to a user's profile.

➤ The My Pictures folder can be a subfolder of My Documents, or it can fall out of the realm of administrative control.

➤ Application Data, Desktop, My Documents, and Start Menu folders are available for redirection.

Administrative Templates Extensions in the User Configuration Node

Figure 14.8 displays the Administrative Templates in the User Configuration node that can be added. They are added using Unicode files with the extension .adm. These files are standalone templates usually provided by the software manufacturer. These template files contain modifications to the registry key *HKEY_CURRENT_USER*. The extensions provide group policies with an additional level of control over software and hardware behavior. The default nodes present are Windows Components, Start Menu & Taskbar, Desktop, Control Panel, Network, and System.

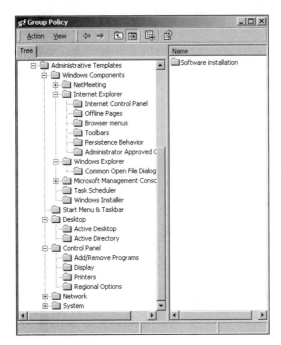

Figure 14.8   The Administrative Templates extensions.

Windows Components Extension for User Configuration

The Windows Components Extensions in the User Configuration node facilitate customization of specific components within Windows. These components can be standalone applications, like Internet Explorer, or applets completely contained within Windows, like Windows Explorer.

➤ *NetMeeting*—The NetMeeting settings for the User Configuration node, shown in Figure 14.9, are quite extensive. At the root of the NetMeeting node, configuration for NetMeeting can be automated using a URL, and the URL for the Intranet Support Page can be set. Directory Services can be disabled, viewing the Web Directory can be prevented, and the adding of Directory Servers can be disabled. The way calls are placed and accepted can be customized as well as the security options and placement methods for calls. File transfer can be prevented, and the size of files transferred can be limited. Finally, the chat and whiteboard features can be disabled. Subfolders can be used to customize application sharing, audio and video, and additional options features. Configuring NetMeeting by using a combination of NetMeeting settings in the Computer Configuration and the User Configuration nodes facilitates complete control of Microsoft NetMeeting.

➤ *Internet Explorer*—As seen in Figure 14.10, the settings in the Internet Explorer subfolder are quite extensive. Appearance settings, such as font and color, can be standardized. Connection and proxy settings can be set. Profiles and identities can be disabled. Even the URLs for Favorites can be

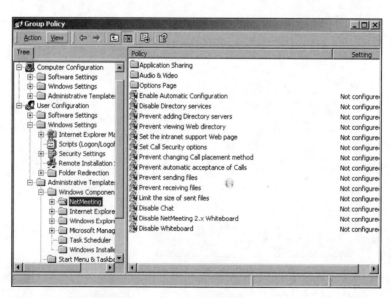

Figure 14.9   NetMeeting customization settings.

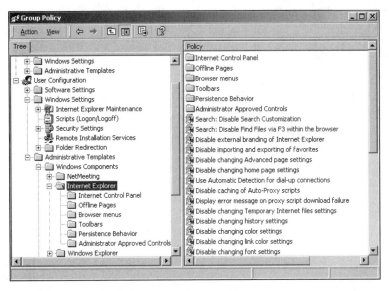

Figure 14.10   The Internet Explorer settings.

preset for all affected users. The Internet Control Panel subfolder can lock users out of any settings tabs within the browser. Offline Pages can be customized or disabled entirely. Certain items in the menus can be disabled. Toolbars can be pre-populated and further customization can be disabled. Controls such as Media Player and Shockwave can be administratively approved or disapproved.

➤ *Windows Explorer*—As Figure 14.11 demonstrates, the Windows Explorer settings allow menu items to be removed or disabled. Customization of the interface can be disabled. Certain items, such as Computers Near Me, can be removed. The shell customizations can be disabled. Recent Documents lists can be limited. Certain tabs, like the Hardware tab, can be hidden. The subfolder for the Common Open File Dialog can be controlled by hiding the recent files menu option and the Back button.

➤ *Microsoft Management Console (MMC)*—The MMC settings ensure proper delegation behavior by restricting users from using Author mode and allowing users to use only permitted snap-ins. In addition, a subfolder that lists all the available snap-ins allows administrators to select which snap-ins are allowed. These are shown in Figure 14.12.

➤ *Task Scheduler*—Figure 14.13 shows the Task Scheduler settings in group policy. The Task Scheduler folder gives administrators the ability to restrict property and advanced settings, run and end tasks, create and delete tasks, and prohibit users from browsing tasks.

14

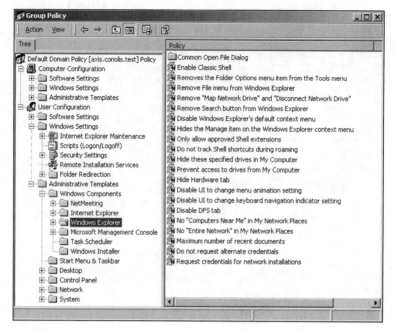

Figure 14.11   The Windows Explorer settings.

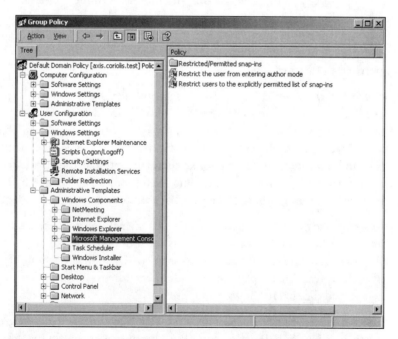

Figure 14.12   The MMC customization settings.

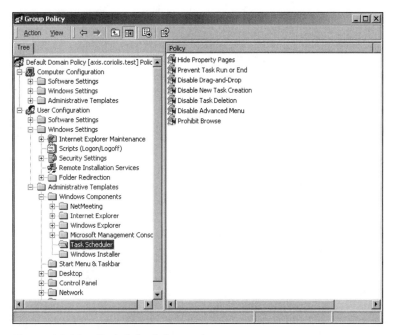

Figure 14.13   Task Scheduler settings.

➤ *Windows Installer*—Figure 14.14 shows the Windows Installer settings for group policies. Windows Installer folder contains settings that you can use to customize the search order for installation files, allow installation to use elevated privileges, and disable rollback and media source selection.

Start Menu & Taskbar Extension for User Configuration

The Start menu and Taskbar can be customized. As Figure 14.15 shows, the Start Menu & Taskbar folder contains numerous customization settings. For example, group policy can remove a user's folders, Windows update shortcut, common programs, recent documents, network and dial-up settings, Favorites, Search menu, shortcut to Help, and the Run dialog box. You can also disable the logoff option, shutdown option, context menus, personalized menu, and user tracking.

Desktop Extension for User Configuration

The Desktop folder allows you to hide all desktop icons or remove individual default icons. Users can be prevented from adding shares to the My Network Places folder and changing the My Documents path. If a user is allowed to customize the desktop, a policy can be set that does not save the user's settings on exit. There is also a subfolder for the Active Desktop that can prohibit users from enabling, disabling, or customizing Active Desktop. The items on the

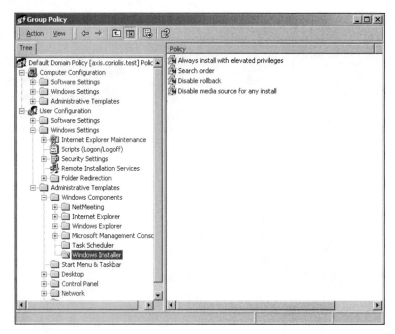

Figure 14.14 Windows Installer customization settings.

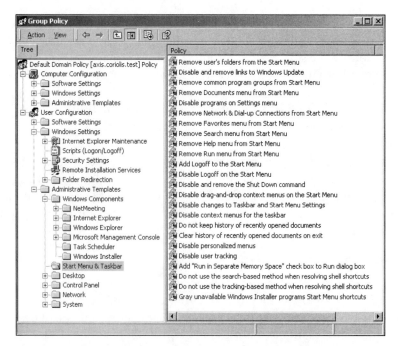

Figure 14.15 Start Menu & Task bar settings.

Active Desktop can be preset, as well as the background. The last folder under Desktop is the Active Directory folder. The Active Directory folder can limit the size of searches, enable filtering searches, or hide the Active Directory folder entirely. Figure 14.16 shows these settings.

Control Panel Extension for User Configuration

The Control Panel folder contains subfolders for Add/Remove Programs, Display, Printers, and Regional Options. From the root of the folder, you can hide the entire Control Panel or just specific applets. In the Add/Remove Programs subfolder, you can hide any of an applet's pages or disable an applet altogether. You can use the Display subfolder to hide any individual Display page or the overall Display Settings applet. The Printers settings can preload specific printers, disable adding or deleting printers, and specify a path to search for printers. Finally, the Regional Options settings can restrict the selection of Windows 2000 menus and dialog languages. Figure 14.17 shows the Control Panel customization settings.

Network Extension for User Configuration

The Network extension contains the Offline Files settings as well as the Network and Dial-up parameters. The Network Extension options provided for the User Configuration node are the same as the Network extension options

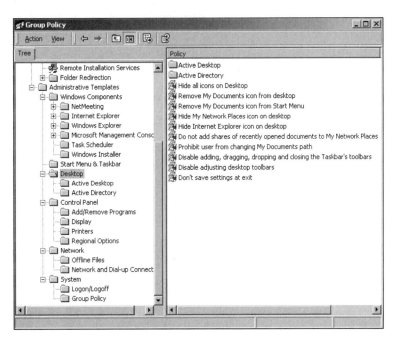

14

Figure 14.16   The Desktop extensions.

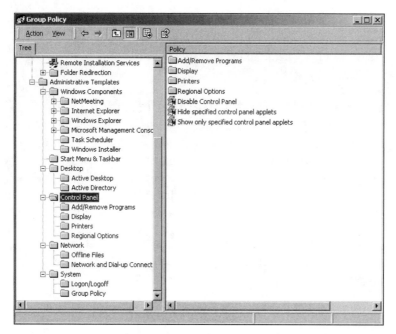

Figure 14.17   The Control Panel settings.

offered for the Computer Configuration node (see the section entitled "Network Extension for Computer Configuration" earlier in this chapter). The only difference is that the Network Extension options are applied to a user at logon, no matter which machine in the scope of the policy they log on to. The Network Settings are displayed in Figure 14.18.

System Extension for User Configuration

The System folder contains the Logon/Logoff and Group Policy subfolders:

➤ *Logon/Logoff settings*—Enables you to disable Task Manager or individual buttons within the Task Manager. Furthermore, you can hide logon and logoff scripts when they run, and you can limit profile sizes. Finally, you can set programs to run at logon, and you can disable the Run Once list.

➤ *Group Policy settings*—Customizes the behavior of group policies. As seen in Figure 14.19, the System settings in group policy provide much-needed customization settings.

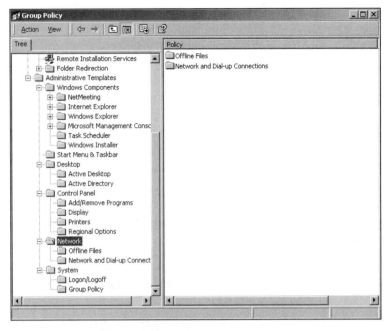

Figure 14.18   The Network settings.

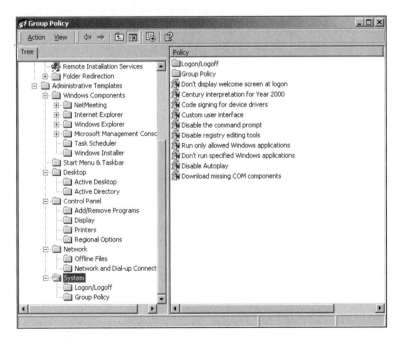

Figure 14.19   The System settings.

GROUP POLICY MANAGEMENT

Group policies are stored in files. As such, they are kept in specific locations on both standalone machines and in the Active Directory. Managing the storage of group policies is critical to the proper performance and behavior of those policies.

Storing Group Policies

Each machine has one local group policy stored in the *%systemroot%*\system32\ GroupPolicy folder, and the Active Directory stores many non-local group policies. You can use a machine's local policy on domain member machines as well as computers that are not domain members. Running the Group Policy Editor with the focus on, or connected to, the local computer will update the local machine policy.

On the local machine, only the Administrative Templates, Security Settings, Scripts, and Internet Explorer Maintenance extensions are available. The local group policy can't be blocked and is always processed first. Furthermore, settings within non-local policies take precedence over local policies.

The non-local group policies are stored in the group policy container on the domain controllers for the domain. Administrators use the Group Policy Editor to store group policies in the group policy container and group policy templates. Each container is identified by a GUID, and each one holds information such as version, status, components, and policy settings. The group policies templates are stored in the sysvol\public folder. At the root of this folder is a file named GPT.INI that contains the client-side extensions, version, and status of the policy. By default, the local Administrators group and the operating system have Full Control permissions, and the Users group has read permissions to the sysvol\public folder. To disable a policy, simply remove the Administrators Read permissions. The local GPT.INI contains the names of the client side extensions as well as the version and status of the policy.

Linking Group Policies

As mentioned, group policies are linked to sites, domains, or Organizational Units. Policies are stored in the storage domain, but a policy isn't effective until it's linked to a container. If a policy is not linked to its storage domain, it does not affect the domain. A policy can be stored in one domain and linked to another domain. Many group policy objects can be linked to one container, and one policy can be linked to multiple containers. Therefore, if a policy is stored in a container but not linked to it, the policy will have no effect.

There are two more ways to manipulate the manner in which a policy will affect a container. Using the no override setting and the block inheritance setting will determine if the policy will affect the container or not.

➤ *No Override option*—Setting the No Override option prevents a policy from being overridden at the level below the No Override setting. If more than one policy has the No Override option set, the links must be prioritized under the Links tab with the highest priority taking precedence. The No Override option takes precedence over the Block Policy Inheritance option.

➤ *Block Policy Inheritance option*—The Block Policy Inheritance option performs the opposite function of the No Override option. Setting the Block Policy Inheritance option at the site, domain, or Organizational Unit level means that the policy will not affect the container or its objects. As mentioned, the No Override option takes precedence over the Block Inheritance option.

Filtering Group Policies

Group policies can be filtered by configuring Windows 2000 security groups on the Security tab in the policy object's properties dialog box. In most circumstances, an entire policy must be filtered. The only exceptions to this are the Folder Redirection and Software Installation settings, which can be tuned within the group policy itself.

If users or groups cannot read the policy, it cannot be applied to them. Therefore, a user or group's permissions to the policy directly affects whether or not the policy will affect a user or group. Discretionary access control lists (DACLs) are used to permit or restrict access to a policy so that it will not affect particular groups. In order for a policy to affect a group, the group members must have the Apply Group Policy and Read access to the policy object itself. The Authenticated Users group has the Apply Group Policy and Read permissions by default. Therefore, the Domain and Enterprise Administrators groups have the Apply Group Policy and Read permissions, because they are members of the Authenticated Users group, and they have explicit Full Control over group policy objects (which allows them to edit policies). Taking the Apply Group Policy and Read access away from security groups that should not be affected not only speeds processing of policies but also ensures that the maximum of 1,000 applicable group policies is not exceeded.

14

Delegating Group Policies

Delegating group policy control is an important consideration for network administrators, because the amount of maintenance required for network administration can become overwhelming. Using delegation, administrators can allow other individuals to manipulate group policies.

Creating and editing non-local policies requires the right to Log On Locally to a domain controller. Therefore, the right to Log On Locally provides one way to restrict the creation of non-local policies. A security group named Group Policy Creator Owner allows the right to Log On Locally to delegate the Create Policy permissions to users.

Administrators and the creator/owner of a policy have Full Control over a policy, thereby allowing them to edit it. Additionally, any user with Read and Write permissions can edit a policy. Policies can't be opened in Read Only mode, which means that the Write permission is needed to open a policy. Control of policies can be delegated using customized MMC consoles. Delegation can also be implemented by creating a specialized console with a subset of snap-ins, saving the console in User Mode, and restricting permission to the customized console.

Processing Group Policies

Policies are processed in a specific order following specific rules. The local policy is processed first and is always processed. The policies linked to sites, domains, and Organizational Units are then processed, in that order. Remember, policies with blocked inheritance or insufficient DACLs will not be processed. Computer policies are processed at startup, and user policies are processed at logon. With few exceptions, computer policies take precedence over contradictory user policies. Group policies are processed by DLLs on the client using a precedence set in the GPOList for the group policy object.

Policies are processed synchronously by default, meaning that the outcome of a policy might depend on the outcome of a previously processed policy. This behavior can be changed to asynchronous processing within the group policy object if necessary.

With the exception of folder redirection and software installation, policies are refreshed every 90 minutes by default, and domain controllers are refreshed every 5 minutes. Both refresh intervals can be changed by configuring the group policy refresh intervals in group policy objects. Although the refresh interval for domain controllers can be set to a value of 0 (meaning 7 seconds), frequent refreshing will cause intolerable overhead. Since users can change some settings that policies affect, by using standard applets in Windows 2000, it is possible to change the process even if group policies have not changed within the group policy object.

Network bandwidth can severely affect the processing of group policy objects. If a slow link is detected, some group policy settings will not be processed, although the security and administrative templates will still be processed. However, the folder redirection, scripts, software installation, and Internet Explorer maintenance settings may not be processed. Each of the settings that will not process on slow links has a toggle that allows the settings to be forced, even on slow links. Unlike Windows NT 4, which uses file system performance as a metric, Windows 2000 pings the server. The first ping is 0 bytes, and the second ping is a 2K uncompressible ping. This process is performed three times to estimate the average network bandwidth. You can define a slow link using a group policy setting. By default, a slow link is defined as 500Kbps, which means that any link that runs slower than 500Kbps is classified as a slow link.

Note: If a server does not have IP support, Windows 2000 reverts to file system performance to detect slow links.

Editing Group Policies

Group policies can be edited from any domain controller. However, by default, all editing takes place on the operations master (PDC Emulator). This centralization prevents loss of data due to multiple simultaneous policy editing by administrators on different domain controllers. You can modify this behavior by changing the options for domain controller settings on the View menu in the Group Policy snap-in. Two additional options in the snap-in allow administrators to opt whether to use the domain controller that is used by the snap-in or use any available domain controller. If the domain controller specified cannot be reached, users receive an error message with the option to cancel or retry using any of the three domain controller options mentioned above. Another helpful setting can be accessed via User Configuration Node | Administrative Templates Settings | System Folder | Group Policy. If this group policy object restricts a user to a specific domain controller setting, the other options are grayed out and the only available option is Cancel.

Using Client-Side Extensions

Client-side extensions are dynamic link libraries that are loaded by a client as needed based on policy settings. These dynamic link libraries are required for proper functioning of policies on the clients. The following are some of the common extensions:

➤ The extension used to access the registry for the administrative templates is userenv.dll.

➤ The file system DLLs include Dskquota.dll for disk quotas, Fdeploy.dll for folder redirection, and Scecli.dll for the encrypted file system settings.

➤ Scripts and IP Security use Gptext.dll.

➤ Software installation uses Appmgmts.dll.

➤ Internet Explorer uses Iedkcs32.dll.

The policy is evaluated as it is loaded, and only the necessary extensions are installed on the client. Each client-side extension can have up to three processing settings, which determine whether to process across a slow link, apply during background (refresh) processing, and process even if the policy has not changed. As previously mentioned, the Administrative Templates and Security Settings will process over a slow link, so no configuration option is necessary. Finally, folder redirection and software installation will not process in the background, because both folder redirection and software installation could interrupt use of files or applications in question.

Using Loop Back Support

Loop back support is useful in homogenous Windows 2000 environments for specifying policies based on the location of a computer rather than a user account. For instance, one policy can apply to a user logged onto their workstation and another policy can be applied to the user when the user logs onto a server. The loop back settings are found in the Computer Configuration/Administrative Templates/System/Group Policy folder. You can choose between two modes of loop back support:

➤ *Merge mode*—Gathers the list of policies that apply to a user when the user logs on, and processes the computer policies last. This means that any settings in the computer policies that contradict user policies will take precedence.

➤ *Replace mode*—Specifies that the user policies are not gathered at all, and only the computer policies are applied.

Addressing Group Policy Issues after Migration

Most existing systems have a mixture of Windows 2000 computers and down-level systems, such as Windows 9*x* and Windows NT. Windows 9*x* and Windows NT computers can be controlled by using policies designed for them. These policies must be created using the System Policy Editor for the operating system in question. The files created are Config.pol for Windows 9*x* and NTConfig.pol for Windows NT systems. These files must be placed in the NETLOGON share of the domain controllers to have an effect.

Group policies use the following behavior, depending on their environment.

➤ If user and computer accounts exist on Windows NT 4 domain controllers, the local group policies are applied at system startup for these computers, and the domain computer policies and user policies are applied when a user logs on.

➤ If computer and user accounts exist on Windows 2000 domain controllers, the Windows 2000 system startup, computer, and user policies are applied.

➤ If a computer account is on a Windows 2000 domain controller and the user account is on a Windows NT 4 domain controller, the local policy is applied, the computer receives the group policy, and the user receives the group policy, but the user does not receive the system policy settings.

➤ If a user has a Windows NT account and the computer has a Windows 2000 account, the group policies are applied at system startup, system policies apply to the user, and any changes to the group policy since the last logon are applied.

When a computer is upgraded from Windows NT to Windows 2000, there might be persistent registry changes from the Windows NT system policy. Therefore, all systems should receive a fresh install of Windows 2000. Also, trusts are not automatically upgraded when domain controllers are upgraded, so all trusts should be broken and reestablished after upgrading a domain controller from Windows NT 4.

CHAPTER SUMMARY

Controlling user environments directly affects the total cost of ownership for networks, and group policy gives administrators the ability to control user environments. Downlevel Windows operating systems support group policies, but they are not secure and their settings often remain in the registry after the policy is removed. Windows 2000 group policies can be applied only to Windows 2000 systems, and they must be applied as a whole. Group policies are applied to sites, domains, and Organizational Units (OUs), in that order. You can exempt security groups from a group policy, however, thereby making them flexible enough for networks of any size.

The Group Policy snap-in for the Microsoft Management Console (MMC) is used to create policy objects. When a policy is created or updated, the effects are automatic without the need to save or commit the policy. Computer policies are applied during startup, and user policies are applied during logon. There is also a refresh mechanism that periodically updates policies. Group policies contain two nodes—Computer Configuration and User Configuration.

14

Both nodes contain Software Settings, Windows Settings, and Administrative Templates folders. However, some of the subfolders within these folders differ between the nodes. The Software Settings folders' subfolders are the same in both nodes. The Windows Settings folder in the Computer Configuration contains subfolders for scripts and security settings. The Windows Settings folder in the User Configuration node contains subfolders for scripts, security, Internet Explorer maintenance, remote installation service, and folder redirection. The Administrative Templates folder in the Computer Configuration node contains the Windows Components, System, Network, and Printers subfolders. The Administrative Templates folder in the User Configuration node contains the Windows Components, Start Menu & Taskbar, Desktop, Control Panel, Network, and System subfolders.

The two types of group policy are local and the non-local. The local policy can't be blocked and is processed before any non-local policies. The non-local policies are stored in the group policy container on the domain controllers. A policy can be stored in a container, but, if it is not linked to the container, it will not affect anything. Policies can be stopped by using the Block Policy Inheritance setting, unless the policy has the No Override switch set. If more than one policy applies to a container, you can prioritize the policies so that the policy with the highest priority takes precedence. Policies can also be selectively applied using discretionary access lists (DACLs). Any security group with Read and Apply Policy DACLs will be affected by a policy, and any security group with Read and Write DACLs will be able to edit a policy. The exceptions to the DACL's rules are the Folder Redirection and Software Installation settings, which can be further tuned within any policy that the affected group has DACLs for.

Network bandwidth is a serious issue with group policies. If a pinging algorithm detects a slow network connection, only the essential policy settings will be applied. Because policies can be edited from any domain controller, steps should be taken to ensure that a policy is not updated with conflicting data by multiple administrators on different domain controllers at the same time. Group policies can be set to use only the operations master domain controller, to use only the domain controller that the snap-ins are associated with, or to use any domain controller. On the client, group policies are implemented using dynamic link libraries, called client *extensions*. When a policy is initiated, it is scanned for required DLLs, and only those required DLLs are installed. Loop back support is useful for applying one policy for a user under normal circumstances and another when the user logs onto certain computers. Loop back's merge mode applies all policies, but applies the computer policies last. In contrast, loop back's replace mode applies only the computer policies.

REVIEW QUESTIONS

1. _____ is a discrete product of the group policy MMC snap-in that contains details of the actual policies implemented.

   a. Group policy object

   b. Local group policy

   c. Non-local group policy

   d. Discretionary access control list

2. What is the name of the object located on every Windows 2000 computer that customizes the operating environment of the computer and every user that logs onto the computer?

   a. Group policy object

   b. Non-local group policy

   c. Discretionary access control list

   d. Local group policy

3. What is the name of the object stored on domain controllers that controls the operating environment of all users and computers in selected sites, domains, or Organizational Units?

   a. Local group policy

   b. Non-local group policy

   c. Group policy object

   d. Discretionary access control list

4. A discretionary access control list is a list of security groups and/or users with the associated permissions to particular objects.

   a. True

   b. False

5. Group policy objects are objects within a Group Policy node that contain settings for a particular section of the operating environment.

   a. True

   b. False

6. What is the name of the object at the root of a group policy that defines an area of effectiveness?

   a. Local group policy

   b. Group Policy node

   c. Group policy object

   d. Discretionary access control list

14

7. What type of applications must be installed on a computer based on a computer or user configuration policy?

   a. Assigned

   b. Published

   c. System

   d. Forced

8. What type of applications are made available for installation based on a computer or user configuration policy?

   a. Assigned

   b. System

   c. Published

   d. Forced

9. What type of policy specifies the scripts that can be run at computer startup or shutdown and user logon or logoff?

   a. Group policies

   b. User policies

   c. Computer policies

   d. Script policies

10. The _____ is a script interpreter that can be used for customizing an environment or automating tasks on Windows computers.

   a. Command Scripting Host

   b. Windows Scripting Host

   c. Prompt Scripting Host

   d. Internet Scripting Host

11. Which of the following extensions are policies that can be set at the domain level to control account lockout, password, and Kerberos policies?

   a. Windows Policies

   b. System Policies

   c. Group Policies

   d. Account Policies

12. Which of the following extensions can be used to control the Audit Policies, User Rights Assignments, and Security Options settings?

    a. Group Policies

    b. Local Policies

    c. System Policies

    d. Account Policies

13. _____ are a set of allowable actions with corresponding security groups and/or users that can commit the actions.

    a. User Rights Assignments

    b. User Permissions

    c. Access Lists

    d. Access Rights

14. Audit Policies dictate the logging of actions taken by a particular security group and/or user.

    a. True

    b. False

15. Public Key Policies dictate the users and/or groups that can recover encrypted files, the list of trusted certificate authorities, and enterprise trust settings for certificate authorities.

    a. True

    b. False

16. Public Key Policies dictate the behavior of computer classes in a secure, non-secure, or mixed security TCP/IP environment.

    a. True

    b. False

14

17. What are the extensible portions of group policies that modify the HKEY_LOCAL_MACHINE or HKEY_CURRENT_USER keys in the registry?

    a. Windows Settings

    b. Security Settings

    c. Administrative Templates

    d. Administrative Settings

18. _____ is the ability to apply a policy based on computer location rather than user or computer.

    a. Loop back

    b. Recurse

    c. Refresh

    d. Reapply

19. Which loop back mode bypasses the user policy and uses only the computer policy?

    a. Replace mode

    b. Merge mode

    c. Refresh mode

    d. Recurse mode

20. Which of the following is not a setting in the Windows Component extension for Computer Configuration?

    a. Task Scheduler

    b. NetMeeting

    c. Windows Installer

    d. Windows File Protection

REAL-WORLD PROJECTS

Consultant Andy Palmer has installed a Windows 2000 network for a client. The client would now like to implement standard desktop environments and software applications while maintaining the ability of departmental administrators to control certain local settings. Andy decides the best way to implement the solution is by using group policies.

Project 14.1
To create a group policy, complete the following steps:

The first thing Andy needs to do is create a group policy for the client's domain.

1. Start the group policy creation process by clicking Start|Run to open the Run dialog box.

2. In the Run dialog box, type "MMC", and then press Enter to access the Microsoft Management Console.

3. On the Console menu, click Add/Remove Snap-In.

4. Display the Stand Alone tab, and click Add.

5. In the Add Snap-In dialog box, select Group Policy, then click Add.

6. As seen in Figure 14.20, in the Select Group Policy Object dialog box, click Browse, and select the domain.

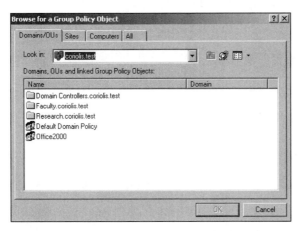

Figure 14.20   Selecting the container for a group policy.

7. To reveal the dialog box shown in Figure 14.21, click Extensions. After doing so, Andy selects the extensions he needs.

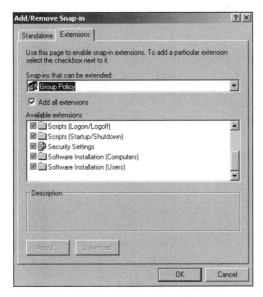

14

Figure 14.21   Adding extensions to the group policy console.

8. Click Finish.

9. Click OK, and the Group Policy snap-in opens with the object selected in focus.

10. After specifying the policies to be implemented, click Save As to save the MSC console file to the desired location.

Project 14.2
To delegate linking control over a group policy, complete the following steps:

After creating a domain policy, Andy needs to delegate group policy linking for an OU to a department administrator.

1. In Active Directory Users and Computers, right-click the OU to be delegated, and click Delegate Control.

2. In the Delegation Of Control Wizard introduction, click Next.

3, When prompted, provide the name of the user (or groups) that will have control, as shown in Figure 14.22.

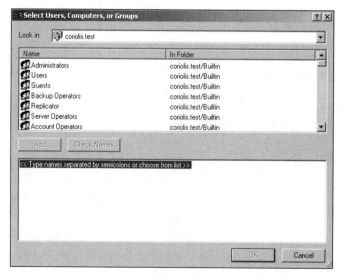

Figure 14.22 Delegating group policy linking for an OU.

4. On the Predefined Tasks list, select Manage Group Policy Links, and click Next.

5. Click Finish.

Project 14.3

To delegate control over group policy creation, complete the following steps:

Once the local administrator had permission to link existing policies to their OUs, a separate administrator needs the ability to create group policies. Andy takes the following actions to delegate this authority.

1. In Active Directory Users and Computers, select the Users container in the root of the domain.

2. Double-click the Group Policy Creator/Owners.

3. On the Properties page, select the Members tab, as shown in Figure 14.23.

4. Click Add, and add the desired users.

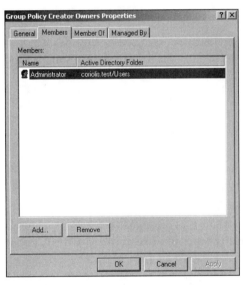

Figure 14.23   Adding members to the Group Policy creator/owner group.

Project 14.4

To delegate control over an existing group policy, complete the following steps:

One of the client's administrators has created a group policy, but he went on vacation before delegating control of the policy to anyone else. Andy takes the following steps to delegate control to a different local administrator.

1. Open the group policy object in the Group Policy snap-in.

2. Right-click the root node, and select Properties.

3. Click Security, then click Add.

4. Select the desired users or groups, then check Full Control.

5. If the policy should also apply to the selected users or groups, ensure that the Apply Group Policy checkbox is selected. Otherwise, deselect the Apply Group Policy checkbox.

6. Click OK to finish.

Project 14.5

To control the domain controller where group policies are processed, complete the following steps:

During the average day, the load on the operations master domain controller appears to be too high. Andy decides that it would be best to change the domain controller that processes group policies to alleviate some of the load. He takes the following steps to do this.

1. Open the Group Policy Editor with the default domain object in focus.

2. On the View menu, click DC Options.

3. To always use the operations master, choose the first selection; to use the domain controller that the snap-in is focused on, choose the second selection; to use any available domain controller, choose the last selection.

Project 14.6

To refresh the group policy from the command prompt, complete the following steps:

Andy has made changes to a policy, but the changes have not taken effect. To refresh the policy on the machine, Andy does the following.

1. Click Start|Run.

2. Type "command", and press Enter.

3. To refresh the Computer Configuration policy, type:

```
secedit /refreshpolicy MACHINE_POLICY [/enforce]
```

4. To refresh the User Configuration policy, at the command prompt type:

```
secedit /refreshpolicy USER_POLICY [/enforce]
```

Note: The /enforce switch refreshes the security and EFS policies, whether there is a change or not. Otherwise, the /enforce switch does nothing.

Project 14.7
To open the local group policy, complete the following steps:

Andy wants to customize the desktop on a standalone computer. To do this, he decides to use the local policy.

1. Click Start | Run.

2. Type "MMC", and press Enter.

3. On the Console menu, click Add/Remove Snap-In.

4. Display the Stand Alone tab, and click Add.

5. In the Add Snap-In dialog box, click Group Policy, and then click Add.

6. In the Select Group Policy dialog box, select the local computer.

7. Click OK.

8. Click Finish. The Group Policy console will be open with the local machine in focus.

14

GETTING A HANDLE ON SOFTWARE DEPLOYMENT

After completing this chapter, you will be able to:

✓ Identify a user's software requirements and create packages to satisfy those requirements

✓ Establish a software distribution point and ensure software is available

✓ Administer software to appropriate users and groups

✓ Install, repair, and update software throughout an organization

✓ Control software distribution with Windows Installer and group policies

✓ Use Terminal Services for software distribution and maintenance

In this chapter we will discuss one of the most costly and most complex aspects of a computer network—software distribution. Since the topic can become quite complicated, we start with a brief introduction to software distribution. We then discuss the software deployment life cycle from beginning to end. Finally, we analyze different ways to distribute software using Windows 2000 technologies such as Windows Installer and other third-party tools.

This chapter covers only the basics of software distribution and remote software installation. Interested readers who want more detailed information are encouraged to consult Microsoft's Web site.

WINDOWS 2000 SOFTWARE DISTRIBUTION

Windows 2000 targets one of the largest areas affecting the total cost of ownership, or total cost for owning a network—software distribution and maintenance. Administrators control software distribution within the organization with the help of various tools and snap-ins. Software distributors use tools like IntelliMirror to customize and control their software. Windows 2000 provides the software installation snap-in for the Microsoft Management Console (MMC) to assign applications forcibly. Windows 2000 can also be used to publish applications so that the Add/Remove Programs applet in Control Panel can be used to install the software based on the needs of the user. On the client side of the software distribution equation, a Windows service called Windows Installer handles the actual installation of the package. All these pieces work together to help control distribution.

Using IntelliMirror to Control Software Distribution

To assist users with software distribution and maintenance, Windows 2000 includes the IntelliMirror utility. IntelliMirror is actually a combination of many technologies that work together to preserve a user's data and environment. Using IntelliMirror, you can manage software from anywhere in an enterprise. You can also control the installation, removal, and maintenance of software, and these responsibilities can be delegated to any administrative level.

Using the Windows 2000 Software Installation Snap-In

In a homogenous Windows 2000 network, the Software Installation snap-in can be used with group policies to administer software. Software can be packaged with a Windows Installer file, which has the .msi extension, and selectively distributed throughout an organization from a single location, called a *distribution point*. Software distribution can be targeted toward users, Organizational Units, or computers. The Software Installation snap-in can be used for the deployment of horizontal market applications (which can be used by any industry), such as Microsoft Office 2000, which will usually have a package file distributed with it. It can also be used to install vertical market applications (which are designed to be used by a specific industry) and locally developed applications by creating package files for the application. The snap-in can also be used for software maintenance tasks, such as upgrades and patches. Finally, software can be removed using the software installation snap-in and criteria such as .msi files and Windows Installer files, as mentioned earlier.

Assigned Software versus Published Software

Two types of software distribution are available—assigned and published. Software installation can be forced by assigning it, or software can be made available by publishing it. The differences between assigned and published software can be summarized as follows:

➤ *Assigned software*—If software is assigned to a computer, the software automatically advertises itself with a shortcut on the Start menu and installs itself when the computer starts. If a package is assigned to a user, the software advertises itself on the desktop when the user logs in. User-assigned software doesn't actually install until a user starts the application by selecting the application's shortcut or opening a document that is registered to use the application.

➤ *Published software*—If software is published, it is not advertised in the Start menu or on the desktop and no documents are registered to use the application. The application is made available to the user through the Add/Remove Programs applet in Control Panel. After it is installed, it is not merely advertised, it is actually installed on the machine.

Basically, if software is published for a user or computer, it is not actually installed, and no evidence of the software's availability appears on the desktop or the Start menu. When the user starts the Add/Remove Programs applet from the Control Panel, however, published software is available in the Add New Programs dialog. This dialog simplifies the user experience, because users do not need to know the network path to the software or have the actual media for software installation. This also simplifies the administrator experience, because administrators do not need to track the permissions on multiple shares for multiple applications. Only the software published for a user or computer appears in the list of available applications.

In contrast, assigning applications does not actually install the application, but it does advertise the application on the desktop or Start menu and registers the application's association with certain file types. If the application is assigned to a user, it is advertised when the user logs onto a computer. If the application is assigned to a computer, it is advertised when the computer starts.

15

The Windows Installer Service

At the heart of software management is the Windows Installer. The Windows Installer service is present on all Windows 2000, NT 4, and 9x systems. The Windows Installer uses *package files*, which have the .msi extension, to control the way software is installed, upgraded, and removed. The Windows Installer service also has an application programming interface (API) so that custom programs can be developed to use the service. The installer keeps track of applications' states so that interrupted installations can be continued or rolled back as necessary. Additionally, because the service knows the state of all applications, it can upgrade, repair, and patch applications as needed.

The Add/Remove Programs Applet in Control Panel

Similar to earlier versions of Windows operating systems, the Add/Remove Programs applet in Control Panel is the main location for most application installation and removal tasks. However, a few new features have been added to the applet in Windows 2000 to assist administrators in software deployment. For example, in Windows 2000, applications can be published to a distribution point in the Active Directory. This means that users do not have to map drives or remember where applications are stored. By pointing users to the Active Directory for applications, the use of CD-ROM drives and floppy drives for software installation can be disabled. This feature helps administrators keep rogue applications from being installed and limits an organization's exposure to offensive code such as viruses, worms, and so forth. Finally, as mentioned earlier, the Add/Remove Programs applet is the tool used to install any published applications.

Software distributed within an organization has a definite life cycle. Windows 2000 recognizes this lifecycle and provides tools to assist the administrator—from distribution, through maintenance, to the eventual removal of the software.

THE SOFTWARE MANAGEMENT LIFE CYCLE

Like any other engineering project, software management should follow a defined set of phases to ensure that software is rolled out in an organized manner with few, if any, surprises. The first phase is, as always, the preparation and planning stage. This is followed by the distribution phase, the targeting phase, and the testing phase. Finally, the installation and maintenance phases complete the cycle.

Preparing for Software Distribution

A thorough preparation stage is necessary for a smooth software rollout. The first task is to identify the software needs of your organization and to formulate your software distribution structure. Ideally, software distribution was a consideration of the Active Directory architect, and the organization's software needs closely relate to the directory structure.

In a well-designed Active Directory, domains provide a number of functions that can be used for software distribution. As discussed elsewhere in this book, a domain is a security boundary as well as a unit of replication. Furthermore, domains are group policy containers. Therefore, domains can be used to dictate the software policies for fairly large groups of users and computers. Organizational Units (OUs) can be used to fine-tune software distribution so that specific containers within a domain can receive additional applications based on their needs. Finally, software policies can be blocked at the OU level if domain-level needs are not appropriate for a specific OU.

After the structure for software distribution is identified, the next task is to collect and license the appropriate software. Distributing applications with these tools can be facilitated in many ways. The software vendor may provide packages, or the application may indicate that it can be made into a package. If all else fails, there is also a method to package noncompatible applications with text files that are created by the administrator.

Native Windows Installer packages are the most reliable and most flexible solutions for software distribution. Many applications have native Windows Installer packages, identified with the .msi extension. (Windows Installer packages are discussed in more detail later in this chapter.) These native packages meet all the specifications set forth by the Windows Installer. In most cases, software distributed with Windows Installer packages can be customized to meet individual needs. The applications are also self-repairing, so any corrupted or outdated files are automatically replaced. Furthermore, Windows Installer packages can be modified using transform and patch files:

➤ *Transform files*—Have the .mst extension and can be used to customize applications' optional components.

➤ *Patch files*—Have the .msp extension and can apply patches and hot fixes to applications that have been installed using the Windows Installer. A patch or hot fix is one or more files applied to an application to fix a particular, immediate shortcoming of the software.

Applications that do not have native Windows Installer packages can be repackaged into MSI packages using Windows Installer utilities. These packages are the next-best solution for software distribution. The biggest drawback is that the repackaged application is installed as a whole. Therefore, no customization can be executed during the installation of a repackaged Windows Installer package.

15

Applications that cannot use the Windows Installer format can also be packaged for distribution. The setup or installation programs for these applications can be defined in plain text files with the .zap extension. Applications distributed via ZAP files cannot use any of the Windows Installer features. They cannot be customized during the installation, and they are not self-repairing after installation. Packages that use ZAP files can be published, but they cannot be assigned. Finally, ZAP applications usually require the user to have local administrative privileges to install the application at all. Applications that do not support Windows Installer can be automatically distributed, but this format has many drawbacks. Listing 15.1 shows a sample ZAP file.

Listing 15.1   A sample ZAP file.

```
; ZAP file for Microsoft Excel 97
[Application]
FriendlyName = "Microsoft Excel 97"
SetupCommand = setup.exe
DisplayVersion = 8.0
Publisher = Microsoft
URL = http://www.microsoft.com/office
; Language for the application
LCID = 1033
Architecture = intel
[ext]
XLS=
XLA=
XLB=
XLC=
XLM=
XLV=
XLW=
```

Most of the code in this file listing is intuitive, but let's take a look at a few lines. "FriendlyName" is the name of the application used in the menus and component associations. "SetupCommand" is the command that is issued to begin setting the application up, though it may call upon other applications to assist with the setup. "DisplayVersion" is the numeric version of the software, which can be used in conjunction with the FriendlyName to identify the application. "Publisher" is the publisher of the software, and "URL" is the universal resource locator used to locate the publisher's Internet site. "LCID" is the language code for this version of the application, and "Architecture" is the type of machine on which it is meant to run. Finally, the last seven lines are simply the file extensions that are associated with this application.

Distributing Software in the Organization

After formulating a thorough plan for software deployment, the distribution phase begins. Software should be stored on designated servers called distribution points. Distribution points can be standard network shares or Dfs shares. Windows Installer packages perform the same tasks from network shares as they do from local media. Therefore, CD-ROMs can be created with the software package and an Autorun.inf file that starts the installation package. The Autorun.inf file is automatically run when the CD-ROM is inserted into the CD player, if the user has the autorun feature enabled on the system.

Two basic models for software installation are available—the pull model and the push model. In addition, you can opt to use Remote Installation Services, which will install both the operating system and the applications in a single step.

Pull Model Distribution

In a pull model distribution setup, Windows Installer distributes software as needed. In other words, software is pulled from distribution points when users actually use the application.

The pull model has some drawbacks. Namely, it affords administrators little control over software distribution, because users choose when to pull the software. Furthermore, the pull model setup could cause unwanted network congestion and might prove impossible for larger applications.

Windows 2000 software distribution features are based on group policies. This means that only Windows 2000 clients can take full advantage of these distribution features. The client-configuration tracking capabilities of Windows 2000 are limited, so the system cannot identify clients that have sufficient client resources for a particular application. Furthermore, Windows 2000 does not have a mechanism to track the number of users that have a particular application, which means that administrators have to maintain license compliance. Finally, software installation features are automatically disabled when a slow link is detected.

Push Model Distribution

Microsoft's System Management Services (SMS) uses a push model for software distribution. In the push model, entire packages are deployed to users and workstations based on an administrator's specifications. Using this model provides a number of benefits, including:

➤ Packages can be rolled out during off-peak hours.

➤ Large applications can be broken down into a number of smaller packages, with the actual installation occurring after all packages are installed. (Due to

15

the level of control that SMS offers, it should be the method of choice for large organizations with numerous large applications to deploy.)

➤ SMS supports Window 9x, Windows NT 4, and Windows 2000 clients, making it the method of choice for systems with downlevel clients.

➤ SMS has built-in client configuration and inventory capabilities, so queries can be written to identify clients that do not meet requirements for a particular application.

➤ SMS has built-in software metering, which automates licensing compliance.

➤ SMS can roll out software over slow links.

The main benefit of the push model is that the installation can be more fully controlled by the administrator rather than pulled by the user without administrative control. The drawbacks of the push model is the lack of user input on the software distribution, and the added cost of the tools necessary to push software.

Remote Installations Services

A third option available to administrators for software distribution is Windows 2000 Remote Installation Services (RIS). RIS is used to install Windows 2000 Professional on PXE-compliant computers. A PXE-compliant workstation is capable of supporting a Pre-boot Execution Environment, which means it can boot to the network without an operating system. When used in conjunction with Riprep and IntelliMirror technology, however, RIS can also be used to install applications. Basically, to use RIS, you must configure a computer with the desired operating system and applications. Then, use Riprep to remove all machine-specific registry entries, and copy an image of the completely configured computer to the RIS server. After the image is on the server, RIS can be used to roll out both the operating system and the configured applications to one or more clients.

Targeting Software to Appropriate Users and Groups

Targeting software involves getting the appropriate software to the appropriate users and ensuring that users don't have access to unauthorized software. This can be accomplished manually by assigning the permissions to shares, but the group policy Software Installation snap-in makes the process easier and more robust. The group policy snap-in for software distribution allows software to be assigned or published to users or computers based on site, domain, or OU membership.

When distributing software, common user scenarios can be implemented to better accommodate organizational needs while keeping the total cost of ownership to a minimum. For example, the average task-based employee uses a specific set of applications to perform required duties. With proper group policies and software installation guidelines, the computing environment for a task-based user has only the menu options necessary to fulfill the job requirements. For this type of user, using the application assignment mode is the best method for software distribution. During the package setup, the least amount of user interaction should be chosen, and the application components should be limited to the set that the task-based user needs. By limiting the complexity of the computing environment, task-based users can have a limited set of computer skills and still be able to perform their duties.

The actual group policy software settings contain many customizations to assist administrators in software distribution. The properties of the Software Installation node, shown in Figure 15.1, affect all packages in this scope (remember that the scope is the area of Active Directory that a policy affects). The main settings you can configure in the Software Installation Properties dialog box, which can be found by right-clicking the Software Installation node, are as follows:

➤ *General tab*—Enables you to configure the default location for packages. Also, the options for new packages can be set to assign or publish automatically, or to display an option box prompting for a choice. User interface options for all packages on the General tab can be set to basic or maximum. Finally, applications can be automatically uninstalled when they fall out of the scope of the group policy.

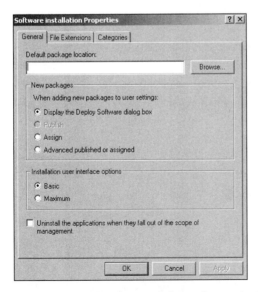

15

Figure 15.1   Properties of the Software Installation node.

➤ *File Extensions tab*—Enables you to customize how applications behave on client computers. File extensions can be associated with particular packages. If more than one package is associated with an extension, the packages can be prioritized to determine which package will be used first when a document with the associated extension is opened.

➤ *Categories tab*—Enables you to customize how applications behave on client computers. The Categories tab allows different categories to be added for software packages. When users open the Add/Remove Programs applet from Control Panel, they must select Add New Programs to display the list of available packages. After the Add New Programs dialog box opens, a drop-down list box, which lists the available categories for packages that are applied to the user or computer, is displayed.

The Microsoft Office properties dialog box, which can be obtained by right-clicking Microsoft Office, contains six basic tabs for customization, as shown in Figure 15.2.

Note: The Upgrades, Categories, Modifications, and Security tabs might not be populated if the installation is the first package being installed.

➤ *General tab*—Provides information like FriendlyName and Version, and includes a text box for the name of the package.

➤ *Deployment tab*—Provides functions based on whether the package is assigned or published. The option to auto-install on file extension activation

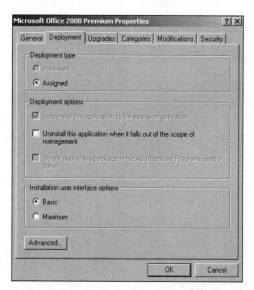

Figure 15.2   Microsoft Office 2000 Properties dialog box.

determines whether the application installs when an associated file is opened. Furthermore, a checkbox is provided that you can use to toggle when an application should be uninstalled if the application falls out of the scope of management. If an application is being published, it can be hidden from the Add/Remove Programs applet. The user interface for the installation can be set to basic or maximum, depending on the user environment. The advanced deployment options can be set to ignore the language of the package when installing as well as to remove previous installations of the product before installing the package.

➤ *Upgrades tab*—Provides options when you are upgrading applications that are already installed. The top text box allows you to add applications that are being upgraded, whether they are objects in the group policy or outside the scope of the group policy.

➤ *Categories tab*—Presents two columns: One column is populated with all the software categories from the properties of the software installation node in group policies, and the other column displays the categories that have been selected for the software package.

➤ *Modifications tab*—Allows you to configure MST files, which contain modifications for existing applications like patches and upgrades.

➤ *Security tab*—Reveals the discretionary access control lists (DACLs) that specific users and groups hold for the package. In order to install the package, the user must be a member of a group with Read permissions to the package. To administer the package, Full Control must be assigned to the user or group.

Multilingual users and software packages require certain special considerations. Previous versions of Windows had a different version for each language, which made compatibility a serious concern. Windows 2000 multilingual support is one version for all languages, which means that operating system compatibility is less of a concern. The setting that affects software installation is the system locale, which determines the code page installed for the operating system. If the Ignore Language checkbox in the Advanced Deployment Options dialog box is checked, the software will be installed whether the language matches the operating system locale or not. If the checkbox is not checked, and the language and locale match, the package is installed without incident. If the checkbox is not checked, and the language is either neutral or English, the package is installed without incident. In any other circumstances, the package might cause errors.

15

Testing the Software Distribution

To ensure that a software distribution will work effectively, a representative sample of the user population should be tested. Testing can take place in a controlled environment, such as a testing lab, a testing OU within the production environment, or with specific groups or users in production containers in the production environment. Unfortunately, it is not possible to define all the steps necessary for testing because they will be different for every application. However, there are some general rules to follow when testing any application.

Though it might not be readily evident, many classes of users have special needs. Mobile users, users who move between different computers, and shared computers can all present challenges to software distribution. For example, when users move from one computer to another, a decision must be made whether to assign the application to the users or to the computers. If all the users use a specified set of computers, assigning the application to the computer is probably the best choice. This means that the application is advertised as soon as the computer starts, and all the users see the advertised applications. If the users move to more than just a limited set of computers, however, assigning applications to the user might be a better choice. Then, no matter which computer a user accesses, the user sees the advertisement of the application. When the user logs off, if the next user is not assigned the same application, the application is not advertised to the new user. Mobile users also present challenges because their computers are not always connected to the network, and, when they are connected, they might be using a slow link. Usually, you should publish applications for mobile users, so they can fully install an application when they are connected with a high-speed link. Remember, software policies will not apply themselves over a slow link, so the group policy settings for slow link speeds might need to be adjusted. If the software being deployed affects any of these types of users, they should have representation in the testing phase of deployment.

Rolling Out the Tested Packages

The actual rollout of packages might involve the installation of new software, upgrading existing software, or patching software. During computer startup, any packages that are assigned to a computer with group policies will be installed. During the user logon process, any packages assigned to users with group policies will be installed. The Windows Installer service continues to monitor the group policies and executes appropriate packages if necessary. With all these processes used for rolling out new packages, the installation phase of deployment can be very complex. Different considerations exist for different rollouts. For instance, if an entire office suite is being assigned to a computer, a significant delay could occur during startup because the icons and associations have to be completed. Some software patches can be quite extensive, so users should be informed of the possible delay during the installation of a patch or upgrade. If the software has been assigned, make sure the user understands that the installation of the package will not begin until the user logs in. Keep in mind that every software rollout will have its own set of requirements and anomalies, and make sure that sufficient planning has been done to avoid any possible surprises.

Maintaining Distributed Software

Simply installing software is just the beginning of the software deployment life cycle. Periodically, some applications might need small fixes, commonly called *hot fixes* or *patches*. Also, applications frequently undergo upgrades that add new functionality to the application. Finally, if a software application is no longer needed in the organization, it will have to be removed from the system. All these maintenance tasks can be accomplished with Windows 2000 software deployment tools.

Patching and Hot Fixing Applications

Patching and hot fixing software can be accomplished with the group policy Software Installation node, although you should keep a few considerations in mind. Software patches and hot fixes usually address a particular software issue. A patch usually requires closing the application and sometimes restarting the machine, whereas a hot fix normally can be applied without disturbing the functionality of the application or system. A software service pack usually contains many patches and hot fixes that are all combined into one package. Sometimes, a service pack contains new features for an application, but, technically speaking, this would be an upgrade and not a service pack.

When patching an application, be sure to test the patch before deploying it. If the manufacturer provided an MSI file for package deployment and the product code for the patch is the same as the product code for the application, simply replace the original MSI with the new one. If the manufacturer provided an MSP file or if the product code on the patch is not the same as the product code for the application, however, the patch will have to be advertised separately from the original package and assigned to all the users that were assigned the original application.

Upgrading Applications

The Windows Installer can also be used to upgrade applications from one version to another, or to perform a competitive upgrade from one company's software to another. For most upgrade situations, a declared upgrade relationship must be established between the applications. In most instances, the

15

manufacturer supplies a new Windows Installer package file that contains the details about the upgrade, including the packages and versions that can be upgraded with the package. If the package is replacing a competitor's software, however, there probably is no upgrade relationship. In this instance, the original package should be removed and the new package installed. If the original application or the upgrade is a repackaged application, you might be able to manually create an upgrade relationship between the packages using the group policy Software Installation snap-in. Upgrades can be specified as optional or required in the group policy. Unless there is a serious security or performance issue, making the upgrade optional is usually best, because it allows the users to choose when to upgrade the application.

Removing Applications

The last operation involving the software deployment life cycle is removing applications. When setting up a new package, you can configure a setting in the Deployment Options to remove a software package automatically when it is no longer in the scope of the policies management. This is a useful setting, but it might be a nuisance if the software is common to many group policy containers. In addition, you can access settings in the properties of a package for software removal. Removal can be forced or optional, and care should be taken when choosing between the two options. If the software should not be used again—for security, licensing, or other critical reasons—then forcing the removal is the best choice. If the software can continue to be used but should not be forced on users, however, optional removal is the best choice. Optional removal not only allows users to keep the software indefinitely, but it also allows users to remove the application at a time and place that is most convenient for them. Although performing a forced removal might always seem the appropriate choice, forced removals should not be taken lightly.

PACKAGING APPLICATIONS WITH WINDOWS INSTALLER AND OTHER TECHNOLOGIES

Packages are created and distributed in several different ways. The Windows Installer is a system service that is built into Windows 2000 to facilitate software installation. For some applications, hosting them on a terminal server to which users connect is the best option. WinInstall can also be used to install applications on Windows-based computers; as a last resort, a ZAP file can be manually created to automate the installation of unsupported applications.

Windows Installer

The Windows Installer service is provided with the Windows operating system, and provides a reliable method for software distribution, maintenance, and removal. By using group policies, Windows Installer can be heavily customized or disabled altogether. Some of the customization settings available are as follows:

➤ Privileges for the service can be elevated for applications that require administrative access to a workstation.

➤ The search order for installation files can be customized.

➤ Start menu shortcuts can be dimmed for applications that have been assigned but are not completely installed.

➤ Windows Installer logging and application patching can be disabled within the scope of a particular policy.

The Windows Installer package, identified by the .msi extension, supplies the necessary details for application installation. The package is actually a relational database that is usually supplied by a software manufacturer, but it can be modified to meet specific needs. The basic information about an application and its manufacturer is contained in the file as well as pointers to the application source files and path to the destination on the client computers. The service itself uses transaction processing, so a failed installation can be resumed or rolled back entirely, thus returning all the files and settings to their previous values.

Windows Installer packages can be created for locally developed applications to facilitate distribution. The in-house application programmers are provided with an interface for creating packages and adding functionality. They can add features such as software maintenance that will periodically check the state of individual program files and replace any that do not meet the verification parameters specified. Packages can also be used for just-in-time component installation so that an application's advanced features are not installed until a user needs them. Packages can be partitioned into a number of compressed CAB files so that the package can be distributed over the Internet or on floppy disks. Because the source code, registry entries, and other information (such as path and shortcuts) are readily available to application developers, package development should be fairly easy. A package should be developed at the same time as the application, however, so that no details are missed.

15

Terminal Services

Windows 2000 Terminal Services can be used for software distribution. Under one model—the thin client—the applications actually execute on the terminal server. In this way, the software is available for use throughout the enterprise, but it is not actually distributed to client computers. Additionally, the terminal server can install the software on the client machines.

In Remote Administration mode, the terminal server installs software on the client just as Windows Installer normally would. In terminal server Application Server mode, however, only administrators can use the terminal server to install software on the client machine. Because user profiles are copied to the terminal server when it is running in Application Server mode, the application might appear as if it is installed. If the user moves to a computer without the application, however, then the shortcuts to a local path will not function properly. Windows 2000 Terminal Services adds flexibility to the software distribution task by allowing applications to execute on the server or, in some cases, actually installing the application on the client machine.

WinInstall

A few software installation programs, made by companies other than Microsoft, are explicitly designed for installing applications on Microsoft Windows operating systems. WinInstall is a product made by Veritas software that is bundled with the Windows 2000 Server CD. This product can be used to create, view, and edit existing package files. WinInstall can also be used for change analysis by capturing critical settings before application installation and then again after software installation. This information can then be used to apply the changes to any machines that will receive the new software.

ZAP Files

One last method of installing applications involves using ZAP files. (One other program, not being discussed in detail in this book, is WISE, an installation program that allows you to package installation similar to WinInstall but is more user friendly.) ZAP files use the existing installation or setup files that come with an application. The ZAP file is created with a text editor (as shown earlier in this chapter in Listing 15.1), and it contains the information necessary to install an application without user intervention. Software can be deployed using third-party tools or simple scripts to automate legacy installation programs. Windows Installer packages are always the safest method for software distribution, however.

CHAPTER SUMMARY

The software distribution features of Windows 2000 assist administrators with keeping the total cost of ownership low for networks. The Windows Installer and group policies combine to perform all functions necessary to install, maintain, and remove software on Windows clients. Software can be forcibly assigned to users or published to the Add/Remove Programs applet for users to install at will.

The software life cycle involves certain discrete phases. In the preparation and planning phase, software packages are collected and licensed, and users' needs are identified. During the distribution phase, the distribution points for the software are strategically placed and prepared. The targeting phase involves defining the users and groups that will need specific packages and evaluating the client machines that they use. The testing phase should involve a representative group of the targeted user community to include any special needs users. Finally, the software packages are rolled out using Windows Installer, group policies, and possibly additional tools, such as Microsoft Systems Management Server or Veritas's WinInstall.

REVIEW QUESTIONS

1. The expenses, including all variables, of owning information systems is the
   _____.

   a. Windows Transform package

   b. Total cost of ownership

   c. Windows Installer package

   d. Vertical market application

2. What is the name of an operating system service that installs, maintains, and removes software from clients?

   a. Windows Installer

   b. Software assignment

   c. Software publishing

   d. Application advertisement

3. A Windows Installer Package is a discrete unit of software distribution used by the Windows Installer service.

   a. True

   b. False

15

4. Which of the following is a utility that assists with the installation and maintenance of software and operating systems?

   a. IntelliMirror

   b. WinInstall

   c. WISE

   d. Add/Remove Programs

5. A _____ is a special unit of software distribution used by Windows Installer to update software packages.

   a. Windows Installer package

   b. Horizontal market application

   c. Windows Transform file

   d. Vertical market application

6. An application used for a specific purpose by a specific industry is known as which of the following?

   a. Horizontal market application

   b. Vertical market application

   c. Windows Installer package

   d. Windows Transform package

7. What is the name of an application that is used for purposes common to many industries?

   a. Horizontal market application

   b. Vertical market application

   c. Windows Installer package

   d. Windows Transform package

8. _____ is a method of distributing software that automatically advertises and registers software.

   a. Software assignment

   b. Software publishing

   c. Application advertisement

   d. Windows Installer

9. Software advertisement is a method of software distribution that makes software available through the Add/Remove Programs applet, but does not advertise or register the software.

   a. True

   b. False

10. _____ is the process of making software available on the Start menu or desktop and registering software without actually installing it.

    a. Software publishing

    b. Application advertisement

    c. Software assignment

    d. Windows Installer

11. What is the name of an update to software that fixes a particular shortcoming?

    a. Software assignment

    b. Service pack

    c. Software patch

    d. Software upgrade

12. A _____ is an update to software that can be applied on the fly to fix a particular shortcoming.

    a. Hot fix

    b. Service pack

    c. Software upgrade

    d. Software assignment

13. A service pack is a collection of patches and hot fixes that fix more than one shortcoming to a product bundled together.

    a. True

    b. False

14. A(n) _____ is a destructive software code spread and activated when its carrier executable files are run.

    a. Autorun.inf

    b. Patch

    c. Macro

    d. Virus

15

15. A _____ is the act of distributing software en masse.

    a. Software push

    b. Software pull

    c. Software assignment

    d. Rollout

16. The _____ is a file placed at the root of a CD that automatically executes a specified application.

    a. Macro

    b. Autorun.inf

    c. Virus

    d. Patch

17. Which of the following is a software distribution method initiated at the distribution point and terminated at the target client?

    a. Software assignment

    b. Rollout

    c. Software pull

    d. Software push

18. _____ is a software distribution method initiated at the client and terminated with the client.

    a. Software pull

    b. Software push

    c. Rollout

    d. Software assignment

19. Systems Management Server is an application used for software distribution and management in large enterprise systems.

    a. True

    b. False

20. _____ is an application created by Veritas software and used for software distribution.

    a. Autorun.inf

    b. Softpatch

    c. Pilot

    d. WinInstall

REAL-WORLD PROJECTS

Andy Palmer has just been contacted by one of his premier clients, the Coriolis company. This time, Andy is asked to distribute Microsoft Office 2000 throughout the organization, while keeping the users' needs and total cost of ownership in mind.

The first step Andy takes is to make the software installation files available on the network. To do this, he uses the Windows Distributed file system (Dfs) to create a software distribution point.

Project 15.1

To create a software distribution point, complete the following steps:

1. Log on to the system and select Distributed File System on the Administrative Tools menu.

2. In the Dfs console, on the Action menu, select New DFS Root.

3. In the first screen of the wizard, click Next.

4. Select Create A Domain DFS Root at the next screen, then click Next.

5. Type coriolis.test or select the domain from the list, then click Next.

6. Enter the name of the server to host the DFS root, or click Browse to find it. Then, click Next.

7. If there is a share on the server to use, select it from the domain drop-down list. If not, select Create A New Share, and type in "DfsRoot." Then, click Next.

8. Enter "DfsRoot" for the name and a comment for the Dfs root, then click Next.

9. Verify the information on the last screen, then click Finish.

10. Select the new Dfs root in the left pane of the Dfs console.

11. On the Action menu, select New Dfs Link.

12. In the wizard, provide the name of the link, path to the share, comment for the link, and a cache timeout for the link. Then, click OK. The new console is shown in Figure 15.3.

15

Figure 15.3 The Dfs console with the new Dfs root and one Dfs link.

13. In the new console, right-click the new Dfs link, and select Open.

14. Place the CD containing the application in the CD-ROM drive, and close any autorun programs that might start.

15. From the root of the CD, press Ctl+A to select all the files and folders, then press Ctl+C to copy the files and folders.

16. Switch to the window with the open Dfs link, then press Ctl+V to paste all the copied files and folders into the new Dfs share.

Project 15.2
To create application categories, complete the following steps:

While implementing the Office suite, Andy realizes that the Office programs are probably the first in a long line of applications that will be implemented for Coriolis. Therefore, to make the system scalable, he decides to categorize applications so that the users can sort the applications by category to more easily find a desired application.

1. First, select Active Directory Users And Computers on the Administrative Tools menu.

2. Open the properties for the Software Installation node.

3. In the Software Installation Properties dialog box, select the Categories tab.

4. Click Add to reveal the Enter New Category dialog box shown in Figure 15.4, and provide a name for the category.

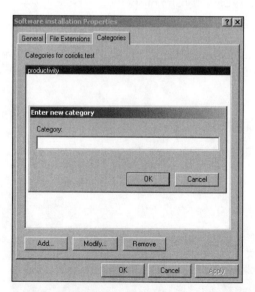

Figure 15.4   Adding a category to the Software Installation node.

Project 15.3
To use WinInstall LE for editing Windows Installer packages, complete the following steps:

When Andy opens the default Windows Installer package for Office 2000, he notices that some of the options need to be modified in order to meet his customer's needs. After researching the topic, he decides to use WinInstall LE, a product developed by a company named Veritas and distributed on the Windows 2000 Server compact disk.

1. Place the Windows 2000 Server compact disk in the machine.

2. Open My Computer, right-click the CD drive, and select Explore.

3. Go to the \ValueAdd\MGMT\WinstLE directory.

4. Right-click SWIADMLE.MSI, and select Install.

5. Open the Veritas Software Console from the Programs/Veritas Software menu.

6. Select Windows Installer Package Editor, and select File | Open.

7. Browse to the desired package file and double-click it.

8. As shown in Figure 15.5, expand the Package in the upper-left pane to select the desired component.

9. In the lower-left pane, labeled *Title*, select General.

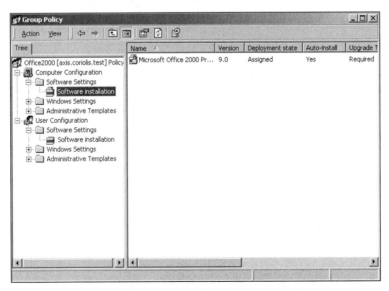

Figure 15.5 Opening a package in WinInstall LE.

10. In the right pane, there are a number of configurable settings that Andy needs to consider, including:

   ➤ *Name of the Application*—Names the application. Andy uses Office 2000.

   ➤ *Favor Advertising*—Allows advertising if advertising is part of the implementation policy. Andy selects this option.

   ➤ *Favor Source*—Keeps the files for unused features at the distribution point until used. Andy also selects this option.

   ➤ *Favor Parent*—Enables attribute inheritance from the parent object in a package. Andy chooses this option.

   ➤ *Do Not Allow Advertising*—Disables advertising, even if specified in the implementation policy. Andy does not select this option.

   ➤ *Do Not Display Option To Be Absent*—Forces the user to install the option. Andy uses this option.

   ➤ *Description*—Allows administrators to add a description of the option. Andy does not use the description.

11. In the lower-left pane, select files. Files can be added or deleted from the distribution if necessary.

12. Use the Shortcuts option in the lower-left pane to customize the shortcuts to be installed.

13. Use the registry section to customize the registry keys for the option.

14. Add any necessary services to the Services selection in the lower-left pane.

15. Finish editing the INI files in the INI Edits selection.

16. Finally, use the Advertising section to customize the way in which the option will be advertised.

Project 15.4

To set up a Windows Installer package in group policies, complete the following steps:

After modifying the package, Andy deploys it. Because the Active Directory is already implemented, he decides to use group policies for this task.

1. Select Active Directory Users And Computers on the Administrative Tools menu.

2. Open the properties for the container for the software package (domain or OU).

3. On the Group Policy tab, click New, and name the new policy appropriately.

4. Edit the new policy, and right-click Software Installation on the Software Settings folder under the appropriate node (user config or computer config).

5. Select New | Package. In the resulting dialog box, browse to the distribution point, and select the appropriate MSI file.

6. Depending on the necessary deployment method, select Assigned or Advanced Published in the packages dialog box (Andy selects Advanced Published), and click OK.

7. On the General tab, name the package (Andy names it Office 2000).

8. Using the Deployment tab, choose to configure an assigned deployment type.

9. Under Deployment options, select Uninstall This Application When It Falls Out Of The Scope Of Management option. Then, select Basic for the installation user interface.

10. Since this is not an upgrade, skip the Upgrades tab.

11. On the Categories tab, select the category (Andy chooses Productivity), and click Select.

12. There will be no modifications (transforms) for the package yet, so skip the Modifications tab.

13. On the Security tab, ensure that the target users have at least Read permissions and the administrator for the policy has Read and Write.

14. Click OK to finish setting up the package. The console should appear similar to the console shown in Figure 15.6.

15

Project 15.5
To install a published application with the Add/Remove Programs applet, complete the following steps:

While the majority of the users have been assigned Office 2000, a limited set of users need to have the option of installing it; therefore, it is published only for them. For these users, Andy installs the software using the Add/Remove Programs applet.

1. Start the Add/Remove Programs applet from the Control Panel.

2. In the Add/Remove Programs applet displayed in Figure 15.7, click Add New Programs.

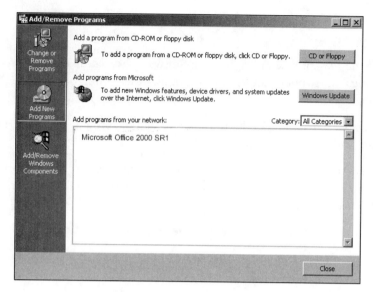

Figure 15.6   Group policy console with a software package installed.

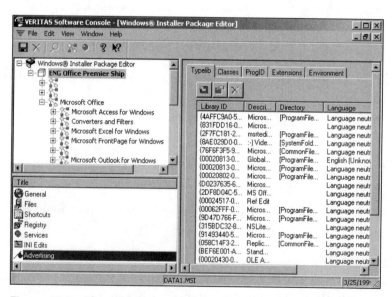

Figure 15.7   The Add/Remove Programs applet showing published applications.

3. Next, select the category for the application using the Category drop-down list (Andy selects Productivity).

4. Finally, double-click the Office 2000 application, and follow the installation wizard.

Project 15.6
To use Riprep to install the operating system and applications, complete the following steps:

As time goes by, Andy sees that new computers with identical hardware and BIOS are arriving without any operating system or applications. To expedite the process of software distribution, he determines that the Remote Installation Services can be used to install the operating system and applications before the computer ever gets delivered to the target user.

1. Install Windows 2000 Professional in one partition on the source computer.

2. Configure and customize the source computer while logged on as the local administrator.

3. Install Office 2000 on the source computer while logged on as the local administrator.

4. Click Start | Run, type "Regedit", and press Enter.

5. Browse through the registry hive to the following key:

```
Hkey_Local_Machine\System\CurrentControlSet\FileSystem\
NtfsDisable8dot3NameCreation
```

6. Change the value from 0 to 1.

7. Save the registry changes, and close Regedit.

8. Right-click My Computer, and select Properties.

9. On the System Properties page, on the User Profiles tab, select the local administrators profile.

10. Click Copy To, enter the path to the All Users profile, then click Change.

11. In the User Or Groups dialog box, grant the Everyone group permission to the profile.

12. Click OK, and then click OK again to close the System Properties dialog box.

13. Click Start | Run, type "\\<RISServerName>\Reminst\Admin\i386\ RIPrep.exe", and press Enter.

14. Provide the name of the RIS server to store the image of the completely configured source computer.

15

15. Provide the subdirectory for the new image. It will automatically be placed under the \\<RISServer>\RemoteInstall\Setup\OS\English\Images folder.

16. Provide the description and help text when prompted.

17. Stop the services on the client machine when prompted to do so.

18. Apply the image to new compatible PXE-compliant systems using the normal RIS installation method.

Project 15.7

To install and use the Windows 2000 Terminal Services Client, complete the following steps:

Andy identifies a few applications that, due to their limited use, can be installed and run by multiple users on a terminal server. Therefore, he decides to install and configure the Windows 2000 Terminal Services Client.

1. On the target server, open Control Panel, and start the Add/Remove Programs applet.

2. Click the Add/Remove Windows Components button, and click the Components button in the resulting windows.

3. Scroll down to Terminal Services, and select the checkbox.

4. Click Next, select Application Server Mode when prompted, and finish the installation wizard. Reboot the machine if necessary.

5. With the terminal server installed, click Terminal Services Configuration on the Administrative Tools menu.

6. Select the Server Settings folder in the left pane. Ensure the settings in the right pane are configured for Terminal Server Mode Application Server, Delete Temporary Folders On Exit is set to Yes, and Use Temporary Folder Per Session is set to Yes. Close the Terminal Services Configuration console.

7. Open Terminal Services Client Creator. Select the appropriate client and disk drive, as shown in Figure 15.8, provide the floppy disks when prompted, and finish creating the client disks.

8. On the client machine, place client diskette number one in the disk drive, open My Computer, double-click the appropriate drive, and run Setup.exe.

9. Provide the name and organization when prompted, accept the license agreement when prompted, accept the default installation path or provide a new one when prompted, select Yes to make the client available to all users of the machine, and finish the Terminal Services Client installation wizard.

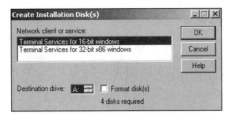

Figure 15.8   Creating the Terminal Services Client Installation disks.

10. On the terminal server, install the desired applications using the Add/
    Remove Programs applet in Control Panel.

11. On the client computer, open the Terminal Services Client application
    from the Terminal Service Client menu in the Programs menu.

12. Select the appropriate server from the Server Connection dialog box. As
    shown in Figure 15.9, enable data compression to reduce network
    congestion and cache bitmaps to improve client performance.

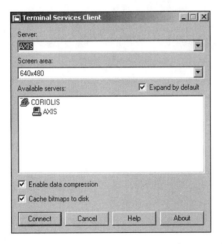

Figure 15.9   Connecting to the terminal server with a Terminal Services Client.

13. When the Terminal Services Client connects, log onto the terminal server,
    and run the desired applications normally. The session behaves as if the user
    is sitting at the terminal server running the applications.

Now that Coriolis has their necessary applications, Andy is ready to tackle his
next client's challenges.

15

CHAPTER SIXTEEN

CONFIGURING REMOTE ACCESS IN WINDOWS 2000

After completing this chapter, you will be able to:

✓ Configure the Routing and Remote Access utility

✓ Use new protocols to secure remote access connections

✓ Configure bandwidth allocation

✓ Create and administer dial-up connections

✓ Create and administer direct cable connections

✓ Create and administer VPN connections

✓ Use policies and profiles to control remote access

One of the greatest challenges facing systems engineers today is the need to secure remote connections for corporate workers. Fortunately, Windows 2000 includes several new features for configuring and administering remote access.

You're likely to find several questions targeting the installation, configuration, and administration of remote access issues on the accelerated exam. Therefore, you should familiarize yourself with the new network and connection wizards, the new protocols, the enhanced management interfaces, and the use of policies and profiles to control network access.

The best place to start involves taking a look at enhancements to the Routing and Remote Access utility and the new protocols that strengthen remote access. Several new protocols are introduced, and each plays a significant role in proper remote access administration.

WINDOWS 2000 ENHANCES ROUTING AND REMOTE ACCESS

The Routing and Remote Access application is a member of the Administration Tools set in Windows 2000. Most Administration Tools are installed with Windows 2000 Server or Windows 2000 Advanced Server.

Administration Tools can be installed or uninstalled using the Adminpak.msi, which is located in the /i386 directory of the Windows 2000 Server and Windows 2000 Advanced Server CD-ROMs. Installing the Administration Tools is a simple process:

1. Double-click the Adminpak.msi file to trigger the Administration Tools Setup Wizard, as shown in Figure 16.1.

2. Click Next to continue the setup, as shown in Figure 16.2. When setup completes, the Administration Tools Setup Wizard confirms the successful installation, as shown in Figure 16.3.

After you install the Administration Tools, you are ready to enable the Routing and Remote Access utility.

Enabling Routing and Remote Access

The Routing and Remote Access utility is enabled using the following steps:

1. Select Start | Programs | Administration Tools | Routing And Remote Access. The Routing and Remote Access interface appears, as shown in Figure 16.4. The local computer is shown, by default. You must click Routing and Remote Access if you want to administer another server.

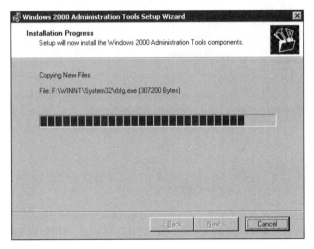

Figure 16.1   The Administration Tools Setup Wizard is used to install or remove Windows 2000's Administration Tools.

Figure 16.2   The Administration Tools Setup Wizard monitors the installation progress.

16

2. Select the server you want to configure in the left panel, or console tree, and right-click it.

3. Select Configure And Enable Routing And Remote Access.

4. The Routing And Remote Access Wizard appears.

5. Answer the wizard's prompts, and the setup completes.

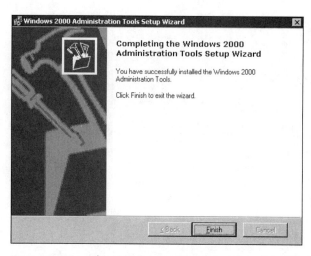

Figure 16.3 The Windows 2000 Administration Tools Setup Wizard confirms that the installation is complete.

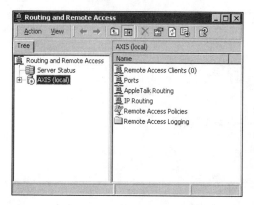

Figure 16.4 The Routing and Remote Access interface is used to configure dial up, virtual private networks, and internetwork connections.

The Windows 2000 Routing and Remote Access Administration Tool supports several types of connections. Routing and Remote Access can be configured for the following:

➤ Dial-up connections

➤ Virtual private networks

➤ Direct cable connections

Both inbound and outbound connections can be set. Before you jump ahead and begin configuring the Windows 2000 Routing and Remote Access settings, however, you should become familiar with new supported protocols.

WINDOWS 2000 INTRODUCES NEW SECURITY PROTOCOLS

Authentication is one of the most important steps in permitting remote access to your network. As the guardian of an organization's data, your responsibility is to ensure that only authorized users access data with the appropriate permissions. Opening a network to remote connectivity, of course, creates the potential for unauthorized access. However, authentication protocols can be implemented to help ensure that the users meant to access data are, indeed, the individuals given permission to do so.

Authentication protocols are used to help protect a network's integrity. The use of authentication protocols shouldn't be new to you. Your previous experience with the Windows NT 4 Server platform undoubtedly acquainted you with the following authentication and connection protocols:

➤ Challenge Handshake Authentication Protocol (CHAP)

➤ Compressed Serial Line Internet Protocol (CSLIP)

➤ Microsoft Challenge Handshake Authentication Protocol (MS-CHAP)

➤ Password Authentication Protocol (PAP)

➤ Point-To-Point Protocol (PPP)

➤ Point-To-Point Tunneling Protocol (PPTP)

➤ Serial Line Internet Protocol (SLIP)

Windows 2000 adds several new authentication and connectivity protocols to help strengthen the defense employed in the battle to protect remote access connectivity and ensure that remote connections are managed properly. They are:

➤ Bandwidth Allocation Protocol (BAP)

➤ Extensible Authentication Protocol (EAP)

➤ Internet Protocol Security (IPSec)

➤ Layer 2 Tunneling Protocol (L2TP)

➤ Remote Authentication Dial-In User Service (RADIUS)

Expertise must be developed with all the new protocols if the full features and benefits of Windows 2000 remote connections are to be realized. Together, the preceding protocols work to manage remote connections properly while also authenticating users connecting to your network and securing the data communicated between your servers and remote users' computers.

16

Bandwidth Allocation Protocol

Windows 2000's Bandwidth Allocation Protocol (BAP) works with the Bandwidth Allocation Control Protocol (BACP) to provide bandwidth as needed. The benefit of dynamic connection management is simple—organizations that use telecommunications carriers that charge the organization based on the organization's use of bandwidth can better control costs by limiting traffic or keeping data transfer rates within specified threshold limits.

BAP and BACP are Point-To-Point Protocol (PPP) controls. Both can maximize an organization's subscribed bandwidth. Both also support multilink functionality.

BAP is enabled on the PPP tab in the Properties dialog box of each server running the Remote Access Service, as shown in Figure 16.5. BAP can also be configured using Remote Access Policies.

Tip: Using Remote Access Policies, an administrator can set an extra circuit to be dropped if the utilization of a link falls below 75 percent for one group and 25 percent for another.

Extensible Authentication Protocol

The Extensible Authentication Protocol (EAP) plays a critical role in remote access authentication in Windows 2000. EAP lets a dial-in client and server negotiate the actual authentication method they will use.

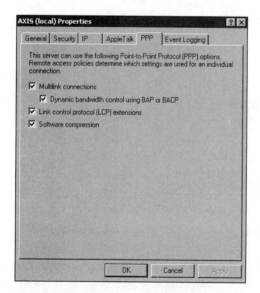

Figure 16.5 BAP is enabled by modifying a server's properties within Routing and Remote Access.

EAP extends the authentication methods used with PPP. New authentication methods can be utilized by third-party software developers as a result of EAP APIs. Thus, EAP can support the use of such security devices as the following:

➤ Biometric security devices, such as retinal scanners

➤ Token cards, which can contain constantly updated codes

➤ Smart cards

EAP also supports these authentication technologies:

➤ MD5-CHAP

➤ Transport Layer Security

MD5-CHAP encrypts usernames and passwords using the MD5 algorithm. Transport Layer Security (TLS) is used by smart card and other security devices.

EAP is enabled by selecting Authentication Methods on the Security tab of the Properties dialog box of each server running the Remote Access Service (RAS), as shown in Figure 16.6.

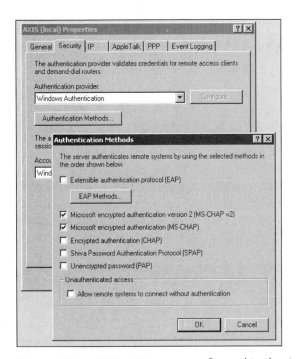

16

Figure 16.6 EAP settings are configured in the Authentication Methods dialog box.

Internet Protocol Security

Communication over IP networks is strengthened in Windows 2000, thanks to the use of Internet Protocol Security (IPSec). IPSec, which is an open standards–based protocol, uses encryption, digital signature, and sophisticated algorithm technologies to secure IP communications from creation to delivery.

IPSec includes a special driver that resides at the IP Transport layer. As a result, security-conscious applications do not need to be used. The IPSec driver assumes the responsibility of decoding the protective security information contained in the encrypted IP data packets. It also authenticates the identities of the sender and the recipient.

In addition to securing IP communications, IPSec provides a powerful defense against network attacks. It is also highly configurable and can be customized to provide varying levels of protection for different types of traffic.

Windows 2000 dedicates a Microsoft Management Console (MMC) snap-in for the exclusive role of administering IPSec policies. Such policies can be configured at user, group, application, domain, site, or enterprise levels.

You install the IPSec MMC snap-in by following these steps:

1. Select Start | Run, type MMC, then select OK.

2. Select Console | Add/Remove Snap-in, and click Add.

3. Highlight IP Security Policy Management, and click Add.

4. Specify the computer the snap-in will manage.

5. Complete the setup by clicking Finish.

6. Click Close, then select OK.

After you've completed the installation, you'll see the IPSec Policy Management tool, as shown in Figure 16.7.

You can access an IPSec switch in the Network And Dial-up Connections dialog box.

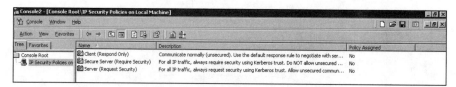

Figure 16.7   The IP Security Policy Management console is used to administer IPSec policy settings.

Accessing the IPSec Switch

To access the IPSec switch, use the following steps:

1. Click Start | Network And Dial-up Connections.

2. In the Network And Dial-up Connections dialog box, double-click the appropriate connection, and select Properties.

3. Scroll down in the Components Checked Are Used By This Connection dialog box until you find Internet Protocol (TCP/IP), and highlight it.

4. Select Properties to open the Internet Protocol (TCP/IP) Properties, and click Advanced. The Advanced TCP/IP Settings dialog box appears.

5. Select Options, highlight IP Security, and click Properties. The IP Security dialog box displays, as shown in Figure 16.8.

Several IPSec policy settings exist:

➤ *Client (Respond Only)*—This setting is for normal unsecured communication. This is the default response. When using this setting, only the requested protocol and port traffic are secured with the server.

➤ *Secure Server (Require Security)*—This setting is for all IP traffic that is required to possess security using Kerberos trust. Unsecured communication is not permitted with clients who are not trusted.

➤ *Server (Request Security)*—This setting is for all IP traffic that is required to possess security using Kerberos trust. Unsecured communication with clients that do not respond to the security request is permitted.

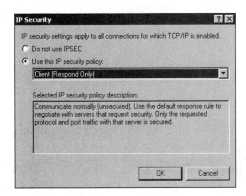

Figure 16.8   The IP Security dialog box permits the option of not using IPSec or selecting an IPSec policy.

16

Layer 2 Tunneling Protocol

The Layer 2 Tunneling Protocol (L2TP) most resembles PPTP from the Windows NT 4 platform. L2TP's purpose is to form an encrypted path over a public network. Like PPTP, L2TP provides *tunneling*, or the creation of a second path within a connection. However, unlike PPTP, L2TP does not encrypt the contents of data packets. Instead, L2TP works with IPSec and other technologies to provide security encryption features. Combining the features of L2TP and IPSec creates a powerfully secure VPN connection.

L2TP works by using PPP to form a data container. It then applies additional headers to the data packet that are responsible for routing the packet. L2TP is installed with the Routing and Remote Access Administration Tool, as is PPTP. As such, these two protocols are one of the three important components required for a VPN connection. All IT professionals should be familiar with the differences between L2TP and PPTP, as described in Table 16.1.

Remote Authentication Dial-in User Service

Remote Authentication Dial-in User Servie (RADIUS) support is introduced for the first time into a Windows platform in Windows 2000. Long a staple requirement for Internet Service Providers (ISPs), RADIUS extends the ability to validate and log the amount of time a user spends on a dial-up network.

RADIUS's authentication and accounting of dial-up networks work by sending user account data to a RADIUS server, where it is verified against a database. Windows 2000 systems can be configured to serve as RADIUS clients, RADIUS servers, or both.

In Windows 2000, a RADIUS client is a server running the remote access service that receives RADIUS authentication requests and forwards the information to a RADIUS server. The Internet Authentication Service (IAS) fulfills the RADIUS authentication role and serves as the RADIUS server on a Windows 2000 network. IAS maintains information about RADIUS accounts in log files.

Table 16.1   Although PPTP and L2TP are similar in that they both form IP tunnels, many significant differences exist.

Function	PPTP	L2TP
Required circuit	IP-based internetwork	Any packet-oriented point-to-point connection, such as permanent virtual circuits (PVC), an X.25 VC, or an ATM VC
Header compression support	No	Yes
Tunnel authentication support	No	Yes
Encryption method	PPP	IPSec

RADIUS clients are configured using the Securities tab on the Properties dialog box of servers running Remote Access Service, as shown in Figure 16.9.

In the Properties dialog box, click Configure, and you'll be prompted to select a server to edit or remove. If no RADIUS server is specified, you can add one, as shown in Figure 16.10.

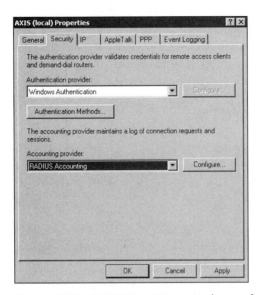

Figure 16.9   RADIUS settings can be configured by selecting RADIUS Accounting in the Accounting Provider drop-down box.

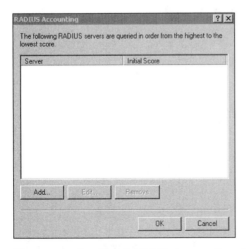

Figure 16.10   The RADIUS Accounting dialog box displays RADIUS servers in the order they are queried.

16

Clicking Add in the RADIUS Accounting dialog box displays the settings box shown in Figure 16.11. The settings that you can configure here include a time-out value and a port. Port 1813 is the default.

IAS, meanwhile, is an optional component installed by selecting Add/Remove Programs in the Control Panel. If IAS isn't included at the time the server is installed, you can install it by double-clicking Networking Services and ensuring Internet Authentication Service is selected, as shown in Figure 16.12.

After you've installed IAS, you can access it by selecting Start | Programs | Administration Tools. Selecting Internet Authentication Service opens the MMC snap-in shown in Figure 16.13.

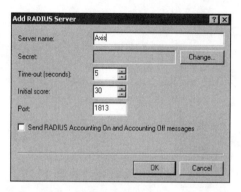

Figure 16.11   RADIUS settings must be configured when adding a RADIUS server.

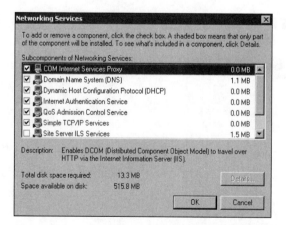

Figure 16.12   Internet Authentication Service is installed by selecting it within Networking Services in the Add/Remove Programs Applet in the Control Panel.

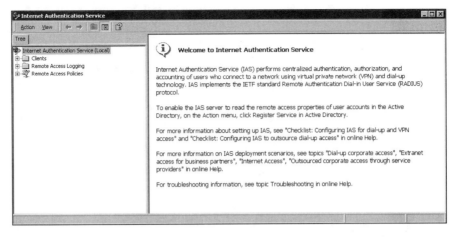

Figure 16.13   Internet Authentication Service is used to perform centralized authentication, authorization, and accounting of users that connect to networks using a VPN or dial-up connection.

CONFIGURING REMOTE ACCESS DIAL-UP CONNECTIONS

Before configuring connections in Windows 2000, you should review the new Network Connection Wizard, as shown in Figure 16.14. The wizard can be used to configure the following connections:

➤ Dial-up connections to a private network

➤ Dial-up connections to the Internet

➤ VPN tunneled connections to the Internet

➤ Incoming connections coming from a telephone line, the Internet, or a direct cable

➤ A direct connection to another computer using a serial, parallel, or infrared port

Connecting to networks often involves the installation and configuration of modems; therefore, you should ensure that you're comfortable with the process of adding and configuring modems in Windows 2000.

Configuring Modems

Windows 2000 automatically detects any modems a system has installed. Windows 2000 dedicates a modem port for each modem it finds.

16

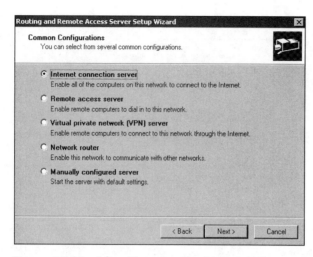

Figure 16.14   After triggering the Network Connection Wizard, you must select the type of connection you want to create.

Modem ports can also be configured manually. To create a modem port, open Routing and Remote Access from the Start | Programs | Administration Tools menu. Then, follow these steps:

1. Right-click Ports, and select Properties.

2. Select a device, and select Configure.

3. Check the Remote Access (Inbound) box to enable inbound connections.

4. Enter a phone number.

5. Finish by clicking OK.

Configuring Inbound Dial-up Connections

The Windows 2000 Network Connection Wizard is used to create an inbound connection for systems that are not members of a domain. Systems that are domain controllers or domain members must use the Routing and Remote Access console.

To complete inbound dial-up connections for a domain member or domain controller, follow these steps:

1. Install the Routing and Remote Access Server.

2. Select Start | Programs | Administration Tools | Routing And Remote Access.

3. Right-click the server you want to enable, and select Configure And Enable Routing And Remote Access. This triggers the Routing And Remote Access Server Setup Wizard. Click Next.

4. Select Remote Access Server, which permits remote computers to dial-in to the network.

5. Next, ensure that the protocols the dial-in connection should use are configured. You have the option of adding protocols, as shown in Figure 16.15.

6. Select whether you want to allow unauthenticated access for remote clients. This is necessary if you want to permit Macintosh Guest Authentication, as shown in Figure 16.16.

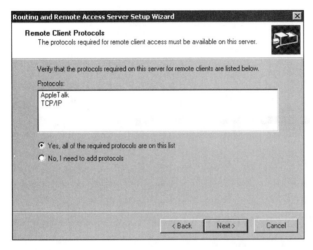

Figure 16.15   Protocols required for communication with dial-in clients must be installed on the server.

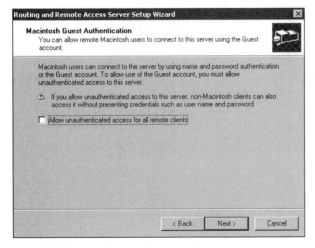

Figure 16.16   Macintosh users connect using name and password authentication or the Guest account. Unauthenticated access must be permitted if the Guest account is to be used.

16

7. Select the network connection you want for the remote clients to access, as shown in Figure 16.17.

8. Select whether IP addresses are to be assigned automatically by a DHCP server or whether IP addresses should be assigned from a specified range (see Figure 16.18).

9. Specify whether the server should use RADIUS, as shown in Figure 16.19.

10. Click Finish to complete the wizard.

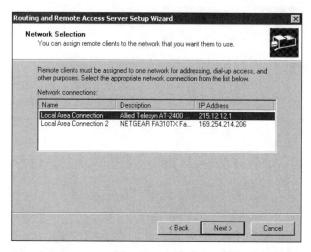

Figure 16.17   Remote clients must be assigned to the network they should use.

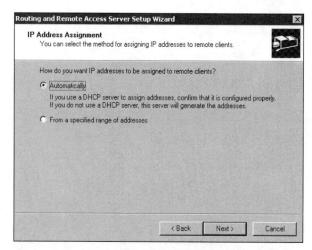

Figure 16.18   The method of assigning IP addresses to remote clients must be specified.

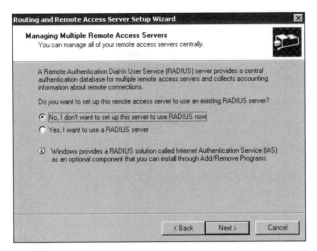

Figure 16.19   The Routing And Remote Access Server Setup Wizard asks whether a RADIUS server should be used to collect accounting information for the remote connection.

Note: Typically, multiple simultaneous dial-up connections are supported using a modem bank or modem pooling hardware. In most cases, a Windows 2000 Server requires a modem bank adapter to be installed to support the use of multiple modems.

Configuring Outbound Dial-up Connections

Outbound dial-up connections are configured using the Network Connection Wizard. Dial-up connections can be configured for dialing up a system whether the system is a standalone unit in a corporate enterprise, in someone's residence, or at an ISP. You can choose to connect either to a private network or a server.

Creating a Connection to a Private Network

To create a connection to a private network, follow these steps:

1. Open the Network Connection Wizard by clicking Start | Settings | Network And Dial-up Connections | Make New Connection.

2. Click Next, and select the Dial-up To Private Network radio button. Click Next.

3. Provide the telephone number the connection should dial (see Figure 16.20).

4. Specify whether the connection is to be used by all users or only by yourself.

5. Check whether Internet Connection Sharing should be enabled for the connection, and whether on-demand dialing should be used, as shown in Figure 16.21.

16

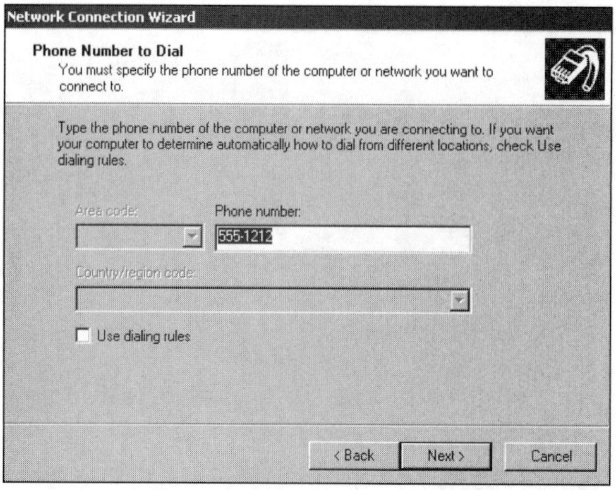

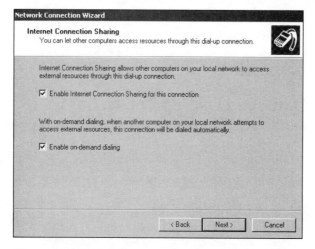

Figure 16.20 The Network Connection Wizard prompts you to supply the telephone number of the connection to be called.

Figure 16.21 Other computers can use the connection if you set Internet Connection Sharing.

6. Click Next, and a dialog box appears explaining which IP address will be used. The dialog box, as shown in Figure 16.22, warns that connections with other computers could be lost and asks if you're sure you want to enable Internet Connection Sharing.

7. Click Yes, and you'll be prompted to select the local network that will access resources through the connection. You can make your selection from the drop-down menu, as shown in Figure 16.23.

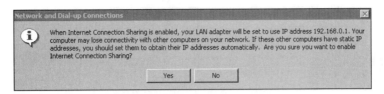

Figure 16.22 A dialog box warns that connections could be lost with other computers and asks whether you're certain you'd like to install Internet Connection Sharing.

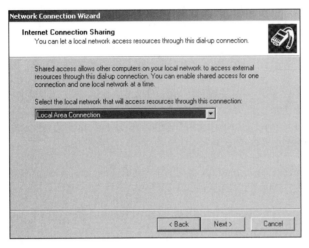

Figure 16.23 You must select the local network that will access resources through the connection being created.

8. Provide a descriptive name for the dial-up connection, select whether you want to add a shortcut to the desktop, and select Finish to complete the creation of the connection.

After you create a dial-up connection, you are ready to configure an Internet connection.

Creating a Connection to a Server

To create a connection to an Internet server, follow these steps:

1. Open the Network Connection Wizard by clicking Start | Settings | Network And Dial-up Connections | Make New Connection.

2. Click Next, and select the Dial-up To The Internet radio button. Click Next.

3. The Internet Connection Wizard appears. You can select whether to sign up for a new Internet account, transfer an existing Internet account, set up

16

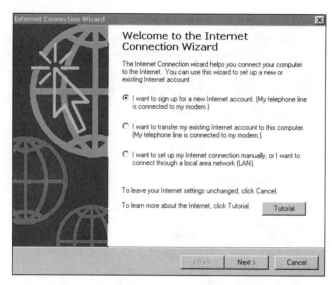

Figure 16.24   The Internet Connection Wizard prompts you to select the type of Internet connection you want to configure.

an Internet connection manually, or connect through a local area network, as shown in Figure 16.24.

4. Select the configuration you want to create, click Next, and follow the wizard's prompts to complete the installation.

CONFIGURING DIRECT CABLE CONNECTIONS

As in Windows NT, direct cable connections can be configured between two systems. Routing and Remote Access automatically creates ports for the parallel and serial cable connections that it finds. Ports for direct cable connections are configured just like modems in Routing and Remote Access.

The Network Connection Wizard is used to configure direct cable connections in Windows 2000. To create a direct cable connection to another computer, follow these steps:

1. Open the Network Connection Wizard by clicking Start | Settings | Network And Dial-up Connections | Make New Connection.

2. Click Next to continue with the wizard. To configure a system as a Host, select Accept Incoming Connections. The Routing and Remote Access console must be used to accept incoming connections if a system is a domain controller or domain member. To configure a domain controller or domain member to connect directly to another system, select Connect Directly To Another Computer, as shown in Figure 16.25.

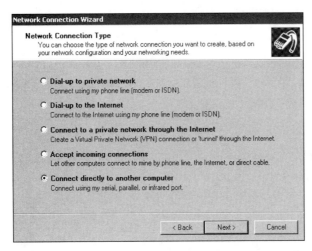

Figure 16.25 Select the Connect Directly To Another Computer option if you want to use a direct cable connection to connect to another system from a domain controller or domain member.

3. Click Next, and then specify whether you want the computer to be a Host or Guest.

Note: *If the system you're configuring is a domain controller or domain member, you must use the Routing and Remote Access console to configure the system as a Host.*

4. Select Guest to permit the computer to access data from a Host, as shown in Figure 16.26.

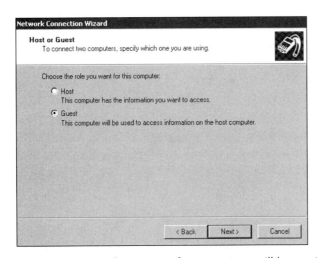

Figure 16.26 Select Guest if your system will be contacting another system.

5. Click Next, and select the device from the Select A Device drop-down menu that should be used to make the connection.

6. Specify whether the connection is to be used by all users or just yourself.

7. Provide a descriptive name for the connection, and click Finish to complete the connection's creation.

CONFIGURING VIRTUAL PRIVATE NETWORKS

As with modems and serial and parallel cable connections, Virtual Private Network (VPN) ports are configured using the Routing and Remote Access console, and you use the Network Connection Wizard to configure a system to connect to a VPN. Windows 2000's Routing and Remote Access Service automatically creates five PPTP and five L2TP ports.

Configuring VPN Ports

To configure VPN ports, follow these steps:

1. Click Start | Administration Tools | Routing And Remote Access, or select Start | Settings | Control Panel | Administration Tools | Routing And Remote Access.

2. Right-click Ports, and select Properties.

3. Select either WAN Miniport (PPTP) or WAN Miniport (L2TP).

4. Click Configure.

5. Select Remote Access (Inbound) to enable inbound VPN connections.

6. Select OK in the Configure Ports dialog box and Ports Properties box to complete the configuration.

Connecting a System to a VPN

The Network Connection Wizard is used to connect to a VPN. VPNs, of course, permit tunneled traffic over a public network to increase security. PPTP and L2TP are used to help strengthen the security by creating the tunneled connection.

To connect a system to a VPN, follow these steps:

1. Open the Network Connection Wizard by clicking Start | Settings | Network And Dial-up Connections | Make New Connection. When the wizard appears, click Next.

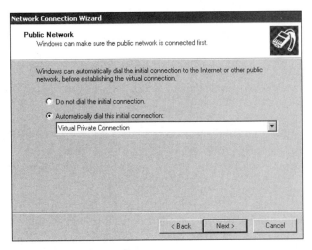

Figure 16.27 When creating a VPN connection, you must specify whether the initial connection should be dialed automatically.

2. Select Connect To A Private Network Through The Internet, and click Next.

3. Specify whether the initial connection should be automatically dialed, as shown in Figure 16.27. Then, click Next.

4. Provide the host name or IP address of the computer or network to which you want to connect.

5. Specify whether the connection is to be used by others or just yourself.

6. Specify whether Internet Connection Sharing is to be used, then click Next.

7. Provide a descriptive name for the connection, specify whether a shortcut should be added to the desktop, and click Finish.

CONFIGURING ROUTING FUNCTIONS IN WINDOWS 2000

Like Windows NT, Windows 2000 provides routing functionality. The Windows 2000 Routing and Remote Access Service provides enhanced routing functionality. Enhanced routing capacities include the following:

➤ Support for routing protocols

➤ IP multicasting, such as might be used for videoconferencing

➤ Network Address Translation (NAT)

➤ Enhanced VPN capabilities, including router-to-router VPN connections

IP routing is configured by clicking the Properties tab of a server in the Routing and Remote Access console. Select the IP tab, as shown in Figure 16.28, to enable IP routing.

Successfully passing the Windows 2000 Accelerated exam will also require an understanding of other routing protocols. You should be familiar at least with the roles that routing protocols ARP, RARP, and Proxy ARP play in Windows 2000.

Support for Routing Protocols

Several routing protocols are supported by Windows 2000. They include:

➤ *Address Resolution Protocol (ARP)*—ARP is used to map IP addresses to media access control (MAC) addresses of hardware devices.

➤ *Reverse Address Resolution Protocol (RARP)*—RARP maps MAC addresses of hardware devices to IP addresses.

➤ *Proxy ARP*—Proxy ARP enables subnetting on networks using older versions of TCP/IP that don't support subnetting.

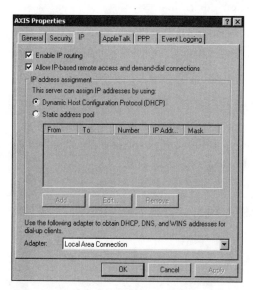

Figure 16.28 IP routing is enabled on the IP tab of a server's Properties within the Routing and Remote Access console.

Network Address Translation

In Windows 2000, you can configure a system's settings so that a system set to provide translation services hides the IP address from machines beyond the system conducting the translation. Network Address Translation (NAT) is used for this purpose.

Proxy Server provides one method of performing NAT. Windows 2000 also performs NAT. Although Windows 2000 provides basic NAT functionality, Proxy Server extends such capabilities further. All you need to know for the Windows 2000 Accelerated exam is that basic NAT functionality is configured from network connections under IP Routing in Routing and Remote Access.

You can specify private versus public NAT interfaces for Local Area Connections. You do so by following these steps:

1. Double-click IP Routing, and then double-click Network Address Translation (NAT) on the console tree.

2. Select the Local Area Connection you want to set, and right-click it.

3. Select Properties, and click the General tab (see Figure 16.29).

Actual NAT settings can be configured by right-clicking Network Address Translation (NAT) in the console tree. Select Properties, and the following four tabs appear:

➤ *General*—Event logging options are provided. They include Log Errors Only, Log Errors And Warnings, Log The Maximum Amount Of Information, and Disable Event Logging.

➤ *Translation*—Settings are presented for removing TCP and UDP mappings, in minutes. The default period for TCP mappings is 1,440 minutes, and the default for UDP mapping is 1 minute. You can also reset defaults and make applications on the public network available to private network clients.

➤ *Address Assignment*—You can configure automatically assigned IP addresses on a private network using DHCP. You can also exclude an IP address range from this tab, as shown in Figure 16.30.

➤ *Name Resolution*—You can specify whether IP addresses should be resolved for clients using DNS and whether NAT should connect to the public network when a name needs resolving. A demand-dial interface is also supplied on this tab.

16

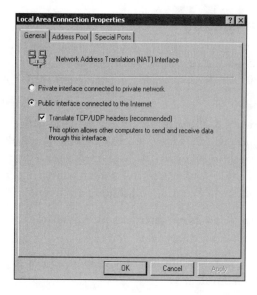

Figure 16.29 The General tab in the Local Area Connection Properties dialog box provides settings for NAT interfaces as well as an option to specify whether TCP/UDP headers should be translated.

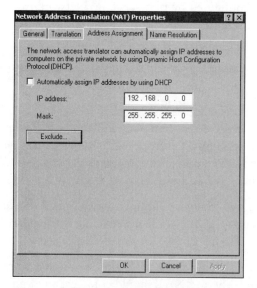

Figure 16.30 You can automatically assign IP addresses using DHCP by using the network address translator, and you can exclude an IP address range, as well.

REMOTE ACCESS POLICY USAGE

Just as user behavior can be controlled using group policies, so too can remote access. Windows 2000 provides default policies to help secure Remote Access Service (RAS) and Internet Authentication Service (IAS). These policies are necessary for the acceptance of user remote access connection requests.

Unlike other policies, Remote Access Policies are not kept in the Active Directory database. Instead, Remote Access Policies are stored on the server running the Remote Access Service.

Remote Access Policies include conditions, permissions, and profiles. These three components work with the Active Directory Service to secure and authenticate remote access server access.

Remote Access Policy Conditions

A Remote Access Policy's conditions are lists of attributes. The remote access server seeks a match for the attributes on the client that is attempting to connect to it. Examples of these attributes include IP addresses, service type, Windows groups, the time, and user groups. You should remember that the first policy possessing an attribute match is processed to see whether its access permissions and configuration information also matches.

Remote Access Policy Permissions

Although the NT platform in the past granted access to remote clients based on settings in User Manager or Remote Access Administration, the user account's dial-in user settings and Remote Access Policies are utilized in Windows 2000. A Remote Access Policy's permission settings combine with the user's Active Directory dial-in permissions to dictate connection requirements.

Confused? Don't be. Learning about Remote Access Policy permissions is easier than learning the hierarchy of user permissions on the NT platform.

For illustrative purposes, let's say you're a member of the Accounting group, and the Accounting group has remote access privileges after normal business hours (from 5:00 P.M. to 8:00 A.M.). And, let's say Mike is also a member of the Accounting group, but he's an employee on probation so his Active Directory user account denies him remote access privileges. Mike's boss, also a member of Accounting, will be able to access the server remotely after dinner, but Mike won't, even though Mike is a member of the Accounting group.

Or, you could have Jan in Accounting who's given permission to access the server remotely during the day, because she's the only employee in a branch office 250 miles away. She could access the server remotely during the day, if she's extended the permission in a Remote Access Policy.

16

Remote Access Policy Profiles

Remote Access Policies include profile settings for such values as authentication and encryption protocols. If a connection setting doesn't match the user's dial-in profile or dial-in configuration, access is denied.

The following values can be provided for a Remote Access Policy Profile:

➤ *Dial-in Constraints*—Used to specify idle disconnect parameters, maximum session lengths, restricted access times, restricted dial-in access numbers, and restricted dial-in media (such as ADSL or Ethernet).

➤ *IP Address Assignment Policy*—Used to define the IP address assignment policy and to indicate whether a server supplies an IP address, the client requests the IP address, or the server's settings define policy. This tab also contains IP Packet Filters.

➤ *Multilink Settings*—Used to enable multilink settings and configure Bandwidth Allocation Protocol settings.

➤ *Authentication Settings*—Used to specify whether the Extensible Authentication Protocol is permitted for the connection and which encrypted authentication protocols are used.

➤ *Encryption Settings*—Used to specify the level of encryption (No Encryption, Basic, or Strong).

➤ *Advanced*—Used to set advanced attributes, such as filter ID, framed compression, service type, and many more.

Remote Access Policy Authentication

Windows 2000 processes a remote connection request by examining policy conditions, user and remote access permissions, and profile settings. If all conditions are met, Active Directory then checks the user's dial-in permission, which overrides the policy's permission setting, unless the dial-in permission for a user account is set to Control Access Through Remote Access Policy In Active Directory. In such cases, the Remote Access Policy's permission dictates whether the user is granted access.

If the connection request matches both the settings provided in the user account in Active Directory and the Remote Access Policy profile, authentication continues. If the request does not match the settings in the user account or profile, access is denied.

Routing and Remote Access creates a default Remote Access Policy named Allow Access If Dial-in Permission Is Enabled. The user's dial-in permission, set in Active Directory, controls access when using the default policy. Conditions for the default Remote Access Policy are any day and time, the Permissions value is set to Deny Access, and no profile is set. The default Remote Access Policy has different implications depending on whether it's being used in a native mode or mixed mode environment.

Remote Access Policies in a Native Mode Environment

If you're working in a native mode environment and you set the dial-in permission on a user account to Control Access Through Remote Access Policy In Active Directory, and the default Remote Access Policy isn't changed, then the user's connection attempts will be denied.

Why is the connection denied? Because the default Remote Access Policy's Permissions setting is set to Deny Access. In order to provide the user with remote access in a native environment, you'd have to edit the dial-in permission in Active Directory to Allow Access or change the default policy permission to Grant Remote Access permission.

If a Windows NT 4 Server running Remote Access Service accesses a native mode server for the dial-in settings of a user account, the Control Access Through Remote Access Policy is seen as Deny Access. Callback settings will work properly.

Remote Access Policies in a Mixed Mode Environment

The default Remote Access Policy is overridden in a mixed mode environment. This is a result of the Control Access Through Remote Access Policy option not being available on all the domain controllers, because non–Windows 2000 servers don't possess the option.

In mixed domain modes, only the Allow Access and Deny Access options are available under Remote Access Permission And Callback Options settings.

Remote Access Policies are applied to users in a mixed mode environment. Should you set a user's dial-in permission to Allow Access, the user won't be granted access unless the user meets the necessary conditions of the Remote Access Policy that's in force.

Note: Permissions for all users with the dial-in setting of Deny receive a setting of Control Access Through Remote Access Policy when converting from a mixed mode domain to a native mode environment. User permissions set to Allow Access, meanwhile, remain unchanged.

16

When connection requests don't match with a Remote Access Policy, access is denied, even if a user possesses a dial-in permission that's set to Allow Access. Thus, you should create and implement Remote Access Policies carefully. Furthermore, you should have a Remote Access Policy in place. If no policy is implemented, no access will be granted by the remote access server.

CREATING AND ADMINISTERING REMOTE ACCESS POLICIES

Remote Access Policies are created using Active Directory and the Routing and Remote Access console. Three steps are involved, which can be completed in any order. They are:

➤ Configure dial-in settings

➤ Create a Remote Access Policy

➤ Edit a Remote Access Policy Profile

Configuring Dial-in Settings

User dial-in settings are configured from within the Active Directory Users and Computers console on an Active Directory server, as shown in Figure 16.31. User dial-in settings are configured from the Dial-in tab of the Properties

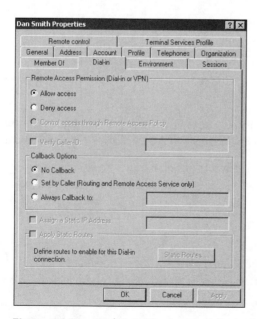

Figure 16.31   Dial-in settings are configured for users from within Active Directory.

dialog box for a user account in Local Users And Groups when operating in a standalone or non–Windows 2000 server. Denying access from Active Directory means a user will not be able to connect remotely.

Setting Callback Options adds another element of security. Callback can be set to Set By Caller or Always Callback To a specific number. Setting a callback requirement means the server will call back the user's system at the respective telephone number.

The Verify Caller-ID box can be selected to verify the user is actually calling from the telephone number the user is supposed to be calling from.

Warning: If you set Verify Caller-ID, and just one hardware peripheral required to complete the connection doesn't support caller ID, the connection request will be denied.

The Dial-in tab also includes IP Routing options. The use of a static IP address can be configured by setting the Assign A Static IP Address option. Static routes can also be specified. If a static route is set, static IP routes are added to the remote access server's routing table. Administrators might find this valuable when working with demand-dial routing.

Creating a Remote Access Policy

From within the Routing and Remote Access console, you can create a policy and set condition attributes for the user. This can be done by right-clicking Remote Access Policies and selecting New Remote Access Policy. Many condition attributes can be set. They are:

➤ Called Station ID

➤ Calling Station ID

➤ Client Friendly Name

➤ Client IP Address

➤ Client Vendor

➤ Day And Time Restrictions

➤ Framed Protocol

➤ Network Access Server (NAS) Identifier

➤ NAS IP Address

16

➤ NAS Port Type

➤ Service Type

➤ Tunnel Type

➤ Windows Groups

Creating a Remote Access Policy entails nine steps:

1. Open the Routing and Remote Access console.

2. Click the server you want to configure, right-click Remote Access Policies, then select New Remote Access Policy.

3. Type a descriptive name for the Remote Access Policy you're creating, then click Next.

4. Click Add to select conditions.

5. Click the attributes you'd like to add.

6. Specify the information needed by the attribute.

7. Add additional attributes you'd like to implement, and click Next when done adding attributes.

8. Grant access to connection attempts that match the attributes you've selected by clicking Grant Remote Access Permission. Conversely, if you want to deny access to the connection requests that match the attributes you've selected, click Deny Remote Access Permission. Click Next.

9. Create a profile, if you'd like one, then click Finish to complete the creation.

Editing a Remote Access Policy Profile

You can edit a policy profile from within Routing and Remote Access. You do so by double-clicking a policy from the right-hand panel in Routing and Remote Access, and then selecting Edit Profile to open the Edit Dial-in Profile interface shown in Figure 16.32.

The Remote Access Policies Profile settings dictate the kind of access a user receives, if all other conditions match. Remote Access Policy Profiles are created in the Properties dialog box of the respective policy. A Profile is edited by selecting Edit Profile on the Properties dialog box, specifying the configuration settings you desire, and then clicking OK.

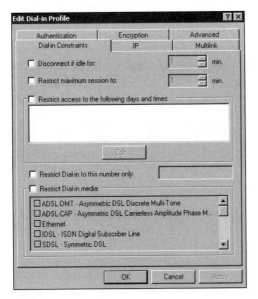

Figure 16.32   Edit Dial-in Profile settings can be configured from the Routing and Remote Access console.

CHAPTER SUMMARY

You're likely to find several questions targeting the installation, configuration, and administration of remote access issues on the Windows 2000 Accelerated exam. Therefore, you should familiarize yourself with the new network and connection wizards, the new protocols, the enhanced management interfaces, and the use of policies and profiles to control network access.

The Routing and Remote Access application is a member of the Administration Tools set in Windows 2000. Administration Tools can be installed or uninstalled using Adminpak.msi.

The Windows 2000 Routing and Remote Access Administration Tool supports several types of connections, including:

➤ Dial-up connections

➤ Virtual private networks

➤ Direct cable connections

Authentication is one of the most important steps in permitting remote access to your network. Authentication protocols are used to help protect a network's integrity. The use of authentication protocols shouldn't be new to you. Your

16

previous experience with the Windows NT 4 Server platform undoubtedly acquainted you with CHAP, CSLIP, MS-CHAP, PAP, PPP, and other protocols.

Windows 2000 adds several new authentication and connectivity protocols to help strengthen the defense employed in the battle to protect remote access connectivity and ensure that remote connections are managed properly. They are:

➤ *Bandwidth Allocation Protocol (BAP)*—Works with the Bandwidth Allocation Control Protocol (BACP) to provide bandwidth as needed.

➤ *Extensible Authentication Protocol (EAP)*—Enables a dial-in client and server to negotiate the actual authentication method they will use.

➤ *Internet Protocol Security (IPSec)*—Uses encryption, digital signature, and sophisticated algorithm technologies to secure IP communications from creation to delivery. IPSec is an open-standards based protocol.

➤ *Layer 2 Tunneling Protocol (L2TP)*—Forms an encrypted path over a public network. L2TP, like PPTP, provides tunneling, or the creation of a second path within a connection. However, L2TP, unlike PPTP, does not encrypt the contents of data packets.

➤ *Remote Authentication Dial-In User Service (RADIUS)*—Extends the ability to validate and log the amount of time a computer spends on a dial-up network.

The Network Connection Wizard can be used to configure the following connections:

➤ Dial-up connections to a private network

➤ Dial-up connections to the Internet

➤ VPN tunneled connections to the Internet

➤ Incoming connections coming from a telephone line, the Internet, or a direct cable

➤ A direct connection to another computer using a serial, parallel, or infrared port

Like Windows NT, Windows 2000 provides routing functionality. The Windows 2000 Routing and Remote Access Service provides enhanced routing functionality, including the following:

➤ Support for routing protocols

➤ IP multicasting, such as might be used for videoconferencing

➤ Network Address Translation

➤ Enhanced VPN capabilities, including router-to-router VPN connections

In Windows 2000, you can configure a system's settings so that a system set to provide translation services hides the IP address from machines beyond the system conducting the translation. Network Address Translation (NAT) is used for this purpose.

Just as user behavior can be controlled using group policies, so too can remote access. Windows 2000 provides default policies to help secure Remote Access Service and Internet Authentication Service. These policies are necessary for the acceptance of user remote access connection requests.

Unlike other policies, Remote Access Policies are not kept in the Active Directory database. Instead, Remote Access Policies are stored on the server running the Remote Access Service. Remote Access Policies include conditions, permissions, and profiles. These three components work with the Active Directory Service to secure Remote Access server access.

REVIEW QUESTIONS

1. Which of the following connection and authentication protocols are supported by Windows 2000 but not Windows NT 4? [Check all correct answers]

   a. PPTP

   b. EAP

   c. ARP

   d. BAP

2. EAP provides authentication support for which of the following? [Check all correct answers]

   a. Token cards

   b. MD5-CHAP

   c. TLS

   d. Biometric peripherals

3. Which features support enhanced multilink capabilities in Windows 2000? [Check all correct answers]

   a. BAP support

   b. BACP support

   c. ARP support

   d. L2TP support

16

4. PPTP requires an IP-based network for transit.

    a. True

    b. False

5. Willard works as a product manager for a regional ISP. His company markets subscriber policies based on the number of hours a customer dials-in to the network each month. Which new feature of Windows 2000 makes the new OS most attractive to his company?

    a. Support for Bandwidth Allocation Protocol

    b. Remote Authentication Dial-in User Service

    c. Support for L2TP

    d. Support for IPSec

6. Ellen is preparing to make changes to an IPSec policy on her network. Which management tool should she use?

    a. Routing and Remote Access

    b. Active Directory Users and Computers

    c. Security Policy Manager

    d. IP Security Policy Management

7. IPSec includes a special driver for decoding protective security information contained in a data packet. At what IP layer does this driver function?

    a. Physical

    b. Data Link

    c. Transport

    d. Session

8. Which service logs RADIUS authentication information?

    a. RADIUS Authentication Service

    b. Active Directory Service

    c. Routing and Remote Access Service

    d. Internet Authentication Service

9. Which features does PPTP share with L2TP? [Check all correct answers]

    a. Both PPTP and L2TP support tunneling

    b. Both PPTP and L2TP provide encryption

    c. Both PPTP and L2TP support header compression

    d. Both PPTP and L2TP use PPP for encryption

10. John needs to create an inbound dial-in connection for a salesperson at his company. He's using a Windows 2000 domain controller. Which utility should he use? [Check all correct answers]

    a. Network Connection Wizard

    b. Dial-in Connection Wizard

    c. Routing and Remote Access

    d. Active Directory

11. Sarah's engineering firm has subscribed to a special telecommunications plan, because it sometimes must send large CAD files quickly. However, the firm doesn't want to pay for a large data pipe 24 hours a day that it might need only five or six times a month. As a result, the engineering firm subscribes to a bandwidth-on-demand plan. Which feature included in Windows 2000 will help Sarah maximize the use of this subscription plan? [Check all correct answers]

    a. Bandwidth-on-Demand Service

    b. Support for the Bandwidth Allocation Protocol

    c. Multilink Service

    d. Pipeline Burst Service

12. George has been tasked with rolling out new laptops to his company's sales force. He wants to use a VPN connection to help ensure sales and pricing information isn't intercepted by others when the salespeople connect to his company's private network via the public switched telephone network. As he prepares a disk he intends to duplicate to quicken the deployment of the new laptops, which utility should he use to create the VPN connection to his company's Windows 2000 remote access server?

    a. Routing and Remote Access

    b. Active Directory

    c. Network Connection Wizard

    d. The VPN Management MMC snap-in

13. The Routing and Remote Access console can be used to create dial-up connections to a VPN in a native Windows 2000 domain mode.

    a. True

    b. False

14. Windows 2000's Routing and Remote Access checks for which of the following when it's installed? [Check all correct answers]

    a. Internal modems

    b. External modems

16

    c. Serial connections

    d. Parallel cable connections

15. Inbound dial-up connections to a remote access server are configured using which utility on a standalone server?

    a. Network Connection Wizard

    b. Routing and Remote Access

    c. Server Manager

    d. User Manager

16. Support for which new Windows 2000 feature hides the IP address of a system from other systems, except for the system responsible for providing translation services?

    a. Proxy Server

    b. RARP

    c. NAT

    d. NTA

17. Kim is having difficulty connecting to her company's remote access server. Her administrator believes her condition attributes and permissions from her connection attempt match the settings on the remote access server, but she's not connecting. What should her administrator check when trying to fix the problem? [Check all correct answers]

    a. Active Directory dial-in permissions

    b. Whether the remote access server's Routing and Remote Access service is running

    c. Kim's profile settings

    d. The times of day Kim is permitted to dial-in

18. Mike is a member of the Marketing group, which is given permission to access the remote access server 24 hours a day. A Remote Access Policy limits access to the server to the hours from 8 A.M. through 5 P.M. When will Mike be granted access to the remote server?

    a. 24 hours a day.

    b. From 8 A.M. to 5 P.M.

    c. Mike will be denied access, due to the Remote Access Policy and Group policy conflict.

    d. Mike's access will be determined by the override settings in Active Directory.

19. Which components are used to form a Remote Access Policy? [Check all correct answers]

   a. Configuring inbound dial-up settings in Active Directory

   b. Configuring inbound dial-up permissions in the Routing and Remote Access console

   c. Creating a policy and supplying condition attributes for it from within the Routing and Remote Access console

   d. Editing a policies profile from within the Routing and Remote Access console

20. Tim has deleted the default Remote Access Policy from the Routing and Remote Access console to ensure unauthorized access doesn't occur on his network. He's configured users' dial-up settings in Active Directory. Then, he enabled the Routing and Remote Access Service. Users, however, are complaining that they cannot connect to the remote access server. What action should he take? [Check all correct answers]

   a. He should call his telecommunications provider to ensure that his data circuit is operational.

   b. He should restart the Routing and Remote Access Service.

   c. He should create a profile in the Routing and Remote Access console.

   d. He should double-check that he hasn't set conflicting condition attributes in Active Directory.

REAL-WORLD PROJECTS

Andy Palmer has no sooner pulled up to his publishing client when he runs into the system administrator leaving for lunch. During a quick conversation in the parking lot, Andy is instructed to install Routing and Remote Access on the publisher's new Windows 2000 Server and to create a Remote Access Policy for the company's traveling sales personnel.

Project 16.1
To install Routing and Remote Access, complete the following steps:

1. Andy sits down at the AXIS server the client indicated should be the remote access server. He clicks Start|Programs|Administration Tools|Routing And Remote Access.

2. He right-clicks on Routing And Remote Access, and selects Add Server, opening the Add Server dialog box, as shown in Figure 16.33. Andy is using the computer he intends to use as the remote access server, so he clicks OK.

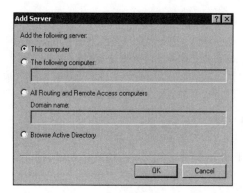

Figure 16.33 In the Add Server dialog box, you can add the local computer, a computer you specify, or all computers in a domain you specify; or you can browse Active Directory.

3. Andy then right-clicks on the AXIS server in the console tree, and selects Configure And Enable Routing And Remote Access, as shown in Figure 16.34. The Routing And Remote Access Server Setup Wizard appears, as shown in Figure 16.35.

4. After clicking Next to continue, Andy is prompted to select the type of connection he wants to create. He selects Remote Access Server to permit remote systems to connect to the server. He then clicks Next.

5. Andy ensures the protocol he wants to use is found by the setup wizard. He's using TCP/IP, which the wizard finds, so he selects Next.

6. No Macintosh machines are supported within the organization, so Andy leaves the Allow Authenticated Access For All Remote Clients unchecked, and clicks Next.

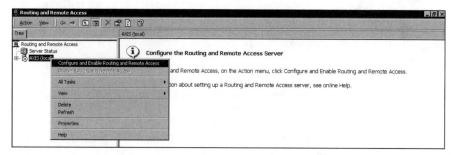

Figure 16.34 You must select Configure And Enable Routing And Remote Access to begin the Routing and Remote Access Service setup.

Figure 16.35 The Routing And Remote Access Server Setup Wizard is used to configure the Routing and Remote Access server.

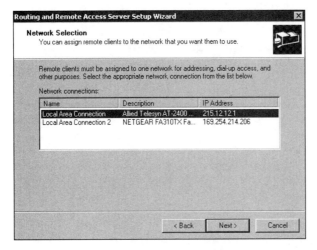

Figure 16.36 You must specify which connection you want the remote computers to access.

7. Andy selects the local area connection he wants the remote clients to use, as shown in Figure 16.36. He then clicks Next.

8. The publishing company indicated that it wants to use a specified range of IP addresses for remote users, so Andy selects From A Specified Range Of Addresses in the wizard's IP Address Assignment dialog box. He then clicks Next.

9. Andy clicks New, provides the range of addresses the company wants to use, and then he clicks OK.

10. He then selects No, I Don't Want To Set This Server To Use RADIUS Now, because the company doesn't want to use RADIUS.

11. He then clicks Finish to complete the installation.

Project 16.2
To create a Remote Administration Policy, complete the following steps:

Andy has been instructed to create a Remote Administration Policy for the company's sales force. Therefore, he proceeds to create a Remote Administration Policy as follows:

1. Andy right-clicks the AXIS server. If he weren't already in the Routing and Remote Access console, he would open it by clicking Start | Programs | Administration Tools | Routing And Remote Access.

2. He selects Remote Access Policies, and selects New Remote Access Policy. The Add Remote Access Policy Wizard opens.

3. Andy types a descriptive name for the connection, which he entitles *Salesforce*. He then clicks Next.

4. He clicks Add to provide conditions. He adds Day And Time Restrictions and permits access during business hours on weekdays, and clicks OK. Andy then clicks Next.

5. Andy selects to Grant Remote Access Permission When Conditions Match, and clicks Next.

6. Andy sets a profile by selecting Edit Profile, clicking the IP tab, selecting the Server Must Supply An IP Address option, and clicking OK.

7. He then clicks Finish to complete the creation of the Remote Access Policy.

Andy reviews the Active Directory settings for the Salesforce group to ensure the users' settings are properly configured. After confirming that dial-in settings don't conflict, he heads out for the day.

CHAPTER SEVENTEEN

UNDERSTANDING WINDOWS 2000 TERMINAL SERVICES

After completing this chapter, you will be able to:

✓ Plan Terminal Services deployment

✓ Install Terminal Services

✓ Administer Terminal Services

✓ Create a terminal session

✓ Install applications for use with Terminal Services

✓ Administer Terminal Services remotely

First, large mainframes were all the rage. Then, client/server systems stormed the enterprise-computing environment. Now, some organizations are turning to thin-clients or less-powerful terminal machines to run applications in an enterprise.

Windows 2000 addresses the need that many organizations have to run applications on powerful servers yet make the applications available to remote-based users, whether the users are in field offices, working from laptops on the road, or using less-powerful client machines or different operating systems. As a result of the reliance on the server's system resources, end-user terminals don't need to possess significant RAM, hard disk space, or super-fast processors.

By installing Terminal Services on a Windows 2000 Server, you can create a multiuser environment enabling users to run applications you've installed on the server, regardless of the power of users' machines. Furthermore, users don't need to be running the same operating systems. The end result of Terminal Services is that it provides the ability to leverage the investment an organization has made in older client-side technology, other legacy systems (including mobile PCs), and Windows terminal units. IT managers, meanwhile, enjoy the improved total cost of ownership (TCO) resulting from a Windows 2000 deployment, which maximizes the use of older and less-powered machines and systems.

This chapter examines how you can plan a Terminal Services deployment, install Terminal Services, administer Terminal Services, create a terminal session, and install applications for use with Terminal Services.

TERMINAL SERVICES COMPONENTS

Three components of Terminal Services work together to extend remote use of server-based applications. The three components are:

➤ *Terminal Services server*—A Windows 2000 Server running the Terminal Services feature. The Terminal Services server assumes responsibility for powering user sessions. It also creates a unique operating environment for each client that connects to it. Each and every client input, whether it's a keystroke or a pointer movement, is processed and run by the Terminal Services server. The Terminal Services server creates the graphical user interface (GUI) and directs the image to display on the remote client.

➤ *Remote Desktop Protocol (RDP)*—An Application layer protocol. RDP enables communication between the Terminal Services server and the remote client device. The protocol is designed to move the GUI elements created by the server quickly to the client. RDP relies on TCP/IP.

➤ *Client*—A local desktop computer or device. Client devices have the responsibility of opening the session as a window. The session with the Terminal Services server is opened from within whatever desktop environment is being used on the client. Actual processing, however, occurs on the server.

PLANNING WINDOWS 2000 TERMINAL SERVICES DEPLOYMENTS

As with any deployment, all Windows 2000 Terminal Services installations should be planned properly. You need to consider the following four factors when preparing a Terminal Services deployment:

➤ Examine which client applications you want to support

➤ Determine the minimum hardware requirements for the remote client devices

➤ Research the required configuration for your Terminal Services server

➤ Obtain the necessary licenses required for your Terminal Services installation

Examine Client Applications

In most cases, applications and programs that run on Windows 2000 will run properly on a Terminal Services server. You should test applications on an isolated Terminal Services server before deploying them, because some programs might require modifications.

Warning: Programs must run properly on the Windows 2000 platform if they're to be considered for use on a Terminal Services server.

Because 32-bit applications run more efficiently, the number of 16-bit client sessions a Terminal Services server can run simultaneously can be as much as 40 percent less when compared to 32-bit applications. Furthermore, RAM requirements can increase by 50 percent when supporting 16-bit applications. For this reason, you should support 32-bit applications whenever possible.

You also probably should adjust settings for your older MS-DOS applications that you want to host on your Terminal Services servers. You'll want to guard against applications that slow the systems with their idle processes. In fact, you

17

might want to simply avoid some applications. The following types of programs might not work, or they might slow your Terminal Services server to a crawl or stop it altogether:

➤ Old, text-based applications not designed to run in multiuser environments

➤ Applications requiring specialized hardware devices, such as bar code scanners

➤ Custom applications

If you must use such programs, be sure to modify the custom applications to run in a multiuser and Terminal Services environment. In addition, if you're using applications that require specialized hardware, be sure the server recognizes the peripherals as keyboard-type devices. You must also ensure the application software and its specialized hardware are supported by the remote client device.

Determine the Client Device's Hardware Requirements

Six operating systems are supported by three Terminal Services platforms. The operating systems Terminal Services supports are:

➤ Windows 2000

➤ Windows NT

➤ Windows 9x

➤ Windows For Workgroups 3.11

➤ Windows CE 3

➤ Windows-based Terminals

The three Terminal Services platforms are:

➤ A 32-bit platform for use with Windows 2000, Windows NT, and Windows 9x

➤ A 32-bit platform for use with Alpha-based systems

➤ A 16-bit version for use with Windows For Workgroups

Requirements for the 32- and 16-bit Terminal Services clients are simply the system requirements demanded by the respective operating system you're using on the remote client. For example, if your remote client uses Windows 98, you'll need 16MB RAM, a 486 processor minimum, and a VGA or better display monitor, which are the minimum system requirements for Windows 98.

In order to use Windows CE Handheld PCs, the minimum hardware requirements are dictated by the Handheld PC specification. HPC requirements vary by vendor. Check Table 17.1 if you need to reference the minimum system requirements for the operating systems supported by Windows 2000 Terminal Services.

Note: All operating systems supported by Windows 2000 Terminal Services require VGA or better display monitors, with the exception of Windows CE, whose system requirements are dictated by the vendor manufacturing the HPC device.

Research the Terminal Services Server Configuration

Because Terminal Services runs client applications on the server hosting Terminal Services, such servers typically require greater processing power and increased RAM. The success of a Terminal Services deployment depends on how well the Terminal Services server can accommodate the number of client sessions it must support.

Two principal factors should be considered when calculating the system requirements for a Terminal Services server. They are:

➤ User characteristics

➤ Server system configurations

Researching User Characteristics

Users can typically be placed into one of the following categories:

➤ *Typical users*—Typical users generally run one application, or two simultaneously. Generally, they utilize few system resources, because they use simple word processing and email programs.

➤ *Task-based users*—Task-based users typically run a single application. Often, this single application is used for simple data entry.

Table 17.1   Each operating system supported by Windows 2000 Terminal Services possesses its own set of minimum system requirements.

Operating System	Processor	RAM
Windows For Workgroups	386	16MB
Windows 95	386	16MB
Windows 98	486	16MB
Windows NT 4	486	16MB
Windows 2000	Pentium	64MB

17

➤ *Advanced users*—Advanced users can cripple a Terminal Services server if you're not careful, because they run three or more applications at the same time. And, many of the applications they run place a great demand on the Terminal Services server. These can include application suites (such as Office 2000), email, and processor-intensive applications such as graphics and database products.

Researching Server System Configurations

Microsoft recommends that Terminal Services be installed on an NTFS partition. Because multiple user sessions are supported simultaneously by the Terminal Services server, enhancing security is important to ensure users don't access data in use by others.

In order not to overwhelm a server's system resources, Microsoft also recommends that you install Terminal Services on a member server, not a domain controller. The enhanced memory and processor demand, coupled with increased network traffic, can overwhelm a domain controller.

You should add a minimum of 20MB of additional RAM for each user you intend a Terminal Services server to host. Typical users require 40MB of RAM. If you're supporting many advanced users, you'll want to add considerably more RAM. One benchmark for advanced users is 80MB. However, if you're supporting only simple, single-task users, you might be able to get by with less.

Disk speed is another important system configuration factor. Consider using SCSI drives, because they offer significantly enhanced throughput than IDE/ EIDE drives. You should also have a minimum of 14MB of disk space available for hosting client installation files.

Also, if you will be supporting multiple users, you'll want to ensure the server's NIC doesn't become a bottleneck. You can do so by adding additional NICs and ensuring they are 100Mbps or faster speed. The faster the better.

Finally, you should also consider adding processors. At a minimum, begin with a server that supports multiple coprocessors. Microsoft says a Pentium II 400 MHz chip can support 15 to 30 users. Of course, the types of users a network supports dictates how powerful the server should be.

As you add support for new users, you might find it necessary to add additional microprocessors. As with all hardware, be sure that the devices you use with your Terminal Services server are compatible with Windows 2000 and listed on Microsoft's Hardware Compatibility List (HCL).

Obtain the Necessary Licenses Required by Terminal Services

The use of Terminal Services raises a few licensing issues, but it's not complicated. Just ensure you possess the following three licenses:

➤ Windows 2000 Server license for the server hosting Terminal Services (the Per Seat licensing mode is usually used when deploying Terminal Services)

➤ Windows 2000 Server Client Access License (CAL) for each client that accesses the server hosting Terminal Services

➤ Windows 2000 Terminal Services CAL for each remote computer or device that connects to the server hosting Terminal Services

The Windows 2000 Server license is included with Windows 2000 Server operating systems. The Windows 2000 CALs and Windows 2000 Terminal Services CALs must be purchased separately. However, Windows 2000 Professional includes a single Windows 2000 Terminal Services CAL for remote administration use.

INSTALLING WINDOWS 2000 TERMINAL SERVICES

After you've dutifully prepared for a Windows 2000 Terminal Services deployment by ensuring that the client and server meet the minimum hardware requirements and systems configurations and that you have the appropriate licenses in place, you're ready to proceed with the installation. Windows 2000 Terminal Services can be installed when you install Windows 2000 Server. To do so, select Terminal Services using the Windows Components Wizard. You can also install Terminal Services after Windows 2000 Server installation is completed. You do so by selecting Add/Remove Programs in Control Panel. If you wait to install Terminal Services, however, you might have to reinstall applications you've previously installed on the server.

When you install Terminal Services, which creates the multiple session environment, two other components are also installed. They are *Client Creator Files*, which includes a wizard for creating installation disks for your Terminal Services clients, and the *Enable Terminal Services*, which permits the starting and stopping of Terminal Services.

Finally, the Terminal Services Licensing component must also be installed. The licensing component configures a system as a Terminal Services license server. This means the server can provide Terminal Services CALs.

17

Whether you're installing Windows 2000 or Windows 2000 Terminal Services, the process is straightforward:

1. Select Start | Settings | Control Panel.

2. Select Add/Remove Programs.

3. Select the Add/Remove Windows Components, fill in the Terminal Services and Terminal Services Licensing checkboxes, and click Next.

4. Specify the mode in which Terminal Services should operate:

   ➤ *Remote Administration Mode*—Permits a limited number of administrators to manage the server remotely. This setting minimizes the impact on server performance.

   ➤ *Application Server Mode*—Allows remote users to run one or more applications. This setting optimizes program response times and requires a Terminal Services Licensing server to be installed within 90 days.

5. Click Next, then select default permissions for applications compatibility. You can select either permissions compatible with Windows 2000 users or permissions compatible with Terminal Server 4 users. The Terminal Server 4 permissions provide an environment in which most legacy applications are supported. Windows 2000 users permissions provide the most secure environment.

6. Select Next. Terminal Services Setup may or may not provide a warning indicating that certain applications might not work properly following the installation of Terminal Services. If you receive a warning, make a note of the specified applications, because you might have to manage them accordingly. Click Next.

7. Specify whether the license server is to provide Terminal Services CALs for your workgroup, domain, or enterprise.

8. Specify the location of the directory you want to use for the licensing server database, then click Next.

9. Wait while Windows 2000 updates your system's files. A dialog box should appear indicating Terminal Services installation has completed. Select Finish.

10. Confirm that you want to restart the server when prompted to do so.

The Terminal Services installation adds several new Administrative Tools:

➤ *Terminal Services Client Creator*—Permits the creation of boot floppies for Terminal Services clients.

➤ *Terminal Services Configuration*—Enables you to manage Terminal Services protocol configuration and server settings. Only one RDP connection can be configured per NIC.

➤ *Terminal Services Licensing*—Enables you to manage Terminal Services CALs.

➤ *Terminal Services Manager*—Enables you to manage and monitor connection sessions and processes on the Terminal Services server.

ADMINISTERING WINDOWS 2000 TERMINAL SERVICES SERVERS

Users must be given appropriate access permissions to connect to a Terminal Services server. Users should have an understanding of how Terminal Services sessions are configured, how applications are installed on Terminal Servers, how Terminal Services sessions are administered, and how Terminal Services clients are configured.

Configuring Terminal Services User Session Settings

You can configure Terminal Services user session settings via the Active Directory. To do so, follow these steps:

1. In Active Directory Users and Computers, right-click the user you want to provide access to, and select Properties.

2. Select the Terminal Services Profile tab, and ensure the Allow Logon To Terminal Server checkbox is filled in, as shown in Figure 17.1. If necessary, check the checkbox, and click Apply.

The Terminal Services Profile tab is also used to specify home directories and user profiles that you want to apply to a user's Terminal Services connections. For example, you might want to use Terminal Services user profiles to disable screen savers and other programs that can utilize system resources that can degrade Terminal Services session performance.

Other Terminal Services session settings can be configured using the Sessions tab, as shown in Figure 17.2. On the Sessions tab, you can configure the following settings:

➤ When to disconnect a session

➤ The active session limit

➤ The idle session limit

17

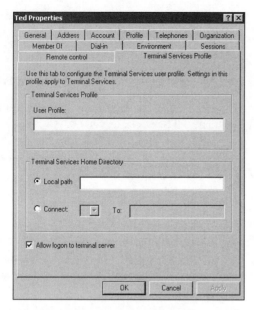

Figure 17.1 Access permissions must be extended to users to enable Terminal Services connections.

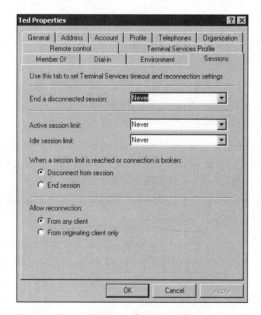

Figure 17.2 Session limits and reconnection settings are configured on the Sessions tab.

➤ What the server should do when a session limit is reached or a connection is broken

➤ Whether reconnection is permitted from any client or the originating client only

Installing Applications on a Terminal Services Server

Before you can install applications on a server running Terminal Services, you must log onto the server using the built-in Administrator account. Only after you've installed an application can you execute a compatibility script to modify an application to run on a Terminal Services server.

Before you begin the installation process, ensure you're installing the application to an NTFS-formatted partition. After you've confirmed the partition that will host the application is an NTFS partition, you're ready to proceed.

Two methods are available for installing applications on a Terminal Services server, or terminal server. You can use the **Change User** command at the command prompt or the Add/Remove Programs applet found in Control Panel. The Add/Remove Programs applet is recommended, because it provides a GUI for the **Change User** command. Microsoft recommends using the **Change User** command, as described in Table 17.2, only after an application has been installed. And then, it should be used only to verify whether multiuser access is operational.

Table 17.2 The **Change Control** command can be used to switch a Terminal Services server between install mode and execute mode.

Change Parameter	Command	Description
Change Logon	Disable	Stops users from beginning logon sessions, but does not disconnect active sessions
Change Logon	Enable	Enables users to begin sessions
Change Logon	Query	Displays the current logon status
Change Port	portx=porty	Maps port x to port y
Change Port	/D portx	Deletes the current port mapping in use by port x
Change Port	Query	Displays the port mappings currently in place
Change User	Install	Installs new applications on a Terminal Services server
Change User	Execute	Triggers applications to be used in multiuser mode
Change User	Query	Displays the current mode

17

Before proceeding with an installation, you must complete two more steps. First, you need to ensure the terminal server is operating in the proper mode. The available modes are:

➤ *Install Mode*—A Terminal Services server should be in install mode when installing an application. Failing to place a terminal server in install mode when installing an application might cause the terminal server to operate improperly. Install mode is used to turn off INI file mapping and to record the application's setup APIs.

➤ *Execute Mode*—After applications are installed, the server should be set to run in execute mode. Execute mode restores INI file mapping and redirects user-specific data to the user's home directory. After a server is returned to execute mode, users will have their respective registry settings automatically returned when they're needed.

The second step after switching to Install mode is to ensure no users are currently conducting Terminal Services sessions. If terminal sessions are active, you should first end them before proceeding with an application installation.

To install an application, the Add/Remove Programs applet should be used, after logging on as Administrator, of course. You should also close all other open programs, including antivirus programs. Follow these steps to complete the installation of an application:

1. After selecting Add/Remove Programs, select All Users Begin With Common Application Settings to trigger the installation for all users.

2. Specify the settings the installation wizard prompts you to provide.

3. If Windows 2000 can't find the appropriate setup program, you can use the wizard's Browse button to navigate to the application's installation program and execute it from there.

4. After you've identified the installation program and selected Next, the installation will proceed. Meanwhile, the After Installation dialog box remains open. When the installation is complete, you'll be prompted to reboot. Do not reboot until you've gone back to the After Installation dialog box and selected Next to proceed to the dialog box where you should select Finish. If the application requires rebooting the terminal server, you should then trigger the restart.

After you've completed the application's installation, you can modify the application to run more efficiently in a multiuser environment. Windows 2000 Terminal Services includes application compatibility scripts for popular programs.

Using Application Compatibility Scripts

Application compatibility scripts modify an application's global registry settings while also disabling features that could harm system performance. You'll find the application compatibility scripts located in the *systemroot*\Application Compatibility Scripts\Install folder, as shown in Figure 17.3.

Note: Using Microsoft Office 2000 on a terminal server requires the use of Terminal Services components included in the Office 2000 Resource Kit.

Follow these steps to execute application compatibility scripts:

1. Locate the script or key file you want to use in the *systemroot*\Application Compatibility Scripts\Install folder. Review the files in a text editor, and ensure you modify the installation path if you've changed the default installation location.

2. Run the script from the command prompt.

3. If a logon script is included in the *systemroot*\Application Compatibility Scripts\Install folder, review it in a text editor, and ensure you modify the path location and drive letter references.

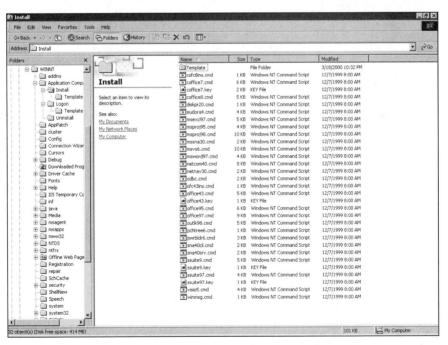

17

Figure 17.3   You'll find application compatibility scripts included for use with several popular applications, including several versions of Microsoft Office.

4. Open *systemroot*\Application Compatibility Scripts\Install\User.cmd in a text editor.

5. Add a call for each logon script you use.

6. Remove the remark command from the lines corresponding to the applications you are installing.

7. Copy the User.cmd file to the *systemroot*\System32 folder.

8. Run Uscron.cmd from the command prompt. (This command enables the use of the User.cmd script when users log on.)

Terminal Services Session Administration

Time limits can be set to ensure sufficient system resources are available to Terminal Services clients. You should use the user account properties in Active Directory Users and Computers to specify client session time limits. The Active Directory user settings can be overridden, however, using the Terminal Services Configuration Administrative Tool. To override user settings:

1. Select Start | Programs | Administrative Tools | Terminal Services Configuration.

2. Click Connections, right-click RDP-Tcp, and select Properties.

3. Display the Sessions tab, as shown in Figure 17.4.

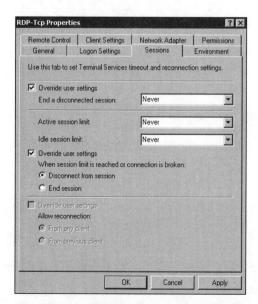

Figure 17.4   The Terminal Services Configuration Administrative Tool permits Terminal Services settings provided in Active Directory to be overridden.

Three settings are available on the Sessions tab:

➤ *End A Disconnected Session*—Specifies when a sessions should be disconnected. Once a session reaches this limit, it will be stopped; it cannot be resumed.

➤ *Active Session Limit*—Specifies the maximum length of time an active session can reach. When an active session reaches the limit, it will be stopped. However, the session can be kept live on the server or it can be reset.

➤ *Idle Session Limit*—Specifies the maximum length of time a session can be left without activity. Once an inactive session reaches the time limit, it will be disconnected or reset.

The Terminal Services Manager Administrative Tool is used to manage terminal services sessions. Terminal Services Manager displays the available terminal servers on a network, which connections are active, which protocols are in use, and which users are connected, as shown in Figure 17.5.

Terminal Services Manager can be used to perform the following functions:

➤ *Find a Terminal Services server*—By right-clicking the domain name in the left pane and selecting Find Servers In Domain, you can find all the terminal servers operating in the domain. You can also find all the terminal servers operating in your enterprise by right-clicking All Listed Servers and selecting Find Servers In All Domains.

➤ *Make a connection to another server running Terminal Services*—Before you can manage terminal session activity, you must first connect to the server hosting the terminal session. This is done by selecting the server you want to connect to, right-clicking it, and choosing Connect. You can also connect to all the servers in a domain by choosing Connect To All Servers In Domain.

➤ *Connect to another session on the server*—With Full Control or User Access permission, you can connect to an active session on another server. You do so by right-clicking the session in the right pane and selecting Connect.

17

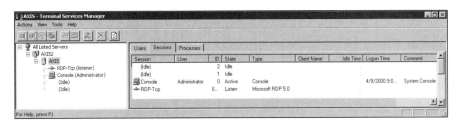

Figure 17.5   Terminal Services Manager is used to administer Terminal Services sessions.

➤ *Manage a connection*—With sufficient permissions in place for the account you're using, you can disconnect sessions, reset them, log off a session, view a connection's status, and more. Terminal Services Manager is also used to end a hung process.

➤ *Disconnect a session*—You can stop a session from passing input and output to a remote terminal, but keep the session running on the terminal server. This is done by disconnecting a session, which helps to prevent data loss. System resources are not freed as a result of a disconnected session, however. Users can disconnect their own sessions. Administrators require Full Control permission to disconnect a user's session.

➤ *Reset a session*—When resetting a connection, system resources are freed and any unsaved information is lost. Resetting a session stops all work that is active. Full Control permissions are required to reset a session.

➤ *Log off a session*—With Full Control permission you can log off a session, thereby freeing any system resources it is using. You can do so by selecting the connection in Terminal Services Manager, right-clicking it, and selecting Log Off. Be sure data is saved before executing Log Off; otherwise, data can be lost.

➤ *View a session's active processes*—Information regarding a session (such as client address, client name, or client resolution) can be viewed using Terminal Services Manager. To view an active process, highlight it in the left pane and click Processes in the right pane. Information about the session can be learned by selecting the Information tab in the right pane.

➤ *Manage user sessions*—You can view and manage current user sessions by highlighting the domain you want to check in the left pane and clicking the Users tab in the right pane.

➤ *Send a message to a session*—Should you want to send a message to a session, you can do so by right-clicking the session or user in the right pane and selecting Send Message. You should do so when preparing to log off a session, for example, to alert a user to the upcoming action and help prevent data loss.

➤ *Control a session*—With Full Control permission, you can remotely administer a computer or device as if you were sitting at it. Controlling a session gives the remote administrator control of the computer or device's input devices and mirrors the user's display. This feature is particularly helpful when troubleshooting problems on the remote system.

Configuring Terminal Services Clients

Two methods are available for installing Terminal Services on a client machine. One method of installing Terminal Services Client involves using Terminal Services Client Creator to create installation disks. The second option is to use a shared folder to make the installation files available to the remote system or device.

Installing Terminal Services Clients Using Installation Disks

The Terminal Services Client Creator is used to create installation disks. Follow these steps to create Terminal Services Client disks:

1. Select Start | Programs | Administrative Tools | Terminal Services Client Creator.

2. Specify which client software you want to create. Terminal Services for 16-bit Windows requires four disks. Terminal Services for 32-bit Intel-based Windows systems requires two disks.

3. Select a destination drive and insert a disk into it. You can also choose to format the disk at this stage.

4. Copy the needed files to the disks, close the Create Installation Disk window, and select OK to continue.

Installing Terminal Services Client Over a Network

If you plan to install the Terminal Services Client over a network, first ensure the intended remote system or device is configured properly. Next, you must share the necessary files.

Follow these steps to install Terminal Services Client over a network:

1. Share the *systemroot*\System32\Clients\Tsclient folder or the folder representing the Terminal Services platform you want to make available on the server running Terminal Services.

2. From the remote system or device, connect to the shared folder on the terminal server.

3. Run the Setup.exe program from the respective system platform you want to install (that is, Win16 for 16-bit Windows platforms and Win32 for 32-bit Windows platforms).

4. Specify and confirm the username and the organization.

5. Accept the license agreement.

6. Specify the folder where you'd like to install the Terminal Services Client files.

17

7. Indicate whether the Terminal Services Client is to be used by all users of the system or just the current user.

8. Wait for setup to complete the file transfer and select Finish.

Creating Terminal Sessions

After Terminal Services is installed and configured on a server, the Terminal Services Client is installed, and permissions are configured for a user on a remote system, you're ready to create a terminal session. Users create a connection using their remote device by creating a Terminal Services connection. Although they'll be presented with a GUI resembling Windows 2000, the fact that the application is really running on the server, and not the client, won't be apparent.

Follow these steps to create a terminal session:

1. Ensure the user is logged onto the client.

2. Start Terminal Services Client by selecting it from the Program menu.

3. Choose a Terminal Services server by providing its name or IP address. You can also specify screen resolution, indicate whether you're using a low-speed connection, and cache bitmaps to disk, which saves desktop display items to the local cache. Select Connect.

4. Specify a valid username and password in the Log On To Windows dialog box.

5. Wait for the Terminal Services window, select Start | Programs, and then select the application you want to use.

Two options are available for ending a terminal session from the remote client. You can either disconnect a session or log off from a session.

If you choose to disconnect, it leaves your session active on the server. You can reconnect and resume the session at a later time, but you continue consuming the server's system resources when you disconnect.

You might also choose to end a terminal session by logging off a connection. When you do so, you should be aware that the active session on the server ends when you elect to log off. Any unsaved data will be lost. However, logging off frees up the server's system resources that were being used by the session.

USING TERMINAL SERVICES FOR REMOTE ADMINISTRATION

Terminal Services can be used not only to provide remote systems with access to applications that run on the server, but also to administer other systems remotely. However, Terminal Services requires a different configuration than that used to provide remote access to applications running on the server.

Configuring a Terminal Server for Remote Administration

When using Terminal Services for the purpose of remote administration, you'll want to configure your terminal servers accordingly. Follow these steps to improve the performance of a terminal server you will use for remote administration:

1. Select Start | Programs | Administrative Tools | Terminal Services Configuration.

2. Highlight Connections, right-click RDP-Tcp in the right pane, and select Properties.

3. On the Sessions tab, set disconnected sessions to end after five minutes.

4. Set idle sessions to disconnect after five minutes.

5. Select Override User Settings and select End Session When Session Limit Is Reached Or Connection Is Broken.

6. Select the Disable Wallpaper option on the Environment tab, as shown in Figure 17.6.

There's also a registry change to be made. Microsoft recommends that when using Terminal Services for remote administration, administrators change the HKEY_LOCAL_MACHINE\System\CurrentControlSet\Control\Terminal Server entry to 0 to keep memory available for other applications, unless you're

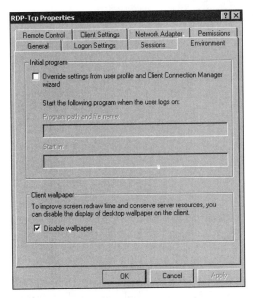

Figure 17.6   Choosing to disable wallpaper saves system resources on the terminal server.

17

also hosting several simultaneous terminal sessions. A value of 1 reserves memory for multiple terminal sessions, which typically isn't needed when performing remote administration. An alternative is to select the remote administration option when installing Terminal Services.

Tightening Security Settings for Remote Administration

You'll also want to ensure you take the following steps to tighten security settings when using Terminal Services for remote administration:

1. Select Start | Programs | Administrative Tools | Terminal Services Configuration.

2. Highlight Connections in the left pane, right-click RDP-Tcp in the right pane, and select Properties.

3. On the General tab, change the encryption level to high. This setting prompts all communication between the terminal server and remote client to be encrypted using the strongest encryption.

4. On the Permissions tab, restrict permission to only the users who must have access to the connection.

5. Minimize the number of connections the connection will support on the Network Adapter tab, as shown in Figure 17.7.

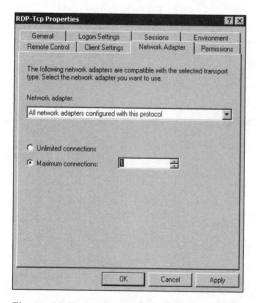

Figure 17.7 You can minimize the likelihood of security failures by minimizing the number of connections a terminal server will support on the Network Adapter tab.

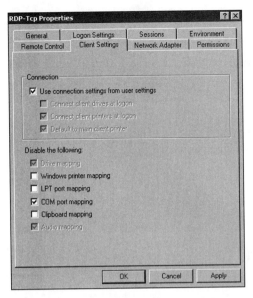

Figure 17.8   Disable Windows Printer Mapping, LPT Port Mapping, and Clipboard Mapping to prevent sensitive server data from being left behind on a remote system or device by the remote administration process.

6. Disable Windows Printer Mapping, LPT Port Mapping, and Clipboard Mapping on the Client Settings tab, as shown in Figure 17.8. Doing so prevents sensitive server data from being left behind on the client.

CHAPTER SUMMARY

By installing Terminal Services on a Windows 2000 Server, you create a multiuser environment enabling users to run applications you've installed on the server, regardless of the power of the machine from which they are connecting. Three components work together to enable Terminal Services' benefits and extend remote use of server-based applications:

➤ *Terminal Services server*—A Windows 2000 Server running Terminal Services

➤ *Remote Desktop Protocol (RDP)*—An Application layer protocol

➤ *Client*—A local desktop computer or device

As with any deployment, all Windows 2000 Terminal Services installations should be planned properly. You should consider four factors when preparing a Terminal Services deployment:

➤ Examine which client applications you want to support.

17

➤ Determine the minimum hardware requirements for the remote client devices.

➤ Research the required configuration for your Terminal Services server.

➤ Obtain the necessary licenses required for your Terminal Services installation.

Six operating systems are supported by three Terminal Services platforms. The operating systems Terminal Services supports are:

➤ Windows 2000

➤ Windows NT

➤ Windows 9x

➤ Windows For Workgroups 3.11

➤ Windows CE 3

➤ Windows-based Terminals

The three Terminal Services platforms are:

➤ A 32-bit platform for use with Windows 2000, Windows NT, and Windows 9x

➤ A 32-bit platform for use with Alpha-based systems

➤ A 16-bit version for use with Windows for Workgroups

Two factors should be considered when calculating the system requirements for a Terminal Services server. They are:

➤ User characteristics

➤ Server system configurations

The use of Terminal Services raises a few licensing issues, but licensing is not complicated. Just ensure you possess the following three licenses:

➤ Windows 2000 Server license for the server hosting Terminal Services (the Per Seat licensing mode is usually used when deploying Terminal Services)

➤ Windows 2000 Server Client Access License (CAL) for each client that accesses the server hosting Terminal Services

➤ Windows 2000 Terminal Services CAL for each remote computer or device that connects to the server hosting Terminal Services

Windows 2000 Terminal Services can be installed when you install Windows 2000 Server. To do so, select Terminal Services using the Windows Components Wizard. You can also install Terminal Services after Windows 2000 Server installation is completed. Terminal Services Licensing must also be installed.

The Terminal Services installation adds several new Administration Tools:

➤ *Terminal Services Client Creator*—Permits the creation of boot floppies for Terminal Services clients.

➤ *Terminal Services Configuration*—Enables you to manage Terminal Services protocol configuration and server settings. Only one RDP connection can be configured per NIC.

➤ *Terminal Services Licensing*—Enables you to manage Terminal Services CALs.

➤ *Terminal Services Manager*—Enables you to manage and monitor connection sessions and processes on the Terminal Services server.

Users must be given appropriate access permissions to connect to a Terminal Services server. You can use Active Directory Users and Computers to configure Terminal Services session settings.

Two methods are available for installing applications on a Terminal Services server, or terminal server. They are the **Change user** command at the command prompt or the Add/Remove Programs applet found in the Control Panel. The Add/Remove Programs applet is recommended, because it provides a GUI for the **Change user** command.

The Terminal Services Manager Administrative Tool is used to manage terminal services sessions. Terminal Services Manager displays the available terminal servers on a network, which connections are active, which protocols are in use, and which users are connected.

Two methods are available for installing Terminal Services on a client machine. One method of installing Terminal Services Client involves using Terminal Services Client Creator to create installation disks. The second option is to use a shared folder to make the installation files available to the remote system or device.

After Terminal Services is installed and configured on a server, the Terminal Services Client is installed, and permissions are configured for a user on a remote system, you're ready to create a terminal session.

Users create a connection using their remote device by creating a Terminal Services connection. Although they'll be presented with a GUI resembling Windows 2000, the fact that the application is really running on the server, and not the client, won't be apparent.

17

Terminal Services can also be used to remotely administer other systems. However, administrators will want to make several changes to ensure maximum performance and security.

REVIEW QUESTIONS

1. Which of the following protocols support Terminal Services communication? [Check all correct answers]

   a. RTP

   b. RDP

   c. RARP

   d. TCP/IP

2. Which components constitute a Terminal Services environment? [Check all correct answers]

   a. A client machine

   b. Active Directory services

   c. Remote Desk Protocol

   d. A Terminal Services server

3. Which of the following should you review when preparing a Terminal Services installation? [Check all correct answers]

   a. Client applications

   b. Domain controller configuration

   c. Standalone server configuration

   d. Terminal Services license requirements

4. If an application doesn't run on Windows 2000, it might still run using Terminal Services.

   a. True

   b. False

5. Bill has four remote systems he intends to connect to his Terminal Services server. Three are Windows 98 machines, and one is a Windows For Workgroups system. Which Terminal Services Clients will he need to install? [Check all correct answers]

   a. The 16-bit Windows Terminal Services Client

   b. The 32-bit Windows x86 Terminal Services Client

   c. The 16-bit and 32-bit x86 Terminal Services Clients

   d. The Multiplatform Terminal Services Client

6. Which types of users should be considered when evaluating the demands a Terminal Services server must support?

   a. Task-based users, typical users, and advanced users

   b. Task-based users, power users, and advanced users

   c. Task-based users, typical users, power users, and advanced users

   d. Typical users and advanced users

7. Barbara is preparing to install a new Terminal Services server on her bank's Windows mixed-mode network. She intends to support four typical users. How many additional MB of RAM should she add to the Terminal Services server?

   a. 50 to 100

   b. 101 to 150

   c. 151 to 200

   d. 201 to 250

8. Frank and Dave are preparing a new Terminal Services server. Performance will be important, because many users will access applications on the terminal server. They are confused as to the best way to configure the server so that it performs as quickly as possible. How should they configure the terminal server? [Check all correct answers]

   a. They should use FAT32 for quicker read times.

   b. They should use NTFS for security purposes.

   c. They should use SCSI drives.

   d. They should set Terminal Services to store desktop elements on the local cache.

9. Which licenses are required when a remote client connects to an application on a terminal server? [Check all correct answers]

   a. Windows 2000 Server license

   b. Windows 2000 CAL

   c. Windows 2000 Terminal Services license

   d. Windows 2000 Terminal Services CAL

17

10. Terminal Services can be installed using which of the following methods? [Check all correct answers]

    a. Network Connection Wizard

    b. Terminal Services Installation Wizard

    c. Windows 2000 Setup

    d. The Add/Remove Programs applet

11. Alison needs to configure a network adapter to accept a connection for a new user for which she just obtained a license. Which Administrative Tool should she use?

    a. Terminal Services Client Creator

    b. Terminal Services Configuration

    c. Terminal Services Licensing

    d. Terminal Services Manager

12. Greg is preparing to create a Terminal Services Client installation disk for a user's Windows 98 machine. How many floppies disks will he require?

    a. 1

    b. 2

    c. 3

    d. 4

13. If Elliot discovers the floppy drive is malfunctioning on his machine, what other options exist for installing Terminal Services Client?

    a. He could take the Windows 2000 Server CD-ROM to the client machine and copy the needed setup files.

    b. He could share out the *systemroot*\System32\Clients\Tsclient folder on the network.

    c. He could use a Windows NT Server to create the require diskette.

    d. No other options exist; Elliot would have to repair the server's A: drive to install the Terminal Services Client.

14. Virginia has been using five applications on her network's terminal server, and she's now heading out to a long luncheon meeting. What should she do before leaving the office?

    a. Nothing, just turn off the light

    b. Disconnect from her session

    c. Log off her session

    d. Shut down her machine

15. Jake is stepping away from his Terminal Services session in which he's been running a query against a large SQL database. Before he steps away, what should he do first?

    a. Save the changes and disconnect his session

    b. Save his changes and log off his session

    c. Disconnect his session

    d. Log off his session

16. Theresa must install an office suite on her Terminal Services server for several users to run simultaneously. Which installation options can she use? [Check all correct answers]

    a. Use the office suite's setup program

    b. Make an Application Installation Disk

    c. Use the Add/Remove Programs applet

    d. Use the **Change** command

17. Lauren installed Microsoft Office on her Terminal Services server, and she wants to modify the installation to best support multiple users. How should she proceed?

    a. She should create an application compatibility script and run it from a command prompt.

    b. She should select the application compatibility script supplied by Microsoft.

    c. She should create a SysDiff file.

    d. She should use the Application Compatibility Wizard.

18. Scott located the application compatibility script for the software he's just installed on his Terminal Services server. He verified that he's installing the script to the correct directory path, and he removed the remarks from the lines corresponding to the software he's just installed. What must he do before the script will execute? [Check all correct answers]

    a. Copy the User.cmd file to the *systemroot*\System32 folder of the Terminal Services server

    b. Copy the User.cmd file to the systemroot\System32 folder of the Terminal Services client

    c. Run the Uscron.cmd.script from the command prompt on the Terminal Services server

    d. Run the Uscron.cmd script from the command prompt on the Terminal Services client

19. Carmella is configuring her Terminal Services server to operate as a remote administration system. How long should she set idle sessions to last before they are automatically disconnected?

    a. 1 minute

    b. 5 minutes

    c. 10 minutes

    d. 1 hour

17

20. Which mappings should Nick disable when using his Terminal Services server for remote administration? [Check all correct answers]

   a. Drive Mapping

   b. Windows Printer Mapping

   c. COM Port Mapping

   d. Clipboard Mapping

REAL-WORLD PROJECTS

The morning has been quiet until our consultant, Andy Palmer, receives a call from a distraught client. Seven new employees have just been hired at the publishing company across town, and the new machines they are to use haven't been ordered.

In order to be productive, these employees need access to an office suite application, but the only computers the firm has available are Windows 95 units. The company knows the machines won't be sufficiently powerful in the long run, but the systems are good enough for at least another year of service.

Andy tells the client not to worry, and he will swing by to install Terminal Services on one of the firm's standalone servers, install the office suite on the server, create Terminal Service Client disks, and install Terminal Services Clients on the Windows machines.

Project 17.1

To install Terminal Services on a standalone machine, complete the following steps:

1. Andy sits down at the company's standalone server, named AXIS, and checks its configuration to ensure it can support seven new employees via Terminal Services. It has a fast processor and plenty of RAM.

2. Next, he selects Start|Settings|Control Panel.

3. From Control Panel, he selects Add/Remove Programs, then Add/Remove Windows Components.

4. Andy then fills in the two checkboxes for Terminal Services and Terminal Services Licensing, as shown in Figure 17.9.

5. Next, Andy specifies the mode in which Terminal Services should operate. Because the server is to provide access to an office suite for users, he selects Application Server Mode, as shown in Figure 17.10.

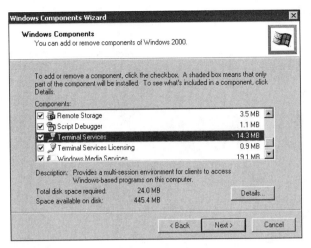

Figure 17.9 You must select Terminal Services and Terminal Services Licensing from within Add/Remove Components.

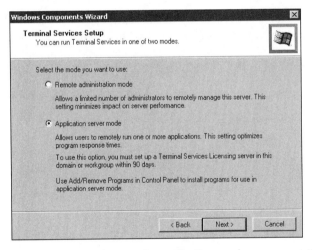

Figure 17.10 You must specify the mode you want the server to use.

6. Andy then selects default permissions for applications compatibility. As shown in Figure 17.11, he chooses Terminal Server 4 permissions, because the system in use is a hybrid network. He then selects Next.

7. Andy reviews the warning Terminal Services Setup provided informing him that the current office suite will need to be installed. Then, he chooses Next.

8. Following the client's instruction, Andy specifies that the server act as a license server to provide Terminal Services CALs for the domain.

17

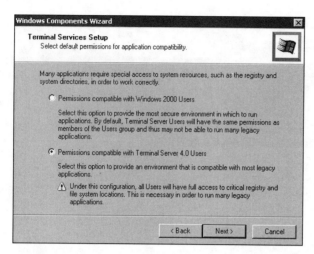

Figure 17.11 When installing Terminal Services, you must specify whether the server should use Windows 2000 or Terminal Server 4 permissions.

9. Next, he specifies the location of the directory he wants to use for the licensing server database, as shown in Figure 17.12. He then clicks Next.

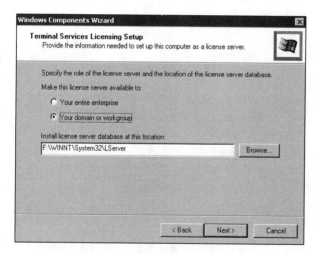

Figure 17.12 When installing Terminal Services Licensing, the setup program asks the installer to specify the role of the server and the location of the license server database.

10. After Windows 2000 updated the system files, a dialog box appears indicating the Terminal Services installation has completed. Andy finishes the installation by selecting Finish, as shown in Figure 17.13.

11. He confirms that he wants to restart the server when he is prompted to do so.

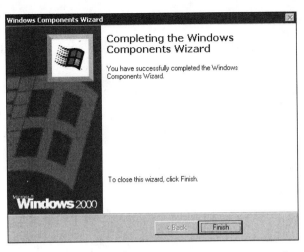

Figure 17.13   The Windows Components Wizard verifies the components have been properly installed.

Project 17.2
To install applications on a Terminal Services server, complete the following steps:

1. After selecting Add/Remove Programs, Andy selects All Users Begin With Common Application Settings to trigger the installation for all users.

2. Next, he specifies the settings the installation wizard prompts him to provide for the respective application he has installed.

3. Because Windows 2000 cannot find the appropriate setup program, Andy uses the wizard's Browse button to navigate to the application's installation program, from where he executes the Setup.exe program.

4. When the application's installation process completes, Andy clicks on the After Installation dialog box, selects Next, clicks Finish, and then reboots.

5. Andy then locates the Windows NT command script file for his office suite application in the *systemroot*\Application Compatibility Scripts\Install folder.

6. He reviews the file in a text editor to ensure he has the correct root drive set.

7. Andy runs the script from the command prompt.

8. Andy verifies whether a logon script is included in the *systemroot*\ Application Compatibility Scripts\Install folder.

9. Andy opens *systemroot*\Application Compatibility Scripts\Install\ User.cmd in a text editor.

17

10. He adds a call for each logon script he plans to use.

11. Andy removes the remark command from the lines corresponding to the applications he has installed.

12. Andy copies the User.cmd file to the *systemroot*\System32 folder.

13. Then he runs the Uscron.cmd file from the command prompt.

Project 17.3

To create Terminal Services Client installation disks, complete the following steps:

Andy then prepares to create Terminal Services Client installation disks, as follows:

1. Andy selects Start | Programs | Administrative Tools | Terminal Services Client Creator.

2. He selects Terminal Services For 32-bit x86 Windows, as shown in Figure 17.14. He verifies that the Destination Drive option displays the server's floppy drive, and selects OK.

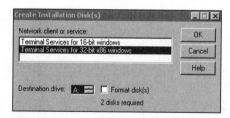

Figure 17.14   You must select the Terminal Services Client Installation disk set you want to create.

3. When prompted to load DISK1 in the A: drive, Andy does so, and selects OK.

4. Andy waits while the disk is created, following the progress displayed in the dialog box shown in Figure 17.15.

Figure 17.15   The Terminal Services Client Creator tracks the disk creation process.

5. The installation program then prompts Andy to load the second disk, as shown in Figure 17.16.

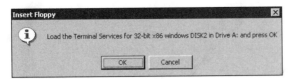

Insert Floppy ☒

ⓘ Load the Terminal Services for 32-bit x86 windows DISK2 in Drive A: and press OK

OK   Cancel

Figure 17.16   The Terminal Services Client Creator prompts the installer to load the floppy disks.

6. Andy clicks OK and again watches as the installation files are transferred to the disk, as shown in Figure 17.17.

Network Client Administrator ☒

ⓘ 2 floppies were created and 21 files have been successfully copied. Press OK to continue.

OK

Figure 17.17   The installation program tracks the Terminal Services Client files as they are transferred to the disk.

7. The Network Client Administrator confirms the number of files that are transferred. Andy selects OK to finish the disk creation process.

Project 17.4
To install Terminal Services Client, comlete the following stpes:

Terminal Services Client installation disks in hand, Andy walks down the hall to the client machines needing access to the office application suite now installed on the AXIS server. Then he installs the Terminal Services Client using the following steps:

1. Andy inserts the Terminal Services Client DISK1 in the floppy drive of the first client. He opens Windows Explorer, navigates to the Setup.exe program, and double-clicks it.

2. The Terminal Services Client Setup opens, as shown in Figure 17.18.

3. He then selects Continue to proceed. The wizard prompts Andy for name and organization information, as shown in Figure 17.19. He enters the appropriate information, selects OK to proceed, and then clicks OK again to confirm that the information he entered is correct.

4. Setup searches for installed components and then prompts Andy to accept the license agreement, which he does by clicking I Agree.

17

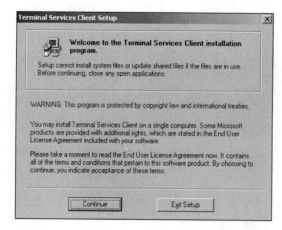

Figure 17.18 Andy used the Terminal Services Client Setup Wizard to install the Terminal Services Client.

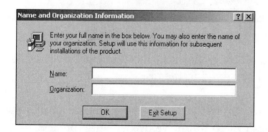

Figure 17.19 Name and organization information must be provided when installing Terminal Services Client.

5. Terminal Services Client Setup then prompts Andy to confirm the installation location. Andy confirms the location and continues by selecting the large button, as shown in Figure 17.20.

Figure 17.20 Before beginning the Terminal Services Client installation, the installer can change the installation directory.

6. Next, Andy is prompted to specify whether all Terminal Services users on the computer are to receive the same initial settings, as shown in Figure 17.21. Andy selects Yes to proceed. Terminal Services Client Setup tracks the files as they are transferred, as shown in Figure 17.22.

Figure 17.21   Terminal Services Client Setup prompts you to specify whether all Terminal Services users receive the same initial settings.

Figure 17.22   File transfer is tracked by Terminal Services Client Setup.

7. Andy is then prompted to install DISK2, as shown in Figure 17.23. After inserting DISK2 and selecting OK, the process continues.

Figure 17.23   Setup prompts the installer to insert the second disk.

8. Andy then receives a confirmation message that Terminal Services Client Setup has completed successfully, as shown in Figure 17.24.

17

Figure 17.24   Terminal Services Client Setup confirms the successful completion of the installation.

CHAPTER EIGHTEEN

PREVENTING AND PREPARING FOR DISASTER RECOVERY

After completing this chapter, you will be able to:

✓ Create a RAID 5 volume

✓ Understand the recovery console

✓ Use the Windows 2000 Backup utility

✓ Understand advanced startup options

✓ Recover from a failed RAID 5 and RAID 1 volume

✓ Describe Windows 2000's protection features

✓ Restore the Active Directory by performing an authoritative restore

A t some time or another, every network professional comes face to face with a failed network server. How devastating a disaster becomes depends on how well the network professional is prepared for the inevitable moment. This chapter explains the tools and processes that you can use to prevent and quickly recover from computer disasters. For this chapter's purposes, a *computer disaster* is defined as any problem that prevents a computer from booting.

Specifically, this chapter describes how to implement stripe sets with parity (better known as *RAID 5*) in order to prevent data loss, and how to recover a RAID 5 and RAID 1 volume if one of the disks in an array is lost. This chapter discusses how to use Windows 2000's Backup utility, which includes a scheduler for scheduling backups to occur automatically. Finally, this chapter discusses the new disaster recovery features included with Windows 2000, including advanced startup options, the recovery console, and the intricacies of restoring the Windows 2000 Active Directory.

Computer failures are caused by a number events, from common hard drive failures to not-so-common lightning strikes and fires to highly absurd reasons— such as small furry animals nesting inside the warm servers. Whatever the reason for a computer failure, proper planning and execution can make the difference between a few hours and a few days of downtime, as well as prevent temporarily missing data from becoming data that is lost forever. Therefore, the first step in managing a disaster starts long before a problem occurs; the first step is to plan for the day disaster strikes.

PLANNING FOR DISASTERS

Inevitably, at some point, every system breaks. Hard drives are the most likely culprit, because they are the most used mechanical component in computers. Whatever the reason, how fast, how well, and how organized your efforts are in correcting the problem will determine the extent of the disaster.

All companies that rely on computer systems today (and what company doesn't?) should have a comprehensive disaster recovery plan. This plan should include the policies and processes currently in place in order to prevent failures. One of the main purposes of a plan is to have a tangible resource to turn to when a network seems to be falling apart. If the entire network staff realizes that a disaster-recovery plan is in place—that a specific procedure to follow in times of crisis exists—they are more likely to not panic when the system goes awry.

What to Include in a Disaster-Recovery Plan

Each disaster-recovery plan will contain different elements due to the nature of networks. Plus, many times, what needs to be done depends on what's "broken." Thus, your disaster plan's documentation must attempt to accommodate all foreseeable failures for your network. In order to create the plan, you must ask yourself, "If *disasterA* happens, what would I need to correct the problem?" and then move on to address *disasterB*. In addition to addressing specific disaster-recovery tactics, all disaster plans should include a few key elements, including:

➤ Network map

➤ Phone numbers

➤ Vendor and equipment contact information

➤ Network baseline information

➤ Purchasing information

➤ Change management process

➤ Backup information

The next few sections discuss each of the preceding elements. Keep in mind that the information presented here is by no means all-inclusive. Each network environment is different in one way or another from every other network. Furthermore, you will find that a disaster recovery plan is a dynamic document that is always changing as the network and network personnel change.

Tip: One point that seems obvious, but is many times overlooked, is that you should not rely on a server to store your disaster recovery documentation. The disaster recovery plan should always exist on paper as well as in electronic formats.

Network Map

The first part of creating a disaster plan should be a well-documented diagram of the network. The network map should include all devices on the network as well as corresponding information about each device. Information such as each computer, switch, router, and any other devices possessing IP or IPX addresses should be included in the map. The location of each network object and who is the responsible party for each device can also come in handy.

The next part of a network map entails compiling a list of servers and each server's specific function. In addition, you might want to document the passwords to each server, router, and so forth. You can publish the passwords, or you can document where passwords to network resources can be found. Having all passwords to network devices documented in a secure location is a good idea. After all, if you are the only one who knows the passwords, you can expect to receive a few phone calls while you are on vacation!

18

Finally, make sure that your network map includes up-to-date configuration information for all servers, routers, switches, and so on. For example, if server1 contains a RAID 5 volume, the drive numbers included in the array should be included. In addition, SCSI device numbers, amount of memory, type speed, number of processors, and number of drives are all examples of information that is critical in a disaster situation and should be stored with your network map.

Phone Numbers

Obviously, the phone numbers of the people to contact in case of emergencies should be published in a disaster document. Document the person or persons who are vendor-specific experts for all types of network equipment and software. For example, calling the Windows 2000 MCSE on staff might not be very useful if the problem is with a failed Cisco router.

Vendor and Equipment Contact Information

Each piece of equipment on the network should be listed in the disaster plan as well as who installed the device, when the equipment was bought and installed, where the equipment was purchased, and any warranty information. Also, remember to include the phone numbers of each manufacturer's and vendor's customer service department.

Network Baseline Information

Creating and documenting a baseline is a comprehensive task; however, the recovery plan should include a baseline of network and server performance. A baseline can be used to help you troubleshoot problems, because you can compare current network and server performance to optimal performance statistics.

Keep in mind that a network baseline is useless if it has not been kept up to date. If the baseline was established and created when there were only three network segments and 200 users and those numbers have now tripled, the baseline will be of no value; this out-of-date baseline will contain utilization information that is no longer relevant to the existing network infrastructure.

Purchasing Information

In large companies, getting approval for purchasing needed equipment can sometimes be a challenge, to say the least. Within your disaster-recovery plan, you should document the proper process for acquiring permission to obtain needed hardware or software. Many times, processes are in place for emergency requisitions that can be used when a network encounters problems.

If your company does not have a process in place for quickly approving emergency equipment, you should initiate one. This might seem difficult at first, until you ask the accounting department how long they could operate if the accounting server failed. You might find it interesting, sometimes (and sometimes not), to see how fast red tape gets cut when a network goes down.

Change Management Process

Few administrators are going to take the time to document all the changes that they are making during an emergency situation; however, in most large companies, a change management process should be in place that documents not only how the change process is approved and managed, but what changes have been made recently as well. Understanding the changes that have occurred on a network is invaluable when problems suddenly arise from what was a perfectly good network just an hour before.

The change management documentation, including the change logs, should always be mentioned in a disaster plan. Your documentation should include location information that details the existence of a change log and where it can be located.

Backup Information

The single most important line of defense in avoiding data loss is a daily backup. All the prevention techniques in the world are simply that—prevention techniques. Prevention means working to prevent an event from happening; after a disaster occurs, prevention is a moot point. Backups are your last line of defense. When all the prevention has failed, you look to your backup tapes.

Documenting your backup procedures in your disaster plan is very important. Knowing what was backed up and when, as well as where the backup tapes are stored is a must. You cannot read the backup log file to find which tape contains a certain file if the backup server has crashed. Proper documentation ensures that you can find the proper tapes in an emergency.

Now that we have looked at how to prepare for a disaster, let's look at ways to prevent as well as recover from disasters using features included with Windows 2000. As mentioned earlier, Microsoft Windows 2000 includes both new and improved features for preventing and recovering from hardware and software failures. This arsenal of emergency tools includes fault-tolerant volumes, advanced startup options, the recovery console, and an improved Backup utility. Each of these new features is detailed in the following sections.

18

Fault Tolerance

Windows 2000 supports RAID 1 (disk mirroring) and RAID 5 (disk striping with parity for preventing data loss from hard drive failures). RAID, which stands for Redundant Array of Inexpensive Disks, is a frequently used technology that prevents data loss by creating multiple copies of data. Each RAID level details a different way of protecting data.

Both RAID 1 and RAID 2 fault-tolerant volumes can be created, viewed, and modified using Windows 2000's Computer Management Administrative Tool. To view a fault-tolerant volume, follow these steps:

1. Within the Computer Management Administrative Tool, select the Storage node and then select Disk Manager.

2. After Disk Manager starts, you can view the current status of all drives and volumes.

Note: *In order to create fault-tolerant volumes, each drive must be configured as a dynamic drive. Basic versus dynamic drives are discussed in Chapter 12.*

RAID 1 Volumes

RAID 1, generally known as *disk mirroring*, can be divided into two subcategories—disk mirroring and disk duplexing. Disk mirroring and disk duplexing perform the same basic functions in order to protect magnetic media; however, they represent two separate implementations of the same technology:

➤ *Disk mirroring*—Disk mirroring is accomplished with two identical volumes on two disks. One disk is called the *primary*, and the other is called the *secondary*. Both drives are represented by one drive letter, such as D:\. Whenever data is written to the D:\ drive, for example, the same data is written to both volumes simultaneously. Because the data is written to two volumes, you always have an exact copy of the data.

One major drawback of disk mirroring is that you have to use two volumes to save data that could be stored on just one volume. Therefore, the cost of using RAID 1 is that you lose 50 percent of your total storage capacity. RAID 1 disk mirroring specifies that the same drive controller control both drives that contain the volumes.

➤ *Disk duplexing*—Disk duplexing uses the same technology as disk mirroring. The only difference is that disk duplexing requires a separate disk controller to control each hard drive that contains a mirrored volume. This setup avoids a single point of failure.

The basic tenet of RAID 1 is that if one disk fails, you always have a redundant copy. RAID is not meant to replace backups. For instance, suppose a fire destroys the server—RAID will do nothing to prevent or recover from a fire or natural disaster. To prevent data loss in situations such as fires or natural disasters, only proper backups with off-site tape storage can save your data.

Creating a RAID 1 Volume

As mentioned earlier, you can create fault-tolerant volumes using the Disk Manager utility within the Computer Management Administrative Tool. To create a fault-tolerant volume, you must use the Create Volume Wizard. To create a RAID 1 volume, follow these steps:

1. On the Administrative Tools menu, start the Computer Management application.

2. In the left portion of the Computer Management window—the console tree—expand the Storage node, and then select the Disk Management folder, as shown in Figure 18.1.

3. Right-click in a free area, and select Create Volume.

4. Click Next. On the Select Volume Type screen, select Mirrored Volume and click Next.

5. Follow the on-screen wizard's instructions.

Repairing a Failed Mirrored Volume

If one of the drives containing a mirrored partition fails, you have a complete redundant copy on the other disk. In cases such as this, RAID 1 performs its job and prevents data loss. However, it is extremely important that you repair or replace the failed drive immediately. You cannot recover data from a RAID array if more than one drive fails, regardless of the level of RAID you have implemented. If more than one drive fails, you have to recover the data from your backup media.

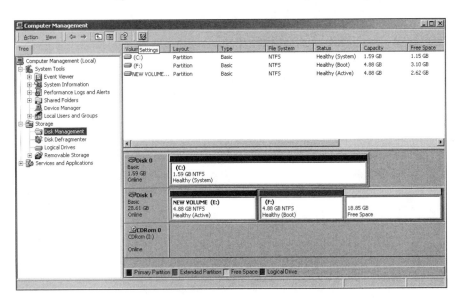

Figure 18.1 The Disk Management folder.

When viewing the status of a failed mirrored volume, you might encounter one of three possible status messages—missing, offline, or errors. Regardless of which status message you receive, the initial process for repairing the volume is the same. To recover a missing disk, offline disk, or a disk that indicates errors, follow these steps:

1. Ensure that the disk is properly connected to the ribbon cable and that it is receiving power.

2. Right-click the disk in question, and select Reactivate Disk.

3. The status of the disk should return to Healthy. If the disk does not return to a healthy status, you should immediately replace the drive.

Replacing a Partition in a Mirrored Volume

If a disk cannot be repaired, you need to replace it. To remove and replace a partition from a mirrored volume, follow these steps:

1. Right-click the failed disk, and select Remove Mirror.

2. The Remove Mirror dialog box appears. Select the failed disk, and select Remove Mirror. Click Yes to confirm your choice.

3. Replace the drive or select a new partition to be included in the mirror.

4. Right-click the volume, and select Add Mirror.

5. Select the second disk (the new disk or another partition), and click OK.

RAID 5 Volumes

RAID 5 volumes provide redundant data by striping files across from 3 through 32 disks and writing parity information to each disk as well. Like mirrored volumes, all partitions that make up a RAID 5 volume are addressed with a single drive letter. Unlike mirrored volumes, data saved to a drive letter in a RAID 5 system is divided equally among the partitions within the array and saved.

Before the data is written to each drive, Windows 2000 performs calculations in order to build the parity information. The parity information is stored on all partitions and can be used to re-create the data on any partition in the array. The calculation used to create the parity information is complex, but is based on a simple algebraic rule. Figure 18.2 illustrates the basic formula used to create parity information.

When a file is saved to a RAID 5 volume, all the bits that make up a file are added together to get a total bit count. As the file is written to each volume, the bits are added to get a per-volume bit count. The total bit count is written to each volume as well as that particular partition's volume bit count. Each volume's

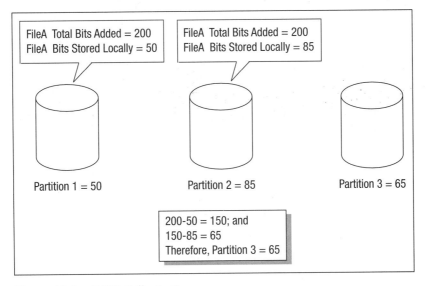

FileA Total Bits Added = 200
FileA Bits Stored Locally = 50

FileA Total Bits Added = 200
FileA Bits Stored Locally = 85

Partition 1 = 50

Partition 2 = 85

Partition 3 = 65

200-50 = 150; and
150-85 = 65
Therefore, Partition 3 = 65

Figure 18.2   RAID 5 illustration.

parity information includes the bit count that is stored on itself and the total bit count for the entire file. Using simple addition and subtraction, you can calculate the information that should be stored on any volume that might fail, as shown in Figure 18.2.

In Figure 18.2, the total bit count is 200. Volume 1 contains a volume bit count of 50, and Volume 2 has a volume count of 85. In this example, the file's total bit count is 200. Subtract the 50 bit count from Volume 1 and the 85 bit count from Volume 2 from the total bit count of 200, and all that remains is 65. Therefore, Volume 3 should have a bit count of 65. If any one volume fails, the operating system can regenerate that data in memory based on the parity information stored on all the other partitions. If more than one volume fails, all data is lost, because you cannot solve for two variables.

Creating a RAID 5 Volume

You can create a RAID 5 volume using the same Administrative Tool used to create a RAID 2 volume—the Computer Management Administrative Tool. RAID 5 volumes require a minimum of 3 partitions residing on separate drives and a maximum of 32 partitions.

18

To create a RAID 5 volume, follow these steps:

1. On the Administrative Tools menu, start the Computer Management application.

2. In the console tree, expand the Storage node, and then select the Disk Management folder, as shown earlier in Figure 18.1.

3. Right-click in a free area, then select Create Volume.

4. Click Next. On the Select Volume Type screen, select RAID 5 Volume. Then click Next.

5. Follow the on-screen wizard's instructions.

Once again, if any drive fails, you need to replace it immediately. Many times, when a volume fails in a RAID 5 array, users complain that the server has slowed down. The server seems to slow down because every time a user requests a file, the operating system must re-create the file in memory.

Recovering a RAID 5 Disk

Steps to recovering a missing disk, offline disk, or a disk that indicates errors are as follows:

1. Ensure that the disk is properly connected to the ribbon cable and that it is receiving power.

2. Right-click the disk in question, and select Reactivate Disk.

3. The status of the disk should return to Healthy. If the disk does not return to a healthy status, you should immediately replace the drive.

Replacing a Failed RAID 5 Volume

To replace a failed RAID 5 volume, perform the following steps:

1. Within Disk Manager, right-click the failed volume, and select Repair Volume.

2. After the Repair RAID 5 volume appears, select the volume that will replace the failed volume, and click OK.

Note: If a disk or volume continuously reports a status of Online (Errors), it might be going bad. You should back up all data on the disk and RAID volume and replace the drive.

RAID Drawbacks

RAID 1 and RAID 5 are both technologies that prevent data loss by creating redundant copies of the data in one form or another. Therefore, both RAID 1 and RAID 5 have some drawbacks.

As mentioned, RAID 1 simply writes the same data twice to two separate volumes. Because all data stored on a RAID 1 volume is stored twice, you lose half your total storage capacity. For example, if you have two drives that both contain a 5GB volume, then you have a total of 10GB of storage. However, if you mirror the drives together, you have only 5GB of total storage capacity. You will always lose half of your total storage resources when the resources are used for RAID 1 mirrored or duplexed volumes.

RAID 5 must have a minimum of 3 volumes and a maximum of 32 volumes, all of equal size. The same data is not stored on multiple volumes; instead, parity information is calculated for each file and stored on all volumes. The amount of storage space used to store parity information is always equal to the size of one volume. For example, if you create a RAID 5 volume consisting of 3 volumes that are all 5GB each, your total storage capacity will be only 10GB. The remaining 5GB will be used to store parity information. In a scenario such as this, you lose one-third of your total storage capacity. In contrast, if you increase the RAID 5 volume to include 4 volumes of 5GB each, you would be losing only one quarter of your total storage capacity. Basically, the more volumes you add to a RAID 5 array, the higher the total disk storage utilization becomes, unlike RAID 1. For this reason, RAID 5 is said to be a more efficient fault-tolerant system then RAID 1.

. . . .

Tip: You should know that RAID arrays can be created only on Windows 2000 volumes, not partitions. In order to create volumes, you must first upgrade your drives to dynamic drives. Differences between basic and dynamic disks, as well as the differences between volumes and partitions, are discussed in Chapter 12.

. . . .

STARTUP OPTIONS

Startup options are not a new feature to Windows 2000. Advanced startup options are available in Windows 95 and Windows 98; however, Windows NT 4 is limited to starting the system in VGA mode only. In order to troubleshoot boot issues for NT, you have to boot from the Emergency Repair Disk (ERD), or modify the boot.ini and add switches, such as the **/SOS** or **/NOSERIAL-MICE**. Realizing these shortcomings, Microsoft has added new options that are specific to Windows 2000.

Understanding Advanced Startup Options

Windows 2000 provides advanced startup options that can be used to troubleshoot server-related issues. Startup options include tools that can be used to troubleshoot and repair boot failures, connect the system to a debugger, and repair the Active Directory. By pressing F8 during the operating system selection phase of bootup, you can access the advanced startup options. The following text describes each of the startup options that are available for Windows 2000.

18

Safe Mode

When Windows 2000 starts in Safe Mode, it creates a log file called Ntbtlog.txt. Safe Mode also loads only the basic drivers needed to start the system. The only drivers that get loaded are the keyboard, mouse, mass storage devices, and a standard video driver. Only the essential system services are started as well.

Systems started in Safe Mode display the text "Safe Mode" in all four corners of the screen. In Safe Mode, the NETLOGON service does not start; therefore, users will not be able to log in.

Safe Mode With Command Prompt

Safe Mode With Command Prompt starts just as Safe Mode does, except the graphical user interface (GUI) is not loaded. The system loads only essential drivers needed and displays a command prompt when booting is completed. In Safe Mode, the NETLOGON service does not start; therefore, users will not be able to log in.

Safe Mode With Networking

Safe Mode With Networking, much like Safe Mode, loads only the basic drivers needed to start the system. In addition, Safe Mode With Networking loads network card drivers and services to enable the network. This option creates a log file named Ntbtlog.txt.

Enable Boot Logging

The Enable Boot Logging option enables the logging of all drivers as they load or fail to load during bootup. This file is named Ntbtlog.txt and is located in the system root folder (C:\WINNT). Other than logging information regarding the loading of device drivers, the system boots normally.

Enable VGA Mode

The Enable VGA Mode option boots the system as normal; however, a basic standard video driver is loaded instead of the installed video driver. This is a useful option if the video settings were changed and now the display is unreadable or if the video card has been replaced with another model.

Last Known Good Configuration

The Last Known Good Configuration option, as in Windows NT 4, loads the registry that is held in the repair directory instead of the current registry. Each time someone logs into a Windows 2000 Server, it is considered a good boot, and the registry is copied to the repair directory. If an incorrect or bad driver is loaded and the system is unable to restart, you can load the Last Known Good Configuration to prevent the problematic device driver from loading.

· · · · · · · · · · · · · ·

Tip: If you suspect that there is a problem with the server, DO NOT log into the server. If anyone logs into the server, the registry is considered to be good and is copied to the repair directory. If the registry is written to the repair directory, then there will be no good Last Known Good Configuration to fall back on.

· · · · · · · · · · · · · ·

Directory Services Restore Mode

The Directory Services Restore Mode option allows you to perform maintenance and restore the Active Directory. Directory Services Restore Mode can be used to restore the SYSVOL folder on each domain controller as well. Active Directory restoration is covered later in this chapter.

Debugging Mode

The Debugging Mode option allows an administrator to connect another machine to the problematic server to receive debugging information. A serial connection between both computers is required. Microsoft engineers can use debugging information to resolve server failures.

THE RECOVERY CONSOLE

Windows 2000 provides a recovery console that can be used to correct a variety of server-related issues. The recovery console is a command-line interface. The recovery and troubleshooting tasks that can be accomplished with the recovery console include:

➤ Reading from and writing to files and directories on the drives. This includes NTFS partitions and volumes.

➤ Starting and stopping network and domain controller services.

➤ Formatting and repartitioning hard drives.

Installing the Recovery Console

The recovery console is not installed during the operating system installation. Therefore, you must install the recovery console manually from the Windows 2000 CD. The installation is a straightforward process; however, after installation, you must restart the server.

To install the recovery console, follow these steps:

1. Insert the Windows 2000 CD.

2. Run the Winnt32.exe application with the **/cmdcons** switch from the i386 directory located on the CD. Windows 2000 installs the recovery console application and informs you that the system must be restarted.

3. Restart the server.

You can also access the recovery console on a system that has not yet installed the recovery console software. To access the recovery console when it has not yet been installed, you must boot from the Windows 2000 CD and select recovery console when prompted to repair the existing installation of Windows 2000.

18

Using the Recovery Console

After the recovery console is installed and the server restarted, you can access the console from the operating system selection screen during bootup. After you select the recovery console option, the system asks you which operating system you want to access, even if only one OS is installed on the computer. The recovery console then asks for the administrator's password. Users must know the administrator's password before they can access the recovery console.

The commands used within the recovery console are, in many ways, the same commands used in Microsoft's previous OS—DOS. The following list details the commands available within the recovery console:

➤ *chdir or cd*—Allows a user to display the current directory or specify a new directory path to change to.

➤ *chkdsk*—Runs a check on the disk specified and displays a report about any errors found.

➤ *cls*—Clears the screen.

➤ *copy*—Copies selected files or folders to a specified location.

➤ *delete or del*—Deletes selected files or folders.

➤ *dir*—Displays a list of files and subfolders within either the current folder or any folder specified.

➤ *disable*—Disables a device driver or service.

➤ *enable*—Enables a device driver or service.

➤ *exit*—Restarts the computer.

➤ *fdisk*—Enables a user to view, delete, or create partitions on hard drives.

➤ *fixboot*—Creates a new boot sector on the system partition.

➤ *fixmbr*—Enables a user to repair the master boot record on the boot sector partition.

➤ *format*—Formats the specified drive.

➤ *help*—Displays the list of commands that can be used in the recovery console.

➤ *logon*—Allows you to log onto a Windows 2000 installation.

➤ *map*—Displays a list of current drive mappings.

➤ *mkdir or md*—Creates a directory.

➤ *more*—Displays the contents of a text file.

➤ *rmdir* or *rd*—Removes a directory.

➤ *rename* or *ren*—Enables a user to rename a file.

➤ *systemroot*—Changes the directory to the systemroot of the Windows 2000 installation you a logged into.

➤ *type*—Dumps the contents of a text file to the display.

WINDOWS 2000 BACKUP UTILITY

Windows 2000 includes an enhanced Backup utility that can be used to protect data in cases of mechanical or software failures. Unlike the version of Backup included in Windows NT 4, Windows 2000's Backup utility includes a scheduler and other advanced features not found in Windows NT. The Backup utility included with Windows 2000 also includes a backup wizard to help make using the utility easier.

Backup Requirements

Before launching the Backup utility, a few requirements must be met. The following text outlines the steps that need to be performed to ensure that you can confidently back up files, folders, and system state data. Namely, you must:

➤ Ensure that all hardware that will be used during the backup process is included on Microsoft's Hardware Compatibility List (HCL).

➤ Ensure that the person performing the backup has the appropriate rights to all files and folders. The user account that is backing up the files must have the Backup Files And Folders user right or be a member of the backup operators group.

➤ Ensure that anyone restoring files and folders has the appropriate rights assigned to them or is a member of the backup operators or administrators group.

Planning for Backup

Before you begin backing up data, you should sit down and create your backup strategy. Your backup strategy should be created to meet your company's needs. Consider the following when creating your backup strategy:

➤ *What files need to be backed up?*—Files that are changed on a regular basis or files that you cannot do without should be backed up regularly. Files that rarely change should be backed up less regularly. For example, the system root directory rarely changes in a stable environment. The files contained in the system root might need to be backed up only once a week; however, user home directories should be backed up nightly. Temporary files should never be backed up.

18

➤ *Should you perform a network backup or have backups run independently on each server?*—Backups that run independently on each server will run faster and will not consume network bandwidth for the backup. However, backups that run over the network can run at night when network resources are not in contention with users. Additionally, if each server runs its own backup, each server will require its own backup hardware, which could be cost prohibitive.

Backup Types

You must consider the types of backups you should run and on which days each backup type is best. Determining the best type of backup depends largely on the amount of files that need to be saved, the amount of time the backup has to run, and the cost associated with the number of tapes, disks, or CDs that will be needed. Before addressing the various backup types, you must first understand the archive file property.

The archive file property, called the *archive bit* (shown in Figure 18.3), is used by the operating system and backup software utilities to determine if a file has been changed. When a file is created, its archive property is selected, as shown in the figure. When the file is backed up, the archive bit is normally cleared to indicate that the current iteration of the file has been backed up. If the file is then changed (or even opened and resaved), the archive bit is checked (sometimes referred to as *turned on*) to indicate that the file has changed and needs to be backed up again. The archive bit for a file can be viewed by right-clicking a file and selecting Properties | Advanced.

Now that you understand the purpose and function of the archive bit, you are more able to understand the different backup types. Basically, you can choose from among the following five backup types:

➤ *Normal*—The normal backup type backs up all files and folders that have been selected for backup. Normal backups clear the archive bit.

Figure 18.3 The file archive bit.

➤ *Copy*—The copy backup type is simply a file copy command. This backup type works just as if you manually copied all the selected files to another drive. The copy type will copy all selected files, but will not change the current settings of the archive bit.

➤ *Incremental*—The incremental backup type backs up only files that have the archive bit checked. If the archive bit is checked, it means that the file has been opened and saved. Incremental backups back up all files that have changed and clears the archive bit.

➤ *Differential*—The differential backup type backs up all files that have the archive bit checked. If the archive bit is checked, it means that the file has been opened and saved (changed). Differential backups back up all files that have changed; however, differential backups do not change the archive bit. This means that if a differential backup is run on Tuesday and a file called txtfileA has the archive bit checked, then it will be backed up during the backup process. Since the differential backup does not change the archive bit, the same file will be backed up on Wednesday because the archive bit will still be checked. Differential backups are cumulative.

➤ *Daily Copy*—A daily copy backup type backs up all selected files that have changed that day. Only files that have changed the same day that the daily copy runs are backed up. Daily does not change the archive bit.

Some backup types, such as incremental, use less tape, which costs less money. Because incremental backups back up only those files that have changed, restoring files takes longer than some of the other backup types. On the other hand, differential backups use more tape, because differential backups back up a file every day until a normal or incremental backup runs and changes the archive bit. However, restoring files from a differential backup takes less time than some other backup types. Choosing among backup types always involves a trade-off of time and money. The differences in backup types tend to confuse even the most seasoned network veterans. Therefore, let's look at a couple of examples.

Differential Example

Let's suppose that the Coriolis company runs a normal backup every Monday and differential backups on Tuesday through Friday each week. On Monday, all files are backed up, regardless of the status of the archive bit. Each differential backup backs up all files that have changed since Monday. Even a file that changes on Tuesday will be backed up on Thursday, because differential backups do not change the status of the archive bit. If a file is changed on Tuesday, it will be backed up on Tuesday, Wednesday, Thursday, and Friday. If a volume fails on Friday, you will need only Monday's tape and Thursday's tape to restore the entire volume. Thursday's tape is cumulative; it contains all files that have changed since Monday.

Incremental Example

In this example, suppose that the Coriolis company runs a normal backup every Monday and an incremental backup on Tuesday through Friday each week. On Monday, all files are backed up, regardless of the status of the archive bit. On Tuesday through Friday, only files that have changed are backed up, and the archive bit will be cleared to indicate that the file was backed up. So, if a file is changed on Tuesday, the file will be backed up and the archive bit will be cleared. Since the archive bit is cleared, the file will not be backed up again on Wednesday unless it is changed again. If a volume fails on Friday, you will need the Monday tape and the incremental tapes for Tuesday through Thursday to restore all files.

Creating Backup Jobs

The Backup utility can be used to back up files and folders, back up system state data (such as the directory), schedule backups, and restore files, folders, and system state data. Windows 2000 Backup can also be used to create an Emergency Repair Disk instead of the rdisk.exe application.

The Backup utility supports a wide array of backup media types, including:

➤ Magnetic tape

➤ Logical or physical drives

➤ Removable disks

➤ Recordable CD-ROM drives

Backup Job Options

Windows 2000 Backup can back up files or folders contained on FAT, FAT32, or NTFS drives. Backups can be created manually, or a wizard can be used if you are unfamiliar with the Backup software. When the Windows 2000 Backup software is started, you are presented with the screen shown in Figure 18.4.

From the Backup utility's startup window, you can select to start a wizard to back up data, restore data, or create an Emergency Repair Disk. Thankfully, Microsoft does not require you to use a wizard to create backup jobs. By selecting the Backup or Restore tab, you can manually create a backup or restore job. In order to create a backup job, you must specify the following:

➤ Drives, folders, and/or files that you want to back up.

➤ Location where you want the backed up files to be stored—either to a tape or file.

➤ Name of the backup file if not backing up on tape. If you are not backing up to a tape drive, you must specify the name of the backup file and the location where the file should be saved.

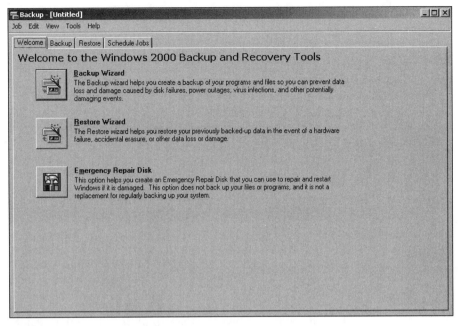

Figure 18.4   Windows 2000 backup.

➤ Backup type.

➤ Log type.

➤ Description of the backup job.

➤ Whether the backup job should append to a file or tape or overwrite an exiting file or tape.

➤ Compression type and verification.

As shown in Figure 18.5, a number of other options are available for you to choose from in the Options dialog box. To open the Options dialog box, click Tools | Options. The Options dialog box enables you to customize the Backup software to meet your needs and preferences. The Options dialog box contains five tabs—General, Restore, Backup Type, Backup Log, and Exclude Files:

➤ *General*—The General tab includes options that determine the behavior of the Windows 2000 Backup utility. The options include:

    ➤ *Compute Selection Information Before Backup And Restore Operations*—By selecting this option, you allow the utility to display file counts and a progression bar during the backup operation. If this option is not selected, the utility will not show a progression bar or the number of files backed up.

18

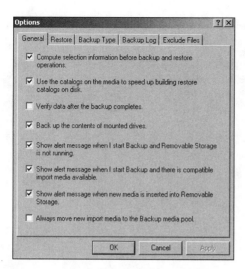

Figure 18.5 Backup and Restore Options.

➤ *Use The Catalogs On The Media To Speed Up Building Restore Catalogs On Disk*—This option allows the Backup utility to use the catalog that is already created on the hard drive instead of creating a new catalog from scratch.

➤ *Verify Data After The Backup Completes*—This option causes the Backup utility to verify all files after the backup is complete. The utility will actually compare all the files backed up to the original files on the drives.

➤ *Back Up The Contents Of Mounted Drives*—This option backs up the data that is on a mounted drive. By selecting this option, you allow the utility to back up the data that is on a mounted drive. If this option is not selected, only the path information for a mounted drive will be backed up.

➤ *Show Alert Message When I Start Backup And Removable Storage Is Not Running*—This option causes the utility to display a dialog box when you start the Backup utility and Removable Storage is not running. You should check this box if you normally back up data to a tape or other media that is managed by Removable Storage.

➤ *Show Alert Message When I Start Backup And There Is Compatible Import Media Available*—This option causes the utility to display a dialog box whenever you start a backup and new media is available in the Import media pool. If you normally back up data to a tape drive, you should check this box.

➤ *Show Alert Message When New Media Is Inserted Into Removable Storage*—This option causes the utility to display a dialog box when Removable Storage detects new media.

➤ *Always Move New Import Media To the Backup Media Pool*—This option causes the utility to automatically move new media that is detected by Removable Storage to the Backup media pool. If you use Removable Storage to manage your media, and you want all new media to be available to the Backup program only, you should check this box.

➤ *Restore*—The Restore tab deals primarily with whether the Restore utility will overwrite existing files. The Restore tab has three options, as shown in Figure 18.6:

➤ *Do Not Replace The File On My Computer*—This option ensures that the restore procedure does not overwrite any files that are already present on the system.

➤ *Replace The File On Disk Only If The File On Disk Is Older*—This option instructs the restore procedure to overwrite any duplicate files that are present on the destination media that is older than the backup copy.

➤ *Always Replace The File On My Computer*—This option instructs the restore procedure to always overwrite any duplicate files located on the destination media.

➤ *Backup Type*—The Backup Type tab allows a user to specify the type of backup that should be run. The options are normal, copy, differential, incremental, and daily copy.

Figure 18.6 Restore Options.

18

➤ *Backup Log*—The Backup Log tab allows a user to specify the level of logging the Backup utility should use. There are three options—Detailed, Summary, and None. The Detailed option logs a list of all files that are backed up, any errors that occur, and any tape changes. Summary logs information regarding only tape changes and errors that occur. The None option prevents the utility from creating a log file.

➤ *Exclude Files*—The Exclude Files tab allows a user to specify which files should never be backed up. An example of this is the file named pagefile.sys. The pagefile.sys is a virtual memory swap file used by the operating system.

Selecting Data to Backup

The Backup utility provides a GUI used to select drives, files, and folders to be backed up. You can select a file, folder, or drive by placing a checkmark next to the file, folder, or drive you want. By doing so, you indicate that the resource should be backed up. You can select individual files for backup, which will automatically place a checkmark next to the folder and drive that the file is located on; however, this checkmark will be grayed out to indicate that only some of the contents of the drive and folder are marked for backup. Figure 18.7 shows the GUI interface used to select resources for backup.

Selecting a Backup Location

With Windows 2000's Backup utility, you can choose to back up to a tape drive or to a file. Backing up to a file requires you to specify the location and name of the file that will be created or appended to by the Backup software, as shown in Figure 18.8.

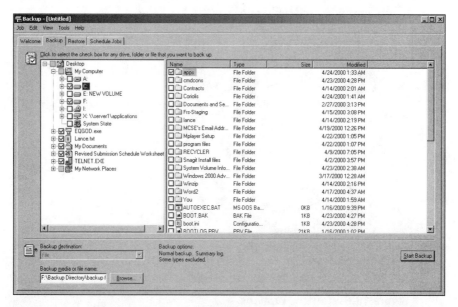

Figure 18.7   Selecting resources to back up.

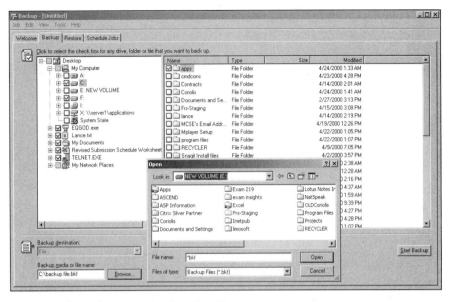

Figure 18.8   Selecting a backup location.

The fact that all Windows 2000 Servers can perform their own backups and they can back up to a file gives network professionals a great amount of flexibility. For example, rather than having a server back up all other servers' data to a tape drive, you could have each server back up its own contents to a file located on a central backup server. This central backup server could then back up all the backup files (received from each server) to a tape drive. Now you have two backups of the same data. The backup files stored on the backup server can quickly and easily be accessed in an emergency, and older copies of all backups are stored on tapes.

Backing up System State Data

The Windows 2000 Backup utility can be used to back up and restore system state data. System state data includes:

➤ Registry

➤ Active Directory

➤ Certificate server database

➤ SYSVOL folder

➤ System startup files

➤ Component services class registration database

Windows 2000 Professional computers do not include a SYSVOL folder, a certificate services database, or an Active Directory database. Only Windows 2000 domain controllers contain a SYSVOL folder and an Active Directory.

18

Separate pieces of the system state data cannot be backed up. For example, on a domain controller, you cannot back up the Active Directory without backing up the registry as well.

To back up system state data, you must place a checkmark next to the System State checkbox located under My Computer when selecting files and folders for backup, as shown in Figure 18.9.

Scheduling a Backup

Finally, Microsoft Windows 2000 includes a scheduler module with the Backup utility. Using the new scheduler module, you can schedule backups to run at any time and at regular intervals. The scheduler module includes a wizard interface that can be used to create scheduled backups; however, the GUI interface can easily be used to schedule backups manually.

You create and name a schedule at the same time you create a backup job. In order to schedule a backup to occur, you must first save the backup job. The backup job and the schedule are saved as separate files so that backup jobs can be attached to different schedules and vice versa.

Creating a Schedule

After all the appropriate files have been selected and the proper options are set for a particular backup job, you are ready to create a schedule. To do so, follow these steps:

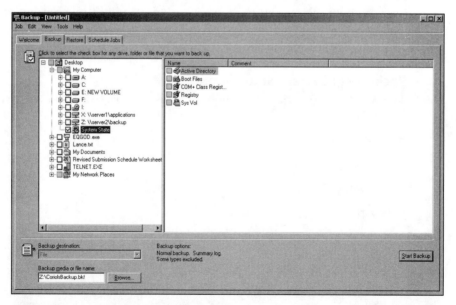

Figure 18.9 Selecting system state data for backup.

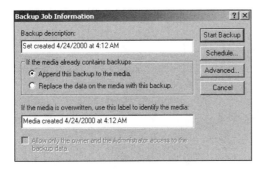

Figure 18.10   Scheduling a backup.

1. Click the Backup button. After the Backup button is clicked, the Backup Job Information dialog box appears, as shown in Figure 18.10.

2. In the Backup Job Information dialog box, select to append the backup to an existing tape or file, or overwrite an existing file or tape. Click the Schedule button, and the system prompts you to save the current backup job if it has not already been saved; click Yes to save the file.

3. After the backup job is saved, the schedule module prompts you for a username and password to use to run the backup job. The user account that is used must have the Backup Files And Directories permission. The scheduler system must have a username and password to run any scheduled event. Enter the username and password for the user account you want to use, and click OK.

4. At this point, the scheduler asks you to name the schedule you are about to save. A good idea is to use a name that describes the times the schedule will run. For example, a good name might be WEEKNIGHT_100am to signify that the job runs every weeknight at 1:00 A.M. Name the file, and click the Properties button to access the Schedule Job dialog box.

5. After you access the Schedule Job dialog box, as shown in Figure 18.11, you can create a schedule for your backup. The Schedule Job dialog box contains two tabs—the Schedule tab and the Settings tab. The Settings tab can be used to control the properties of the schedule. The Settings tab contains the following options:

   ➤ *Delete This Task If It Is Not Scheduled To Run Again*—This setting allows the scheduler service to delete jobs that are no longer scheduled to run.

   ➤ *Stop This Task If It Runs For*—This setting allows the administrator to specify an amount of time the scheduler system should allow a task to run before automatically stopping the task. This could be helpful if the administrator wants to ensure that backups are not running after a specified time period.

18

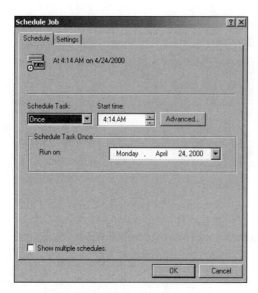

Figure 18.11   Schedule Job dialog box.

➤ *Only Start The Task If The Computer Has Been Idle For*—This setting allows the administrator to configure a task to not run if the system is not idle. Additionally, you can configure the system to keep checking for idle time periodically at configured time intervals.

➤ *Stop The Task If The Computer Ceases To Be Idle*—The administrator can configure the system to start the task only if the computer is idle and to stop the task if the computer does not remain idle.

➤ *Power Management*—Within the Power Management section, you can prevent a backup or other task from starting if the computer is running on battery power or stop a task if the system goes to battery power. You can also configure the system to wake up to start a task if it has powered down before starting the backup.

After the schedule has been configured, you can click the Schedule tab to see a Calendar view of your newly created schedule. By clicking on any icon, as shown in Figure 18.12, you can view a task's schedule.

Restoring from a Backup

A backup is useless unless you can use it to restore missing or damaged data. You can use the Backup utility included with Windows 2000 to restore files and folders that have been backed up with the Backup utility. The Windows 2000 Backup application cannot be used to restore files that were backed up with third-party backup software. Also, you cannot use third-party software to restore files backed up with Windows 2000's Backup application.

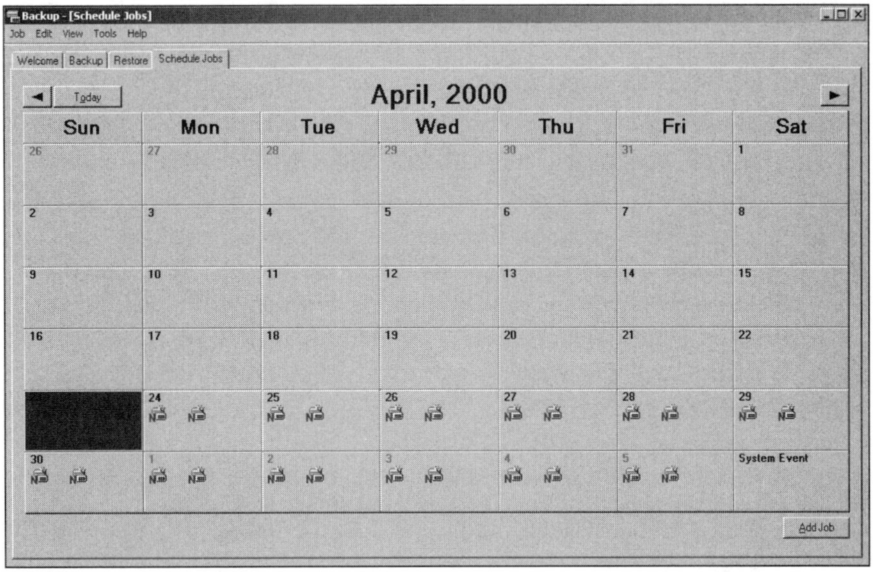

Figure 18.12   Calendar view.

Steps to Restore Data

To restore data using the Backup utility, follow these steps:

1. In the Backup utility, select the Restore tab.

2. Select the backup job or media that you want to restore from.

3. Place a checkmark next to the file, folder, or drive you want to restore. If a catalog has not already been built, the restore process asks if you would like to create one. Select Yes.

4. At the bottom of the window, ensure that the Restore Location setting is correct. You can choose to restore to the original location or a different location.

5. Click the Start Restore button, and click OK in the Advance Restore dialog box. A dialog box appears asking what backup file you want to restore from.

6. Enter the path to the restore file, and click OK. The restore process restores the file.

18

UNDERSTANDING ACTIVE DIRECTORY RECOVERY AND MAINTENANCE

When designing your network infrastructure, you should consider how the Active Directory is going to be maintained and restored in case of server failure. Decisions regarding the maintenance and backing up of the Active Directory can influence design and hardware considerations within your network design. Proper maintenance and backup plans require a thorough knowledge of how Active Directory stores, maintains, and makes changes to its database.

Understanding the Active Directory Store

The Active Directory uses the Extensible Storage Engine, as does Microsoft Exchange. The Extensible Storage Engine provides a fault-tolerant transaction-based database. Fault-tolerance is created through the use of log files where all transactions are written prior to being committed to the database. A transaction is any entry into the log, such as an addition, modification, or deletion from the directory database.

The Extensible Storage Engine includes the following two components:

➤ All objects that are part of the Active Directory database

➤ All the transaction log files used to record transactions to create fault tolerance

Committing a Transaction

Changes to the Active Directory are completed in a three-step process to ensure consistency and reliability. Transactions are first written to a log file. After the transaction has been written to the log file, a separate process writes each entry in the log file to a database page in memory (committed). Another process writes the database page to the hard drive during system idle time or during the shutdown process. This three-step process prevents part of a transaction from being written to the database, which in many cases could cause the Active Directory database to become corrupt. The three-step process is summarized as follows:

1. A change to the directory causes a transaction to be written to the transaction log.

2. The entry in the transaction log is read and then written to a database page residing in the memory buffer. This is called a *committed transaction*.

3. The change is written to the database file on the hard drive (during idle time or system shutdown).

After the change has been written to the database file (Step 3), the pointer in the transaction log file is advanced to the next transaction entry. A database is not fully updated until all transactions listed in the transaction log are committed and written to the database file. If a system is under a heavy load, a significant delay might occur when transactions are being committed and written to the database file.

Active Directory Data Store Files

The Active Directory data store is made up of many separate files that work together to provide a seamless and efficient directory service. You should be aware of each file that makes up the directory store for the purpose of backing up the directory store and properly answering exam questions. The directory store is made up of the following files:

➤ *Database file*—The database file holds all the Active Directory objects and their attributes. The file name is ntds.dit and is normally located in the *%systemroot%*\NTDS directory.

➤ *Log files*—Log files are used to list, track, and maintain additions, modifications, and deletions to the database. Log files are stored in the *%systemroot*\NTDS directory by default. There are four log files, each with its own purpose:

➤ *Transaction log files*—Transaction log files are used to store transactions that already have been or are waiting to be committed.

➤ *Checkpoint log files*—Checkpoint log files are used to hold pointers. Pointers point to transaction logs that have been committed and written to the database file.

➤ *Reserve log files*—Reserve log files are used to reserve hard drive space for use by the transaction log files. Each reserve log file reserves 10MB of hard drive space.

➤ *Patch files*—Patch files are used to manage data during backups.

The Database File

The Active Directory database file (ntds.dit) contains all directory objects and their attributes. The directory database is named ntds.dit and, by default, is located in the *%systemroot%*\NTDS directory; however, you can specify a different location during Active Directory installation. This file cannot be copied or deleted while the system is operational; however, the directory database file can be backed up by selecting the System State checkbox within the Backup utility.

The directory database contains the following three tables used to store information:

➤ *Object table*—Contains a row for each object within the Active Directory. Each row stores an object and all the object's attributes. Storage space is allocated to attributes only if they are not left blank. For example, if a user object's phone attribute is blank, the Extensible Storage Engine will not set aside storage space for that attribute. By not allocating space for unused attributes, Windows 2000 increases efficiency and controls the size of the Active Directory.

18

➤ *Link table*—Contains link information (called *relationships*) between objects stored in the object table. For example, a user object will be linked to the Organizational Unit (OU) that represents the user object's parent object. An OU will have a link to the domain object that the OU resides in.

➤ *Schema table*—Contains a list of all objects that can be created within the Active Directory database. The schema table defines each object as well as the object's attributes. Those familiar with object-oriented programming will recognize the schema table as a class definition table.

The database file size is related to the number of objects, each object's attributes, and the size of the schema table. As objects are added and removed from the Active Directory, the size increases and decreases respectively; however, the reported size of the Active Directory will never change until the system is restarted. For example, if you check the size of the database and it reports 50MB, and you then delete objects from the Active Directory, the operating system continues to report the size as 50MB. To find out the true size of the Active Directory database, you must restart the server and check again.

Transaction Log Files

Transaction log files store transactions that have not been written to the database file as well as transactions that have been committed and written to the database file. The current working transaction log file is named Edb.log and is stored in the same directory as the database file by default. The most current transaction is contained within the Edb.log file. The Edb.log file cannot be opened, deleted, or copied.

The default size for the Edb.log file is 10MB. The number of transactions that each log file can contain is dependent on the size of each change. Storing a large file within the Active Directory could conceivably consume the entire Edb.log file and force another log file to be created. If a transaction is large enough, the transaction could span multiple log files. Normal transaction sizes range from 4K to15K.

When the total size of all transactions within the Edb.log file reaches 10MB, a new transaction log file must be created. When this happens, the original Edb.log file is renamed to Edbxxxxxx.log where x represents a hexadecimal number. A new Edb.log file is then created from a reserve file.

Note: Transaction log files contain information that the NTDS service can read to discover which transactions have been committed; however, the NTDS service normally relies on the checkpoint files for this function.

When a file is renamed to Edb0000001.log, for example, the file is referred to as a previous log file. Once all the transactions in a previous log file have been written to the database file, the file is no longer used by the operating system. During a process known as *garbage collection*, the server deletes previous log files that are no longer needed. The garbage collection service runs every 12 hours on every domain controller.

You can prevent the creation of additional transaction log files by using circular logging. If you do not want the directory service to create additional log files when the transaction log is full, you can enable circular logging. Instead of creating a new log file, circular logging overwrites the oldest file. To allow for greater data recovery ability, circular logging is not enabled by default. In order to enable circular logging, you must change the value of the following registry key to 1.

```
HKEY_LOCAL_MACHINE\CurrentControlSet\Services\NTDS\Parameters\
CircularLogging
```

Checkpoint Files

The checkpoint log file named Edb.chk is stored in the %systemroot%\NTDS directory by default. Checkpoint files provide pointers that allow Windows 2000 Server to recognize which transactions in the transaction log file have been written to the database file. Each time a transaction within the transaction log file is written to the database file, the checkpoint file advances the pointer to the next uncommitted transaction.

At system startup, the NTDS service reads the checkpoint file to discover which transactions have not yet been written to the database file. If the server experiences a sudden power outage, the NTDS service can read the transaction log files and the checkpoint files to find which transactions still must be committed and written. At startup, if the NTDS service finds a transaction that is listed as committed, but finds that the transaction has not yet been written to the database file, the service recovers the transaction and applies the transaction to the database file.

Reserve Log Files

By default, the NTDS directory contains two reserve log files named res1.log and res2.log. Each reserve log file reserves 10MB of space for future log files in cases of low disk resources. When a transaction log file reaches 10MB, Active Directory creates a new log file. If not enough space is left for the Active Directory service to create a new log file, all pending transactions are written to a reserve log file and the Active Directory service shuts down. Then, Active Directory writes an out-of-disk error to the system log.

18

Patch Files

Patch files are stored in the NTDS directory by default and are named with the .pat extension. Patch files are used to store changes that are written to the database file during online backups. While the Active Directory is being backed up, patch files store any changes that are written to the database file. This is an important feature to ensure that a backup of the Active Directory database contains all current changes to the database. The patch files are then backed up as well.

Active Directory Maintenance

As with any file stored on a hard drive, the Active Directory database will become fragmented over time. Fragmentation slows users' access to the directory. Unneeded objects stored in the directory database can also cause performance degradation. The NTDS service automatically runs a process that defragments the disk to optimize disk resources and accelerate Active Directory access. The NTDS service also deletes unneeded files and unused objects from the directory to reduce consumed disk resources. These cleanup processes can also be started manually.

Automatic Garbage Collection

As stated earlier, every domain controller runs a garbage collection service every 12 hours. This garbage collection service deletes unused files, removes deleted objects from the Active Directory database, and defragments the database file.

Unneeded files include the previous transaction logs. Previous transaction logs that contain transactions that have all been written to the database file are removed from the NTDS directory. This process ensures that the NTDS directory does not consume disk resources that are not needed.

Removing deleted objects from the Active Directory is another function of the garbage collection process. When a user deletes an object from the Active Directory, the object is not immediately removed from the database. Instead, any deleted object is tagged with a *tombstone*. The tombstone marker is not visible to users. The object remains in the Active Directory for the period of time defined by the *tombstone lifetime*. The default tombstone lifetime is 60 days. After the tombstone marker surpasses the tombstone lifetime parameter, the object is removed from the database.

The defragmentation of the directory database reorganizes the database in order to provide maximum performance. Online defragmentation does not reduce the size of the database, but it does provide more space for use by new objects.

Manual Garbage Collection

Manual garbage collection is performed while the system is offline. You can use the manual defragmentation tool to defragment and remove unneeded files while the system is offline. This process can reduce the size of the Active Directory.

Offline defragmentation can be performed by restarting the system and then selecting Directory Services Mode during the operating selection phase of boot-up. Once the server is in Directory Service Mode, you can run the Ntdsutil.exe application to create a second defragmented copy of the directory database. This process is normally done only in a test situation where the network engineer wants to view the differences in size of a database after objects are deleted and the directory is defragmented. Under normal circumstances, manual defragmentation is not necessary because the automatic defragmentation process performs this function daily.

The LostAndFound Container

Within Active Directory Users and Computers, you can access a container object named LostAndFound. This container object contains objects that Active Directory does not know what to do with. For example, if an administrator creates a user in the sales OU on server1 and at about the same time another administrator deletes the sales OU, the new user account will be placed in the LostAndFound container object.

RECOVERING ACTIVE DIRECTORY

Planning your Active Directory backup strategy requires you to understand the processes that can be implemented in order to restore the directory database. The Windows 2000 Active Directory can be restored in three ways—an author-itative restore, a non-authoritative restore, and a recovery without a restore.

Non-Authoritative Restore

A non-authoritative restore simply allows an administrator to restore the directory from a backup. The restore is called *non-authoritative* because the domain controller that has its replica database restored will then depend on other domain controllers to replicate any changes that have taken place since the backup was performed. The repaired server's replica is considered non-authoritative because it accepts changes from other domain controllers. In this case, other domain controllers are considered authoritative because they contain the most updated information.

For example, if a disk error causes the loss of the Active Directory on serverA, you can perform a non-authoritative restore of the Active Directory database on serverA; however, the newly restored directory will not contain any changes that have taken place since the backup was performed. ServerA must rely on other domain controllers to replicate any changes that have taken place since the last backup. Only when all changes have been replicated will serverA have a complete replica of the directory database.

18

This type of restore depends completely on the presence of other domain controllers in the domain to replicate changes to the restored directory. If your restore strategy is going to depend on non-authoritative restores, you must install multiple domain controllers in each domain where non-authoritative restores will be used.

Performing a Non-Authoritative Restore

To perform a non-authoritative restore, follow these steps:

1. Start the domain controller that needs to be repaired in Directory Service Restore mode. To do this, press F8 during the operating system selection phase of bootup.

2. Restore the Active Directory database using the most recent backup media.

3. After the Active Directory is restored, restart the system. When the system restarts, the Active Directory is reindexed and a consistency check is run. Then, directory replication replicates any changes to the newly restored directory database.

Authoritative Restore

When you use an authoritative restore, you specify that the restored directory or part of the restored directory is the authoritative replica, and you do not want changes to be replicated to the Active Directory object. More specifically, an authoritative restore allows you to tag specific information that should be considered a master copy and should not be overwritten by replication. You can choose to tag a single object, OU, or an entire directory as authoritative.

For example, let's say you accidentally delete an OU named *Atlanta* that contains a large number of user accounts. You could use an authoritative restore to restore and tag the OU as authoritative. If you perform an authoritative restore, the OU would not be deleted again through replication. If, by mistake, you restored the OU using a non-authoritative restore, the OU would be restored; however, when replication occurs, the OU would be deleted again.

Performing an Authoritative Restore

To perform an authoritative restore, follow these steps:

1. Ensure that the system is in Directory Service Restore mode.

2. Restore the Active Directory using Windows 2000's restore utility.

3. Restart the server. The server must be started again in Directory Service Restore mode.

4. Run the Ntdsutil.exe utility and enter the **authoritative restore** command, as shown in Figure 18.13.

Figure 8.13   Authoritative Restore mode.

5. Enter the **Restore subtree OU=Atlanta,DC=Coriolis,DC=test**
   command, where **Atlanta** is the name of the OU you want to tag as
   authoritative and **Coriolis.test** is the domain name.

6. Exit the Ntdsutil utility. The restored replica database will be updated by
   other replica databases through replication, except for the Atlanta OU. The
   restored replica will replicate the Atlanta OU back to all domain controllers,
   because it is tagged as authoritative.

Recovery without Restore

Transaction logging can be used to restore the Active Directory in the event of
sudden server crashes. If the transaction logs contain transactions that have not
yet been written to the directory, the NTDS service will write transactions to
the database file when the server comes back online.

CHAPTER SUMMARY

Every important aspect of a network begins with a properly documented plan.
Before installing and starting the Backup software, you should design your backup
strategy. Your backup plan should answer key questions, such as What hardware is
going to be used? What type of backup media are backups going to be written
to? What data needs to be backed up and how often? These questions and many
more should be answered as part of your Windows 2000 disaster-recovery plan.

In addition to your backup plan, you should have a prevention plan. Keep in
mind that backups are your last line of defense; the first line of defense is
protection and prevention. Disaster protection and prevention includes many
more aspects of the operating system than just the backup software used. A
disaster prevention plan should include the following tasks:

18

➤ Maintaining servers properly

➤ Using technologies that can prevent network professionals from ever having to restore files, such as RAID levels 1 and 5

➤ Identifying any software that should always be available in case of emergencies

➤ Specifying where backup tapes (or other media) are stored

➤ Determining whether another company should be hired to store the tapes or the administrator be responsible for taking backup tapes off site

Many aspects of disaster recovery and prevention are determined by simply asking questions and implementing policies based on the answers to the questions.

This chapter described the importance of having a solid backup and disaster recovery plan, as well as documents many of the questions and issues that must be addressed before a disaster program can be effectively put into place. This chapter also explained how to understand and use the many disaster recovery tools included in Windows 2000, such as the recovery console. In addition, the chapter described how to back up files, folders, drives, and the Active Directory (known as system state data). The Active Directory store and the files used to create the store were explained in detail. This chapter concluded by explaining the intricacies of restoring the Active Directory through the use of authoritative and non-authoritative restore procedures, as well as recovery without restore.

REVIEW QUESTIONS

1. Which of the following is an example of a fault-tolerant technology?

    a. RAID 6

    b. RAID 0

    c. RAID 1

    d. UPS

2. Which of the following must be true before RAID volumes can be created in Windows 2000?

    a. You are using NTFS 5.5 partitions only.

    b. You are using dynamic disks.

    c. You have more than three drives.

    d. You have SCSI disks.

3. Which of the following statements describes RAID 1 disk duplexing?

    a. Provides redundant data by copying data to multiple disks

    b. Requires a minimum of three volumes

    c. Is better than mirroring because there is no single point of failure

    d. Requires multiple SCSI disk controllers

4. You are the administrator of a server named *Server1* that has a RAID 5 volume spread across 12 SCSI hard drives. Each volume that makes up the RAID 5 volume is 5GB. What is your total available storage capacity?

    a. 55GB

    b. 60GB

    c. 45GB

    d. 50GB

5. You are the administrator of a server named *Server1* that has a RAID 5 volume spread across 12 SCSI hard drives. You open the Computer Management Administrative Tool and notice that one of the drives reports as offline. What must you do to correct the problem?

    a. Right-click the drive, and select Regenerate Volume.

    b. Right-click the drive, and select Break Volume. Format the drive, then right-click the new volume, and select Re-create Volume.

    c. Ensure that the drive is getting power, and click Re-create Volume.

    d. Format the drive, and restore the entire volume from backup.

6. Why is RAID 5 considered to be better than RAID 1?

    a. RAID 5 supports more disk storage.

    b. RAID 5 uses disk resources more efficiently.

    c. RAID 5 is less expensive.

    d. RAID 1 requires more expensive disk drives.

7. You update the network card driver on your network server. After restarting the server, you get an **IRQ EQUAL OR LESS THAN 0** stop error message, and the system locks. What is the best way to correct the problem?

    a. Boot with a Windows 2000 boot disk, and, when prompted, run the emergency repair process.

    b. Restart the computer in Safe Mode With Networking.

    c. Restart the system in Safe Mode, and replace the driver.

    d. Press F8 when the system boots, and select Last Known Good Configuration.

18

8. You update the network card driver on your network server. After restarting the server, you log into the server, and the system locks up. What is the best way to correct the problem?

    a. Boot with a Windows 2000 boot disk, and, when prompted, run the emergency repair process.

    b. Restart the computer in Safe Mode With Networking.

    c. Restart the system in Safe Mode, and replace the driver.

    d. Press F8 when the system boots, and select Last Known Good Configuration.

9. Your server is locking up during the kernel initialization phase of bootup. What is the first step in correcting this problem?

    a. Enable VGA mode.

    b. Enable Boot logging.

    c. Boot to the Last Known Good Configuration.

    d. Start in Safe Mode With Command Prompt.

10. You are creating a backup job to run on Monday and Tuesday nights. You select the System State checkbox so that the backup will include the system state data. Which of the following will not be backed up?

    a. Certificate server information

    b. Transaction log files

    c. Registry

    d. Initialization files

11. Your server's hard drives are all formatted with the NTFS file system. Your system files are located on the D:\ drive. Your system boots from the C:\ drive. The primary volume of your mirrored drive fails, and you must modify the boot.ini file to point to the mirrored secondary volume. How would you accomplish this task?

    a. Boot with a Windows 95 boot disk.

    b. Boot with a Windows 98 boot disk.

    c. Boot with a DOS 6 boot disk

    d. Start the system, and choose Recovery Console.

12. During the process of performing a normal backup, what happens to the archive bit on all selected files?

    a. It is cleared

    b. It is checked

    c. It is left as is

    d. Not enough information is given

13. Andy wants to be able to restore missing files in the least amount of time in case of a hard drive failure. The company requirement is that restoration should never require more than two tapes. Which of the following backup plans should Andy use?

    a. Normal backups on Mondays, and incremental backups every other day of the week.

    b. Normal backups on Mondays, and a daily copy every other day of the week.

    c. Normal backups on Mondays, and a copy every other day of the week.

    d. Normal backups on Mondays, differential backups on Tuesdays, and incremental backups every other day of the week.

14. You need to back up the hard drives on your server; however, you do not have a tape drive or a recordable CD-ROM. What would be the best place to back up your files?

    a. Floppy disk

    b. Local hard drive

    c. Network drive

    d. RAM

15. What occurs when a user deletes an object from the Active Directory?

    a. The object will not be deleted, because user accounts cannot delete anything in the Active Directory.

    b. The object will remain in the Active Directory for 60 days. If anyone accesses the object during the 60-day period, the object will never be deleted.

    c. The administrator must approve the deletion.

    d. The object will be marked for deletion in 60 days. No one will be able to access the object during the 60-day period.

16. The Extensible Storage Engine does not include which of the following components?

    a. Active Directory database

    b. Active Directory patch (.pat) files

    c. Pointer files

    d. Transaction log files

18

17. When a change is made to the Active Directory, a transaction is generated. That transaction is first written to _____ and then written to the _____.

    a. Transaction database, database file

    b. Pointer file, Active Directory

    c. Transaction log, database page

    d. Extensible Storage Engine, Active Directory

18. When a change is made to the Active Directory, a transaction is generated. A transaction is not considered committed until the transaction is written to the _____.

    a. Database file

    b. Database page

    c. Transaction database

    d. Transaction log

    e. Patch file

19. What happens when the transaction log file reaches the 10MB limit?

    a. The transactions in the log file are committed and then deleted from the log file and copied into the reservation log file.

    b. The transaction log file is immediately deleted, and a new log file is created.

    c. The transaction log file is renamed, and a new transaction log file is created.

    d. The transaction log file is renamed, and the reservation log becomes the transaction log file.

20. What purpose do the res1.log and res2.log files serve?

    a. Reserve space on the volume

    b. Reserve space in the Active Directory

    c. Reserve directory database resources

    d. Prevent the log files from consuming more resources than are available on the drive

21. The transaction log file is named _____ and is located by default in the _____ directory.

    a. Edb.msd, NTFS

    b. Edb.txt, NTDS

    c. Edb.log, NTDS

    d. Edb.log, directory database

22. What feature can you enable to conserve hard drive space?

    a. Circular logging

    b. Log file compression

    c. Log file encryption

    d. Automatic database defragmentation.

23. A file named Edb00000234.log is an example of a _____.

    a. Transaction log file

    b. Previous log file

    c. Pointer file

    d. Patch file

24. When an object is deleted from the Active Directory, it is tagged with a _____, and it is removed from the directory when it reaches the _____.

    a. Tombstone, tombstone lifetime

    b. Head marker, tombstone

    c. Deletion marker, tombstone

    d. Deletion marker, tombstone lifetime

25. The boot partition on one of the domain controllers crashes. What type of restore method should you use to recover the Active Directory?

    a. Non-authoritative

    b. Authoritative

    c. Recovery without restore

    d. None of the above

REAL-WORLD PROJECTS

While Andy is drinking his first cup of coffee of the day, he receives a frantic call from his client Coriolis. All that he can ascertain from the conversation is that the domain controller that acts as a file server has crashed and no one at the office knows what to do to correct the problem. Andy quickly finishes his coffee and rushes out to the Coriolis office.

18

When Andy arrives at Coriolis, he finds the office in turmoil. Andy makes his way to the server room and finds that the system is locking up as soon as the kernel initialization screen loads (the blue screen). Andy suspects that a corrupt driver is causing the problem.

In order to find which driver is causing the system to freeze, Andy restarts the system and enables boot logging from the Advance Startup options.

Project 18.1

To enable boot logging, complete the following steps:

1. Restart the Computer.

2. When the OS selection screen appear, press F8.

3. Scroll down and select the Enable Boot logging.

4. Wait while the system continues to boot.

5. Log into the server and open the Ntbtlog.txt file.

At this point, Andy determines that he will have to restart the system by going to Safe Mode so that the corrupt driver will not load and lock the system. While at the command prompt, Andy is able to open and view the Ntbtlog.txt file to find which driver is causing the problem.

Andy finds that the sound card driver is causing all the problems. Therefore, he determines that he has to replace the driver with a new copy.

Project 18.2

To boot in Safe Mode, complete the following steps:

1. Restart the computer.

2. When the OS selection screen appears, press F8.

3. Scroll down and select Safe Mode; the system should continue to boot.

4. Log into the system and replace the failed driver.

The system restarts, and everything seems to be working fine. With everything up and running, many of the users ask Andy what caused the driver to become corrupt. To address this issue, Andy first determines that there had not been any sudden power outages and the server is plugged into a surge protector. Andy becomes suspicious and decides to run a virus scan on the system.

The results of the virus scan are shocking. Within the users' home directories alone, the software finds eight macro viruses within an assortment of Word and Excel files. Andy, however, is more worried about the boot sector virus that was discovered on the server. Andy allows the anti-virus software to clean the viruses from the system; however, because the system had a boot sector virus, Andy decides it would be a good idea to fix the boot sector manually.

In order to fix the boot sector, Andy has to install the Windows 2000 recovery console.

Project 18.3
To install the recovery console, complete the following steps:

1. Insert the Windows 2000 CD into the CD-ROM.

2. Click Start|Run, enter "D:\i386\winnt32.exe /cmdcons" in the Run dialog box, and click OK.

3. Click Yes in the Windows 2000 Setup dialog box. Windows 2000 should install the recovery console and indicate that the system should be restarted.

4. Restart the computer.

Tip: You can also access the recovery console on a system that has not yet installed the recovery console software. To do so, you must boot from the Windows 2000 CD and select recovery console when prompted to repair the existing installation of Windows 2000.

Project 18.4
To fix the boot sector, complete the following steps:

1. Restart the system and select the recovery console at the OS selection screen.

2. Select the installation of Windows 2000 that you want to work with.

3. The next screen prompts for the recovery password for the administrators account. (This password is the password that is asked for during Active Directory installation. Active Directory installation is discussed in Chapter 5.)

4. Enter the **fixboot** command; Windows 2000 writes a new boot sector to the system partition.

5. Type "exit" to restart the system.

Because multiple viruses have been found on the system, Andy decides that now would be a good time to run a backup of all user data, the Active Directory, and the registry of the server. The server does not have a backup tape drive, so Andy backs up the system to a file located on another server's hard drive.

18

Project 18.5
To back up data and the system state, complete the following steps:

1. Open the Windows 2000 backup located under Accessories|System Tools.

2. Select the Backup tab.

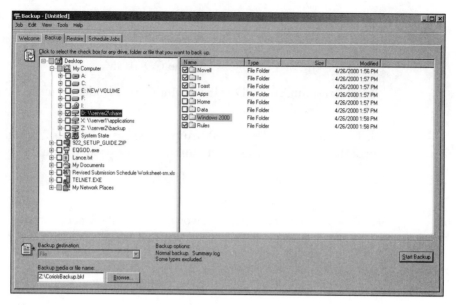

Figure 18.14 Selecting system state data.

3. Ensure that the company shares and the system state data is included in the backup by placing a checkmark in the proper boxes, as shown in Figure 18.14.

4. Click the Browse button next to the Backup Media Or File Name text box.

5. Browse to the network drive and directory where you want to store the backup files.

6. Name the backup file *systemstate.bkf.*

7. Click Open.

8. Click Start Backup

9. Select to replace the data on the media with the backup.

10. Click the Start Backup button.

Project 18.6
To restore system state data, complete the following steps:

1. Restart the computer, and press F8 at the OS selection screen.

2. Select Directory Service Repair Mode.

3. Select the correct operating system.

4. Log in and start the Backup utility. The system should state that it is running in Safe Mode. (Because the system is running in Safe Mode, you must log in with the directory restore administrator's password that you specified during the Active Directory installation.)

5. Select the Restore tab.

6. Expand the entry located on the Restore tab, as shown in Figure 18.15.

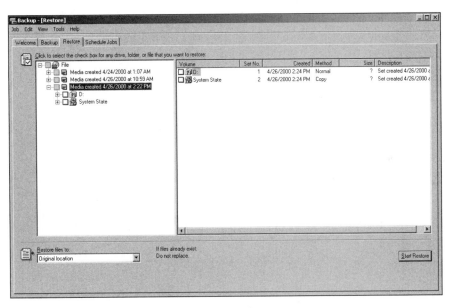

Figure 18.15   Restoring the system state data.

7. Place a checkmark in the System State checkbox.

8. Click OK.

9. Click OK in the Confirm Restore dialog box.

10. If not already correct, enter the path and backup file name, and click OK.

11. When the restore is complete, click Close, and then click Yes to restart the system.

Now that order has been restored at Coriolis, Andy is able to continue on to his next job.

18

CHAPTER NINETEEN

PLANNING AND IMPLEMENTING A WINDOWS NT 4 TO WINDOWS 2000 MIGRATION

After completing this chapter, you will be able to:

✓ Plan the deployment of Windows 2000 in a Windows NT environment

✓ Develop an upgrade strategy

✓ Identify domain controller migration strategies

✓ Identify member server migration strategies

✓ Perform an upgrade

✓ Automate installation and upgrades

✓ Test Windows 2000 using lab and pilot environments

Microsoft has gone to great lengths to make the transition from Windows NT 4 to Windows 2000 easy and seamless. The entire process was thoroughly tested by Microsoft, who developed many tools to help with the migration. This chapter is designed to assist you with questions about migration that will appear on the 70-240 Accelerated exam and also with an actual migration from a Windows NT domain model to Windows 2000 and the Active Directory.

PLANNING FOR SUCCESS

Planning the deployment of Windows 2000 is a critical step in the migration process. A complete deployment plan that considers all variables can make the difference between a successful migration and a system riddled with work-around procedures and shortcomings. Time spent planning will pay back twofold during the actual migration.

Documenting Goals, Resources, and Milestones

The migration to Windows 2000 is time consuming and expensive, so you should have specific reasons for performing a migration. You've learned about the many enhancements and compatibility improvements built into Windows 2000, and specific features should make the migration compelling and necessary. After identifying your objectives, you should prioritize and detail your objectives in the migration plan. Keep in mind that meeting some objectives might require you to complete other objectives earlier in the migration plan. Creating a plan also assists you with limiting the scope of the project. Every project must have defined starting and ending points, and the scope definition of the project identifies these points up front.

To form an accurate plan, the current systems and the proposed systems must be documented. These documents must include the geographical and organizational structure. Mission-critical and strategic processes must be identified and accommodated. The current structure of the IT department and any changes that will have to be made for proper administration should be included. Armed with this information, the standards for the new system can be developed. Identifying the gap between the existing systems and the new systems will assist with forming a list of tasks necessary for the new system to be complete. Finally, during this process, the pilot test systems and users should be identified and contacted.

Armed with the overall migration plan, more detailed requirements can be identified. For example, the people involved in the migration can be chosen to participate on teams based on their specific talents and knowledge base. Also, the documentation creation phase can begin.

The Teams and Their Members

A migration from Windows NT to Windows 2000 can be a large undertaking that will likely involve a number of people with technical specialties, as well as representatives of management and the actual users. When you plan to deploy Windows 2000, you need to create a number of teams. Among the teams you create, you should include the following:

➤ *Coordination team*—A coordination team should contain a wide variety of members. At least one member from each of the other teams mentioned below (the deployment team, the network team, the client team, and ancillary teams) should be part of the coordination team to represent their individual team's interest. In addition, members from outside the IT department with institution-specific knowledge should be members so that the users' needs are represented. If any pieces of the project will be outsourced, a member from the outside company should be involved to ensure communication of needs and goals. Finally, in a mixed environment, at least one specialist from each major system should be on the team to contribute system guard compatibility.

➤ *Deployment team*—The deployment team must have members with specialties in particular computer applications and the company's computer policies.

➤ *Network team*—The network team members should encompass all the skills necessary to keep servers, infrastructure, and security under control:

  ➤ *Servers*—Server hardware, storage, backup, and disaster planning must be considered.

  ➤ *Infrastructure*—Local and wide area network (LAN and WAN) infrastructures including media and connectivity devices usually require a special skill set. For example, application specialists are needed to ensure critical services like DNS and vertical market applications are available on the new system. In addition, interoperability with existing systems might necessitate Unix or NetWare engineers.

  ➤ *Security*—Security is a critical area that requires representation on the team by the highest caliber of network engineer.

➤ *Client team*—The client team must be composed of highly skilled network engineers with specific specialties. For example, because a variety of client operating systems might be incorporated, at least one person who specializes in each operating system should participate. Furthermore, a member of the client team should concentrate strictly on desktop administration and integration, because this area heavily affects the total cost of ownership.

19

Finally, the Help desk department should have representation on the client team, because the members of this department will be the frontline support for the new system.

➤ *Ancillary teams*—During a large-scale, complex migration, ancillary teams will also be required. Ancillary teams deal with issues beyond the technical and implementation issues. For example, for the project to be a success, there must be an executive sponsor. The sponsor could be a group of IT executives or a group of executives from another department. The executive sponsor must have an understanding of the technology as well as the ways in which the new technology will benefit the organization.

In addition, there should be a project management team. These managers should have the same level of knowledge about the technology as the executive sponsor, but their understanding of the project must be more comprehensive than anyone else in the organization. The project management team should have superior organizational skills and the ability to communicate with the executive-level sponsors as well as the implementation team and its members.

Because the new technology will likely deal with cutting edge hardware and software, there might be a need for a dedicated logistics and purchasing team. Finally, there must be a team that documents the new system and trains the user community on the use of the new system.

The Resulting Documentation

The documentation that results from the planning phase should be extensive enough to accommodate the implementation without being so excessive that it restricts flexibility. The project manager should produce documentation with the executive and user communities as the target audience. The project's mission and objectives should be defined, as well as its timeline and budget. Staffing estimates, environmental needs, and the overall risks to the organization must be defined.

The deployment teams should be responsible for more detailed documents mapping out the deployment plan. Included in these documents are the current and proposed systems documentation and the steps to merge the two. The capacity guidelines, detailed risk assessment, and pilot plan also come from the deployment team. Documents on user support, issue resolution, and problem escalation ensure that issues are dealt with in a timely manner. Communication documentation details how information is distributed and how feedback is collected. Finally, the training documents should list the curriculum, schedules, and target audiences for the education of the users as well as the administrators of the new system.

DEVELOPING YOUR UPGRADE STRATEGY

Today, most networks are vital to the productivity of the majority of employees in a company. Because networks are so vital to the productivity of so many people, you must understand the interactions among the various versions of Windows NT and Windows 2000 as well as the proper planning and implementation processes. Before beginning your upgrade, you should ensure that your plan includes the following information:

➤ The upgrade model that matches the existing Windows NT 4 network for your organization.

➤ Migration plans for upgrading the existing Windows NT 4 directory services infrastructure to an Active Directory infrastructure.

➤ Naming strategies for the new Windows 2000 network.

First, let's take a look brief look at the upgrade process and the technical requirements for upgrading a system.

Upgrade Overview

Any computer running Windows 95, Windows 98, and any version of Windows NT 3.51 or later can be upgraded to Windows 2000 as long as the hardware in each system is listed on the Windows 2000 Hardware Compatibility List (HCL). Unlike Windows NT, you can upgrade a Windows 95 or Windows 98 computer to Windows 2000.

When migrating from a Windows NT 4 domain model to the Active Directory, a number of decisions must be made. For example, will the existing domain model be used to upgrade or will the Active Directory consist of entirely new domains? In some situations, both strategies can be used so that the existing domain becomes a part of the new Active Directory structure. If the upgrade must take place in the production environment and the current domain model seems to fit the needs of the organization, then an upgrade of the existing domain is appropriate. However, if the new system can be implemented parallel to the existing system and a significant amount of restructuring will be necessary to meet organizational needs, then an entirely new Active Directory domain structure should be implemented. Finally, if the new system can be implemented in parallel to the existing system and only a few domain structure changes are necessary, both strategies can be used where appropriate.

Every migration requires a specific set of tasks that must be completed in a specific order. Let's take a look at the steps to upgrade to Windows 2000.

19

Steps to Upgrade to a Windows 2000 Network

This section presents the general steps required to upgrade a network to a Windows 2000 network. Each of the following steps can be implemented over time and do not have to be completed all at once:

1. Plan the upgrade

   ➤ Document the DNS requirements for your Windows 2000 network.

   ➤ Develop a naming strategy for all objects within the network.

   ➤ Develop a disaster-recovery plan that includes contingency plans. This should include information regarding how the network can be rolled back in case problems, such as compatibility issues, arise. Chapter 18 provides more details on preventing and preparing for disaster recovery.

2. Establish a forest root domain.

3. Upgrade the primary domain controller (PDC) to a Windows 2000 domain controller.

4. Upgrade the backup domain controllers (BDC) to Windows 2000 domain controllers.

5. Configure the new network from mixed to native mode after all domain controllers, member servers, and client operating systems have been upgraded.

The ability to upgrade directly will depend greatly on the existing hardware.

Hardware Compatibility

Whether upgrading domain controllers, member servers, or client machines, you must complete a number of steps before performing the actual upgrade. First, you must determine the compatibility and capacity of the existing hardware. Check the hardware against the Hardware Compatibility List, and evaluate the additional resources that will be necessary to run the new operating system. Finally, disconnect any uninterruptible power supplies and set the system BIOS to reserve all IRQs for non-PNP ISA devices so that Windows 2000 has complete control over the system resources.

To ensure complete functionality after the upgrade, all software should be checked for compatibility.

Software Compatibility

After checking the hardware's compatibility, you must check the compatibility of the existing software and applications. You can do this via the manufacturer specifications, Microsoft Knowledge Base articles, or testing in a lab environment.

If no compatibility issues arise or if all issues have been resolved, document the current system settings, including BIOS, TCP/IP configuration, and any application-specific settings. Perform a full backup of the existing system, including registry and system files. Check the system log files for any errors that might impede the upgrade, and resolve issues as necessary.

Windows 2000 in Mixed Mode and Native Mode

Any domain that contains both Windows NT and Windows 2000 Servers is known as a mixed mode network, whereas any domain that contains only Windows 2000 domain controllers is known as a native mode network. Mixed mode allows Windows 2000 Servers to emulate and provide the same functionality as Windows NT 4 Servers. Native mode provides many additional features that cannot be used in mixed mode. Table 19.1 compares mixed mode to native mode, and it identifies the features that can be used in each.

A Windows 2000 network running in mixed mode has the following characteristics:

➤ Windows 2000 domain controllers handle requests made to a Windows NT PDC.

➤ Windows 2000 domain controllers handle SAM replication between itself and backup domain controllers as well as answers other server-to-server requests.

➤ Windows 2000 domain controllers assume various services provided by the PDC, such as replication master and trust validation.

➤ Windows 2000 domain controllers handle security issues, such as authentication and password changes, similar to the way in which a Windows NT PDC would handle the security issues.

When all domain controllers are upgraded to Windows 2000, you have the option of changing the operating mode from mixed to native. After a network is converted to native mode, you cannot add any Windows NT domain

Table 19.1 Mixed versus native mode.

Feature	Mixed Mode	Native Mode
Multi-master Replication	Yes	Yes
Transitive Trusts	No	Yes
Group Types	Global, Local	Universal, Global, Domain Local
Nested Security Groups	No	Yes
Password Filters	Installed on each domain controller individually	Automatically installed on every domain controller

19

controllers to the network; however, you can have member servers and down-level clients that are members of a native mode network.

With mixed mode, Microsoft includes legacy support in both the client and server versions of Windows 2000. This compatibility grants network engineers a large amount of flexibility regarding how the network infrastructure is upgraded. A network engineer could decide to upgrade all existing domain controllers first and then focus on the clients and member servers, or the member servers and clients could be upgraded first to gain additional functionality followed by the domain controllers.

Member servers and client computers can be upgraded prior to the migration of servers. The client operating systems are backward compatible, which means that they can be used to connect to legacy Windows NT 4 networks. Because Window 2000 Professional and Server can log into existing Windows NT 4 networks, you can upgrade all client and member server computers prior to upgrading the domain controllers. This scenario allows users and administrators to benefit from many of Windows 2000's new features before migrating the entire network.

Windows 2000 domain controllers running in mixed mode will authenticate legacy Windows NT 4 clients as well as Windows 95 and Windows 98 client operating systems. Because Windows 2000 Server is legacy compliant, you have the choice of upgrading all existing domain controllers before moving to the client and members servers. Windows 2000 Server provides support to legacy clients by use of an operations master called a *PDC emulator*. This is a single computer that has been designated to emulate the primary domain controller of a Windows NT 4 network, so that a Windows 2000 network will be compatible with Windows NT 4 domain controllers.

PDC Emulator in Mixed Mode

Windows 95, Windows 98, Windows NT Workstation, and member servers all look for a PDC when attempting to access a network or make changes to a directory database. Windows 2000 Servers contain a writeable copy of the Active Directory; however, downlevel operating systems are unaware of this feature. To provide support for downlevel operating systems, each Windows 2000 network contains a PDC emulator.

By default, the Windows 2000 Server that is promoted to a domain controller will take the role of the PDC emulator. The PDC emulator operations master fulfills the following requests:

➤ Changes to user and computer accounts, such as a password change

➤ Replication requests from BDCs

➤ Client computers' and backup browsers' requests for information from the domain master browser (this service provides the browser list to back up browsers)

➤ Authentication services for LanManager logon requests

When the PDC emulator is replicating or contacting other Windows 2000 Servers, it uses the Windows 2000 replication protocol; however, when contacting downlevel clients and servers, the PDC emulator uses the NTLM replication protocol and acts as a single master. The PDC emulator also presents all information regarding the accounts database as a flat Windows NT–type database as a Windows NT PDC would. The emulator also allows downlevel clients to use NTLM authentication protocol rather than Kerberos.

You should plan the placement of the PDC emulator carefully. If the PDC emulator fails for whatever reason, downlevel clients will be unable to change passwords or browse network resources.

You can transfer the PDC emulator role to another Windows 2000 domain controller, but there can be only one PDC emulator per domain. If the PDC emulator within a domain fails, you can seize the role of PDC emulator on another domain controller. The seize process is recommended only in situations in which the original emulator has failed.

Even when the Windows 2000 network is running in native mode, the PDC emulator performs network services.

PDC Emulator in Native Mode

Password changes that are performed on other domain controllers are expedited to the PDC emulator. When a user attempts to log onto the domain and access is denied due to a bad password, the domain controller forwards the request to the PDC emulator. This way, if a password has changed but has not yet been replicated to all domain controllers, the user will still be able to gain access to the network.

After all the downlevel clients and servers are upgraded, the network can be converted to native mode from mixed mode. When a network is running in native mode, the PDC emulator no longer has to answer domain master browser requests, allow the use of NTLM authentication, or perform single-master replication.

The backward compatibility of Windows 2000 Server and Professional allows network professionals to plan the upgrade of existing network resources in gradual steps rather than all at once. Additionally, backward compatibility provides the elbowroom needed to perform an upgrade as a natural progression.

19

For example, client operating systems could be upgraded as older systems are replaced with newer computers, and servers could be upgraded as new hardware arrives. By upgrading the network in stages, you can avoid the mad dash to do everything at once, which always seems to lead to disaster.

Logon Service in Mixed Mode

Proper planning for authentication services is an important piece of any upgrade strategy. Windows 2000 clients always attempt to find a Windows 2000 domain controller to log into by querying the DNS server. If the Windows 2000 client does not find a Windows 2000 domain controller, however, it will change to the NTLM protocol in an attempt to find a Windows NT primary or backup domain controller. This process makes Windows 2000 clients compatible with any existing network infrastructure; however, it can also lead to problems on the network.

Windows NT BDCs and PDCs cannot store group policy objects (GPOs) or logon scripts for Windows 2000 clients; therefore, if a Windows 2000 client logs into a downlevel server, the client will not receive any GPOs or logon scripts to process at logon. By ensuring that each site that contains Windows 2000 clients also has at least one Windows 2000 domain controller, you can ensure that all Windows 2000 clients process all GPOs and logon scripts.

File Replication in Mixed Mode

Previous versions of Windows NT used the LanManager replication service to replicate files, folders, and logon scripts to other servers and domain controllers. Windows 2000 does not support Windows NT's version of the directory replication service. In order to have files on Windows NT Server replicated to Windows 2000 Server, you must manually copy or create a batch file that copies files and folders to the proper location.

Microsoft recommends that you upgrade Windows NT export servers last. In most cases, the primary domain controller is the export server and is the first server that should be upgraded. Therefore, you should make another Windows NT Server the export server and delete the export directory on the primary domain controller before upgrading it to Windows 2000. The server that is chosen to become the new Windows NT export server should be the last server that is planned to be upgraded to Windows 2000 to avoid having to re-create the export server on another computer each time you upgrade a server.

When you change the export server, each import server (usually all the BDCs) will have to be configured to point to the new export server. Windows NT's server manager can be used to reconfigure the export server information on all import servers.

Remote Access Server in Mixed Mode

Almost all services that run on Windows NT and Windows 2000 require a username and password configured to allow the service to log into the system and run. The Remote Access Service (RAS) on Windows NT is one of the few exceptions to this rule. Because the Remote Access Service is not required to have a username and password, it is said to use NULL credentials. Windows NT allows a service with NULL credentials to access the security access manager (SAM) and query user account objects to check for remote access permissions; however, the Windows 2000 Active Directory does not allow this functionality.

Because the Active Directory will not allow the RAS service to access the directory database, you might experience problems when users dial into a Windows NT RAS server and the server attempts to query the directory to validate the RAS user's user account. You can solve or avoid this issue on mixed mode networks in three ways:

➤ If the network is running in mixed mode and the RAS server is a BDC, then the BDC already has access to the accounts database locally and does not need to access the directory database on the Windows 2000 domain controller.

➤ If the network is running in mixed mode, the RAS server attempts to verify the user account by querying an existing Windows NT backup domain controller rather than the Windows 2000 domain controller. Because the NT backup domain controller allows NULL services, it will allow the RAS service to query the directory database. Unfortunately, this is not configurable, because you cannot configure which server the RAS service will contact for authentication.

➤ You can loosen the Active Directory security to allow everyone permission to read all user account attributes on all user accounts. This option can also be set during Active Directory installation, as shown in Figure 19.1.

Mixed Mode Security

Windows 2000 and Windows NT both use different system policy and trust techniques. Trust relationships in Windows NT, for example, are one way and non-transitive. Windows 2000 trust relationships, however, are automatically established in both directions and are two way.

Windows 2000 uses two-way transitive trust between all domains within a tree. Downlevel domains do not use transitive trusts. Therefore, in order for downlevel domains to authenticate users that are logging in from other domains, each downlevel domain must have a trust relationship established manually with each

19

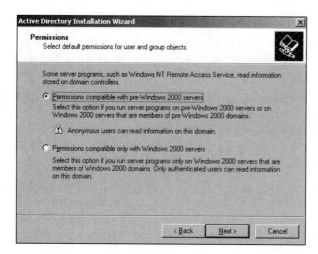

Figure 19.1   Active Directory mixed mode permissions.

domain created. After all domains are upgraded to Windows 2000 and the network has been converted to native mode, the manual non-transitive trusts will not be needed.

Windows 2000 GPOs and Windows NT system policies create another dilemma. In mixed mode, Windows NT Workstations and Servers continue to process policy files (Ntconfig.pol). As those systems are upgraded to Windows 2000, however, they will process Windows 2000 GPOs only by default. An option within GPOs can be configured to instruct client computers to run Windows NT policy files; however, you should be aware of the implications of enabling this option. Windows NT policies are applied at login and therefore will override GPO settings. You should ensure that GPO object settings and Windows NT policy settings are working together to accomplish the same goals and do not contradict each other.

The Security Accounts Manager in Mixed Mode

When a PDC running Windows NT 4 is upgraded to Windows 2000, the contents of the SAM are copied to the Active Directory. The user accounts become user objects, and the group accounts become group objects. Each object is placed in the appropriate container object with the Active Directory database. The following list documents which container object each type of account migrates to:

➤ User accounts migrate to the Users container object.

➤ Computer accounts migrate to the Computers container object.

➤ Built-in local and global groups migrate to the Builtin container object.

➤ Groups that were created manually migrate to the Users container object.

➤ The primary domain controller's computer account migrates to the domain controller's container object.

➤ The current permissions on all NTFS files and folders are retained. Shared folder and shared printer permissions are also retained.

Any user or group accounts that are created on a downlevel computer are automatically placed in the Users container object. For example, if a PDC has been upgraded to a Windows 2000 domain controller and a user account is then created from the console of a BDC, the new user account will be placed in the Users folder.

Because all objects created in a mixed mode are still replicated to all Windows NT BDCs, the Active Directory is limited by the SAM's 40MB limit. If the Active Directory database was to increase beyond the 40MB limit, then the BDC's copy of the SAM would become too large to manage.

Note: *The 40MB limit is not a hard-coded limit. Rather, it is a recommendation. The actual limit of the SAM depends on the hardware resources of the domain controller.*

Rollback Planning

Planning for a rollback to Windows NT 4 is an important part of your upgrade documentation. If you begin the upgrade of all the servers only to find that a critical application will not work, you will be forced to correct the problem or roll the network back to a Windows NT 4 Server–based network.

After converting all domain controllers to Windows 2000 Servers, you might decide to remain in mixed mode for a certain period so that the network can be rolled back if needed. If a BDC is taken offline and stored while all other servers are upgraded, you will have the ability to back out of an upgraded Windows 2000 network.

If the network needs to be rolled back, and the network is still in mixed mode, the stored BDC can be brought back online and synchronized with the PDC emulator. After the accounts database is synchronized, you can promote the BDC to a PDC and reinstall Windows NT Server on all servers.

Upgrade Considerations for Each Directory Service Model

19

Windows NT 4 has multiple directory service models that can be used to facilitate various network requirements. Some networks are relatively simple, while others can become extremely complex for political or technical reasons. To accommodate networks of all sizes, the following network models are identified.

➤ Single domain model

➤ Single master domain model

➤ Multiple master domain model

➤ Complete trust model

The single domain model is the most simple and most commonly implemented directory service model. Larger organizations utilize the single and multiple master domain models many times to accommodate large user counts and to provide for centralized control of the network. Companies in which each department or location developed their own network infrastructure many times implemented the complete trust directory service model.

Any one of the previously mentioned directory service models can easily fit into a single Windows 2000 domain model; however, what is more important than the directory model used is the reason that leads to using a particular directory model. The reasoning behind each directory service model is important, because it might decide the structure of your Active Directory, such as a single domain, multiple domain, single tree, or multiple trees. Domains, trees, and forests, and why they are important, are discussed in Chapter 7.

The first step in upgrading a domain is to upgrade the primary domain controller for the primary master domain. Before doing so, synchronize the domain so that all domain controllers have the same information. To ensure the safety of the existing system and to provide a rollback path, take one backup domain controller offline during the primary domain controller upgrade.

During installation, the Active Directory Installation Wizard appears. For the PDC of the existing master domain, choose the first tree in a new forest. The upgrade process will move the SAM and all its contents to the Active Directory and start the Kerberos protocol for authentication. After the PDC for the primary master domain is upgraded, the upgrades for the BDCs in the domain can take place.

Upgrading the Single Domain Model

The single domain model is the most used and the simplest to upgrade. Because the PDC for the domain already contains all the user accounts, you only need to upgrade the existing PDC to a Windows 2000 domain controller. After the PDC is upgraded to a Windows 2000 domain controller, Organizational Units can be created to divide the network into logical administrative units (see Figure 19.2).

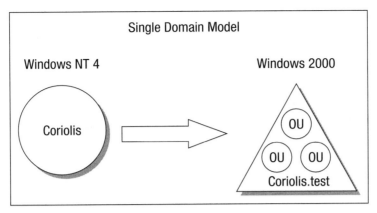

Figure 19.2   Single domain directory service model.

Upgrading the Single Master Domain Model

In Windows NT 4, the single master domain model is used when a network consists of multiple domains combined through trust relationships and centralized control of user accounts is required. Normally, the single master domain model is made up of resource domains and a single master domain that maintains user accounts. Each resource domain trusts the master domain, thereby allowing the user accounts that reside in the master domain to access resources within each resource domain. Resource administration in each domain allows administrators in each resource domain to add resources to the network; however, they cannot add user accounts to the master domain.

The purpose behind the single master is to allow centralized user account and permission administration while continuing to allow resource domain administrators to manage their own network resources, such as printers and file servers. The single master domain can easily be upgraded to a single Windows 2000 domain. Centralized account administration is still possible and resource administration can easily be delegated to Organizational Units with the single domain. However, many times it might make more sense to upgrade the single master domain model into an Active Directory containing multiple domains within a single tree, as illustrated in Figure 19.3.

Upgrading the Multiple Master Domain Model

The multiple master domain model is used primarily for the same reasons as the single master domain model. The two main reasons that a company would decide to use a multiple master domain model instead of a single master domain model are:

➤ A single master domain model is limited to the 40MB limit on the directory database. This will allow only approximately 40,000 or fewer users.

19

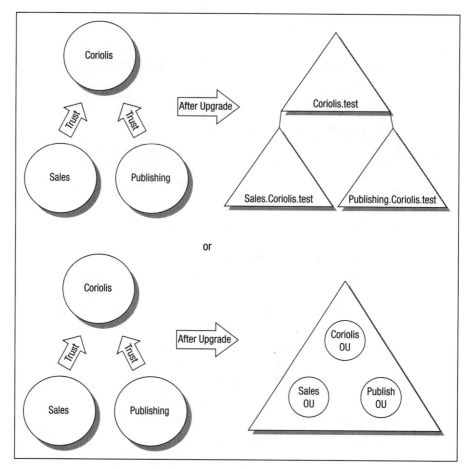

Figure 19.3 Single master directory service model.

Therefore, another master domain model is created, and the user accounts are split between the two master domains.

➤ The most logical domain to become the master domain is the domain in which the IT department resides. Many times, however, the corporate HQ also wants to have complete administrative control over the network. Therefore, the HQ and the IT domains both become master domains in the multiple master domain model.

In a multiple master domain model, each master domain must trust the other, and each resource domain must trust both master domains. In order to upgrade a multiple master directory service network to a Windows 2000 Active Directory network, you must first create a forest root domain. After the forest root domain is established, you can upgrade the PDC in each master domain and install the domain controllers as second-level domains in the new tree, as shown in Figure 19.4.

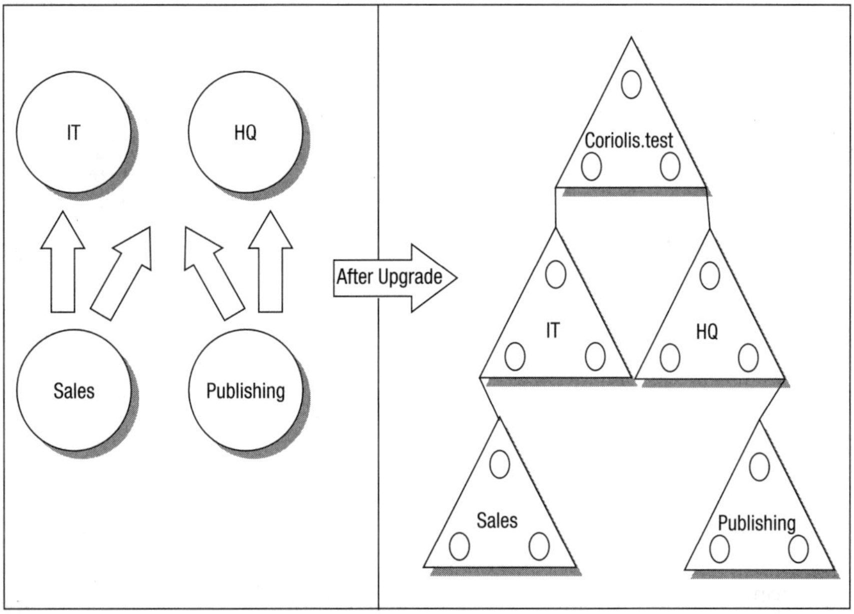

Figure 19.4 Multiple master domain model.

Note: Remember, you are limited to 40,000 user accounts while the Windows 2000 network is running in mixed mode. You must convert to native mode to avoid the 40MB SAM limit.

Upgrading the Complete Trust Model

The complete trust model is the most complicated model to administer. In this model, every domain maintains its own account database, so administration is not centralized; rather, it is split among each primary domain controller in each domain. Every domain trusts every other domain in a two-way non-transitive trust relationship.

Although this model is complicated to administer, it is simple to upgrade. Because all domains within an Active Directory tree participate in two-way transitive trust relationships, the default configuration of the Active Directory creates the same environment as the complete trust model in a Windows NT 4 network. All that must be created is an empty forest root domain. Then, each of the original domains becomes a child domain below the forest root domain, as shown in Figure 19.5.

Planning Organizational Units

Organizational Units (OU) allow an administrator to design a network around the logical structure of a business model. OUs are container objects that can contain user accounts, computer accounts, printers, shared folders, servers, and most any other object that can be stored in the Active Directory.

19

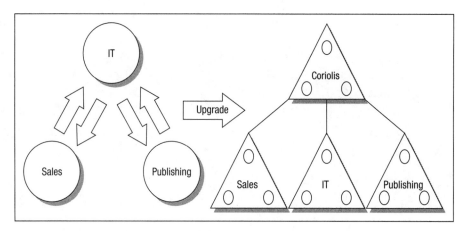

Figure 19.5 Complete trust model.

The fact that OUs can contain any network object makes them appear to be much like a Windows NT 4 domain. A domain is just a logical grouping of computers and users for the sake of security and administration. OUs provide the same functionality, and you can even create administrators that can create, delete, and modify any objects contained within an OU through a process called *delegation*.

Through the proper use of OUs, you can effectively set up domains within domains and subadministrators to manage each OU. Because of this, many multiple Windows NT domain models will be able to create a single domain within Windows 2000 and then use OUs to organize resources according to the logical business model.

Migrating Member Servers, Clients, and Resources

Upgrading member servers and client workstations requires little input from the user, and most operating system settings are preserved. Specific server functions might have issues that must be considered, however. File servers are often specific to particular departments or applications.

Some Windows 2000 network services require special consideration because they are so radically different from the equivalent services under Windows NT 4. One needs to consider planning for the Distributed file system as well as considering Macintosh and NetWare clients, print server considerations, client upgrade paths, and the creation of software distribution points for client upgrades.

Planning for the Distributed File System

Windows 2000 has the Distributed file system (Dfs) service, which means that all file resources can be centralized into one tree model. For instance, if four file servers are named Files, Accounting, Sales, and Marketing, all the shares can be presented under Dfs. To accomplish this, set up the Dfs root on the server named Files, and create Dfs links under the root that point to the shares on the other servers. This allows users to open one share on one server and access file shares on all the servers.

Macintosh and NetWare Client Considerations

Any file volumes that were previously available to Macintosh clients should be upgraded seamlessly as long as they or the AppleTalk protocol aren't removed. To make volumes available to NetWare clients, the Microsoft Services For NetWare must be installed from the add-on utilities for Windows 2000 and Windows NT 4 server package.

Print Server Considerations

The procedure for upgrading print servers is similar to that of file servers. For the most part, printers should come over with the upgrade, but some customization for Active Directory might be in order. Hosting printers for clients with operating systems other than Windows might require special services to be installed on the server. To host printers for Macintosh clients, Services for Macintosh and the AppleTalk protocol must be installed. To host printers that are NetWare 3.*x* and earlier print shares, the Gateway Services For NetWare and the NWLink protocol must be installed. To host printers for Unix or Linux clients, Unix TCP/IP Printing (LPD service) must be installed.

The organization of printers in the Active Directory is also slightly different than in the Windows NT 4 environment. Because most printers are used by departmental and geographical groups of users, OUs in the Active Directory are a convenient method for making printers available. To place printers into an OU, simply open Active Directory Users and Computers, right-click the appropriate OU, and select New Printer. Provide the wizard with the UNC path for the printer. File shares can also be advertised in this manner.

Client Upgrade Paths

Windows 2000 is a valid upgrade path for Windows 95, Windows 98, and Windows NT 4. When implementing a Windows 2000 network, a decision must be made to either upgrade existing operating systems or install Windows 2000 fresh on client computers. If the existing system has upgradeable client operating systems and the existing hardware and software are all compatible, upgrading is the obvious choice. However, significant hardware purchases might

19

be needed and some applications might not be Windows 2000 compatible, in which case a fresh install is often the only option. To assist you in your decision making, Tables 19.2 and 19.3 list the upgrade paths for downlevel server and client operating systems.

Creating Software Distribution Points for Client Upgrades

Whether upgrading or performing a fresh install, an organization with numerous clients will likely use an unattended installation method to expedite the process. First, one or more distribution points for the Windows 2000 installation files must be established. The placement of the distribution points depends on the bandwidth available between the server and the target clients. Table 19.4 details the folder structure of the distribution points.

Table 19.2   Upgrade paths for downlevel server operating systems.

Upgrade From	Upgrade To
Windows NT Server 3.1 or 3.5	Upgrade to Windows NT Server 3.51 or 4 and then to Windows 2000
Windows NT Server 3.51 or 4	Upgrade directly to Windows 2000 Server, Advanced Server, or Datacenter

Table 19.3   Upgrade paths for downlevel client operating systems.

Upgrade From	Upgrade To
Windows NT Workstation 3.1 or 3.5	Windows NT Workstation 3.51 or 4 and then Windows 2000 Professional
Windows NT Workstation 3.51 or 4	Windows 2000 Professional
Windows 95 or 98	Windows 2000 Professional
Windows 3.x	Windows 95 or 98 and then Windows 2000 Professional

Table 19.4   Distribution share contents.

Directory	Content Description
\i386	All contents of i386 folder on compact disk
\i386\OEM	Supplemental files for operating system installation
\i386\textmode	HAL drivers
\i386\$$	Same as \Winnt directory
\i386\$$\Help	Custom help files
\i386\$$\system32	Same as \Winnt\System32
\i386\$1	Same as root of installation drive
\i386\$1\<pnpdrivers>	Specialized plug-and-play drivers
\i386\$1\sysprep	Sysprep.exe, sysprep.inf, and setupcl.exe
\i386\<drive Letter>	Files to be copied to a specified drive
\i386\<drive letter>\Misc	Files to be copied to <drive>\Misc

With the distribution points in place, an installation method must be chosen. A fresh unattended install can be completed in a number of ways, including:

➤ *Syspart method*—If the hardware platforms are not consistent, the syspart method must be used.

➤ *Sysprep utility*—If the hardware is the same on all client computers, the sysprep utility can be used.

➤ *Remote operating system installation*—If the client machines are not accessible, the remote operating system installation can be used.

Develop an Active Directory Naming Strategy

Using the many features that depend on the Windows 2000 Active Directory requires the presence of a well-thought-out naming strategy. An effective naming strategy makes understanding, administering, and using the new network easier.

Planning a Naming Strategy

The first part of creating an effective naming strategy is to determine the number of domain levels you need. The number of domains needed depends greatly on the prior directory service model, which has already been discussed. You must understand that the structure of the directory dictates the naming structure, not the presence of a registered domain name. In other words, you should choose a naming strategy based on the structure of the Active Directory and not just use a name that has already been registered. If the entire Active Directory will be available from the Internet, then the root domain should be the registered name, as in **Coriolis.com**. If only a portion of the directory will be available from the Internet, however, then a subdomain should be the root of the Active Directory, as in **AD.Coriolis.com**. Finally, if no part of the Active Directory will be available from the Internet, then the root should be totally different from your registered name, as in **Coriolis.intra**.

Unique Names

All names in the directory must be unique within the namespace they are used. For example, you cannot have two domains with the same name within the same namespace. Therefore, you cannot use the name **coriolis.coriolis.test**. You could, however, have the name **sales.coriolis.test** and **sales.southeast. coriolis.test**, because each domain shares a different parent domain.

DNS Name Limits

Domain names can contain up to 63 characters (including periods); however, the complete fully qualified domain name of any object in the directory cannot exceed 255 characters. If your network contains a large number of child

19

domains, this could become an issue. Domain names should be kept as small as possible while still explaining their function or location.

Windows 2000 DNS allows letters and numbers, including A through Z, a through z, and 0 through 9. In addition, the hyphen (-) can be used in DNS names. Windows 2000 DNS servers also allow the use of Unicode character sets in order to support languages such as French, Spanish, and German. Care should be taken, however, if you are using DNS servers on platforms other than Windows 2000, because not all DNS applications support the Unicode character set.

Planning for Sites

Sites are an integral part of a Windows 2000 network infrastructure. Sites are used to control replication traffic as well as logon validation traffic. A site is a grouping of one or more TCP/IP subnets that are connected by high-speed network connections. In order to plan for sites properly, you must consider the following:

➤ *Site locations*—Each site should contain only servers and computers that are connected by low-cost high-speed network connections, such as a local area network. Sites are used to represent the physical/geographic structure of your network. Any two servers that are located within the same site will replicate with one another any time a change takes place within the directory. Servers in different sites can be configured to replicate information only during scheduled intervals. User logon validation traffic is normally limited to the site in which the request was generated.

➤ *Site links*—Planning site links is an important step in ensuring that replication traffic is properly passed from one site to another. Replication traffic follows site links to traverse from one site to another site until the information has been sent to all sites and all domain controllers within the forest.

➤ *Subnets and sites*—Each site must represent one or more subnets. Sites can be one or more or even part of a domain; however, a site must contain at least one entire subnet.

PERFORMING AN UPGRADE

After the upgrade plan is in place and all team members are on board, you are ready to begin the upgrade process. As mentioned earlier in this chapter, upgrading the network falls into six distinct steps:

1. Planning the upgrade

2. Establishing the root domain

3. Upgrading the primary domain controller

4. Upgrading the backup domain controllers

5. Switching the network to native mode

6. Testing the new system

Earlier in this chapter, we explained the planning process and documented the information you need to plan your conversion properly as well as some of the technical details involved with upgrading particular types of clients and servers. Now you are ready to establish a root domain for your new network.

Establishing a Root Domain

The root domain is the top-level domain name that is used throughout an enterprise's network. Furthermore, the root-level domain namespace identifies the Active Directory forest. If the root-level domain is not named and con-figured properly, all subsequent domains are compromised as well, because all child domains inherit the namespace of the forest root.

After planning, the first step in upgrading a network is to create the forest root. You can choose from two options when creating the first domain in a network—you can create a new domain, or you can promote a current Windows NT domain controller to Windows 2000 and use the existing NetBIOS domain name. The method you choose depends greatly on the existing domain model you are upgrading. For example, as discussed in the "Upgrade Considerations for Each Directory Service Model" section earlier in this chapter, the multiple master domain model can be upgraded by creating a new root-level domain and then making each master domain a child domain to the new root. If your current do-main model is the single or single master domain, you should consider upgrading the existing domain or master domain to the new root domain.

Upgrading an Existing Domain

When you upgrade an existing domain controller to Windows 2000 and install the Active Directory, the domain becomes the forest root. All user accounts, groups, and permissions will be carried over to the new network operating system. If you upgrade a single master domain to Windows 2000, you can then upgrade all the existing resource domains to Windows 2000 child domains. When upgrading existing Windows NT domains, the following objects are carried over to the new operating system:

➤ User accounts are copied to the Users container object.

➤ Computer accounts are copied to the Computers container object.

➤ Global groups are copied to the Users container object.

19

➤ Local groups are copied to the Users container object.

➤ Default groups are copied to the Builtin container object.

Each of the preceding objects and container objects can be viewed through the Active Directory Users and Computers Administrative tool, as shown in Figure 19.6.

Creating a New Domain

When upgrading a multiple master domain model, you should create a new domain to serve as the root domain. Each master domain can then be upgraded to become a child domain below the new root domain. When creating a new root domain, make sure that the root domain contains at least two domain controllers for fault tolerance. If there is only one domain controller in the root domain and it fails, you will be unable to add any additional domain controllers or domains to the network.

TESTING A PROPOSED SYSTEM

With the necessary documentation and plans in hand, you are ready to test the proposed system. The first tests should be performed in a completely segregated environment called a *lab*. This lab has many requirements—which will be different for every situation—because it should simulate the actual network environment as closely as possible. After thorough lab testing, the pilot systems can be deployed. The pilot systems must be functional, because they will be used for actual production. These tests must be as close to the proposed system as possible, and all issues should be resolved before deploying the new system.

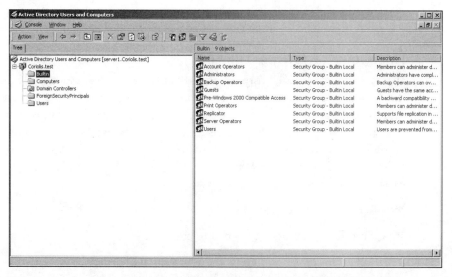

Figure 19.6   Active Directory Users and Computers Administrative tool.

Using a Test Lab for Testing

The first step in the implementation of a new system is to test the system in a controlled environment, or a test lab. For some organizations, one test environment will not be enough. Test environments should include all types of network media and topology as well as a representation of common WAN links.

The complexity of the test environment should closely mirror the complexity of the production environment for accurate and thorough testing. To secure funding for the test lab, management must be able to identify the benefits and return on investment of such a lab. Not only will the lab ensure system functionality, but it might also prevent costly downtime in the production environment. The lab will be useful for the new system implementation as well as testing any further changes to the system after it is implemented.

The test lab should mirror the actual system as closely as possible. The servers in the lab should have the same specifications as the servers that will be used for the new system. Also, any network services that will be used in the production environment should be tested, such as DHCP, DNS, and WINS. Client computers should include all types of clients from the new system, including desktops, notebook computers, and any special devices such as handheld or thin clients. Peripherals of all types should be tested, including printers, scanners, point-of-sale equipment, and any other specialized devices in the production environment. If there are interoperability issues, an effort should be made to expose the lab to these systems or simulate like systems in the lab.

The lab environment should be fully documented to assist with analysis and troubleshooting. The specifications of all the equipment must be detailed, including infrastructure devices. Both physical and logical diagrams should be developed to document the infrastructure and Active Directory structure. Responsibilities for lab maintenance and configuration should be documented, so there are no questions about who should be doing what. Common procedures should be documented to assist with training of new personnel. Finally, guidelines for change management and standard procedures should be included.

Pilot Programs for the Proposed System

After the new systems have been thoroughly tested in the lab environment, you are ready to pilot them in the production environment. The pilot users should be representative of the organization, which means that they should come from different departments with different duties. They should also have various client configurations, including desktop and notebook computers, a variety of client operating systems, and different geographical locations. The IT department is a good place to start with a pilot, because IT professionals tend to be high-end users. After all issues have been resolved for the IT users (or other select pilot users), the pilot can progress to other departments.

19

Communication among the deployment team and the pilot users is critical. Before beginning the pilot program, all pilot users should receive documents out-lining the purpose, scope, goals, and timelines for the program. Periodic newsletters outlining the program's progress should be distributed. Major milestones achieved should be celebrated as victories, and the status of issue resolutions should be shared with the testers. Adequate channels for feedback should be established. Periodic surveys, perhaps anonymous surveys, ensure that the pilot users are accommodated throughout the process. The pilot users must be willing participants, and they should have a representative who has a direct line of communication to the deployment team to help resolve immediate needs. All these elements help to develop a spirit of teamwork and ownership in the project.

The results of the pilot tests should be fully documented. From the initial rollout of the pilot systems to the eventual conclusion of the project, all issues and resolutions should be entered into a customer support database to assist with future troubleshooting. The implementation should be documented, including hardware and software specifications, network services, and infrastructure changes. These details can sometimes be compared to the database with issues and resolutions to form a cause-and-effect relationship between new systems and client issues. After the pilot program reaches maturity and all major issues are resolved, system implementation can begin.

CHAPTER SUMMARY

Performing network upgrades is extremely expensive and time consuming, so there should be adequate consideration of the cost, returns, and risks involved with the upgrade from the beginning. Intimate knowledge of the existing system, as well as thorough training on the new system, is necessary to perform the upgrade with a minimum of system interruptions. The migration will probably involve more than one person; instead, teams of technical experts as well as members of management and a representative group from the user community should be involved to ensure the proper functioning of the new system.

Documentation is possibly the most important requirement for a successful upgrade, and full documentation should be in place before the migration begins. First, documentation of the existing system needs to be collected and analyzed for possible gaps, and then the migration path should be planned and documented in such a way that the documents will assist with the migration without overburdening the migration teams. When documenting the technical requirements for the migration, you need to include hardware and software compatibility.

During the migration, certain aspects of the network and its services will be in flux. Member servers and client machines with compatible hardware and software can be upgraded at any time with little impact on the system as a whole. At least one backup domain controller from each domain should be taken off-line while the migration takes place. If there is a problem with the migration, the old NT 4 domain can be temporarily restored using the offline domain controller. When the first domain controller is upgraded to Windows 2000, the domain will be in mixed mode. Mixed mode is necessary as long as there are domain controllers running Windows NT 4. Mixed mode does not have many of the enhancements that a Windows 2000 domain in native mode has, but it is useful for short-term use during the migration. This chapter has identified migration strategies for most existing domain models to ease the transition. With the Organizational Unit level of delegation, however, some resource domains may be able to be phased out. Finally, there may be additional planning necessary because certain network services have been dramatically changed.

A Windows 2000 network introduces some new concepts and places new importance to some existing concepts. A Windows 2000 network depends entirely on the DNS naming strategy used for the network, which means that the choices made for the naming of the root domain will have a direct impact on the entire network. A new concept called a *site* has also been introduced. Sites are based on physical location, and they are used to control replication traffic in the enterprise.

After these last issues are resolved and the teams are built, the system is ready for implementation. The first implementation should be in a test lab that is representative of the actual operating environment for the new system. After any issues uncovered in the test lab are resolved, the system is ready for some real world trials. A pilot group of users selected specially from specific areas of the company are used for the initial implementation. Finally, once the pilot group has determined that the system is useful and bug free, the final implementation can occur.

REVIEW QUESTIONS

1. When upgrading the first domain controller in an enterprise to Windows 2000, choose _____ in a(n) _____.

   a. Child domain, existing tree

   b. First tree, new forest

   c. New tree, existing forest

   d. Child tree, existing forest

19

2. When upgrading a PDC for the second master domain where both master domains are autonomous systems, choose _____ in a(n) _____.

   a. Child domain, existing tree

   b. First tree, new forest

   c. New tree, existing forest

   d. Child tree, existing forest

3. When upgrading a PDC for a resource domain, choose _____ in a(n) _____.

   a. Child domain, existing forest

   b. First tree, new forest

   c. New tree, existing forest

   d. Child tree, existing forest

4. When upgrading a BDC, choose _____ in a(n) _____.

   a. Child domain, existing tree

   b. First tree, new forest

   c. New tree, existing forest

   d. New controller, existing domain

5. What is the name of the technology that allows file shares from multiple servers to be represented under one logical share?

   a. Distributed file sharing

   b. Domain file sharing

   c. Distributed file system

   d. Domain file system

6. What do you need to install and configure to accommodate file and print sharing for Apple Macintosh clients?

   a. AppleTalk Network Services

   b. Services For Macintosh

   c. Services For AppleTalk

   d. Macintosh Network Services

7. What do you need to install to provide printers to Unix and Linux clients?

    a. Unix Printing Services

    b. TCP/IP Printing Services

    c. Unix Printing Services

    d. Printing Service For Unix

8. The best way to advertise file and printer shares used by a specific department is by placing them into the department's _____.

    a. Network Neighborhood

    b. Network directory

    c. Organizational Unit

    d. Resource container

9. Which of the following operating systems can be upgraded to Windows 2000? [Check all correct answers]

    a. Windows 95

    b. Windows 98

    c. Windows NT 4

    d. Windows 3.1

10. During the planning stages, it is important to keep the details of the new system secret from the user community.

    a. True

    b. False

11. If the hardware platforms are not consistent on a network, which utility must be used for unattended installs?

    a. SMS

    b. Syspart

    c. Sysprep

    d. RIS

12. After the naming strategy for the root domain is determined, changing it requires the re-creation of the primary and secondary DNS zones.

    a. True

    b. False

19

13. Once a domain is changed from mixed mode to native mode, the PDC Emulator is no longer required.

    a. True

    b. False

14. You can create logical domains by creating and delegating authority to _____.

    a. Dfs

    b. Forests

    c. Organizational Units

    d. Child domains

15. The Legacy Limousine Company is in the planning phase of their Windows 2000 Network upgrade. Currently, Legacy's Windows NT 4 network is using a multiple master domain model. How should Legacy plan to upgrade to Windows 2000?

    a. Create a new root-level domain, and add each master domain to the root as a child domain.

    b. Promote one of the master domains to Windows 2000 and make it the master domain. Then, add each additional master domain as a child domain.

    c. Create a new forest for each master domain. Then, add the resource domains as child domains.

    d. Create a new tree for each master domain. Each resource domain will become a child domain.

16. The ACME corporation currently uses a single master domain model. The SAM database on ACME's PDC is currently 41MB. What strategy should ACME use to upgrade their existing Windows NT network to Windows 2000?

    a. ACME should create a new domain as the forest root. Then, ACME should upgrade the existing domain as a child domain.

    b. ACME should upgrade the master domain and add any additional resource domains as child domains.

    c. ACME cannot upgrade until the SAM is less than 40MB.

    d. ACME should upgrade a resource domain to the new forest root, because the SAM database in the resource domains will not be 40MB. Then, ACME should add the master domain as a child domain with all other resource domains.

17. The ANSI Company installed their Windows NT network two years ago as a single master domain model. The company chose the single master domain model because each department wanted to control its own network resources and the IT department wanted to maintain control over all user accounts. Now that the company is upgrading to Windows 2000, what domain strategy should ANSI choose?

    a. The master domain should become the forest root domain, and the resource domains should be eliminated.

    b. The master domain should become the forest root, and all resource domains should become child domains.

    c. A new forest root should be created, and all existing Windows NT domains should become child domains.

    d. A new forest root should be created, and all existing Windows NT domains should be eliminated.

18. Fred is planning the Windows 2000 upgrade for a small college campus. Each building within the network should be configured as a separate site to reduce replication traffic over the switched network. If each building is to be a separate site, then each building must:

    a. Also be a separate domain

    b. Be a member of the same domain

    c. Contain a separate subnet

    d. Be a member of the same subnet

19. Susan is creating an upgrade plan for a small travel company that currently runs Windows 3.1 Server. The network has 50 client computers, of which 30 are running Windows 95 and the remaining 20 are running Windows 3.1. The company wants to upgrade all computers to Windows 2000. What should Susan's documentation include? [Check all correct answers]

    a. Upgrading the server to Windows NT 3.51 and then upgrading to Windows 2000.

    b. Upgrading the computers running Windows 3.1 to Windows 98 and then upgrading to Windows 2000.

    c. Upgrading the computers running Windows 95 to Windows NT Workstation and then upgrading to Windows 2000.

    d. Upgrading the server to Windows NT 4 and then upgrading to Windows 2000.

19

20. The Legacy Limousine Company is upgrading their Windows NT PDC to Windows 2000. The PDC currently has 25 groups that were created by the administrator. When the upgrade is complete, where can the administrator find the group objects?

   a. Groups container object

   b. Builtin container object

   c. Local Groups container object

   d. Users container object

REAL-WORLD PROJECTS

Andy Palmer has been assigned to a new client that would like to migrate their existing system from Windows NT 4 to Windows 2000. They would like to upgrade all the clients, member servers, and domain controllers to gain the full benefit from the new features of Windows 2000.

Andy has evaluated the client systems for the system. He has determined that all the systems use software and hardware that is compatible with Windows 2000. He has also determined that all systems have the identical Hardware Abstraction Layer (HAL). The users do not need to retain their settings or files from the systems, which makes them a good candidate for a third-party imaging tool. To prepare the system for imaging, Andy uses the sysprep tool.

Project 19.1

To use sysprep to install Windows 2000, complete the following steps:

1. Install Windows 2000 Professional on the source computer that has similar hardware as the target computers, and then join the computer to the domain.

2. Log on as Administrator with a blank password, and configure and customize the source computer, including applications.

3. Prepare a sysprep.ini file with the desired customization information for each target computer. Listing 19.1 shows a sample sysprep.ini file, similar to the file prepared by Andy.

Listing 19.1   A sample sysprep.ini file.

```
[Unattended]
OemSkipEula=yes
KeepPageFile=0
InstallFilesPath=%systemdrive%\sysprep\i386
[GuiUnattended]
```

```
AdminPassword=""
TimeZone=20
OemSkipWelcome=1
OemSkipRegional=0
[UserData]
FullName="Joe User"
OrgName="Your Company"
ComputerName="Your-Computer"
[Identification]
JoinDomain=yourdomain
[TapiLocation]
AreaCode=111
[Networking]
InstallDefaultComponents=yes
```

4. Create a directory at the distribution point named OEM\$1\Sysprep and place the files sysprep.exe and setupcl.exe in the directory.

5. Run sysprep.exe with the sysprep.inf file on the source computer. When the process is finished, restart the computer.

6. Use a third-party disk imaging software application to duplicate the source disk to the target disks.

7. Place a floppy disk with the appropriate sysprep.inf file into the target machine's floppy drive and start the machine.

Andy knows that he will need some unattended installation answer files. To create these files, he uses the setup manager tool that is shipped with Windows 2000.

Project 19.2

To use the setup manger to create an unattended.txt file, complete the following steps:

1. Copy the contents of the \support\tools\Deploy.cab to the winnt folder on the host computer.

2. Configure the host computer with the appropriate configuration and customizations.

3. Click Start|Run, type "c:\winnt\setupmgr.exe", and press Enter.

4. When the wizard appears, click Next.

5. As shown in Figure 19.7, choose Create A New Answer File, and click Next.

19

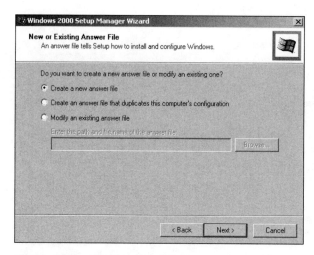

Figure 19.7 Starting the setup manager to create an unattend.txt file.

6. Choose Windows 2000 Unattended Install, and click Next.

7. Select Windows 2000 Professional, and click Next.

8. Select Fully Automated, then click Next.

9. Accept the terms of the license agreement, then click Next.

10. Provide the username and organization name, and click Next.

11. Chose Automatically Generate Computer Names Based On Organization Name, and click Next.

12. Provide an administrator password, then click Next.

13. Accept the default display settings, then click Next.

14. Select Typical Network Settings, then click Next.

15. Chose Windows Server Domain, check Create A Computer Account, provide the domain name and administrator credential, then click Next.

16. Select the appropriate time zone, and click Next.

17. Select Do Not Modify Additional Settings, then click Next.

18. Select No, This Answer File Is For CD Installation, and then click Next.

19. Specify the path to save the file, then click Next.

20. Click Finish. For reference, Listing 19.2 shows a sample unattend.txt file.

Listing 19.2   A sample unattend.txt file.

```
;SetupMgrTag
[Data]
AutoPartition=1
MsDosInitiated="0"
UnattendedInstall="Yes"
[Unattended]
UnattendMode=FullUnattended
OemSkipEula=Yes
OemPreinstall=Yes
TargetPath=\WINNT
[GuiUnattended]
AdminPassword=password
AutoLogon=Yes
AutoLogonCount=1
OEMSkipRegional=1
TimeZone=35
OemSkipWelcome=1
[UserData]
FullName="Andy Palmer"
OrgName=Coriolis
ComputerName=AxisPro
[Display]
BitsPerPel=32
Xresolution=800
YResolution=600
[TapiLocation]
CountryCode=1
Dialing=Tone
AreaCode=502
[RegionalSettings]
LanguageGroup=1
Language=00000409
[SetupMgr]
DistFolder=C:\win2000dist
DistShare=win2000dist
[GuiRunOnce]
Command0=runonce.exe
[Identification]
JoinDomain=coriolis
DomainAdmin=administrator
DomainAdminPassword=
[Networking]
InstallDefaultComponents=Yes
```

19

SECURING A WINDOWS 2000 NETWORK

After completing this chapter, you will be able to:

✓ Plan and implement network security

✓ Secure the authentication and logon process

✓ Control access to resources using trusts and access control lists

✓ Protect network data and communications

✓ Ensure standard security policy implementation

S ecurity is one of the most important issues a network administrator is faced with, but unfortunately security often takes a back seat to the functionality of the system. In this chapter we'll look at some of the facilities that Windows 2000 provides to help secure the network.

PLANNING AND IMPLEMENTING NETWORK SECURITY

Security in a client/server environment is extremely complex due to the distributed nature of client/server systems. Therefore, to secure network communications and resources properly, a thorough plan and meticulous implementation must be used. Providing access to resources so that unauthorized access is prohibited and authorized access is convenient can be a delicate balance. A thorough plan assesses the risks, develops strategies, and details administrative procedures necessary to secure distributed information systems.

Analyzing Common Security Issues

Information systems are subjected to a number of risks on a daily basis. Some of these risks are outright attacks on systems by either professional hackers or amateur thrill seekers. Other attacks are committed by trusted network users who have an overactive curiosity. A good network security plan can secure your network from these risks; it can also help to deter further attacks because attackers will soon learn that the cost of waging an attack—which is necessarily complex—is simply too large. Basically, three elements of a client/server network can be attacked: user accounts, the network, and data.

User Account Attacks

Some attacks seek to gain access to systems by way of a valid user account. A valid username and password combination is like a golden key for a hacker, and hackers can obtain such information in a number of ways. For example, sometimes valid users simply abuse their privileges. In other cases, *social engineering* is used to deceive users into providing information. For instance, an email sent to users notifying them that their passwords will expire if they do not reply with their username and password often seems official enough to garner a response. A phone call from a bogus IT employee asking to verify confidential information can also lead a user to divulge a password or secret key phrase. Other tactics used to gain user account information can be as simple as a *brute force attack*, in which a hacker tries to guess a password. For example, a hacker might enter a user's logon name and then enter significant details from that person's life—such as a child's or spouse's name—as a password. In addition, *keyboard buffer attacks* can capture the keystrokes that a person enters when he or she logs in; a hacker can replay the keystrokes later to gain access to the user's account. Finally, actual data transmissions can be intercepted and decrypted to reveal a username and password combination.

Network Attacks

Some network attacks exploit holes in the authentication and access control portions of a system to intercept data. Two common network attacks are:

➤ *Masquerade attack*—Involves the capturing of packets and manipulation of source address or identity. Once a packet is seen as emanating from a trusted source, many system checks are bypassed and the attacker has access to system resources.

➤ *Replay attack*—Occurs when a transaction or series of transactions are recorded by an attacker and played back at a time when it is convenient to gain unauthorized access.

In addition, simple interception of network transmissions can reveal critical information to attackers, such as marketing or research and development plans. Data can also be manipulated by attackers for their benefit. For instance, the destination of a financial transaction can be changed to a specified bank account where the funds are quickly withdrawn by the attackers.

Data Attacks

The final type of attack—a data attack—can seem pointless, because the aim of a data attack is often simply to interrupt network communication or destroy data. Common *viruses* or *Trojan horses* are actually malicious code inside useful code. After the useful code is executed, the malicious code is released to destroy data or interrupt processing. Users are often trained not to run programs that they do not trust, which quickly circumvents these attacks. *Macro viruses* and *mobile code* follow the same concept as regular viruses, but they exploit the built-in scripting utilities of trusted applications—such as electronic mail readers or World Wide Web browsers—so they are more difficult to control. Finally, a *denial of service attack* uses known exploits in server platforms to overwhelm a system so that it can no longer respond to valid user requests. Although an attacker does not directly benefit from a denial of service attack, the disruption of services can cost the targeted company millions of dollars.

Windows NT Security Models

A security model is a logical diagram of how security is controlled by a system. Multiuser systems, such as mainframes and large Unix servers, use the *centralized* security model in which every user is treated as a remote user. This type of security model is often very secure, because all resources are kept in one place. These systems are limited by geography and scalability, however. Other systems, such as NetWare 3.*x* and smaller distributed Unix systems, allow resources to be distributed to a limited number of powerful servers. These systems overcome geographic and scalability issues by adding the complexity of multiple logons

20

for individual users. In contrast, Windows NT 4 uses the *domain model* of security, which identifies autonomous systems that can be trusted by other systems. NT 4 overcomes geographic limitations without adding unnecessary complexity, but it still isn't scalable enough for modern information systems.

In the late 1980s, an effort was undertaken to interconnect systems through a standard directory of resources. This effort resulted in the X.500 directory model, which can also serve as a basis for a distributed security model. The X.500 standard received limited acceptance in the mainframe and Unix worlds, but it wasn't until the late 1990s that the standard was implemented on a large scale in NetWare 4.*x* and later. With the introduction of Microsoft Windows 2000, parts of the X.500 model and the Lightweight Directory Access Protocol (LDAP) are poised to become the directory and security model of the next generation of information systems. Windows 2000 still uses the domain model, but it is combined with the LDAP and X.500 forest and tree models to provide further scalability. In Windows 2000, the worldwide directory is made up of autonomous systems called *forests*. Each forest is a noncontiguous namespace maintained by a single entity. The forest contains one or more *trees*. A tree is a contiguous namespace based on the Internet Domain Name System. A tree contains one Windows 2000 root domain and can contain additional Windows 2000 domains in a parent/child or sibling relationship with each other. These domains form trust relationships, so resources can be universally accessible and relatively easy to find.

The first interaction most users have with a network is the login process. During this process, the network operating system verifies the identity of the user by one of many ways. Let's take a look at how to secure this process, which is called *authentication*.

SECURING THE AUTHENTICATION AND LOGON PROCESS

The authentication and logon process is the front door to an information system. As such, it is often the focus of attacks. Numerous methods have been used to secure the authentication and logon process, and, up to the current generation of systems, the methods were mostly proprietary. With the growth of the Internet and the acceptance of the X.500 directory model, standards-based authentication and logon protocols have been adopted on a widespread scale. A number of methods are used to secure the login process. Some of the methods vary depending on the type of access, as in local or remote. Other methods add a variable to the login process, using tokens like smart cards.

Kerberos Authentication Protocol

The Kerberos 5 protocol is an Internet standard, and it is the main method for authentication in Windows 2000. Not only does Kerberos authenticate a user, but it also authenticates the resources being accessed. When a user logs onto the system, the user is issued a session ticket, which is like a ticket to get into a movie, except it will let the user into a particular domain, machine, resource, and so forth. From that point forward, new tickets are generated, based on the initial ticket, every time a new network service is accessed. The user is not involved in this ticketing process, so the complexities are almost entirely hidden. Although the user has only one username and password, encryption and the ticketing process makes interception of the username and password much more difficult.

Kerberos is automatically implemented in Windows 2000, but it should be further set as the only authentication protocol. Using Kerberos for Windows 2000 authentication also allows users on Unix systems that employ Kerberos to access Windows 2000 resources. One caveat of Kerberos is that the system clocks must be synchronized for authentication to take place. Although the default trust relationships implemented with Windows 2000 provide for authentication across domains, sometimes adding trusts between sibling domains can speed up the Kerberos authentication process. Kerberos does not allow authentication across separate forests, but Windows 2000 continues to support protocols that support authentication in a separate forest (such as Windows NT Challenge/Response, or NTLM).

Using Smart Card Authentication

A smart card is an item that can be carried by a user to provide another layer of logon security. Network security has traditionally been based on who you are (a username) and what you know (a password). Smart cards add a third variable to the authentication process—what you have (the smart card). The smart card contains a chip that stores critical security information about a user. When a user approaches a machine, the user inserts the smart card into the smart card reader and supplies the personal identification number (PIN) when requested.

The smart card actually stores a user's private key on an embedded chip. The private key can then be used to generate public keys based on the private key's algorithm. This facilitates public key encryption for network communication, Authenticode signatures, electronic mail encryption, and countless other public key infrastructure (PKI) applications. With the smart card system in place, an attacker could gain a user's name and password and still not be able to infiltrate the network.

20

Smart card security comes with certain costs, though, including:

➤ The Extensible Authentication Protocol (EAP) must be enabled for the proprietary format of the smart card to function.

➤ A smart card station must be set up to issue the cards.

➤ A public key infrastructure must be implemented using Microsoft Certificate Server or a third-party X.509 certificate source.

➤ Workstations need to have smart card readers.

➤ Policies must be established for when users lose or forget their smart cards.

As you can see, the implementation of smart cards should not be taken lightly. The real cost and administrative overhead can be quite substantial.

Securing Remote Access Servers

The Remote Access Service (RAS) can provide seamless access to network resources for users that are not directly connected to the network. These services are also provided by the Routing and Remote Access Service (RRAS), but this chapter deals only with general RAS issues. (RAS is covered in more detail in Chapter 16.) Because RAS involves dialing in from a public circuit switched telephone network or connecting from a publicly available packet switched network (the Internet), RAS can be quite a target for intruders. RAS is based on three conditions:

➤ *The system's RAS policy must allow user access*—RAS policies specify rules, such as whether to permit remote access, the protocols to use, and the times of day that remote access is permitted. RAS policies can be applied or filtered by using standard administrative practices.

➤ *Users must have permission to gain access*—Users have permission for remote access. This permission is set in the user properties page using the Active Directory Users and Computers console.

➤ *The authentication between users and servers must take place*—The authentication protocol must match between the user and the RAS server. Windows 2000 supports CHAP, MS-CHAP, PAP, and SPAP. Additionally, EAP can allow Transport layer security and the use of smart cards for remote authentication.

If any one of these conditions is not met, the user is not granted access to the network. In addition, although RAS can be a system's greatest vulnerability, if implemented properly, it can be a safe and convenient method for extending a network.

Once a user is logged in to a network, they usually expect to access some sort of resources on the network. However, different users need access to different resources. Therefore it is necessary to secure the resources on the network.

CONTROLLING ACCESS TO RESOURCE ACLS AND INTERDOMAIN TRUSTS

Access to resources is controlled using access control lists (ACLs). ACLs are lists of users and security groups with associated permissions applied to resources. The security groups used to implement ACLs are particularly important, because they allow administrators to grant or deny access on a widescale basis. Interdomain trust relationships are also important, because they enable users and groups from more than one domain to access a resource. When implemented with care and combined with groups and trusts, ACLs are an administrator's most valuable tool.

Introduction to Access Control Lists

Every resource in a Windows 2000 network has a list of particular users and groups with the permissions for the actions that the users and groups can commit to the resource. Permissions vary for different types of resources. For instance, a printer object has permissions that relate to printing, such as Print and Manage Documents. File resources have file-type permissions, like Read, Write, Execute, and Delete. Even folders have special permissions for listing folder contents.

Access control lists have a few rules that must be followed. This list of permissions can be granted or denied for a particular user or group. This can lead to certain overlapping conditions. For example, when a user has permissions and a group of which the user is a member has different permission, the *effective permissions* must be calculated. Effective permissions are always the more permissive of user and group permissions. The exception to this rule is the Deny set of permissions. Anytime a set of permissions is explicitly denied, the denied permissions take precedence over any granted permissions a user might have. Resources can also have separate access lists for remote users, called *share permissions*. Whenever a set of local NTFS permissions exists for a user or group, and a set of remote share permissions is applied (any time the user accesses the resource through the network), the most restrictive permissions are applied. Of course, if any permissions are explicitly denied through NTFS or share permission, the denial will take precedence over any permissions that are granted.

Implementing Security Groups

The proper design of security groups is critical to the efficient use of ACLs. When a user logs on, a token is generated that details the user's membership in security groups. This token is then used in conjunction with ACLs to determine the user's level of access to network resources.

20

Windows 2000 supports many types of security groups. Each group has special characteristics that make them particularly useful in certain situations. The various types of security groups include:

➤ *Domain local group*—Used to access resources within a domain. The advantage of a domain local group is that it can contain members from any trusted domain in a forest.

➤ *Global group*—Used to organize domain users by common characteristics, such as geographical location or organizational department. The advantage of a global group is that it can cross over to be placed in local groups in trusting domains.

➤ *Universal group*—Used to collect global groups and users from any domain in the forest, and grant access to resources in any domain in the forest. The drawback is that the membership is recorded in the global catalog, which adds significant overhead for frequently changing groups.

➤ *Machine local group*—Used for local machine resources and cannot be used (or even seen) anywhere else in the domain.

Securing Interdomain Trusts

Trust relationships are used to allow interdomain resource sharing. Trusts have certain characteristics that determine their behavior in a network. Trusts can be classified as follows:

➤ *One-way trust*—Provides resources from one domain, called the *trusting domain*, to be available to users in another domain, called the *trusted domain*.

➤ *Two-way trust*—Makes the resources in both domains that are involved with the trust available to users in both domains.

➤ *Non-transitive trust*—Means that a trust relationship between two domains has no effect on the trust relationships between either of the domains and any third domain.

➤ *Transitive trust*—Means that a trust between two domains might have an effect on the trust relationships with a third domain. For instance, if domain A trusts domain B with a non-transitive trust, and domain B trusts domain C with a non-transitive trust, domains A and C have no implied trust relationship. On the other hand, if the same situation exists with transitive trusts, then there would be an implied trust between domains A and C.

Windows 2000 domains use two-way transitive trusts among themselves. However, any trust relationships within Windows NT 4 domains or Kerberos version 5 realms can be only one-way and only non-transitive. Finally, any trusts that traverse forest lines must be one-way non-transitive trusts.

Once the login process and the resources are secured, the actual communication over the network is still not secure. Let's take a look at some methods for securing communication on the network.

PROTECTING NETWORK DATA AND COMMUNICATIONS

Protecting data is necessary at the client machine where the data is used, on the server that stores the data, and on the wire during data transmission across the network. Although authentication and access control are the primary means of protecting resources, data encryption can be used to circumvent many of the intrusion attempts committed by attackers. The Encrypting File System (EFS) is used to encrypt data on client machines or servers, while IPSec (IP Security) is used to encrypt data during transmission over a network.

Securing Data with the Encrypting File System

The EFS uses public key encryption to let users protect their file resources. Once a file is encrypted, only the user with the key or an administrator that is designated as an encrypted data recovery agent can decrypt the file. An encrypted file cannot be recovered without the key, so encryption is often used to secure data on mobile or public computers that are at risk of theft. EFS adds a layer of security by using a public key to encrypt the key that was used to encrypt the file. This user's key can be replaced with the key from an encrypted file recovery agent. If a user's key should be lost, the recovery agent can decrypt the files with a special key. This entire process takes place behind the scenes, with no user intervention. As long as users log onto the network or local machines with the appropriate credentials, they can encrypt and decrypt local files.

The EFS is not automatically implemented. The volume containing the files to be encrypted must be formatted with NTFS version 5 (the Windows 2000 implementation). An X.509 public key infrastructure is necessary for the encrypting file system to be implemented, and certificates must be issued to users as well as the encrypted file recovery agent. After these prerequisites have been met, files can be encrypted by users on their local machines.

Using IPSec Policies to Secure Network Communications

Windows 2000 can encrypt network traffic at the IP layer of the protocol stack. This means that the data is secure on the network wire but the applications at either end are not concerned with this encryption. IPSec policies can be applied to domain or Organizational Units. The policies contain filters that defined the types of traffic that need to be secured. If traffic needs to be secured, the source and destination computers negotiate an encryption format using the Internet Key Exchange protocol. The encryption can use Kerberos, X.509 certificates, or a preshared set of encryption keys. The source computer also signs the outgoing packets to ensure that no one tampers with them.

20

IPSec is a valuable asset in battling data manipulation, interception, and replay attacks. This protection comes at a cost, however. A large amount of overhead is associated with the encryption and decryption of network traffic. Therefore, IPSec is best suited for specific network applications. Peer-to-peer IPSec can protect data for financial- or executive-level communications, and, because it is peer-to-peer, no single server is burdened by the overhead associated with it. Remote access is also a good candidate for IPSec implementation. IPSec can be combined with Layer 2 Tunneling Protocol (L2TP) to secure RAS and WAN communications through nonsecure networks.

With all these different methods of securing the network, there must be a method to keep track of it all. Security policies are used to assist with the administration of network security settings.

ENSURING STANDARD SECURITY POLICY IMPLEMENTATION

To maintain a network effectively, security policies must be standardized and categorized. The standard group policy editor allows certain security settings to be applied to Active Directory containers (such as domains and Organizational Units). Windows 2000 also provides a tool that can apply security settings to certain types of machines. For instance, a template can be made for a public workstation, and then the template can be applied to all public workstations in the organization. With the Windows 2000 security implementation tools, standard security policies can be applied to assist with keeping the total cost of ownership for a network to a minimum.

Using Group Policies to Implement Security

The group policy computer configuration node provides numerous security settings that can be set at various levels. Group policies are normally inherited from the site level, to the domain, and finally to the Organizational Unit, with the policies closest to the target object taking precedence over policies that are more distant. However, with security settings, the policies are applied at either the domain level or the local machine level. We'll start our discussion with the domain-wide security policies.

Domain-Wide Security Policies

Security policies applied on a domain-wide basis apply to account passwords, account lockout, and Kerberos authentication. The password policies include a minimum length and a complexity requirement. Settings relating to password age (such as minimum and maximum password ages) and a password history can be customized. The account lockout policy details the number of failed logon attempts before a user is locked out, the amount of time the account is locked, and the amount of time before the failed logon count resets. Finally, Kerberos settings, such as ticket lifetime and ticket renewal time, are set in this node.

Local Security Policies

Local security policies are applied to computers in the scope of a policy. For example, the audit policy allows auditing of numerous events based on their success, failure, or both. Events that can be audited include account logons, account management, object access, directory service access, and system events. The local policies also include user rights assignments. Rights such as log on local, access computer from the network, and the right to add workstations to the domain can be set in this policy node. Finally, the security options in the local system policy customize items such as shutdown without logging on and pressing Ctl+Alt+Del to log on.

You can also access nodes for customizing event logs, restricted groups, system services, registry, and file system security:

➤ The event log settings can be used to define how large event logs can get and when to begin to overwrite the logs.

➤ Restricted groups allow certain groups to have their membership frozen so that, if additional members are added to the restricted group, the users will be automatically removed from the group.

➤ The system services settings allow the startup method to be customized for individual services on local machines.

➤ Access control lists for the registry and the file system can be set using a policy and applied to all computers in the scope of the policy.

The last security settings in the group policy apply to public keys and IPSec policies. The encrypted data recovery agent is specified here, and new members can be added to the encrypted data recovery agent's group. The policy can be set to request a certificate of a particular type automatically from a certificate authority the next time a computer logs on. A list of trusted root certificate authorities can be built here, and new certificate authorities can be added as needed. Enterprise trusts allow external certificate authorities to be added and trusted for a specified amount of time. The IP Security policies dictate default IPSec behavior for specific classes of machines. By default, client machines will communicate using clear text, servers will request a Kerberos trust, and secure servers will require a Kerberos trust for communication.

Using the Security Analysis Tool and Templates

The Security Template snap-in allows predefined security templates to be created, modified, and saved. Templates are provided for a basic workstation, basic server, and basic domain controller. Furthermore, incremental security templates provide a workstation compatible with Windows NT 4 workstation settings, a secure workstation, and a highly secure workstation. These templates can all be applied using group policies, but the effects should be analyzed first.

To analyze security settings, create a console with the Security Configuration and Analysis snap-in. Create a new database, and analyze your computer's current settings to get a baseline of the current system. When prompted for a template, choose the template that you want to implement. The security analysis tool will compare the current settings to the template and display any differences with a red flag. This allows you to identify the possible impact of the new policies and make changes to the template if necessary before deploying it.

CHAPTER SUMMARY

In the age of the Internet, information systems face many new challenges. Perhaps the biggest challenge for a system administrator is security. Many types of attacks can be aimed toward a network, and each type requires a distinct method of protection. Some attacks are waged by trusted employees who seek to test their bounds. Some hackers focus on direct financial gain, while others simply seek to disrupt a functioning system for some kind of fame or prowess. One of the first methods of protecting a system is defining the boundaries of the system. A number of security models exist, but the most promising is the X.500-based directory model. Windows 2000 uses the Active Directory (which is based on the X.500 standard) to define system boundaries that accommo-date the functionality and scalability demanded by today's companies.

With the boundaries of a system defined, a method to allow access to the system must be implemented. Windows 2000 uses the Kerberos version 5 authentication protocol for this purpose, because it is highly secure and compatible with numerous other systems. In addition to Kerberos, Windows 2000 supports the Extensible Authentication Protocol (EAP), which allows other proprietary authentication protocols to be easily implemented as needed. One use of EAP is smart card security. A smart card is a device that a user possesses. This adds a layer of security to the authentication process, because now the requirements for logging on are who you are (a username) and what you know (a password) as well as what you have (a smart card). The last authentication concern is remote access servers. Since a RAS server is connected to a public telephone network, extra care must be taken to secure RAS servers. Windows 2000 uses RAS policies to apply standard security settings for a RAS server to prevent unauthorized access.

After a user enters a system with appropriate credentials, rules must be in place that control the user's access to resources. These rules are called access control lists, or ACLs. ACLs contain users or groups of users and the permissions that they have for particular resources. To manage large numbers of users effectively, different types of security groups are needed. For groups based on geography or organizational structure, global groups are very effective. To manage access to resources in a single domain, domain local groups are appropriate, because they can contain global groups or users from many domains. Finally, universal groups can contain users and groups from many domains, and they can grant access to resources in multiple domains. To facilitate users and groups travers-ing domain lines, trust relationships can be built between domains. These ACLs, groups, and trusts all combine to make Windows 2000 a scalable and secure network operating system.

Securing networks means securing network data. Data on a network is stored on computers and transmitted across wires. The Encrypting File System (EFS) is used to secure data stored on computers. Each user receives a public key set that can be used to encrypt data. If data should fall into the wrong hands, it cannot be decrypted and, therefore, is of no use to the thief. IP Security (IPSec) policies are used to encrypt data while it is being transmitted on the network wire. IPSec uses public keys, Kerberos, or preshared key combinations to authenticate two computers and encrypt the data transmitted between them. With EFS and IPSec, network data can be secured from unauthorized access, even if it has been intercepted.

Windows 2000 networks can accommodate millions of objects. To ensure that security is standardized in a large system, administrators can use the group policy and security analysis tools. Group policies contain security settings that can be applied from the site level down through the local machine level. Account policies, such as account lockout and password standards, can be applied to domains. On the local machine, features such as the event log settings, file system, and registry can be protected. With adequate group policies, all aspects of a network can be secured with minimal effort. The security analysis tool can be used in conjunction with security templates to analyze current security settings and suggest methods to better protect systems. Finally, the security editor allows changes to be analyzed before they are implemented, so user inconvenience is kept to a minimum.

20

REVIEW QUESTIONS

1. What technique is used by hackers to gain information through the users themselves?

   a. Brute force attack

   b. Masquerade attack

   c. Social engineering

   d. Replay attack

2. What type of attack involves repeated logon attempts with a known username and unknown password?

   a. Brute force attack

   b. Masquerade attack

   c. Social engineering

   d. Replay attack

3. What type of attack involves manipulating data to change the source or destination?

   a. Brute force attack

   b. Masquerade attack

   c. Social engineering

   d. Replay attack

4. What type of attack involves capturing data for use at a later date?

   a. Brute force attack

   b. Masquerade attack

   c. Denial of service attack

   d. Replay attack

5. What type of attack does not directly benefit the attacker but does detriment the company?

   a. Brute force attack

   b. Masquerade attack

   c. Denial of service attack

   d. Replay attack

6. What piece of malicious code hides in an application's scripting interface?

   a. Macro virus

   b. Trojan horse

    c. Packet virus

    d. Mobile code

7. What piece of malicious code hides in an application?

    a. Macro virus

    b. Trojan horse

    c. Packet virus

    d. Mobile code

8. What is the generic name for a mechanism used to form a network boundary?

    a. Domain model

    b. Security model

    c. Kerberos model

    d. Directory model

9. What is the specific name for a mechanism that Windows NT uses to form a network boundary?

    a. Domain model

    b. Security model

    c. Kerberos model

    d. Directory model

10. What is the primary authentication method used in Windows 2000?

    a. Extensible Authentication Protocol

    b. Kerberos

    c. Smart card

    d. EAP-TLS

11. What can be implemented to add a layer of security effectively to the authentication process?

    a. Extensible Authentication Protocol

    b. Kerberos

    c. Smart card

    d. EAP-TLS

12. What is required before implementing the Encrypting File System?

    a. Extensible Authentication Protocol

    b. Public key infrastructure

    c. Smart card

    d. EAP-TLS

20

13. What is required before implementing smart cards?

   a. Extensible Authentication Protocol

   b. Public key infrastructure

   c. Smart card

   d. EAP-TLS

14. What type of group is commonly used to grant access to resources in a single domain?

   a. Global

   b. Domain local

   c. Machine local

   d. Universal

15. What type of group is commonly used to grant access to resources in multiple domains?

   a. Global

   b. Domain local

   c. Machine local

   d. Universal

16. What type of group is commonly used to grant access to manage users based on geography or organizational structure?

   a. Global

   b. Domain local

   c. Machine local

   d. Universal

17. What service provides security for data while the data is transmitted across the network?

   a. Access control lists

   b. Encrypting File System

   c. IPSec

   d. Certificate authorities

18. What service provides security for data while it is stored on local machines?

   a. Access control lists

   b. Encrypting File System

   c. IPSec

   d. Certificate authorities

19. What tool can be used to standardize security based on templates?

    a. Group policy editor

    b. Security configuration editor

    c. RAS policy editor

    d. CA recovery policy editor

20. How many types of security templates does Windows 2000 provide?

    a. 1

    b. 2

    c. 3

    d. 4

REAL-WORLD PROJECTS

Andy Palmer has been contracted to help secure a network for a client that has recently migrated to Windows 2000. Due to recent attacks on major e-commerce sites, the client wants him to ensure the security of their Windows 2000 network. After interviewing the CIO and CFO, and after carefully analyzing the system's current security, he has developed a thorough security plan and has determined that the following procedures will be necessary to secure the network.

Project 20.1

To implement the Kerberos authentication protocol, complete the following steps:

The first thing Andy does is secure the authentication process. To do this, he decides to standardize the Kerberos version 5 protocol for authentication:

1. Open the Active Directory Users and Computers console from the Administrative Tools menu.

2. Right-click the domain (at the top of the tree), and select Properties.

3. On the Group Policies tab of the domain properties, select the Default Domain Properties, and click Edit.

4. Expand the Computer Configuration node, and expand the Account Policies folder within it.

5. Expand the Security Settings folder, and expand the Account Policies folder within it.

6. Select the Kerberos Policy folder, as shown in Figure 20.1.

20

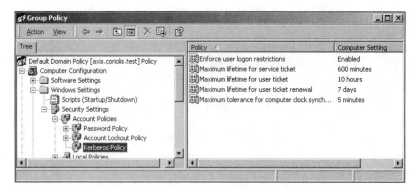

Figure 20.1 The Kerberos settings in group policies.

7. Ensure that Enforce User Logon Restrictions is enabled.

8. Set the Maximum Lifetime For Service Ticket, Maximum Lifetime For User Ticket, and Maximum Lifetime For User Ticket Renewal to reasonable durations for the network environment. Because the workday is 8 hours long, Andy sets the user and service ticket settings to 8 hours.

9. Set the Maximum Tolerance For Computer Clock Synchronization to a reasonable amount of time for user settings in the company.

Project 20.2
To implement RAS policies, complete the following steps:

Andy has identified the remote access server in the Sales OU as a possible target for attackers. He decides that a RAS policy using caller ID is the best way to apply security settings for the RAS server with the least amount of effort and maintenance. To implement RAS policies, he uses the following procedures:

1. Open Active Directory Users and Computers, and select the Sales OU.

2. Double-click the user that needs remote access, and select the Dial-in tab.

3. Select Control Access Through Remote Access Policy, as shown in Figure 20.2.

4. Close the Active Directory Users and Computers console.

5. Open the Routing and Remote Access console from the Administrative Tools menu.

6. Under the server, right-click Remote Access Policies, and select New Remote Access Policy.

7. Provide a name for the policy, and click Next.

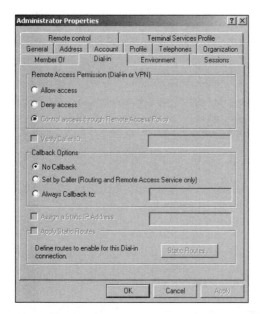

Figure 20.2   Setting a user account to use RAS policies.

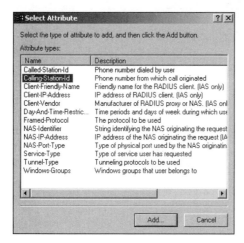

Figure 20.3   Setting a RAS policy for Calling-Station-ID.

8. Click the Add button, and select Calling–Station–ID, as shown in Figure 20.3.

9. Provide the ID of the caller as caller ID will display it, and click OK.

10. Click Next.

11. Select Grant Remote Access Permission, and click Next.

12. Click Finish.

20

Project 20.3

To create security groups and set access control lists, complete the following steps:

While browsing the network, Andy finds that he, as a guest user, has Full Control over the Research share. He asks the department's supervisor which users need access to the share and what type of access they need. The supervisor tells him that all employees should be able to see a directory listing of its contents and be able to read files in the root of the share. Also, all research employees should be able to read the files in the Budget subdirectory, but only managers and executives should have Full Control over the subdirectory. To implement this security, Andy completes the following steps:

1. Open Active Directory Users and Computers, right-click the Research OU, select New, and click Group. Name the group *ResearchEmployees*, select Global for the Group Scope, select Security for the Group Type (as shown in Figure 20.4), and then click OK.

Figure 20.4 Creating a global security group.

2. Double-click the group in the right pane of the console, and select the Members tab. Click the Add button, add the user accounts for the research employees, and then click OK. Click OK to close the group properties.

3. Right-click the domain, select New, and click Group. Name the group *Managers*, select Global for the Group Scope, select Security for the Group Type, and then click OK.

4. Double-click the group in the right pane of the console, and select the Members tab. Click the Add button, add the user accounts for the managers, and then click OK. Click OK to close the group properties.

5. Right-click the domain, select New, and click Group. Name the group *Executives*, select Global for the Group Scope, select Security for the Group Type, and then click OK.

6. Double-click the group in the right pane of the console, and select the Members tab. Click the Add button, add the user accounts for the executives, and then click OK. Click OK to close the group properties.

7. Right-click the Research OU, select New, and click Group. Name the group *ResearchReaders*, select Domain Local for the Group Scope, select Security for the Group Type, and then click OK.

8. Double-click the group in the right pane of the console, and select the Members tab. Click the Add button, add the ResearchEmployees global group as demonstrated in Figure 20.5, and then click OK. Click OK to close the group properties.

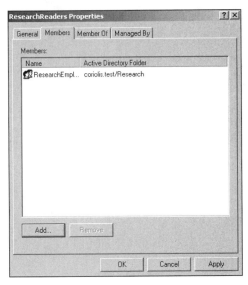

Figure 20.5 Adding a global group to a domain local group.

9. Right-click the Research OU, select New, and click Group. Name the group *ResearchChangers*, select Domain Local for the Group Scope, select Security for the Group Type, and then click OK.

10. Double-click the group in the right pane of the console, and select the Members tab. Click the Add button, add the global groups for Managers and Executives, and then click OK. Click OK to close the group properties. Close Active Directory Users and Computers.

20

11. On the server that hosts the file share, open Windows Explorer, and select the folder that is shared for the Research department.

12. Right-click the folder, and select Sharing. If the folder is not shared, click Share This Folder.

13. Click the Add button, double-click the Domain Users group in the resulting dialog box, and then click OK. Ensure that the group has Read permissions, as shown in Figure 20.6, and click OK. Click OK to close the share properties for the folder.

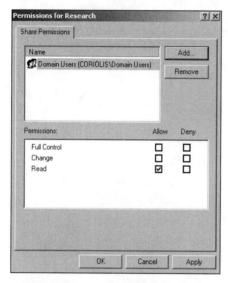

Figure 20.6 Setting the share permissions to allow domain users to read the Research files.

14. In the Sharing dialog box, click the Permissions button. Select the Everyone group, and click the Remove button.

15. Double-click the Research folder to reveal the Budget subdirectory. Right-click the budget subdirectory, and select Properties.

16. Uncheck the Allow Inheritable Permissions From The Parent To Propagate To This Object checkbox, and select Remove in the resulting dialog box.

17. Click the Add button, select the ResearchReaders and ResearchChangers groups in the resulting dialog box, and then click OK.

18. Select the ResearchChangers group, and check the Full Control checkbox in the Allow column. Select the ResearchReaders group. Check the Read&Execute, List Folder Contents, and Read checkboxes in the Allow column. The Budget Properties dialog box should appear as shown in Figure 20.7.

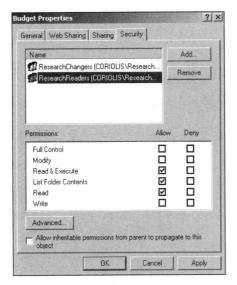

Figure 20.7   The permissions for the ResearchReaders group in the Budget subdirectory.

Project 20.4
To use the Encrypting File System, complete the following steps:

Andy interviews the department managers to find out more about their employees' IT needs. During the interviews, he finds out that some sales users, who have notebook computers, keep Research files on their hard drives when they travel. He is concerned that if the computers should get stolen, secret company projects might be compromised. To prevent such a situation, Andy recommends implementing the Encrypting File System for those users. He dows the following in order to implement EFS:

1. On a user's notebook computer, ensure that all the documents that need to be encrypted are in the same folder.

2. Instruct the user to log on while connected to the network.

3. Ask the user to right-click the folder and select Properties.

4. In the Properties dialog box, click the Advanced button.

5. Under the Advanced Attributes, check the Encrypt Contents To Secure Data checkbox (as shown in Figure 20.8), and then click OK.

6. Ask the user to log off the computer.

7. Log onto the computer as Guest (ensure that the guest account is enabled using Administrative access).

8. Attempt to access the files in the folder logged on as guest. Access should fail.

20

Figure 20.8 Encrypting the contents of a folder for security.

Project 20.5
To use group policies to implement security, complete the following steps:

Andy is analyzing the overall security of the client's domain. He notices numerous potential breeches in security. The password policy does little to protect the system from potential brute force attacks, because no password length or complexity rule is in place, passwords are infrequently changed, and many users have a limited number of passwords that they use repeatedly. Furthermore, the system has no method of detecting attempted brute force attacks and disabling targeted user accounts. To rectify the situation, Andy uses group policies to implement rules concerning account policies:

1. Open the Active Directory Users and Computers console from the Administrative Tools menu.

2. Right-click the domain, and select Properties.

3. Select the Group Policy tab, select the Default Domain Policy, and click the Edit button.

4. Expand the Computer Configuration node, and expand the Windows Settings folder beneath it, as shown in Figure 20.9.

5. Expand the Account Policies, and select the Password Policy folder. Double-click Enforce Password History in the right pane, check the Define This Policy Setting checkbox, set the number to 10 passwords remembered, and then click OK.

6. Double-click the Maximum Password Age in the right pane, check the Define This Policy Setting checkbox, set the number to 30 days maximum password age, and then click OK.

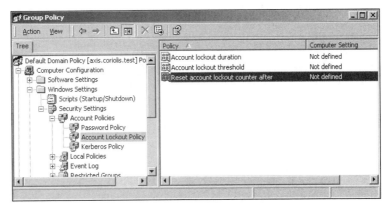

Figure 20.9   Using group policies to set Account Policies.

7. Double-click the Minimum Password Age in the right pane, check the Define This Policy Setting checkbox, and set the number to 15 days minimum password age.

8. Double-click the Passwords Must Meet Complexity Requirements option in the right pane, check the Define This Policy Setting checkbox, select Enabled, and then click OK.

9. In the left pane, select Account Lockout Policy. Double-click the Account Lockout Duration option in the right pane. Check the Define This Policy Setting checkbox, set the number to 60 minutes, and then click OK.

10. Double-click the Account Lockout Threshold option in the right pane. Check the Define This Policy Setting checkbox, set the number to 3 invalid logon attempts, and then click OK.

11. Double-click the Reset Account Lockout Counter After option in the right pane. Check the Define This Policy checkbox, set the number to 4,800 minutes, and then click OK.

Project 20.6
To analyze your system with the security configuration editor, complete the following steps:

Before completing this client's project, Andy decides to verify that his policies are pertinent. Because this could be a formidable task, he decides to use the Windows 2000 security configuration editor to analyze the domain controllers. He takes the following steps to perform this procedure:

1. Click Start|Run, and type "mmx /s".

2. In the Console menu in the MMC, click Add/Remove Snap-in.

20

3. Click Add, and select the Security Configuration and Analysis snap-in.

4. Click Add, then click Close. Click OK to close the Add/Remove Snap-in dialog.

5. Right-click Security Configuration And Analysis in the console tree, and select Open Database.

6. When prompted, provide a name for the database, and select DCSecurity.inf for the template.

7. Right-click Security Configuration And Analysis, and select Analyze Computer Now. Provide an error log path when prompted.

8. Expand the Security Configuration And Analysis folder.

9. Analyze the results for the individual settings. A green checkmark means the current setting and the template settings match. A red X indicates a conflict between the current system settings and the template. No marking at all means that the setting is not affected.

CHAPTER TWENTY ONE

WINDOWS 2000 PROFESSIONAL

After completing this chapter, you will be able to:

✓ Discuss Windows 2000 Professional's new enhancements

✓ Configure Windows 2000 to join and participate in a network

✓ Add, remove, and configure hardware manually and through Plug and Play

✓ Configure Windows 2000 security options

✓ Configure Windows 2000 mobile computing features

Windows 2000 Professional is designed to be a multipurpose operating system for use in small peer-to-peer and large enterprise networks while reducing total cost of ownership and making computers easier to use. The Windows 2000 Professional client operating system builds on preexisting Windows NT technology to make Windows 2000 Professional a well-rounded and complete corporate client operating system. This chapter introduces many of Windows 2000 Professional's new features, including offline folders, increased hardware support, Plug and Play, mobile computing support, and more.

WINDOWS 2000 ENHANCEMENTS

Windows 2000 Professional is easier to use and administer than previous versions of Windows, and it provides greater hardware and software support. Windows 2000 Professional also introduces new features, such as support for mobile computing, improved printing services, enhanced hardware support, better file management, and increased security. One of the more appreciated changes within Windows 2000 Professional for the everyday user is the simplified user interface.

Making Windows Easier

Microsoft modified the Windows user interface in Windows 2000 in an effort to make the system easier to use and understand. The appearance and func-tionality of interface components—such as the Start menu, dialog boxes, and task scheduling—make the user interface easier to use.

Personalized Start Menu

Personalized menus can be created and used so that finding applications is easier. Furthermore, the Start menu keeps track of which applications are used most frequently, and the menu adjusts accordingly. The most frequently used programs display on the Start menu, while less frequently used programs are hidden from view. Program groups that are hidden can be displayed easily, however, by simply clicking the down arrow on the Start menu, as shown in Figure 21.1. As a result of the customized Start menu, finding the appropriate program groups is easier because many of the unused program groups do not clutter the user's view.

Figure 21.1   Expanding the Start menu.

System Dialog Boxes

System dialog boxes—such as the Logon and Shut Down dialog boxes—are redesigned to have fewer and more descriptive options. The new Shut Down dialog box includes a drop-down box to assist users with selecting the correct option. Also, by default, the Logon dialog box does not show the domain name as it did in Windows NT; however, you can change the display by clicking the Options button on the Logon screen.

Task Scheduling

Users can now set up and configure tasks to run at specific times. The Task Scheduler allows system scripts or programs to be scheduled using a graphical user interface (GUI) instead of using **AT** commands at the command prompt.

In addition to making the user Start menu, dialog boxes, and task scheduling easier, Microsoft incorporates many new features in Windows 2000 Professional to help improve mobile computing.

Support for Mobile Computing

Microsoft added the latest laptop technologies to Windows 2000 Professional. For instance, Advanced Power Management (APM) and the Advanced Configuration and Power Interface (ACPI) are both included in the new operating system. After a configurable amount of time, APM and ACPI shut off power to the hard drive and video in order to conserve battery life. The ACPI also allows you to remove or add system devices, such as PCMCIA (Personal Computer Memory Card International Association) devices, without having to shut down or restart the system.

Windows 2000 Professional includes the following mobile computing technologies:

➤ *Network Connection Wizard*—Enables you to configure all network, local area network (LAN), dial-up, and direct connections. All configurable connections are also listed together within the Network and Dial-Up Connections applet found in the Control Panel.

➤ *Offline Folders*—Allows you to copy folders and their contents stored on network servers to your local Windows 2000 Professional computer. After the files and folders are synchronized, you can view and use the files while offline.

➤ *Synchronization Manager*—Compares files and folders on the local machine to the corresponding files on the network server when you connect to the network, and then updates each system. Items that can be synchronized include offline folders, Web pages, and email messages.

➤ *Virtual Private Network Support*—Allows users to connect to a private network through a public network, such as the Internet. Traffic between a user and the

21

remote LAN is encapsulated or encrypted to prevent eavesdropping. Users who frequently travel could use the VPN support within Windows 2000 Professional and Windows 2000 Server to connect to office resources by connecting to the Internet through an ISP. A remote user could even print to printers located at the home offices using the VPN or the Internet Printing Protocol (IPP).

Note: We discuss support for mobile users in more detail later in this chapter.

Windows 2000 Printing Features

Windows 2000 improves on Windows NT's printing configuration and installation, as described in the next few sections. Most notably, Microsoft provides the new Internet Printing Protocol to assist users in printing over public networks.

Internet Printing Protocol

The Internet Printing Protocol (IPP) allows users to send print documents to any Windows 2000 network that is connected to the Internet. For example, using IPP, telecommuters can print documents on office printers from remote locations. The IPP allows users to:

➤ Print to a Uniform Resource Locator (URL) or a private or public network, such as the Internet.

➤ View the status and job-related information regarding the activity of a printer over a private or public network using a standard Web browser.

➤ Download and install a print driver for a particular printer from a Windows 2000 print server while connected to the Internet.

Image Color Management 2

Image Color Management 2 (ICM 2) is a Windows 2000 Professional application programming interface (API) that allows users to print high-color images faster and with more reliability than in earlier versions of Windows. In addition, users can now send high-color image documents to another computer. ICM 2 ensures that the image you see on your monitor displays in the same manner as the printed image.

Add Printer Wizard

The enhanced Add Printer Wizard allows users to add printers without having to specify which port a printer is plugged into or the correct driver model. The new printer wizard also automatically detects the correct printer language.

Enhanced Hardware Support

Microsoft Windows 2000 supports up to 7,000 hardware devices that Windows NT 4 does not support. Devices that Windows 2000 supports include infrared devices, digital cameras, scanners, multimedia devices, and Universal Serial Bus devices. As well as adding support for new devices, Windows 2000 also includes the following new hardware-related features and enhancements:

➤ *Add/Remove Hardware Wizard*—The well-known Add/Remove Hardware Wizard included with Windows 95 and 98 is now included with Windows 2000. The Add/Remove Hardware Wizard allows you to add, remove, and troubleshoot hardware. You can use the hardware wizard to stop the operation of a particular device that is not working, so you can remove the device from the system.

➤ *Plug and Play Support*—Like the Add/Remove Hardware Wizard, Plug and Play support was sorely missed in Windows NT. Windows 2000 supports an enhanced version of Plug and Play, which allows the following:

  ➤ Automatic installation of hardware devices and dynamic hardware reconfiguration

  ➤ Automatic loading of the correct device drivers

  ➤ Support for removable and changeable devices

  ➤ Registration for device notification events (driver signing)

➤ *Win32 Driver Model (WDM)*—Windows 2000 supports the use of the Win32 Driver Model. Beginning with Windows 98, manufacturers could write drivers that were compliant with the Win32 Driver Model. Any existing drivers written to this specification for Windows 98 also work with Windows 2000.

➤ *Power Options*—Power options prevent a computer from consuming power that is not needed by the system. Windows 2000 directs power to devices as it is needed and away from devices that do not. Not all hardware supports this feature; therefore, the available options depend on the installed hardware. The available options include:

  ➤ *Standby*—Allows the hard drive and display to power down so the system will use less power.

  ➤ *Hibernation*—Writes the contents of memory to the hard drive and then turns off the system. When the system is rebooted, the memory contents that were saved to the disk are written back to memory, and the system begins where it left off. This allows the system to boot much faster.

➤ *DirectX*—Windows 2000 supports the use of DirectX 7 and after. DirectX is a set of low-level APIs that provides faster access to system hardware. Programs that require high-performance media acceleration, such as games, frequently use DirectX drivers.

21

Improved File System Management

Windows 2000 now supports all Microsoft file systems, including FAT and FAT32. Additionally, Microsoft incorporates many new features into the existing NTFS (NT file system), such as file encryption and disk quotas. Namely, enhancements to Windows 2000's file system include the following:

➤ *NTFS*—The new and improved NTFS allows the addition of disk space to an existing volume without having to restart the system. Additionally, the file system supports automatic file encryption, distributed link tracking, and per-user disk usage quotas. The new file system also supports the use of volumes rather than partitions. Volumes provide more flexibility in administering storage resources.

➤ *FAT32 File System*—Windows 2000 supports the Windows 95 OSR2 and later file system called FAT32. FAT32 extended the previous FAT16 file system to support disks and disk partitions greater than 2GB in size.

➤ *Disk Defragmentation*—Microsoft includes a disk defragmenter utility with Windows 2000. The disk defragmenter can be used to improve performance on fragmented drives. Defragmentation takes place as files are opened and saved to the hard drive.

➤ *Windows 2000 Backup Utility*—Windows 2000 Professional, like Windows NT, includes a Backup utility that can be used to back up and restore files to prevent data loss. Unlike Windows NT, the Windows 2000 utility includes support for the scheduling of backups and multiple backup device types. Using the Windows 2000 Backup utility, you can back up hard drives to the following devices:

  ➤ External and internal hard drives

  ➤ Logical (network) drives

  ➤ Recordable CD-ROMs

  ➤ Tape drives

  ➤ Zip disks

➤ *Volume Mounts*—Windows 2000 supports the mounting of hard drives to an empty folder, much like many popular Unix systems. No longer are administrators limited to the 24 available letters in the alphabet (A and B cannot be used). Administrators can create a folder, name the folder, and then mount a physical drive to the folder. When this is done, the folder represents the hard drive instead of a drive letter.

Improved Security

Microsoft designed Windows 2000 Professional to be the most secure Windows client operating system available for standalone or network use. Windows 2000 supports Kerberos 5, Encrypting File System (EFS), Internet Protocol Security (IPSec), and smart card authentication. Each of the security features can be used together or independently to secure network and local computer resources. Some of the key security features are summarized here:

➤ *Kerberos 5*—Windows 2000 networks use Kerberos as the primary authentication protocol in order to provide higher security, faster authentication, and faster network response.

➤ *Internet Security Protocol (IPSec)*—IPSec provides the highest level of security over public networks to create virtual private networks (VPN). IPSec encrypts TCP/IP packets to hinder eavesdropping over public networks, such as the Internet. IPSec can be used in conjunction with PPTP to provide additional security and VPN support.

➤ *Encrypting File System (EFS)*—EFS allows users to encrypt files so that only their user account and the recovery agent user account can unlock the files. Encrypting files hinders anyone from reading data from a stolen hard drive or laptop.

➤ *Smart Card Authentication*—Smart cards enable administrators to add an extra layer of authentication security to a network. Using smart cards prevents the need to transmit private information, such as passwords or private keys, over public networks. Windows 2000 security is described in more detail in Chapter 20.

HARDWARE INSTALLATION AND CONFIGURATION

Microsoft Windows 2000 provides a number of new utilities that can assist users and administrators with adding, deleting, and reconfiguring hardware resources. Driver signing and the addition of the Device Manager assist users and administrators in installing and troubleshooting hardware. One of the most awaited additions to the Windows network operating system is support for automatic configuration using Plug and Play technologies.

Plug and Play

Plug and Play is an industry architecture that defines hardware requirements as well as system BIOS and operating system requirements. Plug and Play greatly reduces the headaches associated with the installation and configuration of hardware devices. What once could take hours now takes only minutes.

21

Installing Plug and Play Hardware

Most hardware purchased today complies with Microsoft's Plug and Play architecture requirements. If a device is Plug and Play compatible and the drivers for the hardware are available to operating systems, then Windows 2000 automatically detects, installs, and configures the hardware upon system logon. Not only must the device be Plug and Play compatible, but the system BIOS must also support the Plug and Play architecture.

Installing Non-Plug and Play Hardware

In a perfect world, all hardware would be Plug and Play compatible; however, that is not normally the case. Windows 2000 includes a familiar tool from Windows 9x that you can use to detect and install hardware that is not Plug and Play compatible, known as the Add/Remove Hardware Wizard.

If Windows 2000 does not automatically detect and install a device, or if a device is not Plug and Play compatible, you can initiate the Add/Remove Hardware Wizard to force Windows 2000 to attempt to detect or troubleshoot a hardware device. To start the Add/Remove Hardware Wizard, follow these steps:

1. Click Start | Settings | Control Panel.

2. Double-click the Add/Remove Hardware Wizard.

3. Select Add/Troubleshoot A Device.

4. Click Next, and Windows 2000 searches for new hardware.

Note: *You can also use the Add/Remove Hardware Wizard to uninstall or remove a device from a computer.*

If Windows 2000 does not find any new hardware, it presents an Add/Remove Hardware Wizard dialog box, as shown in Figure 21.2, which you can use to select the type of hardware you want to troubleshoot. After you add new hardware, you can confirm the installation of hardware by opening the new Device Manager utility included with Windows 2000.

Windows 2000 Device Manager

One of the most useful tools included with Windows 2000 to view, troubleshoot, and manage hardware is the Windows 2000 Device Manager. You can run the Device Manager as a Microsoft Management Console (MMC) snap-in, or you can access it via the Computer Management Administrative Tool. The Device Manager utility enables users to view a graphic representation of the existing system hardware resources as well as the status of each device, as shown in Figure 21.3.

Device Manager allows you to view the status of all installed devices within your computer system. Any device that is not working properly is flagged with an

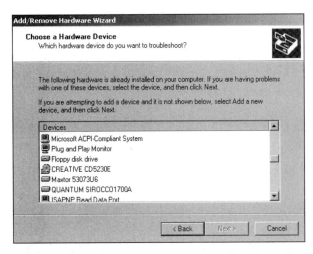

Figure 21.2   Add/Remove Hardware Wizard dialog box.

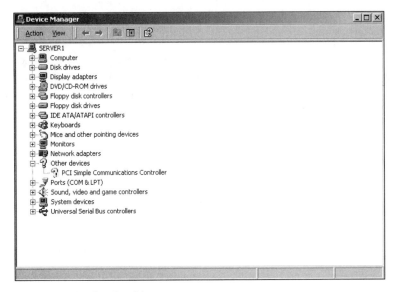

Figure 21.3   Device Manager.

exclamation point or a stop sign. A red X next to a device means the device has been disabled. Device Manager can be used to view used and free resources, such as IRQs, Base I/O addresses, and Base Memory addresses. Device Manager can also be used to reinstall or update device drivers or disable and uninstall hardware devices. In addition, Device Manager can be used to connect to a local or a remote computer.

You must be logged on as a member of the administrators group to make changes within Device Manager, because all changes are written to the registry.

21

The steps to configure or view hardware settings with Device Manager are as follows:

1. Right-click the My Computer icon, and select Manage.

2. Under System Tools, select Device Manager.

3. Double-click the device type you want to view or modify.

4. Double-click the actual device.

The actions that can be performed, as well as which tabs display, depend on the type of device selected. Following is a list of possible tabs and the corresponding information and options on each:

➤ *General*—The General tab displays a device's location, type, and manufacturer. The General tab also displays the status of the device and a Troubleshoot button that will walk you through the process of troubleshooting a problem.

➤ *Device Properties*—This tab lists the properties of a particular device. Device properties are different for each hardware type.

➤ *Driver*—The Driver tab contains information regarding the installed driver for a hardware device. Information can include the driver's file name, version, file date, digital signer, and creator's name. Three buttons are available on the Driver tab:

➤ *Details*—Allows you to obtain specific information about the driver.

➤ *Uninstall*—Allows you to uninstall the driver.

➤ *Update*—Allows you to update the driver the system is currently using for the hardware device.

➤ *Port Settings*—The Port Settings tab allows you to configure COM-port-specific information, such as the bits per second, stop bit, parity, data bits, and flow control.

➤ *Properties*—The Properties tab allows you to specify how you want Windows 2000 to use a device.

➤ *Resources*—The Resources tab lists the current hardware resources that the device is using, such as IRQ, Base I/O, and Base Memory. In some cases, you can use this tab to change the resources that a device is using.

Tip: You should not change the resources used by Plug and Play devices. If the resources that a Plug and Play device uses are changed, then Windows 2000 cannot ever change it again. If you allow Windows 2000 to control the devices and the resources that the devices use, then, when new devices are added, the operating system can change all the settings on all hardware to ensure that the new hardware can be installed.

System Information

Windows 2000 includes a System Information snap-in that can be used to view the local system or remote system hardware configuration. Using the System Information snap-in, you can view information such as the current operating system version and service pack, hardware resources in use, hardware components, currently running software, and Internet Explorer statistics. Table 21.1 lists the nodes within the System Information snap-in and the corresponding information for each node.

Driver Signing

In order to protect operating and driver files, Windows 2000 implemented a new feature called *driver signing*. Many applications overwrite needed operating system files during installation. With the driver signing feature in Windows 2000, you can configure Windows 2000 either to stop applications from overwriting files or to warn you before allowing any files to be overwritten. Overwritten files can cause system failures or problems that are very difficult to solve.

Every driver has a signature that identifies who is the manufacturer of the file. All Windows 2000 operating files and drivers are digitally signed by Microsoft. Using Device Manager, you can look at the signature of each driver to view the current signature.

Driver Signing Options

Using the Driver Signing Options dialog box (shown in Figure 21.4), you can set one of three options, as shown in the following list:

Table 21.1   System Information snap-in nodes.

Node	Node Information
System Summary	Contains operating system version and manufacturer; the system root folder; the computer name, manufacturer, model, and type; BIOS and processor information; local time and time zone; and physical and virtual memory information.
Hardware Resources	Contains current system resources, such as IRQ, DMA, conflicts and sharing, I/O, Base memory, and forced hardware.
Components	Contains information about current hardware, including USBs, problem devices, multimedia, display, infrared, input, modems, network, ports, storage, and printing.
Software Environment	Contains information regarding current processes and applications that are stored in memory.
Internet Explorer 5	Contains configuration settings for Internet Explorer, such as version and build numbers, and provides security and other miscellaneous information about Internet Explorer.

21

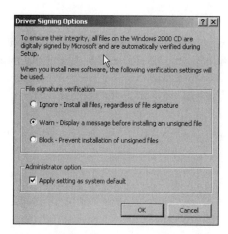

Figure 21.4   Driver Signing Options dialog box.

➤ *Ignore*—Allows applications to overwrite any driver file.

➤ *Warn*—Instructs the operating system to prompt you with a dialog box each time an application attempts to overwrite a file.

➤ *Block*—Prevents the application from overwriting a file.

You can access the Driver Signing Options dialog box by selecting the Hardware tab in the System Control Panel applet and clicking the Driver Signing button.

File Signature Verification Utility

Windows 2000 also includes a GUI utility that can be used to discover which files have been altered by applications. The file verification utility can be used to scan all operating system or specified file types to discover which files are not digitally signed. The file verification utility does not replace overwritten system or configured files. Instead, it presents a list of files that do not have a signature.

The file verification utility can be launched from the Run dialog box or you can create a shortcut to launch the sigverif.exe application. After the application starts, you can click the Advanced button to specify file types that the utility should scan, or you can leave the default, which scans operating system files. The steps to run and use the file signature verification utility are:

1. Click Start|Run, type "sigverif" in the Run dialog box, and press Enter.

2. When the File Signature Verification dialog box appears, click Advanced.

3. In the Advanced File Signature Verification dialog box, you can configure the utility to search only system files or particular file types. Retain the default settings, and click OK.

4. Click Start, and the utility scans all specified file types, as shown in Figure 21.5.

5. When the scan completes, you can view all the files that do not have a digital signature in the Signature Verification Results window, as shown in Figure 21.6.

6. When finished viewing the files, click Close.

Only user accounts with administrative permission can replace system files that have been overwritten. If a Windows 2000 Professional computer is a member of a Windows NT or 2000 network, then any member of the domain admins

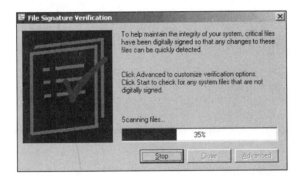

Figure 21.5 File Signature Verification dialog box.

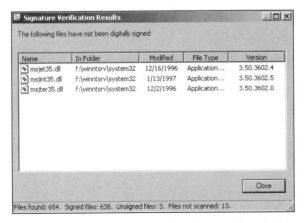

Figure 21.6 Signature Verification Results window.

21

group can add, remove, and configure hardware on any Windows 2000 Professional computer. The next section looks at how to add a Windows 2000 computer to a Windows 2000 network.

WINDOWS 2000 PROFESSIONAL NETWORK CONFIGURATION

Windows 2000 Professional is designed as a client operating system to be used on corporate networks using Windows 2000 Server technologies. Windows 2000 Professional is highly integrated with the Windows 2000 Server family of products developed by Microsoft. Windows 2000 Professional can be joined to a network by installing the correct protocols and configuring the computer to log into a Windows 2000 domain. The Windows 2000 Active Directory structure is built around the TCP/IP protocol suite; therefore, TCP/IP is a requirement for networking Windows 2000 Professional to Windows 2000 Server networks.

TCP/IP and Windows 2000

TCP/IP is an open standard protocol that provides communication across networks of various computer architectures. TCP/IP provides the following benefits when used on Windows 2000 computers and networks:

➤ TCP/IP is a routable protocol that can support even the largest enterprises' networking needs.

➤ TCP/IP can be used to connect dissimilar networks and computer systems.

➤ TCP/IP supports the Windows sockets (Winsock) interface, which makes developing client/server applications faster and easier.

➤ TCP/IP is the only protocol that can be used to connect to the Internet.

Installing TCP/IP on Windows 2000

TCP/IP is installed as a default option during the installation of Windows 2000 Professional or Server; however, if it was not installed during the installation of the operating system, you can perform the following steps to install TCP/IP:

1. Click Start|Settings|Control Panel, and then double-click the Network And Dial-up Connections icon.

2. Double-click the Local Area Connection icon.

3. In the Local Area Connection Status dialog box, click Properties.

4. In the Local Area Connection Properties dialog box, click Install.

5. Select Protocol, click Add In The Select Network Component Type, and click Add.

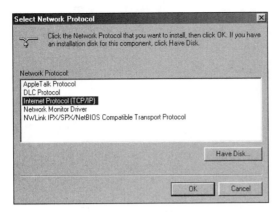

Figure 21.7   Installing TCP/IP.

6. Select Internet Protocol (TCP/IP), and click OK. (See Figure 21.7.)

7. Enter the IP address, or select Obtain An IP Address Automatically.

8. Click OK, and click OK again in the Local Area Connections Properties dialog box.

9. In the Local Area Connection Status dialog box, click Close. The computer does not have to be restarted.

Configuring Static IP Addresses

By default, all Microsoft client operating systems are configured to use the Dynamic Host Configuration Protocol (DHCP) to obtain TCP/IP configuration information. However, you can override this default and manually configure TCP/IP. Some Windows 2000 computers require the use of a static IP address, such as DHCP, DNS, and WINS servers. To configure Windows 2000 with a static IP address, perform the following steps:

1. Click Start | Settings | Control Panel, and then double-click the Network And Dial-up Connections icon.

2. Double-click the Local Area Connection icon.

3. In the Local Area Connection Status dialog box, click Properties.

4. Highlight the TCP/IP protocol, and click Properties.

5. Select the Use The Following IP Address radio button, as shown in Figure 21.8.

6. Enter the IP address, subnet mask, and default gateway.

7. Enter the IP address of your DNS servers.

8. Click the Advance button.

21

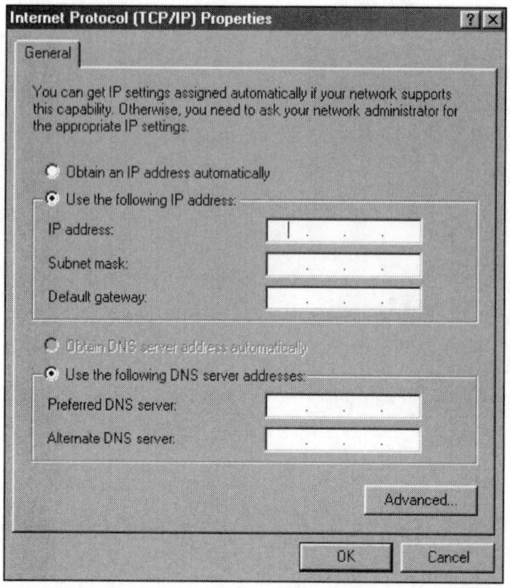

Figure 21.8   Configuring a static IP address.

9. Select the WINS tab, click Add, and enter the IP address of the WINS server.

10. Click OK or Close to close all open dialog boxes. The computer does not have to be restarted.

By clicking the Options tab in the Advance TCP/IP Properties dialog box, you can set configuration options for IPSec and TCP/IP filtering. IPSec is a secure version of the TCP/IP protocol that can be used over public networks to help protect data from being copied. TCP/IP filtering allows you to specify which TCP/IP ports you want to allow or block. (See Figure 21.9.)

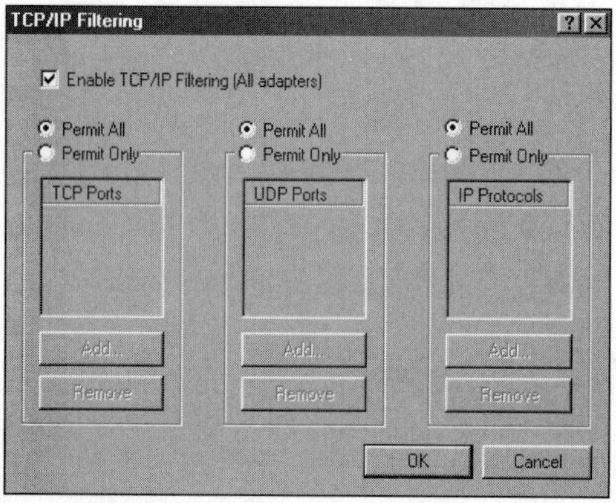

Figure 21.9   TCP/IP port filtering.

Configuring Automatic IP Addressing

If a DHCP server is installed on the local area network, you can enable automatic IP addressing on Windows 2000 computers. To configure Windows 2000 with a dynamic IP address, perform the following steps:

1. Click Start | Settings | Control Panel, and then double-click the Network And Dial-up Connections icon.

2. Double-click the Local Area Connection icon.

3. In the Local Area Connection Status dialog box, click Properties.

4. Highlight the TCP/IP protocol, and click Properties.

5. Select the Obtain IP Address Automatically radio button.

6. Click OK to close all dialog boxes; in the Local Area Connection Status dialog box, click Close.

Automatic Private IP Address Assignment

If a Windows 2000 Professional computer is configured to use automatic IP addressing but is unable to locate a DHCP server, the operating system assigns the computer an IP address of **169.254.x.y**, where x and y are unique numbers from 1 through 254, and a subnet mask of **255.255.0.0**. This is actually a feature of Windows 2000 that allows administrators of small networks to configure each machine to assign itself a private IP address without the need for a DHCP server or a static IP address entry.

After Windows 2000 has the proper protocol installed and it can communicate with the server, you can add a client computer to the domain.

Joining a Domain

To become a member of a Windows 2000 or Windows NT network, each client computer must be configured to join a domain. In order to allow all users within a domain to access the Windows 2000 Professional computer, the computer must become a member of the domain. Before a Windows 2000 Professional computer can join a domain, a computer account must be created for the computer. A computer account represents a computer on the network in much the same way a user account represents a user. Chapter 6 describes the steps to create a computer account.

To join a Windows 2000 Professional computer to a domain, follow these steps:

1. Click Start | Settings | Control Panel, and then double-click the System icon.

2. Select the Network Identification tab, as shown in Figure 21.10.

3. Click the Properties button.

21

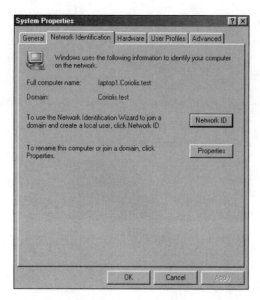

Figure 21.10 Network Identification tab.

4. In the Member Of section, select the Domain radio button.

5. Enter the full domain name, such as "Coriolis.test".

6. Click OK.

By default, once a Windows 2000 Professional computer is added to a domain, any user account that has been created for the domain can log into the Windows 2000 computer. All user accounts that are created on the domain controller become a member of the domain global group named *domain users*. The domain users global group is then made a member of every Windows 2000 Professional computer's local users group. (See Figure 21.11.) Because each Windows 2000 Professional local users group contains the domain's domain users group, any user account in the domain can use the Windows 2000 computer to log into the domain.

If a user wants to gain access to local resources on the Windows 2000 computer, however, the user must have a local user account created on the Windows 2000 Professional computer.

CREATING USER AND GROUP ACCOUNTS ON WINDOWS 2000 PROFESSIONAL

Before any user can gain access to any Windows 2000 computer, the user must first have a user account that has been granted permissions to the computer. Windows 2000 supports three user account types:

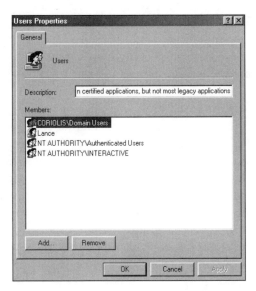

Figure 21.11   Windows 2000 local users group.

➤ *Local user accounts*—Used on Windows 2000 Professional to provide access to the local computer's resources.

➤ *Domain user accounts*—Can be created only on Windows 2000 domain controllers; they are used to provide access to a network's resources.

➤ *Builtin user accounts*—Used to assign system permissions to a user, such as the administrators account.

Local User Accounts

Local user accounts are created on Windows 2000 Professional computers to allow users to log onto the system and gain access to local resources. Without a local account, a user cannot access a Windows 2000 Professional computer. Any Windows 2000 Professional computer that is a member of a domain allows a user to log into the local computer or the domain. If the user attempts to log into the domain, a Windows 2000 Professional computer forwards the authentication request to a domain controller.

Gaining Local Access

Each Windows 2000 Professional computer contains a Local Accounts Security Database that contains all the user accounts and passwords for the user accounts. On a Windows 2000 Professional computer, after a user account is created, the user account is written to the Local Security Accounts Database only, not to the domain accounts database, and the user account is not replicated to any other computers. Creating a user account on a Windows 2000 Professional computer

21

allows the account to log into only the computer that the account was created on and does not allow access to network resources. Windows 2000 Professional uses the Local Accounts Security Database to verify user accounts only when the user has selected to log into the local computer, not the domain.

Gaining Access to Network Resources

Any user attempting to access resources located on a Windows 2000 Professional computer must also have a valid user account on the remote computer. If Windows 2000 Professional is used to create a peer-to-peer network, all user accounts must be created on each computer, because no global accounts database is used, as in a server-based Windows 2000 network. For example, if userA has a local user account only on computerA, userA can log into computerA; however, if userA attempts to log into computerB locally or access resources located on computerB from the network, userA will be denied access. Local user accounts provide access only to the computer on which they are created.

Allowing Domain Accounts to Access Windows 2000 Professional

In most Windows networks, user accounts are created on domain controllers and not on local machines. When creating a domain account, you normally want a user account to have the ability to log into any machine on the network. To enable this feature, Windows 2000 Professional computers send logon requests to domain controllers whenever a user attempts to log into the domain instead of the local machine (see Figure 21.12). Windows 2000 domain controllers do not allow users to log into the machine; all requests made at a domain controller are domain logon requests, because a domain controller, by definition, is the domain.

When a Windows 2000 Professional computer is added to a Windows 2000 network, the domain global groups from the Active Directory are made members of the Windows 2000 local groups. For example, when a Windows 2000 computer is added to a domain, the domain admins group from the Active Directory is added to Windows 2000's local administrators group. This allows a network administrator to gain access to and administer any client operating system on the network.

Domain User Accounts

Domain user accounts allow users to log into any computer that is a member of the domain and provides access to resources on the network. When a user logs into a domain, the username and password are sent to a domain controller in the form of an authentication request. If the user account information is correct, the server builds an access token that identifies the user's unique SID and the SIDs of any groups in which the user is a member. The access token is sent back to the client computer, and the user is granted access.

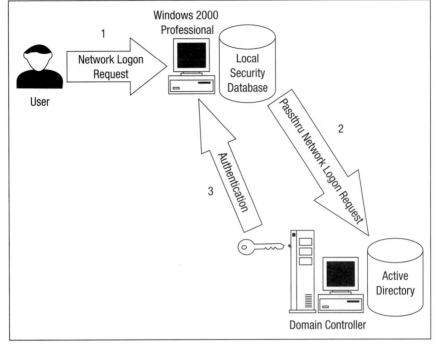

Figure 21.12   A network authentication request.

Domain accounts can be created only on Windows domain controllers. Windows NT 4 stores all domain user accounts in the Security Accounts Database, while Windows 2000 Server stores domain accounts in the Active Directory. Domain user accounts are replicated to all domain controllers within the domain. In some instances, lag time might occur between the time the account is created and the time the account is replicated to the user's local domain controller.

Builtin User Accounts

During the installation of Windows 2000 Professional, the setup application creates two user accounts called builtin accounts. The builtin accounts include the administrators and the guest accounts.

Administrators Account

The administrators account is created to allow access to the computer after the operating system is installed. After the system is up and running, the administrators account can be used to configure and modify system settings and hardware. Only the administrators account can modify the registry or change operating system parameters. Renaming the administrators account is always a good idea, because it cannot be deleted and is a well-known user account name that someone might try to access in an attempt to access a computer without appropriate permissions.

21

Guest Account

The guest account is created during installation and is disabled by default. The guest account is used for occasional access to a local computer system. Users that are hired only on a temporary basis or consultants are usually good candidates for using the guest account. The guest account can be renamed but cannot be deleted.

Creating and Managing User Accounts

To create user accounts on Windows 2000 Professional, you can use the Computer Management Administrative Tool. The Computer Management tool can be accessed from the Administrative Tools menu, or it can be launched as a snap-in to the MMC.

To create user accounts, you must first launch the Computer Management tool, as shown in Figure 21.13. Before creating the user account, you must have the following information:

➤ *Username*—This is the name that the user will use to log into the system. It is not case sensitive and should be no more than 20 characters. Usernames cannot contain the following characters: / \ [ ] : ; | = + , ★ ? < > "

➤ *Full Name*—This is the user's first and last name.

➤ *Description*—This is any information that will assist in identifying the user account, such as the department or location where the user works.

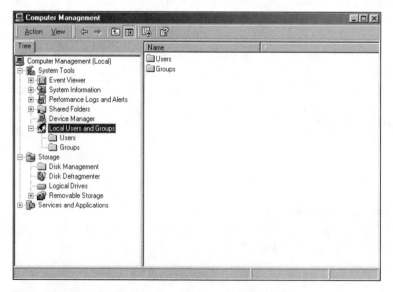

Figure 21.13   Computer Management tool.

➤ *Password*—This is the initial password that you want the user to use. Passwords are case sensitive and can be up to 128 characters. In high-security environments, passwords should be at least eight characters in length and include uppercase and lowercase letters and numbers.

Creating User Accounts in Windows 2000 Professional

To create user accounts in Windows 2000 Professional, follow these steps:

1. Open the Computer Management Administrative Tool.

2. Click Local Users And Groups.

3. Right-click Users, and select New User.

4. Complete the Username, Full Name, Description, and Password fields.

5. Confirm the password.

6. Select whether the user will be required to change the password the next time the user logs on.

7. Select whether the user will be allowed to change the password. Windows 2000 will not allow you to restrict a user from changing the password if you have also selected the User Must Change Password At The Next Logon option.

8. Click Create.

User Account Properties

After a user account is created, you can modify the account's default properties. A user account's properties include information regarding the use of the user account, the user's profile and login script information, home folder location, and group membership. Each setting makes up the user account's properties and cannot be specified during user account creation. Instead, the settings must be modified after the account is created. You can access the user account properties by right-clicking a user account in the Computer Management utility, and selecting Properties.

When you right-click a user account and select Properties, you are presented with the user account properties dialog box, as shown in Figure 21.14. The user properties dialog box contains three tabs:

➤ *General*—The General tab displays the user's full name and description. The General tab also contains options that change the user's password properties. You can select the following options:

➤ *User Must Change Password At Next Logon*—This option forces a user to change the password the next time the user logs onto the network. This option is used to ensure that only the user knows the password. The administrator can change any user's password without knowing the user-assigned password.

21

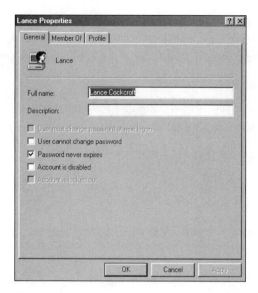

Figure 21.14   A user account properties dialog box.

➤ *User Cannot Change Password*—This option prevents a user from changing the password for the account. You cannot select this option if you have already selected the previous option. This option can be used on the guest account to prevent occasional access users from changing the password.

➤ *Password Never Expires*—This option overrides the security settings for the local machine. Regardless of local password security settings, this option prevents a user from ever having to change the password.

➤ *Account Is Disabled*—This option disables an account. You can use this option when a user leaves the company for an extended amount of time or when an employee leaves the company permanently.

➤ *Account Is Locked Out*—You cannot select this option. The operating system uses this option to lock out user accounts that have repeatedly attempted to log onto the system using an incorrect password. The administrator can set the number of times a user can attempt to log onto the system using an incorrect password before the account is locked out.

➤ *Member Of*—The Member Of tab is used to assign a user account to the membership of a group or groups.

➤ *Profile*—The Profile tab is used to specify the location of a user's profile. Profiles for user accounts can be store locally or on remote computers connected to the network. The Profile tab is also where you can specify the name of the logon script that should be executed when a user logs onto the computer. Within the Profile tab, you can also specify the location and map a drive letter to the user's home folder.

User Profiles

User profiles store users' desktop and application settings. Each time a new user logs into a Windows 2000 computer, a profile is created for that user. The profile stores environment and application data, such as a user's background, colors, sounds, shortcuts, and Start menu options. The profile also stores users' application data, such as Microsoft Outlook email settings and Microsoft Word preferences.

Windows 2000 supports three types of user profiles:

➤ *Local profiles*—Local profiles are profiles that are stored on the local computer. If a user logs into a local computer, the user will see the local desktop and application settings; however, if the user logs into another Windows 2000 computer, the user will see the local profile store on that particular computer. Local user profiles are stored within the Documents And Settings folder on the boot partition and are listed by username, as shown in Figure 21.15.

➤ *Roaming profiles*—Roaming profiles are profiles that are stored on a network server. You can create a roaming user profile by simply copying a profile to a central network share and then specifying the location of the profile in the User Account Properties dialog box. When a user account is configured to use a roaming profile and the user logs onto a computer, the user's profile is downloaded from the network server and loaded on the local machine. Users still have the ability to change their desktop and application settings; however, the changes are made to the profile stored on the server.

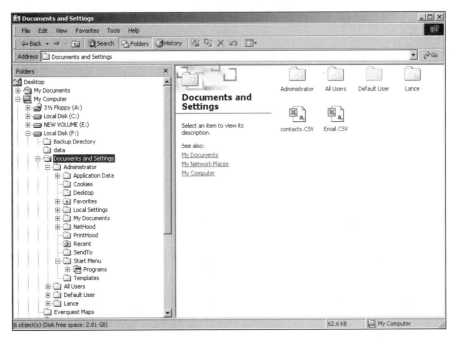

Figure 21.15   Local user profile location.

➤ *Mandatory profiles*—Mandatory profiles are roaming profiles that prevent users from making any changes to the profile. Roaming profiles can be made mandatory by simply renaming the profile's extension. The file that contains the profile information for a user is named ntuser.dat. By renaming the file to ntuser.man, you can prevent users from making any changes to the profile.

Normally, profiles are created on the local computer and then copied to network file servers so they can be used as roaming profiles. Once a profile is created, you can use the System applet in Control Panel to locate and copy user profiles to a central network location. Within the System applet is the User Profiles tab, as shown in Figure 21.16.

Creating and Managing Groups in Windows 2000 Professional

Groups are simply a collection of user and computer accounts. Groups ease administrative burden by allowing permissions to be assigned to multiple users in one simple step. Instead of configuring permission on each user account, an

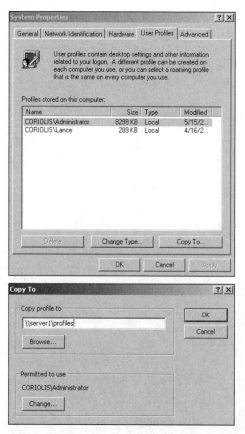

Figure 21.16   Copying user profiles.

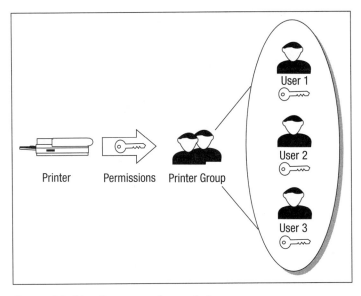

Figure 21.17 Groups and permissions.

administrator can group users according to job function or resource needs and assign permissions to the group. (See Figure 21.17.) Keep in mind that users can be members of more than one group.

Local Groups

Windows 2000 contains a Local Accounts Security Database and, therefore, can contain only local groups. Local groups are created on the local Windows 2000 computer and are used to assign permissions to resources located on the local computer only. Local groups cannot be assigned permissions to resources that reside on the network or remote computers.

Builtin Groups

All Windows 2000 member server, standalone server, and Professional computers contain builtin local groups. The purpose of the builtin groups is to assign system rights to the members of the groups. Builtin groups are used to assign rights, such as the right to back up and restore files, change system configuration setting, and create other groups and users. Builtin groups are contained in the Groups folder within the Computer Management Administrative Tool, as shown in Figure 21.18.

Creating a Group

To create a group, perform the following steps:

1. Open the Computer Management Administrative Tool.

2. Double-click the Local Users And Groups object.

21

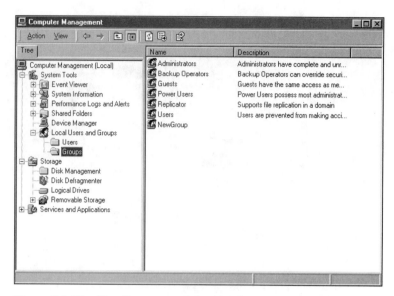

Figure 21.18 The Groups container in Computer Management.

3. Right-click the Groups folder, and select New Group.

4. Enter a name for the group and a description of what the group is used for.

5. Click the Add button.

6. In the Select Users Or Groups dialog box, select the users or other groups that should be members, and click Add.

7. Click OK to return to the New Group dialog box.

8. Click Create to create the group.

9. Click Close.

Windows 2000 Professional Builtin System Groups

Windows 2000 includes a third type of group—called system groups—that is automatically created during normal operations. You cannot modify the membership of system groups; however, the operating system is constantly adding and removing user accounts from each system group. The operating system uses system groups to allow access to computer network resources and to perform specific tasks. Following is a list of the special system groups and their functions:

➤ *Everyone*—The Everyone system group includes all users who are currently accessing a computer or domain. By default, all shared network resources allow the Everyone system group full control access. The Everyone group should always be removed from the access control list for all network and local resources. Instead of using the Everyone group, consider using the Users or Authenticated Users local and global groups; by default, these groups include all user accounts created on the domain or local workstation.

➤ *Authenticated Users*—The Authenticated Users system group includes all users who have been authenticated on the local computer. Consider using the Authenticated Users group instead of the Everyone group.

➤ *Creator Owner*—The Creator Owner system group includes all user accounts that have created or taken ownership of a resource. Any file or resource created by an administrators account lists the administrators group as the owner. Members of the administrators group cannot become owners of files; instead, the administrators group becomes the creator or owner.

➤ *Network*—The Network system group includes any user account that is currently connected to the local machine from the network.

➤ *Interactive*—The Interactive system group includes any user account that is currently logged in interactively to the system. *Interactive logon* means a user is logged in locally to the computer, as compared to being connected over the network.

➤ *Anonymous*—The Anonymous system group includes any users that Windows 2000 did not authenticate.

➤ *Dialup*—The Dialup system group includes any user who is currently connected to the computer via a dial-up connection.

UNDERSTANDING WINDOWS 2000 PROFESSIONAL SECURITY POLICIES

Using the Group Policy snap-in, you can increase the security on your Windows 2000 Professional computer. Password restrictions and policies, as well as account lockout policies, are implemented with the Group Policy snap-in. Local security policies deal with the security setting of the local operating system, such as not displaying the last username and erasing the pagefile.sys file before shutting down.

Account Policies

Account policies can be created to configure password policies for the local Windows 2000 Professional computer. Account policies can also be used to lock out accounts that meet your lockout policy.

21

Password Policies

Password policies can be implemented to assist an administrator in ensuring that users are creating correct passwords as well as changing passwords on a regular basis. Password policies can also be used to enforce unique passwords. By requiring unique passwords, a user cannot change a password to the same as the last or the same as any previous password the user account has had. To create a password policy, you must use the Group Policy MMC snap-in. Password policies allow the following options to be set:

➤ *Enforce Password History*—The number that you enter here determines how many of the previous passwords the operating system will remember and not allow the user to reuse.

➤ *Maximum Password Age*—This option forces a user to change the password whenever the password reaches the specified age, in days.

➤ *Minimum Password Age*—This option prevents a user from changing the password repeatedly to bypass the password history requirements.

➤ *Minimum Password Length*—This option can be used to ensure that all user passwords contain a minimum number of characters.

➤ *Passwords Must Meet Complexity Requirements*—This option forces a user to use both numbers and letters or uppercase and lowercase characters to make passwords harder to guess. Additionally, if this option is enabled, the password cannot contain the username or user's full name.

➤ *Store Password Using Reversible Encryption For All Users In The Domain*—By default, this option is disabled. When this option is enabled, Windows 2000 stores all passwords using reversible encryption. This allows the system to authenticate Challenge Handshake Authentication Protocol (CHAP) requests. This option can be selected only if the Windows 2000 Professional computer is a member of a domain.

To create a password policy, perform the following steps:

1. Open the Group Policy snap-in with an MMC console.

2. Expand the following object:

3. Local Computer Policy|Computer Configuration|Windows Settings|Security Settings|Account Policies|select Password Policy

4. In the display window, select the policy you want to edit.

Account Lockout Policies

To create an account lockout policy, select the Account Lockout Policy object just below the Password Policies object. Following is a list of account lockout options that can be configured and a brief description of each setting:

➤ *Account Lockout Duration*—This specifies how long an account should remain locked out after it has been locked. You can specify an amount of time in minutes that the account should remain locked, or you can allow the account to remain locked until an administrator unlocks the account manually.

➤ *Account Lockout Threshold*—This option allows the administrator to define how many bad login attempts are allowed before the account is locked.

➤ *Reset Account Lockout Counter After*—This setting allows the administrator to specify the amount of minutes to wait before resetting the bad logon attempts counter.

Windows 2000 Professional includes many additional security features that were lacking in Windows NT Workstation. For example, Windows NT Workstation was a poor choice for laptops, because of its lack of support for mobile computing. In Windows 2000 Professional, Microsoft addresses this lack of support by including new features for mobile workers, including the additional security features discussed in Chapter 20.

WINDOWS 2000 PROFESSIONAL GOES MOBILE

One of the areas where Windows NT Workstation missed the boat was in supporting laptop users. Microsoft rectifies this oversight by including many new features in Windows 2000 Professional to assist with the deployment and support of mobile computers. Other than adding support for more PCMCIA devices (as mentioned earlier in this chapter), Windows 2000 Professional includes a new feature called *offline folders*. Offline folders allow users to synchronize the contents of a local folder with the contents of a shared folder on a server.

Offline Folders

Offline folders allow users to continue to work when the network server is down or when users are disconnected from the network. Users or administrators can configure network-shared folders to be automatically synchronized with local folders on the client operating systems. By synchronizing network shares with local folders, users will always have any work files needed, regardless of location or the network's status.

When a user connects a laptop to the network, the files in the local folder and the files in the network-shared folder are synchronized. Any changes made to either copy are replicated to the other copy.

Before any offline folders can be created, the network server and the laptop must be configured to allow the synchronization of files and folders. The client's offline folder is configured for synchronization using the Tools menu in My Computer or Windows Explorer.

21

Configuring Offline Folder Shares on the Server

To allow synchronization between a server's and clients' offline folders, you must first create and configure a shared folder. After the share has been created, you can configure the share for use by clients' offline folders by accessing the Share Properties dialog box (right-click the share and select Share Properties), clicking the Caching button, and then setting the synchronization settings, as shown in Figure 21.19.

After the Cache Settings dialog box displays, you can select the Allow Caching Of Files In This Shared Folder checkbox to enable file caching. Then, you can configure how files are synchronized between the client and the server. The options for configuring synchronization include the following:

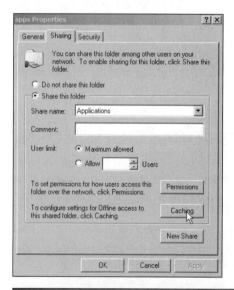

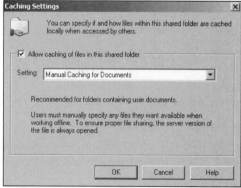

Figure 21.19   Configuring a share for use with offline folders.

➤ *Manual Caching For Documents*—Users must specify each document that they want to include in their offline folder to use when offline. Manually caching for documents is the default setting.

➤ *Automatic Caching For Documents*—Any file that a user opens will be automatically downloaded to the client and saved to the client's hard drive. If the user already has a copy of the file saved on the hard drive, it will be overwritten.

➤ *Automatic Caching For Programs*—Any opened files that are opened by an application are automatically downloaded to the client's hard drive. If there is already a copy of the file, it will be overwritten by the new file.

After you select the appropriate caching settings, click OK in the cache settings dialog box and click OK again in the Share Properties dialog box. After the server's configuration is complete, you must configure the client's offline folder.

Configuring Client Offline Folders

A client computer can be configured to use offline folders by clicking the Tools menu in My Computer or Windows Explorer and then selecting Folder Options. After the Folder Options dialog box appears, select the Offline Files tab, as shown in Figure 21.20.

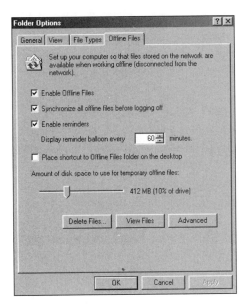

Figure 21.20   Offline folder client configuration.

21

You must select the Enable Offline Files and Synchronize All Offline Files Before Logging Off options to enable offline file caching. As shown in Figure 21.20, you can choose to view the files that have been cached using the View Files button, or you can delete the cached files using the Delete Files button. The Advanced button allows you to specify what your computer should do when you lose your network connection. For example, you could configure the system to begin working offline immediately if the network connection is lost. You can also configure the client to notify you immediately and then begin working offline. Finally, you can specify the amount of disk space to be used by the offline files; 10 percent of total partition space is the default.

After the client and server are properly configured, the client will begin to cache files that are opened from the server's configured shared folder. Which files the client will cache depends on the server's configuration settings.

Synchronization Conflicts

Conceivably, two users could modify the same offline file while away from the network. Both users could then attempt to update the files on the file server when they return to the office. Which file should be copied to the network? If both the local cached versions of a file and the copy of the file on the server are edited, you will be given a choice of how you would like to resolve the issue. You can choose from among the following options:

➤ Retain your edited copy of the file and not update the server's copy.

➤ Overwrite your locally cached file with the copy that's on the network server.

➤ Keep a copy of both files.

If you choose to keep a copy of both files, the edited copy of the file on the network will then be downloaded to your computer, and you will be required to rename your version of the file. Then, your computer and the network server will contain both copies of the file.

CHAPTER SUMMARY

This chapter discussed many of the new features included in Windows 2000 Professional. Furthermore, the text described how to accomplish administrative tasks, such as creating user accounts. This chapter also explained how each user account contains a set of default properties. User account properties specify configuration information about a user, such as whether the user can change the password, whether the user must change the password when the user logs in, and in which groups each user account belongs. Furthermore, this chapter showed how to use the Computer Management Administrative Tool and MMC snap-in to view and modify user properties.

This chapter also described the purpose of groups and how they can be used to ease administration of resource permissions. Builtin, system, and user-defined groups were explained, as well as the steps to create and modify group memberships. Each of the system groups contained in Windows 2000 were listed, as well as their purpose. This chapter also discussed builtin groups and why they are needed on Windows 2000 Professional computers.

Today, as more and more companies realize the importance of the Internet, familiarity with the installation and configuration of TCP/IP is essential. Windows 2000 Professional includes many added features to the TCP/IP protocol, such as the ability to obtain TCP/IP configuration information automatically from DHCP servers on the network. Windows 2000 Professional also supports the automatic assignment of private addresses without the use of a DHCP server on small networks. This chapter outlined how to install TCP/IP as well as how to enable static, dynamic, and self-assigned IP addressing.

In today's business environment, the network is the computer, and the survival of a company often depends on the security of the network. Understanding this, Microsoft provides new security features in Windows 2000 Professional. Included with Windows 2000 is the ability to create password policies to enforce company password policy requirements. Password as well as local security policies are created and configured within the Group Policy snap-in for the Microsoft Management Console.

Managing hardware resources and their associated drivers can be one of the more frustrating administrative responsibilities. Windows 2000 Professional includes many tools to assist administrators with this task. This chapter discussed how Device Manager can be used to view all hardware resources on any Windows 2000 system, how to view driver information, how to view resource information, and how to remove any hardware device. This chapter also discussed the driver signing features as well as how to configure the operating system to prevent any applications from overwriting needed system or device driver files. Many tools are available to Windows 2000 Professional users and administrators to view and modify the digital signatures on each system file. These tools include the file signature verification utility, the System File checker utility, and the Device Manager application.

Mobile computing is becoming more of a requirement in today's fast-paced job markets. This chapter discussed ways that you can provide needed files and folders to a user when the user is disconnected from the network, as well as how to synchronize those files and folders after the user returns to the network. This chapter explained that, before you can implement the offline folders feature of Windows 2000, you must first configure the file server and the Windows 2000 Professional computer as well as resolve synchronization conflicts.

21

This chapter introduced many of the new features of Windows 2000 Professional and described how to install and configure these new and improved features. This chapter touched on many new technologies introduced in Windows 2000; however, it is not, nor is it meant to be, a sole resource for Windows 2000 Professional. Complete books are written on Windows 2000 Professional, and this chapter is included in this book only to assist you in becoming familiar with the new technologies.

REVIEW QUESTIONS

1. Windows 2000 Professional supports which of the following file systems? [Check all correct answers]

   a. FAT

   b. NTFS

   c. CDFS

   d. FAT32

   e. HPFS

2. IPP is used for what purpose?

   a. Printing

   b. Routing

   c. Terminal Services

   d. Hardware configuration

3. When can Windows 2000 Professional use the same drivers as Windows 98?

   a. If the driver is a 32-bit driver.

   b. If the driver is written for Windows 98 release 2.

   c. If the driver is written to the WDM specification.

   d. Windows 2000 cannot use drivers written for Windows 98.

4. Windows 2000 Professional supports the use of Direct X drivers.

   a. True

   b. False

5. The Windows 2000 Backup utility can be used to back up data to which of the following devices? [Check all correct answers]

   a. Zip drives

   b. Recordable CD-ROMs

   c. Network drives

   d. Tape drives

6. What task does the Disk Defragmenter utility perform?

   a. Discovers and repairs bad sectors on a hard drive

   b. Scans for cross-link files

   c. Defragments fragmented files

   d. Creates fault-tolerant volumes

7. What must you do before you can use the Kerberos 5 protocol for authentication?

   a. Enable smart card authentication.

   b. Enable the Kerberos protocol in the Group Policy MMC snap-in.

   c. Disable the NTLM authentication protocol.

   d. Do nothing; Kererbos is enabled by default.

8. Which of the following utilities can be used to view all available IRQ resources? [Check all correct answers]

   a. Add/Remove Hardware Wizard

   b. Device Manager

   c. System Information

   d. Hardware Manager

9. What utility can you use to see whether a hardware device is loaded?

   a. Device Manager

   b. Driver Verification Wizard

   c. Add/Remove Hardware Wizard

   d. Hardware Manager

10. Which of the following utilities can be used to view the current operating system version?

   a. System Manager

   b. Device Manager

   c. System Information

   d. None of the above

11. Driver signing is used to track different versions of a driver for a hardware resource.

   a. True

   b. False

21

12. What function does the file verification utility serve?

    a. Enables you to view only those files with signatures

    b. Enables you to view only those files without signatures

    c. Enables you to view and replace files with incorrect signatures

    d. Enables you to view and replace files without signatures

13. Microsoft's TCP/IP protocol suite supports the use of sockets but does not support Winsocks.

    a. True

    b. False

14. Which of the following does not apply to the TCP/IP protocol?

    a. Can be used to connect dissimilar networks

    b. Can be used in large routed enterprise networks

    c. Can be used to connect to Novell NetWare 3.12 server

    d. Can be used to connect to Unix servers

15. If a Windows 2000 Professional computer is configured to obtain an IP address automatically but there is no DHCP server, then the Windows 2000 Professional computer will not obtain an IP address.

    a. True

    b. False

16. You want any user account to have the ability to log onto any Windows 2000 Professional computer on the network. Each Windows 2000 Professional computer is a member of the domain and has a valid computer account created in the Active Directory. What must you do to enable a user with a valid network account to log onto the domain from any Windows 2000 Professional computer?

    a. Create all user accounts on all Windows 2000 Professional computers.

    b. Copy the domain users group from each server to each Windows 2000 Professional computer.

    c. Copy the users group from each Windows 2000 professional computer to each network server.

    d. This is the default configuration.

17. Which tool is used to create a global group on Windows 2000 Professional?

    a. Computer Management

    b. Active Directory Users and Computers

    c. Group Policy editor

    d. None of the above

18. Fred has a valid local user account on a Windows 2000 Professional computer. The computer is a member of the domain and has a computer account created in the Active Directory on the Windows 2000 domain controller. What resources can Fred access?

 a. Resources located on the local computer or the domain controller.

 b. Resources on the local computer only.

 c. Resources on the domain controller only.

 d. Fred cannot log into a Windows 2000 Professional computer that is a member of the domain.

19. You want to allow all users on the network to have access to your shared printer on your Windows 2000 Professional computer. Your computer is a member of the domain. Which group should you grant permissions to?

 a. The local computer's Everyone group

 b. The local computer's Users group

 c. The domain's Domain Users group

 d. The domain's Everyone group

20. What can you do to prevent users from making changes to their local profiles?

 a. Mark the profile directory as read-only

 b. Mark the Ntuser.dat file as read-only

 c. Rename the Ntuser.dat file to Ntconfig.pol

 d. Rename the Ntuser.dat file to Ntuser.man

REAL-WORLD PROJECTS

Andy Palmer, while updating his résumé to include his newly acquired Windows 2000 Certification, gets a call notifying him that the Coriolis company has finally received all their new computers. Andy is instructed to go to the customer's site and install each new client machine on the network.

Upon arriving, Andy is happy to find that all the new computer systems have Windows 2000 preinstalled, and, anticipating the arrival of these computers, the users have copied all their files to the network server.

Before Andy can add the computers to the network, he must first install and configure TCP/IP. The company is currently using a DHCP server to assign all IP addresses.

21

Project 21.1
To install and configure TCP/IP, complete the following steps:

1. Click Start | Settings | Control Panel, and then double-click the Network And Dial-up Connections icon.

2. Double-click the Local Area Connection icon.

3. In the Local Area Connection Status dialog box, click Properties.

4. In the Local Area Connection Properties dialog box, click Install.

5. Select Protocol, click Add In The Select Network Component Type, and click Add.

6. Select Internet Protocol (TCP/IP), and click OK.

7. Because the network already has a DHCP server installed, Andy leaves the default selection of Obtain An IP Address Automatically.

8. Click OK in the TCP/IP Properties window.

9. Click Close.

After TCP/IP is installed and configured, Andy's next order of business is to connect each new Windows 2000 client to the existing Windows 2000 network. Coriolis's domain name is **Coriolis.test**. Computer accounts for the new clients were added when the network was upgraded to Windows 2000.

Note: See Chapter 6 for information about creating computer accounts on a Windows 2000 domain controller.

Project 21.2
To join a Windows 2000 Professional client to the domain, complete the following steps:

1. Right-click My Computer, and select System Properties.

2. Select the Network Identification tab.

3. Click the Properties button, as shown in Figure 21.21.

4. In the Member Of section, select the Domain radio button.

5. Enter the name of the domain (such as "coriolis.test").

6. Click OK.

Andy knows that the Windows 2000 Server has already been configured to allow offline caching of files and that other Windows 2000 Professional computers on the network are using offline folders. Andy wants to enable offline folders on one laptop that is connected to the network.

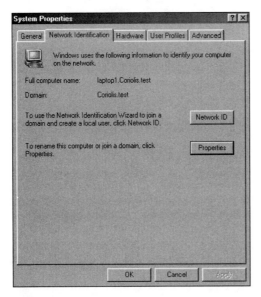

Figure 21.21   System Properties Network Identification tab.

Project 21.3
To enable offline folders on a Windows 2000 Professional computer, complete the following steps:

1. Double-click the My Computer icon on the desktop.

2. Double-click the C:\ drive.

3. Click the Tools drop-down menu, and select Folder Options.

4. Select the Offline Folders tab.

5. Select the Enable Offline Folders checkbox.

6. Use the sliding scale to set the amount of hard drive space you want to allow offline files to consume.

7. Click OK.

Feeling exhausted after having helped so many clients while studying for and passing his certification exam, Andy decides to take a well-earned vaction and heads for the beach.

21

CHAPTER TWENTY TWO

SAMPLE TEST

Question 1

Andy Palmer is trying to add a new class that has mandatory attributes that are also new to the Active Directory schema. When adding a new class to a schema that contains mandatory new attributes, Andy must first add the class with the Active Directory Schema console.

○ a. True

○ b. False

Question 2

Match the appropriate role and property with the corresponding Windows 2000 operation master (items can be used more than once):

Schema Master   _____

RID Master   _____

PDC Emulator   _____

Infrastructure Master _____

Domain Naming   _____

a. There must be one per domain.

b. There is only one per forest.

c. There is only one per tree.

d. Defines all objects that make up the Active Directory.

e. Ensures that all objects have a unique identifier.

f. Contains configuration information for the domain.

g. Is responsible for maintaining DNS names and IP addresses for all computers.

h. Ensures that all domain names are unique within the forest.

i. Provides backward compatibility for legacy client operating systems.

Question 3

Andy Palmer is tasked with synchronizing his client's MS Exchange database with the client's Active Directory. The client needs to administer Microsoft Exchange objects from the Active Directory. What does Andy have to do to facilitate this type of administration?

○ a. Nothing; it is automatic.

○ b. An Exchange-to-Windows directory synchronization.

○ c. A Windows-to-Exchange directory synchronization.

○ d. Two-way directory synchronization.

Question 4

Andy is using Netmon to analyze DHCP traffic. He needs to know how the DHCP server is responding to client requests. In Netmon, which messages sent by a DHCP server to a DHCP client offering a particular set of parameters to the client must he look at?

○ a. DHCPOffer

○ b. DHCPAcknowledge

○ c. DHCPNAK

○ d. DHCPAccept

Question 5

Andy wants to use Netmon to analyze the DHCP server's response to a client's acceptance of DHCP parameters. Which of the following is a message sent from a DHCP server acknowledging the acceptance of TCP/IP parameters?

○ a. DHCPAccept

○ b. DHCPAcknowledge

○ c. DHCPNAK

○ d. DHCPOffer

Question 6

22

Andy wants to ensure that the proper ports are available for Microsoft Exchange and Active Directory database synchronization. What is the default port used for communication between Active Directory and Exchange?

○ a. TCP 839

○ b. UDP 839

○ c. TCP 389

○ d. UDP 389

Question 7

Andy is concerned that the synchronization between the Microsoft Exchange database and Active Directory does not overburden the available network bandwidth. Synchronization between MS Exchange and the Active Directory can be scheduled.

○ a. True

○ b. False

Question 8

Andy has to upgrade an entire department from Windows NT Servers to Windows 2000 Servers. When the project manager asks how much RAM each server will need, what should Andy's reply be?

○ a. 32MB

○ b. 64MB

○ c. 128MB

○ d. 256MB

Question 9

Andy has to make numerous answer files to perform unattended installs of Windows 2000 Professional. Which of the following utilities is used to create and modify answer files?

○ a. Setup Manager

○ b. Setup Wizard

○ c. Sysprep Manager

○ d. Sysprep Wizard

Question 10

Andy has migrated all the servers in a client's system to Windows 2000. Now that he has done that, he wants to gain the extra functionality of nested groups. The DCPromo utility can be used to change a domain from native mode to mixed mode.

○ a. True

○ b. False

Question 11

Tom, a senior manager in the IT department at one of Andy's clients, is amazed that the Active Directory catalog requires such a small amount of disk space. He can't believe that it requires such little disk space, because he believes that the global catalog contains all the attributes for the objects in the directory. Is Tom's assumption true or false?

○ a. True

○ b. False

Question 12

An administrator at one of Andy's clients wants to know how servers replicate. Andy replies that a one-way replication path between two server objects with a point toward the replication source is called which of the following?

○ a. Replication link

○ b. Site link

○ c. Replication object

○ d. Connection object

Question 13

Place the appropriate statements under the respective operating systems (statements can be used more than once):

Operating Systems	Statements
Windows 2000 Professional	Requires Pentium 133MHz or higher (supports up to 2).
Windows 2000 Server	Requires 650MB free space on 2GB hard disk.
	Requires Pentium 133MHz or higher (supports up to 4).
	Requires 64MB minimum RAM.
	Requires 1GB free space on 2GB hard disk (additional space needed if installing over a network).
	Requires 128MB minimum RAM.

Question 14

While consulting for a company that is planning a Windows 2000 migration, an administrator asks Andy Palmer what type of group is best suited for accessing resources in any domain in the forest. Which group does Andy tell the administrator is best suited for this type of access?

- ○ a. Global
- ○ b. Local
- ○ c. Universal
- ○ d. Any of the above

Question 15

A user has called the Help desk at one of Andy's clients because the user cannot access a particular file. The Help desk technician has assigned permissions to an NTFS file for the particular user. The user has been allowed Full Control to the file and denied Read access to the same file. Will the user be able to read the file?

- ○ a. Yes
- ○ b. No

Question 16

Andy serves as the consulting administrator for a company with one network technician, Gary. Andy needs to delegate administrative access for a particular Organizational Unit (OU) so that Gary can add users and computers to the OU. Gary should not be allowed to open more than one window, however, and he should not be able to change the focus of the administrative console. To delegate administrative control for an object, a customized console should be created and saved in which of the following modes?

- ○ a. Administration
- ○ b. Author
- ○ c. Delegation
- ○ d. User

Question 17

Andy calculates that, due to server load, a planned terminal server will need eight Pentium III 800 processors. Windows 2000 Server symmetric multiprocessing supports up to eight processors.

- ○ a. True
- ○ b. False

Question 18

Andy is the architect for a Windows 2000 namespace. He needs to represent the zones on the plan. Which of the following are valid types of DNS zones? [Check all correct answers]

❏ a. Standard primary

❏ b. Standard secondary

❏ c. Incremental

❏ d. Active Directory integrated

Question 19

While designing a Windows 2000 namespace, Andy becomes concerned that the available network bandwidth will be saturated. To limit the amount of traffic that DNS synchronization requires, Windows 2000 supports which of the following zone transfers?

○ a. Partial zone transfers

○ b. Active zone transfers

○ c. Differential zone transfers

○ d. Incremental zone transfers

Question 20

One of Andy's clients has purchased a new departmental server to replace a slightly outdated model. The client would like to give the old server to another department within the organization without reinstalling the operating system. Andy needs to move a Windows 2000 domain controller from one tree in a forest to another one. Andy believes that, once a Windows 2000 Server is converted to a domain controller, it can be moved to a new domain.

○ a. True

○ b. False

Question 21

Andy is developing a fault-tolerance plan for the file servers in a client's system. When he opens the disk management console on a selected server, he sees that the fault-tolerance options in the menu are grayed out. He thinks about the situation and remembers that to create a fault-tolerant volume in Windows 2000, a particular type of disk is necessary. Which of the following types of disks does Andy need?

- O a. Spanned
- O b. Basic
- O c. Dynamic
- O d. NTFS

Question 22

Andy needs to build a test lab that closely resembles a client's production environment. The lab will be completely separate from any other networks. When Andy starts to duplicate a server for use in a test lab environment, he decides that mirroring the disks in the server and then removing one disk for use in the lab is a pertinent method for creating the test lab. To stop mirroring two drives without destroying data, which of the following actions must Andy perform?

- O a. Delete mirror
- O b. Break mirror
- O c. Stop mirroring
- O d. Remove one disk

Question 23

One of Andy's clients wants to implement a file sharing system that has one convenient point of access for users and one convenient point of backups for administrators. Additionally, the client wants to ensure that no single server failure will interfere with the users' access to the files. To create a fault-tolerant shared file system with a single point of navigation for users, which of the following must be implemented?

- O a. Standalone Dfs Root
- O b. Mirrored Dfs Root
- O c. Domain Dfs Root
- O d. Mirrored drives with same share name

Question 24

A client has asked Andy to tighten the security on one of the file servers. The first task Andy decides to perform on the selected shares is to prevent inheritance of NTFS permissions. He knows that, when preventing permission inheritance on NTFS file resources, he has to make a decision ahead of time. Why?

○ a. Current permissions are copied, and future inheritance is prevented.

○ b. Current permissions are erased, and future inheritance is prevented.

○ c. A choice is made to erase or copy current permissions, and future inheritance is prevented.

○ d. Current permissions are manually and selectively copied, and future inheritance is prevented.

Question 25

Folders are provided representing the new names for volumes supported by Windows 2000. Drag the old Windows NT 4 name for each volume type into the appropriate folder.

Windows 2000 folder names:

Mirrored Volume

Simple Volume

Stripe Volume

RAID 5 Volume

Spanned Volume

Old Windows NT 4 names:

Volume

Mirrored Set

Stripe Set

Volume Set

Striped Set With Parity

Question 26

A user, Joanne, calls the Help desk because she cannot change her desktop settings. The Help desk technician, Blake, calls Andy Palmer, because the policy has changed but Joanne has not yet received the additional capabilities. Blake believes that when a group policy is changed, Joanne will not see the effects of the new policy until the next time she logs on. Is this true or false?

○ a. True

○ b. False

Question 27

Andy wants to ensure that all users in a particular Organizational Unit (OU) get a vertical market application installed as soon as possible. He considers assigning the application to the computers in the OU. When an application is assigned to a user or computer, how can it be installed? [Check all correct answers]

❏ a. It is immediately and automatically installed.

❏ b. Start the program from a desktop or Start menu shortcut.

❏ c. Open an associated document.

❏ d. All of the above.

Question 28

Andy is working for a client with a number of publicly shared computers. The decision is made to use group policies to standardize the software on the machines. When adding applications to the computers, a junior consultant, Keith, suggests that publishing an application to a computer is a convenient way to standardize applications on public workstations. Is this true or false?

○ a. True

○ b. False

Question 29

One of Andy's clients wants to add another layer of security to their network. Andy suggests the use of smart card authentication with Windows 2000 to further secure the RAS logons and the interactive logons. Andy is asked what must be done, and in reply he says that the use of smart cards requires a certain type of authentication to be enabled, because it allows the proprietary authentication methods to be added to Windows 2000. What type of authentication does he recommend?

○ a. CHAP

○ b. PAP

○ c. MS-CHAP

○ d. EAP

Question 30

> Reorder the following steps to properly describe the process of creating a dynamic disk on disk 1 using Windows 2000's Disk Administrator:
>
> - Confirm the disks to be upgraded, and click OK.
>
> - Confirm you understand that you will not be able to boot to previous versions of Windows from any volume on the affected disk.
>
> - Confirm you want to execute the operation, which will force dismount all file systems on the disk.
>
> - Open Disk Management, and select disk 1 as the disk you'd like to upgrade to dynamic disk storage. Right-click it, and select Upgrade To Dynamic Disk.
>
> - Confirm you want to upgrade disk 1, and click Upgrade.

Question 31

> Andy Palmer is working for a company with numerous salespeople who access the company network through RAS. The last of the Windows NT 4 Servers has been upgraded to Windows 2000, and Andy decides that the time has come to switch the system from mixed mode to native mode to get additional functionality. In native mode with only the default policy, all users with permissions set to Control Through Remote Access Policy will:
>
> ○ a. Be allowed logon through RAS.
>
> ○ b. Be denied logon through RAS.
>
> ○ c. Be allowed logon through RAS, unless their user account is set to Change Password At Next Logon.
>
> ○ d. None of the above.

Question 32

> Andy is helping to distribute an application that was developed by a client company internally to a number of clients. The application will be used by a small, specific group of users. It is decided that the application should be provided through a Windows 2000 terminal server in Application Server mode for users on 4 Windows NT 4, 8 Windows 95, 9 Windows 98, and 19 Windows 2000 workstations. How many terminal server client licenses must be purchased?
>
> ○ a. 40
>
> ○ b. 36
>
> ○ c. 23
>
> ○ d. 21

Question 33

Andy Palmer is helping to distribute an application that was developed by a client company internally to a number of clients. The application will be used by a small, specific group of users. It is decided that the application should be provided through Windows 2000 terminal server in Application Server mode. The application uses a bar code scanner. What type of bar code scanner peripheral can be used?

○ a. Parallel port

○ b. Serial port

○ c. Keyboard port

○ d. None of the above

Question 34

Andy is helping to distribute an application that was developed by a client company internally to a number of clients. It is decided that the application should be provided through a Windows 2000 terminal server in Application Server mode. Numerous users complain that after accessing the application in the morning, the system will not let them restart the application. If a user disconnects from a terminal server session, all currently running applications are terminated.

○ a. True

○ b. False

Question 35

Andy is a consulting network administrator for a small company. Ralph, a junior administrator who works directly for the company, has accidentally deleted a major portion of the Active Directory tree. To restore deleted portions of the Active Directory, which utilities must be used? [Check all correct answers]

❑ a. Recovery Console mode

❑ b. Directory Services Restore mode

❑ c. AD Users and Computers

❑ d. NTDSUTIL

Question 36

Andy is called to a client because one member of a mirrored set appears to have failed. If a member of a mirrored set temporarily fails, what must be done to restore fault tolerance?

○ a. Reactivate disk, break mirror, reestablish mirror

○ b. Reactivate disk, break mirror, repair volume

○ c. Reactivate disk, delete mirror, reestablish mirror

○ d. Reactivate disk

Question 37

Andy has been tasked with upgrading an entire company's workstations to Windows 2000 Professional. What command will verify a system's hardware with the Hardware Compatibility List (HCL)?

○ a. **Winnt32 /CheckHCL**

○ b. **Winnt32 /CheckHCLOnly**

○ c. **Winnt32 /CheckUpgrade**

○ d. **Winnt32 /CheckUpgradeOnly**

Question 38

Andy has upgraded a member server from Windows NT 4 to Windows 2000 Server. The member provided DNS, DHCP, and GSNW services on the LAN. What should be done immediately after upgrading a member server that runs the Windows NT 4 version of DNS, GSNW, and DHCP?

○ a. Re-create the DNS zone files.

○ b. Reestablish the GSNW gateway groups.

○ c. Authorize the DHCP server.

○ d. Nothing; the upgrade is seamless.

Question 39

A client wants Andy to improve the security for their existing Windows 2000 network. Policies relating to passwords and account lockout can be applied at what level? [Check all correct answers]

❑ a. Local system

❑ b. Organizational Unit

❑ c. Domain

❑ d. Site

Question 40

22

Andy is analyzing the security for a client's Windows 2000 network. How many basic security templates are provided with Windows 2000?

○ a. 1

○ b. 2

○ c. 3

○ d. 4

Question 41

Andy has a new client that manages network printers using the DLC protocol. The client is planning to migrate the network from NetWare 3.*x* to Windows 2000. The client wants to be able to access the printers from the Internet. Which new feature should Andy suggest for the organization's printing needs?

○ a. Active Server Pages

○ b. Internet Printing Protocol

○ c. Simple TCP/IP services

○ d. WebJetAdmin

Question 42

Andy has a remote client who wants Windows 2000 Professional installed on a workstation. The client is not sure which components should be installed with the operating system. Furthermore, the client isn't sure of the network's location setting. What can Andy do to prepare a removable drive that will be sent to the client so that a local network technician can finish the installation and get the workstation on the network?

○ a. Use RIPREP

○ b. Use Sysprep

○ c. Use **Winnt32 /unattend**

○ d. Use **Winnt32 /syspart**

Question 43

Place the following statements under the applicable protocol (statements can be used more than once):

Protocol	Statement
L2TP	Requires an IP-based transmit network
PPTP	Can use IPSec for encryption
	Supports header compression
	Uses PPP envelope for transport
	Provides tunnel authentication when used with IPSec
	Uses PPP encryption

Question 44

The Windows 2000 Active Directory is made up of a hierarchical structure of objects. Each Active Directory object is made up of or can contain other objects. Identify which objects each of the following container objects can contain (items can be used more than once):

Sites   _____

Domains   _____

Trees   _____

Organizational Units   _____

a. Users

b. Domains

c. Organizational Units

d. Subnets

e. Computer Accounts

f. Printers

g Servers

Question 45

Andy is explaining to a junior administrator, Sally, that there is no primary domain controller in a Windows 2000 network, which also means that there can be no backup domain controllers. Sally questions this, because she knows that the Active Directory is a database and there must be a method to control updates and deletions to the database. Andy further explains that the system uses a special kind of operation to accommodate updates and deletions to the Active Directory. What kind of operations are being referred to?

- ○ a. Flexible Signature Multiple Operation
- ○ b. Flexible Single Master Operation
- ○ c. Flexible System Master Operation
- ○ d. Flexible Single Multiple Operation

Question 46

Andy has just finished installing the Active Directory service on the first domain controller, in the first tree, in a new forest. The DNS service has already been installed on the server, and it has been configured with a forward lookup zone and a reverse lookup zone. Andy decides to test the service by checking for the presence of LDAP service type records. What command prompt utility can he use for this purpose?

- ○ a. IPCONFIG
- ○ b. NSLOOKUP
- ○ c. NTDSUTIL
- ○ d. None of the above

Question 47

Andy needs to provide an email distribution list for a new client. The client has an Active Directory forest with two trees, each with four domains. All the domains have Organizational Units in addition to the default Organizational Units. The client needs to be able to send email to all the employees in the company with the least amount of administrative effort. How can Andy accomplish this task?

- ○ a. Andy needs to create global groups in each domain and put the accounts for all the domains users into them. Then, he needs to place the global groups into domain local groups that he creates in the domain where the email server resides.
- ○ b. Andy needs to create local groups in each domain and put the accounts for all the domains users into them. Then, he needs to place the local groups into domain global groups that he creates in the domain where the email server resides.
- ○ c. Andy needs to create global groups in each domain and put the accounts for all the domains users into them. Then, he needs to place the global groups into a universal group that he creates.
- ○ d. Andy needs to create universal groups in each domain and put the accounts for all the domains users into them. Then, he needs to place the universal groups into domain local groups that he creates in the domain where the email server resides.

Question 48

Andy has received an assignment to upgrade a network from Windows NT 4 to Windows 2000. The enterprise has 1,000 client machines running Windows 9*x* with standard hardware and BIOS, and no user settings or data needs to be saved. All servers have the same hardware and BIOS settings. The client has a master domain that contains 1,000 user accounts, a PDC, and 2 BDCs. Finally, the client has a separate resource domain that has three Web servers and two electronic mail servers that must be accessible from the Internet. What machines should Andy upgrade *first*, and what method should he use for the upgrades?

- ○ a. Domain controllers, CD-based upgrade
- ○ b. Domain controllers, Sysprep-based fresh install
- ○ c. Member servers, CD-based upgrade
- ○ d. Member servers, Sysprep-based fresh install
- ○ e. Client machines, CD-based upgrade
- ○ f. Client machines, Sysprep-based fresh install

Question 49

Andy has received an assignment to upgrade a network from Windows NT 4 to Windows 2000. The enterprise has 1,000 client machines running Windows 9*x* with standard hardware and BIOS, and no user settings or data needs to be saved. All servers have the same hardware and BIOS settings. The client has a master domain that contains 1,000 user accounts, a PDC, and 2 BDCs. Finally, the client has a separate resource domain that has three Web servers and two electronic mail servers that must be accessible from the Internet. What machines should Andy upgrade *second*, and what method should he use for the upgrades?

- ○ a. Domain controllers, CD-based upgrade
- ○ b. Domain controllers, Sysprep-based fresh install
- ○ c. Member servers, CD-based upgrade
- ○ d. Member servers, Sysprep-based fresh install
- ○ e. Client machines, CD-based upgrade
- ○ f. Client machines, Sysprep-based fresh install

Question 50

Andy has received an assignment to upgrade a network from Windows NT 4 to Windows 2000. The client has a master domain that contains 1,000 users accounts, a PDC, and 2 BDCs. Finally, the client has a resource domain that has three Web servers and two electronic mail servers that must be accessible from the Internet. In what order should the domain controllers be upgraded?

○ a. Master PDC, resource PDC, master BDCs, resource BDCs

○ b. Master BDCs, master PDC, resource PDCs, resource PDC

○ c. Master PDC, master BDCs, resource PDC, resource BDCs

○ d. Resource PDC, resource BDCs, master PDC, master BDCs

CHAPTER TWENTY THREE

ANSWER KEY

For asterisked items, please see textual representation of answer on the appropriate page within this chapter.

1. b	18. a, b, d	35. b, d
2. *	19. d	36. d
3. b	20. b	37. d
4. a	21. c	38. c
5. b	22. b	39. c
6. c	23. c	40. c
7. a	24. c	41. b
8. b	25. *	42. d
9. a	26. b	43. *
10. b	27. b, c	44. *
11. b	28. b	45. b
12. d	29. d	46. b
13. *	30. *	47. c
14. c	31. b	48. f
15. b	32. d	49. c
16. d	33. c	50. c
17. b	34. b	

Question 1

Answer b is correct. The statement is false. When adding a new class with mandatory new attributes to a schema, the attributes must be created first, then the class. After the attributes are created, they can be added to the class.

Question 2

The correct answer is as follows:

Schema Master	b, d
RID Master	a, e
PDC Emulator	a, i
Infrastructure Master	a, f
Domain Naming	b, h

Question 3

Answer b is correct. To administer Exchange objects from Active Directory, Andy needs to create an Exchange-to-Windows directory synchronization.

Question 4

Answer a is correct. A DHCPOffer is a message sent by a DHCP server to a DHCP client offering a particular set of parameters to the client. Answer b is incorrect because DHCPAcknowledge is used to acknowledge the parameters offered. Answer c is incorrect because DHCPNAK is used to decline the parameters offered. Answer d is incorrect because DHCPAccept is used to accept the parameters offered.

Question 5

Answer b is correct. Andy must look at the DHCPAcknowledge messages. A DHCPAcknowledge is a message sent from a DHCP server acknowledging the acceptance of TCP/IP parameters.

Question 6

Answer c is correct. The default port used by the LDAP protocol is TCP 389. None of the other well-known ports listed have common use.

Question 7

Answer a is correct. The statement is true. Andy is concerned that the synchronization between the Microsoft Exchange database and Active Directory does not overburden the available network bandwidth. Synchronization between MS Exchange and the Active Directory *must* be scheduled.

Question 8

Answer b is correct. Windows 2000 Server requires at least 64MB of RAM for installation.

Question 9

Answer a is correct. The Setup Manager is a utility that can be installed from the Windows 2000 Server CD to create and edit answer files. The other answer choices are incorrect because none of these—Setup Wizard, Sysprep Manager, and Sysprep Wizard—exist.

Question 10

Answer b is correct. The statement is false. The change from mixed mode to native mode is one-way and cannot be undone.

Question 11

Answer b is correct. The statement is false. The reason the Active Directory catalog requires such a small amount of disk space is because the global catalog contains only the attributes necessary to locate an object in the directory.

Question 12

Answer d is correct. A one-way replication path between two server objects with a point toward the replication source is called a connection object. Answer a is incorrect because there is no such thing as a replication link. Answer b is incorrect because a site link is used to connect sites. Answer c is incorrect because there is no such thing as a replication object.

Question 13

The correct answer is as follows:

Windows 2000 Professional

Requires Pentium 133MHz or higher (supports up to 2).

Requires 650MB free space on 2GB hard disk.

Requires 64MB minimum RAM.

Windows 2000 Server

Requires Pentium 133MHz or higher (supports up to 4).

Requires 1GB free space on 2GB hard disk (additional space needed if installing over a network).

Requires 128MB minimum RAM.

Question 14

Answer c is correct. A universal group is best suited for accessing resources in any domain in a forest. Global groups are used to represent the organizational structure, and local groups are for resource access in a single domain.

Question 15

Answer b is correct. Denied permissions take precedence over granted permissions; therefore, the user would not be able to read the designated file.

Question 16

Answer d is correct. To delegate administrative control for an object, a customized console should be created and saved in User mode rather than author mode. Author mode is used for creating the customized consoles.

Question 17

Answer b is correct. The statement is false. Windows 2000 Server supports up to four processors; Windows 2000 Advanced Server supports up to eight processors.

Question 18

Answers a, b, and d are correct. The standard primary, standard secondary, and Active Directory integrated are all valid DNS zone types in the Windows 2000 DNS service. Answer c is incorrect because incremental is a type of zone transfer, not a type of zone.

22

Question 19

Answer d is correct. The Windows 2000 DNS service supports incremental zone transfers, which transfer changes to the zone files, thereby limiting DNS synchronization traffic. Full zone transfers require more bandwidth because they transfer the entire zone file.

Question 20

Answer b is correct. The statement is false. To move a Windows 2000 domain controller to a new domain, Andy would need to use the DCPromo utility to demote the domain controller to a member server, and then move it to another domain.

Question 21

Answer c is correct. A dynamic disk is necessary to create fault-tolerant partitions with Windows 2000. Basic disks, on the other hand, can be used only for fault tolerance in systems upgraded from Windows NT 4 fault tolerance.

Question 22

Answer b is correct. To stop mirroring drives without destroying any data, simply break the mirror. Any other action will destroy data.

Question 23

Answer c is correct. To create a fault-tolerant shared file system with a single point of navigation for the users, Andy needs to implement a domain Dfs. Although Dfs provides one point of navigation for users, only the domain Dfs provides fault-tolerance.

Question 24

Answer c is correct. When preventing NTFS file permission inheritance, an administrator is presented with a choice to either copy the current permissions or erase the current permissions, and then future inheritance is prevented. Since you are presented with a choice, no other answer can be correct.

Question 25

The correct answer is as follows:

Old Windows NT 4 Names:	Windows 2000 folder names:
Volume	Simple Volume
Volume Set	Spanned Volume
Mirrored Set	Mirrored Volume
Stripe Set	Stripe Volume
Stripe Set With Parity	RAID 5 Volume

Question 26

Answer b is correct. The statement is false. If a group policy is changed, the user, Joanne, will see the new settings the next time the policy is refreshed.

Question 27

Answers b and c are correct. When an application is assigned to a user or computer, it is only advertised. The application can be installed by running it from a shortcut or opening an associated application.

Question 28

Answer b is correct. The statement is false. Applications can be published only for users; they cannot be published to computers.

Question 29

Answer d is correct. The use of smart cards requires the Extensible Authentication Protocol (EAP) to be enabled, because EAP allows the proprietary authentication methods to be added to Windows 2000. The type of authentication installed will depend on the type of smart card used.

Question 30

The correct answer is as follows:

1. Open Disk Management, and select disk 1 as the disk you'd like to upgrade to dynamic disk storage. Right-click it, and select Upgrade To Dynamic Disk.

2. Confirm the disks to be upgraded, and click OK.

3. Confirm you want to upgrade disk 1, and click Upgrade.

4. Confirm you understand that you will not be able to boot to previous versions of Windows from any volume on the affected disk.

5. Confirm you want to execute the operation, which will force dismount all file systems on the disk.

Question 31

Answer b is correct. In native mode with the default policy only, all users with permissions set to Control Through Remote Access Policy will deny RAS logon for all users. Answer a is wrong because they will not be allowed through by default. Answer c is wrong because they will not be allowed to logon through RAS, unless their user account is set to "Change Password At Next Logon".

Question 32

Answer d is correct. Twenty-one licenses are necessary, because Windows 2000 provides one built-in license.

Question 33

Answer c is correct. Windows 2000 terminal server requires peripherals to use the keyboard port for communications. Answer a is wrong because Terminal Server does not recognize the Parallel port. Answer b is wrong because Terminal Server does not recognize the Serial port. Answer d is wrong because Terminal Server does recognize the Keyboard port.

Question 34

Answer b is correct. The statement is false. Disconnecting from a terminal server session leaves all applications running. To end all running applications, log off from the terminal server session.

Question 35

Answers b and d are correct. Restoring Active Directory components after deletion requires an authoritative restore using Directory Services Restore mode and NTDSUTIL. Answer a is incorrect because Recovery Console does not provide authoritative restore. Answer c is incorrect because AD Users and Computers does not provide authoritative restore.

Question 36

Answer d is correct. If a disk in a mirrored set *temporarily* fails, reactivating the disk is the only necessary action.

Question 37

Answer d is correct. The **Winnt32 /CheckUpgradeOnly** command will verify system hardware with the Hardware Compatibility List (HCL).

Question 38

Answer c is correct. The DHCP service must be authorized in the Active Directory after upgrading a member server that was running the Windows NT 4 version of DNS, GSNW, and DHCP. Neither DNS or GSNW need any further action.

Question 39

Answer c is correct. Password and account lockout policies can be applied only at the domain level. Password policies cannot be applied at the local, OU, or site level.

Question 40

Answer c is correct. Windows 2000 provides three basic security templates—BasicWK.inf, BasicSV.inf, and BasicDC.inf.

Question 41

Answer b is correct. Andy should suggest the new Internet Printing Protocol for the organization's printing needs. Active Server Pages is used for Web sites. Simple TCP/IP services are used for other services. WebJetAdmin is used for proprietary Hewlett Packard printers.

Question 42

Answer d is correct. Andy can prepare a removable drive that will be sent to the client for a technician there to finish the installation with the **Winnt32 / syspart** command, which will place installation files onto another partition on that drive. None of the other commands will create such a disk.

22

Question 43

The correct answer is as follows:

L2TP

Supports header compression.

Provides tunnel authentication when used with IPSec.

Can use IPSec for encryption.

Uses PPP envelope for transport.

PPTP

Requires an IP-based transmit network.

Provides tunnel authentication when used with IPSec.

Can use IPSec for encryption.

Uses PPP envelope for transport.

Uses PPP encryption.

Question 44

The correct answer is as follows:

Sites

   b. Domains

   d. Subnets

Domains

   a. Users

   c. Organizational Units

   e. Computer Accounts

f. Printers

g. Servers

Trees

b. Domains

Organizational Units

a. Users

c. Organizational Units

e. Computer Accounts

f. Printers

g. Servers

Question 45

Answer b is correct. A Windows 2000 network uses Flexible Single Master Operations (FSMO) to manage replication without formal primary and backup domain controllers.

Question 46

Answer b is correct. The NSLOOKUP command-prompt utility can be used to test the Active Directory service by checking for the presence of service type records. IPCONFIG displays the machine's TCP/IP configuration, and NTDSUTIL is used to manipulate Active Directory.

Question 47

Answer c is correct. Andy needs to create global groups containing all domain users in each domain, and he needs to place the groups into a universal group.

Question 48

Answer f is correct. Andy should upgrade the client machines first, because they are the most time consuming and the impact on production is limited to individual machines. Because the client machines all have standard hardware and BIOS, the Sysprep utility can be used to prepare the machines for disk imaging. Finally, because no settings or data needs to be saved, a fresh install of Windows 2000 is appropriate.

Question 49

Answer c is correct. Andy should upgrade the member servers second, because they can be done individually to limit the impact on production. Although the member servers all have standard hardware and BIOS, meaning that the Sysprep utility could be used to prepare the machines for disk imaging, unique resources are on each, which means that a CD-based upgrade must be performed.

22

Question 50

Answer c is correct. First, the master domain PDC should be upgraded and set as the root domain, then the master BDCs can be upgraded. Next, the resource domain PDC can be upgraded and set as a child domain of the root, and, finally, the resource BDCs can be upgraded.

ANSWERS TO REVIEW QUESTIONS

CHAPTER 1 SOLUTIONS

1. **a.** Intel systems are the only computing platforms supported by Windows 2000.

2. **e.** All Windows 2000 operating systems are built using Microsoft's NT technology.

3. **a.** Support for Windows Scripting Host helps administrators create groups and multiple users quickly.

4. **e.** Security is improved throughout the entire family of Windows 2000 operating systems. As a result, Windows 2000 Professional benefits from the use of IPSec, Kerberos, EFS, smart card support, and more.

5. **c.** Windows 2000 provides a host of new wizards for troubleshooting numerous tasks, including modem configuration, Internet connections, printer installation, execution of MS-DOS programs, Windows 2000 setup issues, and much more. However, wizards cannot overcome installation issues if a device isn't compatible with the Windows 2000 operating system.

6. **a.** IPP enables printing over the Internet via a user's browser.

7. **e.** Active Directory provides a powerful console for the management of users, computers, printers, security, multiple sites, and more.

8. **b.** Windows 2000 Server provides support for physical memory configurations up to 4GB for Intel-based systems.

9. **a.** The Lightweight Directory Access Protocol is an industry standards–based protocol. Its incorporation in Windows 2000 improves security and enhances interoperability with other vendors' operating systems.

10. **a.** True. Windows 2000 supports the dynamic DNS.

11. **a.** Active Directory requires the use of Kerberos version 5 for maintaining objects.

12. **e.** Disk quotas, which help administrators enforce disk space limitations extended to users, require the use of a Windows 2000 server operating system.

13. **e.** The Indexing Service, now incorporated into Windows 2000, helps users find resources on a network. Among the items the Windows 2000 server operating systems index are files and printers. The Indexing Service cannot help a user locate a DNS server, though.

14. **a.** True. Much of the power of the Microsoft Management Console is due to its customizability. MMC can be customized to include Active Directory objects, computer management tools, and performance monitors.

15. **d.** Windows 2000 Server can support two processors on a new installation or four processors when upgrading from Windows NT 4.

16. **c.** Windows 2000 Advanced Server can support physical memory configurations up to 8GB for Intel-based systems.

17. **b.** Windows 2000 provides clustering services for up to two nodes.

18. **e.** Windows 2000 Datacenter Server supports maximum physical memory configurations of up to 64GB for Intel-based systems.

19. **d.** Windows 2000 Datacenter Server extends clustering services to four nodes.

20. **b.** False. While the Windows 2000 NTFS file system is designed for efficiency and security, it requires defragmentation. New utilities are included with the operating system to perform defragmenting operations.

CHAPTER 2 SOLUTIONS

1. **e.** Prior to installing Windows 2000 Professional, you should ensure that the target system possesses the minimum hardware requirements and that each hardware device is supported by Windows 2000. You also must have a CAL for each machine that will connect to the server.

2. **c.** The minimum hardware requirements for installing Windows 2000 Server are a Pentium 166 processor, 128MB RAM, and 1GB of hard disk space.

3. **d.** NTFS does not support dual-booting with Windows 98.

4. **b, c, d,** and **e.** A valid domain name, a computer account, a domain controller, and a server running the DNS service are all required when joining a domain.

5. **a, b, c,** and **d.** Disk duplication, Remote Installation Services, installing from a CD-ROM, and installing over a network are all valid means of installing Windows 2000.

6. **c, e.** The Windows 2000 Setup Wizard prompts the user for information on regional settings, your name and organization, the licensing mode to be used, the computer name and password for the administrator account, and whether you want to install additional Windows 2000 components.

7. **a.** The Microsoft Indexing Service enables dynamic full-text searches of computer and network data.

8. **a.** The **/r** switch is used with the **Winnt.exe** command to specify the installation of an optional folder during Windows setup.

9. **d.** The **Makeboot a:** command is used to create Windows 2000 boot disks.

10. **b.** False. Clients needing to access multiple servers are usually best served by the Per User licensing mode.

11. **a.** The **/s** switch followed by the source path should be used with Winnt32.exe to specify the location of Windows installation files.

12. **c.** The Windows 2000 Setup Manager automates the creation of an Unattend.txt file for customized installations.

13. **e.** The Windows 2000 Setup Manager does not eliminate SIDs. The Sysprep.exe tool is used to eliminate computer- and user-specific information in multiple installations.

14. **b.** False. Windows 2000 includes enhanced support for disk duplication, but third-party disk cloning tools are still required.

15. **d.** The -nosidgen switch is used to specify that Sysprep.exe should not regenerate SIDs on destination systems.

16. **a, b,** and **c.** A DNS server, a DHCP server, and Active Directory Services must be available when preparing to use RIS to install Windows 2000 Professional.

17. **a.** True. RIS must be installed on a different hard disk than that being used to run Windows 2000 Server.

18. **a.** The Sysdiff.exe utility is often used with the Windows 2000 Setup Manager to create a system differences file, later used to create customized installations of Windows 2000.

19. **b.** False. A system does not need to be Network PC compliant to enjoy remote installation benefits.

20. **a, b, c, d,** and **e.** All the options—NIC settings, protocol configuration, domain controller availability, DNS server availability, and whether the computer account has been used before—should be checked when Windows 2000 reports the inability to connect to a domain controller.

CHAPTER 3 SOLUTIONS

1. **d.** A TCP/IP address is 32 bits in length.

2. **c.** The acronym FQDN stands for fully qualified domain name.

3. **a.** The first zone created must be a primary zone.

4. **c.** A mirror copy of a primary zone is a secondary zone.

5. **c.** A standard host is represented by an A type record.

6. **c.** Unicode is the character set designed for international use.

7. **d.** A mail server is represented by an MX type record.

8. **c.** A standard name-to-address translation is a forward lookup.

9. **a, b.** To administer a TCP/IP network with the least amount of effort, DHCP is used to configure clients, and DNS is used for name resolution. WINS is no longer necessary with Windows 2000, and simple TCP/IP services do not assist with network administration.

10. **a, c.** DNS is required for dynamic DNS, and DHCP is required for DDNS with pre–Win2000 clients.

11. **b.** The acronym AXFR represents a full zone transfer.

12. **c.** DNS with redundancy requires setting up a secondary zone server.

13. **c.** When changing the address of a mail server, you must create an MX record for the new address and delete the MX record for the old address.

14. **c.** When resolving a domain controller, the client resolves an SRV record.

15. **a, b, c,** and **d.** Windows 2000, Linux, Windows 9x, and Win NT can all use Windows 2000 DNS servers.

16. **c.** Nslookup can be used to verify the MX record for a domain.

17. **c.** To set up a LAN for a small four-year college connected to the Internet and use friendly names for resources, you must register a second-level domain in the EDU namespace, set up a primary DNS server, and create an MX record for the electronic mail server.

18. **a, b,** and **d.** To help balance the demand for fresh data with bandwidth limitations, DNS uses the secondary zones, caching zones, and Time To Live for records.

19. **c.** Before the Domain Name System was devised, name resolution was based on HOSTS files maintained by a central NIC.

20. **d.** If a DHCP client cannot access a resource by name but it can access the resource by address, IPCONFIG can be used to verify DNS server settings.

CHAPTER 4 SOLUTIONS

1. **b.** The Active Directory uses DNS for name resolution.

2. **c.** The naming format used in email addresses comes from RFC 822.

3. **a, b.** An organizational unit can contain users and computers.

4. **d.** A domain is the core unit in the Active Directory structure.

5. **e.** A tree represents a contiguous namespace.

6. **f.** A forest represents a disjointed namespace.

7. **c.** A site can contain many domains, and a domain can span many sites.

8. **a.** A site is one or more subnets connected by high-speed links.

9. **d.** A high-speed link is at least 512Kbps with 128Kbps available bandwidth.

10. **b.** A domain controller contains a replica of the domain directory.

11. **a.** True. All domain controllers within a domain are peers.

12. **c.** Because the replication path forms a ring, it is fault tolerant.

13. **b.** True. The schema defines classes and the attributes for them.

14. **b.** False. It is not crucial that new schemas be downloaded regularly, because this is not the only way to extend the schema.

15. **b.** All domains within a forest share a common global catalog.

16. **a.** True. Only a domain controller can house the global catalog.

17. **b.** False. More than one server can house the global catalog.

18. **c.** The protocol used for authentication in Windows 2000 is Kerberos.

19. **c, d.** If a two-way transitive trust exists between domains A and B and another exist between domains B and C, then domain A trusts domain C, and domain C trusts domain A.

20. **c.** One-way non-transitive trusts are available to support Windows NT 4 domains.

21. **b.** In a distinguished name, DC stands for domain component.

22. **b.** The Globally Unique Identifier is 128 bits in length.

23. **d.** For backward compatibility, Active Directory supports mixed mode.

CHAPTER 5 SOLUTIONS

1. **c.** The first domain created is known as the forest root domain.

2. **a.** All domains created after the first domain are known as child domains.

3. **a, c,** and **d.** Any Windows 2000 Server can be promoted to a domain controller.

4. **b.** The Windows NT 4 primary domain controller should be the first server that is upgraded to Windows 2000.

5. **c.** In order for a Windows 2000 computer to become a domain controller, it must be running TCP/IP and DNS, and it must have an NTFS partition.

6. **b.** The dcpromo.exe program is the application that is used to promote a Windows 2000 Server to a domain controller.

7. **b.** All Windows 2000 domain controllers participate in a multi-master relationship.

8. **d.** To demote a Windows 2000 domain controller to a member or standalone server, you must run dcpromo.exe.

9. **a, b,** and **d.** Users, computers, and Organizational Units can be child objects to another Organizational Unit.

10. **d.** Using Organizational Units, you can create logical subdomains within your network.

11. **a.** Organizational Units are container objects.

12. **c.** All domains within an Active Directory are automatically configured with two-way transitive trusts.

13. **a, c,** and **d.** Organizational Units are used to organize users and other objects, simplify administration, and divide the network into logical subdomains.

14. **a, b,** and **c.** All computers, users, and groups are examples of security principles. Therefore the Windows 2000 Server, the Enterprise Admins, and all domain controllers are considered security principals.

15. **a.** The discretionary and security access control lists are both contained in the security descriptors of each object.

16. **b.** The DACL contains the SIDs of all users that are granted or denied permission to an object. Each object contains its own DACL.

17. **d.** The SACL is responsible for and contains auditing information for each object.

18. **a.** Modify group membership will allow the user to view current group membership.

19. **c.** Dcpromo.exe can be used to promote or demote a domain controller.

20. **d.** The Security Access Control List (SACL) is contained in the security descriptor.

21. **a.** Enterprise Admins have administrative permissions in all domains within the tree.

22. **d.** Before installing Active Directory you should have a DNS server configured to allow dynamic updates.

23. **b.** False. Domain controllers cannot use DHCP to obtain TCP/IP configurations

24. **a.** The SYSVOL folder is a replacement of the NETLOGON folder from Windows NT 4.

25. **a.** The database and log files must be placed on an NTFS partition.

26. **b.** The NETBIOS domain name is used for backward compatibility.

27. **d.** Microsoft recommends not creating more than 10 levels of OU.

28. **d.** All of the above.

29. **b.** All security principals are assigned security identifiers. User and group accounts are assigned SIDs, but b is a more complete answer.

30. **b.** Existing permissions can be automatically copied or removed.

CHAPTER 6 SOLUTIONS

1. **c.** The Builtin and Users folders are examples of pre-installed container objects.

2. **b.** False. The Builtin folder contains the built-in groups for Windows 2000 and any built-in groups from Windows NT 4.

3. **a.** The ForeignSecurityPrinciples folder holds user accounts from trusted domains that have been granted permissions to the local domain.

4. **b.** False. New user accounts should be placed in the Organizational Units to which they belong. The Users folder is only for users that were present on a Windows NT 4 Server.

5. **a.** True. Organizational Units can contain objects only from within their own domain.

6. **d.** The UPN name is the logon name followed by an *@* and the domain name.

7. **a.** All the characters are allowed in a username for Windows 2000.

8. **a.** True. Usernames can contain spaces, but spaces should be avoided.

9. **b.** User accounts created on standalone or members servers are created with the Computer Management administrative tool in Control Panel.

10. **b.** False. Passwords can be changed by right-clicking the user object and then selecting Change Password.

11. **d.** The UPN suffix is the domain name.

12. **b.** The Account Is Trusted For Delegation option gives a user the ability to delegate authority to other users or groups.

13. **a, b,** and **c.** All Windows NT or 2000 clients must have a computer account. Windows 98 does not require a computer account.

14. **c.** Only the members of the administrators group have permission to add a computer to a domain.

15. **c.** Security and distribution are the two types of groups.

16. **a.** Distribution groups cannot be assigned permissions.

17. **b.** A group's scope determines who can become a member.

18. **c.** A universal group can contain any other group from within or outside the current domain while running in mixed mode.

19. **d.** Universal group membership is replicated to the Global Catalog Server.

20. **c.** Global groups can contain only user accounts and other global groups while in native mode. Global groups cannot contain any other groups while in mixed mode.

21. **d.** Distribution groups are used by applications and for searching.

22. **b.** AGDLP is the proper acronym to describe the proper Windows 2000 group strategy. AGDLP stands for Accounts, Global, Domain Local, Permissions.

23. **b.** Permissions can be set by an object's owner as well as anyone with Full Control permissions. Administrators do not have Full Control for objects they do not create.

24. **b.** Any permissions assigned directly to an object remain with the object.

25. **d.** The DACL contains the SIDs of any security principle that has been assigned or denied permissions.

CHAPTER 7 SOLUTIONS

1. **d.** A forest in its simplest form consists of one domain and one domain controller.

2. **a.** The only way to isolate one administrative control totally is to create a separate domain. Administrators must be assigned permission in the remote domain just as any other user accounts.

3. **a.** The first domain created is known as the forest root.

4. **c.** Because each domain will require a domain controller, your hardware costs will increase as you purchase more domain controller computers and the software for them.

5. **a.** True. Only a limited set of data is replicated between domains.

6. **d.** The first domain created is always the tree root.

7. **b.** All child domains must be part of the same contiguous namespace.

8. **a.** The tree root domain does not have a parent domain; it is the root.

9. **b.** False. Transitive trusts are automatically created between domains within the same tree. Transitive trusts can also be created between domains in different trees or forests.

10. **b.** If domain A trusts domain B and domain B trusts domain C, then domain A also will trust domain C. In this situation, domain A will trust domain B and any domains that B trusts as well. This is an example of transitive trusts.

11. **c.** LDAP queries are used within the local domain only. Outside the domain, the Global Catalog Server is used.

12. **d.** Cross-link trusts are used to create a trust relationship between two domains that may or may not be part of the same tree or forest.

13. **c.** Cross-link trusts are used to speed access between two domains. Cross-link trusts can also be used to speed authentication between domains as well.

14. **a.** True. Cross-link trusts must be configured as transitive.

15. **b.** False. Cross-link trusts can be established between two domains that may or may not be part of the same domain.

16. **c.** Two existing domains cannot be joined into one tree or forest without reinstalling one of the domain controllers. Because each domain was created separately, each domain will already contain a schema. Schemas cannot be joined.

17. **b.** Two or more trees that automatically have a two-way transitive trust are a forest.

18. **d.** When adding a domain to an existing forest, you must specify the full DNS name of the forest/tree root domain controller.

19. **d.** Each tree requires its own unique namespace.

20. **b.** False. No automatic trusts are established between forests.

21. **a.** RFC 2052 describes SRV records.

22. **c.** Integrated DNS zones are replicated only between domain controllers within the same domain.

23. **d.** A caching DNS server does not have a zone file.

24. **b.** An index enables faster searching of a directory database.

25. **a.** Active Directory Sites And Services is used to make a domain controller a Global Catalog Server.

26. **d.** The PDC role acts as a storage location for GPOs.

27. **b.** The RID server assigns a pool of RIDs to each domain controller within a domain.

28. **a.** The infrastructure operation master holds configuration information for the domain only.

29. **c.** The naming context determines how an object is replicated.

30. **b.** The SYSVOL replaces the NETLOGON share.

31. **c.** More catalog servers will speed up searches as well as increase replication traffic.

32. **d.** Multiple forests can be complex to administer and should not be chosen if there are any other choices.

33. **a.** Trusts between forests must be created manually.

34. **b.** Trusts between forests are non-transitive and one-way.

35. **b.** False. Trust between forests can be created between any domains within each forest.

CHAPTER 8 SOLUTIONS

1. **c.** Each Windows 2000 domain controller contains a working copy of the Active Directory database.

2. **b.** Replication ensures that all replicas receive any changes to the directory.

3. **d.** Domain controllers are organized into a multimaster relationship.

4. **b.** False. Changing a password will cause replication to occur.

5. **b.** False. Only the attribute of the object that changed will be replicated.

6. **d.** USN is an acronym for *update sequence number.*

7. **c.** Each domain controller manages its own local USN numbers.

8. **a.** Timestamps are used to break replication ties.

9. **b.** An atomic operation means that both writes complete or they both fail.

10. **d.** USN numbers eliminate the need to perfect time synchronization.

11. **d.** A repaired domain controller must receive all USNs higher than the last one received from each replica directory.

12. **a, d.** Windows 2000 supports originating and replicated updates.

13. **c.** Moving or changing the name of an object is a modifyDN change type.

14. **a.** Any change to the directory through replication is a replicated update.

15. **d.** Changes made to the local directory are originating updates.

16. **c.** A replicated update is made as a result of an originating update.

17. **a.** An originating update applies a stamp to the change.

18. **b.** Propagation delay is used to prevent redundant replication traffic.

19. **b.** Creating a fully looped or meshed topology helps to provide fault tolerance.

20. **d.** The GUID and USN of each change are needed to allow for propagation dampening.

21. **c.** The up-to-date vector contains the highest USN received from an originating server during replication.

22. **a.** The domain name is not included in the metadata.

23. **b.** The high watermark is the highest USN received for any server.

24. **a.** The up-to-date vector is only incremented when replication occurs with the server that performed the original update.

25. **b.** The usnChanged is the highest USN number on the server.

CHAPTER 9 SOLUTIONS

1. **b.** The Directory Information Tree holds a subset of the information in the Active Directory that provides enough information to start and run the service.

2. **a.** The schema container is the part of the Active Directory that represents a discrete unit of replication and contains parameters necessary for the schema to function properly.

3. **d.** The configuration partition is the part of the Active Directory that represents a discrete unit of replication and contains parameters necessary for the Active Directory to function properly.

4. **a.** The Active Directory Services Interface is an application programming interface (API) that provides access to the Active Directory.

5. **d.** The **RootDSE** is an object at the top of every LDAP tree that contains the attributes necessary to extract critical directory data. The **RootDSE** is used to maintain portability in LDAP scripts and applications.

6. **a.** The **schemaNamingContext** attribute directs a query to the location of the schema.

7. **d.** The **subSchemaSubEntry** attribute in the **RootDSE** contains the location of the sub-schema that contains all the attributes and classes in the Active Directory.

8. **b.** The Ntds.dit file contains the domain directory data for a domain. The file is stored in the NTDS share on the domain controllers.

9. **c.** The schema.ini file is used to create and populate a schema.

10. **a.** The **attributeSchema** object, through inheritance, is the parent for an attribute in the Active Directory.

11. **a.** The **classSchema** object specifies the attributes and hierarchy for a class in the Active Directory.

12. **a.** The directory Management Domain is used to create the schema container in the Active Directory.

13. **c.** The **searchFlags** bit indicates whether an attribute should be indexed.

14. **b.** The common name, also called the relative distinguished name, is an attribute for an object within the Active Directory that uniquely identifies the object.

15. **d.** The directory system agent is a system process that controls access to the Active Directory information.

16. **c.** The object identifier is a code that uniquely describes an object within the directory. Issuing authorities' hierarchical systems regulate object ID codes while allowing local administrators to create local object identifiers.

17. **a.** The American National Standards Institute is a regulatory body that sets standards, including X.500 object identifiers.

18. **c.** Flexible Single Master Operations is the method used by the Active Directory to ensure certain changes occur only on one particular machine in the domain.

19. **d.** The CSVDE utility can only be used for bulk additions and deletions in the directory.

20. **a.** The LDIFDE utility can be used for bulk additions, deletions, and modifications in the directory.

21. **c.** The ADSI Edit snap-in can be installed from the Windows 2000 Server CD.

22. **a.** The Schema Manager snap-in is already present and only needs to be registered.

23. **c.** The ADSI Edit utility is used to view the **RootDSE**.

24. **a.** Schema modifications can be enabled using the Schema Manager.

25. **b.** The schema admins group has permissions to modify the schema.

CHAPTER 10 SOLUTIONS

1. **d.** The Active Directory Connector is a configuration and maintenance tool designed to simplify administration between multiple directory services.

2. **b, c.** The Active Directory Connector service can be used to establish connections between the Active Directory service and Exchange Server 5.5 and Exchange 2000 Server.

3. **a, c,** and **d.** Connection Agreements create and maintain connections for the purpose of synchronizing Active Directory and Exchange site directories, link Windows 2000 Active Directory services with other (Exchange) directory services, and create paths for synchronization.

4. **a.** True. One Active Directory Connector can host multiple Connection Agreements.

5. **d**. Connection Agreements can be configured to support one or more objects.

6. **a**. True. The Active Directory Connector service is started and stopped just like other services.

7. **c**. Installing the ADC service on a domain controller reduces the amount of network bandwidth used by the service.

8. **d**. The Active Directory Connector service uses LDAP to connect with Exchange directory services.

9. **a**. The IP address of each server hosting directory services to be synchronized is not needed when defining Active Directory Connector connections.

10. **b**. False. Active Directory Connector synchronization can occur one-way or two-ways, depending on the manner in which it is configured.

11. **a, c**. When using the Active Directory Connector service, bridgehead servers need only be configured and implemented in the locations hosting directories needing synchronization.

12. **a, b,** and **d**. Only Exchange Servers and domain controllers hosting Active Directory services can be configured as bridgehead servers.

13. **c**. Object deletions are configured using the setting provided on the Deletions tab in the Connection Agreement's Properties dialog box.

14. **a, b,** and **c**. Deleted object settings are not configured using the Advanced settings tab.

15. **c**. Active Directory Users And Computers can be used to administer Exchange recipient objects.

16. **a, c,** and **d**. The Active Directory Connector service supports the single site, single domain; single site, multiple domains; and multiple sites, multiple domains models.

17. **b**. False. Deployment should be staggered to prevent network bandwidth from being overwhelmed.

18. **a, b, c,** and **d**. The Active Directory Connector service can be used in all of these environments.

19. **a**. All objects are synchronized by default.

20. **b**. False. The Active Directory Connector service, while using LDAP, can require considerable network bandwidth.

CHAPTER 11 SOLUTIONS

1. **b.** After creating a DHCP scope, activation is the process of making the scope available to clients.

2. **b.** A broadcast is a type of network traffic sent to all nodes on a TCP/IP subnet.

3. **d.** A DHCP server is a computer on a network that provides the DHCP service to clients.

4. **c.** A DHCPDiscover is a message sent by a DHCP client to identify DHCP servers on the network.

5. **d.** A DHCPRequest is a response from a DHCP client wanting to accept parameters.

6. **a.** A DHCPNak is a message sent by a DHCP server denying a DHCPRequest message.

7. **b.** An exclusion range is a range of addresses in a DHCP scope that will not be offered to clients by the server.

8. **b.** IPCONFIG is a utility used from the Windows 2000 client command prompt to display, release, and renew DHCP parameters.

9. **c.** Multicast is a type of network traffic sent to select clients based on their multicast TCP/IP address.

10. **b.** The renewing state is the DHCP state in which the client sends a DHCPRequest message half way through the lease duration.

11. **a.** Scopes are a contiguous range of TCP/IP addresses, usually a TCP/IP subnet, available for use on a DHCP server.

12. **d.** A super-scope is a group of DHCP scopes combined to reduce administrative overhead.

13. **d.** The Session layer protocol used by applications on a LAN is NetBIOS.

14. **c.** A static file that contains NetBIOS name to TCP/IP address mappings is LMHOSTS.

15. **a.** The type of NetBIOS node that uses another host as its primary name resolution mechanism is P-node.

16. **b.** The type of NetBIOS node that can use broadcast, point-to-point (WINS and DNS), as well as HOSTS and LMHOSTS files is H-node.

17. **d.** The process a client initiates to enter its record(s) into a WINS server database is registration.

18. **b.** A server acknowledgement that a record has been entered into the WINS database is a WACK.

19. **a.** The process a WINS client uses to free up a record temporarily is release.

20. **d.** The process a server uses to mark a WINS record available, but not yet ready for scavenging, is tombstone.

21. **a.** The process a server uses to remove records from a WINS server is called scavenging.

22. **c.** A record that identifies a common name for multiple nodes but does not list TCP/IP addresses is a normal group.

23. **a.** A type of record that identifies a common name for multiple nodes and lists their TCP/IP addresses is an Internet group.

24. **c.** A WINS proxy is a WINS-enabled client that intercepts and resolves broadcast queries from non-WINS clients.

CHAPTER 12 SOLUTIONS

1. **a, b.** Windows 2000 supports basic and dynamic disks.

2. **c, d.** Basic disks support volumes, volume sets, mirror sets, stripe sets, and stripe sets with parity.

3. **c.** Windows NT Server 4 stripe sets with parity are known as RAID 5 volumes in Windows 2000.

4. **b.** False. RAID 5 volumes and mirror volumes provide fault tolerance.

5. **c.** Jessica should select stripe volumes for the best possible speed performance.

6. **a, c.** Disk Management is used to configure disks in Windows 2000. Computer Management also includes the Disk Management utility.

7. **a, b,** and **c.** By default, you can access the Disk Management utility by selecting Start|Programs|Administrative Tools|Computer Management, expanding Storage, and selecting Disk Management; or selecting Start|Run, typing "Diskmgmt.msc", and then clicking OK; or double-clicking Diskmgmt.msc in the sysroot\Winnt\System32 directory.

8. **a, b, c,** and **d.** Disk Management provides information on all of these system items.

9. **d.** Both disk quotas and security require NTFS-formatted volumes.

10. **d.** The Adapter Name property reveals which controller a disk is using.

11. **a.** Refresh updates drive letter, file system, volume, and removable media settings within the Disk Management MMC.

12. **d.** Kevin must first format the new disk with the NTFS file system.

13. **b.** False. Volumes containing system and boot files cannot be extended.

14. **d.** Spanned volumes can include up to 32 disks.

15. **d.** If one disk containing a volume that's a member of a spanned volume fails, all the data is lost.

16. **a, c,** and **d.** Disk defragmentation is required for FAT, FAT32, and NTFS. Windows 2000 does not support VFAT.

17. **d.** A Disk Defragmenter report does not provide an estimate of the time needed to defragment a drive.

18. **b, d.** Kerry must click Repair Volume, and, if the mirror set's status is not shown as Healthy, she must right-click the mirror set and select Resynchronize Mirror.

19. **a, b.** Scott doesn't need to do anything, because the only drive letters added by default are A and B. In order to ensure shortcuts aren't interrupted when the disk is pressed into service, Scott can create his own drive letter assignments using the Disk Management utility.

20. **a, b.** Because all data will be lost on the disk when it reverts to a basic disk, Sheila must first back up her data to another drive, and then perform the Revert To Basic Disk operation.

CHAPTER 13 SOLUTIONS

1. **b.** The Computer Management tool is used to share a folder.

2. **b.** False. A folder can be published to the directory before it has been shared. However, users will not be able to access the folder until it is shared.

3. **b.** False. Shared folders do not have to be published to allow access.

4. **d.** The Computer Management Tool can be used to connect to any computer on the network where the user has appropriate permissions.

5. **c.** Device Manager can be used to view the current hardware configuration. Device Manager is located within the Computer Management Administrative Tool.

6. **d.** You cannot create a local account on a domain controller.

7. **b.** The Storage node is used to view disk resources.

8. **b.** Write is not a shared folder permission. Change Permissions is a shared folder permission.

9. **d.** Publishing a share in the Active directory provides a centralized location for accessing the folder, allows all users in the forest to view the share, and eliminates the need to memorize which servers contain which shares.

10. **b.** Active Directory Users and Computers is used to publish a share to the directory.

11. **a.** Dfs centrally locates multiple shares into one virtual directory structure.

12. **d.** None of the above. All the listed operating systems require additional software to be installed before they can connect to a Dfs.

13. **c.** Domain controllers or member servers can host Dfs roots.

14. **b.** Permissions are not affected by Dfs.

15. **c.** Dfs can be created on FAT or NTFS partitions.

16. **a.** Dfs is defined and created by establishing a root.

17. **a.** A Dfs link is a pointer to any shared folder.

18. **c.** The two types of Dfs are standalone and fault tolerant.

19. **d.** A standalone Dfs topology is stored on a single server.

20. **b.** A fault-tolerant Dfs topology is stored in the Active Directory.

21. **d.** Fault tolerance can be created by creating replica shares and adding multiple links.

22. **c.** By default, client computer cache Dfs links for 30 minutes, or 1,800 seconds.

23. **d.** The Modify permission allows a user to perform any function on a file except Change Permissions and Take Ownership.

24. **b.** Ownership of a file cannot be assigned; ownership must be taken.

25. **b.** NTFS permissions are inherited to all subfolders and files by default.

CHAPTER 14 SOLUTIONS

1. **a.** A group policy object is a discrete product of the Group Policy MMC snap-in that contains details of the actual policies implemented.

2. **d.** Local group policies are objects located on every Windows 2000 computer that customize the operating environment of the computers and every user that logs onto the computers.

3. **b.** Non-local group policies are objects stored on domain controllers that control the operating environment of all users and computers in selected sites, domains, or Organizational Units.

4. **a.** True. Discretionary access control lists are lists of security groups and/or users with the associated permissions to particular objects.

5. **b.** False. Group policy extensions are objects within a Group Policy node that contain settings for a particular section of the operating environment.

6. **b.** A Group Policy node is an object at the root of a group policy that defines an area of effectiveness.

7. **a.** Assigned applications must be installed on a computer due to a computer or user configuration policy.

8. **c.** Published applications are made available for installation due to a computer or user configuration policy.

9. **d.** Script policies specify scripts that can be run at computer startup or shutdown and user logon or logoff.

10. **b.** The Windows Scripting Host is a script interpreter that can be used for customizing an environment or automating tasks on Windows computers.

11. **d.** Account Policies extensions are policies that can be set at the domain level to control account lockout, password, and Kerberos policies.

12. **b.** Local Policies extensions are policies that can be set to control the Audit Policy, User Rights Assignments, and Security Options.

13. **a.** User Rights Assignments are a set of allowable actions with corresponding security groups and/or users that can commit those actions.

14. **a.** True. An Audit Policy dictates the logging of actions taken by a particular security group and/or user.

15. **a.** True. Public Key Policies are policies that dictate the users and/or groups that can recover encrypted files, the list of trusted certificate authorities, and enterprise trust settings for certificate authorities.

16. **b.** False. IPSEC policies are policies that dictate the behavior of computer classes in a secure, non-secure, or mixed security TCP/IP environment.

17. **c.** Administrative Templates are extensible portions of group policies that modify the HKEY_LOCAL_MACHINE or HKEY_CURRENT_USER keys in the registry.

18. **a.** Loop back is the ability to apply a policy based on computer location rather than a user or computer.

19. **a.** Replace mode is the loop back mode that bypasses the user policy and uses only the computer policy.

20. **d.** Windows File Protection is a setting in the System extension for Computer Configuration, not the Windows Component extension.

Chapter 15 Solutions

1. **b.** The expenses, including all variables, of owning information systems is the total cost of ownership.

2. **a.** The operating system service that installs, maintains, and removes software from clients is the Windows Installer.

3. **a.** A Windows Installer package is a discrete unit of software distribution used by the Windows Installer service.

4. **a.** IntelliMirror is a utility that assists with installation and maintenance of software and operating systems.

5. **c.** A Windows Transform package is a special unit of software distribution used by Windows Installer to update software packages.

6. **b.** A vertical market application is an application used for a specific purpose by a specific industry.

7. **a.** A horizontal market application is an application used for purposes common to many industries.

8. **a.** Software assignment is a method of distributing software that automatically advertises and registers software.

9. **b.** False. Software publishing is a method of software distribution that makes software available in the Add/Remove Programs applet, but does not advertise or register software.

10. **b.** Application advertisement is the process of making software available on the Start menu or desktop and registering the software without actually installing it.

11. **c.** A software patch is an update to software that fixes a particular shortcoming.

12. **a.** A hot fix is a software update that can be applied on the fly to fix a particular shortcoming.

13. **a.** True. A service pack is a collection of patches and hot fixes that fix more than one shortcoming to a product bundled together.

14. **d.** A virus is a destructive software code spread and activated when its carrier executable files are run.

15. **d.** A rollout is an en masse software distribution.

16. **b.** The Autorun.inf file is placed at the root of a CD that will automatically execute a specified application.

17. **d.** Software push is a method of software distribution initiated at the distribution point and terminated at the target client.

18. **a.** Software pull is a method of software distribution initiated on the client and terminated on the client.

19. **a.** True. System Management Services is an application used for software distribution and management in large enterprise systems.

20. **d.** WinInstall is an application created by Veritas software used for software distribution.

CHAPTER **16** SOLUTIONS

1. **b, d.** Windows 2000 supports EAP and BAP, and Windows NT Server 4 does not.

2. **a, b, c,** and **d.** EAP provides support for all the listed protocols and peripheral devices.

3. **a, b.** Support for both BAP and BACP enhances Windows 2000's multilink capabilities.

4. **a.** True. PPTP requires an IP-based network for data transit to occur.

5. **b.** Willard's company will appreciate Windows 2000 most because of its support for Remote Authentication Dial-in User Service (RADIUS), which can be used to collect the accounting data needed to bill customers based on the number of minutes they utilize each month.

6. **d.** IP Security Policy Management is used to create and configure IPSec policies.

7. **c.** The special IPSec driver operates at the IP Transport layer.

8. **d.** The Internet Authentication Service logs RADIUS authentication information to log files.

9. **a.** Both PPTP and L2TP provide tunneling support.

10. **c, d.** To ensure the salesperson is granted remote access, John must use Routing and Remote Access because he's using a domain controller. He also must use Active Directory to ensure the salesperson has dial-in permissions set properly.

11. **b.** Support for the Bandwidth Allocation Protocol enhances multilink capabilities in Windows 2000 and enables Windows 2000 to dynamically add or release links on demand.

12. **c.** George should use the Network Connection Wizard.

13. **b.** False. The Network Connection Wizard should be used to create a dial-up connection to a VPN.

14. **a, b, c,** and **d.** Windows 2000's Routing and Remote Access Service checks for modems, serial, and parallel cable connections and automatically creates ports when it finds them.

15. **a.** The Network Connection Wizard must be used when configuring an inbound dial-up connection on a standalone server.

16. **c.** Network Address Translation hides the IP address of a system from other computers with the exception of the system that provides the network translation service.

17. **a, b, c,** and **d.** In this case, the administrator should check all the listed components, beginning with Kim's profile settings.

18. **b.** Mike will be granted access from 8 A.M. to 5 P.M.

19. **a, c,** and **d.** Dial-in settings must be configured from within Active Directory, policies and conditions must be set in Routing and Remote Access, and a policy's profile must be edited in Routing and Remote Access to create a Remote Access Policy.

20. **c.** If no Remote Access Policy profile is provided, remote access connection attempts will be denied access.

Chapter 17 Solutions

1. **b, d.** Windows 2000 Terminal Services requires Remote Desktop Protocol and TCP/IP to function properly.

2. **a, c,** and **d.** A client machine, RDP, and a server running Terminal Services are required to create a Terminal Services environment.

3. **a, c,** and **d.** You should ensure you've reviewed the client applications you intend Terminal Services to support, the configuration of your standalone server, and Terminal Services licensing requirements.

4. **b.** False. An application must run on the Windows 2000 platform to run properly with Terminal Services.

5. **c.** Bill will need to install the x86 16-bit and 32-bit Windows Terminal Services Clients.

6. **a.** You should consider the demands task-based users, typical users, and advanced users will place on your terminal server.

7. **c.** Barbara should add 40 MB of RAM for each user she plans to support. She plans to support four typical users, for whom 40MB each would be an appropriate estimate, so she should add at least 160MB of RAM.

8. **b, c,** and **d.** NTFS should be used for security, but SCSI cards and drives and local caching should be used to enhance performance.

9. **a, b,** and **d.** A Windows 2000 Server license, a Windows 2000 CAL, and a Windows 2000 Terminal Services CAL are required when a client connects to a terminal server.

10. **c, d.** Terminal Services can be installed using Windows 2000 Setup when a server is being installed, or it can be installed using the Add/Remove Programs applet in Control Panel.

11. **b.** Alison must use the Terminal Services Configuration Administrative Tool.

12. **b.** The Terminal Services Client for 32-bit Windows platforms requires two floppy disks.

13. **b.** Elliot could share the Tsclient folder and install the Terminal Services Client over his network.

14. **c.** To free up the server resources her five applications have been using, Virginia should log off.

15. **c.** Jake should disconnect his session.

16. **c, d.** Theresa can use the Add/Remove Programs applet and the **Change** command.

17. **b.** Lauren should use the application compatibility script provided by Microsoft.

18. **a, c.** Scott must copy the User.cmd file to the *systemroot*\System32 folder of the Terminal Services server and run the Uscron.cmd script from the command prompt on the Terminal Services server.

19. **b.** To help ensure idle sessions don't drain too many of a server's available resources, you should set idle disconnects to occur after five minutes.

20. **b, c,** and **d.** Windows Printer Mapping, COM Port Mapping, and Clipboard Mapping should be disabled when using a Terminal Services server for remote administration.

Chapter 18 Solutions

1. **c.** RAID 1 is fault tolerant. RAID 0 provides no fault tolerance.

2. **b.** You must be using dynamic disks if you want to create RAID volumes in Windows 2000.

3. **a.** Disk duplexing copies data to two disks like disk mirroring.

4. **a.** The total storage capacity is 55GB. The total size is 60GB.

5. **c.** If a disk reports as being offline, you should check all cables, then right-click the drive, and select Re-create.

6. **b.** RAID 5 provides better utilization of disk resources than RAID 1.

7. **d.** Restart the system and restart using the Last Known Good Configuration Advance Startup option.

8. **c.** Restart the system in Safe Mode and replace the driver.

9. **b.** Enable boot logging in the Advanced Startup options.

10. **d.** The initialization files will not be backed up.

11. **d.** Restart the system, and choose Recovery Console on the OS selection screen.

12. **a.** The normal backup type clears the archive bit.

13. **b.** A normal backup on Monday and a daily backup each day of the week will allow the restoration of all files with only two tapes.

14. **c.** In the described scenario, a network drive would be the best place to store backup files.

15. **d.** If an object is deleted, the object will not be removed from the system for 60 days by default.

16. **b.** Patch files are not part of the Extensible Storage Engine.

17. **c.** Transactions are written to the transaction log and then to a database page in memory.

18. **b.** A transaction is considered committed when it is written to the database page in memory.

19. **c.** The transaction log file is renamed when it reaches the 10MB limit and a new log file is created.

20. **a.** Res1.log and res2.log are used to reserve space on a volume.

21. **c.** The transaction log file is named Edb.log and is stored in the NTDS directory by default.

22. **a.** Circular logging overwrites existing log files and does not create additional files.

23. **b.** Previous log files are transaction log files that have been renamed.

24. **a.** When an object is deleted from the Active Directory, it is marked with a tombstone and is removed from the directory when the tombstone lifetime expires.

25. **a.** A non-authoritative restore should be used when you simply want to restore the Active Directory. Authoritative restores should be used when you want to reverse some action.

CHAPTER 19 SOLUTIONS

1. **b.** First tree in a new forest. The first domain controller becomes the first domain in a new Active Directory tree.

2. **c.** New tree in an existing forest. A tree is already established once the first domain is created.

3. **a.** Child domain in an existing forest. Any new domain added to a tree becomes a child domain.

4. **d.** New controller in an existing domain. When upgrading a BDC, choose a new controller in an existing domain.

5. **c.** Distributed file system. Dfs allows you to combine shares located on any server into one directory structure.

6. **b.** Services for Macintosh provide file and print services for Apple computers.

7. **b.** TCP/IP printing services are needed to print to Unix servers or for Unix servers to print to Windows 2000 printers.

8. **c.** The best way to advertise file and printer shares used by a specific department is by placing departmental resources into the department's OU.

9. **a, b,** and **c.** Windows 95, 98, and NT 4 can all be upgraded to Windows 2000.

10. **b.** False. The users should be directly involved with the new system plan.

11. **b.** The syspart utility is used to create install files for systems that do not contain the same hardware.

12 **b.** False. The root domain name cannot be changed after implementation.

13. **b.** False. The PDC Emulator is still used for authentication in native mode.

14. **c.** Organizational Units can be created to create logical domains.

15. **a.** You should create a new root domain and add the master domains as child domains.

16. **b.** They can directly upgrade because the size of the SAM database does not matter when upgrading to Windows 2000.

17. **a.** In a single master domain model, the master domain should become the forest root and any resource domains should be eliminated. In this case, the only reason for having multiple domains is resource management. Windows 2000 will allow separate individuals to have resource management capabilities through the use of Organizational Units.

18. **c.** Each building will require its own subnet. Subnets are the boundaries for sites, not domains.

19. **a,** and **b.** Windows NT 3.1 must be upgraded to Windows NT 3.51 or better. Windows 3.1 clients must be upgraded to Windows 95.

20. **d.** The Users container object will contain all user accounts and any group accounts that were not created automatically.

CHAPTER 20 SOLUTIONS

1. **c.** A technique used by hackers to gain information through the users themselves is known as social engineering.

2. **a.** An attack that involves repeated logon attempts with a known username and unknown password is known as a brute force attack.

3. **b.** An attack that involves manipulating data to change the source or destination is known as a masquerade attack.

4. **d.** An attack that involves capturing data for use at a later date is known as a replay attack.

5. **c.** An attack that does not directly benefit the attacker but does detriment the company is known as a denial of service attack.

6. **a.** A piece of malicious code that hides in an application's scripting interface is called a macro virus.

7. **b.** A piece of malicious code that hides in an application is called a Trojan horse.

8. **b.** The generic name for a mechanism used to form a network boundary is called a security model.

9. **a.** The specific name for a mechanism that Windows NT uses to form a network boundary is called a domain model.

10. **b.** The primary authentication method used in Windows 2000 is Kerberos.

11. **c.** Smart cards can be implemented to effectively add a layer of security to the authentication process.

12. **b.** A public key infrastructure is required before implementing the Encrypting File System.

13. **a.** The Extensible Authentication Protocol is required before implementing smart cards.

14. **b.** Domain local groups are commonly used to grant access to resources in a single domain.

15. **d.** Universal groups are commonly used to grant access to resources in multiple domains.

16. **a.** Global groups are commonly used to grant access to manage users based on geography or organizational structure.

17. **c.** IPSec provides security for data while it is transmitted across the network.

18. **b.** Encrypting File System provides security for data while it is stored on local machines.

19. **b.** The security configuration editor can be used to standardize security based on templates.

20. **b.** Windows 2000 provides two types of security templates—basic and incremental.

CHAPTER 21 SOLUTIONS

1. **a, b, c, d.** Windows 2000 supports FAT, FAT32, NTFS, and CDFS file systems.

2. **a.** The IPP (Internet Printing Protocol) allows users to connect to and print to printers over the Internet.

3. **c.** The driver is written to the WDM specification. Drivers written to the WDM specification will work with Windows 2000 and Windows 98.

4. **a.** True. Windows 2000 supports the use of Direct X 7 and after.

5. **a, b, c,** and **d.** Windows 2000's Backup utility can write to Zip drives, CD-ROMs, network drives, and tape drives.

6. **c.** The disk defragmenter utility defragments fragmented files on the computer's hard drives.

7. **d.** Kerberos is the authentication protocol used by Windows 2000 and is enabled by default.

8. **b, c.** The Device Manager and the System Information snap-in can be used to view all available IRQs.

9. **a.** Device Manager lists all installed hardware and the status of each hardware device.

10. **a.** System Manager lists information about the computer and operating system.

11. **b.** False. Driver signing is used to verify the manufacturer of a driver.

12. **b.** The file verification utility allows you to view only those files that do not have signatures.

13. **b.** False. Windows 2000 does support the use of Winsocks within its TCP/IP protocol stack.

14. **c.** The TCP/IP protocol cannot be used to connect to Novell NetWare 3.12 servers because Netware 3.12 servers run only IPX/SPX as their protocol.

15. **b.** False. Windows 2000 Professional computers can be used to self-assign private addressing.

16. **d.** The scenario describes the default configuration.

17. **d.** Global groups cannot be created on Windows 2000 Professional computers.

18. **b.** Accounts created on a local Windows 2000 Professional computer do not allow access to network resources.

19. **b.** The local users group on a Windows 2000 Professional computer contains the domain's domain users group when the Windows 2000 Professional computer is a member of the domain.

20. **d.** To prevent users from making changes to their local profiles, you can rename the Ntuser.dat file as Ntuser.man.

Appendix A

OBJECTIVES FOR EXAM 70-240

Installing, Configuring, and Administering Windows 2000 Professional

Installing Windows 2000 Professional	Chapter(s):
Perform an attended installation of Windows 2000 Professional.	2, 21
Perform an unattended installation of Windows 2000 Professional.	2, 21
Install Windows 2000 Professional by using Windows 2000 Server Remote Installation Services (RIS).	2, 21
Install Windows 2000 Professional by using the System Preparation Tool.	2
Create unattended answer files by using Setup Manager to automate the installation of Windows 2000 Professional.	2
Upgrade from a previous version of Windows to Windows 2000 Professional.	2, 15, 19, 21
Prepare a computer to meet upgrade requirements.	2
Troubleshoot failed installations.	2

Configuring Windows 2000 Professional	Chapter(s):
Monitor, manage, and troubleshoot access to files and folders.	13, 21
Manage and troubleshoot Web server resources.	21
Manage printers and print jobs.	21
Control access to printers by using permissions.	21
Configure and manage file systems.	2, 13, 21
Monitor and configure disks.	12
Monitor, configure, and troubleshoot volumes.	12
Implement, manage, and troubleshoot mobile computer hardware.	21

Administering Windows 2000 Professional	Chapter(s):
Optimize and troubleshoot performance of the Windows 2000 Professional desktop.	21
Manage hardware profiles.	21
Recover systems and user data by using Windows Backup.	18
Troubleshoot system restoration by using Safe Mode.	18, 21
Recover systems and user data by using the Recovery Console.	18, 21
Configure and manage user profiles.	21
Implement, manage, and troubleshoot network protocols and services.	21
Connect to computers by using a virtual private network (VPN) connection.	16

(continued)

Administering Windows 2000 Professional (continued)	Chapter(s):
Create a dial-up connection to connect to a remote access server.	16
Connect to the Internet by using dial-up networking.	21
Implement, monitor, and troubleshoot security.	16, 20
Encrypt data on a hard disk by using Encrypting File System (EFS).	21
Implement, configure, manage, and troubleshoot local group policy.	14
Implement, configure, manage, and troubleshoot account policy.	14
Create and manage local users and groups.	6
Implement, configure, manage, and troubleshoot a security configuration.	20

Installing, Configuring, and Administering Windows 2000 Server

Installing Windows 2000 Server	Chapter(s):
Perform an unattended installation of Windows 2000 Server.	2
Create unattended answer files by using Setup Manager to automate the installation of Windows 2000 Server.	2
Create and configure automated methods for installation of Windows 2000.	2
Upgrade a server from Microsoft Windows NT 4.	19
Troubleshoot failed installations.	2

Installing, Configuring, and Troubleshooting Access to Resources	Chapter(s):
Monitor, configure, troubleshoot, and control access to files, folders, and shared folders.	13
Configure, manage, and troubleshoot a stand-alone Distributed file system (Dfs).	13
Configure, manage, and troubleshoot a domain-based Distributed file system (Dfs).	13
Monitor, configure, troubleshoot, and control local security on files and folders.	13
Monitor, configure, troubleshoot, and control access to files and folders in a shared folder.	13
Troubleshoot problems with hardware.	2
Optimize disk performance.	12
Recover System State data and user data.	18
Recover System State data by using Windows Backup.	18
Troubleshoot system restoration by starting in safe mode.	18
Recover System State data by using the Recovery Console.	18

Managing, Configuring, and Troubleshooting Storage Use	Chapter(s):
Monitor, configure, and troubleshoot disks and volumes.	12
Monitor and configure disk quotas.	12
Recover from disk failures.	12, 18

Administering Windows 2000 Terminal Services	Chapter(s):
Install, configure, monitor, and troubleshoot Terminal Services.	17
Remotely administer servers by using Terminal Services.	17
Configure Terminal Services for application sharing.	15
Configure applications for use with Terminal Services.	15

Administering Windows 2000	Chapter(s):
Implement, configure, manage, and troubleshoot policies in a Windows 2000 environment.	14, 17
Implement, configure, manage, and troubleshoot Local Policy in a Windows 2000 environment.	14
Implement, configure, manage, and troubleshoot System Policy in a Windows 2000 environment.	14
Implement, configure, manage, and troubleshoot auditing.	14
Implement, configure, manage, and troubleshoot local accounts.	14
Implement, configure, manage, and troubleshoot Account Policy.	14, 17
Implement, configure, manage, and troubleshoot security by using the Security Configuration Tool Set.	14, 20
Apply upgrades and patches.	15
Remove applications.	15

Securing a Windows 2000 Network	Chapter(s):
Implement, monitor, and troubleshoot security.	1, 13, 20
Encrypt data on a hard disk by using Encrypting File System (EFS).	1, 13, 20

Implementing and Administering a Microsoft Windows 2000 Network Infrastructure

Installing, Configuring, Managing, Monitoring, and Troubleshooting DNS in a Windows 2000 Network Infrastructure	Chapter(s):
Install, configure, and troubleshoot DNS.	3
Install the DNS Server service.	3
Configure zones.	3
Configure zones for dynamic updates.	3, 11
Implement a delegated zone for DNS.	3
Manually create DNS resource records.	3
Manage and monitor DNS.	3

Installing, Configuring, Managing, Monitoring, and Troubleshooting DHCP in a Windows 2000 Network Infrastructure	Chapter(s):
Install, configure, and troubleshoot DHCP.	11
Install the DHCP Server service.	11
Create and manage DHCP scopes, superscopes, and multicast scopes.	11
Configure DHCP for DNS integration.	11
Defining scopes for DHCP servers.	11
Authorize a DHCP server in Active Directory.	11
Manage and monitor DHCP.	11

Configuring, Managing, Monitoring, and Troubleshooting Remote Access in a Windows 2000 Network Infrastructure	Chapter(s):
Configure and troubleshoot remote access.	16
Configure inbound connections.	16
Create a remote access policy.	16
Configure a remote access profile.	16
Configure a virtual private network (VPN).	16
Configure multilink connections.	16
Manage and monitor remote access.	16
Configure remote access security.	16
Create a remote access policy.	16

Installing, Configuring, Managing, Monitoring, and Troubleshooting WINS in a Windows 2000 Network Infrastructure	Chapter(s):
Install, configure, and troubleshoot WINS.	11
Configure WINS replication.	11
Configure NetBIOS name resolution.	11
Manage and monitor WINS.	11

Implementing and Administering a Microsoft Windows 2000 Directory Services Infrastructure

Install, Configure, and Troubleshoot the Components of Active Directory	Chapter(s):
Install Active Directory.	3, 4, 5
Create sites.	4, 8
Create site links.	7, 8
Create site link bridges.	8
Create connection objects.	6, 10
Transfer operations master roles.	8, 9
Implement an Organizational Unit (OU) structure.	4, 6, 7
Back up and restore Active Directory.	18
Perform an authoritative restore of Active Directory.	18

Designing and Modifying the Active Directory Schema	Chapter(s):
Design an Active Directory Schema	9
Modify an Active Directory Schema	9
Replicate the Active Directory Schema	9
Configure the Active Directory Schema Operations Master	9

Installing, Configuring, Managing, Monitoring, and Troubleshooting DNS for Active Directory	Chapter(s):
Install, configure, and troubleshoot DNS for Active Directory.	3
Integrate Active Directory DNS zones with non–Active Directory DNS zones.	3
Configure zones for dynamic updates.	3, 11
Manage replication of DNS data.	3

Installing, Configuring, Managing, Monitoring, Optimizing, and Troubleshooting Change and Configuration Management	Chapter(s):
Implement and troubleshoot Group Policy.	14
Create a Group Policy Object (GPO).	14
Link an existing GPO.	14
Delegate administrative control of Group Policy.	14
Modify Group Policy inheritance.	14
Filter Group Policy settings by associating security groups to GPOs.	14
Modify Group Policy.	14
Manage and troubleshoot user environments by using Group Policy.	14
Control user environments by using administrative templates.	14
Assign script policies to users and computers.	14
Manage and troubleshoot software by using Group Policy.	14
Deploy software by using Group Policy.	14, 15
Maintain software by using Group Policy.	15
Configure deployment options.	2, 15
Troubleshoot common problems that occur during software deployment.	15
Deploy Windows 2000 by using Remote Installation Services (RIS).	2, 15
Install an image on a RIS client computer.	2
Create a RIS boot disk.	2
Configure remote installation options.	2, 16
Troubleshoot RIS problems.	16
Manage images for performing remote installations.	2
Configure RIS security.	16
Authorize a RIS server.	16
Grant computer account creation rights.	2
Prestage RIS client computers for added security and load balancing.	16

Managing, Monitoring, and Optimizing the Components of Active Directory	Chapter(s):
Manage Active Directory objects.	4, 6
Move Active Directory objects.	4, 6
Secure access to Active Directory objects.	6
Delegate administrative control of objects in Active Directory.	6
Manage Active Directory performance.	6
Monitor, maintain, and troubleshoot Active Directory components.	6
Manage and troubleshoot Active Directory replication.	7
Manage intersite replication.	8
Manage intrasite replication.	8
Manage Active Directory Connector	10
Configure Active Directory Connector	10
Monitor Active Directory Connector	10

Configuring, Managing, Monitoring, and Troubleshooting Active Directory Security Solutions	Chapter(s):
Configure and troubleshoot security in a directory services infrastructure.	6, 20
Apply security policies by using Group Policy.	14, 20
Create, analyze, and modify security configurations by using Security Configuration and Analysis and Security Templates.	1, 20
Implement an audit policy.	20
Monitor and analyze security events.	20

Installing, Configuring, Managing, Monitoring, and Troubleshooting Network Protocols and IP Routing in a Windows 2000 Network Infrastructure	Chapter(s):
Install, configure, and troubleshoot IP routing protocols.	16
Update a Windows 2000–based routing table by means of static routes.	16
Implement Demand-Dial Routing.	16
Manage and monitor IP routing.	16
Manage and monitor border and internal routing.	16
Install, configure, and troubleshoot Network Address Translation (NAT).	16
Install Internet Connection Sharing.	16
Install, configure, and troubleshoot network protocols (TCP/IP, NWLink).	2
Configure network bindings.	2
Configure TCP/IP packet filters.	2
Configure and troubleshoot network protocol security.	20
Configure, manage, and troubleshoot IPSec.	20
Configure IPSec for transport and tunnel modes.	20
Customize IPSec policies and rules.	20

Installing, Configuring, and Troubleshooting Access to Resources	Chapter(s):
Install and configure network services for interoperability.	2
Monitor, configure, troubleshoot, and control access to printers.	2
Monitor, configure, troubleshoot, and control access to files, folders, and shared folders.	13
Monitor, configure, troubleshoot, and control local security on files and folders.	13
Monitor, configure, troubleshoot, and control access to files and folders in a shared folder.	13
Monitor, configure, troubleshoot, and control access to files and folders via Web services.	13
Monitor, configure, troubleshoot, and control access to Web sites.	2

Managing, Monitoring, and Optimizing System Performance, Reliability, and Availability	Chapter(s):

Many of Microsoft's objectives for this section were covered in Windows NT 4 and have not changed with Windows 2000. The only item to have changed is how to configure and monitor performance monitor, which is covered in Chapter 8. The other items are not discussed in detail in this book since the authors realize that readers already have the knowledge.

STUDY RESOURCES

BE PREPARED

IT professionals seeking to upgrade their Windows NT 4 MCSE certification to the new Windows 2000 platform have until December 31, 2001, to do so. On January 1, 2002, individuals certified on the Windows NT 4 platform can no longer claim MCSE status.

Two options exist for updating one's certification and preventing it from retiring. A candidate can either sit for seven Windows 2000 tests, or IT professionals can opt to try Exam 70-240: Microsoft Windows 2000 Accelerated Exam for MCPs Certified on Microsoft Windows NT 4.0. After the free 70-240 test is successfully completed, a candidate must pass only a few additional exams to earn the new MCSE designation. The exact number depends upon the electives that were taken to achieve MCSE accreditation.

Sounds great, right? Well, there are a few catches. Microsoft is permitting only IT professionals who have passed the following exams to sit for the 70-240 test:

➤ *Exam 70-067*—Implementing and Supporting Microsoft Windows NT Server 4

➤ *Exam 70-068*—Implementing and Supporting Microsoft Windows NT Server 4 in the Enterprise

➤ *Exam 70-073*—Microsoft Windows NT Workstation 4

Now, here's the real kicker. This intensive and accelerated exam, which is longer and more grueling than any other Microsoft exam in the past, can be taken only once. Pass it, and you're on your way. Fail it, and you're back at square one as if you never passed a single certification exam in your lifetime.

For this reason, it's more important than ever to ensure you've prepared properly for this exam. In addition to reviewing this text, answering all its review questions and sample test, and following its exercises, you should spend several hours with practice exams. You might also want to review other texts covering material with which you're experiencing difficulty. The following list can help you select a few additional resources.

Books

Check out some of the following texts if you're experiencing difficulty or if you seek more information on specific topics.

Active Directory

Blum, Daniel J. *Understanding Active Directory Services*. Redmond, WA: Microsoft Press, 1999. ISBN 1572317213.

Brovick, Ed, Doug Hauger, et al. *Windows 2000 Active Directory*. Indianapolis, IN: New Riders, 2000. ISBN 0735708703.

Coriolis Technology Press. *Active Directory: On The Job*. Scottsdale, AZ: The Coriolis Group, 2000. ISBN 1576106756.

Iseminger, David. *Active Directory Services for Microsoft Windows 2000 Technical Reference*. Redmond, WA: Microsoft Press, 2000. ISBN 0735606242.

Microsoft Consulting Services. *Building an Enterprise Active Directory Notes from the Field*. Redmond, WA: Microsoft Press, 2000. ISBN 0735608601.

Microsoft Corporation. *MCSE Training Kit: Microsoft Windows 2000 Active Directory Services*. Redmond, WA: Microsoft Press, 2000. ISBN 0735609993.

Norris-Lowe, Alistair G. *Windows 2000 Active Directory*. Sebastopol, CA: O'Reilly & Associates Inc., 2000. ISBN 1565926382.

Simanski, Robert. *Windows 2000 Active Directory Black Book*. Scottsdale, AZ: The Coriolis Group, 2000. ISBN 1576102564.

Deployment and Installation

Ferris, Jeffrey. *Windows 2000 Deployment and Desktop Management*. Indianapolis, IN: New Riders, 2000. ISBN 0735709750.

Russel, Charlie, and Sharon Crawford. *Microsoft Windows 2000 Server Administrator's Companion: The Expert Guide to Planning, Deployment, and Maintenance*. Redmond, WA: Microsoft Press, 2000. ISBN 1572318198.

Network Configuration and Management

Microsoft Corporation. *MCSE Online Training Kit: Microsoft Windows 2000 Network Infrastructure Administration*. Redmond, WA: Microsoft Press, 2000. ISBN 0735609527.

Microsoft Corporation. *MCSE Training Kit: Microsoft Windows 2000 Network Infrastructure Administration*. Redmond, WA: Microsoft Press, 2000. ISBN 1572319046.

New Riders Development Team. *MCSE Training Guide (70-221): Designing a Windows 2000 Network Insfrastructure*. Indianapolis, IN: New Riders, 2000. ISBN 0735709823.

Ramsey, James. *Deploying and Supporting Internetworking Services in Microsoft Windows 2000*. Indianapolis, IN: Que, 2000. ISBN 0789722305.

Syngress Media Incorporated. *Managing Windows 2000 Network Services*. Rockland, MA: Syngress, 2000. ISBN 1928994067.

Williams, Vera B. *MCSE Guide to Microsoft Windows 2000 Network Infrastructure*. Cambridge, MA: Course Technology/Thomson Learning, 2000. ISBN 0619015055.

Security

Bragg, Roberta. *MCSE Training Guide (70-220): Designing Security for a Windows 2000 Network*. Indianapolis, IN: New Riders, 2000. ISBN 073570984x.

Internet Security Systems Inc. *Microsoft Windows 2000 Security Technical Reference*. Redmond, WA: Microsoft Press, 2000. ISBN 073560858x.

Mclean, Ian. *Windows 2000 Security Little Black Book*. Scottsdale, AZ: The Coriolis Group, 2000. ISBN 1576103870.

Schmidt, J. *Microsoft Windows 2000 Security Handbook*. Indianapolis, IN: Que, 2000. ISBN 0789719991.

Syngress Media Incorporated. *Configuring Windows 2000 Server Security*. Rockland, MA: Syngress Media Incorporated, 1999. ISBN 1928994024.

Windows NT 4

Hudson, Kurt, Ed Tittel, and James Michael Stewart. *MCSE NT Server 4 Exam Cram, Third Edition*. Scottsdale, AZ: The Coriolis Group, 2000. ISBN: 1576106187.

Hudson, Kurt, Ed Tittel, and James Michael Stewart. *MCSE NT Workstation 4 Exam Cram, Third Edition*. Scottsdale, AZ: The Coriolis Group, 2000. ISBN 1576106209.

Ivens, Kathy, and Bruce A. Hailberg. *Inside Windows NT Workstation 4, Certified Administrator's Resource Edition*. Indianapolis, IN: New Riders Publishing, 1997. ISBN 1562057901.

Microsoft Corporation. *Microsoft Windows NT 4.0 Essential Reference Pack: The 3-in-1 Solution for Complete Details about Windows NT Administration, Management, and Security*. Redmond, WA: Microsoft Press, 1999. ISBN 0735610096.

Microsoft Corporation. *Microsoft Windows NT Server 4.0 Enterprise Technologies Training Kit*. Redmond, WA: Microsoft Press, 1998. ISBN 1572317108.

Palmer, Michael J. *MCSE NT Server Exam Prep*. Scottsdale, AZ: The Coriolis Group, 1998. ISBN 1576102521.

Tittel, Ed, Christa Anderson, and David Johnson. *MCSE NT Workstation 4 Exam Prep*. Scottsdale, AZ: The Coriolis Group, 1999. ISBN 1576102386.

Tittel, Ed, Kurt Hudson, and James Michael Stewart. *MCSE NT Server 4 in the Enterprise Exam Cram Adaptive Testing*. Scottsdale, AZ: The Coriolis Group, 1999. ISBN 1576104478.

Williams, Jeffrey, Jonathan Taylor, Michael Gill, S. Linthicum, and David Johnson. *MCSE NT Server in the Enterprise Exam Prep*. Scottsdale, AZ: The Coriolis Group, 1998. ISBN 157610253X.

Windows 2000 Professional

Boyce, Jim. *The Microsoft Windows 2000 Professional Installation and Configuration Handbook*. Indianapolis, IN: Que, 2000. ISBN 0789721333.

Cassel, Paul. *Microsoft Windows 2000 Professional Unleashed*. Indianapolis, IN: Sams, 2000. ISBN 0672317427.

Dulany, Emmett. *MCSE Prep Kit 70-210: Installing, Configuring, and Administering Microsoft Windows 2000 Professional Exam Guide*. Indianapolis, IN: Que, 2000. ISBN 0789723719.

Honeycutt, Jerry. *Introducing Microsoft Windows 2000 Professional*. Microsoft Press, Redmond, WA: 1999. ISBN 0735606625.

Microsoft Corporation. *MCSE Training Kit: Microsoft Windows 2000 Professional*. Redmond, WA: Microsoft Press, 2000. ISBN 1572319011.

Microsoft Corporation. *Microsoft Windows 2000 Professional Resource Kit*. Redmond, WA: Microsoft Press, 2000. ISBN 1572318082.

Nielsen, Morten Strunge. *Windows 2000 Professional Advanced Configuration and Implementation: A Comprehensive Guide to the New Mainstream Desktop Operating System for Professional Users*. Scottsdale, AZ: The Coriolis Group, 2000. ISBN 1576105288.

Siyan, Karanjit. *Windows 2000 Professional Reference*. Indianapolis, IN: New Riders, 2000. ISBN 0735709521.

Stinson, Craig, and Carl Siechert. *Microsoft Windows 2000 Professional Expert Companion*. Redmond, WA: Microsoft Press, 2000. ISBN 0735608555.

Stinson, Craig, and Carl Siechert. *Running Microsoft Windows 2000 Professional.* Redmond, WA: Microsoft Press, 2000. ISBN 1572318384.

Wallace, Nathan. *Windows 2000 Professional Upgrade Little Black Book: Hands-on Guide to Maximizing the New Features of Windows 2000 Professional.* Scottsdale, AZ: The Coriolis Group, 2000. ISBN 1576107485.

Windows 2000 Server

Boswell, William. *Inside Windows 2000 Server.* Indianapolis, IN: New Riders, 1999. ISBN 1562059297.

Coriolis Technology Press. *Windows 2000 Server Database Little Black Book.* Scottsdale, AZ: The Coriolis Group, 1999. ISBN 1576103927.

Johnson, David, and Libby Chovanec. *MCSE Windows 2000 Server Exam Prep.* Scottsdale, AZ: The Coriolis Group, 2000. ISBN 1576106969.

Microsoft Corporation. *MCSE Online Training Kit Microsoft Windows 2000 Server.* Redmond, WA: Microsoft Press, 2000. ISBN 0735609543.

Microsoft Corporation. *MCSE Training Kit Microsoft Windows 2000 Server.* Redmond, WA: Microsoft Press, 2000. ISBN 1572319038.

Microsoft Corporation. *Microsoft Windows 2000 Server Resource Kit.* Redmond, WA: Microsoft Press, 2000. ISBN 1572318058.

Miller, Chris, and Todd Brown. *Microsoft Windows 2000 Server Unleashed.* Indianapolis, IN: Sams, 2000. ISBN 0672317397.

Minasi, Mark. *Mastering Windows 2000 Server, Second Edition.* Alameda, CA: Sybex Computer Books, 2000. ISBN 0782127746.

Nielsen, Morten Strunge. *Windows 2000 Server Architecture and Planning.* Scottsdale, AZ: The Coriolis Group, 1999. ISBN 1576104362.

Northrup, Anthony. *Introducing Microsoft Windows 2000 Server.* Redmond, WA: Microsoft Press, 1999. ISBN 1572318759.

Palmer, Michael. *MCSE Guide to Microsoft Windows 2000 Server.* Cambridge, MA: Course Technology/Thomson Learning, 2000. ISBN 0619015179.

INTERNET RESOURCES

As more information on Windows 2000 and its associated exams becomes available, the Internet can become one of the most valuable resources available to IT professionals preparing for industry certification. Table C.1 displays some valuable Internet resources for IT professionals.

Appendix C

Table C.1 Valuable Internet resources for IT professionals.

Site	URL	Description
ClNet	www.cnet.com/software/ 0-1497797.html?tag=st.sw.3709. dir.1497797	ClNet's Windows 2000 news and information
Certification Magazine Online	www.certmag.com	Certification news and information
Coriolis	www.coriolis.com	Exam information news, information, and updates
GoCert	www.gocert.com	Certification information and study resources
LabMice	www.labmice.net	Systems administration and certification information for Windows NT/ Windows 2000 professionals
LearnQuick	www.learnquick.com	MCSE exam preparation resources
MCP Magazine Online	www.mcpmag.com	MCP news and certification information and updates
MCSE 2B	www.mcse2be.com	MCSE study site
MCSEHelp.com	209.207.167.177	Infamous brain dump site (use at your own risk!)
Microsoft Knowledge Base	search.support.microsoft.com/kb/ c.asp?fr=0&SD=GN&LN=EN-US	Microsoft's Windows 2000 Knowledge Base
Microsoft TechNet	www.microsoft.com/technet/ default.asp	Microsoft's technical support site
Sylvan Prometric RapidAssess	www.rapidassess.com/test/ default.asp	Rapid assessment online test resources
TechRepublic	www.techrepublic.com	News, MCSE certification tips and tricks, and how-to information for IT professionals
TechWeb	www.planetit.com/techcenters/ windows_2000	TechWeb's Windows 2000 news and information site
ZDNet	www.zdnet.com/filters/ special2000	Ziff-Davis's Windows 2000 news and information

SIMULATION EXAM PROVIDERS

Never enter a testing facility before you've spent seat time with a simulation exam. Never, ever enter a testing facility to take the 70-240 exam without first investing extensive time studying and taking practice tests. There's simply too much at stake. Table C.2 provides some Web sites that can assist you in finding practice exams for the 70-240 exam.

Good luck!

Table C.2   URLs of leading vendors who offer simulation tests.

Site	URL
CiCPrep	www.mcpprep.com
Coriolis	www.coriolis.com/cip/core4rev.asp
Self Test Software	www.selftestsoftware.com/shop
Specialized Solutions Inc.	www.quick-cert.com
Transcender	www.transcender.com

GLOSSARY

access control entry
An entry into the access control list for an object.

access control list (ACL)
A list of all SIDs for all security principals that have been granted or denied permissions for an object.

account lockout
Security feature built into Windows 2000 that allows an administrator to specify a number of failed login attempts before the account is locked. After the account is locked, the account cannot be used to gain access to the computer or the network, even if the correct account information is entered.

account policies
Policies that can be set at the domain level to control account lockout, password, and Kerberos policies.

activate
After creating a DHCP scope, the process of making the scope available to clients.

Active Directory
A centralized database following the X.500 protocol standard. Within Active Directory, all network components become objects of the directory. The directory stores all objects and provides a centralized location of all objects, which simplifies administration.

Active Directory Integrated zones
DNS zone files that have been integrated into the Active Directory. The zone files are held and modified by the Active Directory instead of a primary DNS server. The Active Directory is automatically replicated to all domain controllers.

Active Directory Services Interface (ADSI)
An application programming interface (API) that provides access to the Active Directory.

administrative templates
Extensible portions of group policies that modify the HKEY_LOCAL_MACHINE or HKEY_CURRENT_USER key in the registry.

agent
Program that runs in the background of an operating system and reports events and status information to the user or operating system.

Alias record (CNAME)
Record used to map a domain name to a host name.

American National Standards Institute (ANSI)
Regulatory body that sets standards, including X.500 object identifiers.

application programming interface (API)
Routines that an application can use to make requests to the operating system or to other applications or services.

assigned applications
Applications that must be installed on a computer due to computer configuration or user configuration policies.

AttributeSchema
Object that, through inheritance, is the parent for an attribute in the Active Directory.

audit policy
Policy that dictates the logging of actions taken to a particular object by a particular user and/or security group. An audit policy defines the types of security events that Windows 2000 records in the security log on each computer.

auditing
Process that logs configured information regarding the access or attempted access to a network or network resources by user or group accounts.

authentication
Process of verifying the validity of a user account based on username, password, and account and time restrictions.

B-node
Type of NetBIOS host that uses broadcasts as its primary name-resolution mechanism.

Bandwidth Allocation Protocol (BAP)
Protocol used with PPP and multilink protocols. BAP dynamically controls the use of multilink lines to produce bandwidth on demand.

base I/O port
Memory address used to transfer information between a computer's CPU and a hardware device.

base memory address
Memory that is addressed and used as buffer space by a hardware device.

baud
Term used to describe the amount of oscillations of a sound wave; named after the French engineer and telegrapher Jean-Maurice-Emile Baudot.

baud rate
The amount of oscillations a modem can transmit and receive in one second. The baud rate was previously used to measure the speed at which modems could transmit and receive data; however, modems are currently measured in bits per second (bps) because each oscillation can now carry more than one bit of data.

binding
The establishment of a communications channel between the upper layer protocols and a network interface card (NIC) driver.

binding state
DHCP state in which the server replies with DHCPAcknowledge or DHCPNak.

bit
Term used to describe one bit of binary data, such as a 1 or 0. Eight bits equals one byte.

bits per second (bps)
The amount of bits that a device transmits in one second.

boot partition
Partition where the current operating system files are located.

bottleneck
Term used to describe a device that is unable to keep up with other devices on a network and causes the entire system to slow. The word *bottleneck* can also be used to describe a hardware device that is degrading the performance of a computer.

broadcast
The transmission of information to more than one recipient. A network broadcast is any information that is addressed and sent to all computers on the local subnet.

broadcast storm
Situation that occurs when so many broadcast messages are sent onto a network that the total capacity of the network bandwidth is consumed and the network can no longer accept data.

buffer
Area of RAM that is used as a storage location.

built-in groups
Groups that are installed as part of the installation of the operating system. Built-in groups provide special permissions and rights to allow members to perform operating and administrative functions on a network.

byte
Single character of information. A byte is made up of eight bits.

cache
Special type of memory or part of physical RAM used to hold frequently accessed data to provide faster access to the data. For example, if a file on the hard drive is continually accessed by the operating system, the file can be placed in cache so that the hard drive does not have to be accessed continuously.

callback security
Security feature built into Windows 2000 that allows an administrator to configure the server or workstation to accept incoming calls, verify the user account, and then call the user back at a user-specified or pre-configured phone number.

class ID
Used to identify a DHCP client with a particular class option.

ClassSchema
Object that specifies the attributes and hierarchy for a class in the Active Directory.

client
Any networked computer that requests resources that are located on another computer.

client/server
A network and application architecture that relies on the presence of a server and a client to distribute the processing requirements of an application. The server is known as the back end, and the client is called the front end.

client-side extensions
Dynamic link libraries that reside on the client to assist processing of group policies.

common name (CN)
Attribute for an object within the Active Directory that uniquely identifies the object. A CN is also called the *relative distinguished name*.

compression
Process of reducing the total amount of drive space that a file or folder consumes.

configuration partition
Part of the Active Directory that represents a discrete unit of replication and contains parameters necessary for the Active Directory to function properly.

container objects
Active Directory objects that can contain other objects. For example, groups are container objects, because they can contain other objects, such as user objects.

CSCRIPT
Command-line executable used to interpret Windows Scripting Host (WSH) scripts.

DACL
See discretionary access control list.

Data Encryption Standard (DES)
Algorithm used to encrypt and decrypt files developed by the United States National Bureau of Standards.

deactivate
After creating and activating a DHCP scope, the process of making the scope unavailable to clients.

defragmenting
Process of finding fragmented files and folders. Fragmented files are files that are not stored in one contiguous space on the hard drive. Defragmenting finds and copies all fragmented files and folders to one contiguous space on the hard drive.

delegation
Process an administrator uses to allow other users to perform limited administrative tasks.

DHCP client
Computer on a network that receives its TCP/IP configuration parameters from a DHCP server.

DHCP dynamic updates
Process that allows DHCP to update Active Directory Integrated zone files with the name and IP addresses of all DHCP clients.

DHCP options
Optional TCP/IP parameters that can be provided to DHCP clients.

DHCP server
Computer on a network that provides the DHCP service to clients.

DHCPAcknowledge
Message sent from a DHCP server acknowledging the acceptance of TCP/IP parameters in a DHCPRequest.

DHCPDecline
Message sent by a DHCP client denying parameters sent by a server in a DHCPOffer message.

DHCPDiscover
Message sent by a DHCP client to identify DHCP servers on a network.

DHCPNak
Message sent by a DHCP server denying a DHCPRequest message.

DHCPOffer
Message sent by a DHCP server to a DHCP client offering a particular set of parameters to the client.

DHCPRelease
Message sent by a DHCP client releasing the TCP/IP address for use by other clients.

DHCPRequest
Response from a DHCP client wishing to accept parameters from a DHCPOffer.

digital
Data that is represented by only 1s and 0s.

digital line
Communication medium that carries only digital data.

digital video disk (DVD)
Optical storage medium used to store digital data with higher storage capacity and speed than CD-ROMs.

Direct Memory Access
Allows compliant hardware devices to access the system memory without the assistance of the CPU.

Directory Information Tree (DIT)
Holds a subset of the information in the Active Directory that provides enough information to start and run the service.

Directory Management Domain (DMD)
Class used to create the schema container in the Active Directory.

directory system agent (DSA)
System process that controls access to Active Directory information.

discretionary access control list (DACL)
A list of security groups and/or users with the associated permissions to particular objects. The DACL is contained within the security descriptor and contains all the SIDs of all users that have been granted or denied permissions to a particular object.

disk duplexing
A technology that uses disk mirroring in which each drive that is part of a mirrored volume resides on a separate hard drive controller.

disk mirroring
A technology that allows the duplication of data by writing data to more than one hard drive. Commonly referred to as RAID 1, each mirrored drive has a secondary drive that is an exact copy.

disk striping
A technology that divides data into 64K blocks and writes each block across multiple drives. Disk striping provides no fault-tolerance and is normally only used to increase read and write speed.

diskless computers
Computers that do not have a hard or floppy drive and normally boot from a system ROM and rely completely on network servers for file storage.

distribution groups
Elements used to combine users together for application and searching purposes. Distribution groups can be used by applications such as Microsoft Exchange to send email to all the members of one or more groups. If you need to group users together for a purpose other than for assigning permissions, then you should use distribution groups.

distribution server
Server that contains installation files for an application within a shared folder that is accessible from the network.

domain
Logical grouping of computers and users for the purpose of administration and security.

Domain Name System (DNS)
Distributed database used by TCP/IP hosts to resolve FQDNs to IP addresses.

domain NetBIOS name
The name of a domain in previous versions of Microsoft Windows NT. In order for Windows 2000 Servers to emulate previous versions of Windows NT, Windows 2000 Servers must know the name of the domain that they will authenticate clients for.

downlevel
Term used to describe a lower version application or operating system.

driver
Software component that allows an operating system to communicate with a hardware device.

Dynamic Host Configuration Protocol (DHCP)
Protocol that allows a client computer to receive IP configuration information automatically each time the system is restarted from a DHCP server.

effective permissions
Combination of permissions assigned to a user and permissions assigned to all the groups the user is a member of.

encryption
Act of scrambling or encoding data so that the data cannot be read by anyone without the proper authority to unscramble or decode the data.

exclusion ranges
Range of addresses in a DHCP scope that will not be offered to clients by the server.

Extensible Authentication Protocol (EAP)
An extension to the PPP protocol that allows a client and server to negotiate which authentication protocol to use. EAP works with dial-up connections, PPTP, and L2TP clients.

extinction
Process a server uses to mark a record available but not yet ready for scavenging from the WINS database.

fault tolerance
The ability of a computer or operating system to recover from a fault, such as a failed hard drive.

Fiber Distributed Data Interface (FDDI)
ANSI standard that defines specifications for transmitting data at transmission rates of 100MB over fiber media using a token-passing media access method.

firewall

Software, hardware, or a combination of both used to prevent unauthorized access to a private network from a public network, such as the Internet.

Flexible Single Master Operations (FSMO)

Method used for the Active Directory to ensure certain changes occur only on one particular machine in the domain.

flow control

Term used to describe devices that can send and receive transmissions simultaneously.

forest

Group of Active Directory trees. Active Directory forests are made up of separate trees that do not share a contiguous namespace.

forward lookup query

Normal process for a client to query one or more name servers to retrieve an IP address from an FQDN.

frame

Single package of data sent over an Ethernet network; sometimes referred to as a *packet*.

front end

Term used to describe a client or an application running on a client in a client/server network.

full duplex

Allows simultaneous two-way communication between two network devices. A full-duplex device can send and receive data at the same time.

fully qualified domain name (FQDN)

Multipart name for a particular host that belongs to a particular second-level domain.

gateway

A network device that can connect separate networks using different protocols or architectures.

global catalog

A service and storage location that contains all directory objects and a subset of each object's attributes.

GPT.INI

File that contains a group policy template.

group

A container account used to combine user accounts into one manageable unit, thereby facilitating permissions administration. Members within a group receive all permissions assigned to the group account.

group policy

Object used to customize and control a user's environment.

group policy extensions

Object within a Group Policy node that contains settings for a particular section of an operating environment.

Group Policy node

Object at the root of a group policy object that defines the policy's area of effectiveness.

group policy objects

Discrete product of the Group Policy MMC snap-in that contains details of the actual policies implemented. *See also* group policy.

H-node

Type of NetBIOS node that uses broadcast, point-to-point (WINS and DNS), LMHOSTS files, and HOSTS files as name-resolution mechanisms.

half duplex

Term used to describe devices that cannot send and receive transmissions simultaneously.

Hardware Compatibility List (HCL)

List provided by Microsoft that denotes all hardware that is compatible with their operating systems and is supported by Microsoft.

hardware loopback
A device that can be connected to a network card that allows all transmitted data to be returned to the sender. A hardware loopback is used for troubleshooting network devices.

host
A device, with an address, on a TCP/IP network.

host record
Record used to map a host name to an IP address.

Hypertext Markup Language (HTML)
A text-based language that can be used to develop Web pages.

Hypertext Transport Protocol (HTTP)
Application layer protocol used to transport HTML documents and Web page contents.

Image Color Management 2 (ICM 2)
API included with the Windows 2000 operating system that ensures the graphics and colors seen on a monitor reflect exactly what is printed.

inheritance
A function in which child objects (objects contained within container objects) can acquire the properties and permissions of parent objects (container objects).

Initialization state
DHCP state in which the client sends a DHCPDiscover message.

Internet Control Message Protocol (ICMP)
Network layer protocol used by hosts to send and receive messages concerning network status. The PING utility uses the ICMP protocol, called an ICMP echo message.

Internet groups
Type of WINS record that identifies a number of NetBIOS nodes (from 1 through 25) with access to specific resources.

Internet Protocol (IP)
Network layer protocol used to address and route data across networks.

Internet Protocol Security (IPSec)
Cryptographic security services used to ensure secure private communications over TCP/IP networks.

interrupt request (IRQ)
Mechanism used by hardware devices to gain the attention of the CPU.

IPCONFIG
Utility used from the Windows 2000 client command prompt to display, release, and renew DHCP parameters.

Ipconfig
Windows NT and 2000 utility used to view the current TCP/IP configuration of a computer.

IPSec policies
Policies that dictate the behavior of computer classes in a secure, non-secure, or mixed security TCP/IP environment. *See also* Internet Protocol Security (IPSec).

IPX/SPX
Communications protocol used on NetWare 4.*x* and downlevel network operating systems (a.k.a. NWLink).

jumper
Small plastic and metal connector used to connect electrical circuits on a hardware device. Jumpers are commonly used to configure IRQ, COM Port, DMA, or base I/O addresses.

Kerberos 5 protocol
An Internet standard and the main method for authentication in Windows 2000. It authenticates a user and also authenticates the resources being accessed. It is automatically implemented in Windows 2000 and should then be set as the only authentication protocol.

Glossary

Layer 2 Tunneling Protocol (L2TP)
Protocol used to create private encrypted tunnels through public networks, such as the Internet. L2TP does not encrypt data; it relies on other technologies, such as IPSec, for the encryption. L2TP can be used with IPSec to create virtual private networks (VPNs) across the Internet.

lease
Duration of time that a DHCP client can use the TCP/IP parameters provided by a DHCP server.

LMHOSTS
Static file containing NetBIOS name to TCP/IP address mappings.

local group
Group account that is a part of the local accounts database and can only be assigned permissions to resources located on the local machine.

local group policy
Object present on every Windows 2000 computer that contains customizations to the computer's operating environment.

local policy extensions
Policies that can be set to control audit policies, user rights, and security options.

loop back
Ability to apply a policy based on the location of a computer rather than a user or computer.

M-node
Type of NetBIOS host that uses both broadcast and point-to-point name-resolution mechanisms.

Mail Exchanger record (MX record)
DNS record that identifies a resource as an electronic mail exchanger.

media
Cable or wire used to connect computers to a network. Fiber and twisted-pair cables are types of media.

merge mode
Loop-back mode that processes user policies first, followed by computer policies.

multicast
Type of network traffic sent to select clients based on their multicast TCP/IP address.

name server record (NS)
DNS record that identifies a resource as a DNS name server.

NetBIOS (Network Basic Input/ Output System)
Session layer protocol used for application communication on local area networks (LANs). NetBIOS is an API that can be used by applications to request network services.

NetBIOS name services (NBNS)
Service used to resolve NetBIOS names to TCP/IP addresses. The Microsoft implementation is called WINS.

Network Basic Input/Output System (NetBIOS)
See NetBIOS.

Network Driver Interface Specification (NDIS)
Specification that defines a standard interface for communication between the media access control sublayer and protocol drivers.

non-local group policy
Object stored on domain controllers that controls the operating environment of all users and/or computers in selected sites, domains, or Organizational Units.

normal group
Type of WINS record that identifies a common group name.

Ntds.dit
File that contains the domain directory data for a domain; stored in a share called Ntds on the domain controllers.

object
Collection of attributes used to describe a network resource or user account.

object identifier
Code that uniquely describes an object within a directory. A hierarchical system of issuing authorities regulates object ID codes while allowing local administrators to create local object identifiers.

object properties
Additional information about a particular object. For example, users might have a phone number or department property.

ObjectClassCategory
Method of identifying types of classes; introduced with the X.500 standard of 1993.

operations master
Domain controller that possesses the token that identifies the domain controller as the PDC emulator.

Organizational Unit
Container object that can be used to group Active Directory objects together for organizational and administrative purposes.

P-node
Type of NetBIOS host that uses another host (server) as its primary name-resolution mechanism.

Packet Internet Groper (PING)
Simple TCP/IP utility that can be used to test connectivity and routing. PING uses the ICMP protocol to send an echo request to a remote host on a network; if the host returns an echo reply, then the first three network layers are working properly. The PING utility can be used from the Windows 2000 command prompt to verify the connectivity of a target host.

paging file
A special Windows file located on one or more hard drives and used to create virtual memory. Paging files are commonly referred to as *swap files*.

parallel transmission
A transmission mechanism in which data bits are transmitted side by side.

partition
A segmented area of space residing on a physical hard drive. Hard drives can contain multiple partitions that are presented and treated as separate drives.

peer-to-peer network
A network in which all computers are peers and can act as both servers and clients and there is no centrally managed security.

peripheral component interconnect (PCI)
A 32-bit local bus used in modern personal and Apple computers. PCI devices meet the architectural requirements of Plug and Play.

PING
See Packet Internet Groper (PING).

Plug and Play
A set of application and hardware architectural specifications that allows an operating system and computer BIOS to automatically configure hardware devices that are added to the computer.

Point-To-Point Protocol (PPP)
A Data Link layer protocol used to connect systems via telephone dial-up lines.

Point-To-Point Tunneling Protocol (PPTP)
An extension of the PPP protocol. PPTP is used to connect systems over a public network while encrypting packets' contents to create a virtual private network (VPN).

primary zone
The first zone created for a new domain (or subdomain). The primary is master copy of the zone file.

print device
A peripheral device used to print documents.

printer
Term used to describe the driver used to communicate with the print device.

printer pool
A collection of print devices connected to a computer through multiple ports and managed by one printer.

printer queue
Buffer space located on a hard drive that is used to store print jobs waiting to print.

proxy server
Hardware and/or software device that acts as a firewall between trusted and untrusted networks. A proxy server can filter packets coming into and leaving a trusted network and provide network address translation (NAT).

public key policy
Policy that dictates the users and/or groups that can recover encrypted files, the list of trusted certificate authorities, and enterprise trust settings for certificate authorities.

published applications
Applications made available for installation due to computer configuration or user configuration policies.

Redundant Array of Independent Disks (RAID)
A standard fault-tolerant technology broken into five levels. Each level offers different levels of performance and disk utilization. Formerly, the *RAID* acronym stood for *Redundant Array of Inexpensive Disks*.

refresh
Rate at which a client checks for a change to the group policy objects that apply to the computer or the user logged onto the computer.

registration
Process client initiates to enter its record(s) into a WINS server database.

release
Process a WINS client uses to temporarily free up a name in the WINS database.

Remote Authentication Dial-In Service (RADIUS)
Authentication protocol widely used on the Internet for dial-up authentication and accounting.

renewing state
DHCP state in which the client sends a DHCPRequest message halfway through the lease duration.

replace mode
Loop back mode that bypasses the user policy and only uses the computer policy.

replica
Copy of an Active Directory database.

replication
Process of updating information from one replica to another replica.

requesting state
DHCP state in which a client sends a DHCPRequest message.

reservation
Process that allows an administrator to assign a TCP/IP address to a particular MAC address, thereby ensuring that the client always receives the same TCP/IP address.

resource
Any computer device, computer, or file that is shared on a network.

reverse lookup query
Process in which a client queries one or more name servers to retrieve an FQDN from a TCP/IP address.

rights
Any special authorization that allows a user or group account to perform system tasks on a computer system or network.

root domain
The first domain created in a tree. All additional domains that are part of the same network become child domains to the root domain.

root server
DNS servers at the top of the inverted tree DNS namespace. A root server contains records for top-level domain DNS servers.

RootDSE
Object at the top of every LDAP tree that contains the attributes necessary to extract critical directory data. A RootDSE is used to maintain portability in LDAP scripts and applications.

router
Network device used to connect separate networks and route data packets to the appropriate network.

ROUTER
DHCP option that identifies the TCP/IP gateway for a DHCP client.

RS-232 communications
Serial communication standard that defines signal characteristics adopted by the EIA.

SACL
See security access control list.

scavenge
Process of removing records from a WINS database when the records are no longer useful.

schema
A database that contains a definition of all Active Directory objects and the objects' attributes.

schema container
Part of the Active Directory that represents a discrete unit of replication and contains parameters necessary for the schema to function properly.

schema.ini
File used to create and populate a schema.

SchemaNamingContext
Attribute that directs a query to the location of the schema.

scope
A contiguous range of TCP/IP addresses, usually a TCP/IP subnet, available for use on a DHCP server.

scripts policy
Policy that specifies scripts that can be run at startup or shutdown for a computer and logon or logoff for a user.

SearchFlags
Bit used to indicate that an attribute should be indexed.

second-level domain
Domain assigned to a particular entity within a top-level domain (for example, Microsoft.com).

secondary zone
Mirror copy of primary zone file that provides fault tolerance and load balancing to DNS.

security access control list (SACL)
List that defines which security events can be audited on a particular object.

security groups
Groups used to assign permission to a number of users simultaneously. Security groups were the only type of group used in Windows NT 4.

selecting state
DHCP state in which a client selects one DHCPOffer from one or more offers received.

serial transmission
A transmission mechanism in which data bits are transmitted one behind the other.

Server Messaging Block (SMP)
A protocol developed by IBM, Microsoft, and Intel that is used to display shared files and the transfer of files over a network.

service records (SRV)
DNS record that identifies a resource as a service.

share level security
A security mechanism in which shares are protected with passwords and any user that knows the password can access the share.

Small Computer System Interface (SCSI)
A high-speed parallel interface used to connect hardware devices, such as hard drives and tape devices. SCSI is pronounced "Skuzzy."

Start Of Authority Record (SOA)
First record in a domain. An SOA is a DNS record that identifies the bounds of a zone.

subdomain
Contiguous portion of a second-level domain with separate zone files.

SubSchemaSubEntry
Attribute in the RootDSE that contains the location of the subschema that contains all the attributes and classes in the Active Directory.

super-scope
Group of DHCP scopes combined to reduce administrative overhead.

system partition
Partition that contains the files needed to boot a system.

tombstone
Process a WINS server uses to mark a record for scavenging from the WINS database.

top-level domain
Geographic or entity type delimiter for a namespace. Top-level domains occur between root and second-level domains.

Total Cost of Ownership (TCO)
Term used to describe the total cost associated with the purchase, administration, and maintenance of a computer and/or network.

tree
Group of one or more Active Directory domains that are all part of the same network. All domains within a tree must share the same namespace.

Unicode
Standard character set compatible with many languages.

user rights
Set of allowable actions with corresponding security groups and/or users that can commit the actions.

virtual private network (VPN)
A network of computers that sends encrypted data over a public network. Because the data is encrypted, no one other than authorized users can send or receive data to or from the computers participating in the network, thereby creating a virtual private network.

WACK (WINS Acknowledgment)
An acknowldgement that positively verifies a client registration.

Windows Scripting Host (WSH)
Script interpreter that can be used for customizing an environment or automating tasks on a Windows computer.

WINS
The Microsoft Windows implementation of a NetBIOS name server.

WINS proxy
WINS client that is capable of using a WINS server that will capture and reply to broadcasts from clients that cannot use WINS servers.

WSCRIPT
Windows executable used to interpret WSH scripts.

zone
An autonomous, contiguous portion of a DNS namespace.

INDEX

WHAT'S ON THE CD-ROM

The *MCSE Windows 2000 Accelerated Exam Prep* companion CD-ROM contains the testing system for the book, which includes nearly 100 questions. Additional questions are available for free download from **ExamCram.com**; simply click on the Update button in the testing engine. You can choose from numerous testing formats, including Fixed-Length, Random, Test All, and Review.

System Requirement

Software:

➤ Your operating system must be Windows 95, 98, NT 4, or higher.

➤ To view the practice exams, you need Internet Explorer 5.x.

Hardware

➤ An Intel Pentium, AMD, or comparable 100MHz processor or higher is recommended for best results.

➤ 32MB of RAM is the minimum memory requirement.

➤ Available disk storage space of at least 10MB is recommended.